CHURCH DOGMATICS

KARL BARTH

EDITORS
G. W. BROMILEY
T. F. TORRANCE

THE DOCTRINE
OF RECONCILIATION

CHURCH DOGMATICS

KARL BARTH

VOLUME IV

THE DOCTRINE OF RECONCILIATION

PART 3.1

TRANSLATOR
G. W. BROMILEY

EDITORS
G. W. BROMILEY
T. F. TORRANCE

T&T CLARK INTERNATIONAL
A Continuum imprint

The Tower Building
11 York Road
London SE1 7NX, UK

15 East 26th Street
New York 10010
USA

www.tandtclark.com

First edition copyright © T&T Clark Ltd, 1961
First paperback edition copyright © T&T Clark International, 2004

Authorised English translation of *Die Kirchliche Dogmatik IV: Die Lehre von der Versöhnung 3*, Erste Hälfte
copyright © Evangelischer Verlag A.G., Zollikon–Zürich, 1959

All rights reserved. No part of this publication may be reproduced, stored in a retrieval system, or transmitted, in any form or by any means, electronic, mechanical, photocopying, recording or otherwise, without the prior permission of T&T Clark International

ISBN 0 567 09043 4 (hardback)
0 567 05189 7 (paperback)

British Library Cataloguing-in-Publication Data
A catalogue record for this book is available from the British Library

Printed and bound in the United States by the Data Reproductions Corporation

EDITORS' PREFACE

In *Church Dogmatics*, IV, 1 Barth outlined the doctrine of reconciliation in a threefold form corresponding to the threefold confession of Jesus Christ as very God, very Man and the God-Man. The first form—the theme of IV, 1—deals with Christ as the Lord who humbled Himself as a servant to do the work of atonement (His priestly office). The second—the theme of IV, 2—considers Him as the Royal Man in whom man is exalted and adopted to fellowship with God (His kingly office). Reconciliation is thus effected in two great movements, from above downwards and from below upwards, which together exhaust the material content of the doctrine. Yet if the work of Christ is not to be separated from His person, and if Christology and soteriology are not to drift apart from their application and actualisation, there is also need of a third form—the theme of the present part-volume, IV, 3—in which Christ is treated as the God-Man who is the Mediator and Guarantor of reconciliation (His prophetic office).

Since this third, prophetic form demands no less serious treatment than the first two, the atonement must now be considered in a third dimension in which it manifests, expresses and mediates itself as the truth of all truths, alike the truth of God and the truth of man. Because Jesus Christ, according to Barth's title, is also "the true Witness," the atonement is not merely true; it is active truth shining and revealing itself in the world's darkness and overcoming it. Reconciliation is not closed in upon itself; it moves out and communicates itself, and is the creative source of a reconciled community and a reconciled world. In this third form, it is in the field as the light of life, engaged in triumphant self-demonstration in the enlightening and quickening power of the Holy Spirit.

As in the first and second forms, there are important implications for man. Jesus Christ, the Servant, unmasks the sin of man as pride and achieves his justification. Jesus Christ, the Royal Man, opposes the sin of man as sloth and fulfils his sanctification. And now Jesus Christ, the true Witness, answers the sin of man as falsehood and establishes his vocation. This carries with it the sending out of the Christian community as well as its gathering and upbuilding, and the life of the individual Christian, not only in faith and love, but also in hope. It is in the Church's ministry of witness that the self-revealing and self-attesting of the divine reconciliation to the world is actualised.

An outstanding feature of this part-volume is the attention which Barth has given to the subjective application of reconciliation in the involvement of the Christian community in world history. In this respect, he emphasises strongly that the Church exists for the world, not for itself. Its existence for the world is an essential and masterful aspect of its reconciled life in the light and truth of God. We thus see the universal sweep of God's self-sacrificial and victorious work. We also see the foundations of Barth's understanding of the life and work of the Church as determined by mission, evangelism, witness and service.

The size of the part-volume has unfortunately made necessary its production in two halves after the pattern of the German original. This is, however, a purely technical matter, and so far as possible, e.g., in respect of the table of contents, pagination and indexes, expression has been given to the essential unity of treatment. In spite of the bulk of material, the volume has not presented so many problems as some of its predecessors, and we are particularly happy to have completed the proofs before the appearance of the German IV, 4, so that the whole of the *Church Dogmatics* thus far completed is now available to the English reader. We are again indebted to the Rev. Professor J. K. S. Reid for his invaluable assistance at the proof stage, not merely in correcting errors, but also in smoothing some of the more complicated passages.

EDINBURGH, *Trinity*, 1961.

PREFACE

THIS time the readers of *Church Dogmatics* have had to wait longer than expected for the continuation. The course of production has been slowed up by the fact that my dogmatics class at Basel, with which the growth of the book has always been connected, has now been reduced to three hours instead of four, and had to be suspended altogether in the busy summer of 1956.

And now there is offered only the first half of IV, 3. The second half is almost completed and partly in print, and ought to follow in June of this year. It is not willingly that I have assented to the division, for I set some store by the formal unity of the individual volumes for architectonic and other reasons. However, I can only make an incomplete offering. The shape of what is to follow may be seen from the complete table of contents which is already given. The three indexes will come at the end of the second half.

The compelling reason for this procedure is that the total bulk of the volume has exceeded that which was seriously deplored by so many in the case of I, 2. I still cannot imagine how the men of the 17th century even handled, as they somehow must have done, the far more gigantic tomes sometimes produced in that period. The men of the 20th will surely be grateful that this time they will have two halves which are " bearable " in the literal sense.

The question of the meaning and reach of the prophetic office of Jesus Christ has led me in this third part of the doctrine of reconciliation into a line of study which theoretically and practically, and in the most diverse contexts and under the most diverse titles, stands very much to the forefront in the discussions now conducted in the Church of all confessions. So far as I can see, however, there has hitherto been lacking in these a theological basis strictly orientated on the evangelical centre. In the theology of the Reformation and post-Reformation periods we find little or nothing, and in that of the 19th and 20th centuries very little, concerning the decisive presuppositions on the basis of which we now think that we are free and compelled to pursue the problem of Christ (or the Church) and the world with the zeal displayed in so many different ways on both sides of the Atlantic and in Christianity both old and new. It cannot be my present purpose properly to enter into these discussions, e.g., concerning missions, evangelisation, the work of the laity, the Church and culture, Church and state, Christianity and Socialism, etc. My task is to try to discover the by no means self-evident basic presuppositions, and I have finally been compelled to the insight that the confession before men

xi

which is everywhere to be accepted and made is grounded in the work of the living Jesus Christ Himself, and therefore does not stand on the periphery but belongs to the centre of the life of the Christian in the Christian community, the problem of witness deciding indeed whether the Christian really is a Christian and the Christian community the Christian community. The development of this insight as an essential element in the knowledge of Jesus Christ forms the main portion of the first half here presented. In the second it will be developed more specifically in relation to the Christian and the Christian community. The fact that § 71, on sin as falsehood, brings the first half to an end, whereas the corresponding sections in the two preceding volumes can only be transitional, must simply be accepted as an unavoidably disruptive feature until the second half is available.

As regards the external history of *Church Dogmatics* it may be noted that to the successively growing book of Otto Weber there has now been added the fine and skilful selection and introduction compiled by Helmut Gollwitzer and published by the Fischer-Bücherei in 1957. Mention must also be made of the appearance in the Roman Catholic world of the comprehensive and penetrating expositions and interpretations by Emmanuele Riverso, *La teologia esistenzialistica di Karl Barth* (1955), by Hans Küng, *Rechtfertigung. Die Lehre Karl Barths und eine katholische Besinnung* (1957), and by Henri Bouillard, *Karl Barth* (1957, 3 vols.). All these are characterised by profound learning, by a serious desire to understand within their own ecclesiastical presuppositions, and by actual understanding, though not without some contradictions among themselves.

Looking back more generally over the years since the appearance of the last volume, I am struck by the fact that so many close contemporaries, who have followed my whole course and therefore the *Church Dogmatics* with critical or at least attentive good-will, have now passed from the present scene. First I must mention Arthur Frey, who for many years directed the Evangelischer Verlag, Zollikon, and who always proved a trustworthy adviser and personal friend in critical days. Reference may perhaps be made to what I have already said concerning him in the Preface to III, 4. Shortly before him there died my cousin, the painter, Paul Basilius Barth, who belonged to a very different world, but with whom I enjoyed a late yet warm personal contact on the occasion of his exertions on behalf of a portrait. Again, I must mention my two very different friends Pierre Maury of Paris and Heinrich Scholz of Münster in Westphalia. How I miss to-day the vehement loyalty of the one and the verily humanistic but no less sure and active fidelity of the other! Again, I must refer to my colleague both in Bonn and Basel, K. L. Schmidt, far superior to me in both learning and pugnacity, but always so stimulating. Mention must also be made of the two steadfast Reformed scholars Hermann Hesse and Harmannus Obendiek,

Preface xiii

both associates of the time of the Church conflict in Germany, and also of Lukas Christ of Basel, who in his own different manner proved no less trustworthy. Again, there is Heinrich Held, President of the Evangelical Church of the Rhineland, who as such greeted me on both my sixtieth and seventieth birthdays in such unmerited terms of personal address, and also the Anglican bishop George Bell, an Ecumenicist without guile, who in the summer of 1956 welcomed me in his residence in Chichester with a warmth which I shall never forget. I must also mention Oskar Farner, the Zwingli scholar and expositor, and for many years the acknowledged head of the Zürich Church, Liberal in origin, yet with me on the most important things. Finally, I must refer to Richard Imberg, director of the deaconess house Siloah in Gümlingen, a man of little academic discipline, but for that reason the more mature and forceful a theologian, whose warm humanity opened up to me a whole new side of the community movement. There now shines on them the eternal light in which we, *adhuc peregrinantes*, shall some day need no more dogmatics.

In conclusion, may I express my thanks to Hinrich Stoevesandt for his assistance in this volume too, both in revision and in the preparation of the indexes.

BASEL, *January* 1959.

CONTENTS

	PAGE
EDITORS' PREFACE	ix
PREFACE	xi

CHAPTER XVI
JESUS CHRIST, THE TRUE WITNESS

FIRST HALF

§ 69. THE GLORY OF THE MEDIATOR
  1. The Third Problem of the Doctrine of Reconciliation . 3
  2. The Light of Life 38
  3. Jesus is Victor 165
  4. The Promise of the Spirit 274

§ 70. THE FALSEHOOD AND CONDEMNATION OF MAN
  1. The True Witness 368
  2. The Falsehood of Man 434
  3. The Condemnation of Man 461

SECOND HALF

§ 71. THE VOCATION OF MAN
  1. Man in the Light of Life 481
  2. The Event of Vocation 497
  3. The Goal of Vocation 520
  4. The Christian as Witness 554
  5. The Christian in Affliction 614
  6. The Liberation of the Christian 647

§ 72. THE HOLY SPIRIT AND THE SENDING OF THE CHRISTIAN COMMUNITY
  1. The People of God in World-Occurrence . . 681
  2. The Community for the World 762
  3. The Task of the Community 795
  4. The Ministry of the Community 830

§ 73. THE HOLY SPIRIT AND CHRISTIAN HOPE
  1. The Subject of Hope and Hope . . . 902
  2. Life in Hope 928

INDEXES
  I. Scripture References 943
  II. Names 958
  III. Subjects 960

CHAPTER XVI
JESUS CHRIST, THE TRUE WITNESS

CHAPTER XVI

JESUS CHRIST, THE TRUE WITNESS

§ 69

THE GLORY OF THE MEDIATOR

"Jesus Christ as attested to us in Holy Scripture is the one Word of God whom we must hear and whom we must trust and obey in life and in death."

1. THE THIRD PROBLEM OF THE DOCTRINE OF RECONCILIATION

The twofold development of the material content of the doctrine of reconciliation is now behind us. "Reconciliation" in the sense of the Christian confession and the message of the Christian community is God's active and superior Yes to man. It is God's active Yes to man as it is the fulfilment of the eternal election in which God has determined, determines and will again determine Himself for man to be his God, and man for Himself to be His man. It is God's superior Yes to man as it is the overcoming, in God's omnipotent mercy, of the No, the contradiction, the opposition, the disruption in which man, if he were left to achieve it, would necessarily destroy his relationship to God and his fellows, and therefore himself. God does not permit him to execute this No of his, this contradiction and opposition. God does not abandon him to the mortal peril to which he thereby exposes himself. He takes the lists against man and therefore for him, for his salvation and for His own glory. He stands by His Yes. He accomplishes its actualisation. This is the work of God the Reconciler. "Reconciliation" in the Christian sense of the word—the reconciliation of which we have the attestation in the Holy Scriptures of the Old and New Testament, and in the recognition and proclamation of which the Christian community has its existence—is the history in which God concludes and confirms His covenant with man, maintaining and carrying it to its goal in spite of every threat. It is the history in which God in His own person and act takes to Himself His disobedient creature accursed in its disobedience, His unfaithful covenant-partner lost in his unfaithfulness. He does this as He both abases and sets Himself at the side of man, yet also exalts man and sets him at His own side; as He both vindicates Himself in face of man and man in face of Himself. " Reconciliation " thus means and signifies Emmanuel, God with us, namely, God in the peace which He has made between Himself and us but also between us and Himself. And the one decisive, comprehensive and all-determinative factor is that Jesus Christ is this peace in its twofold form. The history of its establishment and therefore the history of reconciliation is His history. It is the history of His sending and coming, of His life and speech and action, of His death and passion and resurrection, of His ministry and lordship. In Him God is the One who graciously elects man and man is the one who is graciously elected by God. He is the actualisation of the covenant between God and man, both on the side of God and also on that of man.

"God our Saviour . . . will have all men to be saved" (1 Tim. 2$^{3f.}$). The concrete basis of this statement is to be found in that which immediately follows (v. 5): "For there is one God, and one mediator ($\mu\epsilon\sigma\iota\tau\eta s$) between God and man, the man Christ Jesus, who gave himself a ransom for all . . ." In this one man God accomplishes His will, i.e., the salvation of all. Whether the statement is Pauline or Deutero-Pauline, it is matched by 2 Cor. 1^{19}: "For the Son of God, Jesus Christ, who was preached among you by us, even by me and Silvanus and Timotheus, was not yea and nay, but in him was yea. For all the promises of God in him are yea. . . ."

This is the material content of the doctrine of reconciliation. Even when we state it *in nuce*, in a brief outline as here attempted, we cannot contemplate it without being aware of at least the indications of its twofold development. The history of Jesus Christ with which the history of reconciliation is identical is the parallel but opposing fulfilment of two great movements, the one from above downwards and the other from below upwards, but both grounded in His person in the union of its true deity and true humanity. It is a matter of the salvation and right of man established in the humiliation of the Son of God to be the Brother, Representative and Head of all men. And it is a matter of the right and glory of God asserted in the exaltation of this Brother, Representative and Head of all men, of the true Son of Man. As the one Jesus Christ is both true Son of God and true Son of Man, so there take place in His one history both the humiliation of God and the exaltation of man, the conflict and victory of God for man, and therewith and thereby the achievement of covenant faithfulness on both sides, the establishment of peace in this twofold form. On the one hand it is opposed by the sin of man in its form as pride and therefore by the fall of man; on the other by this sin in its form as sloth and therefore by the misery of man. And so in the one work of the omnipotent mercy of God accomplished in Jesus Christ, our concern is with the justification of man before Him and his sanctification for Him, and in the grace of the Holy Spirit of

1. *The Third Problem of the Doctrine of Reconciliation* 5

Jesus Christ with the gathering and upbuilding of the Christian community, with the object of humble Christian faith and the basis of confident Christian love. In all this we are briefly sketching the two first parts of the doctrine of reconciliation as we have presented them in IV, 1 and IV, 2 under the titles " Jesus Christ, the Lord as Servant " and " Jesus Christ, the Servant as Lord."

If we can and will use the expression, this is the inner dialectic of the Christian doctrine of reconciliation. It is self-evident that both as a whole and in detail very different courses might have been adopted, many things being described and formulated and interrelated in a very different way from that adopted. *Methodus est arbitraria.* In each age and by each responsible theologian the best definitions, combinations and conclusions must always be sought and found afresh in dogmatics with a continually new desire for obedience. But however things may be seen or pondered or stated as a whole or in detail, the standpoints from which this must be done are not a matter of arbitrary investigation, discovery and assertion. Apart from all else, they are given in and with the name of Jesus Christ. In God's Yes to man, in the reconciliation of the world with God, it is a matter of this One, and therefore of His deity and humanity, of God's humiliation and man's exaltation, of the justification and sanctification of man, of faith and love. A doctrine of reconciliation which does not present both these aspects with equal seriousness is incomplete, one-sided and erroneous. Even if the two cannot be compared, the one great Yes of God spoken in Jesus Christ includes both the turning of God to man and that of man to God. In all ages and circumstances this must emerge in every theology. If only the one or the other aspect is treated, or one is not given due weight but obscured by the other, too little is said, and therefore in the last resort there is distortion.

The theology of the early and mediaeval Church spoke fairly commonly of a twofold office, a *munus duplex*, of Christ, and to that extent of two problems of the doctrine of reconciliation. In this connexion we are reminded of Rev. $5^{5f.}$ where in the same breath Jesus Christ is described as " the Lion of the tribe of Juda which hath prevailed " yet also as " the Lamb as it had been slain." In the *Testaments of the Twelve Patriarchs* we also meet with the notion that the *Kyrios* descends both from the tribe of Levi and also from that of Judah, the one in His office and work as High-priest and the other in His office and work as King, the one as God (for this aspect is also seen here) and the other as man (*Test. Sim.* 7 and *passim*). By Justin, Athanasius, Augustine and others, and by Peter Lombard in the Middle Ages, He is related to the figures of Aaron on the one side, and David, Solomon and even Joshua on the other, as the One who fulfils their prophetic existence. The question whether this is legitimate or illegitimate allegorising is irrelevant in face of the fact that the material content of the Old and New Testaments is rightly perceived as such. Reformation theology followed the same tradition. Calvin was the one who, imitating the early Church, developed the doctrine of the office and work of Jesus Christ in the way which comes closest to our own reconstruction. It may be noted that he shows a slight tendency to give a certain preference to the kingly office

§ 69. The Glory of the Mediator

of Jesus Christ as compared with the high-priestly (*peculiari regni intuitu et ratione dictum fuisse Messiam, Instit.* II, 15, 2), and that this finds expression in the order of the third book to the extent that justification is there treated within the comprehensive doctrine of sanctification or regeneration. But it could hardly be said that proper justice is not done by him to justification, and therefore to its distinctive presupposition in the high-priestly office of Jesus Christ. The situation was and is very complicated on the Lutheran side. Here, too, the twofold structure (and from the beginning of the 17th century the threefold as it had been discovered or rediscovered by Calvin) was adopted. Yet from the very first an opposing if not alien concern was also appropriated. From the days of Melanchthon's *Loci* of 1521, the tendency was to concentrate on the *beneficia Christi* and therefore not to devote too much attention to the objective presupposition of the salvation accomplished for man, i.e., to Christology. Salvation was predominantly if not exclusively envisaged as a *beneficium*, namely, as the justification of sinful man by faith, and sanctification had only as it were a subsidiary role. Inevitably therefore, to the extent that there was any concern with Christology, the decisive interest was in the high-priestly office of Jesus Christ and His kingly office came in for little more than incidental mention. The tendency was really to merge the latter into the former. Hence we read in Hollaz (*Ex. theol. acroam.*, 1707, III, 1, 3, *qu.* 71) that *strictiori sensu* the whole work of the Mediator is identical with His *officium sacerdotale*, which includes all His other offices. The genuinely Lutheran reservation in respect of a twofold or threefold view of the matter hardened in the *De officio Christi triplici* (1773) of J. A. Ernesti into the formal contention that it is sufficient and alone possible to consider and describe the work of Jesus Christ from the one standpoint of *satisfactio*. Against the background of the genuinely Lutheran preference for the doctrine of justification there could be no consistent distinction and co-ordination of the two standpoints and points of departure. Always there was the menace of a flagrant or secret superordination of the one and subordination of the other. Yet even in this sphere, in spite of the readoption of the protestation of Ernesti by A. Ritschl (*Rechtfertigung und Versöhnung*, Vol. III, p. 394 f.) and F. H. R. Frank (*System der christlichen Wahrheit*, 2nd edit., 1894, Vol. II, p. 201 f.), there has been a continual if not very confident return to this distinction and co-ordination, even Schleiermacher (*The Christian Faith*, § 102) contending for it in the light of his presuppositions and the corresponding lines of argument. That this is the case is an indication that in the union in opposition of the priestly and kingly offices of Jesus Christ (and therefore of justification and sanctification, of faith and love), as this was perceived already in the theology of the early Church, we do not have an arbitrarily invented theologoumenon, but a necessity grounded in the thing itself.

When, therefore, the early Church spoke of this union in opposition, and therefore of a *munus duplex* of Jesus Christ, of His priestly and kingly office, it was justified to the extent that the material content of the doctrine of reconciliation is in fact exhausted by what has to be thought and said from these two christologico-soteriological standpoints. Concerning that which takes place in the history which is the theme of the doctrine of reconciliation there is to be said, with all kinds of expansions or contractions or variations as a whole and in detail, and with equal emphasis upon the two constituent elements, the one fact that it is a fulfilment of the saying: " I will be your God, and ye shall be my people." In our own development we have started with the person and work of Jesus Christ, for to say reconciliation is necessarily to name at once this name in which it is accomplished.

1. The Third Problem of the Doctrine of Reconciliation

But starting from Him and His fulness, we think at once in terms of this union in opposition, and we note at once that there can be no question of anything different or higher or better than what is to be thought and said in these terms. To apply an additional test, no other result could be achieved even if we replaced this name by such material concepts as redemption or the kingdom of God or true life. This is not merely because, if we are not to fill out these concepts arbitrarily, we must always return to the name from which we ourselves have preferred to start. It is also because in their development, presupposing our loyalty to the Scriptures of the Old and New Testament, we are irresistibly compelled first to look and think from above downwards, from God to man, but then also and with the same seriousness from below upwards, from man to God. And we then realise that in the strange twofold movement which we necessarily perceive and follow we are dealing with the whole of the history in which God gives to man salvation but also causes man to give Him glory.

Yet the fact remains that there is a third problem of the doctrine of reconciliation which, if it has to be posed and answered differently, has still to be treated with the same seriousness as the first two, so that if we disregard or fail to develop and answer it the doctrine is just as incomplete in relation to its theme as if one of the first two were neglected in favour of the other, as seems to be the constant threat in Lutheran theology. For the reconciliation which is our concern in this doctrine, i.e., the history of Jesus Christ as the great act of God which the Christian community confesses and by which it may live, itself takes place in a third dimension which we have not yet explicitly considered, and it would not be this history if it did not take place in this direction too. The witness of the Bible, to which theology is responsible in respect of the fulness as well as the accuracy of its discussions and formulations, is in all portions full of traces of a further specific element of the event attested by it, if only we have ears to hear. If this element rests on the distinctness and difference of the two first, it is not identical with either. If it is in unity with them, it is not merely their unity as such, but the one event in a form which is distinct from both and must be considered separately. We could not actually have described it in the first two forms if it did not have this third and if we did not take preliminary account of the fact that it does take place in this form too. But we must now speak of it independently in this third form, in the light of which we must also consider the first two.

What is the point at issue? There can be no question of a further development of our material knowledge of the event of reconciliation. The truth remains that what God did and does and will do as the Reconciler of the world with Himself in Jesus Christ is exhausted in what has to be thought and said from the first two standpoints. But this intrinsically perfect and insurpassable action has a distinct character. For as it takes place in its perfection, and with no need of supplement, it also expresses, discloses, mediates and reveals itself. It is to be noted that there is not revealed anything different, higher or deeper, any independent truth. It expresses, discloses, mediates and reveals itself, not as a truth but as *the* truth, in which all truths, the truth of God particularly and the truth of man, are enclosed, not as truths in themselves, but as rays or facets of its truth. It declares itself as reality. It displays itself. It proclaims itself. It thus summons to conscious, intelligent, living, grateful, willing and active participation in its occurrence. But already we are anticipating what is achieved and effected in virtue of this third element in its occurrence. The basic and all-decisive factor is that, no matter what the result may be or what may be achieved or effected, it displays and proclaims itself as truth, and indeed as *the* truth. For it is the event—we speak of Jesus Christ—in which the covenant between God and man is sealed on both sides, in which peace is established both from above and from below, and in which the justification and sanctification of man are both accomplished, whether or not there is response in the faith and love of a single individual. Its donation sovereignly precedes all reception on our part in the fact that in itself it is not merely real but true, the truth, and that as such it is not dark and dumb but perspicuous and vocal, that it may and will therefore be received, but is independent of our actual reception, being the sovereign basis of all reception and therefore conditioning our reception but not conditioned by it. This is the third element or dimension of the event of reconciliation, the Christ event. And the third problem of the doctrine of reconciliation is to see that it is an event in this character too, and to what extent.

For all our reservations in respect of a possible misuse of the term, this might be described as the formal problem of the doctrine as distinct from the first two material problems. Its concern is with the How of the event in its inalienable distinction from the What. Its relationship to the latter is indissoluble. Revelation takes place in and with reconciliation. Indeed, the latter is also revelation. As God acts in it, He also speaks. Reconciliation is not a dark or dumb event, but a perspicuous and vocal. It is not closed in upon itself, but moves out and communicates itself It is event only as it expresses, discloses, and mediates itself, as it is not merely real but also true, and as true as it is real. Yet the relationship is indissoluble from the other side as well. Revelation takes place as the revelation of reconciliation, as the How of this What, as the self-declaration of this history, as the truth of this reality, and not otherwise. It is the predicate, the necessary determination, of this subject. But it has no independent being in face of it, and it certainly cannot take its place. Reconciliation is indeed revelation. But revelation in itself and as such, if we can conceive of such a thing, could not be reconciliation.

1. *The Third Problem of the Doctrine of Reconciliation* 9

It takes place as reconciliation takes place; as it has in it its origin, content and subject; as reconciliation is revealed and reveals itself in it.

In Jn. 1⁴ᶠ· we read concerning the Logos (who in the Prologue to John is the Revealer whose history is narrated in the Gospel and who is thus concretely the Son sent by the Father, the man Jesus): "In him was life; and the life was the light of men. And the light shineth in darkness." By ζωή R. Bultmann (*Das Ev. des Joh.*, 1950, p. 21 f.) understands "the vitality of all creation" which according to v. 3 (which tells us that "all things were made by him") has its origin in the Logos. And in what follows it is then said that in and with this life of creation light, i.e., the possibility of revelation, is given from the very first and granted to what is created. By "light" and therefore "revelation" (as the revelation of creation) there is thus understood the enlightenment of human existence in order that man should understand himself in his world and find his way without anxiety—an opportunity which is lost ("the light shineth in darkness") through the fact that he lays hold of σκοτία instead of φῶς as another possibility of self-understanding.

On this interpretation our first comment must be that in this passage darkness and light, and therefore revelation, are not described as "possibilities," and certainly not as possibilities of human "self-understanding." But it is said of light at any rate that it is a determination or character of the life which was and is in the Logos Jesus. For in the whole of John's Gospel there is no context in which the word ζωή (whether with or without αἰώνιος) can be understood of a vitality imparted to creation as such. On the contrary, ζωή is the indestructible new life which according to Jn. 5²⁶ the Son and He alone has in Himself when it is given Him by the Father, in order that He, the "bread of God," should impart it to the cosmos and humanity. According to W. Bauer (*Ev. d. Joh.*, 1908, p. 35), ζωή is "the fulness of all the benefits of salvation promised for the Messianic age." We may confidently add that as the essence of all these benefits it is reconciliation. In anticipation of 5²⁶ it is said of this even in the Prologue that in its particularity it was in Him, the Logos Jesus, who according to v. 1 was in the beginning with God and was Himself God. In the further course of the Gospel we then have the saying attributed to Jesus Himself in 11²⁵ and 14⁶: "I am the life." That it is another life which is in question is a notion which is dismissed as soon as it is raised by the differentiating expression ἡ ζωή ("this life"). "This life was the light of men." This life was and is enclosed, or rather breaks through and expresses itself, in its Bearer, as the life given to Him and in Him to the world. By its presence it speaks in and for itself. As such it is light, shining among the men to whom it is addressed, shining in their darkness. It reveals itself. For again in John's Gospel there is no passage in which φῶς could be described as a light shining from creation. According to v. 9 it lightens all men as a light which "cometh into the world" and as the "true light," i.e., as the light of the new life (τὸ φῶς τῆς ζωῆς, 8¹²). For the enlightenment of human existence in the form of a new self-understanding? Why not? Yes, indeed. But above all for the real alteration of the world and man, for his awakening to faith and love, in accordance with the fact that it causes him to recognise his justification and sanctification as they have taken place in Jesus Christ, and therefore his true life in Him, and thus to live anew in the creative power of this recognition. Yet it is not from the fact that it does and achieves all this that it has enlightening power and the dynamic of revelation, but from the fact that it proceeds from the reconciling life actualised in Jesus, that it is the light of this life. How could it help man even to the enlightenment of human existence in a new self-understanding if it were not the light of this life? What is said in Jn. 1⁴ᶠ· is that this life in its determination as light, reconciliation in its character as revelation, is outgoing and self-communicative, so that, as it has taken place in the world, it breaks out and goes into the whole world, to every man (v. 9).

§ 69. *The Glory of the Mediator*

The third problem of the doctrine of reconciliation is thus proposed and set by the simple fact that, as reconciliation takes place, it also declares itself. We may take a quick glance at the whole of the new chapter which opens up before us. The justification and sanctification of man include his vocation, as his pride and sloth also include his falsehood. The gathering and upbuilding of the community include its sending. The faith and love of the Christian include Christian hope. At the end of this third part of the doctrine of reconciliation, when it is a matter of the Christian community and the life of the individual Christian, we shall have to speak of the work of the Holy Spirit in which the event of reconciliation is concretely active and perceptible in this character of self-declaration, establishing knowledge and evoking confession. But, as already indicated, it does not have this character only when it is active and perceptible in this work and there are men whose participation is shown in the fact that they follow the calling issued to them. In itself it is the basis of knowledge even where there does not correspond to it the knowledge of a single man. It speaks, it declares and glorifies itself, it is outgoing and self-communicative, even before it attains its goal in the creaturely world in which it takes place, and to that extent without attaining it. The power with which it does attain its goal in the work of the Holy Spirit rests upon the fact that already in itself it is outgoing and self-communicative, announcing, displaying and glorifying itself. It is not merely light but the source of light. As the light of eternal life it is eternal light in the midst of the darkness of the human world which surrounds and threatens it. It is victorious and powerful even when it is only moving towards its victory. Its actual victory is accomplished in the work of the Holy Spirit. But the work of the Holy Spirit in and to the Christian community and its members, in which it is recognisable and perceptible as self-declaration in calling as well as justification and sanctification, in the sending of the Christian community into the world as well as its gathering and upbuilding, in the hope as well as the faith and love of Christians—this work of the Holy Spirit creates new facts only to the extent that the revelatory character of reconciliation is confirmed in it, and such phenomena as the knowing and confessing community, and individual Christians as its members, are introduced amongst other world phenomena, having their own basis in the revelatory character of reconciliation and to that extent in the event of reconciliation. This objectivity of even its revelatory character must be emphasised so expressly because misunderstanding can so easily creep in, as if the problem of the knowledge, understanding and explanation of reconciliation, or more generally of the doctrine of reconciliation as such, of the question how there can possibly be even the most rudimentary theology and proclamation of reconciliation, were really a problem of the theory of human knowledge and its spheres and limitations, its capacities

1. The Third Problem of the Doctrine of Reconciliation

and competencies, its possible or impossible approximation to this object. Only too easily the reference to the enlightening work of the Holy Spirit can be understood as the final and then, like a *Deus ex machina*, the very doubtful word of such a theory of knowledge. But this reference is the last word of the doctrine of reconciliation itself. It is only as such that it can be meaningful, namely, as a reference to the fact that in the power of reconciliation itself, i.e., of its character as revelation, in virtue of the self-attestation of Jesus Christ, there are world phenomena which have their basis in it. If this reference is not to be left hanging in the air, it is necessary to hold fast not only to the objectivity of reconciliation as such and its occurrence in the world, but also to the objectivity of its character as revelation, to the *a priori* nature of its light in face of all human illumination and knowledge. There is human knowledge, and a theology of reconciliation, because reconciliation in itself and as such is not only real but true, proving itself true in the enlightening work of the Holy Spirit, but first true as well as real in itself, as disclosure, declaration and impartation. This is the basis of certainty and clarity when it is a matter of the knowledge of Jesus Christ and His work through the work of the Holy Spirit. This basis, therefore, must be our opening theme. In this third part, too, we shall have to speak first of Jesus Christ, and only then of the men to whom He is Brother, Representative and Head, only then of their knowledge of Jesus Christ.

We did not complete the New Testament quotations previously adduced. 1 Tim. 2⁶ does not say of the man Jesus Christ only that as the one Mediator between God and men He gave Himself a ransom for all. Beside this statement there is placed another which obviously points to a different dimension, namely, that He gave Himself τὸ μαρτύριον καιροῖς ἰδίοις, to be a necessary witness continually speaking to His times, i.e., the times to be determined by Him. In conjunction with the δούς, therefore, we have a threefold accusative and equation : ἑαυτόν = λύτρον = μαρτύριον. The one mediatorial man is or works or acts both as ransom and witness, both as Reconciler and Revealer, and as the latter as and because He is the former. It is on the fact that Jesus is the latter, τὸ μαρτύριον, that Paul grounds the statement concerning himself in v. 7. It is because the One who accomplishes reconciliation Himself reveals Himself as such that he can say : " I am ordained a preacher (κῆρυξ), and an apostle (I speak the truth in Christ, and lie not ;) a teacher of the Gentiles in faith and verity," and, in the light of what precedes, we must add for the sake of completeness, " in the καιρὸς ἴδιος allotted to me by Him." Thus, it is first Jesus Christ Himself in His person and action who declares Himself to be the Reconciler and as such also the Revealer, and then, on the basis of the latter aspect, there is human *kerygma* and apostolate and διδασκαλία in the Gentile world.

There is an exact parallel in 2 Cor. 1²⁰ : " For all the promises of God in him, i.e., the Son of God Jesus Christ (v. 19), are yea," the Yes of God in Jesus Christ being their sum and meaning and substance. And to this there is added the decisive statement : διὸ καὶ δι' αὐτοῦ (again through Him) τὸ ἀμήν, unto the glory of God by us (the apostle). That the Yes of God is in Him is one thing. But this Yes of God spoken in Him has it in itself to be the power by which there is an Amen to the glory of God. In the Old Testament already Amen is the recognition of a word which binds and commits because it is spoken by God or in His name. Especially it is the solemn agreement in the praise of God as proclaimed and heard, e.g., in a doxology. In the primitive Christian community it seems to have been used sooner or later as a formula of liturgical acclamation by believers in confessional evocation or publication of the name of God in His great acts in Jesus Christ. We may recall the Amen and the Even so, Amen of the salutation of Revelation (1⁶ᶠ·) in response to the recollection of the love of Jesus Christ, of the deliverance effected by Him, and of the creation of the new people of God as His work, and to the announcement of His final and definitive revelation. Amen confirms the certain truth and therefore the trustworthiness of the Yes which it answers. It shows that it is revealed in its glorious majesty and authority to the one who utters it. But according to 2 Cor. 1²⁰ this response to the Yes of God spoken in Jesus Christ is not first pronounced by the world or the community or the apostle. First and properly and basically, as the presupposition of all that follows, it is pronounced by the very One in whom the Yes is also spoken. To be sure, Paul understands all his work and proclamation among the Corinthians as an Amen spoken to the glory of God. But he does not mean that he has taken it upon himself to pronounce this Amen. He is merely following the One who has pronounced it first and properly and basically with His Yes. It is from Jesus Christ Himself that it has power as pronounced by the apostle. It is because it has power from Jesus Christ that Paul can say in v. 18 : πιστὸς ὁ θεός. God Himself is the Pledge to Paul and the Corinthians that His Word among them is not both Yes and No, but an unequivocal because intrinsically certain, reliable and valid Yes. Without this presupposition neither he nor the Corinthians could be sure of his Amen. But on this presupposition they can and should be.

That we are to understand the passage in this way is shown by the remarkable " Amen (repeated in John), I say unto you " with which Jesus does not round off but precedes certain pronouncements both in the Synoptics and John. As and because it is Jesus who makes these pronouncements, Amen may be said to them from the very outset. He Himself makes them valid, and they can and should, therefore, be accepted as valid, sure and trustworthy by those who hear them. H. Schlier (in ThWNT on ἀμήν) has rightly pointed out that " all Christology is contained *in nuce* " in this formula. The Yes of Jesus demands recognition and consent on the part of those who hear it, but it does not need them to be true and valid and thus to claim recognition and agreement with absolutely compelling force. The Yes of Jesus triumphantly bears in itself the positive acceptance proper to it. It triumphantly bears in itself its own Amen. It is for this reason that it is a mighty promise awakening faith and a mighty claim demanding obedience. This is the ἐξουσία which distinguishes His teaching from that of the scribes (Mt. 7²⁹). The people are " astonished " or " startled " because His διδάσκειν, i.e., His announcement of the kingdom of God, His self-declaration as the direct attestation of its presence, His Yes, includes in itself the Amen even as and before it takes place. Hence, and in this sense, the saying : " This is my beloved Son, in whom I am well pleased ; hear ye him " (Mt. 17⁵). Hence, and in this sense, the answer of Jesus to Pilate's question whether He is a king : " Thou sayest that I am a king " (Jn. 18³⁷). But then He adds : " To this end was I born, and for this cause came I into the world, that I should bear witness unto the truth," and in Jn. 14⁶ this is accentuated and sharpened by the declaration : " I am (as the way and the life, so also) the truth." And there is the same accentuation in Rev. 3¹⁴ where Jesus Christ is described as the One who not only speaks Himself the Amen to the Yes actualised in Him, but is Himself, not τὸ but ὁ ἀμήν, *the* Amen, and in this totality " the faithful (i.e., trustworthy) and true witness "—this is where we found the title for the present chapter—and to that extent *the* Apostle (Heb. 3¹) and Prophet (Jn. 6¹⁴).

It is against this background that we may see how even in the early Church

1. The Third Problem of the Doctrine of Reconciliation

the classical doctrine of the *munus duplex* of Jesus Christ, of the twofold form of reconciliation, came to be deepened, and there was asserted a third orientation of the event of reconciliation in Christ and therefore in its totality. Even the Johannine triad already mentioned (Jn. 14⁶), and the declaration of 1 Cor. 1³⁰ that Christ is made unto us wisdom and righteousness and sanctification, must surely have caused them to consider whether Jesus Christ the High-priest and King, the Lord who became a Servant and the Servant who became a Lord, should not also be regarded, in a full evaluation of this being and work of His as very God and man, as " the Amen, the faithful and true witness," the Revealer and Guarantor of His own reality and therefore of the salvation of man and the glory of God ; whether a decisive feature in the portrayal of the event attested in the Old and New Testament witness is not overlooked or obscured, and a decisive question of Christian knowledge suspiciously left open, if it is not seen and formally stated that the Lord and Servant in whom the divine act of atonement takes place is not also the One who declares, makes known and reveals this act and therefore Himself to the community and the world; whether all clear and certain knowledge of this event, all human perception of God grounded upon it, is not primarily His own work and gift no less than the justification of man before God and his sanctification for Him, namely, the work and gift of his calling, as also based upon it. We may refer to Col. 2³ : " In whom are hid all the treasures of wisdom and knowledge." To the indwelling πλήρωμα τῆς θεότητος of which we read in the parallel verse in Col. 2⁹, does there belong only the material fact that He is made unto us justification and sanctification (or in Johannine language that He is the way and the life), and not also the formal fact that He is the truth, that He is made unto us wisdom ? In the decisive context of Jn. 1¹ᶠ· is there not said of Jesus the highly singular thing that as the One whose history the Gospel narrates He is the Logos, the Word, the Revealer of God, that He does not merely become this subsequently in time but is it in the eternity of God Himself, and that as such He has come into the world and been made flesh ?

It is surely because of the actual pressure of such questions that in the 4th century (as first appears in Eusebius of Caesarea, *Ev. dem.*, IV, 15 etc., and then in the 5th century in Petrus Chrysologus, *Sermo* 54) mention is made of a threefold office, Christ being not only Priest and King but also, in the express words of Jn. 6¹⁴, " that prophet that should come into the world." The bringing together of these three functions and titles was not new in itself. Josephus referred to them as the τρία κρατιστεύοντα with reference to the Maccabean hero John Hyrcanus (*Bell. jud.*, 1, 2, 8), probably on the basis of an older Jewish tradition which as *tertium comparationis* could hardly have before it anything but the fact that the dignity and authority of these three theocratic offices in the Old Testament may be traced back to a common anointing. In introducing the threefold scheme Christian theology seems formally to have linked it with the title of Jesus as Christ, the Anointed of God. Yet it is to be noted that in the Cyrilline anathemas of the Council of Ephesus (431) it is obviously not in any connexion with the name of Christ as such, but in dependence on Heb. 3¹, that Jesus is called the ἀρχιερεὺς καὶ ἀπόστολος τῆς ὁμολογίας ἡμῶν (*can.* 10). The threefold schema did not by any means secure general adoption in the early and mediaeval Church. That it was known appears from the reference in Thomas Aquinas (*S. theol.*, III, qu. 22, art. 1, ad 3) : *alius est legislator et alius sacerdos et alius rex ; sed haec omnia concurrunt in Christo tanquam in fonte omnium gratiarum.* But there is no development in Thomas or elsewhere of what is meant by the *legislatio* of Christ as a form of the reconciling grace revealed in Him.

Proper weight was given to this third element in the Christ occurrence and the occurrence of reconciliation only in the theology of the Reformation, or more precisely in the later editions of Calvin's *Institutio* (11, 15) and his *Catechism* (39 and 44, cf. *Heidelberg Catechism*, Qu. 31-32).

§ 69. *The Glory of the Mediator*

Calvin had found it in the theological tradition from which he derived (*sub papatu*), but it had been conceived and presented only *frigide nec magno cum fructu*. His desire was to bring it to light in a completely different way. As he saw it, in Jesus Christ we have to do with the *lux intelligentiae* expected in the Old Testament, as in the confession of the Samaritan woman in Jn. 4^{25}: "I know that Messias cometh, which is called Christ: when he is come, he will tell us all things (ἅπαντα ἀναγγελεῖ)." In distinction from all other teachers, Jesus received and enjoyed the prophetic Spirit in fulness, and that not only for Himself but for His own, for the life of His whole earthly body the Church. He is the revelation of truth in which all prophecy has reached its goal and beside which there can be no other. *En descendant au monde il a été Messager et Ambassadeur souverain de Dieu son Père, pour exposer pleinement la volonté d'iceluy au monde . . . pour être Maître et Docteur des siens*, with the object *de nous introduire à la vraie cognoissance du Père et de sa vérité tellement que nous soyons écoliers domestiques de Dieu*, the Heidelberg Catechism also adding: "That I also may confess his name."

This doctrine of the *munus Christi propheticum*, and therefore of a *munus triplex Christi*, then made its way into Lutheran theology, though hesitantly and with some degree of incompatibility, as already mentioned. It is also found, its introduction obviously corresponding to a generally perceived necessity, in the *Cat. Romanus* (1566, Qu. 194 f.), and more recently it has been adopted by J. M. Scheeben and all subsequent dogmaticians as a well-established element in Roman Catholic theology, Scheeben grudgingly but openly admitting (*Handb. der kath. Dogm.*, 1925, Vol. 3, p. 268) that Protestants had given a lead in this respect, though clearly with the evil intention of ascribing revelation to Jesus Christ alone.

In relation not only to Lutheran and Roman Catholic but also the older Reformed theology (including Calvin), the question can and must be asked, however, to what degree the meaning, importance and relevance of this newly discovered or rediscovered third problem of the doctrine of reconciliation are really grasped and brought out either then or more recently. For in detail there seem to be all kinds of obscurities.

After the example of Calvin, the development of this problem usually preceded that of the other two. In the sense of the ἀμὴν λέγω ὑμῖν of the Gospels, this could draw attention to the fact that everything subsequently said from the other two standpoints had *a priori* certainty from the fact that it is attested and guaranteed by Jesus Christ Himself. But neither Calvin nor any of his successors based the precedence given to the *munus propheticum* upon this. Yet the element of uncertainty regarding the interrelating of the prophetic and other offices could have unhappy consequences. What was supposed to be the theme and content of the prophetic or revelatory action of Jesus Christ? At this point Calvin spoke of the will and truth of the Father and Wolleb (*Chr. Theol. comp.*, 1624, I, 17, 2) referred briefly to *veritas coelestis*. In the Heidelberg Catechism (Qu. 31) it is explained that it is a matter of "the secret will and counsel of God concerning our redemption," and in the *Syntagma* of Polanus (1610, VI, 29) it is stated even more explicitly to be a matter of the true doctrine of eternal salvation, the distinction of the true God from false gods, the indication of the right way to be taken by believers, supremely by the revelation of the Gospel, but also by the true exposition of the Law and the prophesying of things to come. In the *Synopsis* of F. Burmann (1678, V, 12) it is emphasised that what are at issue are the *verba Dei, quae Deum Deique Filium solum proloqui fas est*, and materially the revelation of the whole mystery of redemption. These are the kind of formulations which are given, and they can and must be interpreted *in meliorem* and even *in optimam partem*. The more strongly it was underlined, as by Polanus and many others, that the prophecy or teaching of Jesus Christ is primarily that of the Gospel, the closer was the approximation

1. *The Third Problem of the Doctrine of Reconciliation* 15

to the real heart of the matter. But already in the *Leidener Synopsis* (1624, 26, 39 f.) there is another note : that it is a matter of *veritas legalis et evangelica*, and this is also found in F. Turrettini (*Theol. el.*, 1682, XIV, 7, 5) toward the end of the century. Did this kind of expression denote a real grasp of the subject, or a reference to the self-revelation of Jesus Christ ? Was there not the danger that along the lines of the doubtful expression of Thomas Aquinas Jesus Christ would be primarily understood as *legislator*, i.e., as the authentic exponent of the divine Law and perhaps of general divine law, or more radically as the Revealer, not of Himself in His actuality, nor of the history of reconciliation enacted in Him, but of a principle and system of divine truth with saving significance for man, in which a place could also be found for what had to be said concerning the high-priestly and kingly offices ? The possibility might present itself —indeed, it had been already grasped in the 16th century in the Unitarian theology and church founded by Faustus Socinius, and it was later seized again by the Christian Enlightenment—to gather together the one and total function of Jesus Christ in His prophetic office of witness and teaching, to understand the historical being and work of the Mediator as merely the manifestation, declaration and exemplification of a timeless idea of reconciliation as the true *veritas coelestis*, and thus in short to substitute a Gospel *of* Jesus Christ for the Gospel concerning Him. Self-evidently this was not what Calvin and his Reformed and Lutheran successors had in view. But we can and must say that in their exposition there were no adequate safeguards against this final result.

A second uncertainty arose out of the lack of clarity concerning the inner relationship of the revelation of Jesus Christ and His work. This emerged in the preponderant tendency to understand the relationship of the three mediatorial functions *e ratione executionis*, i.e., as that of different stages in the course of the history of Jesus, and therefore in a historical framework. First, He acted as Prophet in His proclamation of the kingdom of God in Galilee and Jerusalem, then as High-priest in His death and passion, finally as King in His resurrection and ascension. This is the way in which it is presented by Wendelin (*Chr. Theol.*, 1634, I, 17, 3). But in this construction the unity of the event of reconciliation is obscured by the specific actual significance of the individual elements. And if the *munus propheticum* is only the first stage in the history of Jesus, followed by His action in the *munus sacerdotale* and *regium*, it is put in the shade by their superior light as in a sense provisional, and cannot therefore receive the justice due to it. That this problem was perceived is clear from the distinction made by H. Heidegger (*Medulla*, 1696, 19, 19) that, while this sequence is true *ordine executionis* (historically), yet *ordine intentionis* the work of Christ in the *munus propheticum* derives from and follows what He does in the *munus regium* and *sacerdotale*. The reason for this distinction is clear enough, but we are not shown in what sense there is supposed to be an *ordo executionis* which is so very different from the *ordo intentionis*, or in what sense or with what justification the idea of *ordo* (with its necessary ranking) is introduced at all. Is this really necessary or possible as between the reality of Jesus Christ as Servant and Lord and its character as truth ? But it is in the same historical abstraction that the Roman Catholic J. Pohle (*Lehrb. d. Dogm.*, Vol. II, 1903, p. 223 f.) understands the teaching office of Jesus Christ, and he does not even see the necessity to make the reservation attempted by Heidegger.

A third question concerns the way in which Jesus Christ is said to be the " chief Prophet and Teacher " (*Heidelberg Catechism*, Qu. 31, with a verbal parallel in the *Cat. Rom.*, I, 3, 7 : the *summus propheta et magister*). What is meant by the superlatives used at this point by the Roman Catholics, e.g., F. Diekamp (*Kath. Dogm.*, Vol. II, 1930, p. 333 f.) when he says that the teaching office is supreme because grounded on the fullest knowledge and exercised most fully and with supreme authority ? Calvin had said much more succinctly that He is the Bearer of the only revelation, in and with which all others are

§ 69. *The Glory of the Mediator*

superfluous, and Polanus had said more precisely that in His Word a distinction is made between God and idols. All the older Protestants expressed themselves to the same effect, and in the Roman Catholic dogmatics quoted Christ is " our only Teacher to whom the prophets point and from whom all the teachers commissioned by Him derive," B. Bartmann (*Lehrb. d. Dogm.*, Vol. II, 1928, p. 377 f.) describing Him as the " only Prophet " and " absolute Teacher." But were the older Protestant orthodox sure of their ground in this respect ? And can we say of the Roman Catholic theologians that their *summus* really means *unicus* ? How did it come about that so zealous a Reformed teacher as J. Piscator, on the very first page of his aphorisms on Calvin's *Institutio* (1589), could interpret the doctrine of the Genevan master to the effect that, as proved by the fact of heathen religions and the direct terror of man at thunder and lightning, there is a *cognitio naturalis*, i.e., *hominum mentibus a natura insita*, a direct revelation of at least the Creator and of our obligation to honour Him ? How did it come about that at the time of transition from the 17th to the 18th century it proved so easy, even in Protestantism, formally to set alongside or before the theology supposedly based upon revelation a natural theology ? And what are we to make of the loud protestations of Roman Catholic theologians when they have always so self-evidently reckoned with a twofold revelation and knowledge of God ? It is for this reason that Scheeben, rightly from his own standpoint, takes such offence that at this point Protestants seem to be trying to describe Jesus Christ—if only they had done it with more power and consistency !—as the only Revealer of God. The general question must be put whether in the determination to bring to light the *munus Christi propheticum* the cost was really counted or the deductions were considered which must follow if such great utterances are made with genuine seriousness.

A fourth complex of questions is opened up by the definite statement of Calvin that Jesus Christ has received the dignity and commission of the prophetic office not merely for His own person but for His whole body the Church. In exposition of this statement the later Reformed dogmaticians (e.g., the *Leidener Synopsis*, 26, 39, 41) liked to distinguish between His direct exercise of this office by Himself (*per seipsum*) and His indirect through others (*per alios administros verbi sui*), i.e., through the prophets and apostles. How are we to understand this ? We must first ask whether the distinction between *per seipsum* and *per alios* is really possible. Even in the Old and New Testaments, is there really any utterance of Christ *per seipsum* which is not also *per alios* ? Surely He causes Himself to be heard only in the witness of Scripture and its proclamation, and not otherwise. Conversely, is not His whole utterance *per alios* true and authoritative only in virtue of the fact that in this mediation He speaks *per seipsum* ? How could or would the witness of Scripture and its proclamation be true and powerful if He did not cause Himself to be heard in it ? Yet at a pinch we might well have come to an understanding with the older dogmaticians on this point. More serious is the question whether they were right, and especially the Reformed, when they tried to think of the prophecy of Jesus Christ as limited to the Old and New Testament witnesses. The Lutherans (e.g., J. Gerhard, *Loci*, 1610, IV, 322) spoke more freely of the indirect transmission of the prophetic work of Christ in the ministry of the apostles and their successors. Confessional polemics played an open part in the restriction characteristic of the Reformed in the 17th century (cf. *Leidener Synopsis, loc. cit.*). Since only the biblical prophets and apostles can be considered as *administri* of the Prophet Jesus Christ, the *Ecclesia Dei* rejects (*repudiat*) *omnes traditiones quae sacro Codice non continentur*. On this point it is to be observed that the unique dignity of the sacred book consists in the fact that in it and it alone we have the original attestation of the being and action of Jesus Christ as the presupposition of all further proclamation by the Church. Yet there can be no question of the Church rejecting all traditions, its task being to test them by the standard of the

1. The Third Problem of the Doctrine of Reconciliation 17

prophetico-apostolic witness, to weigh their conformity to Scripture, which will not always lead to their total repudiation. The older Dutch who spoke in this way did not really reject all traditions themselves; indeed, at Dort they quite freely added to the old some new ones. And can we truly maintain that only the biblical prophets and apostles are the body which has a part in the office of its Head? A formally parallel question has also to be put to Roman Catholic dogmatics. This recognised and recognises only too well the participation of the Church, and therefore not merely of the prophets and apostles, in the teaching office of Christ. By this J. Pohle (*loc. cit.*) understands the following. At Pentecost Christ instituted the Church as an institution for teaching the truth and imparted to it the Holy Spirit as the Spirit of truth. The infallibility of the Church and Papacy thus rests upon the prophetic ministry of Christ as the infallible Teacher of truth. The teaching office of the Church mediates the full and total truth. Beyond it there can be no spiritual or future " Johannine " Church. Exercising divine authority with the corresponding direct ability, it already possesses all the gifts most adapted to counter its enemies. This view raises the question whether a genuine participation of the Church in the teaching office of Christ can or should imply that its utterances are distinguished by an authority and infallibility similar to those of the Word of Jesus Christ Himself. How, as His body, as His earthly form of existence, did it acquire this similarity of its own function with His? Even though there is this participation, why must it be all or nothing? Is it not enough that it should modestly and penitently and teachably serve Him in the appropriate secondariness of its authority and the obvious and avowed fallibility of its human word? We have also to ask how the assumption is reached that the body which participates in the teaching office of Jesus Christ is limited to the bearers of the ecclesiastical teaching office represented in the Papacy, being restricted to these particular members of the body. Is not the ministry of proclamation, as the concrete form of this participation, the commission, the privilege and the task to be responsibly accepted and humbly executed by the whole community? These Reformed and Roman Catholic constrictions are finely broken through in the statement of the *Heidelberg Catechism* (*Qu.* 32) to the effect that I and not merely the prophets and apostles or a teaching clergy show myself to be a Christian in the fact that " by faith I am a member of Christ, and thus a partaker of His anointing ; in order that I also may confess His name," no one being either excluded or self-excluded. At the end of the century of orthodoxy this statement and the insight which it expresses do seem to have been occasionally accepted by the Reformed, as, for example, when we read that *ex participatione unctionis* all Christians are prophets in appropriation of the Word of God, in the study of Scripture, in the testing of spirits, but also in the instruction of neighbours and courageous witness (P. van Mastricht, *Theor. pract. Theol.*, 1698, V, 6, 26).

A fifth and final question raised but not unequivocally answered by Calvin's restatement is to whom Jesus Christ the Reconciler is really speaking when He is also the Revealer. Calvin's unhesitating answer in *Qu.* 39 of his *Catechism* is that as the sovereign Messenger of God He addresses Himself to the world. Polanus also spoke of His proclamation to the world (*loc. cit.*), and in the same sense J. Wolleb spoke of *totus terrarum orbis* (*loc. cit.*, 19, 6). The same teaching is found in the *Cat. Romanus* (*loc. cit.*): *cuius doctrina orbis terrarum Patris coelestis cognitionem accepit*, as also in the *Theol. did. pol.* (1685) of the Lutheran Quenstedt (III, *c.* 3, 2, sect. 1, *th.* 10), where he says that it is addressed to *omnes et singulos homines, nemine excluso*, and again in *th.* 13, where he tells us that what is at issue is *omnium hominum ad coelestis veritatis agnitionem perductio*. Rather strangely, in *Qu.* 44 of his *Catechism* Calvin also describes Christ as merely the Teacher and Master of His own people. In Wolleb, too, the circle of those instructed by Him is restricted to the *electi* (I, 17, 9), and the *Leidener Synopsis* states emphatically that His Word is addressed only to " His people "

§ 69. *The Glory of the Mediator*

(26, 39). The common rule of the Reformed is to speak indefinitely of " us " as those with whom Jesus Christ has dealings in His prophetic Word. The question is thus posed which of the two understandings we are to follow. Now obviously they are not mutually exclusive as such. We should be happy to think that what is meant is that the Word of Christ applies to " us " the elect, the people of God, as the community of witnesses summoned to proclaim it in the world. But unfortunately this was quite definitely not the meaning of our fathers when in respect of the relationship of the Prophet Jesus Christ to the world they fairly quickly showed themselves to have such strange reservations. They rightly maintained (e.g., Polanus, VI, 29) that by the prophecy of Christ there is to be understood not merely the external *promulgatio veritatis divinae* but also the *interna unctio cordium per Spiritum sanctum*. This being the case, their doctrine of double predestination necessarily acted as a barrier between the people of God, as the elect and exclusive recipients of the witness of the Spirit, and the world. As Christ did not die for all men, in the full sense His Word does not go out to all but only to " us " the elect. As Prophet, too, Christ is and acts only *intra muros*. If this conception had to be accepted, the doctrine of His third office could only end in a blind alley. If we take seriously the fact that the *officium mediatorium* of Jesus Christ, the act of reconciliation accomplished in Him, has this third dimension, then in this connexion, too, we must consider that in sending Him God loved the world and that in Him He has reconciled the world to Himself, so that the specific history of those who hear the voice of the Good Shepherd as distinct from others cannot be the final end of His prophetic work, but can be fulfilled only in the special existence and history of the people of God, i.e., in what Paul calls in 2 Cor. 5¹⁸ the διακονία τῆς καταλλαγῆς. Jesus Christ speaks to this people with the intention and commission that it for its part should speak to the world, that it should be His messenger within it. In fact, Calvin and his disciples were so hampered by their fatal dogma that they were no longer or not yet able to perceive this. But it is comforting and instructive to say that in impulse at least they obviously show signs of looking in this direction.

To ask these questions is not to belittle the significance of this powerful attempt at dogmatic reconstruction which was so influential for contemporary theology, nor to evade the debt of gratitude which we owe to Calvin in particular. There can be no question of trying to resurrect the older doctrine of the *munus Christi propheticum*. Its limitations are obvious, and at all the points mentioned we must carefully and respectfully but boldly and resolutely transcend them. Yet the biblical and then the material considerations with which we have opened this introductory sub-section have shown us that the doctrine of the *munus propheticum*, whatever we may think of the form in which it was presented and asserted, does at least point us to an element in the event of reconciliation which demands individual treatment. It is thus necessary, and will be well worth while, freely to make the same attempt.

We conclude this introduction with a historical consideration. Is it an accident that on the threshold of the modern epoch, which is new even from the standpoint of Christianity, the Church and theology, there should have been this restoration of the doctrine of the *munus Christi propheticum* ? It may well be that in taking up the third problem of the doctrine of reconciliation we are impelled, not merely by reasons of timeless academic accuracy, correctness and completeness, but by concern with a question which has been forced upon us by the historical development of especially the last 450 years, and which a modern theology cannot ignore because it is inescapably presented to it in the destinies, happenings and forms of the modern Church.

From the standpoint of Christianity, the Church and theology, the centuries since the Renaissance and the accompanying Reformation have been and are

1. The Third Problem of the Doctrine of Reconciliation 19

a period of deep shadow. To be sure, the shadow is no greater than that of later antiquity and the Dark and Middle Ages, but it is of a different kind. It must certainly be seen and said that the new element in the modern period, and therefore the distinctive characteristic of the shadow now cast over the whole sphere of Christianity, the Church and theology, did not become visible and effective at a single stroke at the beginning of the 16th century. Intimations of many kinds were not lacking in the later and even the earlier Middle Ages. But the modern epoch is distinguished from those which precede by the fact that certain tendencies which were previously latent, isolated and in the main suppressed have now become increasingly patent, general and dominating. To what do we refer? To take one example, the Church in the modern period has slowly but relentlessly lost its position in the world in the form in which it could previously enjoy it. Perhaps this is because, quite apart from the schism between East and West, in the 16th century it split up even in the West into four different groupings and later into hundreds. Perhaps it is because from the 16th century onwards ostensibly Christian Europe has been brought into increasingly direct contact with the far more numerous non-Christian multitudes of the far West and East, and has found its faith set in co-existence with a plenitude of alien religions, so that not only is the self-evident absoluteness of its Christianity brought under suspicion, but it is subjected to the temptation of recalling pagan possibilities not long since and not very radically discarded. Perhaps it is because —and this is usually regarded as the first impulse—from the beginning of the 16th century, partly under the influence of the rediscovery of ancient Greece, partly under that of the astonishing advances in natural and historical science, and above all under that of technology, it has itself begun to fashion a human awareness and self-understanding based on the autonomy of general reason and even of the individual. More and more the Church has come up against the self-consciousness of modern national and regional powers with a totally new claim to sovereignty, against a modern society recognising and proclaiming its own laws and following its own aspirations, against a modern philosophy, science, literature, art and economics which not only maintain their own particular freedoms and rights against it but silently exercise them without asking any questions. Under the influence and pressure of all these elements and factors in the outside world it has found itself, first imperceptibly and then more and more obviously, thrust aside and pushed into a corner or ghetto. To the more or less educated élite it has become more and more of an offence, or folly, or at any rate an object of mildly tolerant indifference. And to a large extent it has been completely lost to sight by the masses, externally as well as internally. If the consciousness of its irresistibly dwindling or long since forfeited position of religious, spiritual, moral and political power still lingers on in public life, it is either in the form of dangerous recollections of abuses of this power—horrific pictures which provide easy justification both for a pathetic hostility to the Church and an increasing flight from it—or in the clever use which remaining reactionary movements in the state or society are still, and sometimes in quite new ways, able to make of it, to the great hurt of its own cause. And the Church itself seems gradually to have been narrowed down to a difficult choice. It might try to fight for the maintenance or restoration of its vanishing respect and influence with more or less suitable weapons, often in a blind and unfortunate alliance with those reactionary forces. Or it might take the way obviously suggested by these developments and retreat to the reservations of a self-satisfying religiosity, whether in the form of the varied practice of individual piety, renewed or newly discovered liturgics, or dogmatic castles in the air. Or it might accept the increasing secularism on an optimistic interpretation, taking it up into its own self-understanding, working away so critically at the Bible, tradition and the creeds as to appear to be in harmony with the progressive spirit of the age, to justify modern man and to offer to the adult world a suitably adult form of Christianity, thus exposing all the more obviously and palpably the alienation of the life of modern man from that of the Church and *vice versa*. The outbursts of lamentation or scorn which this situation has almost continuously evoked from Christians and non-Christians since the 17th century are only too familiar. Each generation has repeated them as if it were the first to discover the great *diastasis* which is their theme. We shall refrain from adding fresh strophes. But we must soberly face up to the facts. The modern period is in fact the period of Church history upon which the shadow of this *diastasis* lies.

The only thing is that we must not overlook another feature of the situation. It is not at all the case that in these last centuries Christianity has found itself only in the state of this constriction and the execution of these measures of defence, or insulations, or compromises, or apparent truces. There are gloomy and sceptical as well as naive and sanguine falsifications of history, and we should be guilty of such if we were to overlook the fact that most paradoxically the modern period has also seen an original and spontaneous penetration of the world by the Christian community unparalleled in any of the vaunted or criticised periods which precede it. Nor can this process be facilely compared to the despairing sally or counter-attack of a hopelessly beleaguered garrison, and thus explained as one of the phenomena of constriction. On the contrary, the very period when Christianity has been subject to the constriction, and its situation has often enough been very like that of a closely invested fortress, has also been the scene of an awakening which has not been dictated by its enemies, which has been highly original, in which it has shown a new awareness, hardly paralleled since the first centuries, of its commission to the world and mission within it, and in which it has stirred itself in the most different forms to do justice to it. How curious it is that so learned and perspicacious a man as E. Hirsch, in his depiction of recent Evangelical theology, should have succeeded in missing altogether this aspect of the matter and representing it as the history of an unbroken retreat into a kind of Indian reservation!

That Christianity has to say to the world around something strange, unknown and supremely necessary; that it has to pass on to it a message; that it is not there for itself alone but has the responsibility towards those without of confronting them with the Gospel in order that they may participate in the salvation which it thinks or is certain that it has itself; that it owes it to the Lord in whom it in some sense believes, and whom it well or badly confesses, to attest Him to the forces which rule this aeon, all this was a concept which did to some degree move the Christian Middle Ages but was for the most part marginal. There was little room for it in practice, for the mediaeval Church, confined to Western and Central Europe, lived with the surrounding world in the happy illusion that it constituted a *corpus christianum* or Christian world, and could have very little awareness of the existence of a non-Christian world, and therefore of a genuine encounter of the Gospel and man. Since all those in known proximity were supposedly within, there could not really be any who were without. It is true that on the southern and eastern borders of this geographical, political and spiritual kingdom, account had to be taken of Islam standing threateningly *ante portas*, but this problem was easily settled by leaving the border skirmishes *ex officio* to the mendicant orders, when they were not undertaken with the sword. Again, if pagan elements still lived on in the ostensibly Christian European under the cover and guarantee of the sacramental institution, e.g., in the actuality of his private or public life and his conception of right and wrong, which were hardly or not at all affected by the Gospel, or in the practical atheism of both great and small, both rulers and the masses ruled by them, cheap compensations could always be found in persecuting the Albigenses and sporadically the Jews. Even in its own sphere, in its cultus and organisation, in its financial and territorial economy, in its very teaching and preaching and

1. The Third Problem of the Doctrine of Reconciliation

to the very core of its noblest mysticism, did not the Church itself live by innumerable compromises in which the laws and customs of the old aeon maintained an accepted balance against the new aeon of the Jesus Christ venerated in the sacrament of the altar? Was not the whole idea and practice of the *corpus christianum* that of this static counterpoise? We cannot deny that in its own way mediaeval Christianity did believe in the reconciliation of the world with God and therefore in Jesus Christ as its Lord. But in what sense did it do so when it could acquiesce in this counterpoise and accept the continuance and existence of the sacred and secular orders and separations as then established?

The *diastasis* between the Church and the world inaugurated or revealed with the dawn of the modern age has put an end to this state of balance. The outward aspect of the process has been the emancipation of the world from the Church in a whole series of gentle or more violent but ever-increasing disruptions in which the secular world has discovered or rediscovered secularism and successfully attempted to use it, thus turning its back on the Church with which it had contracted that doubtful union in the Middle Ages. It found that it could do this; that it was not committed to the Church in any deep sense; that it had not really adopted the cause which it represented or the Gospel which it preached. What human hands had built, they could pull down again. But this is not the only aspect of the matter. For in the developing *diastasis* inaugurated in the 16th century the Church was not merely an object which was released from that union and forced out of the position of power previously held by it. As this took place, it made its own counter-movement of a very different and positive character, not repaying in kind the rejection, indifference or hostility which it met with, but making a radically new approach to the world, not on the illusory basis of the assumption that it formed a unity or totality with it, but on that of the assumption that it belonged to it in its antithesis to it, and that in its very distinction it could not meet it with indifference or hostility but only with the deepest solidarity and commitment. It is a remarkable coincidence that at the very time and in the very situation when the secular world began to free itself from the Church, the Church began, not to free itself from, but to be unmistakeably free for the secular world, namely, free for the service to its own cause within the secular world which for so long it had for the most part neglected in pursuit of its own fantasies. Which came first, and which followed? May it be that the state, society, culture, the modern man, had first to escape that connexion in order that the Church should finally be set at the distance from the secular world which it needs to perform the service to its own cause within the secular world, and which it so critically lacked in the Middle Ages? Had the world first to become mature in order that in its own way the Church should become mature in a positive sense, achieving an awareness of its own mission in the antithesis and the capacity for its responsible discharge? For our own purpose, however, we need not disentangle what took place, and still takes place, *hominum confusione*, and what *Dei providentia*. It is enough that in these centuries when an unprofitable union with the world has been broken a materially profitable encounter with the world has been achieved. In and with the constriction, and in spite of all the errors of which it has been guilty in what has transpired, the Church's mainly static being and attitude to the outside world has been changed into a dynamic. Certainly, there have been definite limitations in its own insight, volition and achievement. But the fact and the inner necessity of this transformation can be no more ignored than the more striking events which have come upon it during this period in the form of painful rejections, repulsions and humiliations.

In and with the beginning of the great renaissance of paganism, it took place (1) that, very definitely in certain places, although not universally, the Church again took on the form of a Church of the Word. That is, it took on the

§ 69. *The Glory of the Mediator*

form of a Church reformed both by and for the Word of God ; of a confessing Church, i.e., of a Church confessing Jesus Christ and the knowledge of Jesus Christ, and doing this directly and indirectly before civil rulers and in face of the great and very greatest secular authorities ; of a Church fearlessly publicising throughout Europe the name and kingdom and will of its Lord. *Et loquebar de testimoniis tuis in conspectu regum et non confundebar*, was quoted from Ps. 119[46] on the title page of the *Augsburg Confession* in a wholly new consciousness of Christian duty and therefore a wholly new self-consciousness. It was the weak voice of Melanchthon which was heard in this document. But it sounded out loud and clear. Nor was it meant to be the mere expression of human caprice ; it rested on the basis of the new outgoing of the Gospel itself which Luther so often described as the meaning, justification and glory of his work. What gave a distinctive impetus to the whole 16th century Reformation both in its origins and development was that at least the responsible champions of that part of Christianity associated with it believed that they could and should address their contemporaries on the basis of a prior address to themselves by the Lord of the Church and the world as newly recognised in His sovereignty, being free both in face of them but also on their behalf as those who were themselves made free, i.e., free for preaching and teaching. They had something to say to them as the Bible almost spontaneously opened up before them and spoke to them concerning the justification and sanctification of sinful man and the reconciliation of the world with God as it had been accomplished in Jesus Christ, thus claiming the ministry of their lips to challenge accepted Christianity and the supposed Christian West with enlightening, renewing, penetrating and transforming force, demanding and creating a new being in and with Christ. This was how the Reformation spoke to European man at the very time when he was in process of awakening to a new awareness of his secularity. Where had it ever been seen or said or felt or experienced or expressed to this degree, not merely in the Middle Ages but even in the early Church, that everything depends wholly and utterly upon the Word which goes out from the God who acts graciously towards man in Jesus Christ and which is received, appropriated, proclaimed and heard as such, that this Word alone is comfort, direction, help and strength and hope in life and death, whether for individuals or their common life ? The modern man was already born, but he was still sleeping in his cradle, when this took place in the Reformation. And for all the confusion in the later development or failure of the Reformation, the man who then arose was not left to his own devices but was confronted by a witness which, whether he realised it or not, transcended his whole movement of revolt and remained in spite of all the resentment or accusation which led him to oppose or ignore the Church, because, far from being affected by this, it posed and answered the question which, whether he liked it or not, was necessarily put to him, the great hero of this emancipation and secularisation. The remarkable penetration effected at the Reformation has never been reversed. The existence of a community of the Word cannot be erased even in the history of the modern world, whether by its contradiction or silence, or by the weakness, ineptitude, disunity, corruption or baseness of its representatives.

No less noteworthy is (2) the fact that, in movements which were isolated and slow at first but have since become more rapid and general, the new age of apparent Christian regression has become an age of Christian missions unparalleled since the days of the apostles and the time of the christianisation of Europe (which extended well into the Middle Ages in the North and East).

The beginnings of new missionary activity are not to be traced to the Reformation itself, but to a much earlier epoch in the mediaeval Church. They coincided with the frontier struggles against Islam to which we have already alluded, and were conducted by the institutionally commissioned and prepared Franciscans and Dominicans in campaigns which found their literary result in works like the

1. The Third Problem of the Doctrine of Reconciliation 23

Summa contra gentiles of Thomas Aquinas. In practice some of the representatives of the movement carried it far beyond the immediate front of "infidels," for at the time of Mongol dominion in China in 1307 there had been established in Peking under John of Monte Corvino a Catholic diocese of 30,000 souls, although, like the flourishing Nestorian foundation of the 8th century, this disappeared in a comparatively short space of time with the repulse of the Mongols. The discoveries and conquests of the later 15th and early 16th centuries summoned the mendicants to fresh endeavour. They followed the Portuguese to West Africa and the East Indies, and the Spanish to the West Indies, Mexico and South America. Much might be said about the doubtful nature of their spirit and methods in these enterprises. But the simple and spontaneous way in which they engaged in them calls for notice. The resumption of the Mohammedan mission was the original intention behind the foundation of a new order by Ignatius Loyola, though it did not find practical realisation. But Francis Xavier (1509-1552) belonged to the original circle, and what was undoubtedly in its way a genuine missionary impulse and enthusiasm carried him beyond India, Ceylon and the Celebes to Japan (1549), where his followers not only succeeded in winning 600,000 souls for the Church, but brought the Church to political power after the western fashion, even introducing the Inquisition and engaging in organised persecutions of Buddhists, until a radically new chapter opened in the middle of the 17th century. In the ensuing reaction, this Japanese Church produced some staunch martyrs, and remnants lingered on and were rediscovered around 1860. We may thus see that there was not a complete lack of genuine Christian substance in this early effort. Mission, as later taken up by other orders and after 1622 centralised in the special college *De propaganda fide*, has been and is an integrating element in the activities and organisation of the modern Roman Catholic Church. There are obvious objections both to its aims on the one side (its unfortunate confusion of its own cause and honour and power with those of God) and its methods on the other (the distinctively aggressive and superficial nature of its recruitment). But more relevant is the fact that in the modern period, however well or badly, the Roman Catholic Church has also and primarily been a missionary Church, and this far more radically even to-day than the Protestant Churches. This fact throws light on the inner necessity with which modern Christianity, externally attacked and constricted, has also engaged in an original and spontaneous outward movement.

The tardiness of the Reformation Churches in this sphere has often been asserted and deplored. Most surprisingly, these Churches of the Word did not at first, or for a long time afterwards, perceive the opportunity of mission offered by the new discoveries and conquests. Neither on Luther nor Melanchthon, Zwingli nor Calvin, did any deep impression seem to be made by the opening of these doors or the immediate efforts of Rome to pass through them. In explanation, it may be pointed out that the states which accepted the Reformation had no control of the sea-power which was the indispensable technical presupposition of the Roman missions. It may also be argued that the Reformation Churches were so preoccupied with the new and original content of the Word of God and the renewal of the Western Christianity ostensibly before them that in the first instance they had necessarily to stay behind as the Romans confidently launched out across the seas with their Paternoster and Ave Maria, their rigid identification of the Church and the kingdom of God, and their optimistic assurance as to the undeniable correlation of nature and grace, of the old man and aeon and the new. The only trouble is that, even if the time for missionary activity had not yet come for these or similar reasons, there was not even the realisation of the duty of mission. A virtue was made of necessity, and it was explained that the missionary command was given only to the apostles, and had long since been fulfilled by them. Thus the heathenism of the heathen

§ 69. The Glory of the Mediator

was an unalterable judgment of God suspended over them on account of their obstinate rejection of the Gospel as previously offered to them. In any case, it was too late to do anything for them, since the Last Day was at hand and had already dawned. The christianisation of the heathen could now be no more than a civil duty of existing Christian authorities. There could be no question of a mission on the part of the Church. If God did wish to extend His kingdom, this was exclusively His own business and not that of men. An isolated and little known voice to the contrary is that of the Dutchman Adrian Suravia, who was born in 1531 and died in 1613 as Dean of Westminster. In a work on the spiritual office (1590), he declared that, as the promise: " Lo, I am with you alway . . ." applies not merely to the apostles but to all the disciples of Jesus, so, too, does the command: " Go ye into all the world." The apostolic preaching of the Gospel to the nations was only a beginning according to the possibilities of a single generation. In fact, there had always been continuations. Hence the task must be taken up again to-day, not arbitrarily by individuals, but with all the authority of the Church. Suravia was at once and energetically countered by the greatest theological authorities of his day, including Theodore Beza among the Calvinists and J. Gerhard among the Lutherans, and in the main the older Protestant orthodoxy accepted their express repudiation of any outstanding missionary obligation. No impression was made on them by the charge of the Jesuit Cardinal Bellarmine that the Protestant could not be the true Church because it did not engage in any missionary endeavour. Indeed, the bold answer was made that the spreading of Christianity among all peoples is not an essential mark of the Church which in Rev. 12[6] is compared to the woman fleeing into the wilderness. The conversion of Roman Catholics to the Gospel is basically a conversion of heathen. In any case, the teacher must stay by the congregation entrusted to him: " Feed the flock of Christ which is among you " (1 Pet. 5[2]). Previously the command was given to go into all the world, but now it is to stay where God has put us. Individual voices in favour of missions, such as those of G. Calixt, J. Duraeus, P. Spener and C. Scriver, were not able to break through this obduracy even by the end of the 17th century. Even Lord Justinian von Weltz was a voice in the wilderness when in three pamphlets (1664–1666) he called for the formation " of a separate society by which with divine help our evangelical religion might be propagated." So, too, was Leibniz, who discussed the Jesuit mission to China and at whose instigation " the propagation of the true faith " was accepted as an aim, with no practical consequences, in the statutes of the Berlin Academy of Sciences (1700). By this time, certainly, the theory of the missionary duty of Christian colonial authorities had led to some measure of practical action. One such authority was the Dutch East India Company, which for a time commissioned, employed and supported some Dutch theologians (mostly trained in Leiden) in the Far East, unfortunately with a view to mass conversions on the Roman pattern. Naturally, this was not what was needed, and it was perhaps more sincere and objectively better that the English East India Company remained quite indifferent and did not include in its programme enterprises of this nature. In the sphere of the corresponding attempts of the Pilgrim Fathers to do missionary work among the North American Indians, honourable mention is deserved by the far deeper work of John Eliot, which unfortunately was almost completely destroyed in the confusion of the Red Indian wars. It awakened interest in the home country and at the turn of the century provided the impulse for the formation of such societies as the S.P.C.K. and the S.P.G., concerning whose success it is difficult to say anything very significant. Royal missionaries—they were really German Pietists—were also sent out by Denmark into the West Indian colonies. And in connexion with a royal Danish chartered company Pastor Hans Egede began work in Greenland, working patiently for 15 years with very little result.

1. The Third Problem of the Doctrine of Reconciliation

Pietism, in the shape given it by Hermann Francke in Halle rather than Philipp Spener, constituted the stage in the progress of the Evangelical Church in which there took place a more general awakening to missionary duty and the acceptance of missionary action as essential to its very life and being. The limitations of the missionary conceptions and practice of the Pietists need not concern us. What matters is the undoubted fact that the introduction and form of Evangelical world mission as we now know it may be attributed to the influence of Pietism. In face of every kind of opposition, Francke was the first to see and say that Evangelical Christianity as such must be the bearer of mission, to spread abroad knowledge and understanding by means of a periodical, and finally in his orphanage to prepare consecrated workers for missionary service. Yet the true genius of this Evangelical awakening was not that of Francke and Pietism in the narrower sense, but of Count Zinzendorf and his community. By the time of his death, their missionary achievement surpassed everything previously done by Protestantism for the proclamation of the Gospel among the heathen, and in proportion to its membership his community is still unrivalled in this field. This is connected with the fact that Zinzendorf's personal Christianity, for him identical with his love for Jesus Christ, coincided as such from the very first with his irresistible urge to be the Saviour's witness to each and every man and to the whole world. The basic thing which had been spoken by Suravia, Lord von Weltz and Francke was lived out by Zinzendorf. In and with his one " passion " there was directly proscribed for him his action, the way of the Gospel to far and near. As and because he wanted to belong to the One who died for him and for all men, he could not and would not be in debt to any as His messenger. This was not merely his central but his one and only missionary motive. And as he was able to implant it in others, his community, which he had never envisaged or established as a private community but as an *oecumene in nuce*, became in some sense radically and essentially a missionary Church to a degree not yet reached or excelled by any other in the Evangelical sphere. At the same time, in relation to feeling stirred up by the discovery of misgovernment and mismanagement by the East India Company, the last decade saw the foundation in England of three missionary societies in the true modern sense. Again the first and decisive impulse came from a non-theologian, the cobbler and later Baptist preacher, William Carey (1761-1834). When in consequence of the awakening at the beginning of the 19th century there followed a kind of thaw on the Continent, in the first instance it was to these societies that the corresponding associations (e.g., the mission school founded at Basle in 1815) attached themselves, though sooner or later they constituted themselves independent organs of mission. There then followed, not only within all the great Evangelical denominations in Great Britain, North America, Holland, Germany, France and Scandinavia, but also in the colonial Churches, a sudden and irresistible growth of free associations whose fulness corresponds to the number of countries and ecclesiastical groupings and whose achievements in the noble (and sometimes not so noble) competition of the last 150 years have spread with more or less intensity over all parts of the earth.

Our present concern is not with their methods and successes, their strength and weakness, the price which they have had to pay for instruction or the particularly severe problems with which they are now confronted. Nor can we do more than lightly touch on the question whether the missionary cause should continue to be prosecuted by freely constituted societies and associations with the Churches or whether it should be incorporated into the regular ministry of the organised Churches as their own affair (as, for example, in Scotland). Good reasons have been advanced on both sides, but can this still be done in the future or will a decision have to be reached ? What we wish to emphasise at the moment is simply that it was not in the " good old days " of classical Protestantism, but in the time of its regrettable, or not so regrettable, dissolution, i.e., in the 19th century, which was also the time when modern secularism reached its supreme and most conscious maturity, that Evangelical Christianity of all streams could not and would not stop at the position of the Reformers, but saw and accepted with remarkable unanimity its task as a Church of the living and even geographically outreaching Word, awakening and bestirring itself, even if only in the words and actions and prayers of free associations of innumerable individual Christians, to the serious realisation and fulfilment of its mission to the heathen. It is a sufficiently surprising and important statement that this is a period when in part at least the Church has won through to the venture of challenging the might of heathenism with the preaching of the Gospel instead of being influenced and intimidated by it. It has done this in face of all the difficulties in which it has been entangled in the home countries. It has done it at a time when what took place in the home countries, in the so-called Christian West, e.g., wars and world wars, could offer the heathen world no very convincing example. It has done it even though in the attitude and conduct of nominally Christian Europeans and Americans in Africa and Asia it has usually had to expect and experience vexatious hindrance instead of help. It has done it in spite of the fact that it has been severely hampered and compromised and even tempted by the proximity and conjunction of the political and economic colonialism in which it has had to do its work for better or for worse, not to speak of its own confessional division and disunity. It has done it in conflict with continual and virulent prejudices in its own ranks. It has done it, as all keen-sighted friends of missionary work are well aware, with very little pomp or human impressiveness. It has done it in spite of all probability. But it has actually done it. This fact, and the way in which it did it, can be narrated and described. But, so far as I can see, no adequate explanation can ever be given in purely historical terms. We can only say that any picture of modern Christianity is incomplete in which it is not made evident that finally—and " better late than never "—it has ventured in all its weakness to do this.

In the modern period again (3) there has been a new Christian awakening and stirring in relation to what might be called internal paganism, namely, theoretical and practical polytheism, pantheism, atheism or simple indifferentism within what is regarded as Christian society. We have noted already that within the framework of the previous compromise in the older Christian West there were many forms of this inner paganism, some blatant, some subtle and even very subtle, some openly recognised and some concealed, some contested in Church and state and some tolerated or even protected. And in this respect, too, it was the mendicant orders who in the later Middle Ages made it their business to uncover and rebuke the sins of at least the lower strata of society, calling them to repentance and amendment. To some degree, at least, they were thus forerunners of what was to take place in connexion with the Reformation. In Roman Catholicism their successors were the Capuchins among the ordinary people and among the more educated the Jesuits, who became the educators, instructors, counsellors and spiritual advisers of the higher and highest classes. At this point, however, we cannot say that at least the majority of Protestants lagged behind even momentarily. The fight against paganism in the form of a personal and practical renovation of life, now expected and demanded of high and lowly alike in recognition of the will and Law of God as understood in connexion with the Gospel, was from the very first and even in the earliest stages the dominating motive in the preaching, instruction, discipline, pastoral work and ecclesiastical politics of such men as Zwingli, Bucer and Calvin. And from these first beginnings the threads lead us directly to English and American Puritanism and indirectly to P. Spener and the whole of North German Pietism, in which there was a turn to the *praxis pietatis* on the part of a Lutheranism previously more concerned with purity of doctrine than of life, and then in the 18th century to John Wesley, whose violent onslaught on a Christianity which

1. The Third Problem of the Doctrine of Reconciliation 27

was baptised yet in no way converted, but rather in need of conversion, so deeply influenced the moral life of his country that we may not unjustly speak of " England before and after Wesley." Indeed, if we are to be quite fair, we must not forget the moralism of the Enlightenment, which has often been deplored and ridiculed and was certainly very arid, but which in its first stages was not for nothing a child of Pietism, and in many serious representatives was sincerely meant and effectively served the purposes of edification. With the coming of the 19th century and the European awakening which first made itself felt in the stirring of interest in foreign missions, it was inevitable that, as the successive decades saw also an alienation of the masses and the educated classes from the Church, and their adoption of forms more visibly and palpably opposed to its message and belief, the motive of practical renovation of Christian life should again be related to its inner foundation as nourished by the Bible, prayer and fellowship.

These together became the problem and programme of the so-called Inner Mission which in its origins in Germany is associated with the name of J. H. Wichern, and also of the corresponding movements, enterprises and organisations in other lands and even outside the great Churches, together with all their various offshoots for the purposes of practical service, education and evangelism. Among these we may mention the Deaconess Training Schools for Nurses, the international Y.M.C.A., the S.C.M. and also the Blue Cross, in whose slogan we can see very clearly the unity of motives which characterises the more recent form of the whole movement, deliverance from the misery of slavery to drink being also the saving of drunkards by the grace of God and for His service. And if the organ of the Salvation Army is called *The Warcry*, this denotes the militant character of the whole development from Zwingli by way of John Wesley to John Mott. Mention of the latter is also a reminder that there are many material and personal relationships between these home and foreign missions. It is true that, apart from the early days in the Reformed sphere, the organised Churches have been for the most part the sphere of action rather than the subject in relation to this whole outburst, the initiative being taken in the main by voluntary individuals and groups. Here again the question may be raised whether it is healthy that this should continue to be the case. But again the important thing is the fact that this offensive was mounted at the very beginning of the modern period, and that in a plenitude of different forms it has continued right into our own time.

A definite limitation is characteristic of all the movements to which we have alluded. The inner paganism envisaged by them is always the more or less sharply defined alienation from God in the personal life of individuals living in a Christian environment. Their consistent aim has thus been the inward and outward conversion of these individuals, their awakening to faith and the life of faith, their invitation and introduction into a new and active participation in the fellowship of the Church or this or that Christian organisation, in its confession, service and activity. But in all these centuries, apart from a few modest beginnings at the end of the 19th and then in our own century, the awakening and upsurge have never reached the point where Evangelical Christianity has found itself summoned to wrestle with the paganism of the old and new institutions in the sphere and under the pressure and compulsion of which the life of converted or unconverted Christians or of men generally has had to be lived in every age. What are the forces and powers to whose dominion this sphere owes its existence, essence and form ? By what spirit are the existing relationships really determined in which individuals live in such godlessness and within which they are to be called to faith in God and obedience towards Him ? What can and must the existence of these relationships signify for them ? Whether or not they try to be serious Christians, are they perhaps sinful and guilty in adapting themselves to these relationships, and even maintaining

§ 69. *The Glory of the Mediator*

them, as if they were rigidly ordained? These are the questions which were not asked in these movements, or which began to be asked only when matters had been brought to a head from a very different side. The rule was—and very largely is even to-day—that the institutions and relationships, the orders and disorders, within which individuals have to exist, are presupposed as given, and we have simply to attempt and achieve the best possible in these given circumstances. Indeed, all the movements mentioned could give incidental, and sometimes far more than incidental, recognition and approval to the existing or emerging orders and disorders of the period, even lending them their direct or indirect support. Thus the Reformers and their successors did not lay a finger on the traditional patriarchalism of family life, but tacitly and even vocally accepted it with all its curiosities and severities. Again, the Reformed as well as the Lutheran churchmen of the 16th and 17th centuries accepted and supported the older form of authoritarian state, which even when it was republican was not in any sense a democracy, regarding it as not merely given but divinely given, with all its strange privileges and subjections, until at last it met its well-merited end under the pressure of very different forces. And then, of course, their sons quite self-evidently adapted themselves to the newer political Liberalism. Again, Calvinists were not only able to contemplate, without batting an eyelash, the rise of capitalism and the modern industrialism directed and characterised by it, but they proved to be its most determined and audacious and, as it then seemed, progressive promoters, either not considering the question of theocracy in this field or finding to it an answer favourable to these new possibilities. Again, witchhunts and the slave trade and slavery could become established as institutions, and the whole penal code could become notoriously more barbaric in the 17th century than it had been in the Middle Ages, and it was a long, long time before Christianity found any objection in its own sphere to these forms of paganism, or considered renovation of life in connexion with these general relationships, and then for the most part only when others had already taken the lead, as later in the emancipation of women with its supposed encroachment on Christian conviction. And certainly little attention has been paid in our own day to the meaning or madness of the modern national and omnicompetent state, or the right or wrong of war, or the basic condemnation of colonialism (in spite of Christian experience on the mission fields). It is true enough that in connexion with the whole movement to which we refer there has been a remarkable development of Christian philanthropy on a wide front, so that in individual cases, and even assuming the continuance of general political, social and economic relationships, countless tears have been dried and wounds healed, and much necessary help has been offered and given, during these centuries. But when it has been a matter of challenging the dominant orders and disorders, apart from a few eccentrics Pietism and Methodism, the Moravians, the Inner Mission and the Enlightenment, have all acted as if they could no longer have any force as light or salt in this respect, calling a halt and usually leaving it to the children of the world to take up the question of renewal on this level, and only plucking up courage to follow them to some extent at a later date, instead of stimulating and preceding them as they could and should, and as a man like Heinrich Pestalozzi actually did. In the early days of the modern era it looked for a moment as though things might be different. We cannot but admit that in this respect, for all the shortwindedness, over-haste and general weakness of their teaching and practical efforts, the Anabaptists and Spirituals and so-called Enthusiasts of the Reformation period saw much more clearly than the Reformers themselves, being unwilling merely to accept the validity of existing relationships but trying to test them in the light of the Gospel. Were they altogether wrong when they thought that Luther had been moving in the same direction in his 1520 writings? But in the years which followed, and definitively in 1525, Luther was moved by his powerful concern lest Evangelical preaching should

1. The Third Problem of the Doctrine of Reconciliation 29

be corrupted by the admixture of secular hopes and aspirations, by his deep aversion to anything even remotely suggesting revolution, and by his conviction as to the imminence of the Last Day, to call a halt to this aspect and move off in a very different direction. And when Anabaptism itself was segregated and suppressed in other reforming territories, both externally by the political authorities and internally by the Evangelical congregations, the die was cast, and for generations Evangelical Christianity was condemned to lag behind the wiser and more flexible of the children of the world in this field, as behind the Roman Catholics in that of foreign missions. Is there any comfort in the fact that in the last resort it was unrealised Christian impulses and indirect outworkings of the Gospel which came to active expression in all these various spheres, even in reforms inspired and informed by purely secular and humanistic influences? This may well be so. But if it is, surely it is all the more puzzling that it should be blatant non-Christians, men who were not interested in Christian faith and its confession, or who misunderstood or were even inimical to it, who provided the soil in which these impulses fell and flourished, whereas Christians themselves for a long time did not seem to receive them, and even when they did find a place for them, did so only tardily and with great hesitation. We are not for a moment questioning the genuineness and power of the upsurgence effected within this limitation. But we must certainly recognise that it took place only within this limitation.

And even in relation to events in the latter part of the 19th and the first part of our own century, to which we must now turn, it is only with great qualifications that we can say that this limitation has been transcended, i.e., that in addition to the first attempts at the inner and outer christianisation of individual Christian pagans there has been any primarily and spontaneously Christian alteration of general relationships achieved in the light of the Gospel. Certainly, we must not overlook or minimise the various forms of Christian Social work attempted by such men as Adolf Stoecker and Friedrich Naumann under the original inspiration of Wichern and the Inner Mission. Above all, we must recognise the continuing impact of the Religious Social movement which was stimulated by the preaching of the younger C. Blumhardt concerning the kingdom of God, which found in Hermann Kutter and Leonhard Ragaz its most important leaders and teachers, and which unfortunately reflects in its name the terminology of the theology of the day. Nor can we ignore the different Christian peace movements of our age, nor the resistance in the German Churches to the National Socialist paganism widely proclaimed and disseminated among them in the thirties. In connexion with all these movements and trends there has been much new reflection on the relevance of Old and New Testament prophecy, much sharp and even bitter and perhaps exaggerated and therefore unjust criticism of a complacent Church and all previous Christian thinking and conduct, much forceful preaching of political and social repentance, and in detail much bold striving for practical action. From all kinds of new angles there has been revealed, not merely the godlessness and evil of general orders and disorders, but the existence of a public and institutional as well as a private and individual paganism in all kinds of previous Christian activities such as had never before been suspected, let alone made the subject of serious concern or attack. The problem of Christian renovation, and therefore of wrestling with the social principles and powers and forces which rule the life of Christian and non-Christian alike, was now posed in all its rigour. The tasks set for Christianity in this direction were first indicated in powerful sermons and then studied and formulated with greater precision. Nor can we say that all this new work has been futile. It has shocked and stimulated the Christian world in many different ways. The shattering events of the two world wars have caused slogans which it then sought and found, and which were formerly heard and accepted by comparatively few, to become part of the common substance of Christian thought and utterance. The Ecumenical Conferences from Stockholm to Evanston have appropriated them. Where to-day do we not read of the sovereignty of God and His command over all the departments of human life, of the social message of the Gospel, of the responsibility of Christians and the duty of the Church to keep watch in state and society, of the fulfilment of the Church's confession in confessional political action etc. ? What fifty years ago was spoken or more often shouted in the ear, is now proclaimed from the house-tops, and rightly so. Yet we should be wise not to maintain too rashly that to-day Christianity is actually transcending that limitation, or has already done so. Rather we do well modestly to admit that on the Christian side it is a matter of subsequently discovering, making known, bringing to the awareness of Christianity and holding out to it as an example, the Christian significance or impulse of certain more or less purely humanistic, a-Christian or even anti-Christian uprisings such as Socialism. Awakened, unsettled and instructed by these alien uprisings, Christians have maintained that from the standpoint of the active revelation of God attested in the Bible there are far more comprehensive things to be said concerning the peace on earth promised in the Christmas message, or the external as well as internal peace, freedom and righteousness here and now held out to man, than was realised along those older lines or even in the Inner Mission and related movements ; and far better and more radical things than those represented and practised by the non-Christian bearers of this Christian impulse. The point is that the new turning was not primarily and spontaneously Christian in its origins, but has only become such. Furthermore, it is still an open question how far even in its more modern developments it has really made its way in Christianity. In spite of Amsterdam and Evanston, and the loud shouting of slogans and catch-words, is there not even yet a great and compact Christianity or Christendom which is still asleep in this respect, or at very best awake and stirred only on the older individualistic lines ? Again, even to the extent that we see the necessity of the new turning, are we really clear that in making it there can be no question of dropping the concern of the older movement and the Inner Mission, i.e., the problem and problems of the individual, but rather of really taking them up in the greater context, doing the one but not leaving the other undone ? It can lead only to fresh disillusionment if in face of secular unbelief and evil the Christian task is not seen and tackled in its unity and totality, i.e., not merely in respect of the relationships but also of the individual and his personal conduct as it creates and confirms the relationships. Again, we are only at the very beginning in respect of the delimitation of what has to be represented in state and society from the standpoint of the Gospel and command of God as distinct from the originally quite different tendencies to which we have alluded, i.e., in respect of the genuine theological establishment of the relevant Christian word for relationships and events. In this field strong notes will not suffice for long if they are not also pure notes sounded with some degree of obvious if free unanimity. Again, it must be clearly seen that in this whole movement there can be no question of a reconstitution of the mediaeval domination of the Church or its clergy over state and society, but that in the strictest sense the community must stand by its witness and deliver its message both to individuals and also to state and society. The Evangelical Church must avoid clericalist hankerings and aspirations with particular stringency at those points where in the whole process it finds itself in a certain proximity and community of interest with the Church of Rome. Finally, we must not fail to see that the upsurgence in this direction is primarily a movement within the Church and Christian circles and that it has hardly yet gone beyond the stage of serious reflection and lively debate. What those who are trying to be serious Christians think and say in this respect has certainly led on occasion to positive and fruitful contacts between within and without. But so far it cannot be maintained in any general sense that the many true and important things said and thought

1. The Third Problem of the Doctrine of Reconciliation

along these lines have produced real Christian actions transcending the limitations, as the older Reformed, Pietism, Methodism and the Inner Mission certainly produced them within the limitation. For all these reasons, it is right that we should speak with emphasis but also with reserve concerning this final historical phase.

The fact to be pondered is quite simply that with increasing clarity during the last hundred years Christianity has heard, and obviously could not fail to hear, a summons inviting and requiring it to advance further along that older line and therefore to transcend the limitation. Within the limits which cannot be overlooked, this is a fact and must be registered as such.

A new page (4) has also been turned in the last centuries—and this aspect is worth noting in the present context—in the sense that it has seen the rise, unparalleled in the early and mediaeval Church, of a far greater candour of qualified observation, research and thinking in relation to the basis and theme of Christian faith and proclamation, and of a far more serious wrestling with the question of the knowledge of God and therefore that of the right word of human speech concerning Him.

The authority with which God Himself in His revelation has made Himself the presupposition of the life of the Church and its message was known quite well in earlier periods. It was powerfully presented to them in the word of Scripture, in the dogmas which expounded it, and in other traditions of the Church as authentically interpreted by the authentic teaching office of the Church. Century by century they respected, expounded, interpreted (and sometimes misinterpreted) the decisions made and still being made with divine authority, zealously and loyally asserting them in accordance with the needs and language of the different ages. Nor was there any lack of analytical or synthetic acuteness in their attempts to expound the decisions of this authority in terms of the concrete form in which they held them to be prescribed. On the other hand, they made no attempt to investigate how far these prescribed forms—the Bible, dogma, tradition and the teaching office—were really the form of the decisions of God Himself, given to Christianity with His authority. They could not and would not undertake an enquiry and understanding of these decisions which would exercise a critical control in relation to their form and determine their exposition and application. This was the limitation of all earlier wrestling with the question of the knowledge and therefore the true Christian mediation of the divine revelation. It was thought that this could and should be dealt with as with the given features in any other sphere of human knowledge and speech.

But at the very period when new questions of sources were being raised in other spheres, a definite advance was necessarily made in this respect with the Reformation. Now there was to be introduced a Church of the living Word, of the living God Himself proclaiming Himself in His great acts. What was this living Word? There was agreement with the early and mediaeval Church in finding it first and finally attested in the word of Scripture. But how far was it truly expounded and applied in dogma and tradition, or by the existing Church and its teachers and those who were charged to guard its doctrine? Indeed, how far was the word of Scripture itself its attestation? How far was it not merely to be quoted and asserted as a form of the authority of God, but to be understood as the divine address in human speech and therefore as the norm of all Christian utterance concerning God? This new question, and the attempt to answer it, belong to the modern movement of the Church to the world. They demand of the Church an assurance that the theme and content of its witness is really the Word of God and therefore that its witness conforms to that of the word of Scripture. But for the sake of this assurance the Church's exposition of the word of Scripture, while it had not to be abandoned as such, had to be radically relativised and called in question. The question of the Word of God

§ 69. *The Glory of the Mediator*

in the witness of that of Scripture had to be continually answered afresh in independence of tradition and in the light of ongoing investigation. And in the same connexion the testing of the objectivity of the witness of the Church had to become the content of a continual problem. From these standpoints theology as a science acquired a new meaning and purpose. This goal could be understood, as it has often been in various forms, to consist in an answering of the question of the Word of God in that of Scripture and the proclaiming Church according to the measure of the rational, moral, or religious self-understanding of man. In other words, the Word of God in Scripture and Church proclamation is that which is adapted to, or at any rate does not conflict with, the needs and possibilities and limitations of this understanding. It is a fitting and therefore illuminating and acceptable answer at the point where man is forced to see himself as a problem, to project himself. For those who regarded and posed the question in this way, exegetical and dogmatic theology necessarily became an application of the contemporary spirit of the age and therefore a distinctive historical, psychological and practical form of the regnant philosophy. But the question could be understood quite differently. Exegetically it could be understood as the question of what the word of Scripture itself understands by the Word of God attested in it, and how it explains itself in this regard. Dogmatically it could then be understood as the question of the Christian word which proves itself right in the fact that it, too, keeps itself open and fluid in its relation to the Word of God which is to be received where the sovereignty of the word of Scripture over all man's self-understanding is accepted instead of being curtailed and finally suppressed. On this understanding theology achieves its true theme and method as obedience to the living Word of God preceding it in Scripture. Throughout the whole of the modern period there has been theology of both kinds. For our present purposes we need not take up any attitude in their disturbing but salutary inner conflict. Our concern is simply with the fact that these centuries have been centuries of strenuous theological work both exegetical and dogmatic ; and that work of this kind was never previously undertaken in the Church for the obvious reason that it was not affected by the question of the right knowledge of the Word of God and its correct reproduction in human thoughts and words, that it did not think it needed that critical assurance of and by the sources, that it did not feel so acutely in its own day the need not merely to organise and practise a cultus but to speak loudly and clearly, and when it did so, not merely to recite and protest, but to explain and apply in the freedom of direct responsibility. The work of Evangelical theology may have been done in wrong ways as well as right. Its exposition and doctrine may have been dictated by a presupposed hermeneutics or its hermeneutics by its exposition, as also its doctrine. But either way it characterises the modern age as a period when the question of the responsible explication and application of the Word of God attested in Scripture could allow the Church no rest, as the period of a new seeking of the true objectivity of Christian thought and speech to which even great and in their way audacious thinkers like Augustine, Anselm and Thomas Aquinas did not see themselves compelled in times past.

I know of no other explanation of this phenomenon than that suggested in relation to the other phenomena of the age, namely, that as it was the time when the Church was betrayed into great isolation and constriction, so it was also the time of its new outreach, of its new turning to the world between which and itself there now arose and continually increased the *diastasis*. Engaged in this address, it had to speak, and to be able to speak it had to know. And to carry any weight, its knowledge had to be certain. The work of Evangelical (and in isolated instances even Roman) theology in these centuries reflects the struggle of the Church for certainty in its outgoing to men. For this reason the newer theological work, in this case even in its weaker as well as its stronger elements, belongs to the credit side of the total picture.

1. The Third Problem of the Doctrine of Reconciliation

We may also refer (5) to the phenomenon of a turning of the Church to the world which has revealed itself with increasing clarity since the 16th century within the different Christian bodies, namely, the questioning of the classical distinction, taken for granted in the Middle Ages, between a religious and a secular status, between clergy and laity, between theologians and non-theologians.

Significant indication of this development may be found in the existence of the Franciscan tertiaries and later the Brethren of the Common Life, as also in a particular attention to Christ as the Teacher. In the relationship of the Reformation with a popular Humanism it was obvious that in certain strata at least even the so-called secular class, hitherto merely instructed and led, had attained an awareness of its common responsibility for the doctrine and life of the Church, and was prepared on the basis of its own judgment actively to participate in fashioning and practising it either in co-operation with the bearers of spiritual office or in certain cases in opposition to them. When for the first time in 1520 Luther unequivocally stated his doctrine of the priesthood of all believers, this was not a speculative discovery, nor was it merely taken from Holy Scripture, but it also envisaged the actual rise of an educated and semi-educated middle class and nobility and even in some cases peasantry, with whose almost violent interest in the new theological answers the printing presses of the day could hardly keep pace. The political and ecclesiastico-political consolidation of Evangelical Christianity in consequence of the Counter-Reformation did, of course, lead in the first instance to a new over-emphasis even in this sphere on the clergy and theologians. Calvin's doctrine of the Church at the beginning of Book IV of the *Institutio* is in fact a very aristocratic doctrine of ecclesiastical office, or the ministry, or the administration of the word and sacrament, which was to be exercised by an exclusive and special class, and in which the community, represented by the elders and deacons ordained alongside the presbyters and deacons, could only incidentally play any active part. These and similar divisions have officially persisted until well into the 19th century, and even to our own day, in Lutheran and Anglican as well as Reformed circles. But even in the 17th century there were active subterranean movements among the Christian laity which quickly came out into the open in separatist bodies like the Baptists and Congregationalists. Before the theologians Spener and Francke, the conventicles which met independently for Bible-study and devotion in the houses of townspeople, peasants and the nobility were representatives of the variegated movement known to Church history as Pietism. In the age of the Enlightenment a new impulse was given to the emancipation of the laity by the gradual but inexorable development of a general freedom of faith and conscience. In the awakening which inaugurated the 19th century they then played a decisive role, as in the case of the oculist H. Jung-Stilling and the lady of society Juliane von Krüdener. Nor when we think of the contemporaneous revival of Roman Catholicism can we forget the incursion of writers like F. R. Châteaubriand and J. de Maistre, from whom a direct line may be traced to the Catholic Action of modern France and poets like Bernanos, Péguy, Claudel and their disciples. To the association on the Evangelical side of theological untrained and non-ordained elements in the various evangelistic and social movements already mentioned, there corresponds on the Roman Catholic the large number of congregations of Mary, whose membership can now run into millions as in the case of the American Knights of Columbus. On what side to day do not the Churches have alongside their specially called representatives, and often competing with them, more or less spontaneously committed and well-informed fellow-workers from among what were previously the purely receptive congregations ? Where do they not live a most important part of their life in freely formed groups of men, women or young people usually or always coming together *ad hoc* ? Working associations like the Evangelical Academies in Germany (which in their good and less good elements are an unmistakeable fruit of the D.C.S.V. of preceding decades), or

§ 69. *The Glory of the Mediator*

the movement of Church and World which has spread from Holland, have come to the fore during the last years. And individual ecclesiastically minded and theologically instructed doctors, lawyers, teachers, writers and politicians, sometimes much superior to trained theologians in their own field, are no longer a rarity in the main confessions. Yet to see the whole picture we must not overlook the fact that occasionally at least, as theologically represented by such men as R. Rothe and L. Ragaz, there has been the reverse movement from a narrower to a wider form of secular Christian service, whether in the case of the man who at the turn of the century caused a sensation by becoming a factory worker for three months, or the essentially far more resolute action of the French workerpriests who have been temporarily suppressed but will surely come back in some form, or of Albert Schweitzer and the path which he has so impressively taken. The wall which once separated the chancel of the church from the nave has never rested on very solid foundations. And if in the modern period it has not yet wholly disappeared, it has obviously been pierced in places and begun to crumble.

Critical caution is needed in face of this phenomenon too. For one thing, the relativisation of the division is only partial even to-day. We cannot say that a majority, let alone the totality, of Christians has taken part in this advance. Even where it has taken place, it might so easily result, as once in the official Protestantism of the 16th century, in the formation of a new and enlarged clergy with no great significance for the existence of the rest of the community. And even to-day there are ecclesiastical circles where this penetration has either not been attempted at all or only with great timidity, and the old wall of partition has been made the more blatant and effective by the addition of new paint. More noteworthy still is the fact that, while in all ages there has been a more or less culpable and serious resistance on the part of the trained and commissioned members of the Church, which has given good cause and reason for the emancipation of the laity, the laity as such were never the better Christians, so that their emergence cannot be a pure awakening to their joint responsibility and obligation to the cause of the Gospel, nor can it take place and form in this spirit, representing and expressing itself as a necessary reaction and salutary corrective. On the contrary, consciously or unconsciously, directly or indirectly, their emergence has always been, or has always quickly become, a powerful element in the secularisation of preaching, teaching, order and mission which threatens the Church as Church in correspondence with the achievement of autonomy by the secular sphere. The criticism and resistance brought against the movement on the part of the specially trained and commissioned, their reservations even as for good reasons they have desired and stimulated and fostered it, are not then wholly and utterly groundless for all the objections which might be made to them. It might well be that as the awakening " people," appealing to the unquestionable promise of Jer. 31[31f.], has risen against an unprofitable and static distinction between *ecclesia docens* and *ecclesia audiens*, it has also challenged the profitable and dynamic significance of this distinction, attacking and to some extent successfully overthrowing not only the priority of a word of man but also the sacred priority of the Word of God. Speaking of universal priesthood, it might well envisage the sovereignty of man both individually and in the mass. It might rank itself ostensibly with the priest or theologian or preacher, but in reality with the Lord of the whole Church who is perhaps impotently and distortedly proclaimed and represented by it, taking His government into its own hands. In its participation in the exposition and application and perhaps the criticism of the Bible and dogma, and its appeal to the Holy Spirit who blows where He lists, and the conscience to which each is directly responsible, it might theoretically assert the brotherhood of all believers in Christ but practically the association of the *homunculi* who long for life and thought and speech which are not concretely bound, trying to secure for them the leadership of the Church itself. And if the ministers and theologians have often enough failed the people by

1. The Third Problem of the Doctrine of Reconciliation   35

reason of their arrogant exclusiveness, they have just as often shown themselves too weak and yielding, and capitulated too easily to its interests, when for the sake of the whole what was required was vigilance, steadfastness and leadership. When the laity has come to have a part in Church government, with its stronger contact with the spirit and practice and tendencies of the surrounding world, with its more limited knowledge and understanding of Church history, with its formally smaller obligations, with its greater freedom of judgment and imagination in face of tradition, with its cheerfully over-simplified desire for action, it has often proved to be a most important point of entry for the most diverse errors and confusions, which do not threaten only some orthodoxy old or new but the very understanding and progress of the Gospel itself, and in the development of which theology and the official ministry, as shown in Roman Catholicism quite openly by the riotous growth of Mariology and in Protestantism no less openly by certain Liberal outrages culminating in the events of 1933, have often proved to be only the mouth-piece of what is merely presumed to be a pious *vox populi*.

Recognition of these unmistakeably questionable features must not cause us to lose sight of the basic range and positive significance of the whole phenomenon in its historical context. The relativisation, acute since the 16th century, of the distinction which had been so characteristic of the life of Christendom from post-apostolic times until well on in the Middle Ages, is an indication, together with the other phenomena mentioned, of the spontaneous reorientation of the Church outwards instead of inwards, to the world instead of to itself. This reorientation is here fulfilled in the life of the Church itself. For, whatever we might think and say concerning their good or bad points, what were and are the non-clerics and non-theologians who have come to the forefront in their thousands but the representatives within the Church of the world outside it, in relation to which the Church as a whole has now found itself caught up in a newly apprehended responsibility ? What was and is their gradual or more rapid rise and activity but an anticipation of the step beyond itself to which the Church as a whole has now found itself called at the very time when it has come under the great process of constriction within its own frontiers ? And what else but the recognition of a new call, obviously forcing itself even upon the official representatives, leaders and teachers of Christianity, was the reason why, for all the necessary and often neglected reservations which they might have, they could not basically resist the upsurgence of the Christian laity, but had rather to approve and even stimulate and foster it ? The fact cannot be ignored that, in incontestably effective individual forms and more general movements if not in its totality, the Christian people living by the very nature of the case on the frontier between the Church and the world, between the sacred and the secular, has now introduced, as it were, the sacred into the secular, or the secular into the sacred, in the various activities more or less happily conceived and initiated by it. In many cases it has been quite unconscious of its actual aims and achievements. But those who, in either of the two classes which were formerly so sharply distinguished, have now heard and hear the call to move out as a call to obedience to the Church's mission to the world, should certainly realise that in the removal of the inner frontier we have an intimation and preparation for the crossing of the outer, and therefore an indication to the Church to take up its prophetic office.

A final point to be noted (6) is that the ecumenical conception, namely, the conception of the unity of the Churches in the one Church of Jesus Christ, and the desire and striving for this unity, have not merely been latently present in the modern period from the very outset, but have visibly and palpably increased in strength.

Here, again, we must not exaggerate. The beginning of the period saw the great and unavoidable but genuinely regrettable disruption of the Western Church, and this was followed at once by an appalling number of lesser divisions.

§ 69. The Glory of the Mediator

For all the promising understandings in detailed points, the gulf between the Roman and all other Churches is still of frightful depth. Nor are there lacking even to-day all kinds of old and even new emphases and over-emphases on the differences and divisions between the other denominations. Yet from the outset and continuously this centrifugal tendency has been opposed by hopes and efforts of a very different character. In the 16th century we may think primarily of Martin Bucer and more generally of the Church of Strassburg and its theology. In the next centuries we remember men like Georg Calixt, J. Duraeus, Jean Frédéric Osterwald and Leibniz, the many conversations undertaken between the Lutherans and the Reformed with a view to union, the strenuous efforts of the Lutherans particularly to fix on certain basic articles as the epitome of what is essential, indispensable and therefore unificatory, and finally the actual unions achieved in Germany in the 19th century, of which the Prussian is necessarily the most significant. It is not a good sign, perhaps, that the first name which ought to have been mentioned in this list is that of Erasmus of Rotterdam. The weakness in all these attempts, revealed in the fact that they either broke down or led, as in the German unions, to inwardly unclear and therefore unsatisfactory and not very stable results, is to be found in the fact that the *ut omnes unum sint* of Jn. 17[21] was always understood much too formally and the unity of the Church was in large measure conceived as an end in itself. This meant that there could be no escaping the dilemma either of insisting on loyalty to what for good reasons had been previously accepted and confessed as true Christian faith and order and practice, even at the price of confirming and maintaining existing divisions, or of allowing love and friendliness and tolerance to triumph, but at the price of an unprincipled and featureless relativisation or even the surrender of insights and convictions previously felt and declared to be necessary. This older ecumenicism suffered from the fact that it could not detach itself with sufficient clarity from the levelling indifferentism of the developing and then triumphant Enlightenment and later of Romanticism. Even Zinzendorf and his community could be misunderstood in this neutralistic sense. Only in the 19th century and our own, tentatively at first but always in a very definite direction, has it been possible to move away from this deadening conception. This has happened particularly where the union of the Churches has begun to be conceived in teleological and dynamic terms as a union which derives from Jesus Christ and is thus union for Him, namely, for the attestation of His work in the world and for the world. A good individual instance is to be found in the *Theological Declaration of the Synod of Barmen* (1934), which was made in concert by the Lutherans, Reformed and United in their struggle against the German Christians, and the genuinely ecumenical character of which could be questioned only arbitrarily by an over-anxious confessionalism.

It is in relation to this new form that we have to think of ecumenicism in the present context. In our century the various denominations in different countries have everywhere begun to associate for common tasks without affecting their theological and organisational peculiarities. The denominations, too, have begun to transcend national distinctions and unite in great alliances, e.g., of Lutherans, Anglicans, Presbyterians, Methodists and Baptists, on the simple understanding that this is demanded not merely in virtue of their common basis but with a view to their common action. Even earlier, as in the Evangelical Alliance (1846), there had been interdenominational and international unions for concerted activity in the form of evangelical confession. This was followed by the interdenominational work among young people and students to which we have referred already in an earlier connexion, and in 1910 there then took place the most important Missionary Conference in Edinburgh, this being followed in 1914, at the very time of the political disjunction of Christendom in the First World War, by the formation of the World Alliance for International Friendship through the Churches. Under the inspiration and direction of Archbishop

1. *The Third Problem of the Doctrine of Reconciliation* 37

Nathan Söderblom the so-called Conference of Life and Work was then held in Stockholm in 1925, and here for the first time (1600 years after Nicæa) there assembled an explicitly "ecumenical" gathering officially organised by the different Churches and for the first time including representatives of the Eastern Church, though not of Rome. It was now expressly stated that unity is not an end in itself. What was desired was that "in penitence, and with a keen sense of the mischief of socio-ethical confusion and division, the duties of Christians and the Church should be seen in the needs of the age, and a serious attempt made at the following and discipleship of the Saviour" (Söderblom, *RGG*[2], II, 85). For the time being there was conscious hesitation to attempt an organisational union of Churches. This could not even be envisaged, let alone undertaken, except on a solid theological basis. In relation to this distant goal to be achieved, if at all, only in this way, the first movement and conference for Life and Work was accompanied by a second, the Lausanne Conference for Faith and Order (1927), which was closely related by personal links to the former, and in which the question of Church unity, now understood as an inner matter of faith and order, was directly related to that of the Christian message to the world. The Oxford Conference (1937) carried the discussion of this aspect deeper, and later Amsterdam (1948), in which both movements combined, resulted not merely in the formation of the World Council, not as a universal Church but as a covering organisation and alliance of about two hundred and fifty national and confessional Churches, but also—and note the interrelationship of the two motives—in a comprehensive pronouncement concerning "Man's Disorder and God's Design," together with a first message not merely to the Christian public (as at Stockholm, 1925) but to the whole world. The latter example was again followed at Evanston (1954) in respect of its specific theme, "Christ the Hope of the World."

It may well be asked whether the time, or rather the inner situation and spiritual constitution of the Christian societies, is really ripe for such direct apostrophising of the non-Christian or an indifferent Christian world. It can hardly be maintained that what was said at Amsterdam or Evanston has made any great impact. Nor is the reason for this to be found merely in the necessary element of compromise in such common statements (hence the fog of indecision and sterility which envelops from the very first all the ecumenical papers so industriously prepared at Bossey and elsewhere). It is to be found also in the difficulty that as yet there has been no clear apprehension of the concrete things, so earnestly sought in innumerable ecumenical conferences of students, which the Church has to proclaim to the disorder of secular politics and economics as the message of salvation.

Yet in this respect, too, our insistence is simply upon the fact that to-day, if not earlier, the meaning of the Church's strivings for unity has clearly come to be found in this turning of the Church to the world which has so remarkably accompanied the turning of the world from the Church, and which we have had occasion to notice from all the various aspects previously considered. In themselves and as such the Church's attempts at unity would not be a particularly interesting or relevant phenomenon. The practical or in the more general sense missionary teleology and dynamic with which they have been pressed forward so energetically during the last hundred years, and particularly in the last decades, force themselves upon our attention. It is no accident that what is denoted by the peculiar English word "evangelism" seems latterly to have become the focal point of ecumenical interest. Here, too, there is no cause for unrealistic optimism. We are only at the very beginnings, laboriously made and quickly passing. On the other hand, there is no cause for a scepticism which will not recognise these beginnings as such. Certainly, in relation to speech and action undertaken in common with a respect for that which is distinctive yet an avoidance of that which separates, we have no grounds whatever to say that

§ 69. *The Glory of the Mediator*

Church lags far behind advances long since made by the world. In this it is obvious that it has seized the initiative, that it is quite a few steps ahead of the world and can be an example to it. The outlook to-day would be quite different if in some negotiations and conferences there were at least as honest and open and practical a concern for the union of the nations as there has been for the union of the Churches at Edinburgh, Stockholm, Amsterdam, Evanston etc., and as there is continually in Geneva, not in the Palace of Nations, but in *Route de Malagnou*, 17.

We have briefly recalled all these various trends in order to show that dogmatics is challenged, not merely by the underlying reality and Scripture, but by the progress of Church history, to pay particular attention to the character of reconciliation as revelation. If this was once neglected, it cannot be so to-day. The aspect which we have considered may not be the only one, but it cannot be overlooked. Questions naturally arise concerning the astonishing outreach of the community to the world in the different forms mentioned, but it is a fact. And its only final explanation is the fact that the reconciliation of the world accomplished in Jesus Christ does actually have the character of revelation, of the Word of God demanding expression. The occurrence itself is also speech. It is a pure and definite summons to men. Christianity seems to have noted this in quite a new way in the modern epoch. Why only now, and in a period which is so troubled in other respects? This cannot be explained. We are simply confronted by the fact that it does seem to have noted it to-day, that it must obviously be orientated by it, and that however well or badly, and perhaps more badly than well, it has begun to orientate itself by it.

This being the case, it is surely no accident that on the very threshold of this new period of Christianity Calvin should rediscover the doctrine of the *munus Christi propheticum*.

2. THE LIGHT OF LIFE

We begin with Jesus Christ. "The Glory of the Mediator" is the title which we have selected for this first section. And it is by means of the older doctrine of the *munus propheticum Jesu Christi* that we have come to see what is the third problem of the doctrine of reconciliation. In this third part then, in which it is a matter of reconciliation as revelation, we must begin with Jesus Christ. To be sure, we must also continue with Him. But continuation with Him can proceed only from a specific beginning with Him, i.e., from a christological foundation in the narrower sense. This has been our procedure in the two first parts of the doctrine, and it must be so now, not for the sake of systematic consistency, but because there is no alternative. That reconciliation is also revelation is first and decisively event and reality in Him who is its Mediator and Accomplisher in His own person. We cannot first speak generally and abstractly of the fact that revelation, as the revelation of the reconciliation of the world to God, takes place (as it did and will take place), and then come back to Him as the One who is perhaps no more than the prominent Revealer. As the reconciliation is His work, so is its revelation, in its past and present and future occurrence. As the reconciliation takes place in Him, its revelation takes place through Him. It does not take place, and therefore cannot be seen or understood, apart from Him or in any way in itself. For this reason we have to begin with Him.

And we begin with the statement that He, Jesus Christ, lives. This is at once the simplest and the most difficult christological statement. Any child can make it, but the profoundest meditation cannot master it. It says something quite formal and yet it also says the most material thing that is to be said of Him. It says something supremely particular, and yet it also says the most embracing thing; something unique, indeed the one unique thing, and yet also the universally real and valid.

We speak of the Jesus Christ attested in Scripture; of the One to whom the history of Israel attested in the Old Testament moves until it attains its goal and end in the history attested in the New Testament, which is still the history of Israel but also the origin and beginning of that of His community. We speak of the Subject of the history which comes between the one history and the other, the one preceding and the other following, so that, as it is wholly His history, the history of this one Subject, it cannot be separated from the two histories which it integrates, just as conversely these two histories can only precede and follow His, and cannot be separated from it as that which integrates them. The Subject of this central history which controls and determines the whole is Jesus Christ. And He lives. This is where we must begin.

That Jesus Christ lives means quite simply that He exists in the manner of God, and therefore prior to all else that exists, not grounded upon any other, referred to no other existence or support, in unconditional freedom and power. But it also means quite simply that He exists in the manner of a man, and therefore like all other created beings, in the freedom and power of such a being as divinely determined and limited, in the relative dependence of a single member in the natural and historical nexus of the created world. Hence the fact that Jesus lives means concretely that He exists in the manner of the God whose divine transcendence does not find it incongruous but supremely congruous to exist also in the limited manner of the human creature; and conversely that He exists in the manner of the man to whom there is given by God that which He cannot take to Himself, namely, to exist also in the sovereign manner of God. It is thus that Jesus Christ lives. It is thus that He exists. It is thus that He is the Subject of His history as attested in Scripture. This witness implies, however, that who or whatever else exists does so together with Him. The Creator, God Himself, exists only as He does so together with this One who also exists as man, and each and everything in the created world exists only together with this One who also exists as man. As God exists only together with this One, and so too the world, His existence as such is the fact in which God and the world, however they may oppose or contradict one another, are not of course one and the same, but do exist together in an inviolable and indissoluble co-existence and conjunction.

That Jesus Christ lives also tell us, however, that His existence is act ; that it is being in spontaneous actualisation. Primarily and supremely we have again to say *actus purus*, the actualisation of being in absolutely sovereign spontaneity, after the manner in which the Creator, God, actualises Himself, so that His life-action is identical with that of God Himself, His history with the divine history. Again, however, we must add that the actualisation is also after the manner in which it is given to the creature to actualise itself, to exist historically in its conditioned and limited spontaneity. This is its existence as life in particular ; actual existence ; existence in fulfilment. On the one side, then, we have the living God in the fulfilment which has its source in Himself and is freely executed by Himself, in the absolutely sovereign actualisation of His being. On the other we have the living creature in the use of the capacity lent it by God in connexion with all other creaturely life, in the fulfilment of its particular being. As Jesus Christ lives, there takes place in Him both creative actualisation of being, yet also in and with it creaturely actualisation ; creative and creaturely life together, without the transformation of the one into the other, the admixture of the one with the other, or separation or division between them. This is how Jesus Christ is seen and attested in Scripture. And again this implies that God does not live except with this One, nor does any living creature. It is as He lives that the living God lives and all that is by Him and outside Him, so that, in spite of all possible and actual problems in their relationship, they live together (though not in identity) in the indestructible conjunction of the differentiated act in which both Creator and creature exist.

But the fact that Jesus Christ lives, and thus exists in the act of His self-actualisation, is the act of a person. It is not something but Someone who lives. His self-actualisation is not an anonymous process. It takes place as the work of a specfic Subject which is a Subject only as the Bearer of a definite name and is distinct from all other subjects as this Subject. It takes place as the decision, resolve and action of this Subject. " I live." His life is lived in the freedom of this I. It is a matter of the person, or I, of God. God Himself is the One who lives here, who is engaged in the actualisation of His being, who is the free Subject of this occurrence. But it is God Himself as this one man, as the Bearer of His definite human name, as the free Subject of His human decisions, resolves and actions. It is God Himself in the limits to which they are subject in their humanity. It is God Himself in lowliness, temptation, suffering, rejection and death. It is God Himself as the Lord become Servant. But it is also **God Himself in the exaltation and majesty of this one man.** It is

2. *The Light of Life*

God Himself as this Servant become Lord. God does what this man does. Or rather, this man does what God does. But either way this life is fulfilled in a personal act. We have to think of the unity of this personal act when the New Testament calls this living One alone among all others the Lord, but also the Servant. He is the Lord as the One who lives His life in the sovereign power proper to Him as the free Subject of this occurrence. And He is the Servant as the One who wholly and utterly subjects Himself to, and serves, this divine power of life even to the point of obedience unto death. This is how Jesus Christ lives. But we must add at once that with His own life-act, which is directly that of God Himself fulfilled as man, there take place all the life-acts of those who as free subjects (within their determined limits) are the creatures of God. In other words, there takes place all human life. To live as man is to live in the proximity and sphere of this One and therefore of this Lord and Servant. When any of us says I, and in his attempt at life uses the freedom given by the fact that he is I and not It, he declares that in some sense he belongs to the territory in which Another, this One, is Lord and Servant, to the sphere in which God Himself says I in this Other, and as man makes effective and not merely tentative use of His divine freedom. To live as man is to belong to this sphere, to the sphere of the life and activity of this Other, so that, whether we realise it or not, the decision is made that God will accomplish His personal life-act only together with us, and we can accomplish ours only together with God. This co-existence may take different forms. But the fact that Jesus lives as attested in the biblical testimony to this history means that there is this union between God and each of us men, and that it is indestructible.

But the fact that Jesus Christ lives as Lord and Servant implies more than the absolutely solid co-existence between the Creator and His creature, between God and man, to which we have so far confined our reference. Jesus Christ does not live for Himself. His divine-human existence as divine-human act, i.e., His life as we have so far described it, is not an end in itself. What kind of a Lord would He be, and what kind of Servant, if as such, for all that He had His life in common with others, He finally lived it in isolation in their midst, His lordship and servanthood in the creaturely world and humanity meaning only that He was unmistakeably present in their midst, and that by His life the co-existence of the Creator with His creature, of God with man, was inviolably secured? In the New Testament the life of Jesus Christ is naturally not seen in this abstraction. If it were, its witness could not be called good news. It might perhaps be described as the interesting disclosure of an ontological reality. But it could not be called news, and it certainly would not be good news in face of the bitter reality of the disruption and even destruction and corruption of this co-existence by the pride and sloth of man, and the whole ensuing disorganisation and misery of the human situation. The truth is, however, that He is the Lord and Servant who lives, not for Himself, but for the sake of the creaturely world and humanity, for their deliverance. Hence He does not merely confirm the co-existence of God and man, but He creates order in place of the disorder which obtains within it. This Lord and Servant, humiliated and exalted, is the One attested by Scripture. And it is, therefore, as Gospel, i.e., good news, that its witness comes into the bitter reality of the alienation between God and man brought about by the sin of man, into the disorganisation of the human situation. The news is good because it attests the reconciliation of the world with God which has taken place in the person of this humiliated and exalted One, the creation of a new human existence and situation which has taken place in His person. That Jesus Christ lives, as very God and very man, as Lord and Servant in all the singularity of the act of His existence, is only the formal aspect of what has to be seen and said in this connexion. The material question is as follows: What does He live? The answer to this question is given in and with the former. But we must take particular note of it. He does not merely live a general life which is perhaps supremely wonderful but has no particular relevance to the state of things between God and man. The history as whose Subject He lives does not take place merely in a particularity, however distinguished, apart from the rest of world-occurrence or in isolation from even one of the countless life-stories of men. It takes place rather as the history of salvation; as the occurrence of the coming and eventuation of the salvation of the whole world and all men; as the happening which determines all history and embraces all other histories. His life is the life of the grace in which God confirms, restores and fulfils, not merely His co-existence with man as such, but the covenant with Him which man has broken; in which He moves towards man in spite of his No, cancelling this No and pronouncing His own Yes; in which He justifies and sanctifies sinful man; in which He addresses him as His own child and claims him for His service. As the life of grace it is the life both of the Lord and the Servant, both of the Good who condescends to man and the man exalted to God. As the life of grace it is His own life distinct from all others and in this way lived for God and man, given up wholly to the cause of God and man. As the life of grace it is His life, and as such the life of God and that of the world and all men, i.e., our life, the life of fellowship with God and peace with one another and ourselves which is created for us and given us by Him. As the life of grace, reconciling life, it is the life of the One who within the creaturely and human world is really Lord and Servant, and both as its Deliverer. It is this reconciling life of grace which is lived by Jesus Christ. This as such is the act of His existence. Concretely and in its specific content the witness of Scripture to the history of this Subject is the

2. The Light of Life 43

witness to this life of His which reconciles the world, and in the world each individual, with God. And as His life has this meaning, direction and power, the witness to it is good news.

We can now return to our original statement. Even the formal and general truth must be considered that God and man are in any case bound and live together. As Jesus Christ lives, God and man live in this conjunction. We do not have God here and man there; God is the God of man and man the man of God. This is the epitome of the whole order of creation. This order, too, has its dignity, validity, power and persistence in the fact that Jesus Christ lives. But it has its content and fulness in the fact that the life lived by Jesus Christ is the life of grace, that it is the life of the Saviour. From the standpoint of this content and fulness, the one order of God is the order of reconciliation. As such it is more than the order of creation, since it is the order of the free mercy in which God is not content merely to be with man as in some sense his great Neighbour, but in which, even though man is a poor and bad neighbour who has forfeited rather than deserved it, He goes and comes to him, to take him to Himself in His own person, not merely as one who is conjoined with Him, but as one who is His faithful covenant-partner. Yet as the order of reconciliation it is also the confirmation and restoration of the order of creation. The eternal meaning and content of the order of creation are worked out in the one order of God in the fact that this order is also that of reconciliation. The unity of the two, the transcending and restoring of creation in reconciliation, or, as we might say, the unity of the form and content of the one order of God, is event and reality in the fact that Jesus lives. Our present interest is in the life of Jesus Christ as the establishment of the new order of reconciliation, as the act of the God who binds Himself in free mercy with man, as the life of grace, the life of the Saviour. But in the light of the special purpose which leads us to start with it, we do well not to lose sight of our first statement concerning its general and formal significance. In the life of Jesus Christ there takes place, with the establishment of the new order, the reconstitution of the old. As a work of the merciful God, it is also the triumph of His righteousness. As the life of grace, it is also that of nature. As the life of the Saviour, it is also that of the faithful Creator of heaven and earth (Acts $17^{27f.}$) who is "not far from every one of us," but in whom as His creatures "we live, and move, and have our being." This general aspect is grounded—firmly grounded, so that no other ground need be sought—in the particular, this formal aspect in the material, namely, that the life of Jesus Christ is the life of grace, the life of the Saviour. The fact that He lives thus includes in itself the unity and totality of the order, will and act of God.

Before we proceed, three explanatory additions are necessary to this preliminary development of our theme.

§ 69. *The Glory of the Mediator*

1. First, we must refer back emphatically to the starting-point of our previous discussion, namely, that we are speaking of the Jesus Christ attested in Scripture. The One of whom we have said that He lives in the sense described, is not then the creation of free speculation based on direct experience. He is the One to whom the history of Israel moves from the very first as to its goal, and from whom the history of His community springs. He is the One whose own history is the end of the one and beginning of the other. He is the One who is visible, who makes Himself visible, in the documents of this whole historical nexus. He, this One, lives in the figure and role, in the being, speech, action, passion and death, in the work, which are all ascribed to Him in these documents, in the features which constitute the picture of His existence as delineated and represented in these documents. The fact that this One lives, and what it means that He lives, are not things invented or maintained of ourselves. If we say them responsibly, our own responsibility is only secondary. We really draw on the biblical attestation of His existence. For in this attestation He Himself lives, certainly as its origin and theme, but even as such only in the mirror of the picture which is offered. It is He who lives, not the picture. But He Himself lives only in the form which He has in the picture. For it is not a picture arbitrarily invented and constructed by others. It is the picture which He Himself has created and impressed upon His witnesses. When we say that Jesus Christ lives, we repeat the basic, decisive, controlling and determinative statement of the biblical witness, namely, that He, very Son of God and Son of Man, the Mediator between God and man, the One who lives the life of grace, the Lord and Servant, the Fulfiller of the divine act of reconciliation, that He, this One, has risen from the dead, and in so doing shown Himself to be who He is. He lives as and because He is risen, having thus shown that He lives this life. If there is any Christian and theological axiom, it is that Jesus Christ is risen, that He is truly risen. But this is an axiom which no one can invent. It can only be repeated on the basis of the fact that in the enlightening power of the Holy Spirit it has been previously declared to us as the central statement of the biblical witness.

2. "He lives" is very different from an abstract "He has lived" or an equally abstract "He will live." It is not merely that He did live, but now does so no more, being dead and living on only in the recollection of something past and gone. Nor is it that He will live, but does not yet do so, waiting to be born in some mystical fashion or living only with a view to His future and still awaited life. To be sure, He has lived. But the life which He has lived according to this witness, He still lives and will live according to the same witness. To be sure, He will live. But He will live the life which according to this witness He has lived, and still lives as then lived. His life is bordered neither by a No more nor a Not yet. His history did not

2. *The Light of Life*

take place to take place no more. It has not to take place as though it had not yet taken place. It takes place, yet not as one which is merely present at a single point, but in the power of a history which has already taken place and will do so again. This means, however, that the life of Jesus Christ is eternal life which does not extinguish but integrates and to that extent overcomes the differences between what we call past, present and future. For even as human life, it shares the sovereignty of the life of the divine Subject over these distinctions. And the upshot is the same if we say also that it is the life of the grace which was and will be addressed to man as such, and which is addressed to him precisely as that which was and will be.

(3) That Jesus Christ lives is the confession of the faith which knows Him. If we do not know and therefore do not believe in Him, we either cannot repeat this confession or we can do so only without realising its meaning. This does not mean that this confession is an utterance or expression and to that extent a product or work of faith, its favourite child, so that what is confessed is true and real only on the presupposition of faith. It is faith which confesses. But it does not do so on its own initiative or in its own power. It makes the confession, but it does not produce either the confession itself or the reality and truth of what is confessed. He lives, and the believer lives by the fact that Jesus Christ lives, and not *vice versa*. The believer knows that He lives, and in this knowledge he confesses the fact. But it is only in this knowledge that faith in the fact is born, and man is able to confess that Jesus lives. Even the knowledge in which faith is born, so that there can and must be confession, cannot produce what is believed and confessed, namely, that Jesus lives. This knowledge does not add anything at all to the fact that He really and truly lives. On the contrary, in the fact that He lives it has not merely its object and content, but its origin. If we thought that knowledge could even strengthen, let alone condition or produce, the reality and truth of what is known, it would not be the knowledge which is the basis of faith. In this knowledge we for our part are absolutely conditioned and produced. We are first known by the One whom we may know, and it is only then that we may know and believe and confess. The fact that Jesus lives is true and real in itself. It precedes with sovereign majesty all knowledge and therefore all faith and confession that it is so. In face of the fact that Jesus lives there can be no question on man's part of anything but hearing, obedience and discipleship. He can only participate in a repetition in which he has nothing of his own to utter or express or produce, but can only discharge the debt of response to what comes upon him in this encounter. It is in this response that there is achieved the knowledge in which faith and confession occur. In achieving it, man can only confirm that the life of Jesus Christ speaks for itself.

§ 69. *The Glory of the Mediator*

With this third note, and particularly its final development, we have clearly reached the sphere of our particular theme. Everything that has to be said about the glory of the Mediator, and first about the light of life, might well be summed up in the statement that, as He lives, Jesus Christ speaks for Himself, that He is His own authentic Witness, that of Himself He grounds and summons and creates knowledge of Himself and His life, making it actual and therefore possible.

We shall now attempt various descriptions of what is involved. The first is suggested by the title of this second sub-section. We have now to speak of the light of life, of the light which life itself radiates because it is itself light. As Jesus Christ lives, He also shines out, not with an alien light which falls upon Him from without and illuminates Him, but with His own light proceeding from Himself. He lives as the source of light whose shining gives light without. He does not need to receive light from without, from men, the world, or the faith of His community. On the contrary, as He lives He is Himself the light which shines on men, in His community and over the world, revealing Him to men, and men to themselves and also the world to men. As He lives, He is the light which comes and gives sight to all the eyes which as such are created and destined to see Him and everything which He discloses.

We understand His life as His existence, and this leads us to our second description. It is a matter of His existence under a specific name which characterises Him, which marks Him off from all others, and by which He is to be called and addressed. This name is not accidental or capricious. It has not merely been conferred or appended. He Himself pronounces it. In so doing He declares and expresses His inward self. By it He makes known no more and no less than His very being. He gives us to understand who and what He is, His person, will and work. All real acquaintance with Him rests on the fact that He makes Himself known. All adequate conception rests on the fact that He introduces Himself. No other can do this for Him. He does not need the help of any other. He is present Himself, and being present He himself breaks through the impenetrability of His existence to declare both it and Himself.

We understand His life as His history, and this gives us our third description. This history itself, which, as we recall, is His history as attested in Scripture, the history of salvation, is also as such the history of revelation. In other words, as it takes place it makes it clear and certain that it does take place, yet also reveals the meaning, manifests the purpose, and demonstrates the authority and power with which it takes place, indicating the goal to which it moves, the source from which it comes and the ripe fruit which it bears, and all of itself and in its own power, so that all verification of its occurrence can only follow its self-verification, all interpretation of its form and content its self-interpretation. His history is a question which gives

2. The Light of Life

its own answer, a puzzle which contains its own solution, a secret which is in process of its own disclosure. And always it is He Himself who acts in it, and who in so doing reveals Himself, and the fact that He acts, and the source and purpose of His action.

We understand His life as the work of His self-actualisation as Reconciler, Saviour and Mediator, and we thus come to our fourth description. In its high union of action and passion, of lordship and servanthood (in the biblical sense), His work, the will, achievement, commencement and fulfilment, which constitutes His life, takes place in truth and therefore firmly, certainly, authentically, reliably and validly; nor is it hidden or veiled in mystery in this respect, but at once discloses itself with victorious power. It is a work in face of which there can be no solid contradiction, and which has nothing to fear from a host of flimsy contradictions, because it is the truth, and declares the truth. It does not merely bear the necessity of its recognition and acknowledgment within itself, but, as these radiate from it, it carries them in some sense before itself to the men to whom it comes and for whom it occurs, so that they can ignore or deny it only in the form of falsehood, their only normal possibility being to recognise and acknowledge it in its truth and significance.

We understand His life as act, and this gives us our last description. The divine and human act in which He lives is also as such His Word. As He performs it, He constitutes Himself a sign in which He faithfully repeats it in exact correspondence with its reality, meaning and purpose, correctly representing it, authentically sharing it, declaring it in such a way that it demands obedience, making it public and obligatory, calling all those around Him (the whole world and therefore humanity) to the response, not of decision, which might also be decision against Him, but of a right decision for Him, summoning them to correspond with their own Yes to the Yes which He has spoken in His act. In His life, then, there is no place for the well-known dualism of word and act, for the nervous tension between theory and practice. There is no such thing as pure, undynamic or non-actual reason, logic or speech. Nor is there any such thing as irrational, a-logical, mute or mumbling dynamism or actuality. Wholly and utterly in the fulfilment of His life-act, this One is Logos. He is the "Word of life" (1 Jn 1¹), and therefore the "light of life." But in the fulfilment of His life-act He is wholly and utterly Logos, or, as we have said already, light, name, revelation and truth.

In the Bible glory (*kabod*, δόξα, *gloria*) is a characteristic, indeed, it is the supreme chracteristic, of the divine being and action, and it finds its reflection and response in the creaturely sphere in the glorifying (δοξάζειν, or δοξολογεῖν *glorificare*) of God which is proper to man.

The glory of God (cf. *C.D.*, II, 1, p. 640 ff.), however, is the power of God Himself, grounded in His being as free love, to characterise, proclaim and demonstrate Himself as the One He is in all His competence and might, to create for Himself recognition, splendour, honour and worth, to be in and under His name not merely a genuine reality but one which expresses, manifests and reveals itself. And the human action of praising, magnifying, extolling, honouring and glorifying God is merely a confirmation of the divine self-declaration which takes place in and with the divine life-act; the corresponding and appropriate Amen which makes impossible and unnecessary any doubts or questionings. The glory of Jesus Christ embraces both the *gloria* of God and the human *glorificatio* which it deserves and exacts. As the true Son of God, Himself God from eternity with the Father, He is the original and authentic image of the glory of God to the extent that in His life-act there takes place no more and no less than the divine self-demonstration in the time and space of the created world; to the extent that as the love of God seeking and finding man this act is human history; to the extent that His *doxa*, His power of revelation, is concrete event. But as true Son of Man He is also the normative original of the praise to be ascribed to God by man, the prototype of all doxology as the self-evident response to, and acknowledgment of, the self-demonstration which has come to man from God. His glory is indeed that of the Mediator between God and man. It is the glory of the God who humbles Himself to man, and also of the man exalted to God. It is the glory of the Lord who is a Servant and the Servant who is the Lord. It is thus the glory of the fulfilled covenant faithfully kept by both God and man. In this unity and totality it is the light, the name and revelation, the truth, the Word of life. In this unity and totality it is seen by those of whom it is written in John 1^{14}: "We beheld his glory."

And now we can gather together all that we have said from another angle and with reference back to our first and introductory sub-section. To the extent that the life of Jesus Christ as such is also light, name, revelation, truth, Logos; to the extent that glory belongs to it as such, to this extent it is His life, existence, act, work and deed in His third and prophetic office.

In the language of the Old Testament prophets are men in whose spirit, mouth and conduct, and by whose ministry, the will and work of God are declared and proclaimed and disclosed and brought to light in and among His people to instruct and encourage them. Prophets in the Old Testament are specially selected, equipped and called witnesses to Yahweh's acts of grace, judgment and deliverance as they have taken place, are taking place or are to be expected, and as they constitute the secret of the history of Israel. The life of Jesus Christ is a similar expression and attestation of the dealings of God with men. It, too, in the Old Testament sense of the term, but also transcending it, is prophecy.

2. The Light of Life

To the picture of Jesus Christ presented in the New Testament tradition there belong various accounts which show that He was regarded by those around as a Prophet after the manner of the Old Testament. " And there came a great fear on all : and they glorified God, saying, That a great prophet is risen up among us ; and, That God hath visited his people " (Lk. 7¹⁶), is said on the occasion of the raising of the young man at Nain ; and at the entry into Jerusalem " the multitude said, This is Jesus the prophet of Nazareth of Galilee " (Mt. 21¹¹). For " they took him for a prophet " (Mt. 21⁴⁶). Again, the disciples on the way to Emmaus called Him a Prophet (Lk. 24¹⁴), as did also the Samaritan woman (Jn. 4¹⁹) and the man born blind who was healed on the Sabbath (Jn. 9¹⁷). The belief of many is that " one of the old prophets is risen again " (Lk. 9¹⁹), or that as such He is identical with the last prophet, His own predecessor John, or Elias, or Jeremias (Mt. 16¹⁴). Yet the contrary opinion is also met that " this man, if he were a prophet," would have known that this woman " is a sinner " (Lk. 7³⁹), or more basically that " out of Galilee ariseth no prophet " (Jn. 7⁵²). Nowhere do the Evangelists reject the possibility of numbering Jesus Christ with the prophets, nor the right to do so. But we detect a certain reserve in their accounts of these opinions and statements. For is He really just one prophet after and alongside so many others ? He is a Prophet indeed, but in the Messianic confession of Peter in face of these opinions concerning Him (Mt. 16¹⁶) it is maintained that as such He is more than all those who bear this title, and therefore that in relation to them He is a Prophet in a qualified sense. Certain phrases in John's Gospel plainly transcend or correct the ordinary picture, as when it is said that ἀληθῶς He is not *a* prophet but *the* Prophet, not one of those who has come, or one like them, but the One who is about to come afresh into the world (ὁ ἐρχόμενος εἰς τὸν κόσμον, Jn. 6¹⁴), or even more categorically that He is " that prophet " whom many thought that they should recognise in John the Baptist (Jn. 1²¹, ²⁵). The use of the ἀληθῶς and the puzzling definite article in these passages seem to point to the fact that He is indeed a prophet like others, but that as such He is also the One who first discharges their office in its full and proper sense.

There are four points at which the prophecy of the life of Jesus Christ clearly breaks through and transcends the Old Testament concept of a prophet, and is thus characterised as prophecy *sui generis*.

1. It is not subsequently—even if prior to His birth and conception like Jeremiah (1⁵)—that He is elected and called to the exercise of prophecy, i.e., on the presupposition of His wider human existence. He does not acquire the prophetic commission to preach the Word of God as something additional to His existence and action. For its discharge, therefore, He does not need any ecstasies or inspirations. But even as He discharges it, in His own person as such, He is the One who is commissioned and empowered to do so. In Johannine terms, He is the Son who is " sent " by the Father. He speaks the divine Logos as He is Himself this Logos, the truth, revelation, name and light of God. His exercise of the apostolate is identical with His calling to it, and both may be equated with His life as such as the life of the Revealer.

2. While He is Prophet of Israel speaking to Israel, as Israelite He addresses man generally and as such, i.e., all men. According to the Johannine statement, He arises in the suspect territory of Galilee from which no prophet is to be expected. And finally, rejected by

§ 69. *The Glory of the Mediator*

His own people like all His predecessors, He is the Prophet—and this is the new element—who is delivered up by His own people to the nations and the world, and who speaks to the nations and the world as such.

His life is "the light of men" (Jn. 1⁴) come into the world (Jn. 3¹⁹). It is the light of the world, shining in it and illuminating it as such (Jn. 8¹², 9⁵, 12⁴⁶). It is like the light of the sun shining by day, so that there can be no stumbling (Jn. 11⁹ᶠ·). For all its peculiarity to Israel (Mt. 10⁵; Mk. 7²⁷), His prophecy is universal prophecy. This could not be said of any of the older prophets. We might think of the exceptional figure of Jonah, who against his own judgment was sent to preach repentance to the Ninevites, but in Jesus Christ "a greater than Jonas is here" (Mt. 12⁴¹). Again, we must not overlook the many prophetic utterances which from the 9th century to the period of the Exile were delivered concerning or against the nations implicated in the history of Israel. Yet these were not meant as utterances to these peoples, nor are they to be understood as such. Certainly, there is food for thought in the call of Jeremiah (1⁵, ¹⁰): "I ordained thee a prophet unto the nations," and: "I have this day set thee over the nations and over the kingdoms." Is this an exception to the rule? But when and where did Jeremiah really speak to the nations outside the sphere of the people of Yahweh? We do not really find any true fulfilment of the idea of universal prophecy in any of the Old Testament prophets. Their mission and message are to Israel, not to the world.

3. This is connected with the fact that none of the Old Testament prophets can speak in the light of the enacted reconciliation, of the present reality of the kingdom of God. They have it in common with Jesus Christ that they speak on the basis of the covenant. But the covenant seen and attested by them is the unfulfilled covenant, established and maintained by God, but always denied and broken by Israel, and therefore dangerous, since Yahweh, the Lord of the covenant, will not be mocked. They speak as witnesses of the co-existence, but also of the constant and gaping contradiction within the co-existence, of Yahweh with Israel. They speak as witnesses, officers and partisans of Yahweh in His conflict with Israel. To be sure, they speak for His people too. Even in this conflict God is always Yahweh, and He shows Himself God in the fact that He does not weary of recalling through their lips His own will in its sovereign opposition to the opposition of man. But it is only as they are for Yahweh that they are for His people too. They speak as witnesses of the judgments by which the people is threatened, and will be afflicted, and is already afflicted, as the covenant-partner of Yahweh. They do not do this without also being witnesses of the promises which will not fail to be fulfilled on the part of God. But the men of Israel mistake the promises of God and are in serious danger of missing their fulfilment. That is why they must be addressed by the prophets. Hence their word can be only an indication of the glory of God and the salvation of men as the meaning and goal of the covenant. How could they be seers and witnesses if they did not point to this twofold goal in words of judgment no less than those of promise? Yet their indication is made on this side of the abyss of the great contradiction

by which both the glory of God and the salvation of men are seriously challenged. This abyss is the presupposition of their task and its execution. And in no case can their prophecy be more than an indication of this twofold goal. At no stage in the history of God with Israel was it more than this. Now Jesus Christ, too, is a Witness of the covenant. He has this in common with the Old Testament prophets. But what distinguishes Him from them is that He stands on the basis of the fulfilment of the covenant. The abyss of the contradiction is no longer before but behind Him. The " sun of righteousness " (Mal. 3^{20}), the light of the glory of God and salvation of men, has risen and is shining. The kingdom of God on earth, which is the goal of the covenant, is no longer an indicated future. It is the present in and from which He speaks. What He attests is the peace made in the co-existence of God with His people. The prophecy of His life is also a word of judgment and promise, but it rests on the fact that the judgment has been executed and the promise realised in the condescension of God to man and His exaltation of man to Himself. The prophecy of Jesus Christ is no mere indication. It is direct declaration.

4. This leads us to the last and decisive point. None of the Old Testament prophets is a mediator between God and men. They are all men who are called to the side of God from among others, who are charged to be His messengers and champions to others, and who are sanctified and equipped for this task. But they are all men like others. Their prophecy, which is an alien " burden " laid upon them, can consist only in opposing to the contradiction of Israel the superior contradiction of its God, and therefore in revealing unmistakeably the opposition as such, no less in the word of promise than that of judgment. None of them can remove the opposition. None of them has bridged, let alone filled up that abyss. The contradiction is in themselves too. They can only suffer it; not one of them can heal it, not even Jeremiah, nor Deutero-Isaiah, let alone Elijah or Amos. To point from afar to the glory of God and the salvation of men, they must all point beyond themselves. But the prophecy of Jesus Christ is that of the Mediator. It is not, then, the prophecy of a partisan. Nor is it that of a negotiator running to and fro between two parties and now speaking for the one, now for the other. It is that of the One who is both Yahweh and the Israelite, both the Lord and His Servant and the Servant and His Lord, in one and the same person. He does not need to look or point beyond Himself to attest the fulfilment of the covenant, the executed judgment, the realised promise, the present glory of God and salvation of men, the kingdom of God come on earth. In relation to all these things, He cannot abstract from Himself. The actualisation of His own life is coincident with them. In form and content His witness can only be self-witness : " Come unto me " ; " I am " the way, the truth, the life, the door,

the shepherd, the bread, the light which needs no other light or kindling or feeding, but gives light of itself. His prophecy is the direct self-declaration of His life of grace and salvation, of the life of the God who has condescended to man and of the man exalted to God. It is the revelation of His life in the fulfilment of the act of reconciliation. This is what distinguishes Him from all His predecessors. This is why He is (1) the Revealer by His very existence and not on the basis of special election and calling; (2) the universal Prophet who does not speak merely to Israel; and (3) the Proclaimer of the present kingdom of God and not merely that which is to come.

In sum, we do not have in the life of any of the Old Testament prophets a true type or adequate prefiguration of the prophecy of Jesus Christ. The only thing which any of them has in common with Him is to have been also a witness of the true and real covenant of God with man, a proclaimer of this presupposition and contour of the divine act of reconciliation. In their own times and manners, they were all this. Nor is it a little thing that they were. This is what distinguishes them from all the prophets, heralds, teachers, preachers and instructors which have never been lacking outside Israel both before and after them and right on into our own age. Because they were this, even to-day they are to be heard by us as the heralds of the divine act of reconciliation as the fulfilment of the covenant, just as the apostles are to be heard as its later witnesses. For all of them in different ways proclaim the covenant as the presupposition and contour of the divine act of reconciliation. But they do so within their limits. They are witnesses who are only incidentally summoned and appointed in the sphere of the one special people of the covenant. Their witness is borne in face of the breach of the covenant and the rift between its partners. They are witness who cannot speak in their own cause. Their prophecy attains its goal and therefore its end in that of Jesus Christ. It could have no continuation *post Christum*. There can be no more legitimate prophets like them.

According to Ro. 12⁶ the Christian prophets mentioned in the New Testament are bound to the ἀναλογία τῆς πίστεως. This means that they are secondary witnesses of the first and one true Witness. In other words, they are witnesses of Christ. To try to speak in abstraction from His coming and work in the style of Elijah, Amos, Isaiah or Jeremiah, is to be a false prophet *post Christum*. We cannot fail to insist that much preaching which is well meant, and perhaps deeply sincere and moving, even having a touch of inspiration or ecstasy, but prophetic only in the Old Testament sense, is false prophecy. Nor can even the most powerful preaching of the Law in abstraction, whether directed to individual, social or political concerns, escape the same verdict.

Yet this delimitation cannot be our final word concerning the relationship of Old Testament prophecy to that of Jesus Christ. To be sure, in the life and message of no single prophet do we have a true type or adequate prefiguration and therefore a real anticipation of the prophecy of Jesus Christ. We must accept this. But we are mistaken, missing the wood for the trees, if we try to deny that according to the witness of the Old Testament we do have to reckon seriously with such a type and prefiguration and therefore with such an anticipation. Jesus Christ cannot be compared with Moses, or Elijah, or Isaiah, or Jeremiah. Or He can be compared with them only with the four qualifications mentioned. Yet the fact remains that Jesus Christ, the truth of His history, the light of His life, the Logos of His act, can be unconditionally compared—and not merely compared, as we shall see—with the glory of the history of Israel in its totality and interconnexion as planned, initiated, controlled and determined by Yahweh according to the witness of the prophets : in its totality, i.e., in its character both as divine act and as the experience and action of the men of Israel ; and in its interconnexion, i.e., in its character as an unbroken sequence of new events of divine faithfulness in their height and depth as contrasted with the great unfaithfulness of man. Of the history of Israel understood in this way, there must be said positively at all four points that which cannot be said of the prophecy of any one of the Old Testament prophets. We shall reconsider the series from this angle.

1. The history of Israel takes place, and as it does so it also speaks, not additionally and subsequently, but in and with the fact that in its totality and interconnexion it takes place, and does so in the way that it does. For according to the picture given in the Old Testament, the fact that it takes place, and does so in the way that it does, has from the very outset and continually its basis in an address, promise, command, order and summons of Yahweh. " For he spake, and it was done ; he commanded, and it stood fast " (Ps. 33⁹). This basis necessarily attests itself in the fact that the history for its part, even as it takes place, is a speaking, summoning, prophetic history, a history of the Word of God in the flesh. To be sure, there also takes place in it the fact that it is authentically interpreted, explained and expounded by the specially chosen and called human witnesses who are the prophets of Israel in the narrower and wider sense. But it is not their existence and activity which brings to expression the history of Israel. They merely confirm and record that this is what happens. It is really on the basis of the fact that the history of Israel as grounded in the Word of God is itself speech and declaration, out of its abundance as the history of the Word of God in the flesh, that there arises the existence and activity of the prophets. They merely follow the movement in which the history of Israel does not merely occur, but as it does so makes itself perceptible, audible and understandable.

The first point, then, which the prophecy of the history of Israel in its totality and interconnexion has in common with the prophecy, the light of life, the history of Jesus Christ, is that it takes place together with the history.

§ 69. *The Glory of the Mediator*

This is why the Old Testament is everywhere, and not merely in explicit narration, a book of history. In other words, it is the book of witness to what has taken place, is still taking place and will take place, between Yahweh and Israel. It is not a history book of the earlier and later piety and religion of this people. Nor is it a history book of the truths earlier or later perceived by this people, of its earlier and later teachers and cultus forms. We can find these things in the Old Testament only against its own intention and with great uncertainty and very little profit. What interests the Old Testament witnesses, and what they desire should claim the interest of their hearers and readers, are the facts in which the whole, the nexus of common life in the covenant of Yahweh with Israel and Israel with Yahweh, has its structure and contours. They hear, perceive and understand, as these facts speak for themselves. And the purpose of their confirmation and recording of these facts, of their more or less direct reporting, is simply to cause them to speak for themselves to their hearers and readers.

It is in the light of this intention that we are to understand certain features of the explicitly narrative sections. To mention some points to which G. von Rad has recently drawn attention in a most impressive way, there is, for example, the fact that there are so very many accounts which are not interpreted in the texts themselves, and do not impose any interpretation on their readers or hearers. There are accounts of facts, as in the stories of the patriarchs, which are simply allowed to speak for themselves and to be received as such, which do not need any interpretation, and indeed seem to resist any such attempt. Hence we understand and explain them best if we see them as the mute—but not really mute—facts as which they are presented, and we can then incorporate them best, i.e., in closest approximation to the simplicity of the texts themselves, into the totality and interconnexion of what takes place between Yahweh and Israel. Yet because each of these facts is concerned explicitly or implicitly with the totality of the history, we ought not to expect to be able to indicate what might be called a true historical pragmatism in the relationship between the texts. In these accounts that which stands at the beginning takes place with the character of that which comes at the end, and *vice versa*. Promise becomes fulfilment, and fulfilment new promise. Neither an ascending nor a descending line is to be discerned in the accounts of these facts. The only consistent line consists in the fact that under the same presuppositions the same God is at work in and to the same people Israel in facts which are constantly new. Hence we need not be surprised if the differences between past and present events, or past and present on the one side and future on the other, are often blurred or expunged, for this is very much in the spirit and according to the intention of the authors, even though it does not assist a "historicist" understanding. What has spoken for itself to them, and what is meant to speak for itself in their witness—we cannot insist upon this too strongly—is the totality and interconnexion of this history, its unity of before and after, of then and now and one day. The individual accounts of the facts are meant to bring out the structure and contours.

But in this respect we are not to think only of the narrative sections of the Old Testament in the narrower sense. The prophetic writings and those of the third part of the Canon are also books of history. What is the source of the whole series of works from Isaiah to Malachi? It is exactly the same as that of the preceding history books which tell of the so-called *nebiim* or former prophets. What is meant by the specifically prophetic: "Thus saith the Lord," Yahweh, the God of Israel? Not the powerful or intimate or ecstatic influence of a numen present under the name of Yahweh, but the declaration of the past, present and future history of Yahweh with Israel and Israel with Yahweh. What makes the prophets prophets, each in his own time and situation, is the fact that they perceive these declarations and to the best of their ability must

2. The Light of Life

hear and proclaim them. But primarily, and quite independently of their particular commission and its execution, of their existence and activity as prophets, it is the fact that this history makes such declarations. It is by the fact that it does so that both the former and the latter prophets live.

And the same fact is the source of the Psalter. Where did its authors really derive all that they have given us in these poems by way of confession of their praise, their gratitude, their comfort, their confidence, yet also their penitence, their distress in deepest need, their hope and defiance? How do they know what they obviously think they know concerning God and themselves, God and the created heaven and earth, God's relationship to them and theirs to Him? There are Psalms in which the source of this knowledge is specifically treated, as, for example, Psalms 68, 77, 78, 105, 106, 107 and 136, which all consist entirely, or almost entirely, in more or less extended recapitulations of the earlier history of Israel, to which there is attached a longer or shorter or very short consideration of the writer's present and the future to which he moves. There are other Psalms in which the relationship to the history is disclosed only incidentally, and a few others in which it does not explicitly appear at all. If we are to understand the Psalms in the sense in which they were composed, read and sung in Israel before, during and after the Exile, we must remember that, whether they are Psalms of the individual or the whole congregation, they all stand in this relationship. Is this not indicated, incidentally but most impressively, by the fact that the whole Psalter, and some Psalms directly, are brought into connexion with the name whose bearer is the central figure—first as the *terminus ad quem* and then as the *terminus a quo*—of the history of Israel, viz., the name of king David? What we have here is not just wise or pious poetry, but this one in whom so much promise is fulfilled and so much fulfilment becomes new promise, this one whose history is as it were the history of Israel *in nuce*. His knowledge is the basis of the knowledge extended throughout the Psalter. The echo of his voice is heard in it. And as the Psalms live by his voice, or more generally by the voice of the history which moves to him and proceeds from him, even when they have the character of what are called nature-psalms they are not timeless lyrics, but epics which follow and reflect the acts of Yahweh and the experiences of Israel in their totality. *Mutatis mutandis* the same is true of the Book of Job, of Proverbs, Ecclesiastes and finally even the Song of Songs.

The question arises whether the relationship of the New Testament tradition to the history of Jesus Christ is any different from that of the Old Testament literature to the history of Israel. Does not its witness relate to the self-attesting reality, not of a national history, but of the event of the existence of Jesus Christ in the form of a specific life-history, to the facts in which this reality discloses its structure and contours, and speaks for itself? Do we not understand the New Testament best and most authentically, in closest accordance with its own intentions, if we see and interpret it as the attempt to repeat in human words what this reality has to say for itself, what it has said first and directly to the New Testament witnesses? In correspondence with what the prophecy of the history of Israel has in common with that of the life of Jesus Christ, is not the distinctively responsive and repetitive character of the Old and New Testament writings the formally common feature which unites the two parts of the Canon?

2. We have maintained that none of the Old Testament prophets is as such a universal prophet. But the history of Israel in its totality and interconnexion is universal prophecy. Time and again the Old Testament makes it unmistakeably clear that the covenant of Yahweh with the one Israel and Israel with the one Yahweh, that all that takes place in the covenant, including its self-revelation, and therefore its attestation by the prophets, is not at all an end in itself and does

§ 69. *The Glory of the Mediator*

not exhaust itself in this particular relationship, but has significance, relevance and true and dynamic meaning for the relationship between God and all nations, and the men of all nations. If the one God lives in covenant with the one people, and the one people, on the same earth and among all others, in covenant with this one God, then with this event there is created among all nations an example or living model which cannot fail to have a message for these nations, but actively and effectively speaks as such. To be sure, it speaks first to the one people itself, telling it of the unmerited grace of its God addressed to it, of the incomprehensible dignity and distinction accorded to it, of the gratitude and obligation thus incurred by it, and of the glorious future assured by it. But what is the will of the one God when He claims the gratitude and obedience of this one people? To what does He bind it when He binds it to Himself? Does He not bind it to be visible in its being in covenant with Him, and therefore to be active among other nations, to be a real sign to them in its existence as this particular people? What is meant by the glorious future specifically ordained and allotted to it if not a radiant future beaming and shining in the world and therefore enlightening the world? Can this relationship between God and man in all its particularity be a closed relationship, its revelation a secret revelation, the particular history and word merely a particular history and word? According to the recurrent declaration of the Old Testament, the history of Israel as that of the covenant really has the character of an exemplary occurrence which has as such a universal function. And in the exercise of this universal function it speaks to the whole world and to all men concerning that which is for them, too, the plan and purpose and intention of God, concerning the covenant in which they, too, are enclosed, even though they do not realise it, concerning the glory which God will create among them, concerning the salvation which will come to them, concerning the grateful obedience for whose offering they will be claimed. In this universal function the history of Israel is a summons to all peoples. It is an invitation and demand to know and accept and allow to be worked out that which in the decree concerning Israel is decided and already being effected for them, and therefore, as partners in the covenant made with Israel, taken up into fellowship with this one people of the one God, to confess this membership and therefore themselves and their own destiny.

The second point, then, which the prophecy of the history of Israel has in common with that of Jesus Christ, with the light of His life, is that it too, or already, is the city on the hill which cannot be hid. It, too, takes place in order that the blindness of all eyes should be forcefully ended and all eyes should be made to see.

We must now try to review the very extensive passages in the Old Testament which point in this direction. In the Old Testament there is no general doctrine whose content is the truth that one God, the God of Israel, is the Lord of the

2. The Light of Life

whole world. But there is a witness to the decision taken in and with the special history between Yahweh and Israel, and revealed in it, to the following effect: "The kingdom is the Lord's: and he is the governor among the nations" (Ps. 22^{28}); "The earth is the Lord's, and the fulness thereof" (Ps. 24^1); "God is the King of all the earth. . . . God reigneth over the heaven: God sitteth upon the throne of his holiness. The princes of the people are gathered together even the people of the God of Abraham: for the shields of the earth belong unto God: he is greatly exalted" (Ps. 47$^{7\mathrm{ff.}}$); or in the same sense again: "The Lord reigneth" (Ps. 93^1, 97^1, 99^1); "His kingdom ruleth over all" (Ps. 103^{19}); "From the rising of the sun even unto the going down of the same, my name shall be great among the Gentiles" (Mal. 1^{11}); or again: "According to thy name, O God, so is thy praise unto the ends of the earth" (Ps. 48^{10}); "Thou shalt inherit all nations" (Ps. 82^8); "And of Zion it shall be said, This and that man was born in her. . . . The Lord shall count, when he writeth up the people, that this man was born there. As well the singers as the players on instruments shall be there: all my springs are in thee" (Ps. 87$^{5\mathrm{ff.}}$). For "all the people shall see his glory" (Ps. 97^6), and "one shall say, I am the Lord's; and another shall call himself by the name of Jacob; and another shall subscribe with his hand unto the Lord, and shall surname himself by the name of Israel" (Is. 44^5). What is it that tells us all this with such distinctness? It is the history of Israel by its very occurrence.

Again, the history of Israel has in its occurrence the ministerial function of attesting this decision within the world history affected by it. Is not Abraham himself, the father of the race, who lived alone in tents, described as a prophet, the first of all the prophets (Gen. 20^7)? There is no word of any prophetic activity fulfilled by him as such. All that we are told is that he built altars and called upon—but did not preach, as Luther has it—the name of the Lord (12^8, 13^4). He is a prophet, and as such a public person, by his very being among the Canaanites in his special, or, as we might almost say, private relationship to Yahweh. He is not among them for nothing. His name is to be a blessing for all the nations of the earth (12$^{2\mathrm{f.}}$). Similarly, Jerusalem is promised that it shall be "a praise and honour to all the nations of the earth, which shall hear all the good that I do unto thee: and they shall fear and tremble for all the goodness and for all the prosperity that I procure unto it" (Jer. 33^9). The same is true of the spring from under the threshold of the temple, which deepens to cover the ankles, the knees and the loins of a man until he can only swim in it, flowing eastward by the plain to the salt sea, healing the waters of the salt sea, and producing on its two banks the most wonderful trees (Ez. 47$^{2\mathrm{ff.}}$). We may also consider in this connexion the great ordination charge in Is. 42$^{1-9}$: "Behold my servant, whom I uphold; mine elect, in whom my soul delighteth; I have put my spirit upon him: he shall bring forth judgment to the Gentiles. He shall not cry, nor lift up, nor cause his voice to be heard in the street. A bruised reed shall he not break, and the smoking flax shall he not quench: he shall bring forth judgment unto truth. He shall not fail nor be discouraged, till he have set judgment in the earth: and the isles shall wait for his law. Thus saith God the Lord, he that created the heavens, and stretched them out; he that spread forth the earth, and that which cometh out of it; he that giveth bread unto the people upon it, and spirit to them that walk therein. I the Lord have called thee in righteousness, and will hold thine hand, and will keep thee, and give thee for a covenant of the people, for a light of the Gentiles; to open the blind eyes, to bring out the prisoners from the prison, and them that sit in darkness out of the prison house. I am the Lord: that is my name: and my glory will I not give to another, neither my praise to graven images. Behold, the former things are come to pass, and new things do I declare: before they spring forth I tell you of them." Relevant also is the judgment scene in Is. 43$^{8\mathrm{ff.}}$: "Bring forth the blind people that have eyes, and the deaf that have ears. Let all the nations be gathered together, and let the people be assembled : who among them can declare this, and shew us former things ? let them bring forth their witnesses, that they may be justified : or let them hear, and say, It is truth. Ye are my witnesses, saith the Lord, and my servant whom I have chosen : that ye may know and believe me, and understand that I am he : before me there was no God formed, neither shall there be after me. I, even I, am the Lord ; and beside me there is no saviour. I have declared, and have saved, and I have shewed, when there was no strange god among you : therefore ye are my witnesses, saith the Lord, that I am God." We may recall the mission and promise of Israel : " Behold, thou shalt call a nation that thou knowest not, and nations that knew not thee shall run unto thee because of the Lord thy God, and for the Holy One of Israel ; for he hath glorified thee " (Is. 55⁵). For : " It is a light thing that thou shouldest be my servant to raise up the tribes of Jacob, and to restore the preserved of Israel : I will also give thee for a light to the Gentiles, that thou mayest be my salvation unto the end of the earth " (Is. 49⁶). Note should also be taken of the great passage in Is. 53¹⁻¹² concerning the suffering Servant of the Lord, concerning rejected, humiliated, defeated and unattractive Israel. For it is he that " shall be exalted and extolled, and be very high . . . he shall sprinkle many nations ; the kings shall shut their mouths at him : for that which had not been told them shall they see ; and that which they had not heard shall they consider " (Is. 52¹³ᶠᶠ·). The history of Israel as such is at work in this prophetic office. " Their sound is gone out into all lands ; and their words into the ends of the world " (Ps. 19⁴ P.B.V.).

Again, in its occurrence as such it is one long address and summons to the world. " I will give thanks unto thee, O Lord, among the heathen, and sing praises unto thy name " (Ps. 18⁴⁹, cf. 57⁹, 108³)—which carries with it the call : " Magnify, O ye nations, his people " (Deut. 32⁴³), i.e., this people as the people of Yahweh. But strictly this means : " O bless our God, ye people, and make the voice of his praise to be heard " (Ps. 66⁸) ; " O praise the Lord, all ye nations : praise him, all ye people " (Ps. 117¹) ; " Make a joyful noise unto the Lord, all ye lands. Serve the Lord with gladness : come before his presence with singing. Know ye that the Lord he is God : it is he that hath made us, and not we ourselves ; we are his people, and the sheep of his pasture " (Ps. 100¹ᶠ·). Similarly : " Let all the earth fear the Lord : let all the inhabitants of the world stand in awe of him " (Ps. 33⁸) ; " Sing unto God, ye kingdoms of the earth ; O sing praises unto the Lord " (Ps. 68³²). And finally : " Let every thing that hath breath praise the Lord " (Ps. 150⁶).

But is this decision in force ? Does the ministry accomplish what is intended ? Is the call followed ? Does the dynamic of the history of Israel consist only in the fact that it is in some way significant, but not powerful and effective ? The answer is that, as it is this word addressed to the world, it undoubtedly fulfils a real movement into world history as a whole. " And all people of the earth shall see that thou art called by the name of the Lord ; and they shall be afraid of thee " (Deut. 28¹⁰). When they hear of the ordinances given to Israel they shall say : " Surely this great nation is a wise and understanding people " (Deut. 4⁶). Corresponding to the outflow of the stream from the temple there shall be a great inflow of nations into it. " And many people shall go and say, Come ye, and let us go up to the mountain of the Lord, to the house of the God of Jacob ; and he will teach us of his ways, and we will walk in his paths : for out of Zion shall go forth the law, and the word of the Lord from Jerusalem. And he shall judge among the nations, and shall direct many people " (Is. 2²ᶠ·. cf. Mic. 4¹ᶠᶠ·). " At that time they shall call Jerusalem the throne of the Lord, and all the nations shall be gathered unto it, to the name of the Lord, to Jerusalem : neither shall they walk any more after the imagination of their evil heart " (Jer. 3¹⁷). " In those days it shall come to pass, that ten men shall take hold

2. The Light of Life 59

out of all the languages of the nations, even shall take hold of the skirt of him that is a Jew, saying, we will go with you : for we have heard that God is with you " (Zech. 8^{23}). Even more strongly : " The Sabeans, men of stature, shall come over unto thee, and they shall be thine : they shall come after thee ; in chains they shall come over, and they shall fall down unto thee, saying, Surely God is in thee ; and there is none else, there is no God " (Is. 45^{14}). The same movement is more magnanimously described in Is. 60$^{1\text{ff.}}$: " For, behold, the darkness shall cover the earth, and gross darkness the people : but the Lord shall arise upon thee, and his glory shall be seen upon thee. And the Gentiles shall come to thy light, and kings to the brightness of thy rising. Lift up thine eyes round about, and see : all they gather themselves together, they come unto thee," the following verses describing how they fly like a cloud or like doves to their windows, carrying their particular treasures into Jerusalem through gates which are open both day and night. The isolated and striking passage Is. 19$^{18\text{-}25}$ points in the same direction. It speaks of five cities in Egypt " which speak the language of Canaan and swear to the Lord of hosts," and of an altar built to Yahweh in the midst of Egypt as a sign and witness. " And the Lord shall be known to Egypt, and the Egyptians shall know the Lord in that day, and shall do sacrifice and oblation ; yea, they shall vow a vow unto the Lord, and perform it." And finally, and even more radically : " In that day there shall be a highway out of Egypt to Assyria, and the Assyrian shall come into Egypt, and the Egyptian into Assyria, and the Egyptians shall serve with the Assyrians. In that day shall Israel be the third with Egypt and with Assyria, even a blessing in the midst of the land : whom the Lord of hosts shall bless, saying, Blessed be Egypt my people, and Assyria the work of mine hands, and Israel mine inheritance." In short, " I will turn to the people a pure language " (Zeph. 3^9). " And the earth shall be filled with the knowledge of the glory of the Lord, as the waters cover the sea " (Hab. 2^{14}). " The kingdom shall be the Lord's " (Ob. 21). In face of these and other passages there can be no doubt that according to the witness of the Old Testament the *kerygma* which goes out in the history of Israel is powerful and effective.

Certain comments are demanded. It is obvious that this whole witness to the universal significance, scope and meaning of the history of Israel has an eschatological character. It was its future or final course which was presented to the Old Testament witnesses in this universal prophetic character. But we should not lose sight of the fact that it was still the familiar past and present history which was presented to them in this final course and therefore in this character. It was thus, in this teleology, that it spoke to certain men at certain times, as the coming and being together, not only of Yahweh with Israel, but of Yahweh and Israel with the nations, with those near and far, with the whole world. It was as the history which even now hurries relentlessly to this future, bearing it within itself, that there presented itself to them the whole sequence of the facts created by God and experienced by Israel, from the calling of Abraham by way of the sojourn in Egypt, the deliverance at the Red Sea, the conquest of Canaan, the glory and fall of the kingdom of David, the catastrophe of Samaria and Jerusalem, to the new exile and return. This is what disclosed itself to them as its meaning and purpose. This was its apocalypse or revelation. Is it not, then, rather difficult to criticise or bewail the supposed nationalistic tones which may occasionally be found (even in the passages adduced) in the Old Testament witness to this revelation ? And is it not even more difficult to refuse to take this other side seriously because it has here " only " an eschatological character ? What do we mean by this " only " ? Is it not its true importance that it has this side, that it is also witness of the future, of this future of the history of Israel and its prophecy ? To be sure, it is for the most part in the later parts of the Old Testament Canon that this aspect obviously finds expression. It is for the most part the voice of prophecy before, during and after the Exile which is heard in this respect. But the point is that it is the history which leads from the election of the fathers by so many climaxes and crises to this catastrophe, and then to the disillusionments, misery and great bewilderment of this period, which before the eyes and ears of these later prophets discarded the appearance of particularism in which it was previously enveloped, and represented itself as the history in which the one Yahweh of the one Israel was and is and will be on the way and at work not only with Israel but with all men everywhere. It did this at this stage of its development: not at the time of David and Solomon; but at the time when Israel-Judah could recognise itself in the figure of the chastised, stricken and afflicted Servant of the Lord. Could it more clearly demonstrate its prophetic power than by representing itself at this period, and in face of the apparently opposing adversities of this period, in this final character as universal prophecy?

We can see plainly how the Old Testament witness to the prophecy of the history of Israel coincides with the New Testament witness to Jesus Christ as the "light of the world" "which lighteth every man." We naturally accept the fact that it is historically distinct and limited as compared with the latter. It attests "only" the prophecy, revelation and self-witness of the history of Israel. But again we must ask what is meant by "only." If we let it say what it does say in its historical distinctness and limitation, not suppressing or depreciating what in its final phase it has to say concerning the teleology of this history, we shall be astonished at the agreement of these later prophets, not with Jesus Christ, but certainly with His apostles and the New Testament community generally.

For the rest, in comparing the Old and New Testament witness, can we really avoid the impression that the former is richer, more explicit, more patent and more emphatic than the latter in relation to the problem of the universalism of the covenant, the glory of God and the salvation of man as this is envisaged from the very first, and therefore also in respect of the implied missionary task? Indeed, the New Testament passage in which the universalism of the Christian *kerygma* is most plainly and expressly declared, namely, Rom. 9–11, has as its main theme, not an indication that it also applies to the Gentiles, but a recollection that the perverse Israel of the Synagogue must always be numbered among its recipients. The relationship is paradoxical. It can be explained only by the fact that the universalism of the prophecy of Jesus Christ was so plain and self-evident to the New Testament community that there was no need to emphasise it more strongly than is clearly enough done in the missionary command, in Paul, in the Gospel of John, and particularly in the Lucan writings. The Old Testament says what is not self-evident in relation to the prophecy of the particular history of Israel, and for this reason, in order that it should not be overlooked, it says it so much the more forcefully and colourfully. In this respect we cannot be over-attentive to it if we are truly to understand the far less vivid universalism of the New Testament. If there had been this proper attention, there could not have been that fatal stagnation of missionary thinking in older Protestantism.

3. We have described it as a further limitation of the word of all the individual prophets of the Old Testament, as a further mark of their dissimilarity to the prophecy of Jesus Christ, that none of them can speak on the basis of the accomplished reconciliation and the present kingdom of God. But the prophecy of the history of Israel in its totality and interconnexion does not suffer from this restriction. It certainly speaks of the conflict and contradiction between Yahweh and His people. But it does not speak on the basis of this, nor is it

2. The Light of Life

the origin, content and theme of its witness as we have to say of the utterances of all the individual prophets as the great representatives and champions of Yahweh against His people. It speaks synthetically, not analytically, and therefore unequivocally of the grace of the covenant. For this reason it is not merely the reference to a distant future but the declaration of the presence of the glory of God and the salvation of men, of judgments executed and promises realised. It attests itself as a history which even in its climaxes and crises, even in its plumbing of the very depths in constant outbreaks of human sin and guilt, is overarched and stabilised and ordered by the grace of the covenant, so that, notwithstanding all the confusions and disruptions which it includes, the being of God is finally and decisively an affirmation of the people of Israel, and the being of the people of Israel is finally and decisively an affirmation of its divine election and calling. It attests itself as a history in which there is a deeply concealed but very real positive continuum, so that visible fulfilments can never be altogether wanting, and as there is both old and past and new and coming grace, so there is also present grace unreservedly lavished by God and unreservedly experienced and known as such by the people and the men of this people. The revelation which takes place in and with the occurrence of the history of Israel is the revelation of this positive continuum and these representative fulfilments. Even including its inner vacillations and the contradiction exposed by the prophets, in its totality and interconnexion it is Gospel, good news. We must not miss the *cantus firmus* of this positive continuum above the dialectic of the prophets. It is not entirely silenced even in them. That the history of Israel reveals it is the miracle of its utterance, witness and revelation. In this *cantus firmus* it goes out into all lands, to the whole world and all the nations, but it is also perceived continually in Israel itself.

Hence the third thing which it has in common with the prophecy of Jesus Christ is that in its own way it proclaims with the same force and fulness and from the same proximity that God is not merely coming to be but is, and that as the Lord on earth as well as in heaven He is at work as such.

The notes sounded, for example, in the last seven Psalms cannot be regarded as incidental notes which are immediately silenced again or drowned by others. " Happy is that people, whose God is the Lord " (Ps. 144^{15}). " The Lord is righteous in all his ways, and holy in all his works. The Lord is nigh unto all them that call upon him, to all that call upon him in truth. He will fulfil the desire of them that fear him : he also will hear their cry, and will save them " (Ps. $145^{17f.}$). " Happy is he that hath the God of Jacob for his help, whose hope is in the Lord his God " (Ps. 146^5). " The Lord lifteth up the meek : he casteth the wicked down to the ground. Sing unto the Lord with thanksgiving ; sing praise upon the harp unto our God " ($147^{6f.}$). Then in Ps. 148 there follows the great summons, addressed to the whole creation of heaven and earth, to praise the Lord ; in Ps. 149 a similar summons to the congregation ; and finally in

Ps. 150 the call to a great orchestra of trumpets, shawms, cymbals and other instruments to do the same. We misunderstand the Old Testament if we do not realise that this element of praise or doxology is the basic note. But it is first the basic note, not of the Old Testament, but of the history perceived by the Old Testament witnesses. The sign under which, or the bracket within which, this history takes place is the enthronement of Yahweh, which according to a new conjecture was perhaps celebrated every year, but which took place from all eternity, takes place continually in new demonstrations of His power and goodness, and is the event of the ultimate future. Hence this history takes place always under His government exercised from Sinai, from Sion and from heaven. It always redounds to the magnifying of His glory and, however hiddenly, to the salvation of men. This is what is revealed by this history, and it is to this revelation that all parts of the Old Testament respond.

For this reason we must not superciliously or sceptically ignore, not merely the promises, but the very real fulfilments which are disclosed alongside the many acute or chronic accounts of judgment. We may refer to the wealth of Isaac; to the remarkable success of Jacob in the service of Laban; to the glorious rise of Joseph in Egypt; to the preservation of the people in Egypt and its deliverance at the Red Sea; to its protection from so many enemies; to its feeding in the wilderness; to its entry into the promised land; to the victories of David; to the reign of the wise and powerful and gorgeous Solomon, described in almost apocalyptic colours; to the glory of his temple and its festivals; to the similar glory, expressly and emphatically sung in Ps. 119, of the divine commands, statutes, directions and ordinances given to the Israelites; to the almost incredible confidence with which so many Psalmists, for all their penitence and in every contradiction, still rejoice, and, it seems, are forced to do so, in their hidden being at the side of God and therefore in His righteousness, which they find confirmed in their deliverance from sickness or danger or the hands of their enemies; to the happy restoration with which the Book of Job finally comes to a restful conclusion after so much argument and counter-argument; to the wonderful exaltation of Esther and the later triumph of the Jews over their enemies; to the rejoicing on days of sheep-shearing and harvest; to the peaceful enjoyment of a simple life allotted to every man under his vine and fig-tree; to the dignity of ripe old age crowning a long life. All these are fulfilments. They may be very earthly, material, corporal and sometimes uncertain, but they are palpable fulfilments. "Know ye in all your hearts and in all your souls, that not one thing hath failed of all the good things which your God spake concerning you; all are come to pass unto you, and not one thing hath failed thereof" (Josh. 23[14]; cf. 21[45]). And what other fulfilments are we to expect in the history of a nation such as is attested in the Old Testament? These represent the gracious presence and gift of the covenant in which God and a people live together. They only represent them. But in so doing they represent the positive continuum, the final and indestructible meaning and purpose of this history. In them there is declared and revealed and attested what Calvin according to his understanding called the *substantia foederis* identical in both the Old Testament and the New; the power, mercy and faithfulness, the infinite generosity of God addressed to man and experienced by Him, as these are already at work in the totality and interconnexion of the history of Israel, not sparsely or partially, but in all their fulness.

The New Testament witnesses could hardly praise God more highly than is already done in the Old. On the contrary, it is no accident, nor does it rest on an error or confusion of categories, that in its extolling of the grace of Jesus Christ it so often uses the notes and language of the Old Testament praise of God.

4. On this basis we can hardly contest the fact that the history of Israel and its prophecy have a mediatorial character. One aspect in

2. The Light of Life 63

which it bears this character in the Old Testament is that it is a sequence of events in which God and man are together and work together, though naturally it is God who absolutely precedes and man can only follow. Even as sovereign acts and words of God, as His free acts of rule, judgment, salvation and revelation, these events are also human actions and passions, works and experiences, and *vice versa*. If in their Old Testament presentation and attestation now the one side and now the other is given prominence, there is a general acceptance of their co-existence and co-inherence, of their basic unity, though without any confusion or mixture of the two elements, or transformation of the one into the other. And if this history in its totality and interconnexion speaks as prophetic history, it does so in attestation of this living divine-human unity. Its word is prophecy which combines rather than divides, which unites rather than separates, because it comes from the centre and proclaims the centre where what is above and what is below, transcendent God and lowly man, are together. Hence the Old Testament writings respond to the voice of the history of Israel as it derives from this centre and reveals it.

We may take as an example the account of the battle against the Amalekites in Ex. 17⁸ᶠ·. It closes (v. 15) with the report that Moses built an altar and gave it the name Jehovah-nissi, in play upon which there is introduced what sounds like the verse of a very old hymn : " By the banner of Yahweh, Yahweh will have war with Amalek from generation to generation." This obviously means that God Himself is the One who fights and conquers Amalek ; that He is the Hero of this battle. This emerges in the very description. The decisive thing is not what happens on the field, but the fact that Moses on the hill above the tumult, with the rod of God in his hand and supported by Aaron and Hur, holds up his arms and does not let them fall, since when he does so Amalek prevails. The presence and act of Yahweh, with which these uplifted arms of Moses link what happens below, alone achieve the victory, and to them alone must be ascribed the honour of the day. Hence Jehovah-nissi—Yahweh my banner. Hence, too, the slogan : By the banner of Yahweh, or, The hand on the banner of Yahweh. There is required what is done by Moses with the help of Aaron and Hur : on the one side the omnipotent arm of Yahweh ; yet also the impotent but steadfastly uplifted arm of man ; the strained linking of what is above and what is below, of Yahweh and Israel. Nor can we omit what is done by Joshua and those below : " Joshua did as Moses had said to him, and fought with Amalek " (v. 10). Can we not say, then, that what we have here is simply a victory of Israel like so many others ? The intention of the story is not to let this element be lost, but to show how Yahweh alone is Israel's banner, and how Israel can and should lay its hand on this banner. In this unity, more or less clearly disclosed in many other stories of the Old Testament, the history of Israel is an eloquent, prophetic and even mediatorial history, deriving from and witnessing to this centre.

The other aspect which displays it in this character is a kind of reflection of the first. As in its particularity it takes place in the unity of Yahweh's action with that of His people, it also takes place in the centre between the will and plan of Yahweh and the rest of

§ 69. *The Glory of the Mediator*

human history. What we have to say on this point is connected with what we have already called its functional significance. It is the indispensable link between God and earthly history in general. In its particularity it has a microcosmic character. What the one God wills and plans and has done and does and will do with the human world as a whole, He causes to take place on a small scale, but in a way which recapitulates or prefigures the whole, in His history with this one people Israel. The election and rejection of this people, the disclosure of its transgressions and forgiveness of its sins, the fulness of the benefits with which He provides for it and the severity of the judgments in which it is overtaken by His chastisement, the incomparable distinction yet also the contemptible littleness with which He causes it to exist among other nations, the whole *doxa* of the covenant with which He invests it—these are *in nuce*, in compendious form, His action with all humanity. In all these things the history of Israel is a paradigm or model for the history of all nations, and to the extent that it is prophecy, and is known as such, it is the key to the understanding of world history. Hence it is mediatorial history in the sense of exemplary and therefore representative history. It takes place among all other histories, but in such a way that it implies, comprehends, repeats and anticipates their origin, content and goal.

It is the history of the son (Hos. 11^1), indeed, the firstborn son of God (Ex. 4^{22}), who as such is the head of all others, and of whom it is said in Ps. 89^{27} (with special reference to David as the central figure in all that happens) : " I will make him . . . higher than the kings of the earth." On the one side, then, it is inevitable that general history should bring out the contours of this particular history. This is especially plain in the opening chapters of Genesis. In the account of the great universal Sabbath, of the rest on the seventh day with which God completed and crowned the work of creation (Gen. 2$^{1-3}$), there is reflected the Sabbath celebration, freedom and joy of the service of God in which the history of Israel has its meaning and goal. In the account of the appointment of the first man to inhabit, cultivate and keep the Garden of Eden (Gen. 2$^{8-15}$) there is reflected the induction of Israel to possession of the good land of promise, and in that of his expulsion from the Garden (Gen. 3$^{23f.}$) the bitter experience of the Exile. The story of the establishment of the relationship of man and woman (Gen. 2$^{18-25}$) reflects the partnership, often alluded to by the prophets, between Yahweh the Husband and Israel His affianced bride ; that of the Flood (Gen. 6–7) the apparently definitive judgment which came on Israel and Judah with the destruction of Samaria and Jerusalem ; that of Noah's deliverance and the covenant made with him (Gen. 7–8) the preservation of a holy remnant in witness to the mercy of the divine Covenant-partner outlasting all the unfaithfulness of the people and its consequences. The particular history is thus reflected in the general. But on the other hand it is equally inevitable that the particular should bring out the contours of the general. What it means that Israel's history is really a concentration of all history, and to that extent takes place in its stead, for it, as its recapitulation and prefiguration, and the way in which it does this, are brought out with startling clarity in Is. 53$^{4f.}$, where the Servant of the Lord is also Israel as such, if not only Israel. It is the nations and kings who say : " Surely he hath borne our griefs, and carried our sorrows ; yet we did esteem him stricken, smitten of God and afflicted. But he was wounded for our transgressions, he was bruised for our iniquities :

2. The Light of Life

the chastisement of our peace was upon him ; and with his stripes we are healed. All we like sheep have gone astray ; we have turned every one to his own way ; and the Lord hath laid on him the iniquity of us all." And then finally in v. 12 : " Therefore will I divide him a portion with the great, and he shall divide the spoil with the strong ; because he hath poured out his soul unto death : and he was numbered with the transgressors ; and he bare the sin of man, and made intercession for the transgressors."

This, then, is the centre—this time between God and the world—in which the divine-human history of Israel takes place, itself the copy yet also the original of world history. And taking place in this centre, as history at this point, it is revelation, i.e., eloquent, prophetic history.

But this gives us the fourth point which its prophecy has in common with that of Jesus Christ, namely, that it attests itself to be divine-human history which thus takes place between God and the world. And this last and final point is the basis of all the features which, as we have already claimed, it has in common with the prophecy of Jesus Christ : (1) that it, too, is the history of the Word of God in the flesh, an occurrence which declares His will and action in and with men, the history of revelation ; (2) that it, too, is the light of the world lighting every man ; and (3) that it, too, speaks on the basis of the present reality of the lordship of God.

This fourfold statement, however, leads us to very remarkable and far-reaching insight. The prophecy of the history of Israel in its unity is comparable to that of Jesus Christ in an unqualified sense which is not true of the testimonies of any individual prophets, even the greatest of them. We do not say that it is identical ; that would be impossible. But we do say that in and with the prophecy of the history of Israel there takes place in all its historical autonomy and singularity the prophecy of Jesus Christ Himself in the form of an exact prefiguration. In all its autonomy and singularity, and therefore in all its distinction, it is a true type and adequate pattern. To use a much abused but in its true sense valuable expression, it is Messianic prophecy, and indeed complete Messianic prophecy. And when we say this, we mean that as a declaration of the divine wisdom controlling it, it is fore-telling.

We must insist that the reference is to the prophecy of the history of Israel in its unity. It is not a matter of a minute fore-telling in the Old Testament of details of the prophecy of Jesus Christ as attested in the New, nor of ascribing to the Old Testament a mantic capacity for such fore-telling and to the New Testament witnesses a corresponding skill in discovering and expounding it. The Old Testament witnesses do not fore-tell except in so far as they attest the fore-telling prophecy of the history of Israel. And if in their records of the history of Jesus Christ the New Testament texts obviously refer on several occasions to specific details in the Old Testament documents and see a fulfilment of them, these are illustrations of the unity of the history of Jesus Christ with the history of Israel attested in these documents. In the ancient prophetic word of this history the men of the New Testament constantly perceive the new declaration of Jesus Christ, as they also find the latter constantly confirmed by the former. In all probability passages like those in Matthew and Hebrews give us little more than a glimpse of the full and natural way in which they did this.

The truth of the matter is that the history of Israel says earlier what that of Jesus Christ says later. It is Messianic history, its prophetic word being the word spoken by the Messiah concerning Himself, His self-witness. The Messiah is the One who is not anointed by men, but anointed to serve and rule among men. And this means that He is the God-man who is instituted by God Himself, and who in the midst of world history exists in His name, with His authority and in fulfilment of His will, suffering as High-priest, ruling as King and revealing Himself as Prophet. The history of Israel has reference to Him. Its revelation is His, its word and light are His, its glory is His. No other and no less than He exists and acts and speaks later —for He has now become a person—in the history of Jesus whom the New Testament for this reason calls Jesus the Christ, the Anointed, the Messiah. But no other and no less than He exists and acts and speaks earlier in the national history of Israel. He is the mystery which announces itself in it. In all history there is some mystery. But it is only in the history of Israel that this mystery announces itself. And it is because this is the case, because the mystery which announces itself in it is that of the Messiah, the God-man, that its prophecy is true and genuine prophecy as distinct from that of all other history. It can be this, however, only because it is not merely impelled by an idea or conception of the Messiah, but the Messiah Himself exists and takes form in it, so that its witness is His self-witness, and the announcement of its mystery His self-announcement, the announcement of His coming, His appearing. It is as this foretelling, and therefore *realiter* and not merely figuratively as His advent, that the history of Israel is a type ; that it is indeed the true type as we have everywhere seen ; that it is an exact representation and adequate prefiguration of the prophecy of His history.

If we may give to two words which ordinarily bear a weaker sense a rather stronger signification, we can say that the history of Israel is the " pre-history " of Jesus Christ and its word His " fore-word." That is to say, it is the pre-history in which He Himself acts and the fore-word in which He Himself speaks. It was as such a fore-word spoken by Jesus Christ Himself that the apostles and the New Testament community generally listened to the prophecy of the history of Israel. And it was as an attestation of this fore-word of His that they understood and took seriously the Old Testament. In what was said to them by the ancient events concerning Abraham, Moses, David and Jeremiah, or the life and suffering and prayers and hopes of the Psalmists, as they found these attested in the Old Testament, they did not hear the voice of a stranger, but in direct proximity the

2. The Light of Life

voice of the Good Shepherd, of the One who, as the humiliated Son of God and exalted Son of Man crucified under Pontius Pilate, dead and risen again, had spoken and still spoke to them in their own life-time. As the hearers of His Word in this earlier form they thus became followers and fellows of all those who had heard it in times past. Even in those times was not ancient, distant Israel, no less than they themselves as the community of the Messiah who had appeared and come, and together with them, His body, the earthly-historical form of His existence, the only difference being that Israel had taken one form before His appearance, whereas they themselves had necessarily assumed their own form after this appearing? Did not the men of Israel and they themselves belong together as both belonged, the former in the time of His expectation and the latter of His recollection, to Himself as the one Lord and Head, receiving His one Word and having to attest this one Word of His with their own words? For all the difference of time, place and history, could there be any material contradiction between the words of the Old Testament witnesses and those of the New? Deriving from their common source and subject, were not both the earlier and the later witness necessarily given with such agreement that there could be mutual confirmation and explanation, as in the New Testament exegesis of passages from the Old Testament?

Now what came before was not yet what came after. All that we can meaningfully say is that it lived in and by it, that it was perfectly commensurate with it, and that as such it had a part in its light of revelation or prophecy. Thus, the history of Israel was not yet as such that of Jesus Christ. All that can be meaningfully said is that its mystery was already the history of Jesus Christ concealed in it, and that the disclosure of this history in the future event of the birth and historical existence of the Son of God and Son of David was already the goal which cast a retrospective light upon it. Again, even this light, even the prophecy of the history of Israel, was not as such that of the history of Jesus Christ. What is true is simply that it faithfully proclaimed the prophecy of Jesus Christ, saying already everything that He would say and thus preparing the way for Him— His way into world history—as the one coming Prophet. Hence the characteristic feature of what came before, of the history of Israel and its prophecy and the corresponding witness of the Old Testament, is always this " not yet " but also this " already " in the qualified sense in which we have used it.

To what extent is it " not yet "? What is it that qualifies the " already "? What is lacking in this prior sphere and its fore-telling, including its earlier attestation in the Old Testament (Rom. 1^2; 1 Pet. 1^{11})? What is the limit which is never transcended in the Old Testament? It is certainly not the reality of the covenant in all its fulness, least of all its substance in the presence and action of the

Messiah, and therefore not the self-attestation of His by which the prophecy of the history of Israel is made true and genuine prophecy. The only feature lacking is that the reality of the covenant, the presence and action of the Messiah and therefore His self-declaration, is as yet wholly and utterly concealed and hidden. It is concealed and hidden because and to the extent that what came before consists as such only in the history of Israel and what this has to say and says as such. The Messiah was in this. He worked and spoke in it. But He did so mediately and indirectly, not immediately and directly in His own person. Through Him it took place in this national history. But none of its events was the event of His existence, of His coming, of His personal action and speech. He was its origin and goal, but He did not appear in any of its developments. It is palpable that there is fully found within it the gracious presence and gift of God to His own glory and man's salvation, but the Messiah as the Mediator and therefore the Subject of this happening was not one of the many great and small among whom and to whom all this was done and who were the historical bearers of the covenant and witnesses to its reality. The history spoke indeed—or rather, He, the One, who was already Lord, spoke in its occurrence—but it does not tell us with whom we have to do when we hear it. To do this it would have had to be His history immediately and directly. But it was so only mediately and indirectly. It was a national history in which new figures were constantly appearing, some basic like Moses or central like David, but none being more than representative in relation to the whole or to those around, and none obviously constituting its history the history of a single individual. Only as a national history, then, did it speak its word, so that this word is not that of the history, action and experience of a single life, and eloquent as such, but, if we may put it this way, the word of a dumb man which is correctly shaped and spoken by the lips and tongue, but is spoken without any sound and is not therefore uttered. Or, we might say, it is sounded out, but in a language which the hearer does not understand. The One who could not only articulate but pronounce it in understandable form was not yet present. Or He was present only in the form of the national history which included Him as the One promised and expected, or even as its secret Lord and Governor, but concealed Him until His coming and appearance, thus moving around Him only as it were eccentrically, as around a centre transcending itself as this national history. The fathers occasionally ventured the comparison that His body was born, i.e., His people or community in this first form which is unquestionably His body, but not yet He Himself as the Head of this body. His history was announced but had not yet taken place in that of Israel. His word was articulated but had not yet been uttered in understandable form. In the words of Rom. 10[4], He was the end of the Law, but the Law as such was still without this

2. The Light of Life

end. The prophecy of the history of Israel was true and genuine because it was His, i.e., because His was announced in it. But its glory—the glory which according to 2 Cor. 3$^{12f.}$ shone from the face of Moses—and therefore the glory of the Old Testament witness, was still covered by this veil. The veil was that He Himself, who made it for glory, had not yet come and appeared; that there was still lacking the Son who had been promised to Abraham and David and on whose account all Israel could be called the firstborn son of God. The veil was that the authenticity and truth of the prophecy of the history of Israel were not yet confirmed and demonstrated by the One who was coming in it and in whom it had from the very first its basis, content and goal. This is what was missing in all that came before, in that pre-history or fore-word. He Himself was missing. And the fact that He was missing is the great qualification which the "not yet" impresses on everything which is to be seen and understood without reservation as the great distinction of what came before, namely, as its substantial likeness with what comes after. This is what limits any "already" that we may concede it. It was fulfilled and luminous because what comes after is the great event of the incarnation of the Word of God, because it had a part in this and was hastening towards it in its form as national history. But it was unfulfilled and obscure because, while it came before this great event, and therefore intimated it and to that extent had a part in it, it could only intimate it, participating only in the form of the history of the people of the incarnate Word, in the form of the history of Adam, Abraham and David, as the fore-word to the Word of Jesus Christ. The history of Jesus Christ as such, which follows what came before as its goal and end, had not yet begun in it.

But these negative, or critical, or qualifying statements cannot be our final word concerning what came before. It is not a new or different covenant which is established and proclaimed in the history of Jesus Christ. It is the one covenant in a new reality which is only now fulfilled in this form (or, as Calvin would say, in this *oeconomia* or *administratio*) because it is only now immediately and directly conformable to its basis, content and goal as the reality of the Messiah Jesus latent in what came before, in the history of Israel and its prophecy. It is He who, as the electing God and elected man in one person, is the basis, content and goal of the covenant of God with man. It is He who is the one Prophet of this covenant. His coming, appearance, birth and historical existence as this One are what follows that which came before, so that it is broken off and no longer continues as such.

When that which follows comes, the history of Israel and its prophecy find in it their fulfilment and cannot therefore have any continuations. What might seem to be such are only recollections of their former occurrence which is now broken off and concluded. As such they may be very impressive. They may

§ 69. *The Glory of the Mediator*

even be a kind of proof of God, as the history of what is called Judaism has been called. That is to say, they may be a confirmation in world history of the origin and theme of the Old Testament witness. But as abstract recollections they have always a notably unsubstantial and unprofitable character, with no true or genuine prophecy, because even at best their prophecy is only the old without the new, without the fulfilment at which it always aimed even as the old, and which it has long since found in the new.

Yet the fact that the history of Israel can have no more continuations does not mean that it is outmoded, replaced or dissolved. It cannot be outmoded, because already the one covenant between God and man, instituted in the eternal election of Jesus Christ, was its basis, content and goal ; because it was already actualised in it in this first form as national history ; and because Jesus Christ already spoke and acted in it as His type, His pre-history and fore-word. The new thing—His coming, appearance, birth and existence—does not merely follow upon the old as something new and different ; it proceeds out of it as its fulfilment and completion, and therefore in unity with it. If what came before was merely with a view to what comes after, the converse is also true that what comes after follows what came before, so that it could not be what it is, nor be seen and understood as such, without it. The New Testament with its almost innumerable direct and indirect references to the Old makes it unambiguously clear that the apostles and the New Testament community as a whole, in their dealings with the new Word of Jesus as the one Christ and God-man in His coming, appearance, birth and historical existence, could hear and understand it as the Word of His life and action and experience only in harmony with His Word as it had been spoken and received already in the national history of Israel, as the confirmation and fulfilment of this Word. For them as the witnesses of what comes after there was nothing abstract about what came before. The history of Israel was not merely distant, alien, past, mute or foreign. On the contrary, they saw it in its attainment of its goal, in its fulfilment, in its increased rather than diminished presence and reality in the history of Jesus Christ. But conversely, there was for them nothing abstract about what comes after. The history of Jesus Christ was not something in which the history of Israel, its present and living word, did not encounter them with the same immediacy and directness as it had once encountered the Old Testament witnesses. Far from there being any question of the coming and work and Word of Jesus Christ, of His death and resurrection, either commanding or even permitting them to close and file away the book of the Old Testament, leaving behind them its witness and the history attested as though past and done with, the very opposite is true, that the Old Testament is opened up to them by the revelation and in the knowledge of Jesus Christ, and the witnesses of the covenant in its first form speak specifically to them as the witnesses of the history of Jesus Christ as such. For it is now for the first time, and to them specifically, that these witnesses really do speak. They do not speak to those who would like to hear them apart from the revelation and knowledge of Jesus Christ, as though what came before, as attested by them, had nothing following after, as though what comes after had not already arrived, and the promised and expected Messiah had not already come and appeared. For those, but only for those, who have come to participate in the revelation and knowledge of Jesus Christ, it has meant that the veil has been removed from the face of Moses, and they have come to see the life and light of the Messiah in what came before, finding the old in the light of the new because the old was really the same and bore the same witness as the new, in terms of which it has disclosed itself as the old yet also as the same, and with the same fulness, as the new. For the covenant between God and men is one covenant, and its Mediator is the same "yesterday and to-day." In Him the history of what came before and what comes after is one history; the word spoken before and that spoken after is one word; its attestation in the Old Testament and the New is one witness. To be sure, there is no equation of the one with the other. Each has and maintains its temporal and historical singularity and particularity. Above all, each has its teleology, there being an irreversible way or sequence from the pre-history to the history, from the fore-word to the Word, from the first form of the covenant expected in the history of Israel as a goal to its second form in the manifested person of Jesus Christ, from the Old Testament to the New. Yet there is also no separation of the one from the other, as though the temporal and historical particularities either had or came to have the character of individual hypostases. There is no hardening of the difference between the two forms. There is no intensifying of it into the contradiction of two distinct religions. There is no competition between what is called an Old Testament theology on the one side and a New Testament theology on the other. As there is only one Prophet with whom both the Old and the New Testament witnesses are concerned in their different ways, so there is only one prophecy and revelation, one light and word, and therefore one biblical and Christian theology which has to search and present both with equal seriousness, since the New Testament is latent in the Old (*Novum Testamentum in Vetere latet*), and the Old is patent in the New (*Vetus Testamentum in Novo patet*). Such a theology would become irrelevant if it were to try to do the one and leave the other. In such a case, it would fail to do either, and thus destroy itself.

For we have in view the one Prophet of the one covenant in its twofold form, first concealed and then revealed, when we say "Jesus Christ." And we have in view the light of His one life, the name of His one being, the revelation of His one history, the Word or Logos of His one act, the glory of His one and only mediatorship, His one prophecy in its twofold form, when we consider Him more specifically in His prophetic office in life and being and word and act.

But it is high time we posed and answered a basic question which we have so far ignored. Hitherto we have presupposed and maintained that the life of Jesus Christ as such is light, that His being is also name, His reality truth, His history revelation, His act Word or Logos. We have simply ascribed to Him what the Bible calls glory and therefore His prophetic office. On what ground and with what right may we do this?

Have we merely "ascribed" these things to Him, as many historians think that other functions and titles were later ascribed? Is what we have called the light of His life perhaps no more than the light of a "value-judgment" which we ourselves bring as we illuminate Him by giving Him a particular significance, so that the true source of light is to be sought and found in ourselves, namely, in the standard by which we think we can establish what is significant for us, and in this way arrive at His only real and objective "significance"? Is His truth perhaps no more than that of a category under which we try to grasp the importance of His work? Is His revelation perhaps only another word for the creative insight in which, with reference to and therefore with the help of His figure, we achieve awareness of the problem of our own existence, and the solution of this problem? Is His Logos no more than what we regard as the *ratio* of our own life-action? And therefore at bottom is His prophecy no more than the power and authority of our own self-declaration for which we find an evident confirmation and to which we lend dignity and weight by understanding and describing it as the declaration of this person documented in the Bible, investing His declaration with the glory which we really desire for our own? Is this supposed Prophet, who supposedly speaks to us and to whom we supposedly listen, any more than a speaker fashioned and instituted by ourselves in order that by His imaginary existence we may affirm and strengthen ourselves, yet without His really saying or our hearing anything but what we put on His lips and thus say to ourselves? Before we go any further, it is as well that we should face this question, which is, of course, only a modification of the old question of Ludwig Feuerbach.

But we must be very careful how we state and try to answer it. For in so doing we might easily involve ourselves, or be seduced into, an attempted demonstration in the course of which we should deny the very thing which we are seeking to prove, falling victim to Feuerbach in our very attempt to resist him.

For who is it who really asks concerning the right and basis of our presupposition and assertion that the life of Jesus Christ as such has and is this light in which we for our part may and should live, that His work is truth which comes to us as such, His history revelation by which there is made luminous in and to us and our lives that which cannot be made luminous of ourselves, that His act is the Word of God which is spoken to us from above, which we cannot then say to ourselves, but which we can only receive and repeat? Who is it who asks whether Jesus Christ is really the Prophet whom we have not produced as such but who summons us, calling us out of our pride and sloth and falsehood to fellowship with Himself? Who

2. The Light of Life

is it who asks whether it is really the case that in the witness of the Old and New Testament we have, not merely an example and analogy of the witness which we can give ourselves, but the reproduction and propagation of a self-witness which precedes and transcends all our self-witness and by which all our self-witness must be orientated? Who is it who puts these questions? If it is ourselves, then it is more than likely—indeed, it is certain—that, whether or not we accept these things, our answer will follow the lines laid down by that of Feuerbach when he put these questions. For we shall obviously be merely " ascribing " to Jesus Christ, in accordance with the light given to us or generated by us, the fact that He has and is light. But the question which we really ought to put first is whether we should decide, whether we are in any way competent, whether we can imagine that we have some light of our own which constrains and qualifies us, ever to put such questions. Is there any place from which we are really able to ask whether Jesus Christ is the light, the revelation, the Word, the Prophet? Is there any place where we are really forced to ask this for the sake of the honesty and sincerity which we owe ourselves? To ascribe to ourselves a competence to put such questions is *ipso facto* to deny that His life is light, His work truth, His history revelation, His act the Word of God. The most that we can do in such a case is to " ascribe " these things to Him, i.e., to agree that it is so. But this is useless. We may do it with great seriousness and zeal. But this does not alter the fact that we can ascribe to Him only the majesty which we have first ascribed to ourselves by thinking we can and should assign ourselves the competence to put such questions. If we really knew that we were asking concerning His prophecy, the light of His life, the truth of His work, the revelation of His history, the divine Word of His act, our questions would be silenced before we ever came to the point of giving them even inward utterance. We should realise that we cannot ascribe to ourselves any competence to raise such questions. Immunity against the type of answer given by Feuerbach to his own questions begins with the recognition that these are not our questions and we are quite unfitted to play the role of questioners.

Again, what is it for which we are really asking? Is it for some right and basis of our own on which to presuppose and maintain that the life of Jesus Christ is the light in which we can and should live? Is it for an argument to justify our enterprise in our own eyes and the eyes of others like us? Is it for the demonstration that we can and should engage in it? Is it for the kind of demonstration which rests on the results of a hazarded comparison of the influences streaming from the life of Jesus with those shed by the lives of other important figures? Is it for the demonstration of a lack in our picture of the world and history which can be filled only by His existence and significance? Is it for the demonstration of an anthropological problem to which we can find the answer in Him alone? Or more personally, is it for the confessional demonstration of the direct experience which compels us to recognise and proclaim His Word as the Word of God? This kind of demonstration may be sincerely meant, and attempted and executed with great skill. But it means that we are again hastening towards an answer in the spirit of Feuerbach, and on the point of denying the very thing which we are trying to demonstrate. Let us suppose that someone does really presuppose and maintain that the existence of Jesus Christ is light, truth, revelation, Word and glory, and thinks that it is obviously reasonable and incumbent to confess this. Can it ever enter his head to think that he should justify himself in this matter, adducing proofs to convince himself and others, or to assure himself that he is really right, that what he does is necessary or at least possible? Can he ever forget that what he does, he does in a freedom which neither belongs to him nor is to be won by him, but is given him, so that in the use he makes or fails to make of it he is responsible to no other court than that to which he owes it, and certainly not to himself? Does he not betray the freedom which he obviously has if he tries to demonstrate its validity and basis in any other way than by making use of it, i.e., by venturing this assertion and presupposition in such sort that he has no other option in the freedom given him? In all the arguments he might bring in favour of his enterprise, does he not renounce this very freedom? Does he not act as though he did not have it? And does he not make incredible and even deny the assertion and presupposition from the very outset if in his argumentation for its reality or necessity he regards it as an undertaking which he must guarantee—as though he could have any power to do this!— and has thus to produce various reasons in favour of its theme and content? Even more seriously, if he asks concerning such reasons, does he not deny and betray the very thing at issue in this presupposition and assertion, namely, its theme and content as such? Let us assume that Jesus Christ is the light which lightens every man, the truth which affects and convinces every man, the revelation which comes to every man, the Word which is spoken to every man. Let us assume that He encounters every man in this glory of His and that this is the theme and content of the presuppostion and assertion. What does it mean, then, if we try to proceed to a historical, philosophical, anthropological or psychological investigation and exposition with a view to presenting to ourselves or others the fact that the content of the presupposition and assertion is right, that Jesus Christ is thus a Prophet or the Prophet of God to and for all men, that for such and such reasons He must or at least might well be so? As if perhaps He were not, or not at least self-evidently and with axiomatic certainty! What an " as if "! On this procedure, and the more

2. The Light of Life

basically the more skilfully we pursue it, do we not declare the very opposite of what we intend, namely, that we do not really regard as a Prophet the One whom we think we must help in this way, and least of all do we regard Him as the Prophet of God? If we regard Him as such, we shall remember that He Himself has shown and proved Himself to us as such, that He Himself has spoken to us for Himself, so that He does not wait for us to authorise and validate Him as a Revealer and Prophet, nor does He need our reasons to bring true conviction as to His status. What gives us the freedom to venture the presupposition and assertion is simply the sovereignty of the Revealer and Prophet, the free shining of His light, the free clarity of His truth, this free power of revelation. How, then can we suddenly go back on this content, on the event of prophecy? How can we call it in question again in the name of a supposed sincerity and truth? How can we, for our own peace of mind and supposedly to help others, support its reality as this event with various arguments? How can we try to prove its certainty or probability by the different considerations which we adduce? In so doing, do we not notice that we are still speaking, or have begun to speak again, of a very different matter, moving right away from the *thema probandum* by speaking of the light of the life of Jesus Christ as though it had never really happened? Do we not notice that we can experience, demonstrate and prove the truth of this matter only if we treat it in accordance with itself? It signifies dreadful forgetfulness or confusion in regard to the content of the presupposition and assertion if we imagine, or if it appears possible or necessary to us, that we can treat the majestic declaration of God, of which we appear to speak in what we assume and assert, as though it were a little dogma which we had to defend against the doubts, suspicions and objections of ourselves and others, as is necessary in the case of even the very best and the most profound and self-evident of our human propositions. Can we ignore the fact that this includes a surrender, blaspheming and even negation of the divine declaration which, once we are guilty of it, can only make us ridiculous, however seriously we ask concerning the basis and validity of the declaration? For what is meant by sincerity or truth in this connexion? Surely not a procedure which means that, to prove the truth to be such, we must first treat it as though it were not, and then try to recognise it as such when we have found motives for doing so other than the fact that it really is the truth! This is nonsensical. It cannot be excused or justified by any psychological, apologetic, pedagogic or pastoral intentions, nor by any obligation of scientific accuracy. If we think that we are summoned or obliged or even compelled to adopt such a procedure, we do better to admit that we have not yet heard the voice of truth, or that we hear it no longer, so that we are better advised for the moment to occupy ourselves with other matters.

Now there is no doubt that a question is put to us in this respect. Nor is it put incidentally, but urgently and centrally. Nor is it put in such a way that we can evade responsibility for it, but inescapably, so that we cannot proceed with a good conscience without first giving our answer.

But the point is that the question is put to us. It is not that we ourselves have the competence, or find ourselves in such a position in relation to Christ that we can and even must ask concerning the light of His life and the Word of His act. But as His life is light and His act Word, as He is the truth, we are asked by Him whether we are aware of the fact, whether we realise what we are doing when we presuppose and assert that it is so, whether we know the basis and authority necessary to legitimate our action if it is not to be futile. We may well be ready to take it far too easily and lightly because without the necessary legitimation. Perhaps through the influence of someone who has made the same assumption and assertion before us, and under the impression of the assurance with which he has done so, we are surprised into doing it, and then confuse ourselves into thinking that we are doing the same as he. This may well happen. But this kind of surprise or confusion has nothing whatever to do with the light, the revelation of the truth, the Word and prophecy of Jesus Christ. On the contrary, it has very much to do with the darkness of the heart and conscience in which a man can persuade himself, even in ultimate opposition to Jesus Christ, that he is really confessing Him even though he does not have or know the basis or authority for so doing, and therefore does not know what he is venturing and doing with this assumption. It may well be granted that the one who precedes us with his confession, and so impresses us that we feel invited and challenged to follow him, has genuine grounds for making it. But this does not mean that we have. If we think that he can accept responsibility for answering the question of our basis and authority, we have understood him very badly and made poor use of his precedent and example. On the other hand, it may be that he himself is a poor predecessor, with no legitimation, walking in darkness and not in the light of Jesus Christ in spite of his confession. As such he can only surprise and confuse us, leading us behind the light instead of into it. If he has led us into the light, then necessarily we ourselves are asked by the light on what basis and with what authority we boast that we may live in it. This does not mean, of course, that we are asked whether and to what extent we can justify our undertaking to confess Him, or how far we have any aptitude to do this. What we are asked is whether and to what extent His life, not in others but in ourselves, justifies, confirms and demonstrates itself as light, revelation, truth, Word and prophecy. What we are asked is whether and to what extent His presence and action give substance to our presupposition and assertion that this is so. And who but the

2. The Light of Life

living Jesus Christ Himself can give them this substance which they need as our undertaking and action and without which they can only be vain and empty? But to ask whether He Himself is the motive and therefore the legitimation for our confession, presupposition and assertion as our own undertaking and action, is something which we ourselves certainly cannot do because we have neither the competence to put this question nor any point from which to judge concerning it. On the contrary, when we confess Him, He Himself is the One who asks. Hence we do not have to answer ourselves or other men; we have to answer Him. We do not have to give an account to ourselves or other men; we have to give an account to Him. And as, reached by His light, participant in His revelation, conscious of His truth and encircled by the glory of His prophecy, we give an account to Him, not as those who ask but as those who are asked, we know what we are doing in confessing Him, and our confession achieves the substance, the solidity, the specific weight of knowledge, which it must have if it is not to be a futile beating of the air.

Now we have already stated what we are asked. We are certainly not asked whence Jesus Christ has that with which to prove that His life is light. Nor are we asked how it comes about and is self-evident and perspicuous that He can be and is the Revealer of God, the Prophet sent by God to us and speaking to us, and therefore in this respect, too, the Mediator between God and man. If He were subject to this type of question, and an answer could and should first be found to it, He would not be the Revealer, Prophet and Mediator. If there were any need or ability to prove Him to be such, what is to be proved would slip through our fingers. What we are really asked by Him is whether we are men in whose lives He has expressed and shown Himself as Revealer, Prophet and Mediator. And this means concretely whether we act accordingly; whether our being, thinking, willing and speaking derive their bias and orientation from the fact that He has done and still does this, that He is for us light, rule, canon and standard, not just theoretically by way of presupposition or assertion, but in practice; whether we do not merely make ourselves out to be those who know, or more or less seriously believe that we are such, but really exist as such. It is when we do this, and in order to do so, that we can and should presuppose and maintain that His life is light, and He Himself is the Revealer, Prophet and Mediator. If we exist as those who know, we can and should be also those who confess. And in this case our confession will not lack substance, solidity and weight. Nor will it lack veracity. There will then be the desired demonstration of the content of our presupposition and assertion, and therefore its establishment and vindication. But we really are asked by Him whether we act as those who are " of the truth," to use the saying to Pilate in John 18[37]: " Every one that is of the truth heareth my voice." He must not, may not and will not, then, put any more the question of Pilate: "What is truth?" He no longer has the false freedom to ask for special confirmations of the truth from without. Nor does he stand under the false compulsion of having to ask for such confirmations. It has of itself confirmed itself to him. How, then, can he behave as though this had not happened, seeking and enquiring whether the light of the life of Jesus Christ which has shone upon him can really be light, and he himself a child of light? He hears His voice, and his only possible question, put to him by this voice, is not whether and how this voice will show itself to be the voice of truth, but whether and how he himself will show himself to be its hearer. It is not self-evident that he will do this. For even the man to whom the truth has shown itself to be truth, who is thus "of the truth," and therefore hears the voice of Jesus Christ, might very easily deny this in practice by raising again the question of Pilate (" What is truth? ") which he must not and may not raise, demanding and seeking other confirmations and thus being disobedient to the voice which he hears. But is this necessary? Does he have to deny in practice that he is " of the truth " ? Has this impossible thing really to take place? Surely he might also show himself to be a hearer of the voice of Jesus Christ. And what he is asked is whether he will do this, whether he will be obedient. Again, however, it is not self-evident that he will do this properly. There might be a full or only a partial obedience, and therefore a better or worse demonstration. The man freed by the truth for the truth might make only a partial or halting use of his freedom. His use of it might leave much to be desired in the way of clarity and consistency. Hence he is not merely asked whether, but also how, he will prove himself. Yet however that may be, the question which is put to us in respect of our presupposition and assertion that the life of Jesus Christ is as such light, truth, revelation, Word and glory, is the question of our authentication in face of the fact that He is this, of our right conduct in face of the content of this presupposition and assertion, of our obedience to the voice of Jesus Christ. To this question there can be no possible answer in the spirit and along the lines of Feuerbach.

But supposing we set aside once and for all the threatened temptation, what will be the tenor of a sound answer to this question? What is meant by authentication, right conduct and obedience in this connexion? It is obvious that it must be in the whole life of a man that the correctness of our presupposition and assertion must be seen. We show it as we really allow the life of Jesus Christ to be the light of our whole life, and are really prepared to lead our whole life in the light of that of Jesus Christ. In the present context, however, we can only take into account a comparatively narrow but in its way truly significant and decisive sector, namely, how there is to be achieved an authenticating, true and obedient thinking and speaking in which the content of the presupposition and assertion, i.e., that the life of Jesus Christ is as such light, is wholly and evidently and consistently honoured, and we show ourselves to be those who hear His voice and act in correspondence and not in contradiction with this fact. We shall attempt to answer the question in the modest field of dogmatic and to that extent theoretical deliberation. But is there a Christian practice which does not necessarily have also the form of a Christian theory? Again, is there a Christian theory which is not necessarily in itself and as such an element of Christian practice? At any rate, in the deliberations upon which we now enter we have to do with a theory which is to be understood only with reference to its origin and goal in practice.

We take as our starting-point the fact that in the life of Jesus Christ we deal, not with an indeterminate happening, but with that of the presence and action of God. It is for this reason that we say that His life is light, truth, revelation, Word, glory; that it not merely might be, but is; that we not merely suppose that it is, but it is indisputably; that it is so primarily and intrinsically and not just secondarily and derivatively. We say this in view of the fact that in this life God Himself is present as acting Subject. Our presupposition and assertion in respect of this life includes within itself, and has as its basis and authority, the statement concerning God that He is in Jesus Christ. He was this, and will be. This is why it involves such danger and such a betrayal to think that we have to ask something, and particularly that we have to ask how we can prove the content or occurrence of the prophecy of Jesus Christ to ourselves and others. This is why we can see ourselves only as those who are asked. If it were not a matter of God, everything would be different. But it is a matter of God. Hence we can only see ourselves as those who are asked concerning our acknowledgment and respect, concerning our praise of God. And there is no place for the false freedom or necessity in which we might feel compelled, in face of the life of Jesus Christ, and in defiance of its prophecy, to ask concerning its authority, putting Pilate's question as to the truth in defiance of the truth itself. Where God is present as active Subject; where He lives, as is the case in the life of Jesus Christ, life is not just possibly or secondarily but definitely and primarily declaration, and therefore light, truth, Word and glory. A mute and obscure God would be an idol. The true and living God is eloquent and radiant. If He is in large measure mute and obscure to us, this is another matter. In Himself, whether we perceive and accept it or not, He is eloquent and radiant. He does not merely become this when we perceive and accept Him as such. He does not merely become it in His work in creation, time and history. If He is eloquent and radiant in creation and history, this is on the basis of, and in correspondence with, the fact that from all eternity He is not merely the Father, but also the eternal Word as the Son of the Father, and that in the Son He has the reflection of His own glory. Hence it is not accidental or external to Him, but essential and proper, to declare Himself. He does this as He is God, and lives as such. It is in this glory of God that Jesus Christ lives. Now there is no beginning before God, no height above Him, no depth beneath Him, no ground outside Him. But as His life has no whence or wherefore, so His light and speech have no basis or authority, apart from the fact that the life is His life, that as such it cannot be concealed but impels and summons to revelation, that it wills to be recognised and known as such, that it can be recognised and known only through itself, and that it is therefore self-disclosing life. How could it be deduced from any principle that it is self-disclosing and therefore eloquent and radiant? Even the reference which we have ventured to the trinitarian being of God cannot be deduced from any principle, but can only describe and explain the fact that God Himself and He alone is the principle and source from which all that He is, and therefore the fact that He is self-disclosing life, does not " derive " as in the case of a logical deduction, but is eternally repeated and confirmed in the act of His existence as the living God. But it is this life which discloses itself in the act of His existence that is lived by Jesus Christ as the Son of God. This is what is meant when we call His life light. This is the content of our assumption and assertion. This is why it is inviolate against every conceivable doubt or denial. This is why it is equally inviolate against all the related demonstrations and confirmations which might try to buttress it from without. And if the question is put whether and how we can confirm ourselves in this connexion, the first and simple answer is that, in full realisation of what we are doing, we are invited and summoned by what we assume and assert to consider and take seriously the fact that in the life of Jesus Christ we do not have an indeterminate happening, but that of the presence and action of God Himself; that we do not have an incidental Word which might be spoken or not, but the eternal Word; that we do not have any light which might or might not shine, but the eternal light. If we consider this and take it seriously, our conduct will be right, for it will be required by the matter itself. We will thus show ourselves to be those to whom the truth has confirmed itself as truth, who are " of the truth " and children of light. And we may confidently venture our presupposition and assertion. We shall do so in legitimate fashion Our *thema probandum* will be directly before our eyes and crystal clear. Questions like that of Feuerbach will not be even remotely possible. Considering and taking seriously the fact that God is present and active, we have renounced all such questioning from the very outset. We have not merely ascribed to the life of Jesus Christ, or appended to it as a title of dignity on the basis of its value, but really accepted

2. The Light of Life

as its given reality, the fact that in itself and as such it is prophecy. In saying this, we are not advancing a thesis of our own which we then have to defend. We are saying it in response to the thesis which is unmistakeably and incontrovertibly set before us in the life of Jesus Christ as that of God Himself: "I am the light of the world."

To choose another aspect, we now take as our starting-point the fact that the life of Jesus Christ is that of the covenant grace willed and determined by God and addressed and given by Him to the man for whom and to whom it is active. It is for this reason that we call this life light, revelation, Word and glory, with no questions as to whether it might be, with no qualms or hesitation, with no sense of ascribing attributes, but in the sense of a simple statement concerning its essence as this life. Grace, willed and practised by God as His action to man, is as such God's self-disclosure and self-impartation as it takes place towards man but is grounded in His own divine being. It is the choice and act of His own incomprehensible freedom to be the Almighty and the Holy One, not only in and for Himself, not only in His own transcendence and self-originating life, but also beyond this in the depths. In this freedom He is God. He is not untrue to Himself but supremely true, the living, almighty and holy God, in the fact that He is gracious. He is this to man, in His eternal choice to disclose and impart Himself to him, and in the historical event in which He does this, on the basis of the fact that to be gracious, to disclose and impart Himself, is already His own freedom, the freedom of the Father to be in and for Himself, yet not to be only in and for Himself, but eternally to disclose and impart Himself in the Son, and with the Son in the Holy Ghost. No idea of God, no god invented and made by man and exalted to divinity, is gracious in himself or to man. The true and living God is gracious. He transcends Himself. He discloses and imparts Himself. He does this first in Himself, and then and on this basis to man in His eternal election and its temporal and historical fulfilment. And in the life of Jesus Christ we are not dealing with God and His presence and action in the abstract, but specifically and concretely with His election and act of grace, with the election and act of His characteristically and exclusively divine freedom to disclose and impart Himself. Because it is the life of grace, it is this eloquent and radiant life. Grace would not be grace if it were to remain mute and obscure, or could try to be in and for itself alone. It would be a contradiction in terms if it did not mean self-disclosure and self-impartation, or were not eloquent and radiant. As such, it is indeed eloquent and radiant. As such, it is prophecy. This is what is meant when we speak of the prophecy of the life of Jesus Christ. Grace is the election and act of God which is not to be expected or demanded by man, which cannot be provoked, let alone projected or produced by him, but which simply comes to him, which affects and determines him, which is quite undeserved but addressed to him without and in spite of his deserving. It is the inaccessible thing which "eye hath not seen, nor ear heard, neither have entered into the heart of man," but which nevertheless displays itself before his eyes, and makes itself heard, and sinks into his heart, in virtue of the free work of God Himself. Grace means that God expresses Himself before man, declaring Himself as the truth in his existence. It means that He causes Himself to be perceived by this one who is not His equal, who is merely His creature, and who has wilfully closed his eyes and ears and heart to Him. It means the free revelation of God. This takes place in the life of Jesus Christ. In this life it is a matter of God's unmerited good-pleasure, of His free grace, and therefore of His free Word to man. What Jesus Christ lives is God's self-disclosure and self-impartation as inscrutably grounded in His divine sovereignty. It is both the event and the message at one and the same time: God among us; God with us; and God for us. This act and declaration is the content of our assumption and assertion that the life of Jesus Christ is light and prophecy. We do not venture it arbitrarily or at random, but on the basis of the fact that this life is grace, and grace is radiant as such. Hence there is no need to establish or justify its radiance from some other point. Indeed, all attempts to do this are forbidden. Grace itself, and the light of grace, are the election and work of the divine freedom whose action is established and justified in itself alone, but in itself unshakeably. When grace and its light are present and active, as is the case in the life of Jesus Christ, all suspicions and objections against our presupposition and assertion are answered before they are even raised or uttered. They can arise and have force only when the grace of God and its light are not present and active. And if there is one serious question in this whole matter, namely, that which its content addresses to us, the question of our demonstration in obedience to it, the answer to this question, and therefore our demonstration, can consist only in the kind of attitude and conduct to the gracious Word spoken in the life of Jesus Christ which alone are possible in face of it as the gracious Word of God's gracious work. But this means that we can answer it only in gratitude and with thought and utterance which express this. Our freedom to give thanks, and our freedom in thanksgiving, are the consequence corresponding to the divine work and light and Word of grace addressed to us in the life of Jesus Christ. But how can we give thanks except with the freedom, confidence and joy of confession that this light is light, this Word Word, the glory of this life glory? This does not mean any discovery or disclosure on our part. It means that we ourselves are discovered and disclosed as those who are freed for the gratitude of this confession, who may make use of this freedom, and who can make use of it willingly—for otherwise it would not be freedom. How sad it is that the worthy Feuerbach,

2. The Light of Life

like so many other unbelievers and believers, seems not to have had any knowledge of this freeing and freedom, and thus seems to have interpreted the glory of God merely as the self-glorification of man, and the light of the life of Jesus Christ merely as the shining of a light supposedly immanent in man himself, and finally, therefore, to have evaded rather than accepted encounter with it! We must be careful that we venture our assumption and assertion only in this freedom and therefore in grateful thought and utterance. In this freedom it not only can and may but will be ventured. And ventured in this freedom, it cannot be called in question from any quarter.

To select a third starting-point, the life of Jesus Christ, even as the life of God and the life of His grace, is the life of a man who as such, as one of us, as our Fellow, Associate and Neighbour, among the countless numbers of men who have lived, live and will live, is this particular man, the man who even in our human situation and within our human history, has lived and lives and will live this eternal life, this Stranger whom we cannot overlook or remove as such because as such He is at home among us and like us and with us, belonging as we do to our human situation and history. It is because it is the life of this Alien who is so utterly at home among us and so fully belongs to us, of this near Neighbour even in all His otherness, that this life is called light, revelation and Word. As the life of God and His grace, it is not lived in a distant height and therefore in mute obscurity; it is concrete event in the sphere in which this is true of our own lives. It is placed in this sphere, opposed to us in all its singularity and strangeness, yet also set alongside. To be sure, it is new as compared with the accustomed realities of this sphere. It stands in marked contrast with our own life, or what we regard as such. It radically questions all our positions. Yet it is unmistakeably real because, for all its difference from ours, it is the life of a man like us : the name which is hallowed in our situation, time and history ; the kingdom which has drawn near and impinged as it were upon us ; the will of God which is done not merely in heaven but on earth. This happening has as such a voice. It is a declaration. And as it comes to us, it is an address, promise and demand, a question and answer. This is what is meant by our presupposition and assertion that in the life of Jesus Christ we have to do with a Word and prophecy. As the life of God and His grace, it may be perceived and understood by us as it has come and comes and will come to us, bearing quite unmistakeably our human form. It shines in these specific contours. It is near us in these contours. It cannot, then, be confused with any other life. It encounters us, speaks with us, addresses us in terms of I and Thou, and all in such a way that there can be no doubt concerning either the fact that it speaks or the content of what it says, nor any suspicion that we might be merely speaking to ourselves. For as the Bearer, Bringer and Herald of the life of God and His grace, of eternal life, there comes to us Another to speak to us spontaneously and unexpectedly, without any request or requirement on our part. There comes to us this other man whose reality is removed, by the fact that He speaks, from the sphere in which its possibility might be contested or attempts might be made to establish and justify it ; whose reality is truth as such. But there is more to it than this. For when this man encounters us as the Bearer, Bringer and Herald of this life, something happens to us. How do we stand in relation to Him ? We are men like Him, and therefore He can encounter us in His reality as truth, speaking with us. But we are not like Him in so far as the life which He lives is not ours nor that of any other man. For who of us lives an eternal life, the life of God, the life of grace ? Confronted and compared with His life, the life which we live or describe as such is only a vacuum and darkness. Is this the case ? It certainly needs the confrontation and comparison of our life with His ; it needs His encounter with us, to make it clear to us that our life is a vacuum and darkness. There is no human understanding in which we are finally capable even of the perception, and can be clear and certain, that this is so. How can there be ? To achieve even this limiting knowledge, we should have to know the very thing which we lack, namely, this other eternal life, the life of God and His grace. But how can we know this when none of us can live it of himself nor display it to others ? How can we even ask concerning it, or miss it ? The human situation is doubly critical in the sense that we live in a vacuum and darkness but are not even aware that this is so. Our life is not in fact that other life. In no single case is this true. Hence we cannot know that other life. We cannot ask concerning it nor even miss it. Yet this does not alter in the slightest the fact that we do actually lack it and therefore live in a vacuum and darkness. But in this doubly critical situation we are not abandoned. There encounters us at this very point that Fellow, Associate and Neighbour, a man like ourselves, whose human life as distinct from ours is eternal life, the life of God and His grace, the hallowed name, the kingdom drawn near, the will of God done on earth. This means that in His human person there encounters us the fulness which invades the vacuum which we do not yet know, the light which falls upon the darkness of which we are not yet aware. In His person which is not ours—this necessarily means that there is revealed and made known what is not accessible to any self-understanding as such, namely, our being in a vacuum and walking in darkness. This is inevitable, for as the life of this Stranger the fulness of His life is set in contrast with our emptiness, its light with our darkness. And now we cannot fail to see, experience and know what we lack, and who and what we are as those who do not share in this other life which encounters us. Now we become aware of the abyss above which we unsuspectingly moved. But at the same time, again in the human life of this human person, we now

2. The Light of Life   85

become aware of the fact that we are prevented and delivered from plunging into this abyss. For as the Stranger who lives this other life He is at home among us. He is not merely set in contrast with us, but placed alongside as One of us. He reveals the life of God which He lives to be the life of our God, the life of grace to be that of the grace which is directed to us and all men, the eternal life that of the real life ordained and promised to us. As a life lived for us, and clothing and crowning our poor life with the promise of this very different one, it is a human life like ours, lived in the midst of all other human life. And it is not the fact that we lack this life, but that it is given us in Him, which is the bearing, the true and positive meaning, of His encounter with us, the brightness of the light which it causes to shine upon us. We cannot forget our being in a vacuum and in darkness, for it is radically and unforgettably brought before us for the first time in Him. This recollection is a warning against any attempts to confirm it of ourselves. For nothing produces nothing. Even with the greatest perspicacity, we could produce from this vacuum and darkness nothing but further vacuum and darkness. Even less, however, can we confirm the fact which we also cannot forget simply because it is first and decisively set before us, namely, that the life of Jesus Christ is the filling of our vacuum and the light of our darkness. It is the fulness of life. As such it shines forth. And this shining of the fulness of life of Jesus Christ is the content of our presupposition and assertion. We can and must venture it as those who prove themselves in this shining. And from this standpoint, too, the authentication and obedience consist in the fact that we resolutely think and speak as those who have the vacuum and darkness of their own lives directly and unforgettably behind them and the fulness and light of His life directly, dominatingly and convincingly before them. In this transition from the direct past to the direct future, in this Now or present, or, as we might say already, in this presence of the Spirit, we are " of the truth " and hear the voice of the living Jesus. In no form and on no pretext, therefore, can we return to the question of Pilate. The good confession of the prophecy of Jesus Christ is both legitimate and obligatory for us. We can venture it without embarrassment, and need be afraid of no Feuerbach. The only thing is that we must not be ashamed to be like children. We must see to it that we think and speak in this present and not another.

So much by way of answer to the question which has detained us. We can now resume our path and pursue it to the end.

It might help to a better understanding of our answer if we expressly recall that methodologically our line of argument is informed by the true spirit and import of the " ontological proof " of Anselm of Canterbury. The point of our whole exposition is positively: *Credo ut intelligam*, and polemically: " The fool hath said in his heart, There is no God." As we have put it, the declaration of the prophecy of the life of Jesus Christ is valid as and because it is a declaration concerning the life of Jesus Christ. But is not this begging the question ? Are we not arguing in a circle ? Exactly ! We have learned from the content of our presupposition and assertion, and only from its content, that because it is true it is legitimate and obligatory, and in what sense this is the case. *Honi soit qui mal y pense.* Only fools can say in their hearts that this is a *circulus vitiosus*, as though there could not also be, and in this case necessarily is, a *circulus virtuosus* as well.

We have now laid down our main christological thesis that the life of Jesus Christ is as such light and His reconciling work a prophetic Word. We have compared this prophecy of His with that of the Old Testament prophets and related it to the prophecy of the history of Israel as recounted in the Old Testament. We have halted for a moment to discover what is the necessary and only possible demonstration of this thesis.

We must now go on to make an emphasis which is decisive for our understanding of the whole. In other words, we must make a conscious because necessary application of the definite article. Jesus Christ is *the* light of life. To underline the " the " is to say that He is the one and only light of life. Positively, this means that He is the light of life in all its fulness, in perfect adequacy ; and negatively, it means that there is no other light of life outside or alongside His, outside or alongside the light which He is. Everything which we have to say concerning the prophetic office of Jesus Christ rests on this emphasis, being distinguished by it, and by the implied delimitation, from what is also to be said of other prophets, teachers and witnesses of the truth, or of the prophecy entrusted to the Christian community and each individual Christian. " Jesus Christ as attested to us in Holy Scripture is the one Word of God whom we must hear."

It is for this reason that, instead of devising a new formulation, we have chosen as our thesis at the head of this christological section the first statement of the *Theological Declaration* of the Confessional Synod of Barmen in 1934. We have already commented on the historical purpose and context of this thesis in *C.D.*, II, 1, pp. 175 ff., and an important exposition is also to be found in a recent book by Ernst Wolf entitled *Barmen* (1958). In 1934 the time was ripe and necessary for confession not only against a very concrete and threatening situation, but against a long period of very dubious thought and utterance in Protestantism as a whole. There is no need at the moment to speak of the thesis as such. It is quoted to remind us of the relevance of the problem which now concerns us, and particularly of the emphasis and delimitation that Jesus Christ is the *one* Word of God. In the *Declaration* it was explained and given greater precision by the accompanying antithesis : " We reject the false doctrine that the Church can and must, as the source of its proclamation, recognise other events and powers, forms and truths, as the revelation of God outside and alongside this one Word of God."

The basis, the first and final meaning, of the statement that the life of Jesus Christ is the one and only light may be indicated at once.

It is this because His life is the one and only life. Naturally, we shall have to return to this. Our first task must be to develop, understand and estimate the statement as such.

We may begin by saying that, not only for those who are without but initially and constantly for those who have already come to faith in Jesus Christ, it is a hard and offensive saying which provokes doubt and invites contradiction. It is like a hurdle which has to be jumped, and jumped again and again. There are horses which constantly shy at this hurdle and think they should refuse it. Why should we follow only one Prophet? Why should we not give at least a little honour to our own prophecy alongside and in opposition to His?

The basis of the saying is to be found in another "hard saying" (Jn. 6⁶⁰) which precedes it, namely, that "except ye eat the flesh of the Son of man, and drink his blood, ye have no life in you" (v. 53). This was said to the "Jews." But even many of His disciples regarded and described it as a σκληρὸς λόγος, a difficult and even intolerable statement. It evoked muttering and grumbling and murmuring (γογγυσμός) and σκάνδαλον, not only among the Jews, but also among them: "Who can hear it?" Hence what follows cannot fail to give fresh offence: "The words that I speak unto you, they are spirit, and they are life" (v. 63). "From that time many of his disciples went back, and walked no more with him" (v. 66). Hence, too, the question which Jesus can now put: "Will ye also go away?" (v. 67). And the answer of Peter, which is the Johannine counterpart to the Messianic confession of Mt. 16¹⁶, is anything but self-evident, bearing witness to the way in which the disciples overcame an offence which they also had experienced: "Lord, to whom shall we go? thou hast the words of eternal life" (v. 68).

The whole difficulty would be removed if we could be content with the mere assertion that Jesus Christ is one light of life, one word of God: the clearest perhaps; a particularly important one, and of great urgency for us; but only one of the many testimonies to the truth which have been given by others and which have also to be studied and assessed together with His. In short, it could be accepted that He is a great prophet. This could be easily received, and perhaps even with great willingness and readiness. It could be warmly and enthusiastically championed. Many cogent arguments could be found for it. It need not be disputed by the modern Synagogue. It is actually stated in the *Koran*. It can be accepted by Western Idealism. With this message we need not expose or compromise ourselves, or provoke suspicion or unpopularity, or give offence to anyone, least of all to ourselves. Noble rivalry or peaceful co-existence is possible with whose who prefer other lights of life or words of God. And, of course, we maintain our own liberty to hear other such words as well, and perhaps even to prefer them.

But supposing that we cannot be content with this? Supposing that the explicit or implicit meaning of the confession of Jesus Christ is that *Thou* hast the words of eternal life, Thou alone and no other (for there are no others to whom we may go), Thou alone not merely

§ 69. *The Glory of the Mediator*

for me but for all others and all men, yet Thou particularly for me, so that I have no option but to hear these words from Thee? Supposing that the confession excludes as quite illegitimate and prohibited the free and friendly acceptance of many lights of life and words of God among which that spoken by Thee is only one? Supposing that the freedom of the confession consists in thinking and speaking in this way? What will happen when a Christian or the community or theology makes use of this freedom?

The objection to it, and therefore to the statement that Jesus Christ is the one Word of God, is quite obvious even to those who confess it. It has maintained a kind of eternal youth throughout the centuries. And because it does not come upon the Christian only from without, but first and supremely from within, the same is true of the more or less serious attempts made even by the Church and Christianity to suppress this statement, or at least to evade it, to let it drop. Such attempts have always been thought to be necessary and justifiable even within Christianity, and therefore there will always be a future for them.

In what time or place has not the world in its confrontation by the Church finally and basically taken offence at this statement, anxiously or scornfully or defiantly putting to the Church the question whether the confession of Jesus is really to be understood so narrowly or His prophecy so exclusively? In what time or place has not the political, social, apologetic or even evangelistic and missionary situation openly cried out for the removal of this offence and therefore the concealment of this statement, or its dilution by others, or even its abandonment? Even in Roman Catholicism the insight has never been completely lost that this must not take place, but that a genuine attestation and proclamation of Jesus Christ in the world stands or falls with the implicit and sometimes explicit confession of this dangerous statement. Yet the Roman Catholic system, as developed with remarkable consistency throughout the centuries and still maintained against all attempts at reform, is not really based upon this insight or this confession. On the contrary, it is a system of evasion of confession. It is the great attempt to secure the existence of the Church in the world by a comprehensive combination of the truth of Jesus Christ with other comparatively independent truths, such as those concerning Mary, tradition and the teaching office in a first class, the truths of nature and reason in a second, and various political truths in a third and fourth, the essential statement being put under a bushel instead of on a candlestick. At this cost it is possible for the Church and Christians partially and temporarily at least, i.e., to the extent and so long as the revolutionary force of the statement does not reassert itself, to avoid the offence of their existence and thus to escape the assaults which come upon them from without, and primarily rather than finally from within. But this reference to the Roman Catholic system has only incidental significance. It is no more than a single example. For at all times the Church and Christians have been tempted, and exposed to the temptation, to pay this price. How vulnerable they are if they do not pay it but dare to stand, or if through all their attempts at concealment there shines through in their lives the truth that the meaning and content of their confession of Jesus Christ is that He is not merely *a* prophet, not merely a great or the greatest, but *the* Prophet! When this is what it means, and explicitly or implicitly says, the Church speaks and acts as His community in the world. And when this is what Christians mean and say, they prove themselves to be what their name declares, confessing the shame of Christ and undertaking the whole burden of His and their foreignness in the world and in their own hearts. Nothing is more natural than the desire to escape this. It is another matter that it cannot be done. We do well to realise that the desire itself is always imminent, and that it cannot easily be suppressed.

The objection to this statement can take many different forms. Basically, it will always consist in the reproach that it involves an unjustifiable act of caprice. What inexcusable presumption it is to say that we can and must regard and proclaim Jesus Christ not merely as One among many witnesses for the truth (which is quite legitimate), nor even as One who occupies a privileged or even leading place among these witnesses (which might be allowed), nor even as One who is normative for us personally (which is still tolerable), but as the one and only Witness confronting all men with an absolute claim to allegiance! What right have we to go before our fellows with a claim of this nature, however tacitly or indirectly? What authority have we to set ourselves above all others who think they know otherwise? From what exalted place do we think we can violate them with this kind of demand? We have to realise that in making this statement we expose ourselves to this reproach. And inevitably in so doing we feel uncomfortable, secretly making the same reproach against ourselves, feeling its force and effects and wishing that we could evade the necessity of making the statement. The point of the reproach will be only too obvious. On the intellectual and aesthetic side it will be to the effect that it is obscurantist, that it attests and fosters a sorry restriction of the field of vision of human knowledge, and an impoverishment of thought in relation to the plenitude of phenomena, forms and ideas which obviously encounter man and forcefully speak to him, by the demand that one of them should be declared to be divinely and humanly normative, and that this normativeness should be denied to all the rest. On the moral side it will be to the effect that in its arrogance it makes quite impossible the discussion and interchange between those who champion it and those who cannot or will not accept it, that it leads to the breakdown of communication and even in the last resort of fellowship between Christians and non-Christians, and that it implies for its champions an unfitting bondage and constriction. In other words, it is an unfriendly and quarrelsome and evil principle from whose representatives we can only turn away angered and sorrowed by their hardness of heart and deeply bewailing their self-isolation. Politically, it will be to the effect that it is the proclamation of unconcealed intolerance and therefore an intolerable disruption of the co-existence of men of different outlooks and confessions in state and society, signifying either secretly or quite blatantly a radical attack on the freedom of conscience and therefore the potential, and basically already actual, principle of the repression and persecution of those who think or believe differently, with all the accompanying horrors of burnings, religious wars, crusades and similar procedures. And in the background there rolls the ominous question whether those who champion this statement are not to be regarded as pace-makers for totalitarianism. We need hardly say more for the moment. But if we are prepared not to suppress or evade but to champion this statement, we do well to reckon with the fact that all these charges will be brought against us, and that there will be in ourselves an inner voice speaking and arguing and remonstrating along these lines. We do well to realise how great the temptation has been, and still is, either to suppress the statement altogether or to render it so innocuous that it no longer says what it purports to say. But we have no option in this matter. Christian freedom is really the freedom of the confession of Jesus Christ as the one and only Prophet, light of life, and Word of God. It stands or falls by whether it is freedom for this confession. In the exercise of this freedom, in which it has its origin, the statement can and should be explained and established, and it cannot be suppressed or rendered innocuous.

To be sure, it does not need to be expressly reproduced and emphasised in every Christian declaration.

In the earliest of the great symbols it is explicitly made only in the form of the *Filius Dei unicus*. In the Greek version the original εἰς κύριος is strengthened by the description of Jesus Christ as the υἱὸς τοῦ θεοῦ μονογενής—a phrase which was taken from Jn. 1¹⁸ and which passed into the creeds of 325 and 381. It is only implied in the other articles.

Yet it is the common denominator which is accepted in every Christian statement, which marks every such statement as binding and urgent, and the ignoring or obscuring of which causes all such statements to lose their specific weight. It is certainly fashioned and proclaimed arbitrarily, and therefore exposed to reproach, if it is related to the position or opinion or intention of the man who represents it, or to the plans and enterprises and teachings and institutions of the Christian Church as a fellowship of such men, being thus used to declare the absoluteness of this or that form of what is called Christianity or the Church. It is almost inevitable that in the first instance the world will always hear and understand it in this sense. What else can it gather from it but that there are strange people who think that their opinions, convictions and beliefs, and the acceptance of their religious society and tradition, are the only possible and legitimate choice? How can it help resisting this? It would not be the world, but already the community, if it were in a position to receive and interpret it differently. If we are going to represent and champion it, we must see to it that we do so with a clear conscience, that we do not intend or proclaim it with the intention of absolutising our own Christian subjectivity or that of the Church and its tradition, and that we do not therefore give good cause for the reproach which it encounters. Even more, we must see to it that we quietly understand as such the reproach which it necessarily encounters, and are not disconcerted by this reproach. For it rests on a supreme misunderstanding. The statement that Jesus Christ is the one Word of God has really nothing whatever to do with the arbitrary exaltation and self-glorification of the Christian in relation to other men, of the Church in relation to other institutions, or of Christianity in relation to other conceptions.

It is a christological statement. It looks away from non-Christian and Christian alike to the One who sovereignly confronts and precedes both as *the* Prophet. As Jesus Christ is its content, the one who confesses it in no sense marks himself off from those who do not. In face of what it says, not concerning Christians or the Church or Christianity, but concerning Christ, he is in solidarity with them. In distinction from others, he may and must know and declare that in the matter of Jesus Christ both he and they are confronted by the one truth superior to both him and them. Thus the criticism expressed in the exclusiveness of the statement affects, limits and relativises the prophecy of Christians and the Church no less than the many other prophecies, lights and words relativised and replaced by it. It says first and supremely that in relationship to His own community and all its members Jesus Christ is the One to whom it must in no circumstances oppose with any degree of sovereignty its own Christian prophecy, teaching and testimony to the truth. What it says concerning the impotence of all other prophecy which attempts to rival its own is valid only in analogy to, and in consequence of, the fact that first and supremely it is true of the Christian sphere. It cannot, then, be legitimately advanced and stated except as the men who live in this sphere submit themselves first, with all their Christian views and concepts, dogmas and institutions, customs, traditions and innovations, to the relativisation and criticism which come through Jesus Christ as the one light of life. The judgment on the world indicated in this statement begins in " the house of God " (1 Pet. 4¹⁷), and it is from there that it spreads to embrace the world around.

But as the community itself submits to it, it cannot cease attesting it to all. For it has not found or fashioned for itself this statement which its witness declares. It does not exalt or glorify itself in making it. As it bows before the One who alone has authority and alone is the light and truth and Word of God, it declares itself. As it accepts solidarity with all others, and thus brings them into solidarity with it, it brings to them, too, the promise and criticism of this statement. Arbitrary though it may sound, therefore, the statement is not really arbitrary. The consequent opposition to it is thus irrelevant. The only necessary concern of the community and Christians is that they do not make it in any other way but in the submission and humility enjoined upon them, too, by what it says. If this is the case, they

§ 69. *The Glory of the Mediator*

should not allow anyone or anything to deflect or hinder them from making it either directly or indirectly. It would be illegitimate and arbitrary to suppress or deny it. The thing itself, and their own existence in its service, demand that they should not merely recognise but confess and declare it.

That this is demanded of Christians, or better that they have the freedom to do it, is first learned quite simply from the biblical witness. The statement that Jesus Christ is the one Word of God is one which we could not venture on our own authority or responsibility without justly exposing ourselves to the reproach of arrogant prejudice. In such a case, it could be hazarded only with a final anxiety for which there is good cause, and it could not be pronounced with any degree of conviction. Much Christian anxiety in face of this reproach would disappear of itself, however, if we remembered that as Christians we are not summoned or committed to thinking and speaking on our own authority and responsibility, but kept modestly yet steadfastly to the direction of Holy Scripture. It is not a matter of appropriating isolated biblical notions or teachings. But it is a matter of following independently yet loyally the Old and New Testament witness in an attempt to adopt its mode of thought as that which is normative for the Christian community, applying ourselves to learn to think in this mode. Now by "mode of thought" we simply mean the character and style determined by the theme of its witness, the structures underlying its records, speeches, prayers and other utterances. One example is the *circulus virtuosus* in which it always moves in the matter of truth. Another is the self-evident way in which both the Old and New Testament witnesses with equal distinctness count upon and take quite seriously the uniqueness and therefore the absolute normativeness of the revelation imparted to and attested by them. The prophets and apostles do not squint away from but look steadily at the one thing which it always repays us to consider. They do not engage in the uneasy movements of those who try to hear one thing with one ear and another with the other, and would try to hear a thousand things if they had a thousand ears. They listen quietly because the one thing which they hear is enough. And as they concentrate upon this one thing they think and speak accordingly. This prophetic and apostolic mode of thought is the norm in the Canon of Holy Scripture. Applied in detail, it is the school where we are taught how the statement that Jesus Christ is the one Word of God is to be properly understood and legitimately made. As we go to this school, we learn to think and make it humbly yet boldly before God and man. We also learn to avoid lascivious squinting and eavesdropping in other directions, and to rid ourselves of all anxiety in thinking and making it.

The fact that around Israel there were other nations with other histories, religions, pieties, orders and divinities was just as well known to the prophets as is to us the fact that in the world in which

2. The Light of Life

we live there are other conceptions than the Christian and other explicit or implicit confessions than that of Jesus Christ. But to the best of my knowledge there is not a single word in any of the prophets to indicate that this fact made any impression on them, nor any single trace of the notion of a plurality of divine revelations among which the action and speech of Yahweh in the history of Israel is thought to be one of many to which validity might be ascribed. Similarly, the Evangelists and apostles of the New Testament, as we see from their language and terminology, were very well aware of the multiplicity of religious, cultic and doctrinal systems characteristic of the world to which they went with their message of Jesus of Nazareth. But to my knowledge there is not a single indication in the New Testament that its authors understood or respected these systems either individually or as a whole as alternatives to the Gospel proclaimed by them, or that they thought of themselves, as the 2nd century Apologists were so soon to do, as engaged in rivalry and debate with the representatives of these systems. When they speak and write, everything of this sort is already behind them; it is not a problem or task confronting them. From the point where they start there can be no thought of wrestling with strange and in some sense perhaps impressive and normative conceptions of God and the world. As there can be no other sons of God, so there can be no other lords nor witnesses to the truth apart from or side by side with Jesus Christ. If such authorities enter their field of vision, as in the form of angelic or demonic powers, it is always in relation to the picture of the crucified and risen Jesus Christ, who is their Lord and Victor and to whom they are ordered and subordinated, so that even at very best they cannot be more than naughts which are set behind Him as the digit "one." As the history of Israel speaks in the Old Testament, and that of Jesus Christ in the New, the decision is made that other divine pronouncements, no matter where they come from or however they might be grounded or intended, are not to be heard or taken seriously as independent utterances, and can have no claim to our trust or obedience. And with this decision there is also taken the decision that the men of the New Testament must accept this, or that they must represent and attest to the men of all nations the sole authority of the Word of God spoken in the history of Jesus Christ and conducting the history of Israel to its goal.

Quite apart from the content of their witness, the mere fact that the biblical witnesses stand under this determination is an element in their mode of thought. In this framework the statement is so self-evident that only with relative infrequency does it need to be explicitly formulated and pronounced.

By way of illustration I will first choose a passage in which this is not done, but in which the point at issue is the more plainly visible. I refer to the famous introduction to the Epistle to the Hebrews (1^{1-2}). This passage speaks expressly

94 § 96. *The Glory of the Mediator*

of Jesus Christ, yet in such a way that for all the differences the revelation which has taken place in Him is seen as a unity with that which has taken place in the history of Israel. " God (ὁ θεός), who at sundry times and in divers manners (πολυμερῶς καὶ πολυτρόπως) spake in time past (πάλαι) unto the fathers by the prophets, hath in these last days spoken unto us by his Son." It is on the basis and within the framework of our presupposition that the author of Hebrews thinks and speaks. He does not think it necessary to emphasise that this is so. The whole Epistle which opens with these words bears ample testimony. And is it not actually stated in these opening words ? We obviously have a closed circle in God's speaking, and the fathers and ourselves as those to whom He speaks. The fact that God spoke once and then again is the one centre beside which there can be no other. The content of the subordinate or participle clause (λαλήσας) is that He spake in time past. The content of the main clause (ἐλάλησεν) is that He spoke again at the end of the " time past," on the last of the days in which His former speaking began. He spoke in the one whole time which is determined and filled by His speaking and therefore absolutely unique. He first did it on many occasions and in many ways. He now did it once and in one way alone. The fact that He did it in this irreversible sequence means that He did it with an unmistakeable sharpening and an emerging weight and definitiveness, even the manifoldness of His former speaking being determined and revealed as a unity by the singleness and simplicity of the conclusion. He first spoke to the fathers through the prophets, but now He spoke through the Son, through the One promised to the former and fulfilling this promise. Again, the circle of Old Testament expectation and New Testament recollection is for the author of the Epistle a closed one outside of which there cannot be considered, nor is there to be expected, any other speaking on the part of God.

At the same time, there are also passages in which this biblical mode of thought finds expression in explicit statements concerning the uniqueness and exclusiveness of the one Word of God announced in the Old Testament and proclaimed in the New.

In the Old Testament we think first of the remarkable passage in Deut. 18$^{13-22}$. Its most important saying played a very important role, although in the form of a rather over-simplified exposition, in the scriptural proof adduced by the older dogmatics for the prophetic office of Jesus Christ. What is at issue, as stated by Moses, is Israel's distinction from the Canaanite peoples which " hearken unto observers of times, and unto diviners." Because they do this, they will be driven out by Israel. But " thou shalt be perfect with the Lord thy God " (v. 13). He " hath not suffered thee so to do " (v. 14). And then : " The Lord thy God will raise up unto thee (that is to say, continually) a Prophet (that is to say, one prophet after another) from the midst of thee, of thy brethren, like unto me ; unto him ye shall hearken " (v. 15). The statement is repeated as a direct saying of Yahweh Himself in v. 18 : " I will (continually) raise them up a Prophet from among their brethren, like unto thee, and will (continually) put my words in his mouth ; and he shall (continually) speak unto them all that I shall command him. And it shall come to pass, that whosoever will not hearken unto my words which he shall (continually) speak in my name, I will require it of him." In rather a different sense from that of the older exegesis, the passage is truly Messianic if we refer it to the whole series of prophets who—each in his own age and situation—were authorised by Yahweh and thus fulfilled the office of Moses, and therefore if we refer it to the continually articulated voice of the prophetic history of Israel in its totality. These true prophets are then (18$^{20f.}$ and cf. 13$^{1-5}$) distinguished from false prophets like the mantics of the Canaanites. The latter can speak in the name of Yahweh but cannot say what He has told them to say. They can thus speak in the name of other

2. The Light of Life 95

gods and demand that they should be recognised and worshipped: "Let us go after other gods, which thou hast not known, and let us serve them" (13²). And it may even be that their words will be accompanied by signs and wonders (v. 1). Yet they will obviously lack any true content from the standpoint of salvation history, and will thus reveal that they are not really the Word of God (18²¹f·). Between the true and false prophets there is undoubtedly a yawning gulf, with no fellowship nor even the possibility of comparison. "Thou shalt not hearken unto the words of that prophet, or that dreamer of dreams" (13³). "He hath spoken... presumptuously: thou shalt not be afraid of him" (18²²). And even more sharply: "And that prophet, or dreamer of dreams, shall be put to death; because he hath spoken to turn you away from the Lord your God, which brought you out of the land of Egypt, and redeemed you out of the house of bondage, to thrust thee out of the way which the Lord thy God commanded thee to walk in. So shalt thou put the evil away from the midst of thee" (13⁵, cf. 18²⁰).

The command of 18¹⁵: "Unto him ye shall hearken," is expressly taken up in the New Testament (Mk. 9⁷ and *par.*) in the account of the voice from the cloud at the transfiguration. The fact that Jesus is the beloved Son and therefore the object of the divine εὐδοκία, as we are told already in the story of His baptism, is here equated with the command: ἀκούετε αὐτοῦ. The formula reminds us of the whole seriousness and weight of the distinction made in Deut. 18 between true prophets and false. The same thought lies behind the "to whom shall we go?" of Jn. 6⁶⁸. But it is also to be found in the warning addressed to the community in Mt. 23⁸f·: "But be not ye called Rabbi, father, master: for one is your Master; one is your Father, which is in heaven; one is your Master, even Christ." We may also think of the prophecy in Mk. 13⁶ and *par.* that many will come in the name of Jesus Christ with the message and claim: ἐγώ εἰμι. He alone according to John 10³f· is the Shepherd whose voice His sheep hear, who calls and leads them out by name, and whom they follow when they hear His voice. "And a stranger will they not follow, but will flee from him: for they know not the voice of strangers." And then again in v. 16: "Other sheep I have, which are not of this fold (i.e., which do not belong to the Israel to whom I speak in the first instance): them also I must bring, and they shall hear my voice; and there shall be one fold, and one shepherd." The offence in this parable (παροιμία), particularly in the contrasting of the one Shepherd with strangers who are described as "thieves and robbers" or "hirelings," is not concealed in Jn. 10: "They understood not what things they were which he spake unto them" (v. 6). Nor is it removed but aggravated by the claim in v. 11: "I am the good shepherd." This, and everything which underlies the ἐγώ, seems to raise up a σχίσμα among the Jews (v. 19). Can Jesus say this? "He hath a devil, and is mad." Or must He say it? "These are not the words of him which hath a devil." The healing of the man born blind had preceded. Has this not validated the claim of Jesus to be the Shepherd whose voice must be heard in contrast to all others? The drift of the story is plain. Jesus has authority to make this claim to an exclusive hearing. In and with His existence He rightly advances and emphatically exercises and successfully presses this claim. Hence Ac. 4¹²: "For there is none other name under heaven given among men, whereby we must be saved." Hence, too, 1 Cor. 2²: "For I determined (ἔκρινα) not to know anything among you, save Jesus Christ and him crucified."

It is thus incumbent, not that we should merely repeat these or similar biblical texts, but that we should so enter into the biblical mode of thought which underlies and is expressed in them that the thesis of the uniqueness of the prophecy of Jesus Christ impresses itself upon us as no less self-evident than it is presupposed and sometimes stated to be in Holy Scripture. But if we do this, this means that we shall be guided by the direction of Holy Scripture, that we shall not have to champion the thesis in our own strength or on our own responsibility, and that we may thus champion it without anxiety because it is not really exposed to the charge of arbitrariness. There can be no question, however, of merely learning a clever trick of thought. The distinctive thought-form of the Bible is not something which is discovered in that way; it is demanded, enforced and indeed created by that which is attested, namely, by the lordship of Jesus Christ Himself. Hence we have first and foremost to allow ourselves to be confronted by Him through the biblical witnesses in order to learn from the latter, as from older and more experienced fellow-students, how we shall think and speak as those who are confronted by Him. This and this alone is the way in which we can be freed for the fruitful venture of the statement that He is the one Word of God.

We shall now try (1) to understand its more precise meaning by distinguishing what it actually says from what it does not say.

We maintain that it is a christological statement, i.e., a declaration concerning Jesus Christ. It cannot be referred to any other subject. It says of Jesus Christ, announced in the Old Testament and proclaimed in the New, that He is the one Word of God. But it says this of Him alone. There is direct witness to Jesus Christ in the words of the prophets and apostles. In the Bible Jesus Christ declares Himself to be the one Word of God. But the Bible as such is not the one Word of God. Indirect witness is also borne to Jesus Christ in the message, activity and life of the Christian Church, whose whole *raison d'être* is to make Him known as the one Word of God. Again, however, the Church and its doctrine, instruction, worship and whole existence is not the one Word of God. Moreover, there is a history of the gifts and operations of Jesus Christ, and many histories of groups and individuals determined by Him. But neither the history as a whole, nor any one history in particular, is the one Word of God. Jesus Christ shares the uniqueness of God as the Creator of His creatures, the Lord of all His servants, the Doer of all His works, the Giver of all His gifts. He does this even in the luminous sphere in which His attestation takes place and His impulses are in some way visible. He stands alone in face of every light which shines in this sphere. And this is even more true, of course, in the outside sphere where this witness does not take place and these impulses are not seen. The positive thing to be noted is that, even though it is perhaps incontestable that there are real lights of life and words of God in this sphere too, He alone is the Word of God even here, and these lights shine only because of the shining of none other light than His.

2. The Light of Life

We recognise that the fact that Jesus Christ is the one Word of God does not mean that in the Bible, the Church and the world there are not other words which are quite notable in their way, other lights which are quite clear and other revelations which are quite real. We may think of the prophets in the Old Testament and the apostles in the New. We may think of the genuine prophecy and apostolate of the Church. And why should not the world have its varied prophets and apostles in different degrees? As the Bible attests the one Word of God, and to the extent that the Church adopts and repeats this testimony, important human words are spoken, bright lights are set up in the human sphere and great and little revelations occur. Nor does it follow from our statement that every word spoken outside the circle of the Bible and the Church is a word of false prophecy and therefore valueless, empty and corrupt, that all the lights which rise and shine in this outer sphere are misleading and all the revelations are necessarily untrue. Our statement is simply to the effect that Jesus Christ is the one and only Word of God, that He alone is the light of God and the revelation of God. It is in this sense that it delimits all other words, lights, revelations, prophecies and apostolates, whether of the Bible, the Church or the world, by what is declared in and with the existence of Jesus Christ. The biblical prophets and apostles are His servants, ambassadors and witnesses, so that even in their humanity the words spoken by them cannot fail to be words of great seriousness, profound comfort and supreme wisdom. And if the Church follows the biblical prophets and apostles, similar words are surely to be expected of it. Nor is it impossible that words of this kind should be uttered outside this circle if the whole world of creation and history is the realm of the lordship of the God at whose right hand Jesus Christ is seated, so that He exercises authority in this outer as well as the inner sphere and is free to attest Himself or to cause Himself to be attested in it. That there are such words in the inner sphere could be contested only if we were prepared to question the presence and activity of Jesus Christ in the work of His witnesses and that of the Church which follows them. And their existence in the outer sphere could be disputed only if we were to challenge the preservation and overruling of the world by the God who has given all things into the hands of the Son. In both spheres there are human words which are good because they are spoken with the commission and in the service of God. In both spheres there are words which are illuminating and helpful to the degree that God Himself gives it to them to be illuminating and helpful as such words. We live by the fact that we may continually hear good words of this kind in the Bible, the Church and the world.

What we have to contest, however, is that any one of such good words in itself and as such is the Word of God, or can be set beside the Word spoken by God Himself, i.e., Jesus Christ, either by way of supplement or even to crowd Him out and replace Him. The Word of God is His eternal Word which is incomparably and absolutely good and serious and comforting and wise in the fact that it is spoken to us directly by God Himself. As such it does not merely say something valid, but that which is absolutely valid; it does not merely say something which is secondarily useful, but that which is primarily good; it does not merely say that which is provisionally correct, but that which is definitively true. It is not merely an offer and introduction, but creates and renews even as it is pronounced and received. It does not merely instruct a man, or entangle him in discussion, but transforms him. It decides concerning him. It blesses him even as it also judges. It frees him unconditionally yet also binds unconditionally. It is the Word which we must trust and obey in life and death. It is the light of life. Where this Word is heard and received, but there alone, the Word of God is present. No human word, even if it is spoken with God's commission and in God's service, can as such speak in this way or say or accomplish these things. God's direct presence is needed for this. God Himself must come and speak. As He does so, and utters His own Word, this cannot be co-ordinated or compared with any human word: not even the most lofty or profound; not even the most illuminating and helpful; not even that which is spoken with His commission and in His service. But God does speak. What takes place in the existence of Jesus Christ as the true Son of God who is also the true Son of Man is that God Himself is present in person and speaks this Word which cannot be co-ordinated or compared with any human word. It is for this reason and in this sense that Jesus is the one and only Word of God. He is not the only word, nor even the only good word. But He is the only Word which, because it is spoken directly by God Himself, is good as God is, has the authority and power of God and is to be heard as God Himself. He is the only Word which all human words, even the best, can only directly or indirectly attest but not repeat or replace or rival, so that their own goodness and authority are to be measured by whether or not, and with what fidelity, they are witnesses of this one Word.

If we regard and address Jesus as a διδάσκαλος ἀγαθός, then according to Mk. 10[17f.] and *par.* we must ask ourselves if we really know what we are doing: "Why callest thou me good? there is none good but one, that is, God." In other words, in Him we must let ourselves be confronted by the majesty and the total claim of the one God and His command. Was the man who addressed Him in this way prepared and equipped for the fact that in Him he had to do with the one " good Master " ? The passage tells us that he was not. Jesus " loved " this man (v. 21). But " he was sad at that saying, and went away grieved : for he had great possessions." In face of what it entailed, he could not and would not love Jesus as God, and therefore as his one and only and eternal good. Similarly, the scribes (Mk. 2[5f.] and *par.*) who regarded as blasphemy the remission pronounced to the lame man at Capernaum were materially quite right: "Who

2. The Light of Life

can forgive sins but God only?" If it were not blasphemy, what Jesus said to the lame man could really be said only by the one God. The one Jesus thus says what only the one God can say. That He, the Son of Man, has the authority and power to say this is demonstrated and confirmed, however, by the fact that in an addition to the saying He commands the man to arise, take up his bed and walk. Similarly, in 1 Cor. 8⁶f. Paul brings together the " one God, the Father, of whom are all things, and we in him," and the " one Lord Jesus Christ, by whom are all things, and we by him." And, seeing Them together in this way, he advances against the incontestable existence of so-called gods and lords in heaven and earth the statement which is quite decisive for the question of idol-meats, namely, that there is no true εἴδωλον in the world, and that οὐδεὶς θεὸς εἰ μὴ εἷς. The same conjunction is found in 1 Tim. 2⁵, where we read that " there is one God, and one mediator between God and men, the man Christ Jesus." This time it is set in a positive context. Because this is the case, God " will have all men to be saved, and to come unto the knowledge of the truth " (v. 4). This is the basis of the witness in the service of which Paul knows that he is ordained " a teacher of the Gentiles " and therefore a herald and apostle to the heathen. Again, in Rom. 3²⁹f. the statement εἷς ὁ θεός is introduced to prove the assertion that God is the God of the Gentiles as well as the Jews, and the context makes it plain that here, too, the theological εἷς has its root and presupposition as well as its upshot and fulfilment in the christological.

In sum, our statement distinguishes the Word spoken in the existence of Jesus Christ from all others as the Word of God. When we think of these others, we do well to include even the human words spoken in the existence and witness of the men of the Bible and the Church. In distinction from all these, Jesus Christ is the one Word of God. There are other words which are good in their own way and measure. There are other prophets in this sense. We shall return to this point. But there is only one Prophet who speaks the Word of God as He is Himself this Word, and this One is called and is Jesus. This is the substance of our statement, no more but also no less.

We shall now try (2) to fix its more precise meaning by describing what it actually says. That Jesus is the one Word of God means first that He is the total and complete declaration of God concerning Himself and the men whom He addresses in His Word. God does satisfaction both to Himself and us in what He says in and with the existence of Jesus Christ. What He is for us and wills of us, but also what we are for Him and are ordained to be and will and do in this relationship, is exhaustively, unreservedly and totally revealed to us in Jesus Christ as the one Word of God. As this one Word He does not need to be completed by others. If we are to speak of completion, we must say that, as and because He is the living Lord Jesus Christ, He is engaged as the one Word of God in a continual completion of Himself, not in the sense that the Word spoken by Him is incomplete or inadequate, but in the sense that our hearing of it is profoundly incomplete. For He Himself is in Himself rich and strong enough to display and offer Himself to our poverty with perennial fulness. It is not His fault if we see and know so little of God and ourselves. There is thus no need to try to catch other words of God. Indeed, we must not do so, for any such word can only be the word of another god which is *per se* false in relation to the one God, and therefore it can only lead us astray from the truth of the one God and the consequent truth of man as His elect and beloved creature. Who and what the true God is, and through Him true man ; what the freedom of God is, and the freedom given by Him to man, is said to us in and with the existence of Jesus Christ as true Son of God and Son of Man in such a way that any addition can only mean a diminution and perversion of our knowledge of the truth.

That He is the one Word of God means further that He is not exposed on any third side to any serious competition, any challenge to His truth, any threat to His authority. Such a third side could only be a word of God different from that spoken in Him and superior or at least equivalent in value and force ; the word, perhaps, of a *Deus absconditus* not identical with the *Deus revelatus*, or identical only in irreconcilable contradiction. Now we have no cause to reckon with such an alien word, such a self-contradiction, on the part of God. But we have every cause to keep to the fact that He is faithful, and that in Jesus Christ we have His total and unique and therefore authentic revelation, the Word in which He does full justice both to Himself and us. To be sure, this Word meets opposition in the world, and also and supremely, as we must not forget, in the Church. To be sure, its light is resisted by darkness in the many forms of many sinister powers, all of which are connected with the sin of man, all empowered and unleashed by his falsehood, all to be taken seriously as opponents of the one Word of God. Jesus Christ can certainly be unrecognised, despised and rejected in the world and among His own people. He can be partially or even totally unheard as the one Word of God. That did happen, and happens still. But since God does not contradict but is always faithful to Himself, there is one thing that can never take place, namely, that such a sinister power and its lying words, revelations and prophecies should seriously threaten the validity and force of the one Word of God, invading and even destroying it. The living Lord Jesus Christ, risen again from the dead, has no serious rival as the one Prophet of God who does not merely attest but is the Word of God. There is none whose inferiority and final displacement is not already decided by His existence, presence and action. Who or what can rise up against God, or against Him as the one Word of God ? This means in practice that no risk is involved if among the bids made by many supposed and pretended lords and prophets we trust and obey Him as *the* Lord and Prophet. He and He alone is worthy of complete trust and total obedience. None will ever repent of responding to His self-giving, and to the Word spoken in it, with a corresponding self-giving which is resolute and exclusive.

2. *The Light of Life*

"Whosoever believeth on him shall not be ashamed" (Rom. 10^{11}). For, although He has enemies, He has none who can put Him to shame, or who will not be put to shame by Him.

That He is the one Word of God means further that His truth and prophecy cannot be combined with any other, nor can He be enclosed with other words in a system superior to both Him and them. As the one Word of God, He can bring Himself into the closest conjunction with such words. He can make use of certain men, making them His witnesses and confessing their witness in such a way that to hear them is to hear Him (Lk. 10^{16}). He has actually entered into a union of this kind with the biblical prophets and apostles, and it is the prayer and promise in and by which His community exists that He will not refuse but be willing to enter into a similar union with it. Nor can any prevent Him entering into such a union with men outside the sphere of the Bible and the Church, and with the words of these men. Whether in the Church or the world, however, this type of union can be legitimate and fruitful only through His act, as His work, as a form of His free revelation of grace. Conversely, all syntheses which Christians or non-Christians may arbitrarily devise and create between Jesus Christ as the one Word of God and any other words, however illuminating, necessary or successful they may be; all well-meant but capricious conjunction of Jesus Christ with something else, whether it be Mary, the Church, the fate worked out in general and individual history, a presupposed human self-understanding, etc., all these imply a control over Him to which none of us has any right, which can be only the work of religious arrogance, in which we try to invest Him with His dignity as the Lord and Prophet, in the exercise of which He ceases to be who He is, not objectively, but for those who are guilty of this rash assault, and in and with which faith in Him, love for Him and hope in Him are abandoned, however loudly or with whatever degree of subjective sincerity they may be professed. There is no legitimate place for projects in the planning and devising of which Jesus Christ can be given a particular niche in co-ordination with those of other events, powers, forms and truths. Such projects are irrelevant and unfruitful enterprises because as the one Word of God He wholly escapes every conceivable synthesis envisaged in them. They are irrelevant and unfruitful because the men who attempt them will always be content with the revelations of the other elements.

We have here the irresistible and relentless outworking of the "Thou shalt have none other gods but me" of Ex. 20^3. The sin of Israel against the God of the covenant made and continually renewed with the patriarchs did not consist so much in direct apostasy from Yahweh as in the combination and admixture of His service, invocation and acknowledgment in practical obedience, with the adoration of the numina of Canaan and other surrounding peoples. It consisted in the fact that Israel made constant experiments to do the one and not leave

§ 69. *The Glory of the Mediator*

undone, not losing Yahweh yet not missing the Baalim, and therefore between two opinions (1 K. 18²¹). It consisted in the fact that in its ⟨...⟩ to elect in accordance with its own election, it already elected, not electing ⟨Yah⟩weh but deciding against Him and for the Baalim, and thus becoming a ⟨peo⟩ple alien like all others to the command of God. The remarkable but very relevant and accurate reference to the " jealousy " of Yahweh, which according to Ex. 20⁵ is directed against the attempt to worship Him in fashioned images as well as in His invisible majesty, shows us clearly that He radically and automatically refuses to allow His Godhead to be equated with other divinities, or His Word to be heard with other words. Israel can look to Him alone, or not at all. It can hear Him alone, or not at all. The whole prophecy of the history of Israel as attested by the Old Testament, and therefore explicitly and implicitly all its prophets, speak along these lines.

This combining of the Word of Jesus Christ with the authority and contents of other supposed revelations and truths of God has been and is the weak point, revealed already in the *gnosis* attacked in the New Testament, at almost every stage in the history of the Christian Church. The prophecy of Jesus Christ has never been flatly denied, but fresh attempts have continually been made to list it with other principles, ideas and forces (and their prophecy) which are also regarded and lauded as divine, restricting its authority to what it can signify in co-ordination with them, and therefore to what remains when their authority is also granted. Nor is this trend characteristic only of early and mediaeval Catholicism. It is seen in Protestantism too, from the very outset in certain circles, even in the Reformers themselves, and then with increasing vigour and weight, until the fatal little word " and " threatened to become the predominant word of theology even in this sphere where we might have hoped for better things in view of what seemed to be the strong enough doctrine of justification. It needed the rise of the strange but temporarily powerful sect of the German Christians of 1933 to call us back to reflection, and at least the beginning of a return, when the more zealous among them, in addition to their other abominations, awarded cultic honour to the portrait of the Führer. The overthrow of this whole attitude, and its provisional reversal, was accomplished in the first thesis of Barmen which is the theme of the present exposition. But there are other Christian nations in which it is customary to find a prominent place in the church for national flags as well as the pulpit and the Lord's table, just as there are evangelical churches which substitute for the Lord's table a meaningfully furnished apparatus for the accomplishment of baptism by immersion. These externals, of course, are trivial in themselves. But as such they may well be symptoms of the attempt which is possible in so many forms to incorporate that which is alien in other prophecies into what is proper to that of Jesus Christ. If these prophecies are prepared for this—and sooner or later they will make an open bid for sole dominion—the prophecy of Jesus Christ asks to be excused and avoids any such incorporation. If it is subjected to such combinations, the living Lord Jesus and His Word depart, and all that usually remains is the suspiciously loud but empty utterance of the familiar name of this Prophet. " No man can serve two masters " (Mt. 6²⁴). No man can serve both the one Word of God called Jesus Christ and other divine words.

That He is the one Word of God means finally that His prophecy cannot be transcended by any other. It cannot be transcended in the content of its declarations, for it tells us all that it is necessary and good for us to know concerning God, man and the world, embracing, establishing and crowning all that is really worth knowing. It cannot be transcended in the depth with which it speaks the truth, for it is itself the source and norm of all truth. It cannot be transcended in the urgency with which it presents itself to man and demands to be acknowledged, recognised and confessed by him, for everyone who gives it a hearing sees that this is the one thing necessary compared with which all other hearing, however important, must be given a secondary and subordinate place. Above all, it cannot be transcended in the goodness, seriousness, comfort and wisdom of what it imparts, for all other things imparted to us, though these qualities may be ascribed to them, are inferior to it, and in respect of goodness can only be abased and exalted, disqualified and qualified, by it. In one respect alone can there be transcendence. This is not in relation to the content, depth, urgency or goodness of the one Word of God spoken in Jesus Christ. It is not its transcendence by any other word. It is the self-transcendence of Jesus Christ as the one Word of God in respect of the universality and direct and definitive clarity of the knowledge which Christianity and the world do not yet have in the time between His resurrection and ascension, but to which they look and move at His return, i.e., His total presence, action and revelation which will conclude and fulfil time and history, all times and all histories. In this *eschaton* of creation and reconciliation there will not be another Word of God. Jesus Christ will be the one Word and we shall then see the final and unequivocal form of His own glory which even now shines forth from His resurrection into time and history, all times and all histories. The theme of Christian hope, to the extent that it is not yet fulfilled nor cannot be so long as time endures, is the revelation of the fact that neither formally nor materially, theoretically nor practically, can the one Word of God be transcended, as this is now confirmed in and through His self-transcendence, in virtue of which all ears hear and all eyes see all the things which already it is actually given to us to see and hear in Him. The inclusion of the eschatological element, then, does not imply any restriction, but the final expansion and deepening, of our statement that Jesus Christ is the one Word of God.

We now resume (3) our discussion of the question of the basis of this statement. What is it which compels or frees us to make it ? In an earlier connexion we raised the same question rather more generally. We were then asking to what extent the life of Jesus Christ is light, revelation, Word and prophecy. We now put the more specific question to what extent He is the one light, the one Word of God. The more general answer is still true and comprehensive that He is this to the extent that, as God is one, He actually is the one Word of the one God, and shows Himself to be this. This answer means that Jesus Christ Himself guarantees that He is the one Word of God by the fact that He is the only One whom we must trust and obey in life and death, and that He shows Himself to be this by acting towards us as such. Hence, if anyone asks concerning the basis of our statement, we must put the counter-question whether he sees and realises that Jesus Christ actually shows Himself to be the one Prophet of God. This is the question to which we must make answer to ourselves and others. The revelation of God vouches for its uniqueness as it does for itself as such. If Jesus Christ is the one Word of God, He alone, standing out from the ranks of all other supposed and pretended divine words, can make Himself known as this one Word.

" To whom then will ye liken God ? or what likeness will ye compare unto him ? " is the question asked in Is. 40^{18}, and then again in v. 25 : " To whom then will ye liken me, or shall I be equal ? saith the Holy One." The question is as such an answer, i.e., to the complaint and accusation of Israel apparently abandoned and lost in the storms of world history : " My way is hid from the Lord, and my judgment is passed over from my God " (v. 27). In the context the drift of the complaint seems to be that Yahweh is only one of many gods, and a small one among many greater, so that it is not surprising that His people is in this sorry predicament among the great nations. What is the reply of the prophet of the Exile ? Simply to put to those who sigh in this way the counter-question whether, in the face of who and what Yahweh is and has done and still does, in face of His self-evident majesty which reduces to the dust all the majesties of the world in their apparent triumph, there can be even the remotest possibility of the comparison of Yahweh with the gods of the nations—a comparison fatal for Israel and therefore for Himself. " Have ye not known ? have ye not heard ? " (v. 21), and then again : " Hast thou not known ? hast thou not heard ? " (v. 28). What is it that they should have known because it speaks so eloquently for itself ? Again, the answer is first given in the form of further questions : " Who hath measured the waters in the hollow of his hand, and meted out heaven with the span, and comprehended the dust of the earth in a measure, and weighed the mountains in scales, and the hills in a balance ? Who hath directed the Spirit of the Lord, or being his counsellor hath taught him ? With whom took he counsel, and who instructed him, and taught him in the path of judgment, and taught him knowledge, and shewed to him the way of understanding ? " (vv. 12-14). " Hath it not been told you from the beginning ? have ye not understood from the foundations of the earth ? " (v. 21). And again : " Lift up your eyes on high, and behold who hath created these things, that bringeth out their host by number : he calleth them all by names by the greatness of his might, for that he is strong in power ; not one faileth " (v. 26). Yes, Yahweh is the Creator of all things. And with Him there are contrasted (vv. 19-20) the gods of the nations as these are commissioned and executed by men, being moulded and gilded or carved according to their means. This leads us to the positive conclusion that Yahweh is " he that sitteth upon the circle of the earth, and the inhabitants thereof are as grasshoppers ; that stretcheth out the heavens as a curtain, and spreadeth them out as a tent to dwell in : that bringeth the princes to nothing ; he maketh the judges of the earth as vanity. Yea, they shall not be planted : yea, they shall not be sown : yea, their stock shall not take root in the earth : and he shall also blow upon them, and they shall wither, and the whirlwind shall take them away as stubble " (vv. 24-26). " Behold, the nations are as a drop of the bucket, and are counted as the small dust of the balance : behold, he taketh up the isles as a very little thing. And Lebanon is not sufficient to burn, nor the beasts thereof sufficient for a burnt offering. All nations before him are as nothing ; and they are counted to him less than nothing, and vanity " (vv. 15-17). What does this mean for poor little Israel, so impotent by human reckoning ? It means that its complaint and accusation are quite pointless. " The Lord who hath created the ends of the earth is an

2. *The Light of Life*

everlasting God. He fainteth not, neither is weary. There is no searching of his understanding. He giveth power to the faint ; and to them that have no might he increaseth strength. Even the youths shall faint and be weary, and the young men shall utterly fall. But they that wait upon the Lord shall renew their strength ; they shall mount up with wings as eagles ; they shall run, and not be weary ; and they shall walk, and not faint " (vv. 28–31). The train of thought is remarkable. What is at issue—the incomparable uniqueness and therefore the absolute sovereignty of Yahweh, and with this the absolute security of Israel—is not just quietly but with supreme and joyous assurance represented as something which is quite self-evident and speaks for itself. This is how the biblical mode of thought puts the matter. And it is obvious that the comprehensive answer to the question of the uniqueness of the revelation of God in Jesus Christ can basically be no more than that which is so forcefully anticipated in Is. 40.

This does not mean, however, that we cannot and should not fill out this general form of the answer which has to be given ; that we cannot and should not consider and state what is the specific force or point of the one decisive basis of the fact that Jesus Christ is actually the one Prophet, the one Word of God.

We note that even in Is. 40 the uniqueness of Yahweh as the absolute Sovereign over the nations and their gods is not merely laid down but argumentatively expounded. His sovereignty—and here we have one of the most important if not the first forms of an insight rather curiously achieved during the Exile— is that of the Creator of heaven and earth. It is as such that He stands out so unmistakeably above all His rivals and shows Himself to be the one incomparable God. It is as such that He causes eagles' wings to grow for those who wait on Him, for His small and defeated people in an alien land, giving them strength for a journey on which they will never grow weary. This is obviously argumentation. But equally obviously it is argumentation which does not alter the fact that what is proclaimed by God can be proved only by reference to God Himself. Yet the point remains that beyond the mere statement we do also have demonstration, i.e., explanation, elucidation, illustration and comprehension in the form of this reference to God the Creator. We too, then, cannot evade the task of showing why and to what extent Jesus Christ is the one Word of God.

To do this, we simply recall the concrete content of this Word. The light of Jesus Christ is the light of His life. This was our first statement. But His life is His existence as the true Son of God who as such is also the true Son of Man. This means, however, that, as a life lived as a particular existence and occurrence within human history and among the many histories of all other men, it is a life in the covenant which God has not only made but in His omnipotent grace Himself fulfilled and completed with man. It is the life in which God is not only enthroned above man in distant majesty in and above the heavens, in which He is not merely the inconceivable source from which man comes and the inconceivable goal to which he is directed, in which He is not merely the Lawgiver by whose commands his actions and omissions are measured, the eternal good which consciously or unconsciously he misses but to which he consciously or unconsciously aspires, the mystery by which he is encircled on every side. No, it is the life which even in His Godhead, and without its slightest diminution, God lives in terms of our common humanity. Conversely, it is the life in which man, from the very depths of his creatureliness as the grain of dust or drop of water which he is before Him, and from the abyss of his sin and guilt and perdition in the longing of shame and remorse of the one who knows that he is not worthy of such longing, looks up to his Creator as his holy and righteous Lord, consciously or unconsciously seeking to cling and hold fast to Him, not to surrender fellowship with Him, to find and restore the fellowship with Him which has been lost. It is also the life which in this lowest depth, in this abyss, in this longing cry of man for the God before whom he must regard himself as rejected and forsaken, is yet lived in perfect peace with Him, namely, in total harmony with His will, in unqualified surrender to His command, and therefore, as a life which is truly lost, in the most genuine concealment with God, indeed, as a life which is itself divine, as *the* divine life, as the life of the Son beloved of the Father. This is the life of Jesus Christ. It is the life of the God who wholly humbles Himself, and of the man who is wholly exalted to God by this humbling. It is the life in which God justifies man before Him and man is thus sanctified for God. It is the life in which God, for the sake of the justification of man to be accomplished by Himself alone, takes to Himself and thus removes the transgression of man and his ensuing punishment and need. And it is the life in which man, that he may become and be a saint of God, is called and elevated to the side of God, and given his rights there, to reign with Him over all things. It is the life in which God gives Himself up to death and man is made the conqueror of death. It is the life of the Lord who becomes and is a Servant, and the Servant who becomes and is Himself the Lord. It is the life of reconciliation. It is the life of Jesus Christ.

Now Jesus Christ Himself is also the light of this life. In itself and as such this life is Word, revelation, *kerygma*. The life of this High-priest and King is as such also His life as Prophet. This life, and in the form of this life God Himself, speaks with the world reconciled in it. It speaks within human history and all the divers histories of individuals. It speaks with all those who like this One stand under God and before Him, and for and with whom He has acted in this life of His. It speaks with all men. It speaks with us too. It was and is lived for us (*pro nobis*), for thee and me (*pro te et me*). In this life God with us (Emmanuel, *Dominus nobiscum*) is with each of us. What this Word tells us is that *we* are those who are justified and sanctified in this life, that it was *our* place which was taken by God, that *we* are set in His place, that in this life the kingdom of God has come to *us*, that *our* old life is displaced, removed, destroyed and radically transformed in it, that *our* new and eternal life has begun, that *our* deliverance, conversion and even glorification are accomplished, that *we* are already dead and risen again, that *we* are already citizens of the future world, i.e., of the new and true world to be revealed as the dominion of God and His Christ. *We* are those who are eternally loved and elected by God in Jesus Christ, and called to the grateful realisation of their election in time, each in his own time. This is what is said by the reconciliation accomplished in Jesus Christ. This is the light of His life. It is the light of *His* life. He Himself as this light and Word is thus the " everlasting gospel " which " the angel flying in the midst of heaven " had to proclaim " unto them that dwell on the earth, and to every nation, and kindred, and tongue, and people " (Rev. 14⁶). He Himself declares who and what He is, namely, who and what He is for us, for all men, for the world. As He declares His life, Himself, for the world, He is the Prophet Jesus Christ.

We now presuppose that this declaration takes place, that as Highpriest and King He is also Prophet, that His life as such is light, revelation, speech. Our present concern is with the fact that He is the one light, the one Word of God. This is demonstrated by the fact that He is this Word, the Word with this content. For can we think of any word actually spoken, or any conceivable word which might be spoken, that says what the life of Jesus Christ says ? In religious or secular language many words might speak of the majesty, goodness, severity and mystery of God, or the misery and greatness of man, or his destiny and his contradiction of it, yet also of its realisation, or of the glory and terror of the universe. They might point to all kinds of relationships between what is below and what is above, between the things of this world and those of the world to come, usually in the form of the schematic antithesis between reason and nature, soul and body or spirit and matter. They might make various individual or collective efforts to bridge the gap, whether in terms of aesthetic illuminations, intellectual explorations, moral rearmaments or politico-economic ameliorations or renewals. They might say things which in their way are good and which many find illuminating and helpful. But none of them says what the life of Jesus Christ says. They may say certain things which remind us of what this says. But even in so doing they say something different. And since they say these things rigidly and abstractly, this something different is inevitably a corruption. They may wittingly or unwittingly say things which are borrowed from the Word spoken in Jesus Christ, but these lose the meaning which they have in their proper context. Being set in a different context, they cannot fail to be somewhat distorted, or at least different from what is said to us in Jesus Christ. What other word speaks of the covenant between God and man ? What other of its character as the work of God, and indeed of the effective and omnipotent grace of God on the basis of eternal love and election? What other of the fulfilment of this covenant in the humiliation of God for the exaltation of man? What other of a comprehensive justification of man by God and sanctification for Him? What other of the fact that this reconciliation of God with man and man with God is no mere idea but a once-for-all event? What other pronounces that unconditional *Dominus pro et cum nobis*, thus indicating that a new situation has already been created for all humanity, setting each man at this new beginning, and pushing him on from this point? What other knows neither optimism, pessimism nor fatalism? What other does not have to rest on that sorry antithesis of soul and body, spirit and matter, etc., or on that of the individual and society, or man and his fellows, or this world and the world to come, because it embraces and refers to the whole man, and to his whole way from the past through the present into the future as he treads this both inwardly and outwardly, both for himself and in company with others? What other is so penetrating in its simplicity yet also its universality? What other is directed so concretely to each and all men? We may quietly listen to others. We may hear what is said by the whole history of religion, poetry, mythology and philosophy. We shall certainly meet there with many things which might be claimed as elements of the Word spoken by Jesus Christ. But what a mass of rudiments and fragments which in their isolation and absoluteness say something very different from this Word! What strife and contradiction between all these results of one-sided analyses and over-hasty syntheses! It is only on a very facile and superficial view that we think we can range the Word of Jesus Christ and its claim to validity with all other words and their claims, thus believing that any one of them may be normative in view of their multiplicity, or perhaps sorrowfully or cheerfully maintaining that none is normative, but the " true ring "[1] has perhaps been lost. If it were a matter of the word of Christianity among the world religions, or the word of the Christian Church in one or other form, or the words of the Bible in themselves and as such, a view of this kind might be possible. As such, all these may be ranged with many other words. But we are speaking of the light or Word of the life of Jesus Christ. Is it not the case that in the light of its particular content this is quite distinctive in relation to all other words? Does it not say something which we cannot catch in others however attentively we listen? And is this special feature only one particle among a thousand others? Is it not the one thing that raises the question and gives the answer which both begin where the speakers of all other words have not yet begun to ask and answer, and which continue and reach their goal where other questions and answers all usually break off? Does it not have a particular force or point which all others obviously

---

[1] The ring of Lessing's parable in *Nathan der Weise*.—Trans.

2. The Light of Life

lack? Is it not the case that the Word of the life of Jesus Christ is clearly shown to be the Word of God, His one and only Word, even by what it says? Does not this alone authorise, empower and command us to understand and describe it as the Word which needs no completion, which is exposed to no competition, and which cannot be combined with or transcended by others? To refer again to Isaiah 40²¹ : " Have ye not known? have ye not heard? "

This does not mean that we are engaging in apologetics. Or if so, it is only the apologetics which is a necessary function of dogmatics to the extent that this must prepare an exact account of the presupposition, limits, meaning and basis of the statements of the Christian confession, and thus be able to give this account to any who may demand it. We have maintained, and do not cease to maintain, the presupposition of the statement that Jesus Christ is the one Prophet of God. This presupposition is that He actually is this One and shows Himself to be such. Within the framework of this presupposition we have (1) established what the statement says and does not say, and (2) brought out something of its positive significance. And within the framework of the same presupposition that He is the one Word of God and shows Himself to be such, we have now (3) tried to make clear what is the basis of this declaration. We have not added another basis to that which it has (along with its limits and meaning) in the presupposition. The only thing is that we have not been and could not be content merely to denote it again, or to refer again to the fact that it is its own basis. In accordance with the necessary strictness of dogmatic enquiry, we could not stop at mere assertion. In relation to the content of the Word spoken in Jesus Christ, we have tried to describe and explain this basis. The fact remains, however, that it can only speak for itself and show itself to be the basis of our statement. Without counting on the Holy Spirit as the only conclusive argument, even the prophet of the Exile who advanced those arguments and proofs could not have undertaken to proclaim the uniqueness of Yahweh among the gods of the nations.

We have already adduced under (1) some of the passages in which the authors of the New Testament establish the uniqueness of Jesus Christ by simply bringing together and equating the εἷς θεός and the εἷς κύριος (the one εἷς explaining the other). In so doing, they maintain that the uniqueness of the Prophet Jesus Christ has its basis in that of God, and therefore in itself.

We now recall other passages in which they declare the nature and essence of this basis within the framework of the accepted presupposition. The most important statements which call for consideration in this connexion are from Rom. 5¹²f·, in which the significant word εἷς plays so outstanding a role. According to v. 15, it is the grace and the free gift (δωρεά) of God which in the one man Jesus Christ has " abounded unto many." In v. 17 those who receive abundance of grace and righteousness in virtue of the life of Jesus Christ created in them, shall reign through the one Jesus Christ. In v. 18 again it is by the righteous act (δικαίωμα) of this One that there is this justification for all. Similarly, the Epistle to the Hebrews (10¹², ¹⁴) speaks of the one exclusive θυσία or προσφορά which Christ has made for sins, which is followed by His session at the right hand of God, but by which He has perfected for ever them that are sanctified through Him. " One died for all " is the sum of what is stated in 2 Cor. 5[14], and it leads to the conclusion that " they which live (through his death) should not henceforth live unto themselves, but unto him which died for them, and rose again." According to 2 Cor. 11[2] they are engaged to this one man and are to be presented to Him as a " chaste virgin." This corresponds to the fact that in Gal. 3[16] He is the one seed of Abraham. Hence the sayings about the one Spirit in 1 Cor. 12[9, 11, 13] and Phil. 1[27], and about the community as the one body in 1 Cor. 12[13, 20] and Col. 3[15], and the whole series of unities in Eph. 4[4f.], acquire their true meaning and significance. It is in the uniqueness of His works and gifts, of His being for us and to us, that the uniqueness of Jesus Christ as Lord, and therefore the uniqueness of His authority and Word, is manifested. And all this rests upon, and is guaranteed by, the fact that He is the one Lord, with unique and exclusive authority, and that He reveals Himself as such. He alone who is and has life, and can and does forgive, has also the " words of eternal life " (Jn. 6[68]).

Before we conclude, we must be clear (4) what is the relationship between the one Word of God called Jesus and all the other words which according to our discussion under (1), while they are not identical with it, yet even in their whole creatureliness and human frailty either are or may be true words, and are not therefore to be overlooked, let alone rejected. In this respect we think especially of the words of the Bible, i.e., of the Old and New Testament witnesses to Jesus Christ. But we have also to remember the words of the community and Christendom proclaiming Jesus Christ in the world. We have also claimed that there are no good grounds not to accept the fact that such good words may also be spoken *extra muros ecclesiae* either through those who have not yet received any effective witness to Jesus Christ, and cannot therefore be reckoned with the believers who for their part attest Him, or through more or less admitted Christians who are not, however, engaged in direct confession, or direct activity as members of the Christian community, but in the discharge of a function in world society and its orders and tasks. It is obvious that a challenging problem is set, particularly by the third and final form of these words. But before we tackle it, we do well to raise and answer certain general questions which are relevant to all three forms.

(a) What is meant when we say that these words distinct from that of Jesus Christ Himself are " true " ? In other words, how is their truth related to that of the Word of Jesus Christ as the one Word of God ? Does it, or does it not, share the truth of this one Word, and if so to what extent ? In what order are these words to be heard together with the one Word of God ? And therefore, conversely, in what order is the one Word of God to be heard together with them ?

Assuming that there are such words, in what does their general truth consist according to our definition of truth as the faithfulness, genuineness and reliability of what they impart ?

2. *The Light of Life*

To this question our first and general answer must be that in order to be true, and therefore to be words of genuine prophecy, such words must be in the closest material and substantial conformity and agreement with the one Word of God Himself and therefore with that of His one Prophet Jesus Christ. The truth proper to the one Word of God must dwell within them. Applied to such words, " true " must imply that they say the same thing as the one Word of God, and are true for this reason.

(*b*) What will be the formal character of these words, again in relation to the one Word of God ? As human and creaturely words, they can have the same content, but this does not necessarily concur or agree wholly and utterly with that of the Word of God. They can have the truth of this one Word indwelling them, but as the distinct words of other prophets they can hardly have, or arrogantly claim, equal truth for themselves. Even as true words of God, they must still distinguish themselves from this one Word, keeping their distance and conceding and accepting the fact that it alone is truth. They can declare its content and truth, and thus share its content and truth, only to the extent that they declare nothing of their own, but in their utterance and emphasis are prepared to attest this one Word exactly as it is, without subtraction, addition or alteration. It is in this character that they may stand alongside it. Neither objectively nor subjectively may they have any other intention than to correspond to it and thus to confirm it. Only in this relationship to it can they be called true words.

(*c*) Yet how can such words ever succeed in attesting and corresponding to the one Word of God, or even try to do so ? Obviously, this is something to which they can only attain. Those who speak them must in some way be commissioned, moved and empowered to attest it. And what can do this but the one Word of God, Jesus Christ Himself ? He must have encountered in some way those who speak these words, giving Himself to be seen and heard and perceived and known by them. For how else could they attain to this knowledge ? He must have ordained, awakened and called them to take His Word on their lips in the form of witness to Him. And again, if their witness is to be genuine, authentic, and therefore credible and serviceable, He must have acknowledged their word. In other words, it must have pleased the Word of God to allow itself to be in some sense reflected and reproduced in the words of these men. This Word must have demonstrated to these men and their words the grace of its real presence, in the power of which they as men are empowered and authorised, quite beyond any capacity of their own, to declare it with their human words, and thus to show themselves to be speakers of true words.

This is our general answer to the question of the character always essential to such words. If our deliberations are right, we now realise that as these different human words they cannot and will not and must not say anything on their part but the one Word of God, and that it must be by this one Word of God that they are impelled, ordained and fashioned for this function of bearing testimony to it.

It will help to an appreciation of the various elements in this general answer if we pause for a moment to discuss the problem of the parables of Jesus as handed down in the Gospels. παραβολαί are little stories which it seems anyone might tell of ordinary human happenings. But they are called παραβολαί of the βασιλεία, and it is often said expressly that the βασιλεία is "likened unto" (ὡμοιώθη) these events, or, with an obvious view to this equation, that the events themselves, or the leading characters in them, are "like" the βασιλεία. It is also said that the kingdom in its likeness to these events, or these events in their likeness to the kingdom, can and will be heard by those who have ears to hear, i.e., by those to whom it is given to hear (Mk. 4$^{9f.}$). That is to say, they will hear and receive the equations or likenesses as such, whereas those who are "without" will not perceive and understand what is at issue, namely, the "mystery" of the kingdom. Even in these secondary forms of parables, and in them specifically, the Word of Jesus Christ as the light of life, the revelation of the kingdom, the Word of God establishing His lordship in the world, is to exercise its gracious yet judicial power, deciding concerning men and between them. Our present concern, however, is with these secondary forms as such, and therefore with the equations which they make and the resultant likenesses. The one true Word of God makes these other words true. Jesus Christ utters, or rather creates, these parables, speaking of the kingdom, of the life, and therefore of Himself, and doing so in stories which it might seem that others could tell, yet which they are unable to do, because His Word alone can equate the kingdom with such events, and such events with the kingdom, in a way which makes the kingdom really like them, and makes them like the kingdom in which He tells them, so that the narrative is no mere metaphor but a disclosing yet also concealing revelation, self-representation and self-offering of the kingdom and the life, and therefore His own self-revelation. As regards their materials, these are parables in the strict sense, for although they bring before us happenings from everyday life and familiar stories of human action and inaction—the peasant on his land, the owner of the vineyard and his workers, the father and his sons, the capitalist and his stewards, the shepherd and his sheep, the king and his banquet, the children on the streets, the bridesmaids at the marriage—yet the circle of interest is relatively small, many things are not touched upon, and there is obviously no intention of speaking of this kingdom as such and in its totality. Indeed, at the decisive points the materials of the parables of Dives and Lazarus (Lk. 16$^{19f.}$) and the last judgment (Mt. 25$^{31f.}$) are not taken from everyday life at all, but from the imagery of late Jewish apocalyptic familiar to their hearers. Even among the rest there are only a few, e.g., the seed growing secretly (Mk. 4$^{26f.}$), the mustard-seed and leaven (Mt. 13$^{31f.}$) and the drag-net (Mt. 13$^{47f.}$), which have an unequivocally everyday character, and it is to be noted that even here we have to do with more or less hidden processes. Real men, whether peasants, rich and poor, fathers and sons, kings or others, do not normally act and speak as in these stories. They are not really like this. To be sure, there are no miracles in the stories. Yet strange things happen. Hardly any would be in place in an informative newspaper account, because it is obvious that the figures in them are very strangely shaped, and their actions no less strangely directed, by an invisible hand which obviously estranges them from the everyday sphere in which they are set. For this reason, the happenings recorded can hardly lay claim to any purely human interest. It is not intended that the hearers and readers should recognise themselves in them on this level,

2. The Light of Life   113

nor that their consideration and understanding of the human sphere should be expanded by them. It is the kingdom of heaven which is likened unto them, and they to it. This is what is presupposed and declared by all these stories. As other true words they are to accompany and attest the one Word of God. They are not to be witnesses of something old in a specific new form. They are to be witnesses of something new to all men, and to be newly apprehended by them all. How could they be this if on the one side their material did not consist in stories from everyday life ? Yet on the other, how could they indicate that which is new if they were merely photographs of everyday happenings, and we did not see the fashioning and guiding hand which takes events in the human sphere that might well be photographed in theory, though not here in practice, and gives them the mark of the extraordinary, distinguishing them from other events and characterising them as those which are like the kingdom of heaven, and to which the kingdom of heaven is like ? Under this hand, recounted by Jesus, these everyday happenings become what they were not before, and what they cannot be in and of themselves. It is to be noted that even the events taken from the symbolical world of apocalyptic in Lk. 17 and Mt. 25 are brought into resemblance with the kingdom only because Jesus narrates, fashions and transforms them. (This in itself is sufficient reason not to incorporate them into a Christian doctrine of the last things in the raw state in which they are taken up and worked over in these passages.) As Jesus tells them, the material is everywhere transformed, and there is an equation of the kingdom with them, and of them with the kingdom, in which the being, words and activities of labourers, householders, kings, fathers, sons, etc., become real testimony to the real presence of God on earth, and therefore to the events of this real presence.

In sum, the New Testament parables are as it were the prototype of the order in which there can be other true words alongside the one Word of God, created and determined by it, exactly corresponding to it, fully serving it and therefore enjoying its power and authority.

The second main question which we must now answer is whether there really are other words which in this sense are true in relation to the one Word of God. Postponing the most difficult part of the question, our first reply is 1. that the utterance of such true words is the event which the Christian community has always perceived in the proclamation of the Old and New Testaments, from which it has always started, on which it has always built and established its message to the world, and by which it has always to invigorate and orientate itself and its being, life and action ; and 2. that from the very first and right into our own time, as it has let itself be taught and guided by the proclamation of the prophets of the Old Testament and the apostles of the New, the Christian community has always had the promise and commission that it, too, should come to utter such true words. These are the two secondary forms of the Word of God which derive from the primary and are subjected to it in this order. Both are subjected to the first because, while they are true parables, they are and can and should be no more than parables wholly created and determined by it. And they are subjected in this order because the word of the prophets and apostles has its truth from the fact that, as they themselves participated in the history of Israel and that of Jesus Christ, it was directly formed and guided by the one Word of

God, whereas the Church's word can be true only to the extent that it receives its shape in the school of the prophets and apostles, allowing itself to be continually tested, awakened, directed and corrected by their word. By a lengthy detour we are thus brought back to the theme of the Prolegomena to the *Church Dogmatics*, to the doctrine of the threefold form of the Word of God as revealed, written and proclaimed. In this context, we cannot establish, develop and present it again as is done in detail in *C.D.*, I, 1 and I, 2. In explication of the present question it is enough that, recalling our earlier conclusions, we should simply maintain that alongside the first and primary Word of God, and in relation to it, there are at least two other true words which are distinct yet inter-related in the above-mentioned sequence. Their twofold truth—that of the Bible and the Church—stands or falls with, and is wholly dependent on, the fact that the word of the Bible, and taught and corrected by it the word of the community, (*a*) coincides and agrees in content with the Word spoken in Jesus Christ as (*b*) it is ready to be only its attestation, empowered as true attestation by the fact that (*c*) the light of life shines in it as well, Jesus Christ Himself being the Creator and Lord of Scripture, and as such also the Creator and Lord of the community which proclaims Him. Scripture speaks the truth as, impelled by Christ as the Prophet of God, it also presents Him, confirming and attesting His prophecy. And the Christian community speaks the truth to the extent that it perceives and receives the prophecy of Christ attested by Scripture, and thus gives itself to present Christ by its own word. If the words of Scripture and the Christian community can be called a true word in the strict sense, in neither case can there be any question of completing, rivalling, systematising or transcending the one Word. These words do not stand beside it in their own right. The one Word itself sets them there. Similarly, they are not independent, but their relationship with it is one of service, and it is only as they are spoken in this ministry of service that there can be any question of their validity, dignity or truth. To the biblical witnesses, and to all the witnesses of the Christian community, it is promised and given to be parables of the kingdom of heaven.

Presupposing that this is accepted and confessed, we now turn to the more complicated question of true words which are not spoken in the Bible or the Church, but which have to be regarded as true in relation to the one Word of God, and therefore heard like this Word, and together with it.

Are there really true words, parables of the kingdom, of this very different kind? Does Jesus Christ speak through the medium of such words? The answer is that the community which lives by the one Word of the one Prophet Jesus Christ, and is commissioned and empowered to proclaim this Word of His in the world, not only may but must accept the fact that there are such words and that it must

2. The Light of Life

hear them too, notwithstanding its life by this one Word and its commission to preach it. Naturally, there can be no question of words which say anything different from this one Word, but only of those which do materially say what it says, although from a different source and in another tongue. But can it ever pay sufficient attention to this one Word? Can it be content to hear it only from Holy Scripture and then from its own lips and in its own tongue? Should it not be grateful to receive it also from without, in very different human words, in a secular parable, even though it is grounded in and ruled by the biblical, prophetico-apostolic witness to this one Word? Words of this kind cannot be such as overlook or even lead away from the Bible. They can only be those which, in material agreement with it, illumine, accentuate or explain the biblical witness in a particular time and situation, thus confirming it in the deepest sense by helping to make it sure and concretely evident and certain. They can only be words which will lead the community more truly and profoundly than ever before to Scripture. Has it any good reason to refuse this kind of stimulation and direction, whatever its origin or form? In so doing, would it really be obedient to Scripture, which in both Testaments often introduces witnesses to the truth from the darkness of the nations and therefore from outside the community of the elect and called, giving them a serious message to deliver and thus displaying that which is old and familiar in a new guise? Does it not necessarily lead to ossification if the community rejects in advance the existence and word of these alien witnesses to the truth? It must test them by the witness of Scripture. But it must really hear them, although without prejudice to its own mission to preach the one Word of God in its own tongue and manner as grounded in and directed by the biblical witness. We do not refer to words which might tempt it from this task or make it unwilling or incompetent to discharge it. We simply refer to those which make it apparent that the war in which it is engaged has already been fought to a finish by its Lord, that the world in which it has to work has not been abandoned by Him even apart from the action or assistance of the community, that it is not wholly destitute of the Word which the community has been set among it to proclaim. We refer, then, to the words in which the community, when it hears them, can find itself lightened, gladdened and encouraged in the execution of its own task. The community is not Atlas bearing the burden of the whole world on its shoulders. For all its dedication to the cause which it represents in the world, the cause is not its own, nor does the triumph of this cause depend upon it. But the One who has particularly entrusted His cause to it will see to it that it is not left to its own resources in championing it. Even within the world which opposes it, He will ensure that, as there are always acts of His rule in general, so, too, there will be raised up witnesses to its cause, which is really His. This is the message which the community has to learn through these true words of a very different origin and character. In this respect, too, it would be foolish and ungrateful if it closed its ears to them.

But are there really such true words spoken in the secular world and addressed to the community from it? How can we count on this? There is only one decisive answer. We can count on it as and because we come from the resurrection of Jesus Christ, from the revelation of the humiliation of God's own Son to human sin and perdition as this has been crowned by God the Father, from the revelation of man's exaltation to living fellowship with God as this has been achieved in the person of the Son, in short, from the revelation of the reconciliation of the world with God effected in Jesus Christ. It was to the One who, in virtue of His revelation in His resurrection, was and is and will be the Reconciler, that the history of Israel moved, and the prophets of Israel, and later the apostles, bore witness. It is in Him as this Reconciler of the world that the community believes. It is He as this Reconciler who is the theme of its proclamation. It derives from His resurrection in which He was manifested as this Reconciler of the world. It recognises and confesses Him as such. But recognising and confessing Him as such, it does not recognise and confess Him merely as its own, as the man of its own faith, love and hope, as its own Head and Lifegiver and Ruler. It is for all that this One has suffered in His abasement and acted in His exaltation. In Him there has taken place the co-ordination of the whole world with God in disclosure, condemnation, yet also remission of the sin of man. He has taken over the rulership of the world. All things are put under Him. All the powers and forces of the whole cosmos are subjected to Him as He was and is and will be this One who accomplishes reconciliation and makes peace between God and man. In the lowest depths He has triumphed, in the supreme heights He rules at the right hand of the Father, as the One who was crucified, dead and buried for the salvation, justification and sanctification of all men. Neither in the depths nor in the heights does He act in vain, but all that lives and moves and has its being between these spheres lies in the sphere of His dominion, and therefore of that of His Word and prophetic work which are our present concern. Hence, according to the witness of His prophets and apostles grounded in His resurrection, the sphere of His dominion and Word is in any case greater than that of their prophecy and apostolate, and greater than that of the *kerygma*, dogma, cultus, mission and whole life of the community which gathers and edifies itself and speaks and acts in their school. The greater sphere of His dominion and therefore His Word enfolds the lesser sphere of their word of ministry. If with the prophets and apostles we have our starting-point at His resurrection and therefore at His revelation as the One who was and is and will be; if we recognise and confess Him as the One who was and is and will be, then

2. The Light of Life

we recognise and confess that not we alone, nor the community which, following the prophets and apostles, believes in Him and loves Him and hopes in Him, but *de iure* all men and all creation derive from His cross, from the reconciliation accomplished in Him, and are ordained to be the theatre of His glory and therefore the recipients and bearers of His Word. In the very light of this narrower and smaller sphere of the Bible and the Church, we cannot possibly think that He cannot speak, and His speech cannot be attested, outside this sphere. We who in contrast to others have our place and task here, and to whom it is given to know what others do not know, can and must expect that His voice will also be heard without. We can and must be prepared to encounter " parables of the kingdom " in the full biblical sense, not merely in the witness of the Bible and the various arrangements, works and words of the Christian Church, but also in the secular sphere, i.e., in the strange interruption of the secularism of life in the world. In the narrow corner in which we have our place and task we cannot but eavesdrop in the world at large. We have ears to hear the voice of the Good Shepherd even there too, distinguishing it from other clamant voices, and therefore, as we hear it, not moving out of the circle and ministry of His Word, but placing ourselves the more definitely and deeply within it, that we may be the better and more attentive and more convincing servants of this Word.

It will be seen that, in order to perceive that we really have to reckon with such true words from without, we have no need to appeal either for basis or content to the sorry hypothesis of a so-called " natural theology " (i.e., a knowledge of God given in and with the natural force of reason or to be attained in its exercise). Even if this were theologically meaningful or practicable (which it is not), it could not provide us with what is required. By way of natural theology, apart from the Bible and the Church, there can be attained only abstract impartations concerning God's existence as the Supreme Being and Ruler of all things, and man's responsibility towards Him. But these are not what we have in view. What we have in view are attestations of the self-impartation of the God who acts as Father in the Son by the Holy Ghost, which show themselves to be such by their full agreement with the witness present in Scripture and accepted and proclaimed by the Church, and which can be materially tested by and compared with this witness. What we have in view are words which like those of the Bible and the Church can be claimed as " parables of the kingdom." Natural theology would belie its very name if it had any interest in words of this type, while we for our part have no interest in what it thinks it can advance as true words concerning God and man in general. We do not leave the sure ground of Christology, but with the prophets and apostles, and the Christian community established and living by the Gospel and making Christ the object of its faith and love and hope, we look to the sovereignty of Jesus Christ which is revealed in His resurrection and which we find to be attested by the Bible and the Church, but not restricted according to this testimony. Nothing could be further from our minds than to attribute to the human creature as such a capacity to know God and the one Word of God, or to produce true words corresponding to this knowledge. Even in the sphere of the Bible and the Church there can be no question of any such capacity. If there are true words of God, it is all miraculous. How much more so, then, in this wider field! What we have in both cases is the capacity of Jesus Christ to raise up of the stones children to Abraham, i.e., to take into His service, to empower for this service, to cause to speak in it, men who are quite without any capacity of their own. Our thesis is simply that the capacity of Jesus Christ to create these human witnesses is not restricted to His working on and in prophets and apostles and what is thus made possible and actual in His community. His capacity transcends the limits of this sphere. We may thus expect, and count upon it, that even among those who are outside this sphere and its particular orders and conditions He will use His capacity to make of men, quite apart from and even in face of their own knowledge or volition, something which they could never be of themselves, namely, His witnesses, speaking words which can seriously be called true. There is significant and pregnant mention in the Gospels of the fact that Jesus healed the blind, the deaf and the dumb. From the prophets and apostles to ourselves, there has never been a man even in the sphere of the Bible and the Church who has not belonged to the ranks of the blind, the deaf and the dumb, who has not needed, or more strictly does not continually need, to be healed by Jesus. Our present contention is that what was and is possible for Him in the narrower sphere is well within His powers in the wider.

But what is this wider sphere? To whom or what do we refer when we speak of the secular world in contrast with that of the Bible and the Church? If we are to be precise, we must distinguish between a closer and a more distant periphery of this narrow sphere, between a secularism which approximates to a pure and absolute form and another which is mixed and relative. From both, Jesus Christ can raise up extraordinary witnesses to speak true words of this very different order.

We have a secularism which approximates to a pure and absolute form, and which therefore stands furthest from the sphere of the Bible and the Church, when a man or several men stand unwittingly in full isolation from the Gospel in its biblical and churchly form, in which it has never or only very inadequately reached them, and when they are in a frame of mind in which it is to be humanly expected that when it does reach them their reaction to it will be hostile. There are such men, not only in so-called heathen territories not yet opened to missions, nor only—as we must say with qualifications—in Eastern peoples now overrun by an avowedly atheistic culture, education, psychology and ethics, but also in the greatest proximity to the Christian Churches—a proximity which may contain within itself the greatest inward distance. Even in the sphere of Christendom there are many who belong sociologically, by name and baptism, but do not belong at all in practice, being blind and deaf heathen. There is a whole world which for various reasons is not yet or no longer attached to any religion, and certainly not to the Word of God, but obstinately boasts of its own sovereignty. Yet we must not conclude too hastily that this constitutes a limit to the sovereignty of Jesus Christ and the power of His prophecy, so that true words are not to be expected on human lips in this sphere. We are not even to say that they are hardly to be expected, or expected only with a lesser degree of probability. For we must not forget that, while man may deny God, according to the Word of reconciliation God does not deny man. Man may be hostile to the Gospel of God, but this Gospel is not hostile to him. The fact that he is closed to it does not alter the further fact that it is open for him. Nor does the fact that he does not recognise the sovereignty of Jesus Christ, and if he did would perhaps rebel against it in his autonomy, result in its losing any of its validity even in relation to him. How can it be any less probable, or even impossible, that it should actually be exercised and demonstrated in relation to him too? No Prometheanism can be effectively maintained against Jesus Christ. As the One who suffered and conquered on the cross, He has destroyed it once and for all and in all its forms. But this means that in the world reconciled by God in Jesus Christ there is no secular sphere abandoned by Him or withdrawn from His control, even where from the human standpoint it seems to approximate most dangerously to the pure and absolute form of utter godlessness. If we say that there is, we are not thinking and speaking in the light of the resurrection of Jesus Christ. But if we refrain from this inflexible attitude, we will certainly be prepared at any time for true words even from what seem to be the darkest places. Even from the mouth of Balaam the well-known voice of the Good Shepherd may sound, and it is not to be ignored in spite of its sinister origin.

But rather closer to the sphere of the Bible and the Church, there is also secularism in its mixed and relative form. We find it especially in what seems to be the common pattern in so many countries to-day of men who have been reached in some way by the Gospel in its biblical and churchly form, who have been affected by it to varying degrees, who have been influenced and determined by it in some measure, who have a certain deeper or more superficial acquaintance with it, and who either sincerely or not so sincerely accept it, or at least do not deny it, yet whose life as a whole—in the earning of their livelihood, the exercise of their calling, the enjoyment of their great and little pleasures, the thinking of their thoughts, their practice of scholarship, art, technics or politics, the modes and habits and customs which determine their intercourse—runs along lines which, to put it mildly, seem to have no very clear connexion with the kingdom proclaimed by the Gospel, but rather to represent a very different world resting upon and impelled by its own laws and tendencies. What we have here is a world which in some way is concretely confronted by the Gospel in its biblical and churchly form, and at many points affected, illumined, unsettled and modified by it. It is a world which cannot altogether escape encounter with it. In a word, it is the world of mixed and relative secularism which is the distinctive form of the wider sphere in which those who are seriously trying to be Christians jostle with those who are so only in name and appearance and external allegiance. Now on the face of it, it seems much more likely, more easily possible and therefore more readily to be expected, that in this sphere which is closer to that of the Bible and the Church there will be human words which attest the one Word of God and can thus be regarded as " parables of the kingdom." For this sphere can always be explained as an echo or positive answer to the speech of Jesus Christ attested by the ministry of the Christian community. Why should not this speech evoke a reply to the extent that it is sounded forth in the message of the Christian community? Why should we not expect to hear true words from this world which only to a limited extent rests upon and is impelled by itself? Why should we not more readily expect them from this world than from the sphere in which secularism has not been visibly confronted by the Gospel and is thus identical, or threatens to become so, with militant godlessness? Yet we must continually ask ourselves whether this mixed and relative secularism might not be characterised by perhaps an even greater resistance to the Gospel for the very reason that it is used to being confronted by and having to come to terms with it, and is thus able the more strongly to consolidate itself against it, making certain concessions and accommodations no doubt, parading in large measure as a world of Christian culture, but closing its ears the more firmly against it, and under the sign of a horrified rejection of theoretical atheism cherishing the more radically and shamelessly a true atheism of practice. How can there be true words where it is sincerely or insincerely thought that due honour and even reverence should be paid to the Gospel but the art has been long since learned of accepting it without allowing it to intrude upon what are still at bottom secular thoughts and desires, as it can and should if it is really to declare its message? In a meaningful application of what is said about the obduracy of Israel in Romans 9–11, do we not have to think of the particular temptations and dangers of the situation in a " Christian " or " Christianised " culture and society, and in view of these are we not forced to say that, if true words are to be uttered and heard from

2. The Light of Life

such a world of mixed and relative secularism, no less a miracle is needed than where we seem to have the express and unequivocal secularism of militant godlessness? But all this has reference only to the one aspect of the particular situation in this second form of secularism. And when we consider the other, we shall not allow this concern to have the last word, however well-founded it may be. The power and cunning of a wordliness affected, coloured and embellished by Christianity may be as dreadful as we may fear them to be, and as Kierkegaard and others have presupposed. The Church may very properly be asked whether it has really done what is necessary for the true delivery of its message in such a situation, or whether it has not secretly or openly fallen victim to this creeping secularisation, and is now itself howling with the wolves. Yet all these obvious fears must not result in a basic lack of confidence in the power of the message, however well or badly delivered. For there is also a distinctive situation, inward and spiritual rather than external and technical, in which the community and Christianity are found at the heart of secularism, however poor and wretched and strange they may be, so that the world which apes them so cunningly and successfully, penetrating even to the life and thought and speech of Christians themselves, is yet concretely confronted by Jesus Christ as the one Word of God through the instrumentality of the word and preaching, the instruction and worship, the whole life of the community. Is the Church His body, His own earthly-historical form of existence, or is it not? "Lo, I am with you alway" (Mt. 28[20]); "Where two or three are gathered together in my name, there am I in the midst of them" (Mt. 18[20]); "He that heareth you heareth me" (Lk. 10[16])—are these promises true or are they not? And if they are true, are we permitted not to believe them? But if they are true, and we believe them, why do we not also believe in the miracle—as it will always be —that the Word of Jesus Christ as well or badly attested by Christian proclamation, if not the proclamation itself, is stronger than the power and hardihood of the mixed and relative secularism of a "Christian" culture and society which confronts the community and continually penetrates and determines even the community itself? Why should it not be possible for God to raise up witnesses from this world of tarnished untruth, so that true words are uttered and heard even where it might seem that at very best no most than crude or refined deception may be expected? In virtue of the missionary and evangelistic power of Christianity? No, but in virtue of the living and self-developing seed which it sows, namely, the seed of the Word of its Lord who is free to acknowledge its activity, sometimes perhaps to its own very great surprise, by causing it to bring forth fruit and creating for it an echo and response without. For Him neither the militant godlessness of the outer periphery of the community, nor the intricate heathenism of the inner, is an insurmountable barrier.

§ 69. The Glory of the Mediator

In neither case should we have any illusions as to the antithesis between the kingdom of heaven and those of this earth. But in neither case should we have too little confidence in the One who extends His dominion also over the kingdoms of this earth, nor expect too little in the way of signs of this lordship. How many signs He may well have set up in both the outer and inner darkness which Christianity has overlooked in an unjustifiable excess of scepticism, to the detriment of itself and its cause! We are summoned to believe in Him, and in His victorious power, not in the invincibility of any non-Christian, anti-Christian or pseudo-Christian worldliness which confronts Him. The more seriously and joyfully we believe in Him, the more we shall see such signs in the worldly sphere, and the more we shall be able to receive true words from it.

It is evident, of course, that until His coming again, i.e., until the direct and universal and definitive revelation of His glory, there can be no question of anything more than signs of His lordship or attestations of His prophecy, whether in Scripture, in the confession and message of the community, or in such true words as pierce the secularism of the worldly life surrounding it in closer or more distant proximity. If we may compare the truth of the one Word of God, which is called and is Jesus Christ, with the centre of a circle and yet also with the whole of the periphery constituted by it, we shall have to say that the revelation of this centre as such and therefore of this whole periphery, now to the faith of believers and one day to the vision of all eyes, can only be His direct Word, whereas all human words can be true only as its genuine witnesses and attestations. Prior to the song of praise which will ring out on a new earth under a new heaven, the centre of the circle as such and its whole periphery, and therefore the truth of the one Word of God, Jesus Christ Himself, cannot be articulated or expressed by any word or voice of angels, and certainly not of men, whether it be prophets or apostles or very profoundly instructed and instructive fathers, whether it be an enlightened Christian mysticism or a *theologia viatorum* which is ever so notable in its simplicity or dialectic. Self-evidently, therefore, it cannot be articulated or expressed by the words and voices which, in virtue of the sovereignty of the one Lord, Prophet and Revealer, may even now be uttered and heard outside the sphere of the Bible and the Church. In them we have to do with the one truth, and therefore with genuine witnesses and attestations. But, to take up our illustration, they are only segments and not the whole of the periphery, and they are certainly not the centre of the circle which constitutes the periphery. They are true words, genuine witnesses and attestations of the one true Word, real parables of the kindom of heaven, if and to the extent that, unlike segments of other circles with other centres, as true segments of the periphery of this circle they point to the whole of the periphery and therefore to the centre, or rather to

2. The Light of Life

the extent that the centre and therefore the whole of the periphery, i.e., Jesus Christ Himself, declares Himself in them. Hence they do not express partial truths, for the one truth of Jesus Christ is indivisible. Yet they express the one and total truth from a particular angle, and to that extent only implicitly and not explicitly in its unity and totality. As happens even in the different elements of the biblical witness, and as may happen in any act of Christian proclamation and instruction, they manifest the one light of the one truth with what is from one standpoint a particular refraction which as such is still a faithful reflection of it as the one light. But if they are to do this in their particular and individual way, they need to be enlightened by the light of this Word itself, and to draw upon its fulness. Spoken and received abstractly, none of them can be a true word of itself. They are true words only as they refer back to their origin in the one Word, i.e., as the one true Word, Jesus Christ Himself, declares Himself in them. They are true words in their presupposed and implied, if not always immediately apparent, connexion with the totality of Jesus Christ and His prophecy, and therefore as they indirectly point to this, or as this indirectly declares itself in them.

One such true word may, e.g., speak of the goodness of the original creation, a second of its jeopardising, a third of its liberation, a fourth of the future revelation of its glory. Each does this authentically if and as and to the extent that what it says individually and specifically is only apparently and at a first hearing an abstraction, but really declares the goodness, peril, triumph and future glory of the divine work of creation which is enclosed in Jesus Christ, executed in Him and directed towards Him, so that, even though it may seem to be concerned with only individual aspects, it really declares the totality of this work and the whole context of the particular statements. Again, such a true word may speak of the majesty or the mercy or the all-sustaining and directing wisdom and patience of God. In spite of its apparent abstraction, it does so authentically to the extent that the one thing envisaged under all these aspects is the kingdom and deity of the one living God who as the Father in the Son and by the Holy Ghost is at work in the world and revealed in His Word, and therefore to the extent that the life and kingdom of His Godhead are declared in all these statements with their particular orientation. Again, such a true word may speak of the psychophysical or social determination of man, or of his defects, rights or dignity, or perhaps of the forgiveness of his sins, or the marching orders which he is given, or the shadow of death under which he lives, or the joy in which he may live even under this shadow, and it does so authentically to the extent that the abstraction or isolation of what it says is only apparent, since each in its own way points beyond itself to that centre and totality, and therefore to Jesus Christ the true Son of Man, and therefore to the true humanity of God, and therefore, or rather, to the One whom no single human word will declare, but to whom each may well point, so that He for His part may well declare Himself in such words, making them the instruments, signs and attestations of His self-revelation and therefore of His truth.

In this qualified sense there are true human words in the Bible, and there may also be such, not only in the proclamation of the

Church, but even in the words and voices of world-occurrence in its closer or more distant proximity to the Church. The clear task of speaking such true words, and the clear promise of the necessary freedom and power, are given to the Church and thus to ourselves. We have no knowledge of any similar tasks or promises given to representatives of secular history as such. Hence we cannot see or understand how a man may be, or come to be, in a position to speak true words in this qualified sense from the outer or inner spheres of secular darkness. But the circle of what we can see and understand is not the frontier of the sovereignty of Jesus Christ. Even within this circle the speaking of true words implies a miracle. We cannot think that, on the basis of the task accepted by us and the promise given to us, He is limited to this gift and commission of ours. We must thus be prepared to see His sovereignty at work in these other spheres, even though we cannot see or understand it. We must be prepared to hear, even in secular occurrence, not as alien sounds but as segments of that periphery concretely orientated from its centre and towards its totality, as signs and attestations of the lordship of the one prophecy of Jesus Christ, true words which we must receive as such even thought they come from this source. In view of their origin, it is obvious and understandable that we should suspect that they do not have this orientation, that in their abstraction and refraction they have nothing whatever to do with the truth. It is obvious and understandable that we should fear all kinds of lurking dangers which might overwhelm us if we listen to them. These fears and suspicions may often prove to be justified. But in no case must they be stronger than our confidence, not in the potentialities of world history, nor in individual men, but in the sovereignty of Jesus Christ who also understands those who are without. In no case must it be stronger than the readiness to hear, and to test whether what is heard is perhaps a true word which Christianity cannot ignore as such, as though Jesus Christ were bound to its own task and promise, or as though this task and promise were a possession behind which it could and should conceal itself with closely stopped ears. Has it not always been true that the community has always had cause and opportunity to hear in the nearer or more distant world around it words which are at least well worth testing whether or not they are perhaps true words, and in which it will sooner or later recognise with joy something of its own most proper message, or perhaps be forced to recognise this with shame, because by them it is shown and made to realise the omissions and truncations of its own message ? Has it not frequently been set before the fact of a secularism which, even though it may sometimes be openly pagan, has yet made just as clear and definite as itself certain aspects of the truth which it is entrusted to proclaim, and often indeed has attested them far better, more quickly and more consistently than it seems to have done ?

Examples ## 2. The Light of Life

We may think of the mystery of God, which we Christians so easily talk away in a proper concern for our own cause. We may think of the peace of creation, or its very puzzling nature, and the consequent summons to gratitude. We may think of the radicalness of the need of redemption or the fulness of what is meant by redemption if it is to meet this need. We may think of the sobriety of a scholarly or practical and everyday investigation of the true state of affairs, or the enthusiasm with which what is found to be correct is espoused. We may think of the unity of faith and life, of the love of God and the love of man, which can never be taken for granted even in the Christian community at any given time or place. We may think of the totality of human existence as this is continually disrupted by a strict Christianity through too great an emphasis on the spirit or the individual. We may think of the disquiet, not to be stilled by any compromise, at the various disorders both of personal life and of that of the state and society, at those who are inevitably driven to the wall. We may think of the resolute determination, perhaps, to attack these evils. We may think of the lack of fear in face of death which Christians to their shame often display far less readily than non-Christians near and far. We may think of the warm readiness to understand and forgive which is not so frequently encountered even in the Evangelical world just because it has too good a knowledge of good and evil and in spite of its acknowledgment that justification is by faith alone. Especially we may think of a humanity which does not ask or weigh too long with whom we are dealing in others, but in which we find a simple solidarity with them and unreservedly take up their case. Are not all these phenomena which with striking frequency are found *extra muros ecclesiae*, in circles where little or nothing is obviously known of the Bible and Church proclamation except perhaps by very devious ways and in very attenuated forms ? Is there nothing to be learned from these phenomena ? However alien their forms, is not their language that of true words, the language of " parables of the kingdom of heaven " ?

To be sure, what is seen and heard must be tested. This is a duty which is not to be evaded. In this sphere, too, we have to reckon with human pride, sloth and falsehood, with an optimism and pessimism which are terribly far from the truth, with unconscious blindness and only too conscious hypocrisy. But these are encountered *intra muros* as well. In neither case should we be too summary in our judgments. It is no fair test if we dismiss these words in advance on the ground that we have in them only the basically and finally unilluminating insights and virtues of the natural man and therefore *splendida vitia*, or that we see in them hasty conclusions and illusions, or that they are not exempt from the open or secret fanaticism which the children of the world can also display in their best achievements. This may all be very true. But it may also be quite irrelevant if it is nevertheless given to certain children of the world to speak true words, i.e., words which, whatever their subjective presuppositions, stand objectively in a supremely direct relationship with the one true Word, which are not exhausted by what they are in themselves, which may even speak against themselves, but which are laid upon their lips by the one true Word, by Jesus Christ, who is their Sovereign too. Even in Christian circles is it not grace and miracle, and the continual transcending of a whole mass of subjective ineptitude and distortion, if true words are spoken and heard ? Should we not always ask with great attention and the greatest openness whether on the basis of the same miracle true words may not also be spoken without, and seriously recognised as such ?

Criteria are certainly needed to distinguish them from other words which do not derive from the light which lightens the darkness but from the darkness itself, so that they can only be regarded as untrue words. Criteria are needed to distinguish the truth of true words themselves from the untruth which will also cling to them. We have already touched on these criteria, but we must now mention and characterise them more explicitly as such.

First, there is a formal criterion which rightly understood derives its critical force from the fact that it also reveals the decisive material norm which we must apply in this connexion. Wherever we seem to have a true word in some phenomenon of nearer or more distant occurrence, we must always ask concerning its agreement with the witness of Scripture. Naturally, we cannot expect that in its concrete form it will be anticipated and therefore confirmed in a biblical text or passage. But we should expect that, if it is a true word, its message will harmonise at some point with the whole context of the biblical message as centrally determined and characterised by Jesus Christ, that when it is compared with this it will not disturb or disrupt its general line but rather illuminate it in a new way at some particular point. No true word can replace the biblical witness in any respect. It cannot try to suppress or to emulate it. It cannot try to say anything different or new. In the measure in which it shows a tendency in this direction, it will not be a true word. If it is a true word, it will be a good and authentic commentary sounding out the word of the Bible. It will not lead its hearers away from Scripture, but more deeply into it. Whether or not the whole process is right and legitimate may thus be tested in detail by whether or not some artificial harmonisation is needed to bring it into line with the Bible ; by whether or not it is in agreement with the Bible just as it stands, without any adaptation ; and supremely by whether or not the word of the Bible needs to be compressed, truncated or expanded to permit of genuine concord with this word from without. To the extent that the word of the Bible, perceived and understood in the light of its centre, is in evident and easily displayed agreement with these words from without, to this extent we may confidently believe that the latter are true words, and thus be ready for obedience, in the direction indicated, not to the words as such, but to the word of Scripture illuminated and made more pressing by them.

With certain qualifications we must also consider the relationship of these other words to the dogmas and confessions of the Church as a criterion of their truth. They must certainly be tested by this norm. Yet we should not forget that, in contrast to Holy Scripture with its direct authority based on a direct relationship to the history of Israel and that of Jesus Christ Himself, we are now dealing with the secondary authority of the fathers and brethren of the Church, with an introduction to the divine revelation attested in Scripture which is highly venerable but still conditioned by the particular times and circumstances in which these documents had their origin. In due fulfilment of the Fifth Commandment, we can and should take this introduction into account when we test the content of truth in these other words. If they are true words, they will not lead us away from, but more deeply into, the *communio sanctorum* of all ages which is attested in these documents. If they lead to a breach with them, they will show themselves to be false words. But it may well be that the Christian community, assuming that it hears such true words here and now, has still new things to hear and learn which go beyond its dogmas and confessions and which the fathers and brethren could not teach it in the days when these documents were formulated. If these new things, and therefore the truth of these words, are authentic, it may well be expected that their light will somehow be an extension of the line visible in the dogmas and confessions, so that they supplement even though they do not contradict what is stated by them. Indeed, when it is a matter of true words, we can hardly expect that the Church will be spared having to add to this line and therefore to learn something which goes beyond its dogmas and confessions, which is not to be learned directly from them or from its own inner movements, but which it is given by its Lord to learn afresh from without. It will not do to close ourselves to such words, or to question their truth, because they seem to say what is additional to or different from what we already think we know from the dogmas and confessions. For we might at any time be brought to see that these traditional norms of the Church need to be revised, and the Church might perhaps be confronted by the task of a new formulation of these norms. If they are true words, they will show themselves to be such by the fact that, as more or less powerful elements in the progress of the Church, they will guide it, not to break continuity with the insights of preceding fathers and brethren, but in obedience to the one Lord of the Church and in the discipleship of the prophets and apostles to take it up and continue it with new responsibility on the basis of better instruction.

As a further criterion in the question of their truth we may refer to the fruits which such true words have borne and seem to bear in the outside world where they have their more or less strange and puzzling origin, i.e., in the secular world surrounding the community. It is there that they are first heard and have their first effects. And there, in world-occurrence as such, all cats are not grey, but the Church can distinguish, if not the good from the bad, at least the better from the worse. Christianity cannot be blind or indifferent to the question of the significance for world-occurrence as such of the utterance and reception of such words which give even itself cause to think. How do they appear to work in this sphere ? What spirits do they seem to evoke ? In what direction do they impel men ? In what sense do they form their thoughts and aspirations and modes of conduct ? To what enterprises and actions have they summoned them ? Have they led to their greater freedom or their greater bondage ? Have they uplifted them a little, or thrust them deeper into the mire ? Have they united them or divided them ? Have they built up or thrown down, gathered or scattered, quickened or slain ? In relation to world-occurrence generally these are certainly no more than relative distinctions, since they are made and obtain only within the lost condition which marks all that man does as such. Yet in all their relativity they acquire emphasis and significance by the fact that in them, too, the ruling hand of God and His Christ is active and displayed. In the expectation that in them His grace and judgment will at least be sketched in outline, if not revealed, we cannot as Christians escape the task of taking them seriously for all their relativity, and therefore of looking cautiously but resolutely for the difference in the fruits of these words uttered in world-occurrence, and of judging their manner and tendency accordingly. If for the most part we can see and understand these only as less good fruits, we may readily suspect that there is little or no truth in the words which produce them. But if we may cautiously discern better fruits, this may well be a sign that there is a positive relationship between the words which have produced them and the one Word of truth, so that in them we have to do with true words. It will be appreciated that, since we men, even we Christians, are not instituted or endowed to be judges of the world, there can be no question here of a criterion which even with the greatest circumspection can be applied with convincing power. Yet in all its relativity it certainly renders good service of at least a supplementary and auxiliary nature in relationship to the other criteria. In this relationship it may even be an absolute and convincing criterion on some occasions. We have thus to keep our eyes open in this direction.

We return to surer ground when we maintain that these other words may be recognised as true words by what they signify for the life of the community itself, for its activity under the special command and promise of its Lord. If in these words, as distinct from the many others which are uttered and heard in history, we have that which is right, then, in correspondence with what the true word of Scripture means for the community, they will have for it in indissoluble unity the character of affirmation and criticism, of address and claim, of a summons to faith and a call to repentance, and therefore of Gospel and Law. They will show themselves to be genuine parables of the kingdom in this unity. In it they will betray the fact that they are **human words which have their final origin and meaning in the**

2. *The Light of Life*

awakening power of the universal prophecy of Jesus Christ Himself. The community will thus find itself comforted by them as through them it discovers that in and in spite of the strangeness of its message it is not alone nor thrown back solely upon itself, but encounters in the outside world voices which perhaps answer its own, or are perhaps independent and original in their origin and nature, but which with their own particular determination and orientation seem to take up its own word and declare it in their own manner and speech, less strongly and authentically perhaps, yet sometimes more forcefully and in their own way more convincingly than in its own particular manner it has so far been able to accomplish, and at any rate in such sort that it is stimulated and encouraged to give the world its own commissioned word with greater joy and emphasis. If in its weakness and confusion it is comforted and encouraged in this way by these other words, it may surely gather that in them it is dealing with true words. It will be shown, however, that this is genuine comfort and encouragement, and not false temptation and enticement, by the fact that the community is not merely confirmed and approved by these words, but also shamed, frightened, unsettled and corrected. Its proclamation and activity, its whole life, stood perhaps in need of concentration, or extension, or some consolidation or loosening of its present form. And now it seems to have received from without a surprising and perhaps not very welcome but salutary impulse in this direction. Why has it lagged behind when it ought to have been in the van? Why has it not told itself what it must now learn from the children of this world? When Christianity is called to repentance, it is a criterion that, no matter where the summons may come from or in what language, angry and offensive perhaps, it may be couched, it has to do with a true word addressed to it on the commission of its Lord. But we must be cautious. For even as a call to repentance it will be a true and genuine word only if it is also one which affirms and strengthens and upbuilds the community. There can be a respect, an anxious pliancy, in relation to the world's criticism of the Church, which is quite out of place because it is not related to a true word which the Church ought to hear. And it will be shown not to be a true word by the fact that it has no positive content, that it merely denies and destroys or discourages and confuses, that it merely aims at adaptations and compromises which the world desires for the Church. The true call to repentance, whether from within or from without, may always be known by the fact that the law and command critically addressed to the Church are those of the Gospel, by which the community is always raised up as well as cast down, not being plunged into a sterile melancholy, remorse and abasement, but stirred with new resolution and clarity to represent its good cause. The word which criticises the Church is true only if it is one by which the community is comforted in the true and New Testament sense.

Hence we may recognise its truth by the fact that it concerns and activates Christians as Christians and the community as the community in this twofold sense. A word which merely pacified and confirmed, or unsettled and shattered, would by its very nature reveal that it had nothing whatever to do with the one truth of Jesus Christ, that it was not then a true word, and that it should not therefore be heard.

We now turn to the final question which must be put and answered in this narrower context. It concerns the right procedure in relation to such words, the right use to be made of them if they impress themselves upon us as true words and show themselves to be such. Our general answer is that Christianity must avoid any pride or sloth in face of them. It must be ready to hear them, and it must do so. It must let them do the work laid upon them in relation to proclamation, instruction and the whole life of the community. If and to the extent that they are true words, they are free communications of the will of its Lord which it must not stiffly refuse but accept. Rather more concretely, it must receive them, as previously stated, as a commentary on Holy Scripture which is the primary and proper source of all knowledge of the Christian life, as a corrective of the tradition of the Church, and as an impulse to its reformation.

But the more specific point is to be considered that the uttering and receiving of such true words is part of the history of the Church, or better of the history of its overruling, preservation and continual reformation by the One to whom it belongs, whose body or earthly-historical form of existence it is. In this history it experiences, in what must be described as the normal and regular form of the rule of its Head, His self-disclosure by His constant address, in the power of the Holy Spirit, through the witness of His prophets and apostles and therefore by means of the biblical word. But it also experiences, in extraordinary acts of His rule, His free communications in the parables of the kingdom which come to it through the general history of the world around it. By the very nature of the case the correct and prescribed procedure cannot be the same in relation to the latter as to the Bible, i.e., to His self-attestation mediated through the prophetic-apostolic word.

The latter has the character of a constant and universal authority to the extent that, although the Bible is a source and norm which specifically addresses its readers and hearers in the power of the Holy Spirit, it is also an abiding whole which is given to the community throughout its history and in which Jesus Christ accompanies it through this history. Holy Scripture may be compared to the fiery cloud and pillar which in every age precedes the community and all its members as an invariably authentic direction to the knowledge of its Lord, to the gift which He gives and the accompanying task which He sets. It can and should be confessed always and everywhere and

2. The Light of Life

by all. It raises the claim to be heard, to be heard obediently and to be recognised as authoritative always and everywhere and by all. The biblical word is thus the concrete *vinculum pacis* of the Church in every age and place. The community is always and everywhere summoned to regard its claim, to gather around its message, to pursue its investigation, exposition and application. We never do injury to a Christian or the community, nor are we in danger of leading a Christian astray, nor is it arbitrary but always and everywhere salutary and good, if we set ourselves and the community on the way which leads backwards or rather forwards to Holy Scripture. For since in Holy Scripture true words are always to be heard, this way is always the way backwards or rather forwards to Jesus Christ, to the one Word, to the reconciliation accomplished in Him, to the one covenant between Him and man, to the salvation effected and to be found in this covenant. However well or badly it may be followed, this way is always the good way, and to tread it is always and in all places commanded of the community and individual Christians, and is full of promise for them. As I see it, it is the regular way to which we are directed.

The same cannot be said of the free communications of Jesus Christ in world events, or the true words which come to the community through them. Indeed, we must not say this concerning them if we are to estimate them aright. Our handling of them, our listening to them, their recognition and authorisation in the life of the community, their significance and scope for its proclamation and instruction, must be determined and limited by the fact that in them we cannot have more than the voice of certain individual events and elements in world history as it unfolds through the long and kaleidoscopic sequence of the centuries, and in the history of the community within it. Even though they are uttered as products of the omnipotent prophecy of Jesus Christ, and are to be claimed and respected as true words, they lack the unity and compactness and therefore the constancy and universality of His self-revelation as it takes place and is to be sought in Holy Scripture. They are uttered in individual places and situations in which the community and its members find themselves in world history, at individual points in their history in this time which move to its end but still endures. Will what was said then and there be said again here and now in the same way? It might be that something was said then and there to be heard and followed then and there. It might be that it was heard then and there and had its specific and salutary effect and rightly passed into its experience as something learned for the future. But it might also be that the community has still to receive very different words from world events as directed by its Lord, that here and now it must concentrate its attention upon these, and that on occasion it must correct by what is said here and now its understanding of what was perceived then and there, and therefore the experience in possession of which it has come out of the past into the present and is moving to the future. Hence, in listening to what is said to it here and now, it will be attentive and obedient in all good conscience and to the best of its ability, allowing itself to be guided by it in that immediate future. Yet at the same time it will realise that what Jesus Christ says here and now is certainly not His final word of this kind, but that another time, not in self-contradiction but in a very different situation, He may well have another new word of this type. And in any case, it will be conscious of the imperfection and even disloyalty which were shown by itself and the fathers in the hearing of His true words in the past, and which are not so absent from its hearing to-day that it can tie itself and therefore its Lord to what it thinks it receives from Him here and now.

It is also to be considered that, while these communications of Jesus Christ in world events apply virtually and potentially to the whole community and all its members, in this as in other respects (even in their relation to Scripture) it is not at all the case that at every time and in every situation the community is able and ready to hear with a single ear and receive with a single heart and will and understanding what is said to it by its Lord. On the contrary, it is always true in practice that even at best there will only be many, and often very few, who have the openness for such words which the community ought really to have as a whole. There are words which need decades and even centuries to be finally, and even then only approximately, heard and recognised throughout Christendom. Nor is this connected only with the natural stupidity of man generally or the special limitation which is often notably and most unfortunately displayed by the Christian. It is also linked with the fact that the truth of what seems in the first instance to be said only by world-occurrence as such, the character of its words as products of the omnipotent prophecy of Jesus Christ, is nowhere and never self-evident, so that, even though these words may be heard, their truth must always be tested by the criteria to which we have referred. It may be the very conscientiousness of this process of testing, the fear of falling victim to a subjective intuition or audition and therefore to an illusion, which in the first instance allows only a few and not all members of the community to accept and thus to be guided by what is heard. But however we explain it, the community hardly ever presents a unitary picture in its encounter with such true words of its Lord as He rules world history and impresses even the children of the world into His service. As a rule there will be only a more or less feeble vanguard of hearers which is persecuted by a large majority of non-hearers, and an apparently not inconsiderable rearguard of those who never seem to hear aright in this respect. Indeed, is it not even possible that true words may sometimes be spoken and

2. The Light of Life

they are not received at all in the community, or by any of its members?

The distinctiveness of these free communications of Jesus Christ consists (1) in the fact that they come to the Church in a specific time and situation, and are to be heard in these circumstances, but in other times and situations their scope and significance for the Church are an open question to be answered only in the course of its history and not without the utterance and reception of other words of this kind. It consists (2) in the fact that, assuming they are received at all, their reception is never in practice an affair of the whole community and all its members, but they are usually regarded as authoritative only by certain smaller or larger sections and occasionally only by a few individuals. These two characteristics make it quite evident that the right use of these free communications of the Lord can never be regarded as other than extraordinary. But this means that we cannot treat them like Holy Scripture, even though as true words they can only confirm and illustrate Holy Scripture. Hence, even when in a given time and place a few or many or even the majority in the community are convinced of their truth, they cannot be fixed and canonised as the Word of the Lord. That is, they cannot be regarded and proclaimed as a source and norm of knowledge which is valid at all times, in all places, and for all. And they certainly cannot be collected, and assembled as words of universal authority, and as such laid alongside Scripture as a kind of second Bible. They may be issued and received here and there, yesterday, to-day and to-morrow. But neither individually nor corporately can they be given universal and normative authority as a source of revelation. They themselves are opposed to such a process and avoid such a misuse. Their particularity as described above forbids us to handle them in this way. And the consequences of such a misuse might be catastrophic. If the modern Church were to attempt to canonise a free communication of its Lord in this way, it would become a different Church from that of yesterday which did not yet have it and therefore did not know this new canon. And there might well arise a Church which recognised this communication and another which did not, the *vinculum pacis* being broken between them if the former claimed universal validity and obligatoriness for its insight and confession. And since in practice there can seldom if ever be a free acknowledgment of such a communication by all members of the community, the results could only be disastrous if some presented it to others as a binding law, demanding that they should hear it with them as the voice of Jesus Christ, whereas for various reasons the latter could not regard it as anything more than the clamour of secular history. Finally, the possibility cannot be ruled out that we are deceived when we think we have received such an extraordinary communication from Jesus Christ; that we are confusing the voice of a stranger with His voice; that we are regarding a bit of darkness as the true light; or that we are really hearing His voice but either totally or partially misinterpreting it. Supposing that in these circumstances we were permitted or even commanded to declare that what we think we have received is a word of revelation, and to place it as such alongside Holy Scripture? The supposed freedom for this encroachment was and is even to this day the formal possibility of all heresies and schisms, of the formation of all kinds of sects and parties, of all temptations and enticements, of all falsifications of the Gospel and therefore of the Christian life. We may thus conclude that no conviction, however profound or joyous, as to the authenticity of such a free communication of Jesus Christ can authorise either the community or any of its members to give their discovery the exalted status of a dogma or to enforce it on others as if it were such. This is something which the community must not do in any circumstances.

In accordance with the extraordinary nature which always characterises them, these true words can and should be made fruitful in and for the community. If they are really true, and we have certainly to reckon with this possibility, why should they not do this without being given any canonical or dogmatic status? Their work will consist in leading the community at all times and places, and in all its members, more deeply into the given word of the Bible as the authentic attestation of the Word of Jesus Christ Himself. They will make a contribution to the strengthening, extending and defining of the Christian knowledge which draws from this source and is measured by this norm, to the lending of new seriousness and cheerfulness to the Christian life and new freedom and concentration to the delivery of the Christian message. We may let them do this work without the pretension of acquiring from them new tables or of being empowered and obligated by them to proclaim such tables. They do not need this to accomplish what they can and should accomplish. Why should not those to whom it is given to receive these true words confess them with gratitude, sincerity and resolution, yet also with the humility which is required at this point too? Why should they have to claim them as revelations and make of them a law for themselves and others? Is it not enough if they are actually heard and followed? To be sure, those who receive them should stand by their insight to the extent that they are sure of their ground. They should not keep it to themselves. They should hold it up as an invitation and summons to others, to the whole community, to share it with them. But they should do this in such a way that they allow the fact of the instruction received from them to speak for itself. They should show themselves to be such as have heard a true word and been radically smitten by it. They should bring forth the appropriate fruits. And then, with a readiness to be corrected, they should leave it to the power of this true word, by the ministry (and not the assertive claim) of its confession, to cause its truth to shine to others and to awaken its recognition and confession in them too. If it is a true word, the time will inevitably come sooner or later when it can make its way and do its work in and to the whole community. As it is really spoken in world history, and in the measure that it is really received in the community, it will certainly do this work in and to it. The more certain the community or individuals within it are of their knowledge of such a word, the greater should be their confidence in its own power, and the more boldly yet also the more modestly will they make known their knowledge. For in these circumstances it will definitely not have been spoken or received in vain.

> In conclusion, it is to be noted that, surprising though it may seem, in our whole development of the problem of these other words we have not adduced a single example, nor quoted a single name, nor mentioned an event or trend or movement, nor referred to a new and singular or common and general phenomenon in political, social, intellectual, academic, artistic, literary, moral or religious life, to which there might be ascribed the character of a true word of this kind. As distinct from Zwingli, who appealed to Hercules, Theseus, Socrates, Cicero and others, we have deliberately refrained from doing this. This is not because dogmatics, let alone the dogmatician, is forbidden in a particular context to point to this or that person or event or enterprise or book which is obviously outside the sphere of the Bible and the Church, and to draw attention to what is genuinely true in it. And self-evidently there can be no reason why the Christian preacher, teacher or writer, or indeed the Christian generally, should not do so. Our own concern, however, has been with the basic question whether and how far we may reckon with true words of this kind both in theory and in practice. But for a radical investigation of this question we have had to set aside anything that might distract from the matter itself. None of the concrete phenomena which arise in this connexion is as such the matter under consideration. All such phenomena are doubtful and contestable. What is not doubtful and contestable is the prophecy of the Lord Jesus Christ and its almighty power to bring forth such true words even *extra muros ecclesiae* and to attest itself through them. This and this alone is the matter to be treated. Hence it is right and proper that we should avoid giving even the impression that dogmatics can and should make pronouncements on matters on which He has already spoken or will perhaps do so. It is for this reason that no examples have been given.

At the conclusion of this sub-section we must make a delimitation which is essential to a true and keen yet also confident understanding of everything thus far said. In everything thus far said our concern has been with the basic christological form of the event of reconciliation between God and man from its third standpoint, namely, the prophetic work of Jesus Christ. This will still be so in the necessary delimitation. Reduced to the simplest formula, what we have said is that Jesus Christ was, is and will be the light of life, and because the light of life, of His own reconciling life, therefore and to that extent the one light incomparable in its majesty and authority. The implications of this twofold statement have been developed already. Hence we need not recapitulate them, but may take them as recognised and understood. But if this twofold statement is to express and underlie fruitful Christian knowledge and responsible Christian confession, it must be understood both keenly and confidently. This is necessary for its proper distinction in relation to another statement which is different from it, yet also related to it and both possible and necessary alongside it. By "keenly" we mean that it must be made clear how it does in fact differ from this other statement. By "confidently" we mean that it must be shown to what extent it has this other statement with its particular content beside it, not excluding but in the true sense including and necessitating it.

In this second statement we are not concerned with the light of life, with the gracious light of reconciliation, and therefore with the one true light. As we shall see, its primary basis and ultimate meaning are centred in Jesus Christ, and can be understood only in relation to Him. Yet its particular content is not directly but only in this indirect sense christological. First and last it is possible, tenable, fruitful and helpful only in relation to Jesus Christ. It is included in what is to be said concerning Him. Yet in its immediate and most obvious content, in which its distinctiveness consists, it is not a statement concerning Him nor a further development nor description of the assertion that He is the one true light and Word of life. As a specific declaration it rather accompanies and to that extent confronts this statement. If it is understandable only in this confrontation, and therefore in this relationship, it refers to a very different subject. It has to do with lights, and in a qualified sense with words, truths and even "revelations," but not with the self-revelations of God. Thus we are not to think in the first instance of the light of the resurrection of Jesus Christ, nor of His truth as it is to be known in the power of the Holy Spirit, nor of the light of His self-attestation in the word of His prophets and apostles, nor of the extraordinary self-attestations of Jesus Christ in world history—a distinction which must be underlined in relation to the preceding discussion.

It is not at all a matter of the light, truth or word of any specific events. We can speak of the being, activity and speech of Jesus Christ only in relation to specific events, only in the form of the narration of a history and histories. If Christology as the depiction of this being, activity and speech is to be anything more than an obscure metaphysics, in all its parts and aspects it can be only the unfolding of a drama. Nor can we denote or describe in any other way that which is found in Holy Scripture or the extraordinary self-attestations of Jesus Christ. Yet there is also a theatre and setting for His being, activity and speech, and therefore for this history or drama. This theatre is not itself a history. It is not immovable, rigid or lifeless. Yet it is basically the same at all stages in the history. It cannot, then, be described in the form of the narration of a history and histories. If it has life, its life as such is not the reconciling life

2. The Light of Life

of Jesus Christ. It is the sphere in which, the object in relation to which, and the medium by means of which, it is played out. It exists in events. Yet in it we have a sequence and repetition of the same events, or of events which are so similar that there can be no question of a decisive difference between one and another, let alone of any one being comparable or identical with the event of reconciliation, or with any of the events in which the Church lives and there arises the faith and obedience of the Christian. It is only in the *form* of the events in which this theatre or setting also exists, in the form of certain of these events, that against this background there take place reconciliation, the life of the Church and the awakening to faith and obedience. On a theological estimation the important thing in the existence of this theatre and setting is not the fact that histories are found in it too, but that, even when seen and understood as history, it is a sequence and repetition of the same or very similar events. The important thing is that in this field we have dominant lines, continuities and constants which characterise the whole. This theatre cannot be identified with the being, activity and speech of Jesus Christ, nor with its regular mediation in Scripture and the existence of the community, nor with the extraordinary forms of His presence and action. For if there are not lacking lines and continuities and constants in the life and work of Jesus Christ too, the theologically significant thing in this case is that along these lines we are dealing with history, with concrete events, not with the general features which they share but the particularity with which they take place in this way here and now. The problem of the setting of the reconciling life of Jesus Christ, and therefore of His light, of His prophetic Word, certainly cannot be stated, examined or meaningfully answered except with reference to these particular happenings and in the light of them. But in connexion with these it is a problem of its own demanding independent consideration.

We speak of creation, of the *creatura* which is distinct from God yet actualised by Him, of the creaturely world. This was foreseen in the eternal election of Jesus Christ, and specifically called into being in the beginning and as itself the beginning of all things, to be the theatre and setting, the location and background, of the ordinary and extraordinary mediation of His life and work. In the words of Calvin, it is the *theatrum gloriae Dei*, the external basis of the covenant which conversely is its internal basis (*C.D.*, III, 1, § 41). So long as the terms are filled out theologically in this way, it can be called the cosmos or nature. What is meant is the unity and totality of celestial and terrestrial creation, and within this of non-human and human, and within this again of physical and psychical. What is meant is the unity and totality of the reality distinct from God yet willed and posited by Him; creaturely *esse* and *nosse* as mutually related and conditioned. In the setting and framework of this unity and totality there takes place the life of Jesus Christ and therefore reconciliation, the event of salvation. It is the presupposition of this event. It surrounds it on all sides. It is the ground on which and the atmosphere in which it takes place. Indeed, it is the object to which it relates. It is also its indispensable material and instrument. In all these things it is distinct from it. And this persistent distinctiveness of creation, the cosmos, nature, even human nature, from reconciliation, is its constancy. The creaturely world naturally displays many modifications and variations. It has its own dynamic and movements. But it is dominated and characterised by the rotation and return of many things which are the same or very similar. Reconciliation does not take place in this rotation. It impinges upon and determines it from without. It is a new thing in relation to the moving and moved being of the cosmos. Not for nothing is it called a new creation. In the life of the cosmos as such there does not take place anything basically new. Its origin, purpose and goal in God are marked by the fact that it should be steadfast. Even the sin of man cannot shake its constancy, whether by way of diminution, addition or alteration. But as it was and will be, it becomes a corrupted world by reason of man's sin, falling under the divine curse and being enveloped in darkness. Again, its constancy and essence are not altered even by reconciliation, even by the establishment, realisation and fulfilment of the covenant of grace between God and man, even by the life and work of Jesus Christ. But as it was and will be, in Jesus Christ it comes under a new determination. *Creatura*, the creaturely world as such, persists both as the sphere and place of sin and also as the sphere and place of the reconciliation accomplished and being accomplished in Jesus Christ. Elected, willed and posited once and for all by God, it is the one reality of heaven and earth, of space and time, of being and cognition, in dynamic but steadfast and indissoluble relationship. To the faithfulness of the Creator, which is His free grace manifesting itself as faithfulness, there corresponds the persistence and constancy of the creature. The man upon whom and the sphere within which God acts as Reconciler are those elected, willed and posited once and for all by God. As man's Creator, in His faithfulness as such, and as He thus gives persistence and constancy to man and his sphere, God is also his Reconciler. It is with man as he remains the same in his inner and outer nature that God concludes, maintains and fulfils the covenant of grace. If what He does as the Founder and Lord of this covenant is not the same as what He does as Creator, He does not do either without the other, but does both simultaneously and in co-ordination. The work of His creative grace has in view His reconciling grace. But the converse is also true, so that He is always the Guarantor, Sustainer and Protector of His creaturely world, of the cosmos or nature, thus giving it constancy in the being with which He endowed it at creation.

2. *The Light of Life*

It is here that there is to be found the basis, possibility and necessity of the other statement which has its own place and justification alongside the assertion that Jesus Christ is the one light of life, from which the latter assertion is distinct, which is not therefore to be confused or identified with it, yet which is not expunged nor rendered invalid nor meaningless by it, but the proper evaluation of which in relation to it is the theological task to which we must now briefly apply ourselves.

The simple point is that the creaturely world, the cosmos, the nature given to man in his sphere and the nature of this sphere, has also as such its own lights and truths and therefore its own speech and words. That the world was and is and will be, and what and how it was and is and will be, thanks to the faithfulness of its Creator, is declared and attested by it and may thus be perceived and heard and considered. Its witness and declaration may be missed or more or less dreadfully misunderstood. But it is given with the same persistence as creation itself endures thanks to the faithfulness of its Creator. It is given, therefore, quite irrespective of whether the man whom it addresses in its self-witness knows or does not know, confesses or denies, that it owes this speech no less than its persistence to the faithfulness of its Creator. Like its persistence, its self-witness and lights are not extinguished by the corruption of the relationship between God and man through the sin of man, his pride and sloth and falsehood. However corrupt man may be, they illumine him, and even in the depths of his corruption he does not cease to see and understand them. It is true that by the shining of the one true light of life, by the self-revelation of God in Jesus Christ, they are exposed and characterised as lights, words and truths of the created cosmos, and therefore as created lights in distinction from this one light. Yet as such they are not extinguished by this light, nor are their force and significance destroyed. On the contrary, as the cosmos persists in all its forms and media before, during and after the epiphany of Jesus Christ, so it shines, speaks and attests itself before, during and after this event. The truth given it by God in and with its actuality endures. It does not do so independently of the epiphany of Jesus Christ. But it does so independently of man's relationship and attitude to the latter. As the divine work of reconciliation does not negate the divine work of creation, nor deprive it of meaning, so it does not take from it its lights and language, nor tear asunder the original connexion between creaturely *esse* and creaturely *nosse*.

It might be suggested that in order to avoid confusion, to distinguish these lights from God's own self-revelation, and to emphasise their persistence, we should not speak of the lights but rather of the luminosity of the creaturely world, and avoid altogether the use of the term revelation. Now we are certainly speaking of the persistent luminosity of the world as opposed to the obscuring by sin of human vision, yet also as distinct from man's enlightenment by the light of God Himself. But when we remember that in the creation story the account of the fourth day (Gen. $1^{14f.}$), in interesting contrast to that of the first (Gen. $1^{3f.}$), specifically refers to "lights," there seems to be no reason why we should not do the same. The creaturely world, which is only the *theatrum gloriae Dei*, only the place where His own glory shines in the work of reconciliation in which He Himself becomes man, has distinct glories or lights of its own which as such are its own words and truths. And we shall see that there are many of these. It does not have them of itself. It receives them from its Creator. But receiving them from Him, it has them, and they are its own lights, words and truths. Dangerous modern expressions like the "revelation of creation" or "primal revelation" might be given a clear and unequivocal sense in this respect which they do not usually have in common parlance. They are its own revelations, i.e., those of the *creatura* or κτίσις itself. If this expression is to be used only very sparingly, it is not to be totally rejected in this sense and context. There is a luminosity of the creaturely world as and because it is not without lights which constantly shine and words and truths which are constantly perceptible in it, as and because it does not merely have but also does not conceal its persistence and distinctive being, continually disclosing it, making it visible, audible, perceptible and recognisable, and to this extent revealing it. The implied problem is perhaps seen and answered all the more keenly and confidently if we do not try to introduce a new terminology at this point. We are dealing with the light, the Word, the truth of God on the one side, and with the lights, the words, the truths of the world created by and distinct from Him on the other. Two verses of the morning hymn of J. Zwick may be recalled in this connexion:

> "The skies above are full of lights
> To light our life and its delights;
> A beauteous order is displayed
> That honour to our God be paid.
>
> So in the eyes a light is ours
> To seek the good with all our powers,
> To turn and look to God always
> And note how gracious are His ways."

What is (a) the nature and function of these lights, and (b) their relationship to the one light?

On the presupposition and under the condition and limitation that it is created and ruled by God, the world has its distinctive being. It belongs to this distinctiveness, however, that it is not merely *in re* but also *in intellectu*. On the same presupposition and under the same condition, elected, willed and posited as such by God, it is being which is known and knows, is seen and sees, is apprehended and apprehends. The limits entailed by the presupposition and condition appear at once in the fact that strictly and precisely we can understand it only as being which is known by man and knows in the person of man, whereas in the case of all other creatures we may feel and suspect but cannot know that the being of the world is knowable to them, known by them and as this particular being able to know in and through them. We can and must be satisfied to know of man that the being of the world is one which is known by him and in this way knows its own being. In relation to man as *pars pro toto* we may say that the world created by God has truth *in intellectu* as well as in reality. We should be transgressing another of the frontiers set to its being if we were to maintain that it existed merely *in intellectu*, and therefore, since we do not know of any other *intellectu*, only in that of man. But we are on sure ground when we say that it does also exist *in intellectu*; that it is being which is known, contemplated and apprehended by man, and therefore knows, contemplates and apprehends in man. The question whether the same might be true in respect of other creatures obviously cannot be answered in the negative, but since it cannot be answered in the affirmative either, it must be left open.

With this limited but plain object in view, we may now make the further point that the world created by God does not merely exist but also speaks to one at least of its creatures, i.e., to man, giving itself to be perceived by him. And in this creature, in man, it does not merely exist but hears itself speak, receiving the message which it imparts. In respect of man it can and must be said that the world created by God is also (although not merely) a text which may be read and understood, and at the same time its own reader and expositor. Undeniable in the case of man, this quality of divinely created terrestrial being as *esse etiam in intellectu* is what is meant when we speak of created lights which shine and may be seen, of words which are spoken and received, in and with the being of the creaturely world, of the truths valid in the reciprocity of converse between creature and creature. These do not light up the world with the same brightness as God does in His Word or as the world has in His sight and knowledge. But they bring illumination. They prevent the world from being merely dark, or being plunged into absolute gloom by the sin of man. To them we owe it that in the distinctive darkness of the world (as compared with the light of God), and in the gloom caused by the sin of man, there is still a measure of brightness. As words of terrestrial being they are only terrestrial words, and as truths of terrestrial being they are only terrestrial truths. They are not, then, divine disclosures nor eternal truths. But since these words are actually spoken and heard, the world neither is nor can be absolutely dumb or deaf. The fact that they do not cease to be spoken and heard means that it can never be altogether without voice or reason, that even the worst communication does not completely fail to be communication and may perhaps become better. And for all the conceivable and actual error of man concerning God, his fellows and himself, their terrestrial truth in all its relativity is at least an obstacle to the onrush of chaos into the terrestrial life so severely threatened by these errors. For this reason it would be foolish to despise them. And we certainly cannot ignore or deny them. We actually live with them. We cannot live without them. It is as well, therefore, to be grateful to them.

Now the feature common to all these lights, words and truths, to this intelligibility and intelligence of divinely created being, is formally the fact that they point to something lasting, persistent and constant. The very things which speak together endure through every change. On the one side there is the created world which in all its specific forms gives itself to be known, and is actually known, as what it always was and is and will be. On the other side, knowing this world and itself within it (either alone, or perhaps not alone, or it may be representatively), there is the human creature, individually fashioned, yet always as it was and is and will be with eyes and ears, with reason, emotion and conscience. Again, that of which they speak is enduring. What may be and is contemplated, conceived and known between this object which is also subject and this subject which is also object; what is thus bright and audible and true, is always the one in the many, the general in the particular, the steadfast in change, the recurrent in alteration, the identical in the different. It is these lines, continuities and constants, or at least some of them, which the intelligible cosmos makes known to man and the intelligent cosmos actually comes to know and knows in man as it addresses its reason to the grasping of these lines, continuities and constants. It is a matter of making visible and actually seeing certain patterns of creaturely being in the sense of recurrent and ordered qualities and relationships. Declaring these, creaturely being displays its steadfastness; receiving them, it strengthens itself. They cannot and do not have to be mathematical or other rational patterns and therefore " laws." Neither the objective nor the subjective reason of the cosmos is exhausted in the declaration and perception of these. The one order at stake is not just uniform but multiform. It does not exclude the many, the particular, the change, the alteration, the diversity. It includes them, and this quite other than by the operation of a law. The only thing excluded is chaos. What it declares and apprehends are contours, models, orientations which as such have normative as well as individual force, and to that extent a terrestrial and relative though not a divine and absolute reliability—the reliability needed if the cosmos is to be the cosmos and not chaos. This is what is at issue in the converse of the cosmos with itself, i.e., of the intelligible with the intelligent cosmos. This is what is achieved by the lights which shine in this converse, the words spoken, the truths made perceptible. As they point to this order and thus give these orientations, they shed a certain brightness in the darkness and resist the onslaught of gloom. They draw attention to something which counts, and must always be taken into account.

It will be seen at once that they have nothing directly to do with the Word of reconciliation, with the prophecy of Jesus Christ. The guarantee that there is in the world something which counts, and must always be taken into account, does not end the moral strife of man against God, or cancel his sin, or save him from death. One reason

2. The Light of Life

why we might perhaps refrain from speaking of these guaranteeing lights as " revelation " is that no faith is needed to grasp them, but only an obvious and almost inevitable perception, only the application of the good but limited gift of common sense. In the converse which is that of the world with itself, it is not a covenant of God with man which is declared and perceived, but only a kind of divinely ordained concordat between the world and itself. Its result is merely the peace immanent to the world as such in and in spite of every contradiction and conflict. This is not everything. Indeed, it is not a great deal. It certainly cannot be regarded as identical with, or even a parable of, the peace of the kingdom of God. The world as such can produce no parables of the kingdom of heaven. Yet the fact remains that it is something. What would the world be, and we within the world, without it? We must be grateful to the world, and as Christians to its Creator, for the fact that along with many other things it also has and maintains this immanent peace, and that it displays it as a created light of its created stability.

A concept fundamental to all the lights which shine, the words which are spoken and the truths perceived in this whole process of making known and knowing is (1) the simple one of existence. What is meant is a specific existence for one another, namely, the existence of the cosmos which makes itself known for the cosmos which knows and *vice versa*, the existence of the subject which is also object for the object which is also subject and *vice versa*. This existence for one another is the basic form of what is lasting, persistent and constant in the creaturely world. In it, in this relation and therefore relativity, it is real in its own way, which is distinct from that of God but genuine within its limits. In it, it exists not once but continually as an intelligible and intelligent world. For it, it possesses, and in it fulfils, the time given it with its creation. There is no time in which it does not count, and cannot be counted upon, that it is present in this sense, in this encounter, in this making itself visible and audible and actually being seen and heard; that in this sense which is limited but fundamental to its being as the creaturely world, it is secure and secures itself. In this sense it has and is its own basis. This basis is certainly given it by God at its creation. It does not derive from itself. Yet it is its own basis which could be taken away only if God were to revoke His will and choice that it should be created and have this existence. So long as time endures, He has obviously not done this, and therefore we cannot doubt the power of its basis, or its reality. In any case, even the end of time would not necessarily mean that He has done this. What is quite certain is that existence belongs to the content of time, of every time, and therefore that, as we are human creatures in time, we may assume that existence in the form of the existence for one another of the intelligible and the intelligent is a reality which within its limits is impregnable, unalterable and indestructible. This is not everything. It is not even a great deal. But it would be ridiculous to deny that it is something. For it is ultimately the presupposition of every breath we draw, every word we hear and speak, every step we make or refrain from making. The light in which this is declared and perceived is only a created light. But it is certainly a light.

Again (2) it is also light, word and truth that this being for one another of the intelligible and the intelligent is not static but dynamic, yet dynamic in an orderly and not a disorderly way. In its fulfilment there is a definite rhythm which is steady even if it is also multiform. It involves constant repetition, the recurrence of the encounter, the continual resumption of converse. That there is this repetition, and therefore the persistent and constant endurance of the creaturely world, is revealed in the fact that the many forms in which the movement of creaturely existence is fulfilled are always the same and always give evidence of a basic form. There is always speech and hearing, question and answer. There is always beginning, cessation and new beginning. There is constant discovery, concealment and rediscovery. There is continual coming and going. There is no becoming without perishing, but no perishing without new becoming. That which belongs together is distinguished, but that which is distinguished is brought together. The general divides off into the particular and the particular is subordinated to the general. The whole is only in the part, yet the part, too, is only in the whole. Essence is only in the form of existence, existence only in the form of essence. No swing of the pendulum does not evoke and is not actually followed by its opposite. No rest does not also contain and dissolve into unrest. But no unrest does not come from rest and hasten back to it. No over-emphasis is not immediately emulated and corrected. There was and is and always will be " seedtime and harvest, and cold and heat, and summer and winter, and day and night " (Gen. 8^{22}), in the course of an unbroken and never-ceasing cycle. This rhythm of existence is as constant and sure as existence itself. For the concrete fulfilment of its motions terrestrial being in its mutual actuality needs and has its time, and with these motions it fills it up to the very brim, so that there is no time which is not ruled and determined by this rhythm. It is only the rhythm of terrestrial being. But it is the fulfilment in which, within its limits, it exists and is actual. It cannot and must not in any circumstances be confused or equated with the life of God as the Creator and Lord of terrestrial being, or His activity in and to the world. It is quite unthinkable that God Himself should be bound to this rhythm, as myth has always imagined, or that His life and activity should be compared with or measured by it. What moves in this rhythm is not God, but the intelligible and intelligent world. Yet this is the rhythm for the fulfilment of which God has ordained terrestrial being as its Creator. This is the character which He has

2. *The Light of Life* 145

given to the existence of the world. Hence this rhythm counts, and we may count upon it. The flux of the creaturely movement determined by it always takes place, and within the limits of its creatureliness is always to be expected. Whatever this may imply, we can and should always reckon with it. Again it must be said that this is not everything, nor even a great deal. It is not an ultimate answer to ultimate questions. Yet it is something. It is a light, a created light, yet still a light; and since its shining is the presupposition of all terrestrial being, and therefore of our own, it is fitting that we should be grateful for it.

As a further constant of creaturely truth we may mention (3) the fact that the cosmos continually presents itself to man, if not to other elements, with a certain inner contrariety. It is difficult to describe even the rhythm of existence as such in neutral expressions. It has very definite accents, as appears in the first creation story with its significant contrasting of day and night, of the terrestrial and celestial oceans, of land and sea. We have here the encounter and alternation of Yes and No, beginning and end, joy and pain, construction and destruction, life and death. Hence the light of creation as such is a broken light. Existence in this constant movement constantly discloses itself in the twofold form of light and shadow. The accents which indicate this inner contrariety may sometimes be light and bearable, but sometimes so heavy as to be almost intolerable. But in its continual development and reunion, this accentuation is always found, the persistent rejoicing of creation being accompanied by its equally persistent distress and lamentation. The contrariety is intraterrestrial and therefore relative. It has nothing whatever to do with the antithesis of Creator and creature, and certainly not of grace and sin or eternal salvation and eternal perdition. In the same way, the inner peace of creation which is always active and visible beyond the contrariety has nothing whatever to do with the event of reconciliation. Here, too, it is a matter of the setting, not of the event itself. As the event takes place and is revealed, a different picture is naturally given to the setting, and the positive and negative accents acquire the specific character of indications of decisions which are ultimate and a contrariety which is absolute. But this character is not proper to them as such. In the first instance what they indicate, whether they be light or heavy, is simply the imperfection of the world which even as such belongs to its perfection as the creaturely world of God. The glory of existence withstands concretely its disparagement or its dissolution in pure care. Yet equally the jeopardising of its glory withstands any overestimation or establishment by final guarantees. It is in this twofold character that it discloses itself. This belongs as such to the totality of which it is said in Genesis 1[31] that God created it and saw that it was good, and indeed very good. Both aspects count, and we may count on both: not as on an eternal Yes or an

§ 69. *The Glory of the Mediator*

eternal No ; but as on a Yes and No with a validity which is constantly reaffimed and with which we have thus to reckon.

Some attention must also be paid at this point (4) to what are usually described as natural and spiritual laws. It must be emphasised that this is only one aspect of existence among others. The truth of the cosmos is not by a long way exhausted in what is denoted by this concept. But there can be no doubt that it is also to be understood from the standpoint that in the coincidence and converse between objectively intelligible and subjectively intelligent being there is a disclosure and perception, a declaration and apprehension, of laws. These laws are not the basis of existence. But with greater or lesser force, clarity and certainty they constantly show themselves to be the forms of its nature. It is not to them that existence owes its distinctive rhythm and contrariety. They can only confirm the constancy of both in relation to the constancy of their forms. They do not indicate the reality or substance but only the manner of the existence of the created world and the fact that it gives itself to be known and is known. They do not indicate the whole or totality of cosmic existence, but only a part, i.e., the existence of creaturely being in certain specific sections and circles. In relation to the manner of some part of existence, we speak of laws when in the encounter and converse between the intelligible and the intelligent cosmos there are disclosed and discovered and revealed and established certain processes, sequences, courses, connexions and relationships of known being and its knowledge in which constant repetitions of form and therefore rules may be and are discerned. It is a matter of rules which seem to preclude the assumption of accident or caprice in these processes and the rise and persistence of these sequences, so that in their validity they present themselves rather as orders or patterns. It is a matter of rules which apply to being as it may be and is known in a specific circle, and which therefore necessarily extend to its knowledge too. Conversely, it is a matter of rules which apply to the knowledge, and therefore seem to apply to the being which may be and is known in this circle. Laws are formulae for the relative necessity of certain objective and subjective processes and sequences. Such relative necessities have already been disclosed and discovered, or will be. They are thus a fact, and with them the formulae. They cannot claim to be more than relative necessities because they relate only to limited spheres of existence, because even in these spheres the reality and substance of existence are already presupposed and they can only describe its manner, and finally and supremely because it is only in the encounter and converse between intelligible and intelligent cosmos that they can be valid, and this validity is limited and conditioned by the greater or lesser imperfection of the disclosure and discovery and revelation and establishment which take place in this encounter. It is only partially, formally, and above all within the world and the

2. The Light of Life

equivocal nature of all its relationships, that they are valid formulae. And it is only as valid in this way that they can claim to be constant and continual words and truths. They tell us nothing concerning God the Creator and Lord, nor concerning man in his relationship to God. For the Word of God, the revelation of the truth of God and man, is not pronounced by them. Primary and ultimate questions are neither raised nor answered by them. But again, this does not mean that we can ignore or despise them in their relative validity. Not all human knowledge, but an important part of it, namely, the so-called exact sciences built on empirical observation and investigation on the one side and mathematical logic on the other, are constituted in virtue of the knowability and in the knowledge of laws. And human technics in the narrower modern sense consists in the application of laws. We do not live only, but we do live also, by and with the fact that there are knowledge and technics in this sense, namely, that there are, as relatively tenable and usable working hypotheses, these formulae which have partial and formal validity within the world as descriptions of relative necessities, and which really count, and may be counted upon, when they are defined in this way. If not according to "eternal," then certainly according to "brazen" and in their way "great" laws we must "all fulfil the circles of our being." We must and should. For in them we clearly have to do, if not with the light of God Himself, at least with lights of the world created by Him.

We leave out the most important feature, however, if we do not proceed at once to point out that the existence of the created world not only reveals occurrence which takes place in this rhythm and contrariety, and with an obvious measure of regularity, but that from a very different standpoint it is also (5) a summons and invitation to the active ordering and shaping of things, and therefore to a step into freedom. Man at least exists as this call comes to him and he accepts it. He does not accept only this call. Heard and accepted by him there is also the voice of existence as such, over the reality and substance of which he has no power or control ; the voice of the rhythm of being which he cannot escape but which, whether with exultation or the deepest melancholy, he must accept willy-nilly ; the voice of the cosmic contrariety which he may approve or bewail but which is given and within which he must therefore live his life ; and the voice of natural and spiritual laws which he cannot set aside for all his awareness of their relativity, but can only recognise as valid and direct himself accordingly. But as the world gives itself to be known by him in all this objectivity, is he not claimed as one who knows, and therefore as an active subject ? Is he not made responsible for the cosmos which, as he knows it, cannot be remote or alien as though it were a fate, but is his cosmos and therefore a task set for his own life, not merely for his contemplation and apprehension, but for his choice and volition, his decisions and actions ? The encounter of the intelligible with the intelligent cosmos does not mean only that the former declares and makes perceptible to the latter its being, movement, order and forms. It means also that it awakens and stimulates it to a spontaneous work of ordering and fashioning corresponding to the particular way in which it, too, is the cosmos. As the intelligible cosmos exists wholly for the intelligent, it desires and demands that in its own way and work the latter should also exist for it. To put it dramatically, it yearns and cries out to be humanised. As it does this, and as it finds a hearing in accordance with the constant meaning and purpose of the encounter, the action of man as his step into freedom is also a constant element in the cosmos. However it may harmonise or not with the other constants already mentioned, and whatever may or may not be the result of human will and action, through all the being of the cosmos there runs the narrow but indelible and dynamically pregnant line on which, as the being of the intelligent cosmos and therefore as human being, it encounters itself, without separation or dissolution, as self-conscious will engaged in teleological interpretation, planning and creation. This is the line on which the creature acts even towards itself in affirmation and denial, in choice, separation and combination, in defence and attack, and generally in the establishment and execution of human shape and order. On this line the creature is also free in the distinguishing, seizing and realising of its own hidden possibilities. This is also one of its truths. It declares this too. It shines on this side. This is not an illusion or exaggeration. We speak of the freedom of the creature which we know only as the freedom of man and as it is severely compromised as such by the other elements, as it is engaged in continual wrestling with them, with existence as such, its unchanging rhythm, its irremovable contrariety, the nexus of the knowable and known laws of the natural and spiritual world. It is freedom with this limit and commitment, so that it is not even remotely comparable, and cannot be equated, with the freedom of God the Creator and Lord and the freedom given by Him to man. Nevertheless, the world chosen, willed and created by God would not be what it is without this second work of the sixth day of creation, without man existing in the act of his life. The littleness and impotence of man, the measure of his success or failure, the folly and wickedness revealed perhaps even more in his success than his failure, the feeble way in which he actually assumes responsibility for existence—all these do not alter in the slightest the fact that his freedom, too, counts as a cosmic element, and that we may count upon its recurrent offer and command, as we always do. We live as we act. Man would have to deny himself to deny the shining of this very particular light. He has good cause to be grateful for the shining of this light, even though it is not the eternal light.

If the regularity and freedom of the cosmos might be called its

2. The Light of Life

height, the last factor in this series (6) is surely its depth. This is the unfathomable mystery in which it exists as a cosmos which is both intelligible and ordered yet also intelligent and ordering, as a creature which is bound by law yet also freely active. It never reveals itself without new and true concealment. That is to say, every form in which it makes itself known and is known is the form of a riddle. In its dialogue with itself there is no unification or result which is not a new question or a call for fresh unification. What can we really see and say with any true and final certainty, or in any other form than that of obscure outline and intimation, concerning its existence, rhythm and contrariety, concerning its regularity and freedom ? And if what emerges and imparts itself at all these points is something, if it is light, relative yet necessary and helpful light to be welcomed with gratitude, it must not be forgotten that in and with all these lights there is seen a very different one which might be called the light of the universal and unanswered question of the Wherefore both of individual features and the totality, the light of a Therefore which certainly seems to be immanent in the created world but which it declares only by keeping to itself, so that it does not really declare it except as its secret. We do not speak of the mystery of God, but of that immanent in the created world as such. We say too much if we even try to describe this as the mask of God, let alone if we call it His revelation. In itself it has nothing whatever to do with God's silence in His speech or speech in His silence, with the " deep things of God " (1 Cor. 2^{10}). As the creature has its own existence, rhythm, contrariety, regularity and freedom, so it has its own mystery. And in and with all its declarations, it always and everywhere declares also the mystery in which it is itself concealed. Basically, the point is that it is creature, but nothing more ; that it is grounded, but not in and of itself. But we see this as we listen to the Word of God, not as we listen to that spoken by the creature. If the creature itself never tells us that it is more or other than creature, no more does it tell us that it is creature and nothing more. To every question concerning its basis it merely opposes the mute fact of its existence, declaring its mystery in its silence at this point. In this very way, however, it confesses its truth. It would have to be more or other than creature to be able to see, affirm and express itself as such. It can merely confess the fact that it is creature by letting it speak for itself in its very being as such. Otherwise than by its existence, by keeping its secret and thus by declaring it as its secret, it could only deny and not confess its truth. But it does confess it in this way along every line and in and with all its declarations. Now since this secret is its own most proper secret, it is obvious that it is not infinite, absolute, unfathomable or eternal. In the Word spoken in disclosure of the divine mystery, there is also disclosed what the creature itself cannot disclose as its truth, namely, that it is creature, the creature of God, but no more; that it is grounded, yet not in and by itself, but in and by God. It is hidden from itself in this respect. As creature, it can speak here only as it is silent; it can declare itself only in a mystery. The mystery which it declares as such is its limit. It has other ways of speaking besides silence. Its declaration consists in more than the declaration of this mystery or limit. As we have seen, it speaks in many other ways. Nor are we to say that at this point we suddenly come to a chasm which yawns at the very centre, or are confronted by an all-enveloping darkness. None of the other lights of the creaturely world is extinguished by the fact that in and with it the world always and everywhere declares its mystery. On the contrary, we must describe as light, and even as the great light of the creaturely world, this declaration of its mystery, this unmistakeability of the fact that it is simply there without giving any information concerning its basis, its Why or Wherefore. The declaration of this limit is also and particularly a highly important declaration of its truth. For as it always and everywhere makes known this limit, the hiddenness of its basis, it always and everywhere makes known the sphere within which it has its existence and can be satisfied with it, the sphere within which it is hidden. To know that we can know nothing of ourselves, particularly in relation to the creatureliness of the creature, need cause us no searchings of heart, because this ignorance is the signal which the creature may and does continually give itself and in virtue of which it is prevented but also spared from looking beyond itself, from being charged with responsibility for its basis, from accepting as its own the concern for its existence. The truth made known in this signal of the limit of all creaturely being and light makes it quite impossible that we should overestimate the other creaturely lights or entertain any illusions as to their significance. This critical function which it exercises is helpful rather than the reverse. And its positive function is even more important. Warned and restrained by this limit or mystery from any illusions and the corresponding enterprises, the creature, whether instructed or not concerning itself and its creatureliness, can praise its creatureliness and therefore its Creator by simply enjoying and taking seriously its existence within the sphere allotted to it. The mystery of creation gives salutary peace to the extent that it is a direction to keep to what we know and can do within the limit set for us, but also salutary dispeace to the extent that it is obviously a direction within this limit to ask daily what more might be known or what might be done better. This depth of creaturely existence is surely fruitful. Among the creaturely lights, none of which is to be equated with the light of God, it is surely a great and supreme light. It is surely a truth which always counts, and can always be counted upon, so that we have good cause to be grateful for its shining.

2. The Light of Life

We have now developed in its basic meaning, and in some of its more important details, the other statement from which we have to mark off our main thesis that Jesus Christ is the light of life. It speaks of the *theatrum gloriae Dei*, and therefore of the creaturely world as the setting or background, the sphere or location, of the event and revelation of reconciliation as the triumph of His glory. It draws attention to the lights or words or truths which also and already shine in God's creation as such, to the indications of the constant factors in cosmic being and occurrence as chosen, willed, established and overruled by God.

In marking off our main thesis from this other statement, we must also point out its relationship to it. That we cannot be content with a mere assertion of the difference between them, which might well lead to the unfortunate doctrine of two kingdoms, is suggested already by the fact that, while in the one statement we have to do with the one light and Word of the one truth of God, in that which we have just explained we are not just dealing with the many lights and words and truths of the world, but with those of the world created by God. It is thus impossible to allow a simple antithesis to be our one and final word. The more clearly we see the antithesis, the more confused and meaningless and unsatisfactory we shall see this to be. The question thus arises how that can be truth which as the truth of God is different from and even opposed to the truth of His works. Do we not have to accept the antithesis? But then what becomes of the unity of God and His work if the relationship between the *gloria Dei* and its *theatrum*, between reconciliation and creation, is only one of estrangement which may well be actual hostility? To be sure, we have to make a clear and sharp distinction at this point, since the content and function as well as the origin of the one truth are so very different from those of the other if they are taken in isolation. The existence of the cosmos as the existence for one another of the intelligible and the intelligent has in itself nothing whatever to do with that of the existence of God as the Founder and Lord of His covenant with man. Similarly, its rhythm has in itself nothing whatever to do with the life and activity of God, nor its inner contrariety with the contradiction between the holiness of God and the sin of man, between His goodness and man's fall, misery and perdition. Again, the eternal will and decree of God has in itself nothing whatever to do with the laws knowable and known in the cosmos, nor His freedom with the freedom of the intelligent creature, nor finally His mystery with that proper to the creature. But the fact remains that these distinctions become sharp and clear only when they are made with the calm of the common consideration which is demanded and permitted by the fact that the self-declaration of God in Jesus Christ does not take place in a dark and empty and indefinite sphere, but in one which has real existence, fulness, form and brightness thanks to the will and work of the same God. Hence, the critical distinction which has to be made in the relationship between the self-declaration of God in the prophecy of Jesus Christ and the self-attestations of the creature cannot possibly result in the exclusion of the latter, seeing they derive their force from the same God The critical distinction itself entails the search and questing for a positive understanding of the self-attestations of the creature too. It is revealed in the thoughtful inclusion rather than exclusion of what is marked off from the self-declaration of God. Our understanding of the connexion between the one light of God and the many lights of His creation will necessarily be a comprehensive one.

But the terms " common consideration," " inclusion " and " comprehensive understanding " require clarification. Can we really speak in this way ? God and the world created by Him do not exist in the same manner. They are not two elements related on one and same level. They co-exist in such a way that in free grace God gives it to the world that it should be what it is as such in the way it is, deriving its own being and existence only from this gift. The same is true of the relationship between the one light of the self-declaration of God and the many lights which declare the being, existence and nature of the world created by Him. They cannot be compared or considered together as though for all their difference they were only two rays from one and the same light, or two sides, aspects or parts of one and the same truth. This would imply an original truth superior both to the truth of the world and to that of God. The truth of God would then be, like that of the world, a mere manifestation of this original, superior and proper truth. We should be dealing with two words, and in origin with two forms, of a true and unknown kingdom which presents itself on the right hand as God and on the left as the world, and must itself really be both if it is to do this in truth. If we reject such Gnosticism, building on and keeping to the fact that God is the Creator and the world His creation, this very different co-ordination of the being and existence of both forces us to a very different common consideration of the light of God and the lights which shine in the world. In God's self-declaration in Jesus Christ we do not have a mere irruption of some higher, original and true light, and therefore a mere expression of truth, but the one true light of the one truth above or alongside which there can be no other, rival truth. Are there truths outside this one ? Yes, for the creature has its being and existence outside God. But as lights of the creature these truths are irruptions—in this connexion there is a real place for the term—of the one light and expressions—this term is also justified at this point—of the one truth. If they have force, value and validity, these are not independent. Primarily and finally, they are not their own. They are merely those which are lent them by the shining of the one light of the one truth. These are lights and truths of the *theatrum* of the *gloria Dei*. The meaning of the being and existence of the world created by God is to be the fitting sphere and setting of the great acts in which God expresses and declares Himself, i.e., His overflowing love for man, establishing, maintaining, executing and fulfilling His covenant with Him. The revealing of this action, and therefore the prophecy of Jesus Christ, is the one truth and the one light. But as this light rises and shines, it is reflected in the being and existence of the cosmos which is not created accidentally, but with a view to this action and therefore to this revelation. As it shines in the cosmos, it kindles the lights with which the latter is furnished, giving them the power to shine in its own service. The latter cannot do more than become bright in this light. They cannot replace the one light and truth of the divine self-declaration. As self-attestations of creation they do not speak of the great acts of the love of God, nor of His covenant of grace. Their shining, their declaration of truth, is strictly confined to the service which they may render as God declares Himself. But they have a service for which they are ordained, claimed and empowered by the one truth. This is the service of the self-witness of the world that in its existence and nature it is a real world, which is sustained and upheld, which has a basis of constancy as the sphere of the occurrence and revelation of the grace of God in Jesus Christ, and which as such may have continuing essence and existence. What is reflected in them as they perform this service is the fact that the Creator is faithful to His creature with the eternal faithfulness which is active and powerful and revealed in His act and revelation of grace in Jesus Christ, and which He has sworn to it with its very creation. The measure of their force, value and validity is the measure to which they are taken into the service of the self-attestation of God as self-attestations of the creature, and the measure to which they prove to be usable in this service : no more and no less. A true consideration of the *gloria Dei* in conjunction with its *theatrum*, and with the lights of this *theatrum*, will thus necessarily consist in a contemplation of the history in which the one truth of God illuminating the sphere of the creaturely world subjects the many lights of this world which it uses to its critical yet also positive, and positive yet also critical, decision.

Avoiding both dualistic error on the one side and monistic on the other, we have to see and understand both the way in which the truth of God challenges and relativises the truth of the creature and yet also the way in which it institutes and integrates this truth. The acting Subject which challenges and relativises on the one side yet institutes and integrates on the other is God Himself in His self-attestation, the eternal light dawning and giving a new radiance to the world. It is in and from our consideration of the shining of this light that we come to see what we are looking for, namely, its critical and positive relationship to the lights of creation, and therefore the nature and function proper to these lights as such. We shall now try to consider in three ways the history and therefore the action of the truth of God in relation to the truths of the created world. Against the background of what we have said at the beginning and in the middle of this sub-section concerning the prophecy of Jesus Christ, we assume that this prophecy, and therefore the truth of God, is distinguished (1) by the fact that it is completely binding, (2) by its unity and totality, and (3) by its irrevocable finality. It is with this character that it illumines creation and the lights of creation. Our present question concerns its effects upon these lights as it shines with this character. What are the necessary results for them?

(1) As the Word of God gives itself to be heard by man, it binds itself to the man who hears it in a way which is not just incidental, external or partial, but essential, internal and absolute. In a way which is equally essential, internal and absolute, it binds the man to itself, or, as we might prefer to put it, in giving itself to be heard, it gives essential, internal and absolute freedom to the man who hears it. This is what is effected when it is spoken as the Word of Jesus Christ, the kingdom and the covenant of grace through the word of the prophets and apostles, the ministering word of the community, or the word of an extraordinary witness. As God's own Word, it applies to the man himself. He is the one intended and reached by it from all eternity. It takes possession of him and sets him on a new ground and in a new atmosphere and situation. In virtue of its address he is a new man, a man of God, justified, sanctified and called as such. It does not merely enlighten him concerning himself in various relationships. It does this. But it does it only as first and decisively it illumines his heart, namely, himself. Hence he does not need to fear that there is a place where it will not shine with its good news. Nor is there any place to which he might flee to escape the illumination of its law and command. As a bad hearer of the Word of God he might give way to fear or flight of this kind, and therefore sin. But this does not alter the fact that it surrounds him as a hearer on all sides. The witness of Scripture serves it. It gathers, orders and edifies the community. It sends it as its messenger into the world and among the nations. It sends it into the world because, as this binding Word, it is not spoken only to individuals or the community but to the world, in its incarnation binding itself to the world and the world to itself, achieving and granting its freedom and thus making it, whether it realises the fact or not, a new and different world. Thus everything which is to be said concerning its binding quality may be said virtually and potentially of all men. For in virtue of the birth, life and death of Jesus Christ and His revelation in His resurrection from the dead, in virtue of the justification and sanctification achieved in Him, in virtue of the call which has been and is made in Him, every man in His humiliated and exalted and

2. The Light of Life

living person is virtually and potentially a hearer of the Word of God, and therefore claimed, not merely for investigation or experiment, but in a way which is absolutely binding. He has not yet heard it ? He refuses to do so ? He thinks he cannot do so ? Yet the fact remains that he is in the sphere of its sound and voice. Jesus Christ would not be risen if he were not. It is just because he has not yet heard, or refuses to do so, or ostensibly cannot, that he is to be claimed as one who is a virtual and potential, and can and should be its actual, hearer. This is the world to whose existence and nature it also belongs that the prophecy of Jesus Christ has taken place within it and towards it. It is for this reason that it is to be addressed, and indeed addressed with a call to absolute and binding commitment.

As it is confronted by this binding Word of God, it is obvious that what the creature regards as its own truth is challenged and relativised. In their own way, creaturely words and truths are also binding for man. But they do not bind him essentially, internally or absolutely. Nor do they give him freedom as they bind him. They do not strike him from the eternity of God, but merely as self-attestations of His creation, as part of its dialogue with itself. Nor do they strike him personally, as directed to him, but only with a universal application and in relation to qualities which he shares with all men of every time and place. They enlighten him concerning himself, i.e., his possibilities, situation and environment. But they do not illumine his heart and therefore himself. Thus even as he receives them he can and will be elsewhere than in the sphere illumined by them. He possesses them, but they do not possess him. He is not surrounded by them on every side. They tell him nothing of justification and sanctification. They tell him nothing of what he really can and should do. They bring him no shattering news of promise and place him under no shattering word of command. Not really applying to his innermost being, they leave him to his own devices. They tell him nothing new, but merely recall what he already knows and might easily tell himself. In the last resort therefore, for all the gratitude which he cannot withhold from them, they leave him unmoved. He lives with them, but he might equally well live without them. For he does not live by them : neither by the rhythm of the creaturely world, however powerful ; nor by the revelations of its regularity and freedom ; and certainly not by the declaration of its immanent mystery. Of what avail is it to man to know these things ? He has certainly to take note of them. But to what extent do they bind him so that he himself is reached and determined and altered ? In themselves they are only forms with no content, conditions with no fulfilment, presuppositions from and within which good and evil, salvation and perdition, life and death, are equally possible, but no decisions are to be expected in these antitheses. The Word of God shows them to be radical and mutually exclusive antitheses. It makes and calls for decisions. And in so doing, it is a binding Word. Even the brightest of creaturely truths do not do this. In relation to these antitheses they are neutral. They speak only of the constants of existence however it is lived and experienced. Without beginning, end, or time, they are mere hedges on the road which means for man good or evil, salvation or perdition, life or death. They are silent where they should really be pertinent. They carry neither real threat nor real promise. For they speak neither of real judgment and loss nor of real grace and salvation. It is only in relation, i.e., relatively to what might be seriously called real questions and answers, possibilities and realities, that they shine as truths. But this relation is not immanent in them. In themselves and such, unless they are set in this relation, they are merely bodies or forces of light, i.e., lights which are not yet kindled, or have been extinguished, and do not therefore burn and shine. In themselves and as such they certainly point—but only into the void and the unknown. It is for this reason that they cannot finally bind as does the Word of God. And this is at least an aspect of the way in which they are called in question when confronted and compared with this Word.

Yet we have also to speak of their institution and integration. For what they lack may be acquired by them as the absolutely binding Word of God, the Word of Jesus Christ and the Word of the covenant of grace, is spoken among them, and they are thus confronted with and set alongside this one true light. It must be remembered that we are not referring to another message given by the creaturely world, but to the one declaration of its Creator and Lord, who as such has intervened in His own person to save and keep it, to give it peace in peace with Himself, Himself becoming a creature, man, and in this solidarity with it acting for and towards it. It is not an alien who now begins to speak His absolutely binding Word within it, so that He and the world with its self-attestations are not to be thought of as at cross-purposes. And it is certainly not an enemy whose word contradicts its own and may rightly be contradicted by it. On the contrary, the One who now, as its Creator who is also its Reconciler, begins to speak His Word, is One to whom as such its own words and lights can be neither indifferent nor obnoxious, but who wills only that His absolutely binding Word should go forth and be heard. This being the case, it is only natural that its own words, however they may run as its self-attestations, should be taken up and used in the service of His Word, and given a part in its work. The positive thing which takes place in the confrontation of the little lights of creation with the great light of its Creator is that they are not passed over or ignored, let alone destroyed or extinguished, but integrated in the great light. They are not incapable of this integration. How could they be? They are created by Him, and were certainly not created accidentally or without purpose. They are even binding to a limited

2. The Light of Life

yet unmistakeable degree. They tell of orders in which the life of man and all other creatures is lived, of limits which are set for him and directions given. We have seen that these are not absolute orders, limits or directions. Their force, value and validity are only in terms of this world. They have as their object only the presuppositions, conditions and forms of human thought and action, not the thought and action themselves, not their orientation and content, and not therefore man. Yet they are still orders, limits and directions, and to the extent that these are declared the words of creation are also binding. For good or evil, man must keep to the sphere allotted by them. And the integration, the conscription to service, which comes to the self-witness of the creature in its encounter with the self-witness of God, consists in the fact that it is taken up by the latter, and that its limited power to bind can be invested with the absolute power of the Word of God, or conversely that the absolute power of the Word of God can invest itself with the limited power of creaturely self-witness. The eternal Word of God, which concerns and affects man himself, which radically changes and renews the world, which decides and demands decision, which is the Word of the kingdom and of the covenant of grace, can change its form and find expression in the apparently claimless form of this or that self-witness of the creature which in itself speaks only of various orders, limits and directions, of various presuppositions, conditions and forms of human thought and action. It can conceal its divine force, value and validity in the relative force, value and validity of such creaturely self-witness, and yet in this very concealment be God's self-declaration and as such absolutely binding. In the course of this action of the Word of God the eternal light can shine, the Word of the covenant of grace be spoken and the saving truth of God be uttered in the lights, words and truths of creation. The latter can thus be integrated by the Word of God and achieve what they could not be or do of themselves, but can be and do as the Lord of creation wills it. They are instituted into His direct service and set in a relation in which they do not stand of themselves. They can thus be truths which shine as expressions of the one truth. All the declarations of the cosmos, from that of its existence as such to that of its mystery, can in this sense acquire absolutely binding force in the change of form which takes place with the self-declaration of God. This is the positive note on which to end our first consideration.

(2) We begin the second by asserting the full and undivided and indivisible unity of the Word of God, and its totality which neither needs nor is capable of any addition or emulation. When we hear it as it gives itself to be heard, or see its light as it gives itself to be seen, we no longer need to crane our heads in an attempt to catch other sights or sounds in other directions. We must not and indeed we cannot do this any longer. The voice of Jesus Christ does not

scatter but gathers man and men. The whole wealth of the omnipotence of the divine mercy is the one necessary thing in His Word beyond which or in addition to which we need nothing more, and cannot fittingly ask for more. It is one as God is One in the infinite fulness of His divine life, yet also as man is one in the appropriate finite plenitude of his possibility. It is one as Jesus Christ Himself is One as the Mediator between God and man. It is in this unity and totality that the Word of God is spoken and also received when it is heard as such. Holy Scripture does not say many things; for all the many forms of its witness it finally says only the one thing which as such is also the totality. Built upon the witness of the prophets and apostles, and serving the Word of God, the community in all its legitimate and more particularly its illegitimate variety of form can live only by the one thing, and try to declare to the world only the one thing, which is also the totality. In every time and place it is *sancta* only as it is *una* and *catholica*. So, too, these extraordinary witnesses of revelation must show their genuineness by saying one thing and not many. For the Holy Ghost, in all the multiplicity of His gifts and powers, is One—the totality outside and alongside which there are no other holy gifts and powers. It is the content of the Word of God which gives it its exclusiveness: the one Lord over all; His all-embracing kingdom; the one and total justification and sanctification of man. Necessarily the Word which has this content is a Word which cuts, distinguishes and decides with a final sharpness. Necessarily Jesus Christ as this Word of God is also the One who " shall come to judge the quick and the dead."

Again, it is obvious that everything which creation can say of itself is relativised and called in question by this Word of God. It is not for nothing that we can speak only in the plural of lights, words and truths. The voices uttered and heard in creation are many, and none of them speaks in such a way that its message can be recognised in what is said by others. Our only option in this sphere is constantly to listen and look in every direction, so that if we hear the voice of constants, they are different cosmic constants which seem to contradict one another, as in the case of the regularity of the cosmos on the one hand and the freedom which obtains within it on the other. It continually seems as though one or other of the different lights is pointing to one constant as that which determines and controls the whole. But which of them can really fulfil this role? Even the questions which they raise and the riddles which they put cannot be reduced to a single form, let alone the answers and solutions which they propound. Attempts are continually made to bring them to a common denominator which can then be proclaimed as the world *logos*, whether it is matter, spirit, energy, act or existence. If only we could recognise this to some degree at least in a significant series of the attempts to establish it! But even in the series, let alone in the

2. The Light of Life

individual factors and elements proclaimed as the one and all in the various attempts, it has not given itself to be known in such sort that these statements are not able and even forced in constant interaction to dissolve and mutually suppress one another. It is obvious, of course, that there are world *logoi*, but it is equally obvious that there is no world *logos*, i.e., no word in which creation expresses itself in its unity and totality. From this angle, the problem of all creaturely truths is that there are so many of them, that they make themselves known only as partial truths, that none of them is the one whole truth. If we do not know the one whole truth, the light of life, we cannot concede that we have discovered it in one of these lights, or that we expect the day to come when it will be seen as the one great light in all of them. We can only resist such a view. To those who perceive it, the shining of the one whole truth, the light of life, which is the Word of God, Jesus Christ, always proves itself to be the standard by which the relativity of all creaturely lights is unequivocally manifested.

Yet where the relativising Subject is God Himself in His self-declaration rather than a relativising principle, in this respect, too, relativisation means institution and integration. What is lacking to the self-attestations of the creature as such, in this respect, too, they can acquire as and when God Himself begins to speak and claims and uses them in His service. They are not in themselves witnesses of His one and total Word which is spoken in the resurrection of Jesus Christ from the dead and which reveals His reconciling action. But as they are taken up into association by Him, they can attach themselves to His Word, and in all their multiplicity and ambiguity, both alone and with greater or lesser completeness together, they can acquire and assume its distinctive orientation and to that extent its character of unity and totality. If not alone, nor in any conjunction or synthesis of their own, yet in connexion with the action of the one Word of God, they can point beyond their disparate statements to a unity and totality of creation, and to that extent speak of that which will not differ from the unity and totality declared in the Word of God. They can blend their voices with that of God. He could hardly be the God who has lent them these voices if they could not do this as commanded and empowered by Him. What they say can so harmonise with what He Himself says that to hear Him is to hear them, and to hear them to hear Him, so that listening to the polyphony of creation as the external basis of the covenant, to its questions and answers, its riddles and solutions, is listening to the symphony for which it was elected and determined from eternity and which the Creator alone has the power to evoke, yet according to His Word the will also. Nor has He only the will. For when He speaks His one and total Word concerning the covenant which is the internal basis of creation, this symphony is in fact evoked, and even the self-witness of creation in all the diversity of its voices can and will give its unanimous applause.

(3) In a third consideration which will gather up the threads we shall again begin by thinking of the character in which the Word of God gives itself to be received in the event of the prophecy of Jesus Christ within creaturely existence and its lights and words and truths. Under our previous heads we have thought first of its binding force and then of its unity and totality. We must now think of its finality. Finality means that it has a validity which cannot be qualified or conditioned by any end or limit, which cannot be contested, questioned or transcended, which constitutes a threat to every other validity. The Word of God is final in this strict sense. It is the eternal light. It always shines now. There never was nor will be a time when it does not shine. It shines as the light which makes all other lights what they are, and without which they would have no power to shine, and would not actually do so. In it there is no darkness. Indeed, outside it there is no darkness to which it is not superior in its shining, which it cannot penetrate and illumine with its shining. It is an irrevocable Word. There is no fault in it, nor does it contradict itself. It cannot be recalled and replaced by any other Word of God. In face of it all contradiction is ill-grounded, impotent and untenable, and therefore condemned to be silenced and removed. It is the prototype of Word—the Word which makes all others possible as such, from which they derive and to which they return, to which they approximate, which they would like to emulate but cannot, alongside which they cannot therefore range themselves. It is the declaration both of first and original and last and final truth. It is the truth itself and as such. It cannot then be subjected to any criterion of truth different from itself. It is itself the criterion of all different truths. Declared by God, it authenticates itself. If any other truth authenticates itself, it does so in the power of this self-authenticating truth. It is with a final Word in this sense that we have to do in the prophecy of Jesus Christ. It is in this character that it is the light of life. It is this as and because the life of which it is the light is first and last, eternally and indestructibly, life in itself. Behind and above its life, i.e., behind and above the election made in it from all eternity and fulfilled and revealed by it in time, behind and above God's covenant of grace with man established and sealed by it, behind and above the justification and sanctification of the sinner accomplished in its life and death, there is no one and nothing save the free God Himself. And the free God is personally present and active in the being and activity of Jesus Christ. His life is not actually lived behind or above the reconciling life of Jesus Christ. In virtue of the resolve of His omnipotent mercy, and in its actualisation, His life is this reconciling life. Its declaration, revelation and prophecy are thus the light and Word and truth of the free God Himself. It is not at all the case that

2. *The Light of Life*

they are perhaps finally called in question by another declaration, revelation and prophecy of a free God existing somewhere behind or above them. On the contrary, it is the free God Himself who gives to the declaration, revelation and prophecy of Jesus Christ this character of finality, or rather, who is present in them with the finality of His own light and Word and truth. It is with this finality that His Word goes forth in Jesus Christ and is received as it causes itself to be heard, and is heard. For those who receive a final word—this final Word—" finally " means absolutely true and trustworthy. It means that he can and should hold to it in all circumstances as a Word spoken with once-for-all validity. It means that he need have no fear that at some point or in some respect it will not authenticate itself. It means that he cannot hope to escape what is said to him in it. It does not compel or even permit him to test its foundations by other considerations. It is the Word which does not entangle in disputation those who receive it, but takes them out of the sphere of disputation, sparing them the anxiety and futility of proving what is said in it. In relation to it any serious or less serious intellectual, moral, aesthetic or emotional questionings, doubts, suspicions or objections which may arise can have their basis only in the recipient and not in the Word itself. Either individually or as a whole, its promises and threats and admonitions, its offers and commands, its disclosures, are all perfect in themselves and therefore perfectly reliable. The Word of God cannot be the object of genuine questioning. On the contrary, it is the Subject which puts the only genuine question which can arise in this respect, namely, whether and to what extent its reception by those to whom it comes is true reception, a reception which corresponds to its declarations, and therefore the only reception which can be seriously called reasonable. In true and reasonable reception of the Word of God, those who receive it achieve an absolute confidence grounded in its own finality, in its eternity as light, its irrevocability as Word, its original and definitive character as truth. Without taking up the points in detail, we may add that it is in the light of this finality that we have to understand that which in our previous deliberations we have called its binding force and its unity and totality. It is in its eternity and irrevocability, in its original and definitive character, that it has the power to bind and loose men, and is enabled to say the one thing which is also the totality. First and last in its finality it is what all delineations of its character can only describe, namely, the Word of God.

When it manifests itself in this character, and particularly in this finality, this implies and effects the challenging and relativising of all created lights and words and truths. Whether and to what extent the validity of these is doubtful or relative may seem to be contestable so long as we are not aware that both individually and collectively they are all confronted by the final Word of God, and exposed to the work of His revelation. If we think we can know these lights abstractly and not in their confrontation by the Word of God, we are forced on to the way which leads from radical scepticism to radical dogmatism or *vice versa*, and on which the dubiety and relativity of all creaturely disclosures and perceptions are concealed. But if they are knowable and known in this encounter and confrontation, they are unequivocally known in their lack of finality. What can they make known ? Something to be sure ! To a radical scepticism we must reply, with reference to this confrontation, that they do in fact make known in their own way the existence of creation as willed and posited by God. Yet to a radical dogmatism we must also reply, with reference to the same confrontation, that they do not make anything known definitively in eternal light, in an irrevocable way, or in first and final truth. Creation can never declare itself as God does. Otherwise it would not be creation. It does declare itself, but in correspondence with its limited, conditioned and finite being, existence and nature, i.e., with a limited, conditioned and finite declaration. This is true, as we have seen, even in relation to its mystery. It does not know itself as God knows Himself and it, but only in the limits within which it may know itself in its continuing dialogue with itself, and which carry with them the constant threat of error. Only in radical self-deception can it ascribe finality to what it actually declares on the basis of its own knowledge concerning the constants of its being, existence and nature. The same is true of the necessity and freedom with which it should keep to what is imparted in this way. They can be only a conditioned necessity and freedom. We can and should count on its disclosures, but only in a limited way. There can be no question of an absolute trustworthiness of the disclosures of creation even in relation to itself. Even when what is said shines and illumines us with general validity, we are not to expect a first and final declaration from it. General validity is not necessarily the same as final validity. We must not forget that it is man by whom the disclosures of creation may be known, and who for his part knows them. When we speak of general validity, we refer to the agreements and common statements of many or all men. The certainty of these disclosures thus stands or falls with the self-certainty of man, and confidence in their validity with his self-confidence. Centrally, therefore, it is the self-confidence of man, of all men, which, if it is not negated or destroyed or even shattered by the Word of God spoken to him, is certainly called in question and relativised, being set in its limits and as it were bracketed, so that in these brackets, but only here, it may have its own place and sphere of action within the continuing self-converse of creation in which it is proper to the creaturely nature and determination of man to be both receptive and productive. This means, however, that, if this dialogue leads to results, and therefore to lights, words and truths as the emergence of certain knowable and known constants of intelligible

2. The Light of Life

and intelligent cosmic being, these can and should, as hypotheses, provide foundations and materials for the continuation of the dialogue, but, in sharp contrast to the definitive Word of God, they cannot claim final validity, since the end of the dialogue is not yet in sight, it must proceed further from the point now reached, and the goal can be reached, if at all, only with the end of the whole of the present form of the cosmos and its self-witness. Obviously, they are provisional assumptions to which man is invited and constrained but which he is summoned to transcend, deepen, amplify or correct by similar assumptions. None of the agreements or common statements reached in this dialogue, whether speculative, logico-empirical, moral, aesthetic, scientific or mythological, can pretend to be a final and authentic declaration concerning existence. They are not to be underestimated. As lights, words and truths of problematical and relative validity, they have great practical value, force and significance in the time and situation in which they are knowable and known with greater or lesser clarity. They can be counted upon within the limitation which marks their witness and that which it attests. But they all lack final validity. We can and should and must live with them in this sense, but we certainly cannot live by them. Is this so, or is it not? Even more clearly, it may be stated that where they are considered abstractly, and not in confrontation with the Word of God, doubt is thrown on their own dubiety and their relativity itself appears to be relative. In these circumstances the discussion between those who view them sceptically and those who view them dogmatically can and must proceed. This discussion is brought to an end, and the dubiety and relativity of these creaturely lights and words and truths are unequivocally seen, only when they are seen and understood in the context in which they stand, i.e., only when it is seen and understood that the self-attestations of creation are challenged and relativised by the final self-declaration of God.

But this critical consideration is possible only if it is accompanied by some awareness at least of what is to be seen and understood of their institution and integration in this respect, too, by the final self-declaration of God. To relativise means critically to set something in its limited and conditioned place. But it also means positively to set it in the relationship indicated by the limits of this place. When and where God causes His own final Word to go forth within the cosmos and its lights and words and truths, the latter are set in their place but also in the appropriate relationship, i.e., in what we have called their context. Their context, however, is creation as the external basis of the covenant which is itself the internal basis of creation. It is the setting of the glory, i.e., of the omnipotent love of God. In their own place and way, with the provisional, problematic and relative character commensurate with the nature of their theme, these lights speak and tell of creation, and laud and praise it as the work of God. But supposing that that happens for which creation has the being and existence attested by its own lights and words and truths. Supposing that Jesus Christ is born and lives and dies and is raised from the dead within it, so that " the sun of righteousness " arises, the eternal light, the irrevocable Word, the definitive truth of the election and the covenant and therefore of the glory and love of God ? To be sure, their provisional nature is then disclosed and they are divested of any claim to absoluteness. But they are also invested with the glorious finality of God and His action towards man as this is now revealed. They still shine and speak and bear witness concerning creation. But they no longer do this abstractly. They do it concretely, in the context of and in harmony with that which God Himself says concerning His action towards man, concerning what He is and does for man, and what man may be and do for Him. And as the being and existence of creation itself are glorified rather than destroyed by the events of which it is ordained to be the theatre, so its words and truths, far from being contradicted or given the lie, acquire in this context and in harmony with God's definitive Word a similar final force and value and significance. For now the self-witness of creation can also speak and tell of what God says, and therefore speak as from God Himself, praising and glorifying Him : " The heavens declare the glory of God ; the firmament sheweth his handywork " (Ps. 19^1). To be sure, "there is no speech nor language," i.e., they have no power to do it of themselves. But they acquire this power. The final and trustworthy thing which they cannot say of themselves concerning their being and existence, they now say as they reflect the eternal light of God, as they answer His word and as they correspond to His truth. In other words, they speak of the meaning and determination of the creaturely world for what God is and does for man and what he may be and do for God. In the mirror of this final self-declaration of theirs we have a reflection of the final self-declaration of their Creator in His great act of peace. In this sense they are taken, lifted, assumed and integrated into the action of God's self-giving and self-declaring to man and therefore to the world made by Him. And in the power of this integration they are instituted, installed and ordained to the *ministerium Verbi Divini*. Nor are they unworthy of this ministry, for by the *Verbum Divinum* itself they are made worthy. Nor are they incapable of it, for by the same Word they are made capable. Nor are they unwilling to accept, for by this Word a new will is awakened within them, namely, the will to do it. In their discharge and execution of this ministry " their sound is gone out through all the earth, and their words to the end of the world " (Ps. 19^4) ; and the words and the sound are final and definitive.

This, then, as we have tried to indicate it under our three headings, is the critical but also, since it is genuinely critical, the positive relation-

3. Jesus is Victor

ship of the light of life to the lights which the God who[...] action is revealed by the one light does not withhold from His [...] as such but gives them in His eternal goodness.

3. JESUS IS VICTOR

The statement which has so far occupied us is the simple equation of life as such with light. In other words, the covenant of God with man and man with God as fulfilled in Jesus Christ is not a dumb fact but one which speaks for itself. The reconciliation of the world with God accomplished and consisting in Him is revelation in its very reality. To use the terminology of the older dogmatics, as the High-priest and King, as the humiliated and suffering God and exalted and triumphant man, He is also the Prophet, Herald and Proclaimer of the name hallowed in Him, the kingdom come in Him, the will of God done in Him on earth as it is in heaven. This equation, however, must now be developed and explained in a specific way. A presupposition decisive for its meaning must be particularly emphasised. It must be stated expressly and considered with great precision that in this equation we have the description of a history. In the " is " which links the life with the light, the covenant with the Word of God, the reconciliation with the revelation, Jesus Christ the High-priest and King with Jesus Christ the Prophet, there is concealed a drama. The " is " is thus to be understood in dynamic rather than static terms. This is what calls for emphasis.

All the concepts used refer to a history, whether life, covenant and reconciliation on the one side, or light, Word and revelation on the other. Life, covenant and reconciliation all " are " as they take place. Similarly, light, Word and revelation " are " as that which is denoted by them occurs. Only as they happen, therefore, " are " they in this equation. That life is also light means that as true life it shines and radiates and gives light from God and for God. That the covenant is also Word means that in its institution, execution and fulfilment it makes itself known as it is enacted. That reconciliation is also revelation means that in its accomplishment, which establishes, orders and guarantees peace between God and man, it also reveals and proclaims itself as divine-human truth. But life, covenant and reconciliation are only material descriptions of the being, work and activity of Jesus Christ. We must thus continue that as true God and true man, as the One who accomplishes all that is described in these terms, Jesus Christ is not only the High-priest and King but also the Prophet, Herald and Proclaimer of this accomplishment. That is to say, He works and acts as such. He exists in the actual discharge of this specific office, in the corresponding rendering of service and confirmation of lordship. But this means that He exists in this special form of His history. Hence in this third form too, as a doctrine of Jesus Christ the true light, Word and Revealer, as a doctrine of His prophetic office, Christology is a narration of His history, and specifically of the shining of His light, the real speaking of the covenant, the revelation of reconciliation, the action of the Prophet Jesus Christ.

The specific obligation to develop and explain our equation in this particular sense originates in two different respects from the matter itself. The first is formal, though not on that account any the less important or noteworthy. The second is material, and even more important and decisive in the ensuing discussion.

The relationship between God and man denoted by the terms life, covenant and reconciliation does not rest on any necessity immanent in either the existence and nature of God or those of man. God does not owe it to man. And man has no claim to it. From the standpoint of both God and man it seems rather to be excluded and impossible. It exists as it is created and takes place in Jesus Christ. Seen from above, it is actual in the free act of grace for which God determines Himself and upon which He resolves in Jesus Christ. Seen from below, it is actual in the free act of obedience in which man acknowledges the doing of the will of God active in the divine act of grace. In this its actuality as a free act of grace and obedience, it is a new thing between God and man. It is the sphere and character of this new thing, in that the life is also light, the covenant Word and the reconciliation revelation. It is still a matter of Jesus Christ and His activity, but now in His prophetic office and work. Here, too, nothing is self-evident, given or necessary. As the actuality of the relationship takes place, so its truth, i.e., its self-declaration, and therefore the grounding of its recognition, can only take place. Its occurrence is the prophecy of Jesus Christ. That He Himself, and in Him the life, covenant and reconciliation, shine out and are disclosed and made known, is an event, and can only be understood as such. It is a drama which can only be followed, or rather experienced and recounted.

The necessity of a historical understanding of the equation results supremely from the fact that His light, Word and revelation no less than His life, covenant and reconciliation, are challenged by an opposition which encounters them, and His prophetic no less than His high-priestly and kingly service and rule thus consist practically in the overcoming of this opposition and answering of this challenge. They occur in an environment to which they are superior in right and might, but which is either hostile or alien, or at any rate strange. The " world " is this environment : humanity ; man in and with the cosmos ; man in his creaturely and historical nature. But we do well to think also of the Church and individual Christians in this respect. By this environment the Son of God and Man, Jesus Christ, is Himself challenged and assaulted as He challenges and assaults it by His existence and with His Word. His life is constantly confronted by death, the covenant by unfaithfulness and apostasy, reconciliation by strife. But this is also the situation of His prophetic office and work, ministry and action. His Word is met by the contradiction and His truth by the falsehood of His environment, and they consist in the exposing, resisting and overcoming of the falsehood and contradiction. This does not mean that absolute and final limits are set to Him, but it does mean that He has to contend with limits of relative and provisional seriousness. He is noticeably though not invincibly confined. And as His Word contradicts the contradiction, it seems for its part to subject itself even to a certain bondage and conditioning, and to be spoken with a relative and provisional but unmistakeable restraint. We recall the expression in John 1^5: "The light shineth," but it shineth "in darkness" (whatever this may signify in detail). Yet we must not forget the continuation: "And the darkness overcame it not." This light which streams into the world is still the eternal light which cannot be vanquished or extinguished. Nevertheless, this does not alter the previous statement that it shines in a place or environment which is certainly illumined by it, but does not even partially shine itself, not corresponding to its shining with any brightness of its own, but being differentiated from it as darkness, and as such negatively opposing it with its own limited power. In face of this environment it does not yield but makes its way. Yet, in order finally to exclude and destroy it, it must do so step by step and therefore in a history. Or, as we might say, the Word of the covenant is uttered, going out through all lands, to the end of the world, like the voice and sound of Psalm $19^{4f.}$ Yet is it not something self-evident, given or necessary, but a new and special and wonderful thing both as a whole and in detail, if this does not take place in vain, if the Word achieves its object, if it finds ears which are open or even partially open. Or again, reconciliation is revealed in all its clarity. Yet, as it is itself an event, it can only be an event if in the place where it happens, in the reconciled world of humanity, its revelation is confirmed by the fact that it is perceived in its truth and clarity, and it is thus recognised as the reconciliation of the world of humanity. Comprehensively, the great Prophet Jesus Christ is certainly present and at work, pronouncing authoritatively the first and last and total truth concerning the name and kingdom and will of God. Yet like the prophets before Him, and even in the circle of those who are with Him, He is a lonely Newcomer and Stranger, a Messenger who has something to say to the world which it does not and cannot know of itself, which is closed to it as it arbitrarily or indolently closes itself against it, which it is neither willing nor ready to receive, so that it is something which has to happen, and only can happen, if He does not remain lonely, if His message is not in vain but wins a hearing and obedience, if the seed

§ 69. *The Glory of the Mediator*

sown by Him is not scattered to the winds but germinates and brings forth fruit.

Hence we cannot in any sense understand in static terms the relationship between Him and the surrounding world of darkness. It is certainly not dualistic. We do not have the equilibrium of opposing forces, as though darkness had the claim and power finally to maintain itself against light, as though its antithesis, opposition and challenge to light, its restricting of it, rested on an eternal and lasting order. On the other hand, it is not monistic. The power of light is not so overwhelming in relation to that of darkness that darkness has lost its power altogether, as though its antithesis were already removed, its opposition brushed aside, its challenging and restricting of light of no account. The only alternative is to think of it in terms of dynamic teleology, namely, in relation to the power of light, Word and revelation as this is active in great superiority yet has not so far attained its goal but is still wrestling toward it, being opposed by the power of darkness, which even though it yields in its clear inferiority, is still present and even active in its own negative and restrictive way. A history is here taking place ; a drama is being enacted ; a war waged to a successful conclusion. If from the very first there can be no doubt as to the issue of the action, there can also be no doubt that there is an action, and that it is taking place, and can thus be described only in the form of narration.

In connexion with what has just been said concerning the necessity of a historical understanding of the prophetic work of Jesus Christ (particularly from the material standpoint last mentioned), and before we go on to present and therefore to narrate its occurrence in its various dimensions, we must first undertake two basic discussions the results of which will necessarily be with us in all that follows.

I have chosen as the title for this sub-section the statement, or rather the challenge : " Jesus is Victor," for the simple reason that this statement, which is really to be heard and read as a challenge, is the sign under which a presentation and therefore a narration of the prophetic work of Jesus Christ must always stand. It tells of the issue but also of the beginning of the action, and in so doing of the dynamic and teleological character which marks it from its commencement to its goal. " Jesus is Victor," is the first and last and decisive word to be said in this respect.

It has been popularised by the story of the Blumhardts, and first and supremely by that of J. C. Blumhardt the elder. It should not be overlooked that in content, far from having the character of a new revelation, it merely sums up and succinctly formulates many New Testament sayings behind which there may be seen either directly or indirectly the central witness of the whole of the New Testament. We may think of Jn. 16^{33} : " In the world ye shall have tribulation : but be of good cheer ; I have overcome the world " ; or of Col. 2^{15}, which tells us that when God " spoiled principalities and powers, he

3. *Jesus is Victor* 169

made a shew of them openly, triumphing over them," i.e., in the resurrection leading them in His triumphal march as subjects and prisoners; or of 2 Tim. 1[10], where there is ascribed to Jesus Christ a completed abolition (καταργεῖν) of death; or of Heb. 2[14], where He is said to have destroyed "him that had the power of death, that is, the devil." The things seen and heard in the Apocalypse may also be called to mind. Perhaps it is hardly relevant to think of the rider on the white horse who in 6[2] "went forth conquering and to conquer," since like the other three horsemen he seems to represent one of the unleashed forces of destruction. But we may certainly refer to the other Rider on a white horse who in 19[11f.] is called Faithful and True, the Word of God, the King of kings and Lord of lords, who "in righteousness doth judge and make war," whose eyes are "as a flame of fire," who has on His head not one but many crowns, whose vesture is "dipped in blood," and out of whose mouth "goeth a sharp sword, that with it he should smite the nations; and he shall rule them with a rod of iron: and he treadeth the winepress of the fierceness and wrath of Almighty God." Similarly 5[5]: "Behold, the Lion of the tribe of Juda, the Root of David, hath prevailed"; and also the answer from heaven when the seventh trumpet is sounded: "The kingdoms of this world are become the kingdoms of our Lord, and of his Christ; and he shall reign for ever and ever" (11[15], cf. 12[10]). We may naturally recall as well Paul's saying in 1 Cor. 15[54] about the swallowing up of death in victory, which is for Paul the goal of all history already actualised here and now in the resurrection of Jesus Christ; or his saying in Rom. 8[37] that Christians are "more than conquerors through him that loved us"; or the saying in 1 Cor. 15[57] that the Lord Jesus Christ "giveth us the victory"; or the saying in 1 Jn. 5[4]: "For whatsoever is born of God overcometh the world: and this is the victory that overcometh the world, even our faith"; or Paul again in 2 Cor. 2[14]: "Thanks be unto God, which always causeth us to triumph (θριαμβεύοντι) in Christ." But where does not the New Testament finally look in this direction? Where does it speak on any other basis? It would not be witness to the risen Jesus Christ if things were otherwise.

Yet in the summary formulation: "Jesus is Victor," we do not have the witness of the New Testament, but that of J. C. Blumhardt. To be sure, he did not assert and declare it as a slogan which he himself had coined. He took it from a very curious source. In a formal report given in one of his church courts he tells us that he and many others first heard it in Möttlingen on December 28, 1843, at the climax of the two-year story of suffering, now about to become a story of healing, of someone called Gottliebin Dittus who was entrusted to his pastoral care. It was not from Gottliebin herself that he heard the words, but from her sister Katherina who for a time had become implicated in her situation. With notable sobriety but great definiteness and astonishing concreteness, he tells us—I am summarising—(1) that this story of suffering unmistakeably had for him and all around the form of demon possession so often mentioned in the New Testament, (2) that his pastoral intervention was only participation in a conflict properly and decisively waged by Jesus rather than himself, and (3) that the story of healing which followed had no less unmistakeably the form of a victorious encounter of the living Jesus with the alien demonic power which tempted, dominated and tormented this person. Hence he heard and quoted the saying: "Jesus is Victor," not as a saying of her sister, but as a cry of despair—Blumhardt refers to a shriek "which is almost inconceivable on human lips"—which the demonic power uttered through her lips at the very moment when a superior opponent forced it to yield its control over Gottliebin— this power being cautiously described by Blumhardt as "presumably," i.e., according to its own final self-characterisation, an "angel of Satan." We are forcibly reminded of the story in Mk. 1[23f.] about the man ἐν πνεύματι ἀκαθάρτῳ who cried out, saying: "What have we to do with thee, thou Jesus of Nazareth? are thou come to destroy us? I know thee who thou art, the Holy One of God."

§ 69. *The Glory of the Mediator*

Like similar events in the New Testament, the occurrence during which Blumhardt heard this cry: " Jesus is Victor," has three aspects. On the first, it is realistically explained in the sense of ancient and modern mythology. On the second, it is explained in terms of modern psychopathology, or depth psychology. On the third, it is not explained at all but can only be estimated spiritually on the assumption that the two former explanations are also possible and even justifiable in their own way.

Its spiritual estimation is possible on the basis of the influence exerted by this story of suffering and healing, and especially by the saying heard by Blumhardt and those around him on this decisive day, upon his own future life and activity and that of his son Christoph. However we may explain the battle of those two years and its issue, the fruits of the occurrence and the results of the saying are still unambiguously before us in the story of the Blumhardts as it commenced at that time : in a new and unhesitating action in the light of the superior life of the risen Jesus Christ ; in a new power and joy in the proclamation of the remission of sins as it has taken place and is found in Him ; in a new and self-evident apprehension of the reality of the kingdom of God as it has come in Him, and the lordship of God as it has been set up in Him ; in new intercession with the unquenchable expectation and indestructible hope that there will be fresh declarations of this lordship and a fresh outpouring of the Holy Ghost on all flesh (of which Blumhardt saw the beginning in this event and the utterance of this cry) ; in a powerful challenge : " Die, that Christ may live " ; in a life of powerful confidence in the coming and revelation of a new heaven and new earth ; and therefore in new and disturbed yet also comforted thinking in relation to world history and men in their sin and need, and in relation to that to which they are called, whether they realise it or not.

These were the consequences which flowed from the experience of the elder Blumhardt with Gottliebin Dittus and which marked the whole movement centred in Möttlingen and later in Bad Boll. They were all a development of the disclosure and recognition which came to Blumhardt at this moment : " Jesus is Victor." It was not that he then believed and realised for the first time that this is the case. His whole narration of this two-year battle shows that he had entered it with a realisation of what this statement says, and with faith in it. This emerges in the sense of dread yet also the daring resolution with which he undertook the struggle. " Lord Jesus, help me. We have seen long enough what the devil can do. We now desire to see the power of Jesus." This was from the very first his prayer with and for the sufferer. Nor did he meet with anything new—except the new thing of the New Testament—at the crisis of the battle. Yet the fact remains that this well-known truth was then much more to him than the confirmation of an existing conviction or the success of his pastoral venture in the strength of this conviction. It came as a new thing and in an unexpected way when he heard that simple statement : " Jesus is Victor," at the beginning of the healing of the afflicted in demonstration of the power of Jesus. It is to be noted that there is no question of a kind of divine inspiration. It was not mediated by a voice from above, but very much from below through the lips of a girl. It came as the wild and despairing surrender of the opposition, as its declaration of impotence, as the final cry of a routed angel of Satan, and therefore from within the darkest darkness of the world. For Blumhardt the new and surprising thing in the issue of the conflict, which necessarily found immediate expression in new insights and impulses and directives, was the fact that the victory of Jesus is " eternally settled," as it is put in a later hymn, that it is objectively decided even in the darkest darkness of the world, and that it is now manifested, known and declared.

It did not necessarily follow, but was actually the case, that in his own time, too, this was a new word and for long enough an isolated word. That Jesus conquers was not stated nor known, and certainly not " settled " in this way

3. Jesus is Victor   171

among the contemporaries of Blumhardt, whether *extra* or *intra muros ecclesiae*, whether in the world of Goethe or that of Hegel, whether in official circles, pietistic groups or theology, whether by the Rationalists, Supranaturalists and Pietists of the 18th century or the Romantics, Speculatives, Biblicists or theologians of the Awakening of the 19th century. In the first instance it was merely the content of his own particular perception and confession. To be sure, many important things were then seen and said concerning Jesus the God-man of the early dogma, Jesus the supreme vehicle of eternal reason, Jesus the Friend of humanity and Teacher of ethics, Jesus the Saviour of souls, Jesus the centre of Christian piety, and, after the fabulous discovery of D. F. Strauss, Jesus the mythical personage. If we turn to any secular or Christian book of the period, and among the Christian books it makes little difference whether it is a work of scholarship or edification, the two words said about Jesus in this declaration, namely, that He " is Victor," could be put on the outer margin of any of them, but they could not have the decisive and comprehensive significance, the emphasis, which they have for Blumhardt. They would represent an intrusion in this sense. Even Christian missions, which took a new turn at this period and in which Blumhardt played an important part, did not in the main stand under this sign. No cause was seen from a reading of the New Testament to fashion this or a similar slogan nor to draw the consequences which it held for Blumhardt. Many years must elapse, and many things take place, be learned and forgotten, before what might almost be called the underground stream of the insight achieved by Blumhardt could come to the service and become increasingly influential over wide areas of Christian life and thought. Nor by a long way can we expect that all Christians even to-day are really awake to the movement which then began, let alone seriously implicated in it.

But however that may be, the source of this thing which was new for Blumhardt, for his contemporaries, and for our modern world, is to be found in the strange happening of the Möttlingen struggle at whose decisive hour the cry : " Jesus is Victor," was uttered and heard. The really strange element in this struggle does not in fact lie at the point where it is usually seen by the hostile, confused and curious eye, namely, in the aspects of Blumhardt's account which call for explanation and perhaps find it in terms of mythology or medicine. Quite apart from the manner of its coming or the resultant interpretations, the really strange element is to be found in the utterance at the conclusion of this thing which is new, or which declared itself anew, and therefore in the cry which was then uttered and which came as a summons to Blumhardt, to his age, and to ourselves as its successors. The only question which is finally relevant in relation to the incident is the spiritual one whether or not we will hear this saying.

What does this saying mean in the context of the discussion in which we are engaged ? For the understanding of the prophetic work of Jesus Christ, of the concepts light, Word and revelation which now concern us, it means that the occurrence or action of which we are to think has a definite bias or orientation which we have to take into account and to which we have to do justice even as we present and therefore narrate it. In our preceding deliberations we have made it quite clear that this occurrence has the character of a conflict to the extent that the light shines in the darkness which resists it, the prophecy of Jesus Christ taking place in relation to an opposition and challenge on the part of the world. And already we have indicated at least that there can be no question of an equality between the two factors which here confront and conflict with one another, but that their encounter can be understood and described only as that of a greatly superior and a greatly inferior, and therefore a struggle concerning the issue of which there can be no doubt. But this must now be emphasised for a true evaluation of the theme of this sub-section. And we are reminded of this by the story and cause of J. C. Blumhardt as summed up in the saying : " Jesus is Victor." The saying refers us to the Subject of the action, the dominating Character in the drama and the Hero in the conflict which here concerns us. It tells us that the One at work here as Prophet, light, Word and Revealer, is not One for whom his resisting and restraining opponent might prove too much, who might be too seriously jeopardised and held in check by the challenge and opposition presented. In relation to the issue of the conflict, as it is unforgettably brought before us in the Blumhardt story, and even at its very commencement, He is characterised as the One who is greatly superior in relation to His greatly inferior adversary. In some degree the saying analyses the name of Jesus, and it gathers up this analysis in the simple equation : Jesus=Victor. This tells us that from the very outset, and come what may, the dynamic and teleology of the prophetic ministry and rule of Jesus Christ are unshakeably stamped by the fact that He is this One, Jesus. From the very outset it is clear and certain what will be the result of His ministry and rule, namely, that His right and might will triumph in opposition to the resistance and challenge offered to Him, removing the challenge and destroying the resistance. The equation made in this saying thus forbids us to take with equal seriousness both light and darkness, both Jesus and the contradiction and opposition which He meets. It certainly forbids us to take the contradiction and opposition even more seriously than Jesus. It commands us simply yet resolutely to count on it that, although the contradiction and opposition are to be taken seriously, yet we are to take infinitely more seriously the One whom it encounters, or rather who encounters, contradicts and opposes it, i.e., Jesus, and the dignity and power with which He does this as the One against whom the adversary can bring nothing corresponding, equivalent, or even similar. He and He alone is *Kyrios*. It is with this bias or orientation that there is enacted the history, action, drama, or conflict of the prophetic work of Jesus Christ, the shining of light in the darkness. As and because He, Jesus, is the acting Subject, the dominating Character, the warring Hero, it has this orientation. And because it has it, this declaration concerning Him is the first and final word to be said about it. If it is to be presented correctly, we must also say that the opponent which contradicts and resists the prophecy of Jesus Christ is also revealed as such and will be taken seriously in its own way. Otherwise it could not be a history, and could not be narrated as such. Nevertheless, the first and decisive requirement in the narration is that it should manifest the One who acts in it, and

3. *Jesus is Victor*

that He should be revealed throughout as the Lord who does not need to fear the storm on the lake, but possesses and uses the power to still it with His Word of command. The title of this sub-section is designed to emphasise this decisive requirement for an understanding of what is to be said at this point.

A critical delimitation is demanded. Might we not adopt instead the title and slogan : " The Triumph of Grace " ? This would actually indicate what falls to be indicated. Grace is undoubtedly an apt and profound and at the right point necessary paraphrase of the name Jesus. As Jesus conquers, there triumphs in Him the manifested grace of God (Tit. 2^{11}). But the statement needed is so central and powerful that it is better not to paraphrase the name of Jesus, but to name it. " Triumph of Grace " might at any rate give rise to the impression that what is meant to be indicated is the victory of one principle, that of grace, over another which is to be described as evil, sin, the devil or death. But we are not concerned here with the precedence, victory or triumph of a principle, even though the principle be that of grace. We are concerned with the living person of Jesus Christ. Strictly, it is not grace, but He Himself as its Bearer, Bringer and Revealer, who is the Victory, the light which is not overwhelmed by darkness, but before which darkness must yield until it is itself overwhelmed. He Himself is present as the Victor from the very outset. He is life ; in Him the covenant is fulfilled ; in Him reconciliation is effected ; in Him is everything which, again in Him, shines out into the world around. He makes Himself known as He makes known the name and kingdom and will of God on earth. It is in this self-declaration that He is superior to the contradiction and opposition brought against Him. In this context, therefore, " Jesus is Victor " is better than " The Triumph of Grace."

It is not by accident that I refer to this alternative and emphasise that I prefer not to choose it. *The Triumph of Grace* is the title of a book by G. C. Berkouwer which appeared in Dutch in 1954, in English in 1956 and in German in 1957, and which under this slogan dealt with my previous theological work, and particularly with the *Church Dogmatics* so far as it was then in print. Already in the Preface to IV, 2, I have referred to this work with the respect which it deserves. I can only join in according it the recognition which it has won in many different circles on account of its wide range of knowledge and reading, its perspicuous and penetrating mode of exposition and the sharpness and balance of its criticisms. And Berkouwer has undoubtedly laid his finger on an important point. I must admit, however, that I was taken aback when I saw the title given to his book. If I am in a sense understood by its clever and faithful author, yet in the last resort cannot think that I am genuinely understood for all his care and honesty, this is connected with the fact that he tries to understand me under this title. If my guess is right, it was an incidental remark of H. U. von Balthasar, to the effect that Christianity is for me an absolutely " triumphant affair," which inclined Berkouwer to adopt this title. This is something which can be said, though I should prefer not to say it of Christianity. Nor can we describe the expression as unbiblical in view of the Pauline θριαμβεύειν. Yet understood thematically, and in connexion with the concept of grace, it does not seem to me to say with sufficient acuteness what should be said at this point. In trying to understand me under this title, it is perhaps inevitable that Berkouwer should develop the suspicions to which he gives utterance in this volume.

He has well seen my initial and constant concern to display the superiority of God and His saving will and Word and work over the ruinous defensiveness and rejection, over the power of chaos, which meets Him on the part of the creature. But he asks whether this is justifiable. Do I not take the sting out of the whole problem of triumphing over this opposition? In my presentation is not the " triumph of grace " in danger of leaving us with nothing more than a sham-fight, in opposition to the witness of Scripture? Do I not fix the issue from the very first, and thus see and understand the whole movement too unilaterally? For me are not grace and its triumph a decision which is not merely resolved already in God Himself and His eternal will but also taken prior to all history and even creation, so that it predetermines the contest between God and evil, and this contest, with all that takes place in the creaturely world and therefore in time, can only develop irresistibly, like a piece of clockwork, with no real threats or genuine problems? Berkouwer thinks that I have given him the occasion for this objection in my discussion of " God and Nothingness " in *C.D.*, III, 3, § 50, where I deviate from the language of the Bible by describing evil as an " impossible possibility " or an " ontological impossibility," thus being guilty not merely of a minimising of its significance and power but of a basic denial of its reality. As " nothingness " it can do nothing against grace. It need not then be feared. The " triumph of grace " is somewhat cheaply assured from the outset, for it has no reality. It is empty in an *a priori* and ontological sense, in and with a speculative rather than a theological conception of it. Its utter emptiness is presupposed. That is to say, it is posited in God and His eternal will, in relation to which history, sin, unbelief, and the divine judgment, but also the act of grace and faith as man's act of obedience, can no longer have for me any serious meaning. Hence there arises the sinister and in its systematisation unbiblical *triomfantelijkheid* with which I allow myself to speak of the whole relationship between God and evil and therefore between God and man.

This is an objection which deserves to be weighed and answered. On a rather less comprehensive basis, it is in fact often made, especially in the north of Europe. Substantially, it is of a piece with the objection which Heinrich Vogel has long been urging against me. If I am not mistaken, it also links up with the question raised by Eduard Buess, particularly in relation to my view of predestination. Some explanation may thus be given, though within the context of Berkouwer's criticism. For this purpose I distinguish and interrelate four points which need elucidation.

1. Berkouwer has clearly perceived and continually emphasised that I find, or try to find, a christological basis for what I say concerning the will and Word and work of God on the one side, the evil which strives against these on the other, and finally their relationship to one another. The question is whether he and I mean the same thing by " christological " thinking and the related investigations, definitions, conclusions and foundations. I can only speak for myself, and I maintain that for me thinking is christological only when it consists in the perception, comprehension, understanding and estimation of the reality of the living person of Jesus Christ as attested by Holy Scripture, in attentiveness to the range and significance of His existence, in openness to His self-disclosure, in consistency in following Him as is demanded. In this formal definition I am confident that Berkouwer and I are in agreement, and I also think we can agree that christological thinking in this sense is a very different process from deduction from a given principle. I underline, however, that we are not dealing with a Christ-principle, but with Jesus Christ Himself as attested by Holy Scripture. Again, there is surely agreement between Berkouwer and myself that christo-

3. Jesus is Victor

logical thinking must always be a matter of the perception, apprehension, understanding and estimation of the person who according to the witness of Holy Scripture discloses Himself as the crucified and risen Son of God and Son of Man, as the one almighty Mediator between God and man, indeed, between God and all creation, and therefore as the One to whom as such all power is given in heaven and on earth (Mt. 28^{18}). We do not really speak of Jesus Christ, of His self-disclosure, of the witness of Holy Scripture, if we do not assume from the very first that we have to do with this person. There can hardly be any disagreement between Berkouwer and myself on this point. And surely we also agree that within theological thinking generally unconditional priority must be given to thinking which is attentive to the existence of the living person of Jesus Christ (just because it is this existence), so that *per definitionem* christological thinking forms the unconditional basis for all other theological thinking, even that which deals with the relationship between God and evil. It is thus quite out of the question to start with certain prior decisions (e.g., concerning God, man, sin, grace etc.) and then to support these christologically. We cannot do this even with decisions for which we think there is a basis in Scripture, as though Scripture would give us any other foundations than the one laid in Jesus Christ. The only decisions which can have any place are those which follow after, which are consistent with thinking which follows Him, which arise in the course of christological thinking and the related investigations, definitions and conclusions. The obligation to give to christological thinking this unconditional precedence, this function of a basis in the strict sense, seems to me to be imposed quite simply by the character of the living person Jesus Christ as the almighty Mediator whom it must follow. Yet I have doubts whether Berkouwer does agree with me in respect of this obligation, and therefore this unconditional precedence of christological thinking within theology generally. Perhaps he cannot do so because he is more deeply rooted than I am in the older Reformed tradition which would have it, on what are thought to be good biblical grounds, that already in the doctrine of election we have a principle which has priority over the person and work of Jesus Christ, so that Jesus Christ is to be understood only as the mighty executive organ of the divine will of grace, and only a secondary place can be given to christological thinking. Again, it may be that he cannot do so because, so far as I can see, the story and influence of the Blumhardts have not yet penetrated effectively the very Calvinistic environment to which he owes his development. Thus Berkouwer can explain my conception of the relationship between God and evil only by thinking that I, too, proceed on the basis of a prior decision, and am thus ensnared in the unilateral and one-sided manipulation and development of a principle. But this is not how I myself understand my intention. I am not trying unilaterally to think through the principle of grace to the point at which I reach the " triumph of grace " in this relationship. I should regard such a procedure as quite illegitimate. My desire is that from the very first, at every point, and therefore in answering this question too, we should take with unconditional seriousness the fact that " Jesus is Victor." Surely Berkouwer cannot really have anything against this. For, on the basis of Holy Scripture at least, there is nothing that can seriously be alleged against it.

2. If we start at this point, what will be the resultant picture of the encounter between God and the evil which strives against him on the side of the world ? Berkouwer is concerned lest it should present itself to me far too triumphantly as the encounter with an opponent who is from the very first absolutely inferior, as an action concerning whose issue in the overcoming of this opponent there can be no doubt since it is decided at the commencement. Now in my view this is a picture which might well arouse suspicion if it were gained deductively and constructively, by following through a principle supposedly given, from a prior decision concerning the nature of God, or that of evil, or the perfection of grace ;

if the encounter were imprisoned in a conceptual synthesis in the discovery and formulation of which it might be imagined that the antithesis were really grasped. We should be arrant fools to believe that something of this sort ought to be attempted. There cannot and should not be any question of an enterprise of this nature. According to the biblical witness the partners in this encounter are not a God *in abstracto* and evil *in abstracto*, nor is their relationship fixed by a grace *in abstracto*. On the contrary, the living person of Jesus Christ in His character as the almighty Mediator between God and man is the one person, and that which contradicts and withstands this person is the other. But the fact that this person is envisaged as such means that the reference to the absolute superiority of this person cannot mean that we can grasp and master either Him or the whole situation. We can trust a person, and in the case of this person we must do so unconditionally and with final certainty, as Blumhardt did when he accepted that battle. But we cannot grasp a person, and especially not this person, in the sense of conceptual apprehension and control. Hence, we cannot grasp the whole situation in this sense, and there is no cause for anxiety in this respect. It is in the free act of this person, which cannot be comprised in any synthesis nor brought under any control, that the divine and therefore absolute superiority of this Partner is worked out and the situation between Him and His opponent is settled—and not otherwise. Blumhardt never even dreamed that He could control Jesus. He did something which is very different, and which is the only thing possible in relation to this person. He called upon Him for two years. He did so with absolute confidence. But he still called upon Him. It is thus a matter of confidence in this person, of His free act, of calling upon Him. Yet the counter-question has to be put to those who are concerned about this matter whether confidence in Jesus can be limited or assurance in calling upon Him restricted. Do we not forget or deny that we are dealing with this person in this character if we regard caution or a limited confidence as the better part ? Yet if we do not forget or deny this, we must agree with Blumhardt that it is "eternally settled" that, no matter what may be thought of His opponent, this Partner is in any case absolutely superior to him, that the action between them can end only in His triumph, and that we have thus to say that the issue of this action is in fact decided from its very commencement in view of the fact that the One who is the First will also be the Last. In relation to Him there is no justification for doubt. Is this a bad thing ? Is doubt so attractive that it must always be regarded as justifiable ? After all, our statement is simply to the effect that Jesus is Victor. In relation to all other real or supposed victors, especially ourselves, there is place enough for doubt. And in the description of such victors there is plenty of room for the paradox so highly estimated by H. Vogel, and for every type of "counterpoint." But there can be no qualifying or calling in question the statement that Jesus is Victor. At this point there is no room for counterpoint. The statement does not contain any paradox. It is incontrovertible. It gives no ground for suspicion. Where does the Bible teach the contrary ? With reference to a logical principle of grace and its triumph, I concede that it might be doubted or that something might be said for the assertion of paradox. But in relation to the name of Jesus I see no alternative to my understanding.

3. But we must now turn to the opponent of God in this relationship. Berkouwer is right when he maintains that, when I use such formulae as "nothingness," "impossible possibility," and "ontological impossibility" (especially the latter) to denote and describe this opponent comprehensively designated as evil, I am not merely speaking of its obscure, unfathomable and baffling nature from the standpoint of human knowledge, but saying something very definite about its nature and existence as though it were not at all concealed from human knowledge. And it is for this reason that he objects, dismissing the formulae used by me and finding in their application an indication of the dubious nature

3. *Jesus is Victor*

of my whole presentation. As he sees it, I am guilty of intellectual or speculative arrogance, but also of robbing evil of its sting, in my attempt to explain it by the use of such formulae. Above all, I am guilty of introducing formulae which almost seem to suggest or imply a denial of the reality of evil. There are passages in Berkouwer's book from which it may be gathered that, as he sees it, the conception of nothingness characterised by these formulae is really the basic article and decisive fulcrum of my whole doctrine of what he calls the "triumph of grace," and perhaps even of the whole of the *Church Dogmatics*. What am I to make of this?

First, I should like us to be agreed that we can achieve a true and relatively clear definition of evil only as we pursue thinking which is controlled by the living person of Jesus Christ in His self-disclosure and which is thus consistently "christological," but that along these lines we surely can achieve it, so that it is neither arrogant nor dangerous to seek the *intellectus fidei* in this respect instead of renouncing all understanding, and thus to strive at least for a true and clear conception. If I may presuppose agreement on this point, it is surely not impossible to show that the construction of the formulae which I have selected— and I might have chosen different and better ones, though they would have amounted to the same thing in substance—is materially quite unavoidable. Nor should it be too difficult to show what is meant, and what cannot be meant, by them. It is not speculation, but a description which even the veriest child can understand, simply to say of evil in the first instance that it is what God does not will. But to say this is also to say that it is something which He never did nor could will, nor ever will nor can. It is thus that evil is characterised, judged and condemned in the self-disclosure of the living person of Jesus Christ. As opposition to God, it is that which is simply opposed to His will, and from eternity, in time and to all eternity negated, rejected, condemned and excluded by this will. To be sure, we cannot first erect this or a similar definition of evil and then proceed by means of it to praise of the "triumph of grace." On what grounds could we do this? But on the basis of the recognition that Jesus is Victor we can and must arrive at this definition. Is this to deny its reality? No, for when we see it in this light, in its concrete opposition to the will of God active and revealed in Jesus Christ, and in the counter-opposition to which it is thus exposed, we acknowledge and recognise its reality. But we recognise what kind of reality it is. We do not see merely how baffling it is for our human comprehension. We see rather the nature of its existence. It will always be obscure, unfathomable and baffling that something which is merely opposed to the will of God can have reality. We do not understand how this can be. But it is of a piece with the nature of evil that if we could explain how it may have reality it would not be evil. Nor are we really thinking of evil if we think we can explain this. Yet the nature of the reality of what God has simply denied is shown up in the light of the One who withstands it as Victor. Hence it can and must be denoted and described by those who know the reality of this Victor. It can and must be known and defined in and with His reality. Berkouwer, too, can and must define it in some way. Has he some better starting-point and therefore some better proposal? And is it really the case that the sting of evil is withdrawn when, starting with God and Jesus Christ, we define it as that which is opposed to the will of God, so that it is not merely later but from the very outset negated, rejected and excluded by this will, its nature being thus understood as perversion, its greatness as that of mischief, its power as that of impotence? Is there any sharper discrimination of evil or warning against it, any stronger recognition of its sinister character, than that which is pronounced with this definition in accordance with the condemnation obviously passed on it in God's own attitude towards it in the existence of Jesus the Victor?

I now turn in detail to the formulae used in this connexion. It is obvious that I have fashioned them myself, and that they are not to be found in the

Bible. Nowhere does Scripture itself speak of "nothingness," of "impossible possibility," or especially of "ontological impossibility." Yet in theological language in every age (even in that of the Reformers and Berkouwer himself) terms and formulae are used which have no direct equivalents in the Bible, but which we do not reject or suspect for this reason alone. Such formulae are fashioned when it is necessary to summarise briefly, tersely and strongly, in delimitation against misconceptions and mistakes and for continuing use, insights which have been won from the Bible and are to be developed in accordance with it. They are to be interpreted in the light of the insights, and not *vice versa*. In the best sense of the expression, we must take them *cum grano salis*. The *homoousios* of Athanasius is of this character, and so too, on a different level, are the terms which I use to describe evil. They simply gather together what I am trying to develop in this respect.

When I speak of nothingness, I cannot mean that evil is nothing, that it does not exist, or that it has no reality. I mean that it exists only in the negativity proper to it in its relationship to God and decisively in God's relationship of repudiation to it. It does not exist as God does, nor as His creatures, amongst which it is not to be numbered. It has no basis for its being. It has no right to the existence which to our sorrow we cannot deny to it. Its existence, significance and reality are not distinguished by any value nor positive strength. The nature underlying its existence and activity is perversion. Its right to be and to express itself is simply that of wrong. In this sense it is nothingness.

"Impossible possibility" is another term for the same thing. If it is a paradox, it is used in the sphere to which paradox properly belongs. What it denotes is the absurd possibility of the absurd. Since evil has and is reality in its fatal manner, we have to reckon with its possibility, with its power to be real. What kind of a power is this? Can it be described as any other than the power of impotence and therefore the possibility of the impossible? Evil exists only *per nefas*, in the fact of a revolt which has no positive basis, which can have its *ratio* only in the abyss, which as such can be no more than the product of unreason. It lacks any justifying *raison d'être*. This is why we cannot explain either the fact that it exists, or the way in which it does so. This is why its reality is so baffling to our understanding. But as this baffling reality it is known, and therefore needs to be, and can be, denoted and described. Those who dislike the formula "impossible possibility" are at liberty to suggest an alternative.

Particular offence is taken by Berkouwer at the third suggestion, namely, "ontological impossibility." I have no great affection for this myself, but do not see that it is so wholly inappropriate. What it means is that the nature of evil as the negation negated by God disqualifies its being, and therefore its undeniable existence, as impossible, meaningless, illegitimate, valueless and without foundation. If we are to speak of a class or level of being which might properly be ascribed to evil in all its shapes and forms as distinct from the being of God and that of His creatures, we can describe it only as the class or level of the being which, in radical distinction from that of creation, is negated, rejected and excluded by God. When we weigh and understand the formula in the light of everything which has gone before, is it really so speculative and therefore dangerous? It may well be that mysteries are discovered in it which it does not contain in my own usage. For instance, on the grounds of a linguistic misunderstanding, Berkouwer thinks that in its attempt to bring out the vigour of the rejection of evil as it is to be seen in Jesus Christ, and thus to understand its absolute inferiority, this formula must always refer in some form to a self-differentiation within the being of God which underlies the ontological impossibility of evil, whereas what I myself had in view was simply the original self-differentiation of God from evil, i.e., His original turning aside from the possibility of chaos mentioned in Gen. 1[2]. Evil is what it is according to the divine

3. *Jesus is Victor*   179

sentence, no other, no more and no less. Hence, it is—but only in the character of " ontological impossibility."

4. Do these presuppositions really mean that the historical character of the encounter between God and evil is threatened or even destroyed ? Instead of a real history, does it become a mere process, which can finally be reduced to conceptual analysis, if the overcoming of evil is resolved and actually accomplished in the eternal will of God, if the evil to be overcome in the encounter is nothingness, and if on both sides the issue is thus decided at the very commencement ? Berkouwer is particularly critical of my use of the phrase " from the very outset " in this connexion. But I am unrepentant. We surely do not see the wood for the trees if this kind of objection is raised and pressed here. For to what do we refer when we speak of God's encounter with evil, and with this reference count upon it " from the very outset " that God is infinitely greater and stronger than evil and evil is thus mean and despicable in relation to the One who encounters it ? Are we speaking of two principles, a positive arbitrarily endowed with the highest possible qualities, and a negative no less arbitrarily endowed with the lowest possible ? If this were so, there might be force in the criticism. No history would be possible nor even conceivable between two such principles. In an easy conceptual triumph, their very opposition would mean at once that the first would *per se* consist in the destruction of the second, and the second would *per se* be destroyed by the first. But this is not at all the case. We speak of Jesus as Victor, of the God active and revealed in Him, and of evil as known in confrontation with the God active and revealed in Him. How do we know that the overcoming of evil is resolved and even accomplished in the eternal will of God, and that the evil which opposes this will is nothingness ? We know it quite simply because we have before us the conflict which takes place between them in Jesus, in His encounter with the world. We know it because we take seriously the manner in which the conflict is waged in Him as the source of our sure and certain knowledge of this matter. In other words, we know it because we try to be consistently christological in our whole thinking on the subject. Jesus ! And we cannot avoid using such words as " conflict " and " event " to describe what is before us. To say " Jesus " is necessarily to say " history," His history, the history in which He is and does what He does. In His history we know God, and we also know evil and their relationship the one to the other—but only from this source and in this way. But at this point a way is trodden. A question is raised and answered. A sentence is pronounced and judgment is executed and suffered. A faith and obedience are demanded and displayed. Prayer is offered. A cross is borne, and on this cross suffering is endured. From the deepest depths a cry is raised to heaven. Nothing is self-evident, obvious or matter-of-course. The day must be carried against the fiercest opposition. A war is waged against sin, death and the devil. It is in this war that Jesus is Victor, even though He is the almighty Mediator between God and man, and the eternal will of God fulfilled in His faith and obedience is absolutely superior to the contradiction and opposition which are only contemptible nothingness in face of this towering opponent, and the issue is thus certain at the commencement and therefore " from the very outset." The One who treads this way, who causes this situation of conflict seriously to fall on Him, who accepts and endures this conflict, who acts in it, and in this way, in His free act, overcomes the enemy and is thus the Victor, is the living Jesus Christ. And it is as He does this in His life and death, demonstrating and revealing what is resolved and fulfilled in the eternal will of God, that He also demonstrates and reveals the impossibility, absurdity, valuelessness and impotence of evil. The crucified and slain Jesus is the One who triumphs, demonstrating and revealing what is on the right hand and what on the left. He does this, and we must keep to the fact that He does. But how can we ever imagine that this is an easy " triumph of grace " ? How can we overlook or deny that we have to

§ 69. *The Glory of the Mediator*

do here with encounter and struggle, and therefore with history ? Indeed, we may note at this point that the disciple is not above his Master. We, too, must enter into this history and therefore this conflict of His. We have clear confidence concerning its issue. Only victory is to be expected in view of its commencement, in view of Jesus, who has already fought the battle. Yet we have this confidence only with the last and bitter seriousness enjoined and demanded by this commencement, by Jesus. Neither hesitant qualifications nor rash or slothful assurance are possible at this point. The only possibility is perfect confidence in the perfect, yearning, yet resolute expectation of that on which it is grounded. How can we pray : " Thy kingdom come," if we do not start with the sure and certain fact that in Jesus the kingdom has already drawn near in all its glory ? Conversely, how can we start with the sure and certain fact if on this basis we do not pray and implore and beseech : " Thy kingdom come " ? What option have we but to recognise in the history in which Jesus exists what is from the very outset real and true on the right hand and on the left, and where else but in this history can we recognise from the very outset what is real and true on the right hand and on the left ? Can we not say that in the last resort there is no reason for the anxiety which seems to be felt by Berkouwer and others on this point ?

The second basic discussion to which we now move concerns the context in which emphatic reference must now be made to the historical, dramatic and warring character of the reconciliation of the world with God. Our concern is with this event of reconciliation as an event of revelation. It is with the life which shines as such, the covenant which speaks for itself, the reality of the fellowship of God and man restored in Jesus Christ as this declares itself to be also truth. It is with Jesus Christ Himself in His prophetic office and work, as He confesses and makes Himself known as the humiliated Son of God and the exalted Son of Man, and therefore as the Mediator between God and man, and therefore as the One who restores fellowship between them and accomplishes the justification and sanctification of man. In this context, therefore, our problem is that of knowing the atonement. How is it that its occurrence is not hidden but may be and actually is perceived ? How is it that it does not remain alone, but achieves significance, regard and acknowledgement in the world and among men ? How is it that the cosmos reconciled in Jesus Christ realises how matters stand with it ? How is it that men come to see in Jesus Christ their Fellow and Brother ? How is it that they are discovered, and discover themselves, as the people who have their own life, and are justified and sanctified, in Him ? It is in this connexion that the prophetic office and work of Jesus Christ are relevant as an integrating factor in the event of reconciliation. A " prophet " in the biblical sense is one to whom it is given to see and understand the doing of the will of God on earth, and who is also charged to declare, expound and explain, and thus to mediate, his understanding, thus enabling others to participate in what takes place. Jesus Christ is the Prophet who knows and proclaims the will of God which is done in His existence. The Synoptic statement that " the kingdom of God is at hand," materially identical with the

Johannine "I am" (ἐγώ εἰμι), is the sum and substance of His prophetic message and therefore of the knowledge mediated by Him. This is the context in which the historicity of the atonement now calls for particular emphasis.

It can be no more than a question of particular emphasis. Reconciliation as a whole is history which as such can only be recounted. History is the life of all men actualised in Jesus Christ. It is the history of the covenant fulfilled in Him. That the Son of God humiliated Himself to be with us and for us in order that He could uncover the pride of man and positively accomplish his justification, the gathering of His community in the world and the awakening of faith in Him; and again, that the Son of Man should be exalted to fellowship with God in order that He should uncover the sloth of man, and positively accomplish his sanctification, the upbuilding of a community of God on earth, and the awakening of love, all this was worked out on the dramatic way of conflict from Bethlehem to Golgotha, and was and is therefore history. Salvation takes place in this salvation history. There cannot, then, be intended an exclusive but only a special emphasis, to be undertaken *in parte pro toto*, if we underline the historicity of the atonement specifically in relation to the fact that in its fulfilment this is itself the answer to the problem of its declaration and knowledge, or if we point out that in its prophetic element it has a specifically historical character. All that can be meant is that in our present context, in its prophetic element, its historical character forces itself upon us with a special and direct insistence acquired only at this point, and is thus to be firmly grasped. How far is this really so? How far does the historicity of the atonement particularly impinge upon us at this point, in relation to the prophetic work and office of Jesus Christ, so that it is meaningful to give it particular attention in the present context?

The general answer to this question must be to the effect that, as the event of reconciliation is also that of revelation or prophecy, as the life as such is also light, it emerges from the apparent distance in which it is played out for us men, and comes to affect us directly, so that we are not merely implicated in its occurrence, but realise that this is the case. As it is heard and perceptible as Word, it engages our attention and we men see that the event of reconciliation of which it speaks is an event for us and to us, and that we are implicated in such a way that we can no longer exist at all without being implicated. "We men" means all the men who have not yet perceived, or who have forgotten or denied again. It means all the men who in the first instance think that they are not directly, properly and seriously implicated either in the history of Israel or in that of Jesus Christ as first its intimation and then its enactment. It means all the men who can be and actually are of the opinion that they belong to another sphere than that in which it has taken place that the kingdom of God has drawn near, that God has reconciled the world to Himself, that He has established and maintains and fulfils the covenant between Himself and man, that He makes a reality of true life in fellowship with Himself. No matter what has taken place according to the witness of the Bible, as they see it they themselves are not affected in their own sphere, but are remote from it, being at best only spectators of a rather unusual drama or hearers of rather a strange message, and therefore free either to regard the matter as so much more history or myth, or to turn away from it with a complete lack or disengagement of interest to pursue their own more pressing thoughts and affairs. Are we not all men who think that they can treat the occurrence of reconciliation, the history of salvation, in this way? In the first instance, and continually, does not the story seem to affect us in this way, and therefore not really to affect us, because it does not seem to refer in any sense to ourselves? But in so far as the event of reconciliation is also that of revelation; in so far as the justification and sanctification of man (as we shall see in greater detail later) are also his vocation; in so far as Jesus Christ is not only High-priest and King but also Prophet, this appearance is torn aside and this opinion is made untenable. For as reconciliation is also revelation, the life light, the covenant Word and Jesus Christ Prophet, the sphere is burst wide open where we shut ourselves off from Him, the distance which we think that we can and should keep is overcome, the water pours over the dam behind whose shelter we believe that we have solid ground under our feet apart from the being and action of Jesus Christ, and, putting an end to our mere seeing and hearing, to our evaluations in terms of history and myth, and to our unconcerned hastening past Him to very different thoughts and affairs, He brings us right into the picture, namely, into His picture, the dynamic picture of His action. No safeguard, protest or shrugging of the shoulders can help us here. Whatever it may or may not mean for us subjectively; whatever may be its reflection in our consciousness, the fact that reconciliation is also revelation and Jesus Christ lives and works as Prophet means that objectively we can no longer be remote from Him in a private sphere, but that we are drawn into His sphere, into what takes place in Him. This occurrence becomes objectively our own experience. We experience here what takes place there in the supposed but only apparent "there" which in reality encloses our here and in which our here is also there. That man's here (and he himself in his here) is truly there; that the there of that history is here in reality man's own history—this is what is disclosed as reconciliation is also revelation and Jesus Christ acts also as Prophet. In His prophecy He draws the logical conclusions of His own well-founded claim to lordship over the whole world and all men. In His prophecy He comes "unto his own" (Jn. 1^{11}).

This is the general answer to our question. To what degree is the

3. Jesus is Victor

historicity of the atonement particularly distinguished in its character as revelation ? To the degree that in this character it proves itself to be a history which encroaches and impinges upon us men no matter who we are or what we may think of ourselves, thus showing itself to be not merely *a* history of the usual historical or mythical type, but history in the supreme sense, history in which we have a share whether we realise and like it or not, history in which our own history takes place. But we must consider the matter more closely.

In the occurrence of the prophecy of Jesus Christ, in His being as God's Word to us men, there takes place (1) the mediation and establishment of a specific knowledge, namely, the knowledge whose subject and content is neither directly nor indirectly the man who knows, but He Himself, who also mediates and establishes it. He Himself is the reconciliation of the world to God which He declares. As He declares this and therefore Himself (ἐγώ εἰμι), as in the discharge of His prophetic office He mediates and establishes knowledge of Himself, He encounters man, approaching and confronting him, setting Himself over against him as the One who is for him but is not known, regarded or valued by him, as the One whose existence is filled with a salvation which man has overlooked, as the One who is the true life of man as yet unknown and unrecognised by him, as the One who comes to him as to an alienated possession, as the One who is thus to him a new and strange Counterpart. That man experiences this confrontation with Jesus Christ ; that he comes to have dealings with this new and strange Counterpart ; that he cannot avoid wrestling with Him, is the basic form of the revelation, of the event in which reconciliation overcomes and destroys man's distance from it, approaching man, encroaching and impinging upon him, disclosing itself to him and making itself the subject and content of his knowledge. Being itself history as the subject and content of his knowledge, its revelation, the knowledge mediated and established by it, is also history as man's confrontation with the new and strange Jesus Christ. In this fulfilment which is also history, the history of Israel known in it, and the history of Jesus Christ which fulfils it, show themselves to be man's own history, his salvation history. It is in the particularity which consists in this demonstration that the revelation of reconciliation has its specific historical character.

We cannot impress upon ourselves too strongly that in the language of the Bible knowledge (*yada*, γιγνώσκειν) does not mean the acquisition of neutral information, which can be expressed in statements, principles and systems, concerning a being which confronts man, nor does it mean the entry into passive contemplation of a being which exists beyond the phenomenal world. What it really means is the process or history in which man, certainly observing and thinking, using his senses, intelligence and imagination, but also his will, action and " heart," and therefore as whole man, becomes aware of another history which in the first instance encounters him as an alien history from without, and becomes aware of it in such a compelling way that he cannot be neutral

§ 69. The Glory of the Mediator

towards it, but finds himself summoned to disclose and give himself to it in return, to direct himself according to the law which he encounters in it, to be taken up into its movement, in short, to demonstrate the acquaintance which he has been given with this other history in a corresponding alteration of his own being, action and conduct. We can and should say even more emphatically that knowledge in the biblical sense is the process in which the distant " object " dissolves as it were, overcoming both its distance and its objectivity and coming to man as acting Subject, entering into the man who knows and subjecting him to this transformation.

Israel is to know in its heart that " as a man chasteneth his son, so the Lord thy God chasteneth thee," and it is thus to keep His commandments, to walk in His ways and to fear Him (Deut. $8^{5\text{-}6}$). It is to know the greatness of Yahweh, " his mighty hand, and his stretched out arm, and his miracles, and his acts, which he did in the midst of Egypt," at the Red Sea and in the wilderness, and it is thus to obey His Law (Deut. $11^{2\text{-}8}$). A similar awareness of God's activity in and to Israel and among the nations, is also intended when it is said that there is perception that " the Lord is among us " (Josh. 22^{31}), that His hand is strong (Josh. 4^{24}), that He alone is most high (Ps. 83^{18}), and that as such He " ruleth in the kingdom of men, and giveth it to whomsoever he will, and setteth up over it the basest of men " (Dan. 4^{17}) ; or even more simply when reference is made to the knowledge that " I am God " (Ps. 46^{10}, cf. 100^3) or to the knowledge of the name of God (1 K. 8^{43}). There is never any suggestion in all this of merely an objective seeing and understanding of the divine nature and being. What is always meant is to know His ways (Ps. 67^2), to know that the Lord has done this or that (Is. 41^{20}). And this knowledge of God in His past, present or future action according to the direct or indirect contexts of these developments always implies a new human action corresponding to the divine and altered in relation to it. In this regard, note should be taken of Is. 11^9, where in the depiction of the coming Messianic reign of peace it is said : " They shall not hurt nor destroy in all my holy mountain : for the earth shall be full of the knowledge of the Lord, as the waters cover the sea." This is the alteration which the knowledge of God does not merely entail but necessarily encloses. " As the eyes of servants look unto the hand of their masters, and as the eyes of a maiden unto the hand of her mistress ; so our eyes wait upon the Lord our God, until that he have mercy upon us " (Ps. 123^2). This is how it is with the knowledge of God. The " knowledge of the Holy One " according to Prov. 9^{10} is practical understanding. That is, the willing and doing of the Holy One, as it is known, creates for itself a counterpart in the history of the one who knows. If man knows God, this includes and primarily implies the fact that God acts towards man as the One who knows. It is thus inevitable that the human knowledge should have a total reference and claim and alter the whole man. This is dramatically expressed in the fact that the same word *yada* is obviously used to denote the act of sexual intercourse.

Now in the New Testament the terms γιγνώσκειν and γνῶσις can also be applied to intellectual and contemplative apprehension. Yet nowhere can it be said that knowledge is merely of this type, having its theme and content in abstractly objective things or essences. Here, too, since everything characterised and described as an object of knowledge is to be understood as a description of the divine action and therefore historically, it is a matter of the salvation which comes to man (Lk. 1^{77}), of the truth which discloses itself to him (1 Tim. 2^4), of the grace of God directed toward him (Col. 1^6), of the love which He has for us (1 Jn. 4^{16}), of His legal decision which alters our whole situation (δικαιοσύνη, Rom. 10^3), of what is given us in Him (1 Cor. 2^{12}). The contexts show, and usually state, that it is a matter of the knowledge of the Son of God (Eph. 4^{13}), of knowing Him " and the power of his resurrection " (Phil. 3^{10}), of knowing that He is in or among us (2 Cor. 13^5). He, Jesus Christ, is the mystery of God (Col.

2³). Knowledge of the one true God is identical (Jn. 17³, ²³) with the knowledge that He has sent this One, Jesus Christ, that the Father is in Him and He in the Father (Jn. 10³⁸), but also that we are in Him (Jn. 14²⁰), or according to the most succinct formulation quite simply that " I am " (Jn. 8²⁸). The ἐπίγνωσις αὐτοῦ is thus the work of the Spirit of wisdom and revelation (Eph. 1¹⁷) for whose gifts we pray. And again and supremely the history marked by this name expresses itself in the history of the one who knows. The terms faith and love and obedience are always near when reference is made to knowledge. Knowledge in the biblical sense directly includes, indeed, it is itself at root, μετάνοια, conversion, the transformation of the νοῦς, and therefore of the whole man, in accordance with the One known by him. Note should be taken of what is included in the knowledge of Jesus Christ according to Eph. 1¹⁸f·: " That the eyes of your understanding should be enlightened ; that ye may know what is the hope of his calling, and what the riches of the glory of his inheritance in the saints, and what is the exceeding greatness of his power to us-ward who believe." To know Him is to come into the sphere of this incomparable power of His. To know God in Him is thus to be known of Him, according to the bold expression of Paul (Gal. 4⁹ ; 1 Cor. 8³, 13¹²) in which the object becomes the Subject. Or, according to his even bolder expression (1 Cor. 2¹⁶), it is to receive and have the νοῦς of Jesus Christ Himself, and thus to know in fellowship with the One who is known and in whom are hid all the treasures of wisdom and knowledge (Col. 2³). So radical is the transformation which comes on man in this knowledge, so full of content is his own history in it, and so far is this *intelligere* from a merely ratiocinative, argumentative or even contemplative process which might be described as intellectualistic and the results of which might be attacked and denounced as empty *gnosis* ! Paul was well aware what he was about when among the various things for which he gives thanks or prays in relation to his churches he almost always gives pride of place to *gnosis* (πᾶσα γνῶσις, which is included in the one), and when he says that for his own part he counts everything loss compared with the ὑπερέχον of the one knowledge which includes all others, the knowledge of Jesus Christ His Lord (Phil. 3⁸).

As the prophetic work of Jesus Christ takes place, and the atonement is thus revealed and known, there also emerges (2) the opposition of the world and man towards it. We have to do with the world reconciled to God in Jesus Christ, and the man justified and sanctified in Him, but with the world which for its own part has not yet found itself in what has been done in Jesus Christ to it and for it, and with the man who on his side still lags behind the justification and sanctification accomplished for him in Jesus Christ. In other words, we have to do with the world and man which have not yet followed up with their own decision the gracious decision of God concerning them. It is in this " not yet " that there is place for futile resistance to the name of God already hallowed in Jesus Christ, the kingdom of God already come in Him, the will of God already done in Him on earth as it is in heaven. And in the sphere left by this " not yet " it is always and everywhere present, as creaturely being is always and everywhere determined by it as well as by what the gracious God has already done on its behalf. At what point in space or time can we ever say that in this place left to it resistance is not present ? Can we ever say this even within the sphere of the community of Jesus Christ ? Its presence and influence characterise the creation which in the death of Jesus Christ and in virtue of His resurrection from the dead is already reconciled to God, but is not yet redeemed and consummated by His coming in glory, i.e., in His final, definitive and universal revelation. Life, the covenant, and reconciliation are one thing, but ranged against this there are also nothingness and evil, which in their impossible mode and existence still have their own shape and freedom of action in the world and among men, and can thus assert themselves as a real factor to be taken in all seriousness.

Latently, this factor is always and everywhere present and active. But when the prophecy of Jesus Christ takes place, when reconciliation is heard as the Word of reconciliation and knowledge is established, it becomes open contradiction. As such it opposes the prophecy of Jesus Christ, meeting it on its own level, calling in question the declaration and recognition of what God has done and achieved for His creature in Jesus Christ at the very point where it comes to the world and man as the proclamation of His saving grace. As the light of life shines out into the surrounding darkness, the question arises whether the darkness will yield before it or resist it. But it would not be the not yet dissipated darkness which can only hate the light as such if it did not resist it. And as the light shines in it, there is revealed, in the fact that it cannot dissipate or overcome it, the power which it still has to resist, to continue to be darkness. Again, as the world is told, not merely what is resolved concerning it, but what has already been done for it, for its total renewal and transformation; as it is thus given news concerning itself, it has to decide whether it will accept this information or not. But how could it be the unredeemed world on this side of the final coming of Jesus Christ if it did not seriously reject this information which is so diametrically opposed to its own understanding of itself? Again, as there begins this process of the knowledge of the true and living God in His acts; as that which, or rather the One whom man would like to regard as a distant object to be regarded, studied and contemplated only at a distance, now threatens to come to him and even into him, overpowering him and subjecting him to a total alteration and renewal, it must be shown whether or not he will accept the proffered liberty of the children of God. Will he allow the process of knowledge which begins on this basis, and therefore his own alteration and renewal, to take its course? Or will he resist and evade this new and strange Subject, and His claim to lordship, and therefore the development and consummation of the knowledge established in His power, and even the establishment of the knowledge itself? Will he not set against what takes place and what is to be made of him a final hindrance in the name and exercise of what he regards as his own freedom? How could he be the being which continually thinks that by saying " I " it places itself on the basic rock of all reality, if in this situation he did not find himself incited

3. Jesus is Victor

and summoned to resolute opposition? What does it mean to him that this Other says " I am " ? How can he accept the fact that he knows only on the basis and according to the measure of his being known by this Other? *Hic Rhodus, hic salta!* Who has any desire for the necessary *saltare*? And who will not base his lack of desire on his incapacity? Who will not think that at this point he is confronted by a kind of emergency, and is thus justified in opposing the requirement made of him?

It is in the question of knowledge posed by the Word of reconciliation, i.e., by reconciliation in its form as revelation, by the prophetic work of Jesus Christ, that man's opposition to the gracious will and work of God is brought to expression in the form of his contradiction. As we have seen, the revelation and knowledge of Jesus Christ is the history in which He confronts man with Himself, in which man and his history are thus drawn into the history of Jesus Christ. With man and his history, there is thus drawn into the same history of Jesus Christ the resistance which he brings against Him, and therefore concretely the contradiction with which he rejects His revelation and knowledge, the obstruction with which he tries to hamper and suppress it at its very commencement and in its progress and completion. With man and his history, therefore, there is drawn into the history of Jesus Christ the nothingness or evil still present and active in the world which is not yet redeemed. As Jesus Christ confronts man, He confronts with His prophetic Word this element which is quite unworthy in its sinister sordidness and shame, integrating it into His own history, letting it play the role of His opponent, allowing it to show its nature, desires and ability in contrast with Him, exposing Himself to its opposition yet also constituting Himself the Opponent of this opposition, causing this adversary to put to Him the question and problem for which He has the answer. It will be a far superior answer. It will confound the adversary. It will remove the question and show the problem to be ridiculous. But it will still be the answer to the question put by the existence of this adversary. As He reveals Himself and gives Himself to be known, His history, as that which also encroaches and impinges upon ours, acquires the specific character of a drama consisting in this conflict. As He reveals Himself and gives Himself to be known as the One in whom God's gracious decision has been made concerning the world and man, the devil is let loose on the side of the world and man.

It is for this reason that most strikingly the New Testament speaks with great emphasis not only of a knowledge but also of an ignorance of God. In the Old Testament already the saying of Isaiah (11⁹) about the knowledge of Yahweh which will fill the earth to the exclusion of all wicked action is accompanied by the complaint of his contemporary Hosea (4¹) that "there is no truth, nor mercy, nor knowledge of God in the land." It is in this light that we have to understand the sharp assertion of Paul in 1 Cor. 15³⁴: ἀγνωσίαν θεοῦ τινες ἔχουσιν.

§ 69. The Glory of the Mediator

What is meant is not decisively—though this is also included—a mere lack of acquaintance with God or uncertainty as to His nature or existence, nor is it merely a lack of knowledge or misunderstanding of God which is excusable and and can be set right by enlightenment and suitable instruction. As Paul tells us, he is speaking to the shame (ἐπιτροπή) of the community in Corinth in which such ἀγνωσία is possible. And in order to overcome similar ἀγνωσία amongst those around according to the will of God, Christians are not told in 1 Pet. 2¹⁵ to undertake academic instruction, but simply to do good. What is meant by ἀγνωσία is a suppression of the knowledge which has already been disclosed and commenced to dawn in men. This suppression is startling in its inexplicable factuality, for it is quite inexcusable. It is a " holding down " (κατέχειν) of the truth in ἀδικία (Rom. 1¹⁸). The Gentiles are strikingly enough described as already γνόντες τὸν θεόν (Rom. 1²⁰f.) to the extent that God is undoubtedly present, perceptible, conceivable and therefore knowable to them in His works of creation. But of what avail is this ? As those who know in this sense they are in practice those who do not know, since they do not give God either glory or gratitude, but are vain in their imaginations (λογισμοί), their foolish hearts are darkened, and professing to be wise they are fools. According to 2 Cor. 10⁴ there are strongholds (ὀχυρώματα) of such imaginations, veritable high things (ὑψώματα), which exalt themselves against the knowledge of God and which have to be pulled down if matters are to be brought to a successful issue. According to Rom. 10²¹· the Jews are guilty of similar self-exaltation when they do not recognise the judicial decision made and revealed by God Himself. It is manifest and known in virtue of the present self-declaration of the history of Israel and the apostolic witness to them concerning the history of Jesus Christ. But of what avail is this when they will not submit to it but seek their own righteousness instead of that revealed and promised by God ? A puzzling knowledge which is also ignorance ! Similarly, the " savour " of the knowledge of Christ which God spreads in every place by the witness of the apostles can be to some " the savour of death unto death," and to others " the savour of life unto life " (2 Cor. 2¹⁴f.). It can be the former, not regularly, but irregularly and *per nefas*, in virtue of the perversity of those who share this knowledge. This was the complaint against the lawyers of Israel in Lk. 11⁵² : " Ye have taken away the key of knowledge (which is obviously in your hands) : ye entered not in yourselves, and them that were entering in ye hindered." The reason why Jesus wept over Jerusalem in Lk. 19⁴¹f· was because, when He approached it, it did not know τὰ πρὸς εἰρήνην, because it was hid from its eyes that the kingdom of God had drawn near. In the power of its own wisdom the world has not known the wisdom of God (1 Cor. 1²¹). If it and its rulers had known Him, " they would not have crucified the Lord of glory " (1 Cor. 2⁸). Hence it is no mere rhetorical device that Paul so often uses expressions like " Know ye not ? " or " I do not will that ye should be ignorant." His intention is to show that both as a whole and in detail his communities are continually threatened by the possibility of this kind of ignorance.

It is quite natural—and will serve as an illustration which intensifies the mystery—to think at this point of the parable of the Sower (Mt. 13³⁻⁸) and its interpretation (vv. 18–23). The interrelationship of the two passages is doubtful. It may be that the interpretation, like that of the Wheat and the Tares in vv. 37–43, belongs to a later stratum of the tradition. In favour of this view, it may be argued that it one-sidedly rivets our attention on only one of the many elements in the rich content of the parable, namely, the difference in the soils on which the good seed falls, this being allegorically related to the different reception which the Word has among different listeners. On the other hand, reflection on this side of the matter is not only not forbidden by the parable itself, but seriously occasioned by its nature and wording. And what the interpretation offers in this respect must surely be regarded as a very old, indeed, as the first

3. *Jesus is Victor*

commentary on the parable. It certainly does not say anything which might not be intended by the parable itself. And quite apart from this, it certainly does say one thing which is quite definitely intended by the parable. The parable speaks (1) of the proclamation of the Word, (2) of the hearers of the Word, and (3) of the differentiation between them.

The Word goes out (1) as the one message and summons to all men. As is rightly observed in v. 19, it is the λόγος βασιλείας, i.e.—and here the most literal translation is also the most meaningful—the Word in which the imminent kingdom of heaven declares and proclaims itself to man. All those to whom it comes hear exactly the same as others. No matter who the hearers are, the enlightening and renewing power of this Word, the fruitfulness inherent in this seed, is the same : *quia hominum vitio et pravitate non eripitur verbo sua natura, quin seminis vim retineat* (Calvin, *C.R.*, 45, 364). Nor is it the case that it does not reach all, or reach them with the same seriousness. Calvin is again right to point out that neither in the parable nor the interpretation is there any reference to those who reject the Word from the very first, but only to those *in quibus aliqua videtur esse docilitas* ; and that in v. 19 it is called that which is sown " in the heart." *Dei enim respectu seminatur in cordibus verbum*, not then as a Word which has merely an external influence, but as one which effects man internally. The interest of the passage is in the reception which the full and true and living and effective Word of God finds in its hearers.

But it is also concerned (2) with the hearers of the Word proclaimed, and with the One who proclaims it, the Sower who sows the seed. For this Sower there are not four different fields in which to sow but only one. The statement in the interpretation of the parable of the Wheat and the Tares may be equally well applied in this case too : " The field is the world " (v. 38). To the cosmos as such, and to all its representatives, the kingdom self-declared and proclaimed within it is new and strange. But the Word of the kingdom is directed to it, and to all its representatives, with the same intention and hope in the case of all its hearers. To the one field traversed by the Sower belong alike the path, the stony ground, the thorny ground, and the good ground. Men constitute a homogeneous community in relation to the Word of the kingdom addressed to them. They are ἀκούοντες and therefore they are foreseen, foreordained and able to be those who receive and accept the Word, who are begotten again of the Word of truth (Jas. 1[18]), who are doers of the Word (Jas. 1[22]). All of them are described as such in the interpretation, in conformity with the parable itself. " God our Saviour . . . will have all men to be saved, and (therefore) to come unto the knowledge of the truth " (1 Tim. 2[4]).

We now come (3) to the point of the parable. If the truth, the Word of the kingdom, the kingdom itself, is so new and strange to the world and all men, so is what follows, i.e., the inner difference revealed in the one field, from the standpoint of the Word and the One who speaks it. In some cases the seed is hindered from growing and is thus sown in vain, but in others it brings forth fruit and thus justifies the work of the Sower. There is thus a division within the one world to which the Word of the kingdom is spoken and among the men to whom it is declared without distinction. Yet according to the tenor of the passage, the account of this division ought to startle us as a new and sinister factor. It cannot be taken for granted. On the contrary, it has no real place in the story. It is the very thing which ought not to happen. Indeed, it is the thing which is both objectively and subjectively impossible. It is the possibility which from the standpoint of the Sower and the seed is excluded and impossible. The only trouble is that it is a reality. The general ἀκούειν is followed by a certain συνιέναι, but not by one which it seems may be expected in every part of the field. This latter verb is to be rendered as strongly as possible, almost in the sense of *intelligere*. " Understand " does not suffice. Everywhere there is understanding of what is heard according to the context : even where the Word immediately vanishes as though it had never been, as the seed which falls on the harder soil of the beaten path is picked up by the birds ; but more particularly where it falls and springs up and flourishes on the ground which is stony or thorny but still intrinsically receptive. Of all the hearers to whom it comes we may say that they have understanding. But in the συνιέναι (v. 23) which takes place where the seed falls on good ground, growing unhindered to maturity and bringing forth fruit, we have to do with something more than mere understanding. What we have here is reception, acceptance, appropriation and comprehension. It is true inner apperception of the Word heard and understood. It is knowledge which corresponds to the Word and in which the hearer is begotten of the Word and becomes a doer. This knowledge is the normal case correlative to its proclamation and to the determination of the hearer. It is to this that the conclusion of the parable refers (v. 8) when it says that the seed " brought forth fruit, some an hundredfold, some sixtyfold, some thirtyfold." It is to be noted that this conclusion is simply repeated and not expounded in the interpretation (v. 23), and it would be foreign to the purpose of the parable to try to explain the new differentiation which it introduces. The emphasis lies on the fact that beyond mere hearing and understanding we here have true knowledge, i.e., the knowledge which appropriates and does. As in the parable of the pounds, we have a quantitatively different but qualitatively identical alteration corresponding to the nature of the Word no less than to the world situation created by its proclamation. It is the normal case that the seed should bear this fruit, that there should be this knowledge in the hearing and understanding of the Word. Yet the point of the parable does not lie in the depiction of this normal case which is only the conclusion and in which reference is merely made to the " good ground " in indication of its presupposition. The real point is to be found in the fact that the normal case is confronted by so many unforeseen and startling abnormal cases in which, contrary to every rule, intention and hope, this knowledge does not arise and the true and living and effective Word of the kingdom does not accomplish in the world that which it should accomplish in accordance with its nature and the world situation created by its proclamation. The differences between the wayside, the stony ground and the thorns certainly invite us to consider, as is done in the interpretation in vv. 18–23, the many different forms which the abnormal case usually assumes. On the one side, there is the man whose hardened self-will causes him to escape the Word immediately he has heard and understood it. Again, there is the man of cheap enthusiasm who thinks that he has grasped what he has not really grasped at all, as is revealed by the first serious opposition which arises. Again, there is the man who is decisively claimed by very different forces, amongst which the interpretation (v. 22) numbers not only carnal passions and ideological ties, but with great realism " the care of this world, and the deceitfulness of riches." We must all consider the different ways in which we, too, might become abnormal cases. In itself, the differentiation of these possibilities is simply an indication of the terribly wide variety in which they may crowd in upon us, so that in face of them the normal case seems almost to be a fortunate exception to the general rule.

There is no doubt that in all these cases there is depicted the great threat to which the work of the Sower is exposed. It might seem that the result of this work is inevitable. Is not the world in which it takes place the world which is known by God ? Has it any option but to know the One by whom it is known ? Yet the fact remains—and it must be recognised as a fact—that in large measure it seems to have a very different option, namely, the sinister possibility of the ἀγνωσία τοῦ θεοῦ in whose actualisation the exception threatens to become the rule, and the rule the exception. It may well be " eternally settled " that the Sower should not go forth to sow in vain, that Jesus should be Victor. Yet in face of this threat to His work, this is by no means self-evident. It has to take

3. Jesus is Victor

place that He conquers. The enemy who aims at a different result, who is also intent to triumph, is truly present in all the absurdity of his nature and existence. It has to happen that he is driven from the field. Precisely from this standpoint the parable throws light on the historicity of the prophecy of Jesus Christ.

We have now established two preliminary points. The first is that the prophecy of Jesus Christ is the history in which He establishes in the world reconciled by Him to God knowledge of Himself, and therefore of the saving action which He has accomplished toward it, of the kingdom of God which has drawn near in and with His existence, of its own alteration as effected by Him. The second is that the prophecy of Jesus Christ is the history in which, as He establishes this knowledge, He meets the meaningless and unfounded opposition of this world, the absurd fact of ignorance of Himself, of His action, of the kingdom of God, of the accomplished alteration of the whole world situation. In both cases, namely, in the work of Jesus Christ as the living Word of the living God on the one side, and in the work of its hampering and questioning on the other, we have an event. It may thus be seen already in relation to both these preliminary points that in the prophecy of Jesus Christ we are dealing in a most emphatic way with the historicity of the atonement in general and as such.

This historicity of the atonement, and particularly of the prophecy of Jesus Christ, emerges even more definitely (3) in the fact that it impinges upon and includes within itself all history, the history of each and every man, and concretely in the fact that it involves all world history, and each and every man, in the antithesis of knowing and not knowing. As reconciliation is reconciliation of the world, of all men, it applies to the whole world, to all men, whether in terms of its self-declaration to all in Jesus Christ, or in terms of its hindering and questioning by the opposition and obstruction offered to Him as the Word of God. That it applies to all in this twofold sense means that as the light of life *shines* in the darkness, the world and all men come within the reach of its beams, but as it shines in the *darkness*, the world and all men are still in the sphere of darkness. As a creature of the God and a fellow of the man who speaks, every man, whether he realises it or not, is actually and objectively confronted by the proclamation of Jesus Christ, yet also by the limitation of this divine and human Word by the contradiction which encounters it from the abyss of nothingness. But " confronted " is too weak a word in this connexion. The proclamation of Jesus Christ and its dreadful limitation are together the history which embraces and comprises, and thus controls and determines, the history of the world and the history of each and every man. Man is not unaffected by the fact that he finds himself in the sphere both of light and of darkness. The whole world and each and every man is marked and determined in the light of this twofold confrontation. Man is, and can only be, that which he is with Jesus Christ, and with the adversary of Jesus Christ. Whether he realises it or not, he is set in this antithesis. He does not exist without belonging to Jesus Christ, and therefore without having to do with His adversary; without sharing in the knowledge established by His Word, but also without being bound to the ignorance established in this limitation of His Word.

There are, of course, important differences. Within the world which the Word of God, declared once and for all, has set in this antithesis, and which is therefore determined by this antithesis, there are the community and the non-community, Christians and non-Christians, believers and unbelievers, confessors and deniers of the truth. Again, there is a sleeping knowledge, unborn, withheld and apparently only virtual, and in face of it a wakeful, living, and apparently unbound and totally dominant ignorance. Again, and conversely, there is an actual, unmistakeably wakeful and living, and apparently cheerful and triumphant knowledge, and in face of it an apparently dispersing ignorance active only as a dwindling remnant. Yet as between the community and Christians on the one side, and the rest of the world on the other, there is a distinct yet not an absolute but only a fluid and changing frontier, which thus holds out a constant threat to Christians but a constant hope to non-Christians, so those who know and those who do not know, for all the important differences between them, are ultimately or primarily, i.e., in relation to the sovereign revelation of the Word, in exactly the same position and under the same determination. That is to say, in very different relationships, they are all both those who know and those who do not know, all being determined by the great antithesis that the light shines, but that it shines in the darkness. If the Word of God spoken in Jesus Christ had completely destroyed the opposition and contradiction which withstands it; if it were thus no longer spoken in this antithesis, this would necessarily mean that we should all be those who know, and nothing more. Conversely, if the opposition and contradiction were a match for, or even superior to, the Word spoken in Jesus Christ, this would mean that we should all be those who do not know, and nothing more. But neither of these assumptions is valid. There is no opposition or contradiction which is superior to the Word of God, or even a match for it. Yet the Word of God has not so far removed the hindrance and questioning, but is still spoken in this antithesis. It thus follows that, since it is the Word of God (spoken in this hindrance and questioning), which controls and determines the situation of all men, we may all be said to be, in very different relationships, both those who know and those who do not, those who do not and those who do. The only serious distinction between us men is that in the one case, as among believing Christians gathered in the community, it is knowledge which is predominant and ignorance is giving ground, whereas in the other, as among the theoretical and practical ungodly or idolatrous of every type, it is ignorance which is predominant and knowledge is held in check. In neither case, however, can it be said that there is wholly lacking that which is rightly or wrongly rejected, denied, suppressed or concealed, whether an alien ignorance in Christians or in the rest a suppressed yet dawning knowledge established objectively in the divine revelation. On the contrary, this other element is always vocal and active, always asserts itself, and always plays a significant and distinctive role in their existence. Within and among us men there is no such thing as either an angelic and therefore exclusive knowledge or a devilish and therefore exclusive ignorance. As those who know, we always exist in face of the abnormal and sinister possibility of ignorance, and as those who do not, in face of the normal and bright, yet not completely lacking, but present possibility of knowledge. We exist under the threat of the one possibility and the promise of the other. We are warned against seizing the one and summoned to seize the other. We exist in this antithesis. And we do so because the prophecy of Jesus Christ is the history in which our history is comprised and by which it is marked and determined. Its fulfilment as the *shining* of light in the darkness, but also its limitation as the light shining in the *darkness*, is the law under which our history, the history of the world and of each and every man, necessarily stands and which it has no choice but to follow. As the prophecy of Jesus Christ is historical in this concrete sense, so is human existence in the same concrete sense. The prophecy of Jesus Christ gives us a part in the existence in which it takes place itself, and in so doing it palpably displays its own concrete historicity.

In this exposition we have in view the two lines which characterise the structure of the biblical witness both in the Old Testament and the New.

On the one side, our concern is with the assumptions made in both the prophetic and the apostolic proclamation with respect to the hearers and readers. Who are the people who are addressed by the authors of the Bible and from whom an understanding of what is said is expected ? In the Old Testament it is obviously members of the national community of Israel who are to be told what is good, and what Yahweh requires of them (Mic. 6[8]), by means of the narration, and the reflective and even poetic description and interpretation, of their own history as established by Yahweh's election and calling and constituted by His acts of grace and judgment. In the New Testament it is the members of the community of Jesus Christ to whom He is present and revealed as their Lord and Head, living in virtue of His resurrection and reigning and ruling at the right hand of the Father yet also among them in the power of His Spirit, and to whom He is now " set forth " (Gal. 3[1]) and brought to remembrance by these witnesses in the accounts of His words and deeds, His death and passion, and in the corresponding exhortation regarding the significance of His existence for theirs. Behind Israelites and Christians, however, there also stand in a more distant circle the men of the surrounding world of the nations to whom it is the meaning and ordination of the narrower circle of those first addressed in the biblical testimony to be witnesses of what has been said to them. Obviously, then, the assumption of the prophetic and apostolic address to all these men is twofold. In both cases it is assumed (1) that they can, and normally must, hear and

§ 69. *The Glory of the Mediator*

understand and accept what is said to them, not because they have any capacity or disposition to do so, but because the attested truth of the history of Israel and of Christ is the truth of their own most proper reality, and they thus come from the place to which they are directed by the prophets and apostles. They have no pre-eminence, but they still have their origin in the election and calling of God, in the acts of grace and judgment which He has done for and to and among them. What is said to them verbally or in writing is simply an appeal to the knowledge already established in and with the fact of their specific existence, a recollection of what is recognised in and with their election and calling and the ensuing divine acts of salvation. The covenant made, the life manifested among them, the accomplished reconciliation, has spoken, and continually speaks, its Word to them even before it is attested by the prophets and apostles. We recall Ro. 15^{14}: " I myself also am persuaded of you, my brethren, that ye also are full of ἀγαθοσύνη, filled with all knowledge, able to admonish one another." We also remember 1 Jn. 2^{27}: " Ye need not that any man teach you . . . even as it hath taught you, ye shall abide in him." These sayings are not in any sense ironical. What the witnesses of Yahweh and Jesus Christ have to say can only be an appeal to what their hearers and readers already know directly through the One of whom the witnesses speak. But it is also assumed (2) that those who are addressed by the witnesses need to be reminded and therefore need this witness, not merely occasionally, but seriously and decisively. The Word of Yahweh in His acts may be loud and clear in Israel, yet this national community needs prophets, historians, psalmists and wise men to expound and emphasise it. The community may be established and continually upheld by the Word of Jesus Christ Himself, yet in the same sense it needs apostles and evangelists. The time of salvation announced in Jer. 31^{34}, when " they shall teach no more every man his neighbour, and every man his brother, saying, Know the Lord : for they shall all know me, from the least of them unto the greatest of them "—this time has secretly dawned in the history of Israel and the history of Jesus Christ, but it has not yet come openly or in such a way that there is in fact no further need of a " Know the Lord." There is a real knowledge established in the power of the great acts of God and the prophecy of Jesus Christ. Yet in the New Testament no less than the Old (even in Romans and 1 John), it is strangely but undeniably accompanied by an ignorance which is potent even within the community of the elect and called and therefore of those who are solidly enough instructed by the acts of God. Neither the prophets nor the apostles fear nor respect this fact. Yet they do not ignore it. They know how chronically and acutely dangerous it is. They know that it must be destroyed. They thus reveal it. They attack it. They treat it as a serious enemy. There are no writings in either the Old Testament or the New in which the authors do not reckon seriously with this opponent : not so seriously as with the reality whose truth they have to proclaim ; yet with the seriousness appropriate to it. It is because of it, and to resist it, that they are empowered and commissioned by God to speak their word. In relation to Jesus Christ Himself, in the hearing of His prophecy, and therefore on the assumption that knowledge is already established in and among their hearers and readers, this word cannot fail to be one of pure and consistent grace. Yet in relation to the opposition and contradiction active among their hearers and readers, and therefore in relation to their ignorance, it must necessarily assume the pure and consistent form of a word of admonition, warning, accusation, invective and threat, i.e., the form of the Law as that of the Gospel. These are the two assumptions made in the biblical witness in respect of its hearers and readers. And it hardly needs to be said that the same assumptions apply where in the fulfilment of the determination of the inner circle this witness moves into the outer circles of the nations which in the first instance are envisaged only indirectly in the writings of the Old and New Testaments. Here, too, we have to reckon both with the prophecy of Jesus Christ and with the opposition and obstruction which it meets. Men are addressed by the biblical witness both as those who already know (in virtue of the power of the Word of Jesus Christ) and as those who do not yet know (in virtue of this fatal counter-action).

On the other side, following the second of the two relevant lines which characterise the structure of the biblical witness, our concern is with the basis of this twofold address. It does not rest on any remarkably persistent caprice on the part of the witnesses. They have not elected of themselves to speak to others, and therefore to do so in this twofold way. Nor does its basis lie in their better or worse experiences with those to whom they turn. They have such experiences. But how could such experiences, which are only relatively normative, give them the right or the freedom to address others so seriously and decisively both as those who know and those who do not ? It is in relation to the object and content of their witness, and under its compelling direction, that they must see and address them in this way. For all of them it is a matter of the light, truth and revelation of God, of service to His Word, and therefore of the proclamation of the covenant, and of the great acts of God which have taken place for its establishment, execution and fulfilment. It is in the service of the divine Word concerning the divine work that they can never see or claim those to whom they turn with sufficient definiteness, seriousness or joy as those for whom and to whom this work has been done and this Word is spoken. Again, as loyal servants of this Word of God they cannot overlook or neglect its concrete form, namely, that though it was and is spoken with divine glory, majesty, authority and effectiveness, it is not spoken in a vacuum, but to the world and men, and therefore not without being exposed to assault, but as a Word which is continually contested in view of the blindness and deafness of man, and which continually strives against this blindness and deafness. They have received it in this character, and if they really want to serve it they take it seriously in this character. It is from this that there derives the earlier assumption with which they approach men as witnesses of the Word of God. They receive it as the Word of power which upholds all things (Heb. 1^3). How else, then, can they see and address men but as those who are reached and upheld by its power, and who therefore know ? But they receive it also as the Word of the One " who endured such contradiction of sinners against himself " (Heb. 12^3). How else, then, can they see them but as those who are still imprisoned and closed against it, and who therefore do not know ? The realism with which God expresses Himself and His work consists in the fact that His Word is gloriously directed above all norms and therefore to sinful man resisting His glory. And the biblical witnesses do justice to this realism by understanding those to whom they have to address this Word under this double aspect and therefore both as those who know and those who do not, by recognising that their existence is existence in this antithesis, and by addressing them accordingly. Does this mean that we must apply to them the term " dialectic " ? The answer is a decided negative if by " dialectic " we mean thinking in contradiction or in reconciliation of two principles. But the term might be used if what we have in mind is the alternation of divine speech and human answer indubitably envisaged by the Old and New Testament witnesses. Yet even so this does not bring out the true compulsion under which they stand in seeing and describing human existence under this twofold aspect. Hence it is better to abandon the term " dialectic " and to replace it quite simply by that of history. In itself and as such the Word of God is historical. It takes place in glory, but also in conflict with the opposition and contradiction of the world before it is heard in the world and there is converse between God and man. It is because the biblical witnesses receive and must attest it in its own historical concreteness that they must understand and address the existence of the men to whom they speak, not dialectically, but in the historical concreteness corresponding to that of the Word of God itself, so that they are seen to be both those who already know and those who do not yet know, and their existence is regarded as existence in this antithesis, existence on the way characterised by this antithesis.

This feature in the structure of the biblical witness constitutes the background against which our previous exposition is to be understood.

It is obvious that the rise of this antithesis is not the final thing which takes place in the occurrence of the prophecy of Jesus Christ and the human knowledge which results from and corresponds to this prophecy. The antithesis can arise only to show that it has no solidity and therefore (4) to move to its overcoming. In the event of reconciliation as the restoration of peace between God and man there is no static counterpoise, vacillation or balance. Again, in the justification of man there is no immobile *simul* of the *homo iustus* and the *homo peccator*. In sanctification, too, there is no armistice between the being of the new man and that of the old. But the same is no less true when we come to the event of the revelation of this reality and the knowledge thus established by the Word of God. In accordance with its theme and content, it is a transition, turning and decision in a very definite direction, namely, in that of the consummation which is from the very first the meaning and purpose of its execution. It is certainly a history of battle. But as such it is a history of triumph. God is not God in vain. Nor is it in vain that the One who acts in this history and therefore conducts this war is the eternal Son of God. Nor is it in vain that as the Son of Man He is man exalted to fellowship with God. It is not in vain that He is the great Prophet, the living Word of the living God. The fact that He allows opposition does not mean that He accepts it. The fact that He attacks and defends does not mean that this exhausts His work, or that He will be continually engaged in conflict. There can, of course, be no question of a merely temporary struggle, and certainly not of a final armistice or treaty with the adversary. He would not be the One He is if this were possible or even conceivable. We do not know Him if we consider such possibilities in relation to Him. Nor would His adversary, the opposition or contradiction which resists the omnipotent Word of God from the side of the world, be what it is if it could prevail or even maintain itself in this warfare. It is the sum of folly and futility that the world already reconciled with God continually resists the Word in which it is told the truth concerning itself. This folly and futility are very really and dreadfully present. Yet they have no true value or power. They cannot put in the field more than the reality and dread of a reactionary usurpation. This adversary has no power to triumph over the Word of God, or even to achieve equality with it, to oppose to it the law of a continuing resistance. " One little word can fell him." He can only be felled and destroyed, even from the standpoint that he can never leave the Word of God alone, nor finally nor even temporarily make peace with it, but only constantly deny it.

3. Jesus is Victor

What we have in view, from both angles, is only his finite overthrow. Yet this is inevitable from the very start of the conflict, and is declared in the course of it. Complete and utter victory is with the Word of God. Its negation and denial will be completely and utterly eliminated. From the standpoint of the struggle itself, there will be the steady but relentless emergence and disclosure of the superiority of the one contestant and the inferiority of the other.

Our reference is to Jesus, to His warfare and victory. Now in relation to Him, the situation in the sphere of knowledge on the part of those to whom His prophecy is addressed cannot be seen or understood in any other way than in terms of the antithesis between knowledge and ignorance as played out in the world and human existence. Yet in this respect we have also to note and consider the fact that the occurrence of the prophecy of Jesus Christ includes and therefore dominates, marks and determines the history of the world and of each and every man. If we have a part in the problem of the Christ event, we also have a part in its solution in Him. Neither with sighing nor scorn, therefore, can we accept the idea of an equilibrium of our knowledge and ignorance, nor of an eternal conflict nor an armistice nor treaty between the two. What takes place in this antithesis and conflict is not any history. It is not any history of conflict, indefinite as to its meaning or issue. It is the history of the " good fight " in the sense of 1 Timothy 6^{12} and 2 Timothy 4^7, of the fight which is good because it is laid upon us by the model and example of Jesus Christ and is to be entered and waged in His discipleship, so that from the very outset it can be accepted and fought step by step with the promise and guarantee of victory. For in relation to Jesus Christ it has a definite *telos* and direction in which it cannot result in defeat or stalemate but only in the triumph of knowledge over ignorance. This means that the antithesis which determines the existence of man can be understood only dynamically and teleologically. Even as man knows, he does not know. In his very knowledge he is hindered and hampered by his ignorance. Yet in his ignorance he is visited, startled and set moving in the opposite direction by his dawning knowledge. Darkness still threatens his light. But with a far more serious threat, the light now threatens his darkness. This is our history as seen in the light of that of Jesus Christ. What we have in the antithesis is a " still " and " already," not the equivocal balance of a " partly-partly " or a " both-and." The movement is quite definitely from ignorance to knowledge. The conflict is still in full course, but already in the course of it there can be no doubt as to the outcome. Knowledge and not ignorance is in process of gaining the upper hand. It is to knowledge that the future belongs. This is the human situation as determined by the prophecy of Jesus Christ under the sign *Christus victor*.

§ 69. The Glory of the Mediator

The biblical background to this fourth and final element in our discussion may best be illustrated by the transformation of Saul of Tarsus, the Pharisee and persecutor, into Paul the apostle. In Acts no less than three express accounts are given of this event, and though they differ in details they agree in substance. In addition, it is often and very significantly mentioned, and briefly characterised, by Paul himself in his Epistles. It is usually called his conversion. This is a very fitting description so long as we remember all that is meant by the New Testament word μετάνοια, and so long as we realise that what is envisaged is the total transformation which takes place with the rise of specific knowledge. What happened to this man was that now he could and should receive something which he had not previously been able or willing to receive, and that in this transition from non-reception to reception he became a new man and moved from an old way to a new. We have to consider this incident in the present context because in it there is unmistakeably revealed (1) the radical meaning of what is called knowledge in the Bible, (2) the historical character of this knowledge, and in particular (3) the teleological orientation of this history as we have just considered it.

In all the passages in question all these three elements, and their indissoluble unity, are brought before us by the fact that the primary and proper subject of the event described in them is not the man of Tarsus but the man of Nazareth, the living Jesus who encounters him. It pleased God by His grace to reveal, not a truth, but His Son in me (Gal. 1¹⁵f·). " In the face of Jesus Christ " Paul knows the glory of God shining upon him (2 Cor. 4⁶). He appeared last of all to him (1 Cor. 15⁸). It was Jesus the Lord whom he saw (1 Cor. 9¹). Jesus had pity on the one who persecuted Him (1 Tim. 1¹³). It was He, Jesus of Nazareth, who met him in the way before Damascus (Ac. 22⁸). He was made a witness of Jesus (Ac. 22¹⁵, 26¹⁶), and immediately became His " slave " (Rom. 1¹). We miss completely the import and meaning of these passages if, instead of referring them primarily and properly to this different Subject, to His appearance, speech and action, to what He does to Paul, we emphasise Paul's own experience and evolution and therefore regard Jesus only as a motive or exponent or cipher. As presented in all the texts, this is Paul's very personal history, but as such it has an " eccentric " character. It speaks of his decision, but this is a decision which can only follow that already made concerning him by Jesus. He knows only as one who is known by Him. This is why his knowledge has the power, not merely to give him new information, but radically to transform his life, himself. This is why his knowledge itself is genuine history, and especially history which is teleologically orientated, the history of warfare, history which from the very outset is victorious. The great event of this transformation can be understood only in relation to the One in face of whom, in the powers of whose invasion of the existence of Paul, it takes place according to the declaration and meaning of the texts. With constant attention to this centre which motivates and organises the event in its totality, and keeping as closely as possible to the statements of the texts themselves, we shall now attempt a brief analysis of this transformation.

Its *terminus a quo* is the man Saul of Tarsus on this side of the transformation before Damascus, and on the threshold of the history which constitutes his knowledge of Jesus. The picture is not absolutely unequivocal. It cannot be. Yet there can be no doubt that his knowledge dawns in the powerful and dominant darkness of his ignorance. In a later passage (2 Cor. 4⁶) Paul himself described the dawn of light in his heart in clear allusion to Gen. 1³. The God " who commanded the light to shine out of darkness " (ἐκ σκότους) by His Word had spoken to him the same creative Word with the same effect. As in Rom. 7⁷⁻²⁵ he sees his justification begin in all the darkness of sin (cf. C.D., IV, 1, p. 581 ff.), so he now sees his knowledge of Jesus Christ arise in the darkness of his ignorance. His history is particularly instructive in this regard because in his case

3. *Jesus is Victor*

we do not seem to have merely a common instance of darkness, but darkness in its supreme and at a first glance impenetrable form. The man who is now converted is not a worldling abandoned in his unbelief, or superficial belief, to his own lusts and passions. He is certainly not a godless man, or an open malefactor. From the human point of view, he seems to be in every way creditable. The justifiable pride of this earlier man is still clearly reflected in what he says of himself in Phil. 3[5] : " Circumcised the eighth day, of the stock of Israel, of the tribe of Benjamin, an Hebrew of the Hebrews " ; and there can be no doubt that his attitude and conduct (ἀναστροφή, Gal. 1[13]) accorded with the mode of Jewish life (ἐν Ἰουδαισμῷ) as then expected. In the righteousness of the Law he not only seemed to be but actually was " blameless " (Phil. 3[6]). In this respect he emulated most of his contemporaries of the same age. He was a strict Pharisee (Phil. 3[5]), a pupil of Gamaliel, " taught according to the perfect manner (κατὰ ἀκρίβειαν) of the law of the fathers, and zealous toward God " (Ac. 22[3]). He thus deserved the praise which later he did not withhold from his own people even in its continued rejection of Jesus Christ (Rom. 10[2]). Compared with heathenism and much secularised Judaism, should not this really be called light rather than darkness ? In what sense is this the work of ignorance ? In what sense is it the groping of a blind man on a way of destruction ? It is noteworthy that these passages do not include any criticism of Pharisaism, of its legalism, self-righteousness, pride, hypocrisy and human obstinacy, such as we have in Mt. 23, although this might have been apposite in a context like that of Gal. 1. They seem to have no interest in this, but press on to the statement that the man who trod this path became and was a persecutor of the community. The Epistles simply mention the fact (Gal. 1[13], 1 Cor. 15[9], Phil. 3[6]), but in 1 Cor. 15[9] it is added that because of it Paul is the least of the apostles and is not worthy to be called an apostle. Even the more extended accounts of Acts are concerned only with this aspect. Paul was present at the stoning of Stephen and gave his consent (Ac. 8[1]). " Breathing out threatenings and slaughter against the disciples of the Lord," he succeeded in expelling many of them from the Jewish synagogues (9[1]) and in his fury " persecuted them even unto strange cities " (26[11]). Finally, he secured a commission from the high-priests (9[1], 22[5], 26[12]) to hunt out supporters of this " way," both men and women, even in distant Damascus, and to arrest and bring them bound to Jerusalem. This is what Paul has in mind when in 1 Tim. 1[13] he calls himself a " blasphemer " and " malefactor." No explicit mention is made in the texts of any particular motive for this line of action. No apparent necessity is seen for this in view of what precedes. Care must be taken not to try to make good the deficiency with such suggestions as that of a sadistic desire to persecute for its own sake, or the intolerance of a man who regards his own way as right and all others as pernicious, or the excited resistance of one who is not sure of his own ground and is thus driven to lash out all the more fiercely. There is no need of any such suggestions. From what has been said, it is clear that this man is an opponent and persecutor of the community simply because (cf. Rom. 9[4f.]) he stands for Israel, for its election and calling, for its mission to the world, for the course and development of its history as the history of salvation, and therefore for the faithfulness which is to be shown to God in the form of the faithfulness of Israel, its obedience to the Law which He has given it and its trust in the promises which He has made to it, in short, for faith in the Word of God which has been spoken and is to be received in and with its existence. He persecutes Christians because he sees that this economy of reconciliation and revelation is questioned, transcended, relativised and outmoded by them, i.e., by their proclamation of the person, work, lordship and authority of the Jesus of Nazareth rejected by Israel and delivered up by it to be crucified, by their declaration of His Messiahship, election, calling and commission, of His history as salvation history, of the demand to obey Him, to trust in the promise given in Him, to believe the Word spoken in His existence.

§ 69. *The Glory of the Mediator*

He hates these men and seeks to destroy them and their witness because this witness tells him that the way of Israel which he is resolutely prepared to share and follow to the end is already at an end and therefore cannot be pursued further. He thus has a zeal for God, but, as he later says of the Jews who try to pursue this way, it is a zeal οὐ κατ' ἐπίγνωσιν, in lack of understanding, or ignorance (Rom. 10²). What was it that he did not then know ? According to the same passage, it was the δικαιοσύνη τοῦ θεοῦ, i.e., of God, of the God of Israel, of the God of the fathers, which does actually transcend and relativise and outmode both his own righteousness and all the righteousness of Israel. It was the sovereign sentence in which God fulfilled His covenant with Israel, and led the history of Israel to its goal, by Himself coming as the Deliverer of His people in the person of an Israelite, of a son of Abraham and David, by intervening powerfully on its behalf, by taking into His own hand the cause which its unfaithfulness had ruined. What he did not know was what took place for Israel in this way. What he did not know was the necessity of radical conversion thus laid upon Israel, its obligation to accept this divine decision which actually precludes all seeking of its own righteousness. What he did not know was the urgency of the command, in the best and only possible understanding of the Israelitish economy of reconciliation and revelation, to recognise in this decision of God His helping action and binding Word, and to give to it all the faith and obedience required of Israel. This was what Saul of Tarsus did not know. What it all amounts to is that he did not know Jesus. Looking back later (2 Cor. 5¹⁶), he said that he then knew Christ κατὰ σάρκα, i.e., in a carnal way, as the author of a sect which despised all that was most holy, which destroyed the Israelitish economy of reconciliation and revelation, and which was thus guilty of serious apostasy from God. This was how he saw and understood Him from the standpoint of an unrepentant Israel ignorant of its own peace. And seeing and understanding Him in this way which necessarily made him a persecutor of the community, he did not know Him at all. To know Christ in this or some other carnal way is not to know Him at all and thus necessarily to hate the witness concerning Him, and those who bear it. Saul of Tarsus did not know Him and therefore did not know the divine election resolved for the deliverance of Israel in the existence of this Israelite rejected by Israel. He could interpret His existence only to the detriment of Israel and therefore as hostile to God. This was the ignorance of his unbelief (1 Tim. 1¹³). It was in this darkness of ignorance that in his zeal for God he finally went rushing to Damascus.

Yet we have not correctly seen the *terminus a quo* of the event which awaited him on this journey if we try to see and understand him merely from the standpoint of the ignorance which then dominated and determined him. According to Ac. 26¹⁴, Jesus Himself in the words which He addresses to this Saul makes mention of a κέντρον, a spur or goad, against which it is " hard " for him to kick like a wild horse. That he still resists even when it is made so hard shows that the Word has come to the Pharisees and other persecutors. In the event, he will give up his resistance. It will be made not merely hard but impossible. But it is already hard. To suspect that he suffers pangs of conscience does not help us much. It is perhaps better to start with the fact that in 2 Cor. 5¹⁶, where Paul speaks of his earlier, carnal and empty knowledge of Christ, he does in fact speak of knowledge (γινώσκειν). He can do this because even then, in that ignorant knowledge, he was in fact dealing objectively and factually with the living Lord Jesus Christ, with the δικαιοσύνη τοῦ θεοῦ in all its scope and fulness ; just as men generally are confronted objectively and factually with the works of creation in contemplation of which they have to do objectively and factually with the true God, so that to this extent they can be called γνόντες θεόν (Rom. 1¹⁹ᶠ·), even though they are very far from the knowledge of God which is actually offered them. As the glory of the Creator does not begin to be glorious only when received by man, so with the glory of the Mediator. Hence the fact that

3. *Jesus is Victor*

Paul made nothing of the knowledge suggested to him, but regarded Jesus as a rightly rejected deceiver and treated His witnesses as worthy of condemnation, did not alter in the very slightest what Jesus was objectively and factually for him, namely, the Messiah who had now come, the true Son of God and Son of Man, the Inaugurator and Revealer of the dominion of God and of reconciliation between God and man. Nor did it alter in the very slightest what Christians were, namely, those sanctified by the Holy Spirit, the members of the body of which He was the Head, His obedient servants, whose offensive action was the only true and unequivocal well-doing and whose Word was the Word of truth affecting and binding Paul no less than others. It did not alter in the very slightest the fact that in this community of His saints Jesus was already present to Saul in his ignorant zeal for God, was already objectively and factually knowable and even known by him, as the One He was and is and will be. To this extent his ignorance was not absolute. It was fully in control. But it was already limited by the knowledge which was already before him waiting for him to exercise it. The same result is reached if we consider Paul's then relation to what we have called the Israelitish economy of reconciliation and revelation. He did not know this in resisting the knowledge that the history of Israel is the preparatory history of Jesus Christ, or, as he later put it (Rom. $1^{1f.}$), " the gospel which he had proclaimed afore by his prophets in the holy scriptures." He did not know that Christ was the *telos* of the Law, fulfilling the Abrahamic, Sinaitic and Davidic covenant (Rom. 10^4). He did not know the prerogatives of the Jews which were so familiar to and so highly valued by him, and which even later he recognised and praised so solemnly (Rom. $9^{4 \cdot 5}$), Israel's adoption to sonship, the glory of God in its midst, the institutions of the covenant, the giving of the Law, the service of God, the promise, the fathers, the Messiah Himself who as man should be one of them, in short, the whole tradition in which he desired so consistently and passionately to live. He knew it only as he did not know it. But what difference did his ignorance, his false view and understanding, make to the fact that objectively and factually the old covenant meant something very different from what he thought, and that in the most sacred things which he thought he had to defend against Christians and their supposed Christ he really had to do with Jesus of Nazareth as the true Christ, and in Him with the God of the covenant made with the fathers? To adopt the words put in the mouth of Ananias in Ac. 22^{14}: "The God of our fathers hath chosen thee, that thou shouldest know his will." What does his ignorance and its predominance signify in face of the fact that he is chosen to know by the God of his fathers, whom he served with so great a lack of understanding? The reality in this respect, too, was the limitation of his overabounding ignorance by the knowledge objectively and factually secured to, though not yet exercised by him. And the words of Ac. 22^{14} already point to the dimension to which Paul himself refers in Gal. 1^{15} when he speaks of himself as one who is separated by God and for God not merely before Damascus but from his mother's womb, this being the basis of his calling by grace on the Damascus road. In Ac. 9^{15}, too, he is called a σκεῦος ἐκλογῆς. Elected by God long before the eighth day of his circumcision and therefore his entry into the tradition of Israel, and certainly long before his first encounter with Jesus in the members of His community, he was obviously known by God long before he had even the opportunity to exercise his own knowledge. In defiance of his ignorance, this knowledge was already offered in and with his creaturely existence as such. It was, as it were, laid in his very cradle. In virtue of his election he could only know. It is of all this that we are reminded by the κέντρον against which the wild horse may lash out but by which it is restrained, so that it cannot lash out with any success. Its rider is in the saddle and cannot be thrown off. And in view of this whole aspect we must not form a one-sided picture of the *terminus a quo* of this great change in the life of Paul. The impression of the undisturbed dominion of his ignorance is opposed necessarily—

§ 69. *The Glory of the Mediator*

for otherwise it would not be Jesus Christ whom he did not know—by that of the knowledge which he does not exercise, which he indeed repudiates, but which is powerful in virtue of its object, Jesus Christ. Light was already near to the darkness of his way, and ready to shine out from within this darkness.

The Damascus event is clearly that of the knowledge which Paul was shutting out on his way to the city and which he did not therefore exercise even though it was objectively and factually presented to him on every side. It was brought to him by the One whom he did not know on the way, and whom he would never have known of himself, as plainly indicated by both the Lucan and the Pauline references. In spite of the clear witness of the history of Israel and the Christian community, he would have gone storming along this way if on it there had not encountered him in person the One of whom he was elected to be a witness from his very birth and who had continually spoken to him in the tradition of the covenant with Israel which meant so much to him, namely, the Christ Jesus vainly attested to him by Christians. It was in the power of the self-witness of Jesus Christ that he passed from ignorance to knowledge. Jesus Himself met him before Damascus. This is the new factor in relation to everything that goes before. This is the decisive element in the story. It was solely and simply in the power of the fact that Jesus met him that the event became that of his conversion.

We shall first try to seize on the essential feature in the event. It consists in the fact that Jesus Himself makes Saul acquainted with Himself, enlightening him concerning Himself, namely, that He is the One for whom Saul is elected from his very birth, that He is the *telos* of the Law and covenant so vehemently asserted by Saul, that Saul has to do with Him in the witness of the Christians whom he persecutes. Formally this means that the Owner and Bearer of the name Jesus of Nazareth, whom formerly he viewed and understood and treated in a wholly inadequate and perverted way (κατὰ σάρκα) as an object, now gave Himself to be perceived by him, in making Himself known, as acting Subject. Did He give Himself to be viewed and understood and treated as such? Yes, and to that extent He gave Himself to be perceived "objectively" as a distinct Other. But at the same time He made it quite impossible for Saul to view and understand and treat Him merely as an object and therefore at a safe distance from Saul as the acting subject. For He encountered Saul as Himself the Subject acting on him, thus giving Himself to be known in the biblical sense of the term. It is He who, acting as Subject, enlightens Saul. There is an encroachment by Him upon the human existence of Saul. Saul in his subjectivity can no longer maintain his distance in relation to the existence of this Other, this acting Subject. Nor is this all. For the activity of this other Subject on him is to make Himself known to Saul, to give him enlightenment concerning Himself, to reveal Himself, His being, His competence and authority, His will and work. It is as the Lord that Jesus gives Himself to be known. And as He gives Himself to be known to him, it is as his Lord, as the One for whom he is elected from his very birth, who demands obedience in the Law which he so painfully keeps, and who is rightly and not wrongly attested as Israel's and therefore his own Messiah by the Christians whom he persecutes. But if it is this Subject who enlightens Saul concerning Himself as his Lord, this enlightenment, this encroachment upon Saul's existence, necessarily means that Saul must give place to this Other as his Lord, that he must accept His lordship, that he must end his headlong rush as a persecutor of this Subject, or more positively that he must bend to His rule, subject himself to His will and work, and thus in a right-about turn become a disciple, a witness and an apostle instead of an enemy of this Jesus. The call which overtakes him when this Jesus makes Himself known and he is brought from ignorance to knowledge is a summons to leave his former path and to enter and tread the new and opposite path which is indicated to him as one who now knows Jesus and which he cannot hesitate to take as such. Saul of Tarsus does not live any more. Christ lives in him. To the extent that he still lives, it is in faith in the Son of God (Gal. 2²⁰). He is now free to obey this superior Other. He is the prisoner, the slave, the apostle of Jesus Christ. The whole process typifies the event designated in the New Testament by the terms γνῶσις and μετάνοια. It thus typifies the prophetic work of Jesus Christ. We shall now turn to certain details which emerge in the accounts.

The accounts of the incident given directly by Paul himself are marked by the terseness with which he sums up its decisive content by bringing the self-revelation of Jesus Christ into immediate connexion with his own institution to the apostolic office. It pleased God " to reveal his Son in me, that I might preach him among the heathen " (Gal. 1¹⁶). The Resurrected appeared to him, too, as the last of the apostles, and therefore quite plainly as one of them (1 Cor. 15⁸). " Am I not an apostle ? . . . Have I not seen Jesus Christ our Lord ? " (1 Cor. 9¹). Christ had pity on His persecutor, treating him as a believer and taking him into His service (1 Tim. 1¹²f·). The Lucan accounts read like analyses of these compressed Pauline statements. Yet even in the speech before Agrippa and Festus (Ac. 26¹⁶f·) the calling to be an apostle is a constituent part of the message addressed by Jesus Himself to Saul in the encounter before Damascus, the intermediate role of Ananias being completely ignored : " For I have appeared unto thee for this purpose, to make thee a minister and a witness both of these things which thou hast seen, and of those things in the which I will appear unto thee, delivering thee from the people, and from the Gentiles, unto whom now I send thee, to open their eyes, and to turn them from darkness to light, and from the power of Satan unto God." And after repeating these words of the Lord Paul adds at once (v. 19 f.) : " Whereupon, O king Agrippa, I was not disobedient unto the heavenly vision : but shewed first unto them of Damascus, and throughout all the coasts of Judaea, and then to the Gentiles, that they should repent and turn to God, and do works meet for repentance." In this third account in Acts the appearance of Jesus, the calling of Saul as an apostle and the beginning of his work as such constitute an integrated whole which is presented rather more expressly than in the Pauline sayings already quoted.

In the two first Lucan accounts, however, the happening clearly takes place in two acts. The first is the direct encounter of Saul with Jesus Himself before Damascus. The second is the indirect encounter with Jesus through the mediation of the disciple Ananias. The two acts are closely related, but each has its own emphasis and distinctive character.

What is first recorded in these accounts (Ac. 9 and 22) is obviously a development and description of what Paul himself denotes in 1 Cor. 15⁸ by the phrase ὤφθη κἀμοί: " He was seen of me also " (as previously by Cephas, the five hundred, James and all the apostles). The use of the term " appearance " shows that even if the incident is a kind of postscript it is numbered with the events of the 40 days which are constitutive for the existence of the community. (The same term is also found in the summarised statements of Ac. 26¹⁶, ¹⁹.) Yet according to the accounts given here the structure of the incident is not quite the same as that of the appearances of the Resurrected in the Gospels. For we cannot assume from these accounts that Saul saw Jesus of Nazareth in the same way as did the two on the road to Emmaus. The decisive verses in all three versions tell us that what Saul saw (and those with him according to 22⁹) was a light suddenly shining upon him from heaven above the brightness of the noonday sun. And as he saw this he was stricken to the ground and blinded, so that he saw it no more. In 9⁹ we are then told that for three days he neither ate nor drank. In seeing what he then saw, he seemed to have been struck down. He certainly saw the Just One (22¹⁴) in His personal self-revelation. But in this first part of the event he saw Him only in His δόξα, in the strange and even frightening irresistibility of His majesty, in a way which could only annihilate all his previous vision and call in question all his earlier existence, so that when He gave Himself to be seen Saul was first reduced to impotence and totally routed from the field. Even that which he actually hears does not go beyond this according to the first two records. An anonymous voice puts to him the question : " Saul, Saul, why persecutest thou me ? " It discloses the emptiness and futility of all his previous action. As a question from heaven, it tells him that, checked by the Unknown whom he persecutes, he can no longer tread this persecuting way. But who is it that puts this question to him ? Who is it that checks him ? " Who art thou, Lord ? " It is evident that the One who has met him is a Lord clothed with supreme authority and acting with supreme power. But who is this " Lord," the Bearer of this authority and power. He does not know, and cannot imagine. He might be an unknown third party intervening between him and the Damascus Christians whom he was going to attack. Perhaps it is a sheer mystery that he is confronted with the overwhelming fact that he can no longer be a persecutor. " Why persecutest thou me ? " But who is this One whom he persecutes ? He does not know. He has to be told : " I am Jesus, whom thou persecutest." But he has been persecuting the community. Yet now the One by whom he is unequivocally prevented from doing this any more tells him that he has been persecuting Himself, Jesus. This identification of the unknown Lord, however, does not wholly solve his problem. For the question remains what is to become of him. Perhaps he will be left lying where he has fallen. Perhaps he will be swept from the board like a captured chess-man. Perhaps he will be brushed aside as a troublesome obstacle by the *Kyrios* Jesus whom he has tried to resist. Hence the further question (22^{10}) : " What shall I do, Lord ? " Even though he now knows with whom he has to do, he does not yet know what he is to do now that his previous work of persecution is brought to an end. Hence his knowledge of the One who restrains him increases rather than lessens his bewilderment. And according to 9^6 and 22^{10} the final thing which Jesus tells him in this context of a blinding and shattering appearance of light is simply that he should arise and go to Damascus, where he will be told what to do. He is not rescued from all the consternation into which he has been plunged by what he has seen and heard. Although " his eyes were opened, he saw no man." In this condition he was led by the hand and conducted into Damascus by his former companions. " And he was three days without sight, and neither did eat nor drink " ($9^{8f.}$).

We must not be led astray by the negative aspect of this first picture. It simply shows the reverse side of the highly positive event in which Jesus acts and reveals Himself as Victor in the life of this man. " As Victor " always means necessarily as the One who is absolutely superior to the ignorance by which he is ensnared, so that He can and does break its dominance with a word. The one who is smitten down, who lies blinded on the ground, who as an invalid is led forward to an unknown destiny still to be disclosed, who cannot even eat or drink, who is at the end of himself even though he still lives—this man is no longer the ignorant Saul, the Pharisee filled with mistaken zeal for God, the rejecter of the witness concerning his own election and the covenant with Israel and the community, the persecutor of the community and therefore of its Lord and Head, to whom he still belongs. A total and effective No is said to this man. No future is left to him. An end is made of him. He is driven from the field. Jesus has done this—the One to whom he belongs. He has proved to be infinitely stronger than this one who does not know Him ; and He has shown this one to be infinitely weaker than Himself. With overwhelming and irresistible force His light has burst into the darkness of the opposition and contradiction which dominated him. Confronted with Him, the false and pretended light of his whole seeing, understanding, thinking and willing has been changed into darkness. No future has been left to him. Jesus, who has done this, has made Himself known to him as his superior Antagonist. He has told him that in this

3. Jesus is Victor

defeat and destruction he has to do with Him, that He is his Conqueror. Hence he does not merely know the κυριότης, the superiority, of this Other as such. Suffering defeat at His hands, he knows His name. He is the One against whom all his opposition and contradiction were directed. He is the One whom he persecuted. As Jesus makes Himself known, he knows Him as the One whom he did not know but who has now radically set him aside as the one who did not know Him. He knows Him, not merely objectively as he did before, but subjectively. This is the positive element even in the first and negative picture. The picture is negative because in fact it reveals only the setting aside of the old and ignorant Saul, Jesus being the One who sets him aside and his knowledge of Jesus being knowledge of the victorious Jesus who does this. Yet, true though this is, the decisive thing is not that he knows Jesus in this way, but that in this way, in the No spoken to him, he does actually know *Him*, and that in and with Him he knows the Word of God which is already uttered to him in his own election, in the proclamation of the covenant with Israel, in the witness of the community, but which is rejected by him in his ignorance. The decisive thing is that the turning from ignorance to knowledge does actually take place as brought about by Jesus. As a turning away from ignorance it has to have the form which it is given here. It must also be revealed as a turning to knowledge. It must have a positive continuation, expressing and clarifying itself in its consequences. But whatever may follow will do so in fulfilment of this turning. It will take place under the directive and power of the One who here causes it to take place as Saul's turning away from ignorance, as the negation of his negation. It is the One who here meets him on the way in his ignorance, and takes away from him any possible future in ignorance, who will determine his future as one who is engaged in the turning away from ignorance and therefore in the turning to knowledge, or rather who has already determined and ordered it as one who is no longer ignorant but knows.

Paul's entry into the future, determined and ordered with the dissipating of his past by the One who removes it, is brought before us in the second part of the narratives in Ac. 9 and 22. The content of the shorter of these (22^{12-21}) is as follows. Saul is now in Damascus. He is there sought out by a Jewish Christian called Ananias. At the word of this disciple his sight is restored. Ananias bears witness that what has happened was pre-determined by the God of Israel. Saul was to know the will of this God in contrast to his own, to see the Just One and to hear His voice, in order that he should be a witness of what he had seen and heard to all men. Hence he must be baptised and wash away his sins, " calling on the name of the Lord." It is presupposed, though not explicitly stated, that Saul did this. He then returned to Jerusalem, but was at once told by Jesus, who appeared to him ἐν ἐκστάσει, that he should leave the city, since his witness would not be received there. " And he said unto me, Depart : for I will send thee far hence unto the Gentiles." The account given in 9^{10-30} is the same in substance, but adds many details. An important point is that Ananias does not go to Saul on his own initiative, but only when the " Lord " has come to him in a vision (ὅραμα) and commanded him to do so, in spite of his own reference to what Saul has done and to what he plans to do in Damascus, and therefore his own opposition to this command. The information which causes him to go is as follows : " He is a chosen vessel unto me, to bear my name before the Gentiles, and kings, and the children of Israel." And Jesus will lead him along a path on which he will have to suffer many things, but for His name. Thus charged, Ananias goes to Saul, addresses him without further ado as " brother," and lays his hands upon him, that he should receive his sight and be filled with the Holy Spirit. As this takes place, Saul lets himself be baptised, takes food and is refreshed. Then after a few days, to the general astonishment, he begins to preach Jesus as the Son of God, and to show that He is the Messiah of Israel, in the synagogues of Damascus. Threatened by the

Jews, he leaves the city by the extraordinary method recounted in 2 Cor. 11[33] and goes to Jerusalem, where he is led to the apostles by Barnabas, begins to dispute with the Hellenistic Jews, is finally threatened here too with death, and thus returns to his own city of Tarsus.

The first point of theological importance in these two accounts of the second act of this story of conversion is that, whereas in the first Saul apparently has to do directly and solely with Jesus, the community now enters into consideration in the person of Ananias. Jesus Himself in His closing words (9[6]) promised it a definite function in the ordering of Saul's future. If it is not expressly mentioned, this is certainly intended when he is told : " Go into the city, and it shall be told thee what thou must do." He is now to encounter the community in a very different way, with all the initiative on its side rather than his. And it is as he does so, his past done away and his future opened up, that there is revealed to him what was previously hidden, namely, what is to become of him and what he is to do. It is by the community that there is shown to him the only possible way now that he is at an end of his former way. Through the word of Ananias he is told that the goal and purpose of his election is His calling to be a witness to the Jesus now seen and heard as his superior Antagonist. And as the consequence rather than the presupposition of this commitment to service he is commanded to be baptised, the forgiveness of his sins and the fulness of the Holy Spirit are promised and imparted, and even physically he is given a fresh possibility of life with the restoration of his eyesight and liberty of nourishment. Yet Ananias has also to tell him (9[16]) that his way will be one of suffering. In the third Lucan account no mention is made of this intervention of the community in the story of his transformation (Ac. 26), nor does it seem to be implied by the relevant Pauline passages. Indeed, the record of this intervention seems to be in direct contradiction to the assurance of Paul that he was " an apostle, not of men, neither by man, but by Jesus Christ (Gal. 1[1]), and that he did not receive the Gospel which he preached of man, " neither was I taught it, but by the revelation of Jesus Christ " (1[12]). Is this an instance of the so-called primitive Catholicism of Acts ? Yet we must not be over-hasty or over-confident in criticising or correcting one Scripture by another in this regard. Neither Ac. 9 nor Ac. 22 speaks of any instruction imparted to Saul by Ananias or the apostles in Jerusalem. Saul knows at first hand all that is necessary. Known by Jesus Christ, and taken by Him out of the darkness of his ignorance, he is also one who knows Him. He is taught by Jesus Himself concerning Himself as his Lord, concerning his election, concerning the meaning and *telos* of the covenant with Israel, and therefore concerning the truth of the Christian witness which he had hitherto scorned. Indeed, the texts themselves tell us that he can at once proceed to proclaim the Son of God and the Messiah, and thus practise his calling as soon as he has received it. This, too, he receives from Jesus Himself even in these passages. From this angle the noteworthy feature of these analyses of the event which he himself later described in so compressed a way is that he receives it from Jesus Himself through the mediation of His community. There is no question of anything in the nature of an ecclesiastical office. Acts agrees with Galatians that the Jerusalem apostles played no part in the conversion and calling of Paul. It was only later (9[27]) that he was introduced to them. And as far as concerns Ananias, who bore the same name as the ill-fated Christian of 5[1f.], he is certainly described in 22[12] as a man who according to the Jews in Damascus lived devoutly according to the Law, and in 9[10] rather more simply as a μαθητής or member of the community, but in this whole affair he does not act in virtue of any ecclesiastical dignity, but in virtue of a direct command of Jesus Himself. If it is asked how the community can and must act in the person of Ananias, a first and general consideration is that in the thinking of the New Testament there is no exclusive distinction or antithesis between Jesus Christ and His community, nor rigid either-or between His being and action and the being and action of the community. Notwithstanding the real difference, Jesus Christ and His ἐκκλησία constitute an interrelated totality, so that He can represent His community and it can represent Him. The most obvious illustration in the three passages before us is to be found in the question of Jesus: "Saul, Saul, why persecutest thou me?" In persecuting the community, he really persecutes Jesus as the Head of the community and therefore as the One who is not merely incidentally but primarily and properly affected. And it is as this Head of His community, representing His own, that He encounters Saul directly, enveloping him personally with the light of His glory, and speaking with him man to man. Invisibly, therefore, it is also the community itself which encounters, withstands and checks him. In the same relationship, he now has to do directly with the body and members of this Head in this matter of his apostolate, of his legitimation and authorisation for the new action deriving at once from this source. The relationship is the same. It is not reversible. The community does not now take the first place and Jesus the second. The word and act of Jesus are not as it were absorbed into those of the Church as in Catholicism falsely so-called. They do not disappear in those of the Church. Jesus is still the ruling Head and the Church His ministering body. But while this distinction remains, the fact is that Saul is now directed and introduced into the service of Christ through Ananias and therefore through the community. No early reader of Acts could possibly have imagined that on this account he did not receive his apostolate by Jesus Christ, but of and by man. For in the men whom he had encountered as a persecutor, and who now encountered him in this function, he was dealing with the "saints" of Jesus (9^{13}) and therefore with those who were directly His. And above all the initiative of the community towards him was only secondarily its own and primarily and properly that of Jesus Himself. This is the explanation in $9^{10f.}$ of the account in $22^{12f.}$ which is itself quite unambiguous in spite of its brevity. Ananias does not act arbitrarily or autonomously. He goes to Saul on receiving from Jesus Himself a direction which in the first instance he resists. What he says is according to the instructions of Jesus and on the basis of, and with respect to, His primacy. After executing his important mission, he fades out of the picture and is never again mentioned either in Acts or in the rest of the New Testament. Obviously it is only in this ministering function that the body and members can represent their Head or the community its Lord. But in this function they can and must do so. Even when the community comes on the scene, Jesus Himself is no less the acting Subject than in the first act where He alone was present. It is He and not Ananias who converts Saul in this positive aspect as well. It is He who orders his future and calls him to be an apostle and therefore a Christian, to be baptised, to receive the remission of sins, and to be filled with the Holy Spirit. Ananias, and in him the community, merely lays before Saul what Jesus wants with him and of him, pointing him to Jesus as his future. But the community has to come on the scene at this point and with this function, laying all this before him. Just as it was the community which in Christ's stead suffered under his persecution now concluded, so it is the community which, again in Christ's stead, points and introduces him to the service of Christ. And since Saul, in accepting this service, accepted for Christ's sake full responsibility in relation to the community already engaged in it, for Christ's sake, too, the community must accept full responsibility for his service. This is what it did in the person of Ananias. The Lord who showed Himself as such to Saul, and whom Saul recognised as such, was also the Lord of the community. On the way on which he was now set, therefore, Saul could not help coming up at once against the community and recognising himself as a member and brother. And as the community saw him take this step on the basis of the self-demonstration of the One who was its Lord too, it had to recognise his gift and commission as those of a brother, and thus to summon him to baptism and to the promise of the remission of sins and the Holy Spirit. This is what Ananias did, not on his own account, but at the direct command of Jesus. The one who in his ignorance had been against the community and thus against Jesus could now be the new man he was in his knowledge only in and with the community, for the community, and in this way for Jesus. This is what we are told in Ac. 9 and 22. Paul himself would have been the very last to reject this explanation of the short formulae in which he describes his own conversion.

It is obvious, however, that, important though this consideration of the mode of the ordering of his future way may be, it is only a side-issue in the passages (Ac. 9 and 22) upon which it is based. The really decisive thing which we learn from these passages, as from Ac. 26 and Paul's own statements, concerns the content of this order. This consists in the fact that the man of God who is " delivered from the power of darkness " and " translated into the kingdom of his dear Son " (Col. 1¹⁸), is immediately claimed and set to work in the διακονία of this kingdom (1 Tim. 1¹²). We are told in Ac. 9¹⁹ᶠ· how promptly he began to exercise this ministry. The vacuum which opened up at the end of the first act of the drama was filled with astonishing speed. Indeed, it was filled immediately. He had been decisively checked in his previous activity as a persecutor of Jesus only in order that he should be no less decisively enlightened, empowered and liberated for his new activity as a witness and preacher of Jesus. Of what avail would it be to suppress his dominant ignorance if it were not at once replaced by dominant knowledge ? Ἀγνωσία can be truly and effectively suppressed only by γνῶσις, blasphemy only by praise. As we are perhaps shown by the saying in Mk 9⁴⁰, those who are restrained by Jesus Himself and can no longer be against Him can only be for Him, and as they were wholly against Him so now they cannot but be wholly for Him. The one who can no longer be a persecutor has no option but to be an apostle. This is what is represented in Ac. 9 and 22 as the second act of the drama. Nor can it be merely literary pretension or catechetical requirement which stimulates this narrative exposition of what Paul himself says so succinctly. What is described is the transition to dominant knowledge, the rise of the new being of Saul for Jesus, his institution as an apostle. It is described as a special act in which Jesus as the all-dominating Subject speaks a new Word not yet uttered in the first act. It is quite obvious that what we have here is the result of what took place before, the reverse side of the page on the first side of which what took place before is written. Yet it is also clear that in this result, in the turning of this page, we do not have the automatic and inevitable functioning of a mechanism. The positive consequence was not contained in the negative presupposition in such a way that it must now proceed necessarily and as a matter of course. The presupposition did not have to have this consequence. Saul might have lain blinded where he was, or have been swept aside as the wreckage which he was at the end of the first act. A second act—this second act—did not have to follow the first. What we have here is history in which both the presupposition and the consequence, both the passing of the ignorance of Saul and the rise of the knowledge of Paul, are the work of the free act of the all-dominating Subject, of the *Kyrios* Jesus. It is in this *Kyrios*, in His will, in His glory, in His prophecy, and not in any inner and autonomous causality, that this history has its continuity. It is one history in its two acts as and because it is human history in participation in His history, taking place in consequence of His decisions and words. Paul himself says that he is what he is by the grace of God (1 Cor. 15⁹ᶠ·), and in relation to the place from which he derives he thinks himself, yet cannot think himself, constantly unworthy to be called an apostle. It is the free and gracious character of the transition to this status which is emphasised by the presentation in Acts with its division into two acts. Grace and apostleship were later for Paul himself (Rom. 1⁵) synonymous descriptions of what he had received from Jesus Christ.

But the apostolic office into which Paul is directed and instituted by Jesus, not self-evidently nor automatically, but in a new and free act of grace, yet

3. Jesus is Victor

immediately and with unassailable factuality and irresistible effectiveness, consists in the fact, as he himself sees and understands it, that he is made a witness of Jesus (22^18, 26^16). As such he is sent to all men (22^15) with the task of bearing His name to all. He is thus enabled and commissioned to say and prove to the Jews, in exposition of their own book, the Old Testament, that He is the Son of God, the Messiah of Israel (9^20, 22). And then when he is rejected and threatened by the Jews, who are foremost in making his path one of suffering, he can go to the Gentiles (22^21) that their eyes should be opened, that they should be brought out of darkness to light, that they should be delivered from the power of Satan to God, that they should come to faith in Jesus Christ, to the remission of their sins, and to participation in the inheritance promised to the sanctified of God (26^18). If the path to be trodden by the witness who is thus empowered and sent out is to be a path of suffering (9^16), he is yet promised that the One who calls and sends him will deliver him from both Jews and Gentiles (26^17). The ἀποστολή and therefore the χάρις which are described in this way, and given to Paul with such inconceivable reality, have thus the twofold implication (1) that he should be baptised, and receive the Holy Ghost with personal remission of sins, and thus become a μαθητής (9^26) or Christian, and (2)—a point which is not to be overlooked or despised—that he should eat and drink again, and find refreshment, and thus continue the existence in time and space as a creature of God which seems to be so severely jeopardised at the end of the first act.

All this in its unity is from the positive standpoint the conversion and transition of Saul to Paul, of his ignorance to knowledge. Nor must we fail to appreciate the theological significance of the proportions in which it is presented in these passages. Precedence is obviously given to the calling of this man as a witness and his sending out to the work of proclamation. The restoration of his physical being is plainly co-ordinated with, or subordinated to, this primary factor, as is also his personal reception as a Christian. In relation to many later ideas, and to those which are dominant to-day, this is no doubt very strange. In our doctrine of the calling of man we shall have to remember that many things will perhaps have to be corrected if they are really to correspond to the way in which the matter is expounded here. Paul himself surely never conceived of any other possible order. But we must leave this for the moment. In the present context it must suffice to look beyond this subsidiary result to the main point in the stories, namely, that Jesus is Victor in the history of His persecutor and apostle. He is this both as the One who overcomes him and as the One who ordains, arms and sends him forth to overcome, enabling him to participate as a future victor in the fellowship of His own victorious being, action, suffering and triumph, in the fellowship of His own warring and all-conquering prophecy. "If any man be in Christ, he is a new creature: old things are passed away; behold, all things are become new" (2 Cor. 5^17).

It simply remains for us to put the concluding question whether and how far, at the *terminus ad quem* of the history of Saul or Paul, i.e., on the new way, the way of the apostle Paul, which he now enters, there remains together with or behind his dominant knowledge an ignorance which is defeated and subjugated and cannot therefore rule, but which is active all the same. In other words, to what extent, if at all, do we have to say that he exists in this antithesis? Can it be claimed that the *post tenebras lux* which we witness as readers means that henceforth there is only *lux* in his life and there can be no more *tenebrae*? The picture of the *terminus a quo* was not monochrome, as we have seen. It was not the picture of pure, unbroken, undisturbed ignorance. Can we claim, then, that we now have a monochrome picture on the other side? There can be no doubt, as we have stated already, that in relation to those whom they addressed, to the communities to whom they turned in their Epistles, neither Paul nor the other biblical witnesses had any such picture in view. We are thus forced to

§ 69. The Glory of the Mediator

assume that Paul did not regard himself merely as a figure of unbroken light. Nor do we need such a conclusion *a posteriori* to maintain that even as an apostle Paul did consciously exist in this antithesis, still active in its own way and within its own limits. He never referred to this day as belonging to an evil or glorious but in any case distant past. It was always for him the νῦν of the transition from darkness to light which on this basis accompanied and characterised his whole course. If he was aware of the presence of the καινά which came into being on that day, he was also aware of the ἀρχαῖα which passed away on that day. He recalled the former with gratitude, the latter with horror. But he really did recall both, even if in a relationship which could not be reversed but was unshakeably fixed. To be sure, he was confident that Jesus Christ is Victor, that His Spirit is all-powerful, and therefore that his own way and warfare would be crowned with victory. But he still had to tread this way and fight this war. He did not yet enjoy a peaceful because relaxed perfection of knowledge. It was in this spirit that he proclaimed the justification of man by faith alone, love as the fulfilment of the Law (Rom. 13¹⁰), and the hope which "maketh not ashamed " (Rom. 5⁵). For after all, why is it that hope particularly can be understood and proclaimed only as a genuine anticipation of the " manifestation of the sons of God " (Rom. 8¹⁹) to which even these sons of God, in whom the Spirit is a first ἀπαρχή, can only look forward with groaning like the rest of humanity and all creation (Rom. 8²³f·) ? It is because there is still present, and obviously known at first hand, an ungodly φρόνημα τῆς σαρκός, a possibility of being or walking ἐν σαρκί which is continually to be assigned to nothingness but which continually returns and threatens (Rom. 8⁴f·), an ἐπιθυμία τῆς σαρκός which resists the Spirit and which the Spirit for His part must also resist (Gal. 5¹⁶). It cannot be taken as a matter of course that man will sow to the Spirit and reap everlasting life, and that he will not sow to the flesh and reap φθορά. At the very height of his apostolic career Paul can and must write in the present tense and in personal terms a passage like Ro. 7⁷⁻²⁵, in which the contradiction in his existence is plainly to be seen in all its menace, and which closes with the ταλαίπωρος ἐγὼ ἄνθρωπος which, although it is matched and transcended by the χάρις τῷ θεῷ διὰ 'Ιησοῦ Χριστοῦ, can still lead on to the final and dominating conclusion: " So then with the mind I myself (αὐτὸς ἐγώ) serve the law of God ; but with the flesh the law of sin " (v. 25). We are not to isolate this passage, but always to bring it into relationship with the opening verses of the chapter (7¹⁻⁶), and especially to see it in the greater context of chapters 5–8. Otherwise we shall fail to see where the way leads. Yet in face of the negative elements in the apostolic self-consciousness as they emerge so unexpectedly at this point in the whole sequence, we cannot conceal the fact that Paul and his communities are still on the way on which he was led before and into Damascus, i.e., the way from ignorance to knowledge. We remember that in 1 Cor. 13¹² Paul calls his present seeing (as distinct from seeing " face to face ") a puzzling seeing in a glass, and his present knowledge (as distinct from one commensurate with his being known by God) a knowing in part. That he does this surely rests on his awareness of the antithesis which is not resolved even in his existence. There can be no doubt, of course, that this antithesis is teleogically ordered in the irreversible movement from ignorance to knowledge. There can be no stopping or hesitating, for it is the antithesis of the history of the apostle as inaugurated and determined by Jesus Christ. It is an antithesis which goes down to destruction ; to the destruction of all ignorance by knowledge. Nor can there be any question of a retreat in this history. Yet it is a history which takes place in this antithesis. That the antithesis is not yet removed, but Paul can still regard the history as one of triumph, we learn from Phil. 3¹²f· : " Not as though I had already attained, either were already perfect ; but I follow after, if that I may apprehend that for which also I am apprehended of Christ Jesus. Brethren, I count not myself to have apprehended : but this one thing I do, forgetting those things which are behind, and reaching forth unto those things which are before, I press toward the mark (σκοπός) for the prize of the high calling of God in Jesus Christ." This, then, is how we are to understand, so far as we can, the situation of the converted and holy apostle Paul, and therefore the *terminus ad quem* of the history of Saul who became Paul. It is clear that what we have here is a history of triumph, but also that it is genuine history.

We have now answered the question as to the historicity of the prophecy of Jesus Christ, i.e., of His revelation and of the knowledge of the reconciliation effected in Him as this knowledge is established, awakened and fashioned by His revelation. We may conclude that the reconciliation of the world to God is in every respect history. But there is particular reason to emphasise its historicity at this point, in relation to its third form. In this form, in its character as light, Word and truth, it is historical in a distinctive and outstanding way. Generally speaking, this is because, as revelation which is the basis of knowledge, it here bursts from within and in its own strength its apparent restriction and isolation as that which has occurred in a specific time and place, transcending itself and moving into world-occurrence and the occurrence of each individual life, in order that it may there show itself and its occurrence to be the origin, meaning and goal of all occurrence and thus seize all occurrence and refashion it for participation in itself, impressing upon it its own law and giving it its own direction. It is the reconciliation of the whole world, of all men. Yet as such it must, it wills to be understood and grasped by the whole world and all men. It sees to it itself that this should happen in its third form in which its reality is also truth, the act of God in Jesus Christ is also the Word of God, the life is also light. As atonement takes place in this dimension, too, as it is also revelation establishing knowledge, it expresses and asserts what it is for the whole world and for each and every man. It thrusts down its roots and wins for itself form and existence in this outside sphere. It becomes the beginning of a corresponding wider and new history : of a wider to the extent that it takes place outside in the world and in and among men ; and of a new to the extent that its occurrence is something novel and different and strange in relation to other events in this outer sphere.

This wider and new history following and corresponding to the event of atonement is the Christian knowledge established, awakened and fashioned by the revelation, manifestation and prophecy of Jesus Christ. In accordance with the event of reconciliation in Jesus Christ as its origin, theme and content, it, too, is history, salvation history. In it, it can and should and must take place that what is done in Jesus Christ for all should express and assert itself, that the power and relevance of the Word of God as the third integrating element of His action and work in the world and humanity which receives it should be effective and visible, that the seed of the message of reconciliation, the covenant and the kingdom should be sown and bring forth fruit. But Christian knowledge is also history in the fact that its fulfilment in the world—in this again it resembles its origin, theme and content—necessarily comes up against non-recognition, resistance and contradiction. In the same correspondence, it is also history in the fact that it is always and everywhere achieved in the form of opposition to this contradiction and conflict with it. It is history finally and supremely in the fact that the victorious outcome of this conflict, and therefore its fulfilment, is decided from the very outset by Him who is its theme and basis, by Jesus the Victor. As the history of salvation enacted in Jesus Christ imparts itself as such, and is thus the history of revelation, it reproduces itself. Invading the history of the world and men, it again creates salvation history in the form of Christian knowledge. It creates the history whose course and content we have schematically indicated under the four heads of the preceding discussion. The supreme and distinctive feature of the historicity of reconciliation in its character as revelation, which is the theme of our present enquiry, might well be defined as follows. In this character, under this aspect of the prophetic office and work of Jesus Christ, it is self-multiplying history. For it does not merely take place in its two basic dimensions as man's justification before God and sanctification for Him. In so doing, it also transcends itself in a third dimension grounded in the first two. It evokes its own reflection in the world and among men in the form of Christian knowledge of what has taken place in Jesus Christ. In this reflection, it is made clear that not for nothing did it happen that the relationship of the world and men to God, and therefore their whole constitution and situation, were made quite different in and through Him. Nothing less or other than reconciliation itself is made present and takes place wherever and whenever it establishes, awakens and fashions knowledge of itself and therefore Christian knowledge. This is what it does in this third dimension. As the divine work of justification and sanctification, it achieves its own real presence in the world and among men by revealing itself in the totality of its occurrence and establishing Christian knowledge. Or, to put it the other way round, the real presence of reconciliation, i.e., of the living Lord Jesus, is the theme and basis and content of Christian knowledge. This, then, is the supreme and distinctive way in which Jesus Christ is historical in His prophetic office and work. In His prophecy He creates history, namely, the history enacted in Christian knowledge. And the fact that He does this in His prophecy gives us good reason to emphasise His historicity (the historicity of reconciliation) both in its totality and specifically in relation to His third mediatorial office and work. It gives us good reason to set on a candlestick in this particular context the fact that Jesus Christ is Warrior and that as such He is Victor.

If this emphasis is correct, it has certain basic and pregnant

3. Jesus is Victor

consequences for all Christian thinking, and therefore for all the spheres of ecclesiastico-dogmatic investigation and presentation, and indeed for the meaning, task and fashioning of Church proclamation in all its forms. These may now be briefly indicated.

1. There is first confirmed and authenticated in this way the distinction between the history of reconciliation and salvation which took place once and for all *illic et tunc* in Jesus Christ, and which is the basis of Christian knowledge as effective also in its character as revelation, and the actual history of Christian knowledge which is established by and related to it, participating in it *hic et nunc* and taking place in this participation. We might also say that there is confirmed and authenticated the distinction between the one reality of reconciliation and its verification in the world and among men as this now takes place in Christian knowledge in virtue of its intrinsic truth. Or, to adopt more familiar terms, we might say that there is confirmed and authenticated the distinction between the ontic and noetic or objective and subjective elements in the intercourse between God and man inaugurated and ordered in Jesus Christ. Or we might say very simply but aptly that there is confirmed and authenticated the distinction between Jesus Christ as the Word of God and us Christians who receive Him as the Word of God. This distinction, however described, is confirmed and authenticated in our answer to the question of the particular historicity of the prophecy of Jesus Christ. There is urgent reason never to abandon but always to maintain it. There is cause, therefore, wisely to refrain from identifying what is distinguished. The revelation of reconciliation as the act of God in Jesus Christ does not disappear and is not dissolved in any form of its knowledge, but underlies Christian knowledge in all its forms. Conversely, its knowledge does not disappear and is not dissolved in its revelation but is established in it as a distinctive event by which it is awakened and fashioned. The Sower goes forth to sow on the field which is the world, and even where the richest fruit is produced He is not identical either with the field or the sowing. Conversely, the field, whatever its nature, is dependent on the alien power and work of the Sower and His seed if it is to be ground which bears fruit. Jesus does not really identify Himself with Saul of Tarsus when He calls him. In calling him, He confronts him as a very different Other, as the *Kyrios*. Again, Paul does not merge into the *Kyrios* Jesus who encounters him. By His calling he is set on his own feet in relation to Him, and stirred to freedom and action as His apostle. Thus in the history in which knowledge is grounded, and in the Christian knowledge grounded in it, neither the ontic and objective nor the noetic and subjective element is absorbed or swallowed up by the other. Both are elements in a relation which has and maintains and continually acquires the character of an encounter in which neither robs the other of its autonomy and distinctiveness, nor

indeed of its specific place and function in the encounter. In the real intercourse and exchange between them their mutual relationship is always irreversible and their connexion unequal. Precedence is always taken by the *esse*, by the objective occurrence of reconciliation in its first and second dimensions as the justification and sanctification of man and in its third as revelation, by Jesus Christ in His high-priestly, His kingly and also His prophetic work. He is always the primary acting Subject. He can only be followed by the *nosse* as the work of His prophecy, by the subjective occurrence of knowledge, by Christians. They can be present and active only as secondary acting subjects. In the history between God and man there is no doubt an intimate relationship and reciprocity between establishing and establishment, imparting and participation, truth and verification, leading and obeying, enlightening and enlightenment, address and answer. Yet these are still very different and inconvertible elements. The history of Jesus Christ embraces that of the world and all men. But it is impossible that the history of the world or any man should embrace, control or determine that of Jesus Christ. Such history can take place only as that which is embraced, controlled and determined by His, and not *vice versa*. Those who know Him owe to Him their knowledge and their name as Christians. His name cannot, then, be understood or declared as a mere vehicle of their knowledge or traditional sign of their Christian existence. He remains the Head and they the members of His body. This is something to be kept strictly before us as we consider the further implications of the results yielded by our previous deliberations.

2. A second implication which no less definitely demands consideration is apparently contradictory to the first but is really correlative. Our earlier discussion also entails relationship and reciprocity between the reconciliation which in its character as revelation establishes Christian knowledge and the knowledge which is established by it and thus participates in its occurrence. Reconciliation does not happen in vain in this character. It is not for nothing that it has this dimension. For in this whole happening, and therefore in its occurrence in this character, in the work of His prophecy, Jesus is Victor, as we have seen, in relation to the resistance and contradiction offered Him by the world and men. But this means that the revelation of reconciliation, and therefore, since this is an integral element in its occurrence, reconciliation generally and as such, does not merely take place for itself in a special sphere closed off by the resistance and contradiction which it encounters. On the contrary, it takes place as it establishes Christian knowledge in the world and in and among the men who are reconciled in its occurrence. There is, of course, no knowledge of reconciliation which is not grounded in the event itself as that of revelation. Any abstract consideration, reflection or statement of only the first or the second elements in the intercourse between

God and man inaugurated and ordered by Jesus Christ ; any abstract use of such terms as ontic and noetic or objective and subjective ; any separation at the point where distinction is certainly demanded but only for the sake of clarifying the existing relationship, can only be evil and give rise to new confusions and false identifications. Neither of the two histories, i.e., of reconciliation in its self-declaration or of the Christian knowledge of it, takes place autonomously or in isolation from the other. As reconciliation in its character as revelation establishes, creates, guarantees and orders Christian knowledge, it takes place in relationship to it, and sets it in relationship to itself. Relationship is thus essential on both sides, though different on both sides ; and it must be strictly taken into account for all the difference. The ontic or objective element implies as its consequence the noetic or subjective established by it. Conversely, the noetic or subjective element implies as its presupposition the ontic or objective which establishes it. If the implication is different on the two sides, it is still implication, and if we ignore it we cannot see or grasp on either side what is to be seen and grasped. A reconciliation which did not have Christian knowledge as its consequence would not be that which reveals itself ; and a knowledge which did not have this self-revealing reconciliation as its presupposition would not be Christian knowledge. If Jesus Christ is not High-priest and King without the whole people of those justified and sanctified in Him, He is not Prophet without the Christians called by Him to a knowledge of His high-priestly and kingly work and therefore of their justification and sanctification, together with others still to be called to this knowledge through their ministry. Similarly, there can be even less question of Christians apart from the Prophet Jesus Christ who calls them to knowledge of the reconciliation which has taken place in Him and therefore of their Christian standing ; and even less question still of a Christian existence which either rests in itself or oscillates between its own heights and depths, but either way understands, interprets and declares itself in terms of itself and finds in Jesus Christ only its symbol or slogan. It is just because true theological thinking and utterance must not try to exist in either form of monism, but make a genuine distinction, that there must be no separation or abstraction, no exclusive contention or definition either on the one side or the other. Whether we think down from Jesus Christ to His people, or up from His people to Jesus Christ, we must respect and bring out the relationship and reciprocity which always characterise the intercourse between God and man inaugurated and ordered by Jesus Christ. To be sure, there is inequality. This is inevitable when on the one side we have as the primary acting Subject Jesus Christ in His prophecy and on the other as the secondary acting subjects those who receive His Word ; when on the one side we have the divine work of self-revealing revelation and on the other the human work of

Christian knowledge. But for all the inequality they are mutually related. It is not that either the one or the other in isolation is salvation history. In virtue of the dimension in which it takes place, the one, reconciliation, is salvation history for and in relation to the other, imparting itself to, impressing itself upon and taking up its dwelling within the other ; and in virtue of the fact that it is reached, determined, ordered and fashioned by reconciliation, the other, human perception, appropriation and comprehension, is salvation history through the former, as its dwelling-place and by participation in its fulness. Salvation history is the going forth of the Sower, yet also the sowing and fructifying of the seed together with the being and action of the Sower. Salvation history is the history of the Jesus of Nazareth who encounters Saul of Tarsus, yet also the history of the apostle Paul who recognises and proclaims this Jesus as the Christ. Salvation history is both the establishing and establishment, the truth and the verification, the enlightening and the enlightenment, the address and the answer, each in its own relationship to that which is below or above it, yet each also with and in relation to the other, and not apart from it. Salvation history is the totality both in its dynamic differentiation and yet also in its unity. Salvation history is the history of the *totus Christus*, of the Head with the body and all the members. This *totus Christus* is *Christus victor*. This is the second implication of our previous discussion which we must not allow to slip from our grasp.

3. Our third implication is that reconciliation thus takes place also in the Christian knowledge grounded in its revelation. In the course of its breaking out from the *illic et tunc* and breaking into the *hic et nunc* of the Christian who knows it, it does not become a neutral truth maintained for no very obvious reason, nor does it become a tedious construct of thought, nor a static principle or system, nor a mere doctrine, however soundly constructed or endowed with ecclesiastical authority. In this third form and dimension, as it establishes, awakens and fashions Christian knowledge, reconciliation takes place as God's act of salvation to and in man. The living Jesus Christ Himself is reconciliation. Not a mere something, but He Himself is revealed with its revelation. It is all real in Him, and therefore all that it includes is revealed as He is revealed. But He Himself is at one and the same time the Son of God who humbles Himself and justifies all His human brothers in His humiliation, and yet also the Son of Man who is exalted to fellowship with God and sanctifies and draws after Himself all His human brothers in His exaltation. This event of salvation is Jesus Christ, and Jesus Christ is this event of salvation. And if Jesus Christ, who is Himself this event of salvation, reveals Himself and therefore this event of salvation ; if He makes Himself and therefore this event of salvation the theme, basis and content of Christian knowledge, this means that to the man who

3. Jesus is Victor

participates in His revelation, and knows Him in its power, a gracious share is given in the being and action which are first His own, and therefore in the event of salvation which is first God's act of salvation fulfilled in Him and taking place in His person for the whole world and for all men. And the prophetic work in which He gives this man a share in Himself, and therefore in the divine act of salvation fulfilled in Him, consists in the fact that He comes to him. He encounters him. He thus overcomes the temporal and spatial distance which at first seems necessarily to come between. He does not exist only primarily in His *illic et tunc*, but also secondarily with this man in His *hic et nunc*. He makes Himself the object, and as a living and acting " object " the basis, and as a basis which underlies knowledge of Himself the content, of the contemplation and apprehension of this man. He makes his contemplation and apprehension serviceable to Himself in this way. He thus presents Himself to this man. He appears to him. To be sure, He does so in a secondary form. Yet He does so *realiter* and not just *nominaliter*. It is He Himself who appears. Secondarily but really He exists also in this man and his knowledge. And He Himself is reconciliation, the justification of all men as the Son of God and their sanctification as the Son of Man. He Himself is this event of salvation. What applies to Him applies also to it. As He is not only High-priest and King but also Prophet and Revealer of His work, this event cannot remain only an event fulfilled in Him. It is also revealed in its occurrence. In and in virtue of His revelation, it becomes the object, basis and content of human knowledge. It makes itself present in this. As the event of salvation it thus takes place, not just primarily there and then in Him, but also secondarily and no less really in the knowledge of salvation created by Him. It is thus the case that the one who participates in this knowledge participates in the event of salvation itself. The event becomes the living seed and therefore the fruitful element in the events of his own life. Conversely, the events of his human life become the fruit-bearing field and therefore the confirmation and authentication of the event of salvation which comes to him. God's Word as the object, basis and content of his knowledge demonstrates and confirms itself in him as the act of God which it declares and in which it gives him a share. Hence as it takes place primarily, the act of God also takes place, not primarily but secondarily, yet in all its reality, in the one who knows the Son of God and Son of Man in His prophecy, in His Word. The work of Jesus Christ, the High-priest and King, did not merely take place for him as for all men. In the power of His prophecy, demanding his gratitude and obedience and service, it also happens to him and in him. "In Christ," as Christ in His prophetic Word gives him a part in Himself and therefore in the fulness of His high-priestly and royal work, he becomes a new creature, a justified and sanctified child of God, in the further sense that he may find and know himself as such, that he must respond as such, that he is summoned and directed to orientate himself and act accordingly. In the power of its revelation, reconciliation thus takes place also in the Christian knowledge established by it, and therefore to and in the men whom it, or rather He Himself as the great Mediator between God and man, causes to participate in its revelation.

4. The fourth implication is the converse of the third. Yet we do not introduce it merely for the sake of completeness, but because it includes a further and materially important insight. It is to the effect that in the Christian knowledge established by the revelation of reconciliation, reconciliation does actually occur. What we have rather brusquely to oppose in this insight is a constant and widespread devaluation of the concept of knowledge. It is not the case that Christian knowledge can be regarded and described as a mere acceptance or reflection, as mere thought, as mere conviction of perhaps a profound and even emotional nature. In this case it would be (1) only a subjective attitude which would leave open the question of the truth and reality of its object, and therefore of its basis and content, as if this were a completely separate issue. And it would be (2) only one subjective attitude among others, so that the question of its significance and relevance for the other possibilities and problems of human existence would still have to be raised and answered. If we understand Christian knowledge merely as a subjective human attitude which is only partial in its subjectivity, we can have no very high conceptions in this whole matter. When we come to speak of it, our most important concern will be to draw attention to the difficulties involved in so limited a human attitude. We shall lay our finger either on the preliminary question of an objective content corresponding (or not corresponding) to this acceptance, reflection, thinking or belief, or on the fact that knowledge is nothing more nor better than knowledge, i.e., on the open question of man's other and perhaps more essential inner and outer life, of his will and action, of the spiritual and moral *praxis pietatis* corresponding (or not corresponding) to his Christian knowledge. It may well be that in both respects we shall prefer not to proceed beyond a critical consideration and exposition of the situation, beyond an amateurish and dilletante enquiry concerning what is lacking in Christian knowledge as such. Or it may be that on both sides, with a greater emphasis on our supposed realism, we shall think that we can supplement this knowledge, our realism taking either a metaphysical form in relation to the dubious theme, basis and content of the knowledge, or perhaps a moral, sentimental or aesthetic, or possibly a sacramental or existential, in relation to its limitation as compared with other and perhaps more genuine and serious possibilities of human existence. Whatever the course adopted, the root is always a devaluation of the concept of Christian knowledge. In other words, when we think or speak along these lines, we do not yet

3. *Jesus is Victor* 219

envisage, or do so no longer, the true Christian knowledge established in the revelation of the reconciliation effected in Jesus Christ and therefore by the prophecy of Jesus Christ. If we really had this in view, we could not think or speak in this way. For our own part, we recall the usage and significance of the term " knowledge " in the Old and New Testaments. And we are reminded by our own systematic discussions that we are not speaking of any kind of even " religious " knowledge, in relation to which reservations and proposed additions might well be in place, but of the Christian knowledge grounded in and related to the prophecy of Jesus Christ. We thus maintain that this knowledge is not vulnerable either to enquiry concerning an objective being or content corresponding to and justifying the subjective attitude or to that concerning other subjective possibilities by whose greater genuineness or seriousness it might be transcended and put in the shade. True Christian knowledge cannot be subjected to meaningful criticism on either side. Nor does it need any realistic amplification on either side. For its theme, which as such is its basis and as its basis its content, is the real happening of reconciliation in its character as revelation. Once we have seen and pondered and estimated that something happens in true Christian knowledge, and what it is that happens, we shall refrain from critical depreciation in the sense indicated, or from realistic inflation in the sense indicated. True Christian knowledge defies both these courses. It takes place as it is set in motion by its living object which seizes and retains the initiative in relation to man ; as from the very outset and continually (for this is a living object), it has in this its basis ; and as in the basis (for it makes itself known in this knowledge), it has its content. Since it takes place in this way, the question of a corresponding objective factor, and therefore the question of truth, is answered at the very beginning. The serious question of truth which has to be put to it cannot be whether or how far there is really a corresponding objective factor, and therefore whether or how far it can clear itself of the suspicion that it is a subjective illusion. The question of truth which must seriously be put to it is whether or how far it corresponds and does justice to the object by whose initiative it is set in motion and can alone remain in motion, and which is itself its basis and content. In virtue of this object, basis and content, there is no need of any attempt at metaphysical realism. Such an attempt can only lead to confusion, obscurity and evacuation of real content. Only by missing the object which totally claims it can this knowledge try even incidentally to seek a supposedly more real object of this nature. In the measure in which it does this, it ceases to be Christian knowledge. As it takes place, however, in the power of the initiative wrested from man by its object, there need be no fear that the claiming of man which it entails will be only partial and not total. The object itself sees to it that the act of contemplating and grasping it, of accepting and considering it, cannot possibly be purely intellectual. What takes place in real Christian knowledge is rather—here we are reminded again of the New Testament concept of *metanoia*—that the whole man with all his possibilities and experiences and attitudes is grasped by the object which takes and retains the initiative in relation to him, and turned right about to face this object, to be wholly orientated upon it. In the event of Christian knowledge, therefore, the question of perhaps more genuine and serious human attitudes and experiences which surpass mere knowledge is answered from the very first, and all attempts in this direction are rendered superfluous. Christian knowledge is the one genuine and serious attitude and experience. It stands in no need of moral, sentimental, aesthetic, sacramental or existential amplification. As it takes place, there also takes place— much better and far more profoundly—all that is perhaps rightly envisaged in such attempts. At a pinch it can itself be described and understood as the moral, sentimental, aesthetic, sacramental or existential happening *par excellence*. In the power of its theme, basis and content (of its object in this sense), it does not take place in isolation or poverty, but in the totality and fulness of its subject, the man who knows. For its theme, basis and content is the reconciliation between God and man effected in Jesus Christ and also revealing itself in Jesus Christ. As a human action it takes place in participation in His action. It has not grasped at this participation; it can only receive it. Nor can it control this participation; it can only be continually given it. But as it takes place in this participation, His action, i.e., that of Jesus Himself, takes place in it as a human action. If it does so secondarily and not primarily, it does so no less really, and no more and no less as the work of reconciliation itself. In virtue of the fact that the event of salvation is also as such the revelation of salvation in the power of which it becomes the object, basis and content of human knowledge, Christian knowledge, as it receives this object, basis and content, and takes place with reference to it, is the knowledge of salvation. As such, however, it is obviously itself an event of salvation. It is a secondary event, related to the primary event fulfilled in the one Jesus Christ and participating in this on the ground of His free address of grace. Yet with no less reality it is itself also an event of salvation. In Christian knowledge Jesus Christ comes to be and is really present to man. What He does for him He also does to and in him. He gives him the freedom, permission and command to be the man he is in Him, the new creature, the justified and sanctified sinner, His brother, the child of God, the responsible witness of the atonement which has taken place in Him. Less than this we may not think or say of the event of true Christian knowledge. What takes place in it is that through Christ, through the power of His prophetic Word, man becomes in the full and not merely the conventional sense of the term a Christian.

3. Jesus is Victor

Having clarified the presuppositions, we shall now make our attempt to sketch the history in which light shines in darkness and the prophetic work of Jesus Christ is done in the form of the disclosure of completed reconciliation and man's opening up to it. Where does this history begin? How does it begin? What course does it take? How does it reach its goal? These are the questions which must now be answered.

It begins as in the created world God sets among men a fact which speaks for itself. This is the fact of the existence of Jesus Christ, who as the Mediator between God and man is also God's Word to us. It is the fact of the light which shines as such, of the reconciliation which declares itself as it takes place. We shall not now return to the divine positing of this fact as such, nor to its nature and significance. We dealt with these questions in the first two parts of the doctrine of reconciliation, and earlier in that of election. The history now under consideration begins with the special truth that this fact which God has set among us is not a mute but an eloquent fact; that it is a fact which speaks for itself, which indicates and explains itself; that it has and uses the power adequately to proclaim and therefore to communicate itself in its truth, to impart itself in its reality. Our reference is to the third dimension in which Jesus Christ is His own Prophet, light is its own light and reconciliation its own revelation. Not every fact has this character. The fact of the covenant which God has set in the created world and among men has it. It has it, indeed, in supreme and exemplary fashion. There are many other eloquent facts. But strictly speaking, we can say only of this one that directly as fact it is also statement, word, *kerygma* and light.

Above all we must insist that even in this essential character it is still a specific fact, i.e., a fact which is singular, individual and distinct from thousands of others, indeed, from all others. To be sure, God posits it in many forms, but as and when He does so these are all limited by their place and time and manner. Hence it is not identical with the fact of the totality of the divinely created world. In face of it there is a whole world of other facts. It does not, therefore, exist and speak everywhere. As God posits it and it is thus an eloquent and radiant fact, always, in all its forms and in face of all other facts which occur and even speak always and everywhere, it constitutes something completely new which proclaims good and yet also unexpected and vexatious news. It encounters the world and all men as the disclosure of what would be secret apart from this encounter. It speaks and shines among them from without, declaring what could not be known of itself either to the world or to any individual. The fact of the covenant is materially the fact of the intercourse which God has freely willed and instituted between Himself and the men who are certainly ordained for it by God but who of themselves have no claim to it nor any power to receive and enjoy it. The unexpected, inconceivable reality of this intercourse is declared and represented by this fact—the overcoming of the distance, but also the distance itself, between God and man. It is thus a singular fact with its own time and place and manner as distinct from all others, not in order that it may remain alone, but in order that as such it may speak and enlighten and impart itself. As an individual, self-existing and self-disclosing fact it attests the particularity, uniqueness and sovereignty with which God has His divine nature and essence in face of all other reality and the false reality of nothingness, not to be isolated in this high majesty, but from it to pursue His cause in the depths of the world, to leave it for these depths, to make the cause of the world in these depths His own cause, and to prosecute it as such. We must not fail to note the distance from which He declares and imparts Himself, overcoming it as He does so. Not the cosmos is the Son or Word of God, but the unique One whom He sends into the world as His Son and therefore His Word. Not every man is a Christ, but Jesus of Nazareth alone. Salvation is for all, but the covenant, which as such is God's glad tidings, is not concluded with all. It is the covenant of Yahweh with Israel fulfilled in the Christian community as the body of Christ. Not all peoples are Israel. Not all societies are the community of the Lord. Not all writings are Holy Scripture as the document of this covenant. In each case there has had to be a particular positing for the addition of new documents of the covenant which as such can be called holy. Not every revelation is revelation of reconciliation. Not every attestation of revelation is thus witness of this revelation. Not all knowledge, therefore, is Christian knowledge, nor all confession, however true or significant or clear or brave, Christian confession. Not all men are Christians. There are many kinds of prophets and apostles, true and false, those who speak in the name of the Lord and those who speak in their own name ; and we have to reckon with the fact that even among the false there may be many noble and impressive figures who still cannot be accepted and heard as true. Of a piece with this is the fact that theology is not universal science but can only be quite unpretentiously a particular discipline. The divinely posited and eloquent fact of the covenant is distinguished from all other facts, which may also be eloquent and notable in their own way, by a line which may not always be visible, which may be lost sight of for long periods, but which is intrinsically sharp. And we must add that in its particularity and individuation in relation to the many other mute or eloquent facts, it is something which, if appearances do not deceive, is externally modest and unimpressive for all its inward glory. It may well be asked in every time and place whether its minority voice will ever be successful, or even make itself heard, in face of the majority of countless other statements, revelations, witnesses and confessions, and in face of so much only too eloquent silence. We must also add that its voice is not only

3. *Jesus is Victor*

directly and immediately that of the Son of God and His Holy Spirit, but also indirectly and immediately that of the servants of His Word and therefore of all kinds of fallible, confused and confusing men who have little or no adequacy for their task, so that it has a broken, anxious and afflicted sound and therefore seems to hold out little promise of successfully winning a hearing. But we mention this only to illustrate that the divinely posited fact of the shining light and eloquent covenant is in the totality of the world and human life one fact alongside and among many others of a very different nature and significance. It is a special fact which is called in question by them, and indeed compromises and calls itself in question in relation to them. It is precisely as such that God posits it alongside and in face of them. In the sphere of all these other facts, and to all the men in this sphere, it has to shine as the light of life and speak as the Word of the covenant. How could it shine, or speak, or present the intercourse of God with men, if it were not a special fact among many others with all its limitation, modesty and even vulnerability? We must not be worried about this. In positing it, God Himself is not worried that He becomes a special instance, the great special instance, and as such our God, the Lord and Saviour of all men. It is as He speaks to and with us as such that He posits the special fact in which He is not everything in the world and among us, but this one thing among others, and therefore in the minority, and surrounded and burdened by the problems of this minority. In the confrontation of this particular fact by all others the history of the prophecy of Jesus Christ, the history of the shining of light, continually begins in darkness.

But the word " fact " which we have provisionally used to denote the commencement of this history is one which in its rather crude exclusiveness might finally give rise to error. " Fact " certainly means: *quod factum est*, that which has happened. And that which, posited by God, shines and speaks and declares itself as the beginning of this history, is certainly something which has happened. It has, indeed, happened ἐφ'ἅπαξ, once and for all. What is meant by the word fact in this context is first and last, essentially and properly, the history of Jesus Christ in all its forms. This is the covenant of God with man and man with God, and also its shining, its Word to the world as the covenant made and fulfilled for the world's salvation. It has in fact taken place once and for all. But what is meant by " once and for all " when we refer to His history? It certainly bears a linear chronological sense. That is, it happened once as this unique history. It also means that, as the history of the way of Jesus of Nazareth to Jerusalem in the days of Caesar Augustus and Tiberius, it is revealed and shines and speaks as the history of salvation. But the " once and for all " as applied to this history cannot be intended or meant restrictively. What took place did not only take place then. It has not become past. It is not an event which is not present, or present only in the recollection of its happening then. Its shining and speaking cannot be reduced to the *historia docet* which is basically proper to all recollected history. It cannot be said of Jesus Christ that He merely has lived. It must also be said that as the One who has lived once He lives and will live. To avoid misunderstanding, we add that He does not merely do so spiritually but physically, in the very spatio-temporal form of His then history. As the One who has lived, He has no need of later recollection to live continually. Risen from the dead, He has appeared and been manifested to His own. His history has been, but it has not passed. It is the promise given also to our histories that one day they will have been, but will not have passed. As the history which overlaps all others, that of Jesus Christ takes place primarily, but in the particular history of Christian knowledge it also takes place again and again secondarily. As that which took place *illic et tunc*, it also takes place *hic et nunc*, in the present of other times, of our time. And present immediately in this way, it speaks and shines, not in distant echo of an old Word, but with all the clarity and urgency of a Word which, whether it is received or not, is spoken here to-day and is distinguished by its unique declaration. In all forms of the beginning of the history of the light shining in darkness we are thus dealing primarily with this fact which is not exclusive but open because constantly self-disclosing. As history, it begins with history. But although this history of Jesus Christ took place once, in its very singularity it really takes place, and therefore shines and speaks, for all times and in many other times.

It is as such a history that it constitutes the " specific fact " in relation to the whole world and in face of all other facts. Its occurrence is the distinctive and differentiating secret of the existence, content and declaration of the Old and New Testaments among all other books, of the Christian community among all other societies, of its knowledge, confession, witness, message and even theology among the many formally similar phenomena, even of Jews and Christians alongside and among the other men from whom they can hardly be distinguished and seldom to their great advantage. This distinctive element is simply the occurrence, shining and speaking of the history of Jesus Christ in all its external modesty and all its inner yet outwardly pressing glory, in all its supposed littleness yet also its true superiority in relation to all other events in the cosmic and human sphere, in its burdening and obscuring by all the affliction, caprice and corruption of the men who know and confess and therefore represent it, but also in the sovereignty with which it makes its way in spite of the resultant and perhaps most serious obstacles, continually overwhelming or penetrating the feeble and confused voice of Christians and our equivocal witness and dubious theology in such a way that this voice is made strong in its weakness. What would have become of the history of Jesus Christ in the world if in all this it had not constantly shone and spoken in its own strength? It uses human voices. These can and should serve it. But it is not bound to them. It is not at their mercy. It is not determined by their faithfulness or unfaithfulness, by their perfection or imperfection, by their cleverness or folly. In and in spite of all its good or bad human representations, it still shines in its own light, utters its own sound, speaks its own Word. Continually taking place in and among us Christians, it continually meets us in sovereign power, constraining us to new and more obedient attention, or rather setting us in freedom, giving to our knowledge and confession and witness and even to Christian theology a continually new and at first unexpected form in which it then continually confronts the rest of the world with a new orientation and as the content of a new message. Like Israel, the Church could and can grow secular. That is, it can lose its particularity in face of the world around. It can set its light under a bushel, or lose its savour. But the history of Jesus Christ which underlies and controls that of the Church cannot itself become secular history. It remains always light and salt, shaming but also awakening the Church, judging but also saving and astonishing the others among whom it is represented by the Church. It does not cease to represent itself, and therefore to see to it that it does not merely maintain its particularity in relation to the facts of other occurrence, but that it continually stands out from them in sharper and more distinct contours, so that, come what may, it shines the more brightly, it speaks the more clearly, and the history of the shining of light in the darkness can continually begin again.

We take another step backwards when we go on to say that in the reality in which this history begins the positing must be that of God. Jesus Christ is the Son of God, Himself very God from all eternity, and as such also the Son of Man, and therefore the Mediator between God and us men. It is God who in Jesus Christ reconciled the world to Himself. It is God who is the Founder and Lord of the covenant. What is told the world by the fact of the covenant, by the history of Jesus Christ, is the Word of God. This statement means that the beginning to which we refer, although it takes place in the world and has the character of a world event, is not one of the many beginnings within the world in the sense that its basis can be found in worldly forces and movements or that it results from worldly relationships and can be explained by them. On the contrary, it rests on a new positing of its own distinct from all the forces and movements and relationships of the world. If we were to abstract from God, and to look only to the created world and the possibilities and realities effective within it, we should have to say that the history of Jesus Christ comes from nowhere and has no basis. It would then be contingent in the strictest sense. It would have no presuppositions of any kind. It would be a puzzling and paradoxical fact in relation to the world created by God. Its shining would be comparable to that of a meteor for whose descent and appearance there is no ground or explanation at any rate in the earthly sphere. It would have to be called mere fate or chance that in the world we do actually have the Christ event and its self-declarations. But neither here nor elsewhere is it advisable to abstract from God. The rise of light in the darkness does not have this random character. If things were as described, it would necessarily mean that the self-declarations of this Christ event would give rise to a limited astonishment, and even compel a certain attention, but could not enjoy or claim serious authority. In effect they would not really differ from an event grounded in and explicable by the world, for even a paradox or mere fate or pure chance can only accidentally kindle anything like respect. Hence, the measure of regard devoted to them would depend upon the arbitrary choice of the individual. It might be great, or small, or non-existent. In reality however, this beginning is neither one which is grounded in the world and its possibilities, nor one which has no basis at all. On the contrary, it is posited by God and therefore has its basis and explanation in Him. It certainly takes place in the cosmos. But its basis and explanation are to be found neither in heaven nor earth, neither in nature nor history, but in God alone as their Creator. In relation to all the created bases of the world and their consequences, it is a new positing to the extent that as a new creation it takes place on the same level as the old, i.e., on the level of the God who is distinct from all reality and to whom alone reality owes the fact that it is and is not not. It takes place within reality. But it is not its work. It is not one of the products or positings of which it is capable. What is posited in it, the history of Jesus Christ, is not a further creaturely reality which is therefore distinct from God. It is a reality which in its creatureliness, its humanity and therefore its distinction from God is also united with Him, so that it is not merely human and creaturely but divine-human and divine-creaturely. As such it could not possibly proceed from the reality which is distinct from God. As divine-human and divine-creaturely it is a new reality in relation to it. Its positing is a new one in relation to creation. It belongs to the created world, yet not to this alone, but first and foremost to the reality of God Himself. And as the work of this new divine positing, it has and enjoys in declaring itself a distinctive authority in relation to the created world. It is not any light, but the eternal light, which here shines to give a new radiance to the world which it cannot achieve of itself and which it cannot escape, but to which it can only subject its own lights. It is not any word which is here spoken from man to man and therefore from flesh to flesh, but in the flesh the Word of the One before whom every man, all flesh and all creation can only be silent. It is not any lordship which is established, exercised and proclaimed, but the lordship of

3. Jesus is Victor

the Lord without whose creative Word there would be no worldly powers and authorities and in face of whom no such power or authority can thus lay claim to independent force or significance. That which God as its Creator wills and willed from all eternity in and with the world; that which alone it can serve as the world made by Him; the great *prius* which heaven and earth, and man on earth and under heaven, can only follow as *posterius*—this is what is event and revelation in the history of Jesus Christ. Its direct origin in God's eternal election, decision and act is what gives its voice authority. This is its distinctive feature. This is what gives it the contours which mark it off from other facts. This is the mystery of the awakening of Jesus Christ from the dead, and therefore of His unconquerable and indestructible life, and therefore of the newness and originality with which He confronts the world and primarily and supremely Christians, and therefore of the beginning of the history of light shining in darkness. God Himself is the Beginner in this beginning. The history which here begins cannot grow old in time. It cannot become past history. In every age it begins with the same and indeed increasing power, for God Himself and His election, resolve and action are at work in its beginning.

In further clarification of this beginning we must now underline the fact that its positing is a work of divine freedom. What God does, He does with no other necessity than that of His own good and holy but also sovereign election and will. He does it as and because He is God. There can be no question of any other reason. He does not owe to the world or man His covenant and its revelation. He does not even owe them their creation. He certainly does not owe them His coming to take up their cause in His own person. Nor does He owe them the fact that, instead of acting over their heads and confronting them with a *fait accompli*, He condescends to speak with man concerning these things, bringing them to his notice in the form of an offer, claiming his hearing and obedience and awaiting his response and reaction, when we might have thought that He could have much more directly and surely reached His goal by dumb and unilateral action. Man has no right or claim to any of these things, from the very first to the very last. This whole order, not least to the extent that within the framework of God's foreordination it implies and respects man's self-ordination and therefore his freedom, rests on the sovereign disposing of God and not on any imposed obligation to deal with man as is done and revealed in the history of Jesus Christ and its revelation. Man does not deserve that God's order should take this form. From the very outset he resists it. He breaks the covenant. He sins against God. He hardens himself against Him. He closes his ears to His voice. And in so doing he characterises himself as a being which does not deserve that God should deal with him as He does, but deserves the very opposite. If

§ 69. *The Glory of the Mediator*

God does not allow Himself to be diverted by this attitude of His partner; if He swears and keeps new faith despite and on the presupposition of man's apostasy, this merely discloses how doubly great and incomprehensible is His freedom. He is not dependent on man, nor is He referred to him, but acts on His own initiative, when He deals with Him in this order. He wills of Himself to be the God of man and to have man as His man. He determines of Himself to begin this history common to Himself and His creature, to create man with the determination of being His partner in this history, to maintain him in this determination in spite of his sin, to turn to him even as the sinner he is, to give Himself to him, to take up in earnest rather than to break off His conversation with him, to give value to his knowledge, faith, praise, thanksgiving and prayer, to call him and unweariedly to claim his service as though he were worthy and capable of it. Why is this the case? " What is man, that thou art mindful of him? " Only one answer can be given, namely, that it was and is the good-pleasure of God to be mindful of him and to act towards him in this way. In other words, it is not accidentally, nor arbitrarily, nor under any constraint or compulsion of a reality distinct from Himself, but in His own freedom that He is this God, that He is God in this way and not another. It is in virtue of this free and basic kindness that He is the God who makes Himself the Partner of man, and man His partner, in this covenant and conversation, even though He does not owe him this, even though man has no right or claim, even though man deserves the very opposite of His address and self-giving. He is mindful of man because to Him as the God He is, His own glory and man's salvation, man's salvation and His own glory, are not two things but one. The freedom in which, determined by nothing and no one else, He was and is and will be this God and not another; the execution and revelation of His own divine election—these are our concern in the history of Jesus Christ and therefore in the fact with the positing of which the history of light shining in darkness begins. But the awkward term " positing " needs clarification as follows. It does not result from a systematic view of the essence of God or the existence of man or the relationship between them. It is not in any sense the fulfilment of a necessary postulate. It does not arise from any necessity, even that of the freedom of God to be this God and not another, or to be God in this way and not another. It is a free gift of this free God. Hence it is not subject to man's control or even to the reflection whether or not He might have refrained from it and therefore been another God. It is the gift to which there can correspond only the gratitude of man in respect for the divinity and therefore the wisdom and righteousness and therefore the inner basis of His election. The result is—and this is the particular point to be elucidated—that the history here to be narrated begins with

3. *Jesus is Victor*

the pure gift of the existence and history of Jesus Christ and therefore of His Word.

The word "gift," correctly suggested and interpreted by the word "positing," reminds us, however, that in the history of Jesus Christ, with which there begins the history of light shining in darkness, we have to do with the work of the free grace, goodness and favour of God, with His love for man, with His action for the supreme good of the world and man, with His work of salvation, deliverance and glorification on our behalf. As the gift of God the beginning of this history is *per definitionem* good. Indeed, it is very good, unequivocally good. The covenant has in view the life of the people with whom God has made it. The reconciliation of the world has in view its righteousness, peace and joy as imparted thereby. The act of the free God establishes our freedom. The history of Jesus Christ is the unmerited but unconditioned and unmistakeable Yes of God to man. It is as the Proclaimer of this divine Yes, and therefore as the light of life, that Jesus comes. Hence He is Victor from the very outset. The content of His prophetic Word is the Gospel, good news. There are no ifs or buts in the *kerygma* of Christmas. To be sure, even though its content is good news, it awakens evil resistance and morose contradiction as it is proclaimed. It enters the antithesis of darkness. It comes to Herod and Pilate, to the Pharisees and Sadducees, even to drowsy and unbelieving disciples. In this antithesis, it necessarily has the form of a Word of strife and contention, of the Law which warns and accuses and threatens and condemns, of the preaching of God's wrath and judgment. Reference will be made to this later. But it belongs to the continuation of the history to be narrated, not to the distinctiveness of the light in its dawning. And even in this antithesis it will still be Gospel, the message of God's Yes to man, the Word of life, the positive preaching of righteousness and peace and joy and freedom, in its true and decisive statements. It would have to bow to the opposition and contradiction which meet it, to cease to be good and joyful news, to yield before its enemies, if it were to be to them a word of very different content, negative rather than positive, or partially negative and therefore only partially positive. Even in this antithesis it is only formally that it becomes the Law and thus proclaims the necessary divine No. The change is only in the husk, not in the kernel. And even in the husk of the Law the grace and goodness and favour of God are declared and revealed. Even under and with the divine No the divine Yes is pronounced as its meaning and purpose. Even the wrath of God is seen to be the burning of His love. Hence it is all the more important to realise that at the very beginning it is free from any relationship to this antithesis, being good and joyful news beyond any possibility of anxiety or suspicion. According to Matt. 10^{16}, did not Jesus send forth His disciples as sheep among wolves? It must be so. For when His Word speaks of the will of God done on earth, of the coming of His kingdom, of His condescension and man's exaltation, of the justification and sanctification of man as the act of God, it speaks of that which in itself and as such is a work which is good, which in its significance for the men to and for whom it is done is positive, which is saving and healing and comforting and quickening, which makes the sick well and awakens the dead and forgives sins, which creates only righteousness and peace and joy, which establishes freedom. How could the Word, the revelation, the self-declaration of this work in itself and as such be a Word which contains both Yes and No and is therefore self-contradictory? How could it speak, like so much poor preaching, half of grace and half of judgment, half of life and half of death, half of the love of God and half of the power of the devil? But obviously it does not go forth in this form even in the antithesis. And in its beginning, in the origin from which it comes, it is pure Gospel. It does not even have the form of Law. It speaks only of grace and not of judgment, only of life and not of death, only of the love of God and not of the power of the devil. The light shining in darkness is in its dawning, to which we now refer, pure and unadulterated light as an unreserved and unconditional indication of the gift laid in the hands of the world and men in the history of Jesus Christ. From the height of its purity it plunges into the darkness of the opposition and contradiction which encounter it. In these depths it necessarily assumes the character of light striving with darkness and therefore of broken light. It does not cease even as broken light to shine in these depths. In its origin, however, and even in the continuation of its history, it is in itself pure light. Otherwise even as broken light, in the vestment of Law, it could not shine victoriously and dispel the darkness. At this point there is no alternative. It is kindled by God, "the Father of lights, with whom is no variableness, neither shadow of turning." He Himself has set it on a candlestick. The Word of truth with which "of his own will he begat us," is His "good gift and perfect gift" (James $1^{17f.}$). We do not merely set on an inadequate foundation our knowledge of this Word and therefore our faith and love and hope, but we ascribe ambiguity and contradiction even to the begetting will of God Himself, if we question the clarity with which His Word comes to us as such and the work of His Word begins to be done in the world and us. This is something which we must never do. In the Word spoken in the history of Jesus Christ we have the first rays of eternity. By His might He dispels our night. The message is one of day-break. It is the disclosure of the perfect gift which God in His grace has put in our hands. It is a message of salvation.

We may sum up the conclusions thus far reached as follows. At its beginning, the history of the prophecy of Jesus Christ is one which (1) in and with its own history, (2) which speaks for itself and (3) is distinctive in relation to all other events, (4) does not merely belong to the past in its singularity, but is divinely present (5) within the world, (6) inaugurated by God in His sovereign freedom and (7) unequivocally revealing His grace. We must not overlook any of these characteristics if we are to understand correctly the commencement and therefore the continuation of the prophetic work of Jesus Christ, of the dawning of His light, and the declaration of His Word as the Word of the covenant. We are not suggesting, of course, that any of these characteristics in isolation can set us on the way to true understanding but rather that all of them are essential in the unity in which they mutually condition and supplement each other. No word or name or concept must be used to denote this unity apart from the one name of Jesus Christ. None of them, therefore, can point to any other reality than that of Jesus Christ Himself. But if the reference to Him is to go beyond the mere naming of His name, which in the last resort is alone adequate and comprehensive, it is hard to see how in this context any of the characteristics mentioned can be left out in substance, however we might enumerate or define them in detail.

As they have been here adduced and cursorily described, I have tacitly taken them from the total witness of Holy Scripture, with constant reference both to its Old Testament form and also to the way in which the work of the prophecy of Jesus Christ begins in its secondary form in Christian knowledge as it is to be understood according to the guidance of the New Testament. Whether the proposals and descriptions attempted really fit the facts and are accurate and satisfactory can be decided and judged only in relation to the relevant witness of Scripture in the same totality. But I do not think that on this basis we shall quickly come to conclusions on this matter which differ essentially or decisively from those advanced.

In view of the importance of the question, however, it is perhaps not wholly superfluous that we should check at least one element in the biblical witness which particularly demands our attention, namely, the Gospel of John. By means of this we can show in outline that the seven characteristics adduced were not selected and presented at random, but in the light of the source by which Christian theology must always orientate itself and be authoritatively instructed in what it must venture to say and not to say. It is especially relevant that we should consider the verdict of this Gospel in the present context because the terms Word, light, revelation, speech and witness denote the specific angle from which the history of Jesus Christ is seen and recounted in this Gospel. Epigrammatically, we might almost say that the Gospel of John is the Gospel of the Gospel itself, i.e., of the prophetic work of Jesus Christ. Our present concern, however, is with what we learn from it concerning the beginning or initiation of this work.

1. It is crystal clear that everything here begins with the entry, speech and action of Jesus Himself among men. " I am " is both the presupposition and the epitome of what He has to impart and of what the Evangelist has accordingly to say to the community and the world. I am the way, the resurrection, the life, the door, the bread, the vine, the Shepherd, and also the truth, the light, the Word. Accordingly the Baptist, with whom the author seems in some sense

to identify himself under the name John, has no witness to bear except to the fact—and he points away from himself in a way which is exemplary for all true witnesses—that " this (οὗτος) is he." And it would be difficult to contest that the same οὗτος is not already announced in the Prologue : " The same was in the beginning with God " (1^2), i.e., the Word which was made flesh (1^{14}) and to whose presence the Baptist later points ($1^{15, 30, 34}$). From the very moment when John sees Him "coming unto him," His history absorbs that of the Baptist. He is the Son of Joseph of Nazareth (1^{45}), and concrete features are occasionally mentioned to make it clear that He is a real man. Yet He is an absolutely dominating and almost more than lifesize figure beside whom the disciples, the hostile " Jews," the people, Nicodemus, the Samaritan woman and finally Pilate, with all their speeches, questions, answers and attitudes, seem to have only the function of giving Him occasion to express and present Himself. In everything that takes place and is said and done it is a matter of His person and the work accomplished in His existence. For all others, for the world and His disciples, it is a matter of what He is for them and among them, of His mission and coming and going and abiding and coming again ; and on their side of their positive or negative attitude to Him, of their being as His friends or enemies. To have faith, and in faith eternal life, means quite distinctly to believe in Him ; and not to have faith (and therefore to be condemned) means not to believe in Him. Eternal life (17^3) is to know the one true God, and with Him Jesus Christ whom He has sent.

2. His work, the sum of the work laid upon Him by the Father who sent Him, and accomplished or still to be accomplished by Him as the One who has been sent, consists in His being the light and Witness and Revealer of the glory which He has not usurped and which is not in this sense His own, but which has been given in all its fulness by the One who sent Him and which is therefore His own (1^{14}). As soon as He appears in the Fourth Gospel He is this Revealer. The Baptist has only to see Him and at once—not on the basis of spontaneous knowledge ($1^{31, 33}$), but on the basis of the immediate revelation of Him who sent Him—he describes Him as " the Lamb of God, which taketh away the sin of the world." And it is with the recognition that He is the Messiah " of whom Moses in the law, and the prophets did write " (1^{45}), " the Son of God . . . the King of Israel " (1^{49}), i.e., with the knowledge later expressed by Peter at Caesarea Philippi, that those who are to be His disciples come to Him and on this basis are called to follow Him. Here, then, His prophetic work is already being done even before He commences His teaching and miracles. In the beginning of all beginnings with God (1^1), namely, in the disposition of God which precedes history, and as Himself God, He not only spoke but was the very Word by which all things were made and without which nothing was made that was made. In Him was life. He was the light of life which lightens man. He was the power of the saving work of God to speak for itself as it is accomplished. As He was this light, He now is, and He thus shines in the darkness and cannot be overcome by it. The Baptist, too, can be called a " burning and a shining light " (λύχνος, 5^{35}), yet He is not that light (φῶς), but can only be called its witness, the witness of this incomparable Witness. He Himself was this Word and light. He did not have to become a Witness and Revealer. He was so from the very first. With His present " I am " He reaches back even behind the time of Abraham (8^{58}). He shares the glory of the Father before the world was (17^5). He is loved by the Father before the foundation of the world (17^{24}). And it is thus that He raises His voice, the voice which the dead shall hear and live (5^{25}). He really does raise it. The beginning does not make the continuation superfluous, nor His history as such empty and meaningless. The Gospel of John recounts the history of works, of revealing words and acts, of genuine encounters and decisions. But it recounts them with the orientation and dynamic proper to this history from the very outset, i.e., in the light of its basis in God Himself and

3. *Jesus is Victor*

then in the first beginning in time, of the unity in which the being and action of Jesus as such are also His word, or rather the Word of Him that sent Him. Far from this weakening the history of the prophecy of Jesus Christ, it is the very thing which gives it its clear and distinctive light and thus enables it to be told as illuminating history.

3. It is inevitable that in John's Gospel the prophetic work of Jesus should be differentiated and marked off quite unmistakeably from all other prophecies, revelations, witnesses, voices, words and lights. The acknowledgment of the Baptist is plain : " He bare witness unto the truth " (5^{33}). " But I have greater witness than that of John " (5^{36}). Indeed, the witness of John himself points consistently in this direction : " After me cometh a man which is preferred before me : for he was before me " (1^{30}). " He that cometh from above is above all : he that is of the earth is earthly, and speaketh of the earth " (3^{31}). In this respect the Baptist has his own place, and his own task and authorisation within these limits. " I am not the Christ, but am sent before him. He that hath the bride is the bridegroom ; but the friend of the bridegroom, which standeth and heareth him, rejoiceth greatly because of the bridegroom's voice : this my joy therefore is fulfilled. He must increase, but I must decrease " ($3^{28f.}$). Again, there is a plain acknowledgment of the Old Testament, which also precedes and points to the prophetic work of Jesus Christ. " Search the scriptures ; for in them ye think ye have eternal life : and they are they which testify of me " (5^{39}). " Your father Abraham rejoiced to see my day : and he saw it, and was glad " (8^{56}). " Do not think that I will accuse you to the Father : there is one that accuseth you, even Moses, in whom ye trust. For had ye believed Moses, ye would have believed me : for he wrote of me. But if ye believe not his writings, how shall ye believe my words ? " ($5^{45f.}$). It is in this positive presentation of the place and function of other genuine witnesses that the basic particularity of that of Jesus emerges. " No man hath seen God at any time ; the only begotten Son, which is in the bosom of the Father, he hath declared him " (1^{18} cf. 6^{46}). Hence He is the Way, the Truth and the Life, and no man comes to the Father except by Him (14^6). Hence the disciples, having believed on Him and known Him, cannot go to any other, for He and He alone has the words of eternal life (6^{68}). Hence they cannot confuse His voice with any other. As He calls them by name and leads them out, they hear Him and " follow him : for they know his voice. And a stranger will they not follow, but will flee from him : for they know not the voice of strangers " ($10^{3f.}$).

4. In recounting this history, the Fourth Gospel does not narrate a past history, but one which is present in its unique content. To be sure, it speaks not only of His coming and existence, but also quite emphatically of His going, of His exaltation from the earth, of His return to the Father. To be sure, His presence among His own and in the world seems to be limited in a way which seriously threatens His whole work by the irruption of His suffering and death as they are ever more plainly intimated after the great uproar of the seventh chapter. Yet it would be quite inadequate to describe as " parting words " the content of the three chapters (14–16) which stand supremely under this shadow of the cross. Already in $6^{56f.}$ we read : " He that eateth my flesh, and drinketh my blood, dwelleth in me, and I in him. As the living Father hath sent me, and I live by the Father : so he that eateth me, shall live by me," and this twofold living in and with one another, which obviously cannot be broken by any parting, is the tenor of the later passages too. The One who to-day is " the resurrection and the life " (11^{25}), will also be this to-morrow. The One who can promise to those who believe in Him that they will live though they die, will also Himself live though He dies. And it is not just in spite of His departure but because of it—for it is the completion of His life—that He will be definitively present to His own and to the world, and they to Him, and also and precisely on the far side of this departure. " Now is the Son of man glorified, and God is glorified

in him," is the boldest possible anticipation of 13^{31} immediately after the unmasking of the purpose of Judas and therefore at the commencement of the story of the passion. This glorifying is indestructible by its very nature. In the light of it we cannot be too faithful to the positive content of the parting discourses. " Let not your heart be troubled : ye believe in God, believe also in me " (14^1). " For all things that I have heard of my Father I have made known unto you " (15^{15}). " Now ye are clean through the word which I have spoken unto you " (15^3). " I will not leave you comfortless : I will come to you " (14^{18}). " A little while, and ye shall not see me : and again, a little while, and ye shall see me " (16^{16}). " But I will see you again, and your heart shall rejoice, and your joy no man taketh from you " (16^{22}). " He that loveth me shall be loved of my Father, and I will love him, and will manifest myself to him " (14^{21}). " Whatsoever ye shall ask in my name, that will I do " ($14^{13f.}$, 15^7, $16^{23, 26}$). The Holy Spirit, sent by the Father and Himself, will be the " Comforter " who will make all this true to them, who will continually glorify Him afresh, who will teach them all things as He takes of His and shows it to them, who will lead them into all truth, but who will also convince the world of the sin of their unbelief, of the meaning of His death (cf. 12^{31}) and of the judgment already executed on its prince (14^{26}, $15^{26f.}$, 16^{7-14}). Hence : " In the world ye shall have tribulation : but be of good cheer ; I have overcome the world " (16^{33}). For after He has lived His life to the final point of self-offering, He does not live any less, but really lives and is really present to His own and to the world. This is how His history continually becomes a new reality to His own and to the world.

5. All this can and must be the case because it is the history which here below, on earth and among men, is inaugurated from above, from heaven and by God. The man who speaks in it is not alone (8^{16}, 16^{32}). He does not speak of Himself (5^{30}, 12^{49}, 14^{10}). He has not come to do His own will (6^{38}), nor for His own glory (8^{50}), like those who speak of themselves (7^{18}). Again, He does not bear witness to or of Himself, for otherwise He would not be a true Witness (5^{30}, 8^{14}). Yet He does not need human witness or honour (5^{31}). As the Son of the Father, He speaks what He has heard of Him ($8^{26, 40}$), what He has been commissioned by Him to speak (12^{49}), and as He has been taught by Him (8^{28}). He gives His own the words which He has received from the Father (17^8). His meat is to do His will and to finish His work (4^{34}). Hence He does not do His own works, but those of the Father who sends Him (9^4). It is the indwelling Father who does them (14^{10}). He Himself does them only in His name (10^{25}). Only as He does them in this way do they bear witness (5^{36}), the Father thus witnessing to Him and for Him (5^{37}, 8^{18}). As the One who glorifies the Father, He Himself is glorified by Him (12^{23}, 13^{31}, $17^{1f.}$). This twofold glorification, however, takes place as He is in the Father and the Father in Him (10^{38}, 14^{10}, 17^{21}), as He and the Father are one (10^{30}), so that to see Him is to see the Father (14^9) and to honour Him is to honour the Father (5^{23}). It is in this fellowship of action and being with God that the man Jesus is the Revealer, the Light, the Witness of the truth. To believe in Him is thus to know that what He says and does is said and done in this fellowship.

6. It is at this point that the mystery of the divine freedom must be considered. The fellowship of action and being with God in which the man Jesus is the Revealer rests, of course, as regards its basis and possibility, on the divine disposition which precedes all history and indeed before the creation of the world, and which is the theme of the Prologue and of later passages which either refer to this or are in harmony with it. But since the inner divine disposition as such is grounded in the freedom of God and not in a compulsion to which He is subject, so is its historical actualisation, the temporal event of the incarnation of the Word. This is the absolutely sovereign act of God which in John's Gospel is continually described as the Father's sending of the Son or the Son's being sent

by the Father. It cannot be taken for granted that this self-revealing work of God among men not only can take place on the basis of that divine disposition, but that it actually does take place, that the concrete fellowship of God and man there decreed and sealed in the height of the divine counsel is in fact enacted and manifested here in this one person. That the Word itself was once and once-for-all as we are, that it tabernacled among us, that its glory was perceptible to and perceived by us (1^{14})—this is the unexpected and therefore absolutely majestic declaration, transforming our whole situation, of a Messenger from another sphere imparting and bringing what we neither have nor can have, namely, eternal life. As we read in the clear-cut saying in 3^{16}, God gave His Son " that whosoever believeth in him should not perish, but have everlasting life." Like the life itself, the revelation in the world which makes faith possible is a free gift of God, grounded only in the fact that He loved the world which was and is quite unworthy of such love. But it is again a free gift of God, according to the emphatic declaration of the Fourth Gospel, when His Messenger is heard and obeyed. " No man can come to me, except the Father which hath sent me draw him. . . . Every man therefore that hath heard and hath learned of the Father, cometh unto me " ($6^{44f.}$). Hence the disciples whom He finds and who find Him are called those who are given Him out of the world. " Thine they were, and thou gavest them me " (17^6). They are born, " not of blood, nor of the will of the flesh, nor of the will of man, but of God " (1^{13}). Those who do not believe are not thereby excused. Nowhere in the New Testament are such sharp and stern sentences passed on unbelievers who despise and reject the gift of faith as in the Fourth Gospel. And yet according to the same Gospel those who may believe can never doubt for a moment that they owe to the divine freedom both the objective presupposition and the subjective fulfilment of this action and therefore their whole existence in this circle, so that they can receive and honour not only the Son but also their faith in Him only as a free and quite unmerited gift made over to the world and to them.

7. What does Jesus reveal according to the Fourth Gospel ? What is the positive thing which He makes known, which He causes to shine as the light of the world, as He reveals Himself and His own glory (1^{14}, 2^{11}) ? We look back for a moment to our fifth point, and must first reply that He reveals Himself as the One who as the Son of God exists in this fellowship of action and being with the Father, by whom the Father's work is done, and who for His part wills to do and does this work. His glory consists in the fact that He glorifies the Father and in so doing (showing Himself to be sent by Him) is Himself glorified by Him. It consists in the fact that the Father is in Him and He in the Father, that He and the Father are one. But the expression " fellowship of action and being " is too weak to describe what Jesus reveals as this glory of His. The Gospel characterises what takes place in this fellowship with greater force and content when it speaks of the love of the Son for the Father and of the Father for the Son. Their fellowship, unity and indwelling are thus described as their action and being in free and mutual affirmation and surrender, the Son loving the Father and being loved by Him, and *vice versa*. This love is the content of the Word or declaration of Jesus, the positive thing which He makes known to the world. In the perfection of its movement it is the light which in His person shines in the darkness. Is this, then, the revelation of the inner divine mystery ? It is this, too, and it is because it is the revelation of perfect love in God Himself that even in its conflict with darkness it has and maintains its positive character, its superiority and invincibility. But the revelation of this mystery can and does take place only because it does not remain this inner divine mystery, but discloses itself within the reality distinct from God, the Word being made flesh, the Son who loves and is loved by the Father becoming identical with the man Jesus, so that Jesus is the One who is in the Father and the Father in Him, who glorifies the Father and is glorified by Him, who does

the work of God and by whom this work is thus done. He, the man Jesus, the son of Joseph of Nazareth, can and does reveal love in God because He Himself exists in its perfect movement. In His human person therefore—and this outbreaking of the divine mystery is the point and true content of His revelation—the world is brought into this movement as the world which loves God and is loved by Him. What took place (3^{16}) in the sending and giving of His only begotten Son, who loved and was loved by Him, was that God did not love Him alone but also loved the world, and that He was not loved by Him alone but also by the world. It is as this man loving and loved by the Father, sent by Him into the world (10^{36}, 17^{18}), coming out from Him and coming into the world (16^{28}), that He speaks in and to the world (8^{26}, 17^{13}) and is the light of the world. The world does not know Him, nor the light which shines in Him, nor His sending, nor His intervention for it, nor what it is therefore in Him (1^{10}, 17^{25}). But this does not alter the fact of what He is for it nor the fact that in His person it is drawn into the movement of the love of God as the world which is loved by God and loves Him in return. In spite of its ignorance He Himself is the pledge that it is this world. And with Him, as His disciples, those who believe in Him, the community of His followers, are a similar pledge. As they follow the drawing of the Father to the Son (6^{44}), the mutual love and fellowship and union, the reciprocal affirmation and surrender of the Father and the Son, are also in them. As they believe in Jesus, there is realised in them that which He achieves by His intervention as the One sent by God. Believing in Him, they have eternal life. Believing in the light, they are " the children of light " (12^{36}). For their own sake ? Certainly for their own sake, yet primarily and decisively that they should shine in the world with what is realised in them by faith in Jesus, that they should love one another (13^{34}, $15^{12, 17}$), that others should believe in Him through their word (17^{20}), that the world should believe " that thou hast sent me " (17^{21}). From the body of those who believe in Him there are to flow rivers of living water (7^{38}). It is, therefore, the love which is in God Himself, which goes forth and breaks into the world in the existence of the man Jesus, and which is first actualised in those who believe in Him that they should be its witnesses—it is this love which the Jesus of the Fourth Gospel reveals as He manifests His glory. He reveals the self-affirmation of God as His affirmation of the world. He reveals Himself as the One in whom this affirmation of the world takes place, as the Saviour of the world (4^{42}), the Bread of God which gives life to the world ($6^{33, 51}$), the fulness of life, so that what He gives and what is received from Him is absolutely unequivocally and exclusively grace, " grace and truth " ($1^{14, 17}$), " grace for grace " (1^{16}), inexhaustible, victorious grace which can be followed only by more grace. " Whosoever drinketh of the water that I shall give him shall never thirst ; but the water that I shall give him shall be in him a well of water springing up into everlasting life " (4^{14}). Τετέλεσται : " It is finished, the goal is reached," is the last saying of the Johannine Jesus (19^{30}). In Him, therefore, there is no negative alternative foreseen by the Father who sends Him and the One sent by Him. This can arise only contrary to all plan and purpose as No is said to the unconditional divine Yes pronounced in His sending, as the hour of the clock which stands already at completion is wilfully pushed back, as the world already saved by Him acts as though it were not, as though it were not nourished by Him. This impossible No must be negated by the divine Yes, by the Yes of Jesus. It recoils upon those who are guilty of it. " He that believeth not is condemned already " (3^{18}). " He that rejecteth me, and receiveth not my words, hath one that judgeth him : the word that I have spoken, the same shall judge him in the last day " (12^{48}). " He . . . shall not see life ; but the wrath of God abideth on him " (3^{36}). " This is the condemnation, that light is come into the world, and men loved darkness rather than light, because their deeds were evil " (3^{19}). To this extent the sending of Jesus becomes in fact a sending for the omnipotent execution of true and righteous

3. Jesus is Victor 237

judgment ($5^{22, 27, 30}$, 8^{16}), making a distinction in which the blind are shown to see and the seeing to be blind (9^{39}). It is to be noted, however, that it only becomes this in its conflict with darkness and in its relation to those who ignore and reject. It is so unavoidably as it must negate their negation. It is so in its *opus alienum*. But it is not so in itself, in its *opus proprium* which cannot be altered by any darkness, by any human opposition, nor by its own opposing of this opposition. " I judge no man " (8^{15}). " God sent not his Son into the world to condemn the world ; but that the world through him might be saved " (3^{17}). And therefore " he that heareth my word, and believeth on him that sent me, hath everlasting life, and shall not come into condemnation ; but is passed from death unto life " (5^{24}, 3^{18}). He has judgment, condemnation and death behind him, and not as an alternative ahead. For in the revelation of the glory of Jesus, in the love of the Father for the Son and the Son for the Father, in the light of love which shines in the darkness, there is no alternative, since this light is absolutely, unequivocally and exclusively the positive light of life.

And now we must give a brief account of the course of the history of the prophecy of Jesus Christ. In its course, though not its commencement, it is a history of conflict. Indeed, among the many such histories in which human existence is only too rich both on a larger canvas and a smaller, it is strictly the only absolutely necessary, important and relevant history of conflict. Beside it all the rest seem to be little more than shadowy caricatures. For all the bitterness and bitter consequences which they entail, they merely point to the fact that the only great and serious history of conflict, that of the prophecy of Jesus Christ, has not yet been concluded but is still pursuing its course. If it had reached its goal, this would have meant the end of all the other human histories of conflict which in the long run, both as a whole and in detail, rest on misunderstandings and are waged in misconceptions. Since the great and true history of conflict still runs its course, these others, too, cannot yet be terminated, but in thousands of forms must be experienced in all their bitterness. " Till Thy love conquers, there can be no peace."

This love and its light are not lacking. In it there is only peace, and in the event its light is the pure light of grace. But dawning as such, it shines in the darkness, and its history is thus one of conflict against darkness. Darkness is the sum of all discord. Hence there can be no peace between it and the love of the Father and the Son. The light of this love can only fight and repel and destroy it. In relation to it Jesus and His Word bring a sword on earth (Mt. 10^{34}). We could not speak even of the beginning of His prophecy without incidentally considering its continuation in opposition and strife. Nor could we develop the basic problem of its historicity except in relation to the conflict in which it takes place. It is this occurrence in conflict which now demands more detailed discussion.

To understand it, we must above all things avoid an error to which we are in continual danger of falling victim in an anxious concern for the relationship of Christianity and the Church to the world around. In this conflict it is primarily a matter of the attack of light on darkness and not *vice versa*. Only secondarily, and under the law imposed by the attacker, is it a matter of the defence of darkness against light. At the commencement of this struggle it is Jesus who lifts the sword—the incomparable, living, effective and penetrating sword of Heb. 4^{12}—against which sin, death and the devil are forced to defend themselves as best they can and with what weapons they can, though we may surmise that these will prove to be no better than the toy swords of children.

It is not the case, then, that what we have here, in a hostile, self-contained and self-assured world, is a truth which is right and beautiful and good, which even claims to be the primary and ultimate truth of God, but which only occasionally raises its voice, which for the most part is simply there modestly and quietly, which continually asks itself rather bashfully whether it will secure approbation and applause, which has indeed the task of finding this. It is not the case that we have a truth which is confronted and opposed by the great and little validities, certainties, powers and forces of the world around in all their unconcern, their basic because self-assured indifference, yet also their mounting suspicion and sometimes their open hostility. It is not the case that we have a truth which unfortunately secures little or none of the approbation and applause which it seeks, but more often rejection and hatred and even worse contempt, so that under attack it has either to yield or to reply in self-defence and self-justification. It is not the case that what is possible or impossible, what is actual or non-actual, what takes place or does not take place in the circumstances of this conflict initiated and dictated by its opponents, is what really constitutes the shining or warfare of light in darkness.

What we have first to realise is that this picture, which might correspond to an anxious view of the history of Christianity and the Church in the world, does not correspond in the least to the battle history of the prophecy of Jesus Christ. In this history we do not have an intrinsically right and beautiful and good truth modestly confronting a hostile and autarchic world. In it we do not have the mere raising of a claim or making of a bid. In it there is no question as to the outcome. In it there is no recognition of an adult world capable of affirming or rejecting its declaration. In it there is no waiting for agreement and no surprise if it is not forthcoming. In it there is no preceding initiative or offensive on the part of the opponent. In it every opponent is first attacked. He is attacked even before he realises it, or resolves and rouses himself to act as an opponent. In it he is known, exposed, challenged and dealt with as such and thus given his character as an opponent. In it there can be no question of replies or self-defences or self-justifications, because there are no courts where such are required. In it the conflict with the opponents and their indifference, suspicion, hatred or contempt consists rather

3. *Jesus is Victor*

in the fact that without any sign of respect and with no chance of success they are summoned to make answer, forced to justify themselves and pressed back upon the defensive. In it light is wholly and utterly light and darkness is no more than darkness, having no light, dynamic, authority or dignity of its own, existing and known only in virtue of its opposite, having only the substance and significance still left to it by this opposite. If we are to give an authentic account of the nature and power of darkness in this conflict, and therefore of the various incidents, hindrances and repulses which it brings, then, whatever else we may say, our first and never-to-be-forgotten affirmation must be to the effect that it is Jesus Christ in His Word who opens the conflict, that He is the Aggressor, that the law of His action is imposed on His opponent, and not *vice versa*.

What is the origin of the anxious view of Christianity and the Church in the world which tempts us to take a similar and perverted view of the prophecy of Jesus Christ? The answer is quite obviously that Christianity does not dare to understand itself in and in face of the world as the people or body of Jesus Christ and therefore in terms of His mission and prophecy, so that in the warfare imposed upon it, it cannot be of good heart but must always take a tragic view of itself and its opponents, and might even make a bad situation worse by making common cause with the wolves of historical philosophy in relation to the prophecy of Jesus Christ, and thus constructing a relativistic picture which corresponds to its own anxious self-consciousness. This is what Christianity should never do even though the diagnoses and judgments of historical philosophers on its own state are ever so imposing and even though its own uneasy conscience tells it that they are ten times right as far as concerns itself. If it admits this, it must still ask itself why it is that its uneasy conscience tells it that they are right only in so far as it must see and understand itself with such anxiety. And it must never in any circumstances transfer the anxiety of its self-understanding to the understanding of its Lord. Whether its circumstances are good or bad, and whether it may have optimistic or pessimistic views concerning itself, the decisive thing is that its Lord is the man who in His warfare—which it has to fight with Him and may really do so with good heart—is the superior Aggressor, in face of whom darkness, however thick, is only darkness. Its regard must always be to Him as this man.

Our account must begin, therefore, with the attack opened and made by Him. In general, He conducts it quite simply but powerfully by seeing, addressing and treating the world, i.e., humanity as such, each individual man, and the whole creaturely world which shares the existence, activity and destiny of man, from a standpoint which is incomparable in critical force, namely, as the world which is reconciled to God, which is delivered from destruction, which in His person is loved by God and loves Him in return. Is this a bold illusion? No, it is the sober truth. He takes the world as it is, i.e., as it is for Him and therefore in truth on the basis of the fact that, as the Son sent into it by the Father, He is for it, He intercedes for it, He has accomplished its reconciliation to God. He reveals, proclaims and attests to it that within it God has established and introduced

His lordship over it and that it finds itself under this lordship. It does not know this, It cannot know it from any other source. But He knows it, and He tells and shows it to it. Self-evidently, this is a new and strange message. Even more self-evidently, it must hear it, and must hear it from the One who alone can guarantee it. Hence He Himself tells it. What else could He say to it? If He were to say anything else, it would not correspond either to what He is for it or to what it is for Him. It would not be in accordance with reality and therefore would not be the truth. He naturally tells it in order that it should hear and be obedient, accepting what He is for it and it for Him. But He tells it as the truth, and therefore independently of its hearing or non-hearing, of its obedience or disobedience. There may and must and will be a distinction between belief and unbelief, between the way of hearing and obedience and that of non-hearing and disobedience. But it does not lie in what He says, or in any ambiguity or limitation of His Word. This is quite unequivocally and unconditionally to the effect that in Him God has loved the world and reconciled it to Himself, that He has established and introduced His kingdom within it. He does not debate this declaration with it, for on what grounds could it make a judgment? He simply shows that all things are as they are and as He says they are. He sets it in the light of the love of the Father and the Son. He illumines it as the world which in His person is drawn into this circle. Any pronounced or trivial indifference, any deep-seated or superficial suspicion, any foolish or malicious hatred, any more or less serious contempt which it may advance against him, is no doubt very menacing —for those who are guilty of it. But it is always too late. It cannot outbid or qualify the declaration which He has made concerning the whole world. It cannot call in question its content. Even less can it change it. It cannot overwhelm or shake or shatter the rock of His declaration but can only dash itself in pieces against it. This is the attack by Jesus with which the struggle of light in and against darkness is opened. It is not merely a declaration of war. It is at the same time His decisive stroke in the war. It is a remarkable stroke in a strange and remarkable war. For the attack is that of the love of the Father and the Son. It is the attack of the grace of God. It is the attack of His affirmation of the world, of His generous self-giving to it, of His intervention for its salvation, of His pledging and guaranteeing of its life. This is what the Prophet Jesus proclaims to the whole world and to all men. It is with this that He encounters all possible or actual opposition. It is in this way that He met and attacked it long before it could rise up to defend itself, which is all that it can attempt in relation to Him.

But to what extent is this to be described as an attack? To what extent is opposition envisaged and provoked? We are still speaking generally when we say first that in the Word of the grace of God there

3. Jesus is Victor

is attack to the extent that in it there is proclaimed and indicated a decisive, radical and universal alteration of the whole situation and constitution of the world and therefore a future very different from its past and even from the present in which this Word is now spoken. And this change is proclaimed and indicated as one which has already taken place, so that the only option—this is why it is proclaimed and indicated—is to take note of it and to orientate oneself by the fact that it has irrevocably taken place. Now that the grace of God is manifested in the world, the great divine Yes has been spoken, salvation and life have taken place and are revealed in the midst and this change has been accomplished, things cannot, must not and will not go on as before in the world and in human life, in its relationships and orders, in the interconnexions of men and their inner and outer existence. On the basis of this alteration they can and will tread new and corresponding paths. In and with the Word spoken by Jesus, like the last stroke on New Year's Eve, there strikes the final hour for the continuation of the form in which the history of the world has always run in the past and is still doing so in the present in which this Word is spoken. Yet this means that there also strikes the first hour of a new time, of a new history in a new form, which begins in the same present. There can be no trifling with the establishment of the kingdom of God and the deliverance and reconciliation of the world as proclaimed to it in the Word of Jesus. To the continuance of its history in the first form there is presented a command to halt behind which there is a corresponding and no less imperious command to advance. This aeon is at an end. The world and its relationships and orders, and man both individually and in interconnexion with others, can have a future only in the new aeon determined by the deliverance and reconciliation accomplished and revealed and the lordship of God established and proclaimed within it. To be sure, we are still dealing with the world which God created good, and the man whom God created good. The faithfulness of the Creator has not failed. In this transition from the old aeon to the new literally nothing in His creation will be broken or extinguished or destroyed. His faithfulness will triumph in the fact that in form it must and will undergo a total and radical and universal transformation. Now that His grace is revealed, and the fulfilment of the covenant with man is declared in the Word of Jesus, to think or speak or proceed along the old lines is meaningless, unnecessary and dangerous, for there is absolutely no future in it. The only meaningful, fruitful and wholesome thought and speech and action are along the new way now disclosed and indicated by God's grace as Jesus speaks His Word. This total inversion is the content of His prophetic Word. " Now," is what this Word says, and in so doing it unreservedly distinguishes in the present between what is past and what is future, declaring what is past to be unconditionally and irrevocably ended and what is future to be unconditionally and ineluctably imminent and even pressing in already. " No," is what this Word says, and in so doing it forestalls the decision of those to whom it is spoken by confronting them with this accomplished inversion, this decision which is so pregnant for their own existence, as one which has taken place without any agreement or co-operation on their part, which their own decision in freedom must follow, but which it can only follow as a decision which is truly free. It is of this that the Word of the grace of God speaks as pronounced in Jesus Christ. We need not say for the moment who or what is attacked by this Word. The point is that it is quite unmistakeably an attacking Word which as such puts all other attacking into the shadows of supreme innocuousness. Someone is envisaged and challenged. And it is obviously someone who does not know, and presumably and quite understandably refuses to know, about the accomplished change which is to be realised " now " because it " now " gives unasked but without qualification a new direction, about the halt and advance which are commanded with the event which is here proclaimed. It is someone who would rather close his ears as the clock strikes and not accept its message. This someone is roused from his rest and calmed in his unrest by the Word of Jesus. He is the goal of this attack. He is invaded and challenged. He is envisaged, and he cannot evade the fact. He is plunged into conflict and must arm himself for this genuine emergency. What are all intellectual, moral, artistic, social or political revolutions, all wars and world wars, but limited, particular and passing domestic squabblings compared with the revolution and conflict which are here accomplished and proclaimed in all quietness and friendliness, yet for all the friendliness with a final radicalness and universality?

But we must now try to examine more closely the character and significance of this attack.

On the first and negative side, the Word of grace spoken by Jesus Christ means that in the present a whole interconnected and for all its differentiation unitary type of human thinking and speech, action and inaction, is described and treated as belonging to the past and therefore as without a future and quite impossible. It is to be noted that there is no criticism, blame, accusation or judgment. The Word of grace is not the Word of divine morality in conflict with human immorality. Only indirectly, secondarily and incidentally does it say of the being and attitude in which man finds himself engulfed that it is evil or bad or at least imperfect and in need of correction. What it is really concerned to say is that this being and attitude rest on a presupposition which is no longer present. Ignoring its removal, they are already outmoded, overtaken and can lead nowhere. Like the carriage-way on a broken bridge, they lead only into the void. What it says, therefore, is that it is folly to try to proceed on this way as though nothing had happened. For something has happened. God has established His lorship on earth. He has reconciled the world to Himself. He has justified and sanctified man. He has taken him to Himself in grace. He has thus removed the presupposition of his previous action and done away with the man who can proceed along that way. The Word spoken in Jesus Christ tells us that this has happened and that there is thus no future for man's previous being and attitude. What kind of being and attitude are these? They have many aspects, but one thing is common to all, namely, that we have here an action in which man continually but impotently and vainly regards himself as free, capable and strong, whereas this is no longer true on the basis of what has taken place for him in Jesus Christ. We shall describe this under two heads.

He regards himself as free to take into his own hands and order for himself his relationship to God, the world and himself, to justify and sanctify himself, and therefore to be his own reconciler, renouncing any other forgiveness than that which he lavishes on himself or any conversion other than the different turnings which may seem to be necessary or desirable to himself. The Word of grace does not tell him that this is false, perverted, godless, inhuman and the root of all evil. Or it does so only indirectly and in the more radical form of showing him that what he is trying to accomplish is already accomplished, that it has been done without him, against him and therefore for him, that it cannot then be done again, that he is no longer free, capable and strong. It tells him that he cannot help himself because he is already helped. It thus tells him that all his activity in this respect belongs to the old aeon, that there is no place for it now that this has passed, and that everything he might attempt along these lines is a futile snatching at the wind. Proclaiming quite simply but impressively the grace of God addressed to the world, it asks him what is the point of his life and thought and speech apart from and even against the grace of God, or what he thinks to accomplish by his action or inaction. The presupposition for this has been removed, and therefore further steps along this road are impossible and certainly cannot lead to any near or distant goal.

A further point is that, in relation to the first delusion, man also believes that he is free to live in a suppressed but continually re-emerging anxiety before God, his fellows and himself. He believes that he is free to make of this anxiety a constant questioning, worrying, complaining, accusing and protesting against God and the world, to be constantly upset about something, to be constantly voicing his concerns and troubles, constantly to be engaging either forcefully or quietly in the corresponding quarrels, and more or less noticeably to extend these quarrels to those around. In this respect, too, the Word of God does not meet him on a moralistic level. It does not merely tell him that things are not as bad as they seem, that he must not give way to anxiety and that he must not provoke or trouble others as he does. It tells him something far more basic, namely, that he *cannot* do this, that he does not have the freedom, capacity or strength for this anxiety and its explosions, since the only convincing ground for it is removed, destroyed and overcome in and with that which has taken place as the reconciliation of the world. Another has long since borne and borne away his anxiety. He is too late to think that he must still endure and bear it. He is too late with all that he thinks he should carry and express to his own sorrow, to that of others, and above all to the outraging of God. The Word of grace tells him that whatever he does along these lines is outdated, that it belongs to the old aeon whose end and passing mean that there is no further place for it, that it is a futile snatching at the wind. Proclaiming the grace of God addressed to the world, his fellows and himself, it asks him very simply but most emphatically why he now acts as though it were not addressed to the world, his fellows and himself, and what right or authority he has for his sighing and protesting. The presupposition of all this has gone. The way on which it is done leads nowhere.

A further point is that the man who tries to be his own reconciler, and as such, not without reason, falls victim to anxiety and the corresponding unrest, stills believes that he is free to adopt the alternative role, in lively or morose resignation, of a comfortable spectator of the good Lord and His world, of the joys and sorrows of others and last but not least of his own life. In other words, he can give perhaps a few scattered thoughts to those questions, limiting himself to what is most obvious and essential and for the rest waiting to see whether and how God will succeed with the world and people and himself, whether and how things will finally turn out right or not. In this respect, too, the Word of God does not address him on a moralistic level. It does not hiss out the question whether he does not see how cheap and indolent and careless and unloving and unworthy is such an attitude. It merely issues the quiet but definite challenge whether he has any freedom for it. It merely shows him that this attitude again is too late. For in virtue of the establishment of the lordship of God on earth in Jesus Christ, it is decided that there is no further place for the existence of a non-participant who is neutral towards others and himself, who accepts no responsibilities nor duties, who at any rate takes partial leave of absence, who is a mere spectator. Outside fellowship with the living God, and therefore otherwise than with Him, as a living participant in His action, there is no place for him to think or speak or act, or even to observe God, the course of the world, his fellows and himself. This alternative, too, belongs to the old aeon which will not return. The man who takes this way of escape is told that the indifference which he might finally choose as

3. *Jesus is Victor*

the better part is deprived of all presupposition, that it too, and above all, is a futile snatching at the wind. In this respect again he is softly but firmly asked by the Word of grace what he is aiming at, and whether he does not see that the very first step on this way is impossible, quite apart from the fact that the way itself cannot lead anywhere.

It is to be noted, of course, that the Word which says this is not the mere expression of a powerful religious movement or of the profound religious reflexion of an individual Christian, nor is it the mere word of serious preaching or sound biblical and theological instruction. Our reference is to the Word spoken by Jesus Christ, to His present declaration concerning these and similar presuppositions which have been done away in and with His existence, concerning the future which is blocked up in His person and work for all those who still try to live by such presuppositions. Our reference is to the Word of God as the revelation of the act of God in the light of which man is no longer capable of all these well-known basic attitudes, of all the thoughts and words and works of self-assurance, anxiety or unconcern, because the man who thinks that he has this freedom or capacity is long since dead and buried in this act of God and is thus no longer present as an acting subject. If we only see clearly for a moment that we have to do with this Word which is so distinct from all old or new, orthodox, liberal or neo-orthodox attitudes, constructions, ideas or theories, with the Word of what was done on the cross of Jesus Christ, then we cannot fail to see the attack which is launched in such depth on so broad a front. Against whom or what is it launched? A better question would be: Against whom or what is it not launched? But we can still leave this question unanswered. We may imagine that this Word will be experienced as an attack, and will thus provoke astonishment, hatred, scorn, head-shaking, complaint, ridicule, protest, contradiction, opposition, in short reaction. But before this reaction emerges and develops, it is already attacked by this Word. And it can develop only in relation to this attack, not from any substance of its own, nor by any other act of God, and therefore not with divine dignity nor radiance, but only in opposition to the one Word and light of the one God. Reacting against this Word, it lives only by the fact that this Word is spoken, and it would rather not hear it, or would prefer that it had not been spoken. From the very first, therefore, it can orientate itself only by this Word. The Word of grace as the divisive Word concerning what was and can be no longer has all the advantage as well as the glory of the aggressor in relation to all possible and actual opponents and all their efforts.

But we must also consider what the prophetic Word of Jesus Christ declares on the positive side, namely, that again in the present there is intimated and proclaimed, as the only possible way forward at the end of all past ways, the future, or more strictly, the arrival, advent, manifestation and incursion, of a new, complex but unitary reality of human thought and speech, abstention and action, i.e., the presence of a new man. It is to be noted that what is announced in this way is not a new possibility which may or may not be chosen, but a new reality diametrically opposed to the old man who is now outmoded and removed. The new aeon whose dawn is declared by the Word of grace is no mere radiant idea, related to the reality of the old like the mirage to a caravan plodding through a desert which is only too real. On the contrary, it is the form of human existence and history which, arising or arisen already in the great transformation of the world, is now the only reality, and can alone lay claim to the term, in relation to the form which perishes or has already perished in this transformation. No wonderful Utopian dream is recounted, nor is there proposed a clever and practically illuminating and helpful programme for the amelioration of the world or men either generally or in detail. No enthusiastic movement is initiated, nor is there accomplished a new organisation of the different forces for good with a view to creating for humanity both individually and collectively a more worthy future. The Word of grace tells us something incomparably more basic and helpful because quite simply far more true, namely, that the future has already begun, not an empty future still to be fashioned, but a future already filled and fashioned in a definite way, the future of the man who lives here and now just as the old past was his past, the future into which he here and now has the freedom, capacity and power to enter as his own most proper future. This future has begun with the fact that God has fulfilled His covenant with man, that He has loved the world and reconciled it with Himself, that He has introduced the justified and sanctified man as the second Adam (who was before the first). " Behold, I have prepared my dinner : my oxen and my fatlings are killed, and all things are ready " (Mt. 22[4])—not just some things but all things, and not all things in a state of preparation but all things ready. The new man is born. It is worth noting that our Christmas carols tell us this in every possible key. If only our Christmas preaching would bestir itself no less distinctly to say the same ! Since the enslaved man who was can be no longer, all that is needed is that he should now be the man he is. It is just as though a newly tailored and ornamented garment were ready and we had only to put it on, with no possibility of delay since the old one has already gone to the ragman and is no longer available. This new being of man, which is the only one to be considered now that the old is removed, has of course different aspects, though it is one and the same in all of them. We shall now attempt to describe it from various standpoints.

Man is now free to set out from or continually to begin with the fact that his relation to God, his fellows and himself is ordered, and indeed ordered for the best, to the extent that in all these interconnexions he can now live only by the justifying and sanctifying grace of God, but may actually and unhesitatingly do so ; that he can now live only by the remission of sins, but may do so quite unconditionally ; that he can now live only in daily conversion, but may do so quite unafraid. He is free to let himself go, and not to try to take himself into his own hands again. He is free no longer to be the servant he was, and to be what he was not and could not be, namely, a child which has life before it. He is free to be himself in the hand of God, in Jesus Christ. He is this as He is already in the hand of God, in Jesus Christ. In speaking of this order, therefore, the Word of grace does not tell him that the humility possible in this order is pious and good and beautiful, that it is best for his own inner peace and for peace with his fellows and the world, and that with the help of God he should thus resolve upon such humility, thus converting himself, and living as another man in virtue of this self-conversion, as though as he were not already humbled and ordered and set at peace in the most salutary way. No, the conversion which it ascribes to him consists rather in the exercise of the freedom which he does not need to assume or give to himself because this is not necessary, since it has been already given in what God has long since done for the world and for his own salutary humbling and therefore for his peace and that of the whole world. The Word of grace simply tells him that the table is spread for him and for all, but that a few places—his own included—are still vacant, and would he be so good as to sit down and fall to, instead of standing about and cleverly or foolishly prattling. Everything else will then be discovered, or is really discovered already. With this positive disclosure the Word of grace speaks as it were from advance into man's present.

A further point is that, in connexion with the order in which he is now free to be salutarily humbled, man is also free supremely to rejoice. He is also free to become finally serious and thankful, to obey, to think and speak and act responsibly, to believe and love and hope, to serve God and man. But above all, in a way which is basic, decisive and normative for everything else, he is free to rejoice. In clear and sharp distinction from the past which now passes, the future of the new man now breaking into his present is a time of rejoicing. It is as such that it is announced by the Word of grace, the image of the marriage feast being often used in the New Testament for this purpose. Naturally there is no impossible, or only rhetorically possible, demand that those who cannot rejoice on any real grounds should still do so. Naturally it does not merely raise a universal hymn to joy. What it does is rather to speak of the reason why in all circumstances man can go forward, not sadly or indifferently, but merrily. It is itself glad tidings as an indication of this reason, of the sun which smiles on us above. There is no third thing between care and joy, and therefore there can be no tarrying between them. If on the same ground, i.e., the proclamation of the reconciliation and lordship of God, care is expelled, the only positive option is joy, not as an empty and abstract cheerfulness, but as thanksgiving and obedience, and therefore as thinking, speech and action, as faith, love and hope, as responsibility and service, which correspond to the concreteness of this reason for joy and which on this basis are to be undertaken and executed with gaiety. Their deep seriousness will consist and be demonstrated in the fact that they are done in this way. And the test or standard by which we may know that man's joy as that of the new man really rests on this basis will be whether or not this joy radiates itself with the same self-evident necessity as it is his joy, whether or not it extends to others as to himself, whether or not in their case, too, it demonstrates itself at once in cheerful thoughts and words and actions. We may also put it like this. As the Word of grace is Gospel, having outmoded care and locked the door against it, it opens up the only remaining path to the future of an evangelical life. But this means a life which is nourished by the glad tidings, or rather by their theme and content. It means a life which also attests the glad tidings and their theme and content. It thus means a cheerful life in this twofold sense. It means the life of the new man already here in the present and standing at the door and knocking that it should be opened, yes truly opened, to him.

A further point is that man is now free to range himself with others, to live in contact, solidarity and fellowship not only with God but also with the world reconciled to Him, and therefore with his fellows not merely as fellows but as companions in the partnership of reconciliation, as brothers and sisters in the fulfilled covenant of God. He is now free for unqualified participation in the cause of God and therefore in the cause of the world and men. He is free. Hence there is no question of an imposed duty, of the observance of a compulsory law which must be kept but with at least the mental reservation that in some depth of his existence he can still be a camp-follower and therefore a spectator of the good Lord and other men and finally himself. No one wills that he should now participate. No one forces him to do so. He simply does. God has reconciled and bound the world to Himself, and him with the world, but only in and with the world. This means, however, that, in the determination thus given to the world, its existence and that of men concern him no less directly than the existence, will and action of God. No less directly! He cannot then be alone under a glass-case or behind asbestos sheeting. No, God has him now, and so, too, the world and men. For he has God, the world and men, and therefore he cannot be alone but only in contact, solidarity and fellowship both vertically and horizontally. He can now be a lord only as in his own place and manner he is a servant. This is his future as a new man as now disclosed—and not just proposed or prophesied to him by the Word of grace. This is the given and only future intimated to him. For the fact that this future is given him as his only future is the work of grace itself addressed to him, his justification and sanctification as attested by the prophetic Word of Jesus Christ.

In face of this positive side of the declaration it is quite natural to wonder whether after all this is not an illusionary idea, theory or programme, since what is here said to man is far more radical than any plans for his future development with which it might be compared. Indeed, the message of the coming of the new aeon and man is if possible even more strange than that of the passing of the old. In what conceivable form of self-understanding can man think of himself as one who is really the old man no longer but this new man with the child in the cradle of Bethlehem? In face of this declaration concerning his free future, is he not constrained to laugh as did once the aged Sarah when it was told her that she should bear a son? Or, if he takes the announcement seriously, has he any option but to understand it eschatologically as the description of his pure, supra-temporal, transcendent future to which he can only look forward with longing, thus agreeing in practice that it has not yet arrived and that the positive (and therefore the negative) declaration of the Word of grace has no validity for us here and now? But we cannot dispose of this declaration so easily. Whether we laugh or sigh, the Word of grace does not say that man will be this new man, but that he already is. It speaks of his eternal future, but with the eschatological perspective of the Bible, and therefore with no restrictive " only," it speaks also of the present irruption of this future, of the advent of the new man here and now, of his peaceful and merry life in fellowship within the present, as it also speaks of the present passing of the old man. Whether the one seems to be more strange to our ears than the other or *vice versa*, or whether both are equally strange, what we have here is a royal Word which as such we cannot shake or twist. It is not a word of religious, ecclesiastical or theological teaching. It is not a word of man at all. If it were, we would have to admit that it could express and formulate no more than an idea, and a highly illusionary one as the veriest child could see. It has validity, however, even in all its strangeness, because it is the Word of God spoken in Jesus Christ—a Word which speaks of the end of the old man in the power of His cross and the coming of the new in the power of His resurrection: " Because I live, ye shall live also " (Jn. 14^{19}). For this reason, it is distinct from all illusions. All the realisms supposedly asserted against it are themselves shown to be illusions on this basis. And we have only to realise and accept for a moment that it is uttered on this basis to see what an attack is mounted by it. There is no more sharp and incisive attack than this.

§ 69. The Glory of the Mediator

We might imagine the conversation to which it gives rise and some of the forms which it necessarily takes.

The man to whom it is said thinks and says that he is not this new, peaceful, joyful man living in fellowship. He asks leave honestly to admit that he does not know this man, or at least himself as this man.

The Word of grace replies : " All honour to your honesty, but my truth transcends it. Allow yourself, therefore, to be told in all truth and on the most solid grounds what you do not know, namely, that you are this man in spite of what you think."

Man : " You think that I can and should become this man in the course of time ? But I do not have sufficient confidence in myself to believe this. Knowing myself, I shall never become this man."

The Word of grace : " You do well not to have confidence in yourself. But the point is not that you can and should become this man. What I am telling you is that, as I know you, you already are."

Man : " I understand that you mean this eschatologically. You are referring to the man I perhaps will be one day in some not very clearly known transfiguration in a distant eternity. If only I had attained to this ! And if only I could be certain that even then I should be this new man ! "

The Word of grace : " You need to understand both yourself and me better than you do. I am not inviting you to speculate about your being in eternity, but to receive and ponder the news that here and now you begin to be the new man, and are already that which you will be eternally."

Man : " How can I accept this news ? On what guarantee can I make bold to take it seriously ? "

The Word of grace : " I, Jesus Christ, am the One who speaks to you. You are what you are in Me, as I will to be in you. Hold fast to Me. I am your guarantee. My boldness is yours. With this boldness dare to be what you are."

Man : " I certainly hear the message, but . . ." In this perplexed and startled " but " we see the attack, and who it is that is attacked.

For in all its forms, and in every nook and cranny, what is attacked is a something in man in which he thinks he knows about himself and the possibilities of his own future, and thus resists any other information concerning himself through the indication and disclosure of his real future. It may be supposed that, quite irrespective of the determinations of this real future, this something will necessarily offer radical resistance to anything of this nature. For under its domination man thinks that he can and should live in and by the realisation of what he regards as his possibilities. The new man as whom he is addressed by the Word of grace is not one of these possibilities and cannot be realised by him. Yet quite apart from all his possibilities, and in contradiction of his self-understanding, this new man is shown to him as his own truest reality. The something in man which compels him radically to reject this is attacked by the work of grace before it is aware of the fact. In self-preservation it has to defend itself. It is obvious from the very first that it has nothing original, no other reality, to oppose to it. The law of its action is dictated by the attacker and not *vice versa*. It can only be and declare the No to the Yes spoken by the Word of grace. However ferocious its air, the glory and advantage in the battle can never be on its side.

3. *Jesus is Victor*   251

For better or worse, we must now speak of that which is attacked and of its self-defence. It is painful to have to do this, but the time has now come to do so.

All things considered, we do well to speak only of " something in man " which is attacked and forced on to the defensive. It is undoubtedly man himself who is addressed by the grace of God and the Word of grace, who feels that he is affected by this attack, who in face of it conceives the corresponding thoughts, utters the corresponding words and makes the corresponding movements, who is the den in which there lurks the No to the Yes of God spoken in Jesus Christ, in which this No realises what it is when the light of God's Yes streams in, and from which it emerges to give battle in the armour and with the weapons of human emotion, argument, volition and action. It is man who is responsible and guilty and in mortal peril at this point. We shall have to consider more fully how he defends himself and what this implies for him. For the moment, however, our concern is with the prophetic office and work of Jesus Christ as such, and therefore with its historical relationship to the opposition and contradiction offered to it. There is no doubt that man is the representative and champion of this resistance since he finds a place for it. But it would be too simple to identify him with it and thus to say what Scripture does not say, namely, that he is this opposition and contradiction, that he is sin and falsehood. He opposes, contradicts, sins and lies. With serious enough consequences, he thus makes himself the battleground on which darkness resists with all its force the light by which it is attacked. He is dark and in darkness, and darkness is in him. He loves darkness more than light (Jn. 3^{19}). This is bad enough. But he is not darkness. The Word of God speaks of the grace directed to him. But God has no grace at all for darkness. He has not reconciled darkness to Himself, not made any covenant with it. He attacks it in His Word, not to spare and preserve, but to destroy. He does not attack man. He attacks the darkness which envelops and indwells him for man's sake, for his good, for his salvation. Man is his creature to whom He has sworn faith and with whom He keeps faith in the attack against darkness mounted in His Word. The world is the world which is really loved by Him in the giving of His Son.

Thus it is something in man which is unmistakeably and unequivocally attacked by the Word of grace, by Jesus Christ in His office and work as a Prophet, and which must defend itself accordingly. This resistance is necessary because it cannot bear what is here said about the passing of the old man and the coming of the new. Especially it cannot tolerate without opposition the urgent " now " of this message. It would be all up with it if the man around and in whom it has its being were to hear and accept and ponder this. It can only stop its own ears and those of man to this Word and sound. It cannot silence and therefore it must try to drown it. This is what it attempts. The assailant is thus faced by a defender, and the history of the prophecy of Jesus Christ becomes a true history of conflict.

How are we to define and describe this something in man which is attacked, and therefore the darkness which defends itself against light? Since its being is supremely non-being, we cannot do it the undeserved honour of a positive definition. Yet we must bring out the fact that its being does not exist as non-being, and that it is related as darkness to light.

It is obvious enough that the nature and therefore the power and action of this opposing something in man can be understood only in its diametrical opposition to the Word of God spoken to man and therefore only as its negative reflection. It is in confrontation by it that it has its place, in its negation that it has its basis, in relation to it, attacked, illumined, shaken and assailed by it that it appears, in conflict with it that it is what it is in the way it is. But we have defined and described the Word of God spoken in Jesus Christ as the Word of grace, in which grace expresses, attests and proclaims itself, in which God has loved the world and taken it to Himself and radically altered its situation, by causing the old aeon and man to pass in Jesus Christ and a new to come. If this is correct, it is also correct to describe that which resists in man, opposing the Word of God by which it is challenged, as that which resists the grace attested by this Word. It is that which will not have the free kindness of the free God, and therefore God Himself, and therefore the man who lives by His free kindness. It has no use for a liberation of man which is wholly and utterly the work of God, nor for a freedom which he owes wholly and utterly to God, and in which he has to live in fellowship with His freedom and can thus be free only in obedience to Him. It resists the cycle in which there can only be the giving of God on the one side and on the other the receiving and therefore the thankfulness of man. It hates this Giver, this giving, and this being given. It hates grace and gratitude. Or, in approximation to such positive terms as are possible, it desires a different reality of the world and man from that which exists in this cycle of giving and receiving. It wants a God or fate or Supreme Being which does not stoop to the being of man but is self-sufficient; and it wants this God as a supreme symbol for the self-resting and self-moved sovereignty, autarchy and self-sufficiency of human being. It rejoices in the independence of this being and therefore in an aseity of God which confirms this, projecting it as it were into infinity. It wants an unloved world, loving only itself and therefore loved only by itself, neither sharing nor needing the love of another. For this it needs a loveless God, neither willing nor able to love another. It is the mortal enemy of grace in the pride which is perhaps its most positive feature

3. *Jesus is Victor*

—the pride of a freedom which is not given but usurped. It has the splendour and power of this pride. It commends, develops and expresses itself as this pride. It is the darkness which is discovered and characterised as such by light, the opposing element in man which is attacked and challenged by the Word of grace and asserts and defends itself against it. Controlled, determined and possessed by this element, in its service and hire, as its representative and champion, it is man himself who does this by finding a place for it as it finds its own place in him. We thus deal with this element as we find it in man as such. However distasteful the theme, we must now try to consider some of the basic forms of the attitudes in which it tries to resist the Word of grace. It belongs to the nature of the case that we shall have to speak for the most part in mythological terms. For apart from all else, in this resisting element in man we are dealing with the ontic presupposition of all mythological thought and utterance.

Its first and crudest, yet in its own way not inconsiderable, attempt is to resist and silence the Word of grace by a kind of factual demonstration, by its own silent but tenacious clinging to existence, by its ignoring of this Word and what it says. The opposing element in man is assailed. The light of grace has shone into its den. It is exposed and wounded in its pride. Its dominion in man and the world is challenged. It must see that the situation has altered to its own detriment. It is forced to do something about this, to react and intervene. If it is not to yield, as it certainly will not, it must come out of its den and take action. And the simplest and most obvious thing to do consists simply in acting as if it had not heard the Word, as if it had not been spoken, as if that which it says has happened had not happened. In other words, it sets one fact against another: against the fact of accomplished reconciliation, of the fulfilled covenant, the fact of indifference to what this Word proclaims, to the divine Giver and His divine giving and gift; against the fact of grace the fact of the calm but all the more effective continuation of pride; against the fact of man's liberation from his old being for a new the fact that he can obviously continue to exist in his old and usurped freedom and make no use of the new freedom which he is given; against the fact of the drowning of the old Adam the fact that the rogue is an expert swimmer; against the fact of the new birth of man in the mystery of Christmas the fact that the old game of self-reconciliation and anxiety and indifference still goes on, so that the news of the irruption of the new aeon with its peace and joy and fellowship is easily given the lie by this very continuation; against the fact of the Bible, as we might say, the fact of the liberal newspaper; against the fact of the " now " the fact of a " not for a long time yet." What cause is there for alarm? The disruptive truth of the new and true reality will soon be blunted by the fact that the old familiar and supposed reality is still maintained and demonstrated against it. This will prove more lasting than the newcomer and finally win the day as though the latter had never been. It has only to display itself publicly like a rhinoceros in the sun and everyone will see that it is just as real as it always was. This, then, is the first reaction of the opposing element in man under attack. It does not consist in any special action, but is all the more illuminating for this reason. It is simply left to the facts of the case to show that there is no reason for panic. The wild beast does not even need to switch its tail to remove the threatened danger. It has simply to act as if the danger were not there. It has simply to continue in error, in stupidity, in wickedness, without love, according to the course of the world, as it always did and will. However crude this may be, and just because it is so crude, we are forced to ask rather anxiously whether the attack of the prophecy of Jesus Christ as the attack of light on darkness will not be arrested already by this first form of opposition, so that even at best only an unending war of position may be expected.

It is worth noting, however, that the element of resistance in man is not content with this. Does it know that it cannot survive in this way, that its supposed factual demonstration will prove to be mere appearance and illusion, that it cannot in this way resist the Word of grace as the Word of God? However that may be, it certainly adopts another and more aggressive attitude as well as that of mute reaction. In its own way it, too, can think and speak and act. It can produce its own little prophecy in opposition to that of Jesus Christ. It can try to undercut this. It realises what is said by it concerning an accomplished reconciliation, a covenant made and fulfilled, a man justified and sanctified by God, the passing of the old man and the coming of a new. It has no thought of capitulating, of adapting itself to this message. It would not be what it is if it were to do this. It cannot be converted. It can only be set aside, dissolved and destroyed by what is said. But it knows too well the greatness and threat of what is said to be content to meet it merely by passive resistance. And so it undertakes to introduce a counter-truth which will be innocuous, which will correspond to its own interests, which will be more obvious and more easy to see and grasp than that attested in the Word of grace, which will not have the sharp edges of this truth, which can be combined with its pride because with the certainty that there need be no revolution, that nothing old need pass nor new come, that the *status quo* may be maintained, a being in smooth transition from an indefinite past to a similar future. The opposing element in man grasps at the possibility of a world-view. We need not go into details. There are many different world-views, magical, naturalistic, idealistic, sceptical, historico-political, aesthetic and moral. There are also religious world-views, and at decisive points all the others contain open or concealed religious elements. Common to all of them in their relation to the prophecy of Jesus Christ are the following basic characteristics.

In all of them, as the term itself implies, man grasps (1) at the possibility of viewing, of making images of things and finally of the totality, from a certain distance. When the Word of grace is spoken and causes itself to be heard, it immediately removes this distance and thus leaves no place for man and his contemplation of images. It takes, in fact, the form of a forceful prohibition of images. To view the world is the glorious possibility of resisting this command and its urgency. Within this sphere the Word of grace itself becomes like everything else an object of contemplation, a detailed picture (perhaps called Christianity or the Church or theology) which, so far as such a picture can, may also speak at a suitable distance and among and alongside many others, but only in the context of a total picture whose author, in creating it, has taken good care that it will say nothing to affect him too closely.

In world-views (2), as the word again implies, it is the world which is viewed, the great totality of an *intelligere* and *intelligi* more or less closed both in detail and in its nexus, of nature and history, of the multiplicity and unity of their phenomena, of the laws perceptible in them and the direction and meaning of their discernible processes. Even in world-views man will obviously take a central place, and under some name or other God can also be given an important position. The Word of grace speaks of an activity of God in the world, and in so doing it speaks also of man in his relationship to this activity, which also entails in some fashion his relationship to his fellows and himself. A world-view is the glorious possibility of escaping the oppressive atmosphere of this triangle of God, fellow-man and oneself, of the ultimate decision which is here proclaimed with unbearable tension to have been already taken and thus to be in process of fulfilment. The more the world is viewed in a world-view, the more there dominates the temperate climate of a panorama in which there is much to see and study and consider and take seriously and compare and co-ordinate instead of just the one thing— what poverty, limitation and one-sidedness !—which takes place with its exclusive claim in that triangle.

In world-views (3) it is a matter of the supposed reality of general states and relationships and consequences, of the truth of finitely perceptible sequences and their infinite extension both backwards and forwards, of the truth of that which is always and everywhere the same and thus recurrent. The Word of grace speaks of a unique and highly particular event, of its bearing on all things and everything, of the negative and positive sign which with its occurrence and revelation and perception is set before all general truths and also as a concluding sign behind them. A world-view is the glorious possibility of relativising this like all other particular events and revelations and perceptions, of blunting the edge of its claim to absoluteness, by putting it in the series to which it belongs. Will not every proper world-view know the concept of the contingent, the individual, the concrete, the singular and unique, and find a place for it in its seeing and understanding? In this sense this particular event may thus be honoured in it. But every world-view will insist that it is unique only in its own way, and it will thus co-ordinate it with and interpret it by a corresponding and ultimately a comprehensive generality instead of adopting the crude and arrogant process—which no world-view would ever do—of setting the generality in the light of this particular event. In world-views it is the principle which counts and not any one thing, even though it were the most important.

World-views are (4) doctrines which the man who views the world from a particular standpoint deduces from the many things which he has seen or thinks he has seen. Usually it will be a doctrine which includes some kind of practical ethics and perhaps politics, but it will be one that can be set against others, that can be compared with them, that can be debated academically with those who represent others, that can even be passionately defended or advanced against them. The Word of grace is not a doctrine of this kind. It is a declaration and a summons: the declaration of a decision already taken, and the summons to orientation by this, since only obedience or disobedience is possible in relation to it. It is a message according to which something has happened and a corresponding happening is thus claimed from those who hear it. A world-view is the glorious possibility of learning from this as from so many other messages, and from phenomena generally, from a particular standpoint, i.e., of comfortably criticising, modifying and finally formulating them to produce a doctrine which can be related to others and more or less cautiously adopted and expounded and marketed quite irrespective of what would necessarily happen if it were heard and accepted as a genuine message. A world-view is the art of avoiding the latter. It is the cheerful and consoling possibility of being content with talk, and basically with endless talk.

World-views are (5) the attempt of man to come to terms with himself concerning himself. He thinks this necessary. He also thinks it possible. But how can he do it without viewing himself in the world and therefore without viewing the world, his world, the world from his standpoint? He thus goes to work in his threefold capacity as observer, constructor and manager, bringing to bear his eyes, his capacity for apperception, his freedom of choice and will, his needs and aspirations, the particular conditions and tendencies of his age, his agreement or disagreement with the spirit of the time, his primitive instruments or his more or less developed and assured scholarship, his originality and loneliness or his association with others in the stream of a movement or orientation or perhaps even as the tool of a collective, but always he himself in sovereign mastery. The Word of grace has the dangerous force of an offence which strikes man from without and from a superior height, and in virtue of which he must only try to understand himself, and can only understand himself, as he is understood. Revealing to him this understanding, it sets him at the summit of the pass between what he was and what he will be, leaving him no possibility of retreat but only of advance. It does not say No to him, but Yes, and indeed the most radical, warm and unconditional Yes that could ever be conceived. Hence it does not forbid him to say Yes to himself in his own place and time and manner. It allows him, however, to say to himself only the Yes which is an answer to the Yes said to him. This is its dangerous force. This is why it is an offence to him. A world-view is the glorious possibility of evading this offence, of fleeing from it. So long as man, viewing the world, is observer, constructor and manager, he is safe, or at any rate thinks he is safe, from this offence.

This, then, is the second strategem which the resisting element in man employs as though the first, the passive resistance of factual demonstration, were not quite enough. He sets against the truth the counter-truth, the little prophecy, of world-views. It is obvious that this does not violate but reaffirms the pride which is the essence of this element. It is obvious that in its undercutting of the prophecy of Jesus Christ something may be accomplished. When is there not a powerful temptation to slide off from evangelical into philosophical thought and speech and attitude? The essence of this possibility, in which all the aforesaid characteristics combine and which is identical even with their external marks, is that no world-views can find any place for Jesus Christ. Of course, they can find room for an abstract God and an abstract man, but not for Him, the God-man. Of course, they can find room for a supposed historical Jesus distilled out of the witness of the New Testament, or for a Christ-idea attained by a similar process of abstraction, but not for the living Lord, for the High-priest, the King and especially the Prophet Jesus Christ. This Jesus Christ is of no value for the purposes of a world-view. He would not be who He is if He were. And so He is absent among the detailed images and in the total picture of all world-views. This, then, is a not insignificant reason why it is always tempting to listen to the little prophecy of the various world-views. They offer plenty of pictures, panoramas, generalities, doctrines, human attempts at self-understanding. But His voice—and this is the decisive reason why we so easily resort to them—is not heard in any of them. This is why man is so urgently and almost compellingly invited by the resisting element within him to seize this possibility. And again we might anxiously ask what will become of the Word of grace when this offer is so tempting. Can it really maintain itself against this defensive manoeuvre on the part of its opponent?

Is there worse to come? Yes, one thing at least is much worse. The resisting element in man may realise that all its attempts at rivalry and competition are inadequate and futile. It may thus pretend to abandon its opposition. It may formally accept the Word of grace, though only in its own way and with a view to rendering it finally innocuous. As we shall have to show in a special section, it may become religious. Nor do we mean only religious in a pagan or humanistic sense, but in a Christian sense, in the sense of the Church. It may come to life and vigour particularly in Christians. It may seduce them into building up and setting forward the work of the church of Antichrist. It may establish Christian communities and establish Christian worship and preaching and theology in a work which looks as though it is supremely concerned with grace and its Word. There may be much zeal, and great loyalty in big things and small, and genuine subjective sincerity on the part of the Christians engaged in the service of this resisting element. There may be serious and attentive reference to the Bible. The kingdom of God as coming and already come, the forgiveness of sins, conversion, the new life, the expectation of eternity, the viewing of time in the light of eternity, the Gospel as a message to the world— all these may be declared and represented and emphasised and honoured in preaching and instruction and pastoral care, in dogmatics and ethics and other praiseworthy forms. And the name of Jesus Christ may not be entirely suppressed, but introduced as at least a third or fourth word which has always to be heard. What is really lacking in such a case? It seems as though nothing is lacking. We may sigh when we come across the slight variations in ecclesiastical and theological movements, but we can console ourselves with the thought that all our different words ultimately mean the same thing and basically we are brethren. And, naturally, there is no lack of reference to the resisting element in man. With no attempt at demythologisation, some at least will mention and characterise the devil and his minions by name, asserting and branding their work both at home and more particularly abroad, but always discerning again that the bow of reconciliation, of the victory of Christ and therefore of hope arches peacefully over the whole. No, it seems as though nothing is lacking. The only thing is, perhaps, that for sharper ears, and ultimately and basically though perhaps unconsciously for all ears, all these very right and proper things, all these good words and songs and assurances, for all their seriousness, have a rather empty, tinny or wooden sound, as though we were listening to the lifeless clatter of an idly turning mill-wheel. We do not see anything evil, nor hear anything palpably false. It is just that a grey mist of puffed up mediocrity, of pathetic tedium and of important unimpor-

3. *Jesus is Victor*

tance lies over the whole. It is just that nothing really takes place, nothing really works even inwardly let alone outwardly, whether in the participating Christianity or in the world around. The church is still in the middle of the village. It is still a topic of conversation. It is still treated with great respect. But the silent and sometimes the vocal question cannot be suppressed either without or within : " I know not what it meaneth." What is it that has happened ? It is perhaps that the Word of grace, as proclaimed and championed and presented by Christianity and the Church, has been rendered basically innocuous. It is perhaps that it has been cheapened, so that it is declared cheaply and may be heard and had cheaply. It is perhaps that those who are charged to attest it have quietly given it a structure and character which assimilate it to the Christians and worldlings to whom it is addressed by the careful blunting of its rough edges and the suppression or softening of the strangeness of its declaration, so that it is now trivial and familiar, and the divine Yes has become curiously like the Yes which man is always about to say to himself, and it has become a kind of world-view, facilitating, supporting and even furthering man's evasion and escape from its message in perhaps the most respectable and unchallengeable form. Everything will still sound great and august and holy. But it will no longer be the indicative and imperative which impinge incisively upon the present. It will no longer give offence. It will no longer be engaged in attack. It will wound no one, and therefore it will not really help anyone. It will no longer spread unrest, and therefore no longer give rest. The most cunning of all the strategems which the resisting element in man can use in self-defence against the Word of grace is simply to immunise, to tame and harness. It is politely to take its seat in the pew, cheerfully to don the vestment and mount the pulpit, zealously to make Christian gestures and movements, soberly to produce theology, and in this way, consciously participating in the confession of Jesus Christ, radically to ensure that His prophetic work is halted, that it can do no more injury to itself, let alone to the world. May it not be that this most cunning of all defensive movements is also the most effective ? We speak in the conjunctive. Even this most cunning and effective of all the defensive movements has no guarantee of success. But whenever and wherever the prophetic work of Jesus Christ, the work of grace, is proclaimed and heard by us Christians, us Christian men, it balances always on a razor's edge whether its human proclaimers and hearers really have to do with this Word or only with the imitation whose clever and powerful author is the resisting element immanent and active not only in man generally but also in the Christian. Is there not good cause for serious concern at this point ? Yet how great is the superiority of the Word of God, which allows Paul—and the context seems to indicate that he has in view a particular form of this possibility—to write to the

Christians in Rome (16[20]) : " The God of peace shall bruise Satan under your feet shortly "—not immediately, but shortly (ἐν τάχει).

In what has been said enough honour has surely been paid to the opponent of the prophecy of Jesus Christ. The Word of the grace of God which Jesus Christ declares by revealing Himself as the One in and by whom God's name is hallowed, His kingdom has come, His will is done, man is justified by God and sanctified for Him—this Word is met by a resisting element in man which will not accept at any price the news of what God has done in Jesus Christ to His own glory and for man's salvation. It is this which is attacked in the work of the prophecy of Jesus Christ. It is this which is forced and challenged to defend itself. It is in opposition to this that the history of the prophecy of Jesus Christ becomes the history of a battle waged for man and on his behalf. We have learned to know the stratagems and movements of this resisting element in their distinctive points. The crudest is man's attempt to remain indifferent to the Word of truth spoken to him, to act as though nothing had happened, to bury his head in the sand like the ostrich. A more refined policy is to try to create an apparently water-tight alibi by the creation of world-views. The supreme and most dangerous is to immunise this Word by pretending to be a Christian adherent, confessor and preacher and thus escaping it the more surely. The resisting element in man knows what it wants. And it also thinks it knows what to do or where to lead man in order to attain it.

But have we really paid it enough honour ? Has it become sufficiently clear in this description that the history of the prophecy of Jesus Christ is not that of a sham fight but that of its encounter with a serious enemy, so serious indeed that all things considered its victory at every stage would seem to be unlikely and can be said to be sure only because it is the prophecy of Jesus Christ ? More than this it is surely unreasonable to ask. Yet we can easily deceive ourselves. For what do I read in a book published in 1957 by Gustaf Wingren under the title *Die Methodenfrage der Theologie* (p. 38) ? " In Barth's theology there is no active power of sin and tyrannical power of perdition holding man in bondage and overcome by God in His work of salvation. There is thus no devil. This is a distinctive feature from the very commencement of his work." I make no complaint or protest against this scarifying report, alongside which one might set many others from his new book as from earlier writings. But since I notice that he is particularly concerned about the devil or a devil, I might perhaps take the opportunity to make the following express statement.

What has been defined and described in the present context as the resisting element in man is naturally identical with the being which is not systematically or consistently taught in Holy Scripture, but in the New Testament especially is frequently mentioned as the " devil," the *principium* or *princeps* of darkness, Satan (the adversary), the διάβολος (who throws everything into confusion), the evil or wicked one κατ' ἐξοχήν. The devil certainly exists and is at work. We have to reckon with him. We cannot possibly recount the history of the prophecy of Jesus Christ without thinking of him, for in his self-defence against it, having nothing more to oppose to the completed work of reconciliation, he finds his final sphere of operation. The ancient foe, or however we might describe him, cannot alter the justification and sanctification of man actualised in Jesus Christ. But he still has space to resist the Word of reconciliation, to hinder its understanding, acceptance and appropriation on the part of man. It is to the story of his opposition in this sphere that we now refer.

But if we think and speak of the devil in this context, we must keep clearly before us the passage in Jn. 8[43f.] which to the best of my knowledge is the only one which gives any exact information concerning his nature. In these verses we learn that the " Jews " cannot hear the Word of Jesus because the διάβολος, who throws everything into confusion, is their father, and their will is necessarily to do his lusts (ἐπιθυμίαι). From the very beginning, from his origin, from the very outset (ἀπ' ἀρχῆς) this διάβολος has been a murderer (ἀνθρωποκτόνος), abiding not in the truth, there being no truth in him. Only as he tells lies does he speak of his own (ἐκ τῶν ἰδίων), manifesting his nature. He is nothing but a liar and the father of lies. The passage indicates at once that the devil and his work are indeed relevant to our present context. Those who have him as their " father," who are his children, who are dominated, tempted and led astray by him, cannot and will not hear the Word of Jesus as the Word of truth, but only resist it as did the Jews in this passage. Even more important is the material fact that the one who leads man astray in this fashion, is from the very first and by nature nothing but a liar destitute of all truth and a hater and murderer of men. It is in this way and in this way alone that he exists, not as God, nor as man as God's creature, nor as even the lowliest of God's creatures, but in contradiction to the truth of God and His creatures, in a mode of existence which as such can only be a lie and the source of all lies. He exists only as the epitome of the active power and malignity of that which in and by itself is nothingness, of that in relation to which faith in God can have only the form of the most resolute unbelief. This has to be remembered when we think and speak of the devil. If we do remember it, however, we shall think and speak of him only reluctantly, infrequently and with great reserve. Thinking and speaking about the devil can only result—except when we have a handy ink-pot to throw at him—in our turning our backs on him; and Luther would sometimes have used a much more expressive gesture. Time should not be devoted to considering, contemplating or conceiving of the devil, or to concrete interest in him, for he is not worthy of it. He cannot really be given a proper place or *locus* in theology, just because he has to be reckoned with so seriously. He can be mentioned and taken seriously only in such a way that he who is myth in person is demythologised and delivered up to ridicule. Believing in God and not in him, theology bids him an immediate ὕπαγε. This is how he is treated in the Bible. This is how he is in effect treated in J. C. Blumhardt's struggle with him. This is how theology must handle him. It must not be betrayed into regarding him otherwise than as the hypostatised falsehood which can only stand in a negative relationship both to God and man, and can therefore exist only negatively. For this reason reserve is necessary in thinking and speaking of him—a reserve which will be manifested not least in the fact that neutral expressions like " the resisting element in man " are usually preferred to personal (though these are not debarred) in describing him. What is essential is simply that his power and malignity as the alien force which dominates, seduces and deceives man, but is absolutely subject to God, should be known and revealed in the limits in which, as the light shines in darkness, it may be seen and known in its encounter with Jesus the Victor.

This is how I have tried to treat the devil from the very first. This is how I hope to treat him in the future. And I must simply accept it as best I can if G. Wingren really thinks that he fails to find him at all in my theology. He has many other ideas concerning me at which I can only shake my head in astonishment.

Concerning the prophecy of Jesus Christ a final word has still to be said. This is only provisionally the final word. He Himself will speak the definitively last Word in His concluding return in glory. This Word does not belong any more to His work of reconciliation. It belongs already to His work of redemption. Hence we cannot speak of it except in the sphere of eschatology. What we can say is a provisionally final word—which points to the definitively final—in relation to the history of His prophecy which is our present concern.

§ 69. The Glory of the Mediator

We have spoken of the beginning of this and also of its course as an attack with the resultant opposition. Its issue and end cannot yet be told because it is not yet concluded, the conflict being still in progress. Jesus is Victor already both in the beginning of His prophecy and in its present course right up to the present day. He suffers no defeats. He is never at a halt or in retreat. But He is not yet at the conclusion of this warfare which, so far as He and His action are concerned, is always victorious. He is already known by, because revealed to, those who believe in Him as the Victor who marches to this goal. But He cannot yet be manifested to the world or to them as the One who has completed His prophetic no less than His high-priestly and kingly work, and is thus at the goal. He is not yet at this goal. Light still battles with darkness, with the resisting element in man, with the prince of darkness. Place is still left for him—his final place—in and with the fact that the Word of truth must still be spoken and received in opposition to falsehood. Hence the light is still light shining in darkness. The victory of Jesus the Victor is not yet consummated. This is the limit of our sphere or circle of vision. We shall have to face and answer the problem of this " still " and " not yet " in the fourth and final sub-section of our present section.

But there is now needed a provisionally final word in respect of the certainty with which we may look back on the history of the conflict of light with darkness as so far recounted and with which we may thus take up the problem of its incompleteness. When we had to describe the power of darkness and the work of the resisting element in man, did it perhaps seem as though the cause of the Word of grace and therefore of the prophecy of Jesus Christ were seriously threatened ? Were not the probabilities against its victory ? Did we not see how great are the force and cunning brought against it ? Could we have painted any blacker picture ? Do we really see any way in which the strategems and efforts of the enemy can be frustrated ? Even in our strongest faith in Jesus Christ, are we not helpless in face of supreme indifference, of the constant jugglery of world-views, and finally and above all of the dreadful possibility of mock Christianity, of the church of Antichrist ? But if we are helpless, how can there be any certainty that Jesus not only is the Victor, but will prove Himself to be the victorious Aggressor in face of this apparently triumphant defence ? This is the problem of the incompleteness of the history of His warfare. We have to reckon not only with the triumphant attack of Jesus but also with what seems in its own way to be this equally triumphant defence of the enemy. What certainty can we have that this defence is succumbing and will finally do so ? What certainty can we have that there will be no reverses or halts or retreats on the part of the Aggressor ? What certainty do we have of His final victory ? In relation to the " still " and " not yet " which are our sphere and circle of vision there seems little prospect of the continuing advance and final triumph of Jesus. Of what use are all the positive things which might be recalled and said in relation to this " still " and " not yet " if we can have no certainty from the very outset that Jesus cannot and will not fail to be both the final and the continuous Victor in all circumstances ? The whole meaning of the conflict between light and darkness, but also of our being in the sphere of the incompleteness of this conflict, depends upon the fact that we have certainty concerning it, the prior, basic, direct and unconditional certainty of victory. We must now try to say a word on this.

The decisive and comprehensive answer to the question of this certainty can consist only in a reference to the living Jesus Christ Himself, who as the One He is, if not known by all, is revealed and knowable for all, Christians and non-Christians alike, so that all without exception may be referred to Him with the demand and invitation to know Him. In Him it is manifested and therefore knowable for all that He and not the resisting element in man will finally conquer. As the living One, the Risen from the dead, He is not only Victor at the beginning but will also be at the end. We have said and must say again that He is not yet at this end when His prophetic work will be completed. His prophetic work is thus reconciliation in its transition to consummation in redemption. He cannot yet be revealed and knowable to any as the One who is already at the goal, but He can be revealed and knowable to all as the final Victor, i.e., as the One who as the Finisher of His prophetic work and therefore the Conqueror of the resisting element in man will achieve this goal, and thus finally prove to be the Victor He is. To know Him as the living One, the Risen from the dead, is to receive and have at once, from the very outset, basic, direct and unconditional certainty of the final victory which is still awaited but which comes relentlessly and irresistibly. He cannot be known as the One He is if this certainty does not immediately arise and persist. But if it does arise and persist as certainty of His final triumph, in the same direct and unconditional way it includes the lesser certainty that He cannot experience any reverses, halts or retreats on the way to this goal, but that the *vexilla Regis prodeunt*. Every step on this way, being taken on the way to this goal by the One who will finally have conquered as the Victor He is, means that in the continuous fulfilment of this transition He approaches this goal and therefore the final triumph. It means the constant increase of light in darkness. To know Him as the One who takes His steps along this way of His is thus necessarily to know Him continuously as the One who irreversibly and ineluctably marches forward to this goal. Again He is not known as the One He is if this certainty does not immediately arise and persist, namely, the certainty that He the Victor, who will also be

§ 69. *The Glory of the Mediator*

the final Victor, marches forward to this goal at each moment and therefore at this very moment of His existence and presence.

This decisive and comprehensive answer to the question of certainty must be properly understood if it is to be able to prevail and to be a genuine answer to the question. We shall have to try to develop it later. But it can be rightly understood in every development only if it is first and comprehensively and exclusively understood and taken seriously as a reference to the living Jesus Christ. This reference cannot be exchanged for or replaced by any other conceivable, and within its limits permissible, reference.

Manifestly inadequate is, of course, the reference to an imaginable human goal and the discernible progress of the human race towards such a goal. The eighteenth and nineteenth centuries were very partial to ideas of this kind and the supposed evidences of progress seen by them. Our own century, which has less resemblance to this period than to the Middle Ages, has good reason to view such notions with less favour and even with disfavour. Things may alter again in the years ahead. But the alternation shows that with such ideas and evidences we are only at very best in the field of strong and fluctuating conjectures rather than certainties. Pictures of the race and its history cannot drive away the darkness which obscures its goal and way, or the resisting element in man (which for once let us call the devil), as a power which seems to be equal if not far superior to what is regarded as light. How can such a picture give us any certainty of victory worthy of the name? It is not that there is no such certainty in respect of the goal and way of man. But if this is to be true certainty it can consist only in the certainty which is grounded in the knowledge of the Jesus Christ who intervenes and acts for the race, namely, the certainty of His future victory and of the victory which even in its futurity is already present and effective. There can be no reversal at this point. The victory of Jesus Christ, and therefore the serious victory of Light over darkness, cannot with genuine or tenable certainty be deduced from any victories of the race.

Nor is it of any value in this respect to refer to the goal and way of the Church, of Christianity, of its mission and work in the world, or at least of its inner development. Encouraging and continuous lights may be seen at individual points in this sphere, but no certain picture emerges of what it will finally be as the people and body of Jesus Christ, or of its way to this goal, or of the assured attainment of its future, or of a sure advance towards it even in the best moments of its history, not to speak of the others. In this matter we are far more cautious, especially in relation to the success of missions, than were our predecessors fifty years ago. The outlook may become brighter again than it now is. But no sure ground is given us at this point. It would be mischievous ecclesiastical optimism to try to overlook the work of the resisting element in man even in the sacred

3. *Jesus is Victor*

sphere, or the anti-Christian element which continually obscures the goal and way of the Church even within Christianity itself and the various developments of Church history. There is, of course, an unconditional certainty of victory for the Church too and for its goal and way. But if it is to be genuine, it can be only the certainty which is received in the knowledge of Jesus Christ its Head, namely, the certainty of His victory in which He will finally cause it to participate, and already does so on its way towards it. Again there must be no reversal. There must be no certainty of the cause of Christianity or the Church which even temporarily or partially abstracts from the reference to Jesus Christ and looks to its own past or present.

Inadequate, too, is the reference to the inner certainty of faith in Jesus Christ. In itself, this is a human work, humanly conditioned and limited, like any other. In it man can have only such certainty of his cause—and this is not saying much—as he can have of himself in his other works. The resisting element in man acts and reacts even in those who believe in Jesus Christ. And this means that this faith and its certainty, as all true believers know full well, is a precarious thing only too easily shaken to the very core, so that we cannot refer to it with any direct or unconditional certainty when it is a matter of the triumph of light over darkness. There is, of course, a direct and unconditional certainty of victory for faith and for its goal and way. But it is not at all the inner certainty of faith which is proper to man himself and thus to be confirmed by his self-certainty. It is the certainty which is proper to the origin and subject of faith and therefore again to Jesus Christ. It is the certainty which can be received only from Him and as the certainty of His victory, and which if it is genuine will have to be sought and found continually in Him. Again, there must be no reversal. The certainty of faith as such is not a certainty of victory which endures against assault. Our faith overcomes the world only as and because Jesus Christ does so— the One in whom it believes, who is its basis, theme and content.

These delimitations are necessary, not to discourage us, but to encourage us to keep to the reference which alone is of any real value in this question of certainty. None of the other references, as we have seen, is altogether futile. But none of them can or should be confused with or substituted for the reference to the living Jesus Christ Himself which gives us the only true answer to the question of certainty. None of them indicates the point where our helplessness in face of the machinations of the enemy is overcome. There is a true certainty of victory in respect of the goal and way of humanity, the Church and faith, so long as it is grounded like a rock in the fact that Jesus Christ is the Lord of humanity, the Head of the Church and the basis, theme and content of faith. It is neither humanity, the Church nor faith which radiates, capacitates, awakens and maintains this certainty, however, but the living Jesus Christ Himself.

He and He alone is the Victor who will finally triumph and who is even now relentlessly and incontrovertibly engaged in the transition from reconciliation to redemption, and therefore in triumphing. He is this for the race, the Church and the faith of those who believe in Him; but He and He alone. To know Him is to know the coming and indeed the continuous and unequivocal victory of light over darkness which cannot be arrested by any resisting element in man, by any devil. To know Him is to know this victory with direct and unconditional certainty, with no unsettlement in face of the incompleteness of His warfare as Prophet of the Word of grace and with no doubt in respect of our being in the sphere and circle of vision of the "not yet" and the "still." Unsettlement and doubt can arise only if we try to have regard to other certainties than that of His triumphing.

Whatever may be added to this decisive and comprehensive answer can consist only in developments or confirmations. It might be left as it stands. Its content, the reference to the living Jesus Christ as the source of genuine certainty of victory over the enemy, or rather the living Jesus Christ might be allowed to speak for Himself. But the point at which we stand is too important to allow even the impression to be given—as Lavater's confession did with Goethe—that we are in the sphere of a kind of magic, and that in this reference we have a mere assertion which cannot be established or explained but is dogmatic in the bad sense. It may be presupposed that our answer is cogent and compelling only when the living Jesus Christ to whom it refers does speak for Himself. It is not only possible, however, but necessary that we should consider what He who establishes certainty of victory says, and what we hear from Him. The certainty to be received from Him is distinguished from others by the fact that it is not blind, ignorant or amorphous, but a seeing, knowing and fashioned certainty which confirms itself and can be explained by those who have it.

Generally speaking, it is an unconditional certainty of victory in the fact that it is clearly based on the unconditional superiority of Jesus Christ to His opponent, to the resisting element in man. In this context to know Him is concretely to know the superiority of His prophetic work to the being and machinations of the defender attacked by Him. It is to know the superiority of His light to the opposing darkness, of His truth to lying, to the liar and to all the liars dominated and deceived by him. It is in this superiority that He exists, that He is Lord of humanity, Head of the Church and basis, theme and content of faith, that He speaks as the Prophet of the reconciliation accomplished by Him, the covenant fulfilled by Him, the kingdom of God drawn near in His person. If He is known, it is in the superiority proper to Him as the One He is, in His unconditional superiority. And this is the point of reference and foundation of the unconditional certainty of victory to be received from Him in respect of the history of His conflict. This unconditional superiority is proper neither to the race, the Church nor faith. Hence none of these can spread or mediate unconditional certainty of victory. But it is proper to the living Jesus Christ. Hence this certainty may really be received from Him, and from Him alone. This general truth must now be elucidated along three specific lines.

The superiority of the living Jesus Christ which gives the certainty of the victory of His prophetic work consists first and quite simply (1) in the fact that He is the Word of God. He does not merely speak or attest or proclaim this Word, as is done also by faith, the Church and in a wider and indirect sense the history of the race and even the existence of the whole creation of God. He is this Word. It is as this Word that Jesus Christ in His prophecy takes the offensive and is resisted. This is the situation. And this is His superiority in it. To know Him is to know God, the Creator and Lord of heaven and earth, the One who is incomparably free and loving. It is to know Him as the God who speaks to us men, who enters into dealings with us, who establishes and maintains fellowship between Himself and us. It is to know His nature and existence, His power and mercy, His will which is done and His lordship which is established among us. It is to know all this in His action in the Word which is addressed to us, which comes to us, which does not leave us alone, which claims our hearing and obedience and therefore ourselves. God in person enters the battlefield in the living Jesus Christ and His prophetic work. It is not any light which shines in darkness, but the eternal light. It is not any truth which confronts the liar and his lies, but His truth.

This is what gives Jesus Christ absolute pre-eminence in relation to the whole race as such, to the Church in all its members and works, and to even the most profound and serious Christian faith. As these are all in their own ways the creatures of God, they all have to do with God, and above all God has very much to do with them. But neither the race, the Church nor faith is the Word of God. Jesus Christ is. This gives Him immediate superiority. It is for this reason that the reference to Him cannot and must not be confused with nor replaced by the reference to the race, the Church or faith.

But as the Word of God He has even more imposing superiority in relation to the enmity which He encounters and therefore the resisting element in man which has nothing whatever to do with God nor God with it, which is not in any sense the creature or work of God but only a devastating interposition between Him and the world, which can be addressed only as nothingness.

We shall illustrate by referring to the last and worst of its machinations, namely, the construction, maintenance and prosecution of a sham church in which it may have dealings with man and be active even in the Christian as the adversary and opponent of the grace of God. We can hardly exaggerate the serious nature of this threat. But no matter how great, when it is measured by the Word of God spoken in Jesus Christ, it obviously lacks all greatness, all power and significance of ultimate or even provisional account. Are not all lies, and therefore even the worst, the Christian lie, unsubstantial, and will not this emerge sooner or later, and basically at once, when they are confronted by the truth of God which they can neither imitate nor disarm ? But the synagogue of Antichrist in all its forms is confronted with this truth when it is attacked by the living Jesus Christ and tries to deploy all its forces against Him. How can it win the day in this battle ? Must we not ask indeed whether the game which it plays with so much power and cunning is not finally more dangerous to itself than the One it attempts to resist ? Can it really do itself any lasting good by trying to use that which is Christian as its mask and instrument ? May not this most powerful machination recoil upon itself ? The Christian things behind which it hides, and which it tries to turn against Jesus Christ, can still maintain in hidden form something of their own distinctiveness as they are misused by it, and suddenly revolt against their misuse, escaping from the Babylonian captivity in which they are held and maintaining their freedom against the power and cunning of the tyrant. Within the anti-Christian church as well as against it, the living Jesus Christ Himself can suddenly emerge in all the superiority of the Word even from the Bible which it has suppressed and falsified, even from its corrupt traditions and liturgy and practice, even from all its secret or blatant perversions (e.g., from the text of even the most dreadful preaching), and greatest honour can thus accrue to Him where the greatest dishonour is done. More than once things have happened in Church history in such a way that, against all the clever intentions of the enemy in the attempted prosecution of his cause under Christian cover, the voice of Jesus Christ and therefore the Word of God have quite unexpectedly rung out, and there have necessarily been strange resurrections and revivals of the true Church in the midst of the false. If we are properly to consider the superiority of Jesus Christ as the Word of God, have we not to reckon with the fact that this may happen at any moment even when the assault of Antichrist seems to be at its most serious either on a larger scale or a smaller ?

There can be no doubt that the relation between the Assailant who is the true Word of God Himself and the defender who is simply the liar is so unequal that those who know the former can have nothing less than the most complete certainty of victory even in respect of the as yet unconcluded conflict of light with darkness. If they know anything at all, they know that a single saying of this Word can and will fell the one who opposes it, the axe being already laid to the root of this tree.

The superiority of the living Jesus Christ which radiates and mediates certainty of victory consists (2) in the fact that He is the Word of the act of God. He is not the mere expression, or reflection, or manifestation of an idea of Godhead, but the eloquent work in which the transcendent God, to take the world and man to Himself, to make common cause with His creation, has Himself come into the world as a human, creaturely, historical factor, and as such has dealt and still deals towards us and with us in grace. To know Him is to know Him as the claim of this act of God which has taken place in Him. And as this claim of the act of God which has taken place

3. *Jesus is Victor*

in Him, He stands in conflict with the resisting element in man. The latter tries to withstand and evade this claim, the light of this life, the truth of this reality. This is the situation. It points to the superiority of Jesus Christ from a new angle.

A first point which is clear is His precedence on this side, too, over humanity, the Church and even the most vital faith in Him. These can, of course, acquire and have a share in the expression of the act, the reconciling act, of God. They may be summoned to attest it, but only because its expression has first taken place, and still takes place, authentically and originally in Jesus Christ Himself. It is not they which do what is certainly expressed through their ministry. They cannot, then, give any direct or reliable information of their own concerning it. To the extent that they are entrusted and commissioned with the task of witnessing to it, their witness even at best can be only secondary, indirect and apparently very broken. We are still referred to the self-witness of the One who has done that to which they bear testimony. In itself and as such, therefore, their witness can mediate no certainty of victory. Jesus Christ can and does as He expresses the divine act of reconciliation accomplished in Himself.

But even more clear on this side, too, is His superiority to the contradiction and resistance which He meets. For what stands behind the resisting element in man in virtue of which it tries to compete with Him as the Word of the act of God? It certainly exists as a kind of expression. But it does not express any act in the true sense, not even a creaturely act which would give to what it expresses at least the power of creaturely life and creaturely reality. From the great vacuum of falsehood it has nothing to declare. It is a hollow, empty word. And it is trying not merely to rival the word of a creature but to compete with the Word of God, to oppose the prophecy of God Himself. Again, the act of God accomplished and expressed in Jesus Christ is the justification and sanctification of man. It is thus the act in which man, whether he realises it or not, is objectively alienated, separated and torn away from this resisting element in him, because he is already set in the liberty of the children of God. It is the act in which the right of domicile and lordship in man is once and for all taken from this element, so that the ground is objectively cut from beneath its feet. It is the Word of this act of God which it ventures to contradict and withstand. What can and will become of it in this conflict and collision? What has Jesus Christ really to fear from this adversary as the Word of this act of God?

We may illustrate this aspect of the situation by considering its attempt to construct world-views, i.e., its attempt to make it easy and desirable for man to withstand the Word of grace, to evade the decision which it requires, to relativise it in its particularity, to conceal its practical claim under harmless theory, and to understand and reconcile himself, by the offering of all kinds of pictures,

§ 69. *The Glory of the Mediator*

panoramas, general truths, doctrines and human self-interpretations. This is a vast and influential undertaking, yet one which for all its splendour is from the very first foredoomed to failure in relation to what is to be attained by means of it and in relation to the One who is to be warded off and arrested by it. In distinction from the Word of the grace of God, world-views are only ideas and ideologies which must make themselves as impressive as they can. They are only analyses, insights, explanations and interpretations of the reality of man, the world and even God, which may perhaps be attempted and carried through with great perspicacity and profundity from particular standpoints. But they are not expressions or authentic self-declarations of this reality. They are not words which have directly the power of the truth of this reality. Even at best they are only thoughts and words concerning it which are relatively and partially apposite. In particular, they are not words or expressions of the reality of divine action. They are not self-documentations of the life created and maintained by God. They are not words or expressions of the act of love and grace and reconciliation. They are not self-revelations of the divinely established peace between God and the world, of the glory of God and the salvation of man in the covenant instituted and fulfilled between them. Is not the deception attempted by the adversary in this enterprise apparent at once when we realise that he ventures it in this conflict and in face of this Assailant? What has he to set against the living Jesus Christ? However glistening the soap-bubbles which he blows up in the attempt to deceive man concerning himself, what can he accomplish against Him? When we consider against whom he is contending, how can we be seriously alarmed at his efforts even in relation to the present state of the conflict, let alone its final outcome?

There can be no doubt that where we have on the one side the Word of the act of God, of this act of reconciliation (and the living Jesus Christ is this Word in His prophecy), and on the other empty word of falsehood (and this is the weapon and power of the resisting element in man), the relation between Aggressor and defender in this conflict is so unequal that in relation to it there can and must be the fullest certainty of victory, and it would be sheer folly not to find a place for it. From this standpoint, too, we may confidently and very definitely affirm that one little word will fell the adversary.

For an appreciation of the superiority of the living Jesus Christ which awakens this certainty, we must look in yet another direction. His superiority consists (3) in the fact that His prophecy as the Word of God revealing the act of God appeals directly to the real man. It appeals directly. That is to say, it overlooks and by-passes, as it were, the resisting element in man, the devil. It disregards the fact that man is tempted, deceived, controlled and possessed by the devil. It does not recognise that man has given himself to the service of falsehood. It appeals to the real man, to the man whom it may and can address directly, and irrespective of the resisting element in him, because even as its slave, even under its domination, he has not ceased and cannot cease, in relation to the illusion and deception to which he has fallen victim, properly and essentially to be real man, the man whom God created and whose divinely created nature has not perished even in the alienation in which he now exists, the man who in this reality of his is still the nearest and most direct object of

3. *Jesus is Victor*

the love of his Creator. The reconciliation which in the Word of Jesus Christ is shown to have taken place in Him is, as man's sanctification no less than his justification, not merely the actualisation of the freedom and the establishment of the right and claim of God in face of this real man, but also the gift of the freedom and the establishment of the right and claim of this real man in his relationship to God. Negatively formulated, reconciliation is God's solemn non-recognition of the incident which separates Himself from man and man from Himself. Positively formulated, it is God's solemn recognition of the faithfulness with which He loves man as His creature and confesses the determination of His creature to love Him in return. And the Word of divine reconciliation grounded in the existence and crucifixion of Jesus Christ and uttered by Him as the Resurrected is God's solemn proclamation of this non-recognition of the incident, of this scorn of the devil, of this demonstration of the divine faithfulness in which He does not cease to draw real man, notwithstanding his self-alienation, into the covenant of peace with Himself, and to treat him seriously as a partner in this covenant. This real man is thus directly the one who is intended, addressed and taken seriously in the Word of Jesus Christ as the Word of reconciliation. It is to him that this Word appeals directly quite irrespective of the resisting element in him. It can sound alien only to the alien element in man, to man in his self-alienation. But for all that it is so unexpected, for all that it does not arise from within man but comes from without, from a great height and distance, it reaches and strikes the real man as a call from the Father's house, from the home to which he belongs and which belongs to him, as a summons from his native place, as the gift of his freedom and the ascription of his right and claim to be there and not elsewhere, to be a resident in his own land and not a stranger abroad. The great superiority of the prophetic Word of Jesus Christ is that it is this call to the real man. It is with this superiority that He attacks the resisting element in man and is necessarily opposed by it. This is the situation.

In this respect again we see first the pre-eminence of Jesus Christ in relation to anything which might be said to man by the history of the race, or the Church, or faith. For even though these have voices and can speak, how can what they have to say to man appeal directly to what he really is, and not therefore to the various masks or costumes with which he clothes himself and thinks and maintains that he is identical, but to the real man whom God has created and loved and who is not at all identical with the external appearance in which he exists ? In the history of humanity, even in the history and present activity of the Church, even in faith, even and especially in personal faith, the speaker is always the man who is burdened by the resisting element in him, and he is always speaking to the man whom he cannot perceive or reach except as similarly burdened.

Even if he is given a word, this word of man as such has no power to penetrate the twofold armour of the resisting element in himself and the other and to strike him where he is truly and properly man, namely, man for God, and before God, and therefore in truth. Hence we men and even we Christians usually talk past one another except when a miracle occurs. We do this even when we are talking to ourselves. We cannot, then, derive certainty, the certainty of victory, from any genuine superiority in us. But Jesus Christ in His Word can and does. He is the Neighbour who can and does really speak to the other as Neighbour to neighbour, and therefore in this sense, too, He is superior and radiates certainty. For to radiate certainty there is needed the power to appeal to the real man. He and He alone has this power. Hence in the question of certainty we are warned from this angle, too, that the reference to Him must not be confused with or replaced by any reference to the human race, the Church or faith.

But our present concern is with His superiority to the resisting element in man. This, too, is palpable. We maintain that this element is something in him which possesses and dominates him, which powerfully and cunningly induces him to attempt all those machinations against the Word of grace. But we insist that it is not man himself, the real man. It can and does alienate him from himself, so that he no longer knows himself in his reality but as an only too docile negator of the Word of God. But it cannot destroy him, or as it were consume him, or transform him into a devil. Nor can man himself do this, even though he renders the resisting element in him devoted and zealous service and perhaps makes a compact with the devil in his own blood. The real man, created good by God, loved by Him, and ordained to love Him in return, remains alien to the resisting element in him and is opposed to it even in the worst forms of the slavery in which he has become its victim. However oppressed he may be, however little he may know himself, however much he may have foolishly or deliberately yielded to the alien power, he is still the man he is, awaiting his hour and somewhere straining at his bonds. The Word of grace is for this man. And this man is for the Word of grace. Between these two there is an original and indestructible agreement. And it is in this agreement that there consists from this third standpoint the superiority of the One who speaks this Word in face of the whole world of opposition and contradiction brought against Him. The resisting element in man is a strong power and enjoys very great and fateful successes. But it cannot boast of agreement with the real man nor of his agreement with it. It cannot work in the power of this agreement. Jesus Christ can and does. He works not only in the power of the Word of God which is the Word of His reconciliation, but also—because it is this—in the power of its agreement with the real man and as an appeal to him. It is on this

3. Jesus is Victor

basis that He assails the resisting element in him. It is in this power that He ignores it, treating it with scorn. He will have dealings only with the real man, and He does so in superior power. He speaks on the well-founded presupposition that this real man, even though he is oppressed and does not know himself, is on His side whether he realises it or not, having his natural Covenant-partner in God as God has in him, the creature of God. What can and will become of the resisting element when this is the situation ? What has Jesus Christ to fear from His encounter with it ?

By way of illustration we may again consider the defensive measures adopted by it, or by the man whom it has dominated and deceived. And in this case we turn to the crudest which is also the most massive, namely, that which causes man to set against the call of God the fact that, instead of meeting it with active counter-measures, he simply takes no notice, excusing himself as absent. We have seen that his resistance to the Word can take the form of simple indifference, lack of interest, unconcern, neutrality. Will this form of defence succeed ? Well, there can be no denying that indifference is possible and practicable, because subjectively or objectively more or less well founded, not only to religion in general but also to Christianity both as a whole and in each of its manifestations, as, for example, the public worship of God or theology. Nor need we suppose that this is merely a phenomenon of the last centuries and particularly of our own period. There is also, and always has been, a no less widespread indifference to such things as politics, art and philosophy. Indifference to Christianity, too, is quite possible, although it has its limits and may quite unexpectedly—whether for good or evil—turn into its opposite, as has happened in the last decades in spite of all the conjectures which might have been made in the eighteenth century and the prophecies everywhere noised abroad in the nineteenth. Our present reference, however, is not to indifference to Christianity ; it is to indifference to the Word of God spoken in Jesus Christ. And of this we may say quite definitely that it is a defensive manoeuvre which in spite of every appearance to the contrary can have no prospect of success. For the real man is not uninterested or unconcerned or indifferent or neutral in face of this Word. Jesus Christ appeals to the real man on the self-evident and well-founded assumption that he is not identical with the resisting element in him, that he cannot identify himself with this, that he is really in basic agreement with what He has to say to him, however great his entanglement in opposition and contradiction to it. He may, of course, ignore or refuse to answer it like an unwanted call. He may be won over to this attitude by the resisting element in him. He probably will be, and this applies in no little measure to the Christian too. But the fact that he ignores it does not mean that he is dead to it, nor does his refusal to answer it mean that he is not at the place where it visits him, i.e., not at home and within its reach. Man would have to cease to be what he is if he were to be able to escape the reach of the Word of God and to attain an actual or—let us say for once—an ontic indifference or neutrality to the Word of God, or to allow himself to be forced into this by the resisting element in him. He can do many things, but this is something which he cannot do. As the man he really is, he is on its side. He can only play at indifference falsely, hypocritically and in pretence. He does this. He does it persistently. But the very persistence with which he does it bears witness that he is not so uncommitted as he pretends to be. We must not overlook the advantage which the Word of God spoken in Jesus Christ enjoys against this stratagem of its opponent as well.

In considering this third aspect, too, we may conclude that the conflict in which the living Jesus Christ in His prophecy is still engaged is an unequal one for all that it seems to be and is so serious. The relation between Assailant and defender is such that there can be no doubt as to the issue. As the Word of God spoken in Jesus Christ is not against man but for him, so man for his part, as the one he really is, cannot be radically against the Word spoken to him but only for it. The battle continues, but it bears this aspect. Again it is the case that one little word can fell His adversary. From this angle, too, there is certainty, the perfect certainty of victory, in relation to the issue of the battle and the course which it takes towards this issue.

This, then, is what must be said in development and confirmation of the decisive and comprehensive answer to the question of certainty in relation to the final and continuing victory of Jesus Christ as the Prophet of the Word of grace. There is need that we should expressly recall the content of this decisive and comprehensive answer. It consists in the reference to the living Jesus Christ Himself, to His superiority in the campaign launched and conducted by Him, and therefore to His self-witness which awakens, establishes, creates and maintains certainty, the certainty of victory. He Himself is and gives the guarantee that He will triumph, and is already engaged in triumphing. Even what we have tried to say in development and confirmation of this answer must not be understood as a substitute for the guarantee which is given in and with Jesus Christ Himself, but only as an attempt to explain and concretely to describe it. No exposition of this basic text can replace it. None of the three lines of presentation along which we have explained the superiority of Jesus Christ and the certainty awakened by it can pretend to be this superiority or to give this certainty in itself. We have to consider to what extent Jesus Christ does in His warfare represent and give Himself in a superiority which gives rise to certainty. But we must always expressly presuppose that to do this is His own work and not that of our own explanatory and confirmatory argumentations. These can be effective, illuminating and helpful only in so far as they point to Him and He Himself places Himself behind them in the superiority which is His alone, developing, confirming and explaining Himself, Himself awakening, establishing, creating and maintaining certainty, Himself saying what even the best theology can only stammer after Him, namely, what He is and will be as Prophet, as the Word of His work, as what He will show Himself to be even here and now, Jesus the Victor.

4. THE PROMISE OF THE SPIRIT

We must now draw to a close this first section of the third part of the doctrine of reconciliation. In it our concern has been and is with the christological basis, content and horizon of the whole matter under consideration. We remember the title under which our

4. *The Promise of the Spirit* 275

reference to the basis, content and horizon of this whole matter is set. The Mediator is Jesus Christ who, as very God humbled to be man and made like us men, and as very man exalted to fellowship with God and made like God, as the Accomplisher of reconciliation, as the Fulfiller of the covenant, is in His own person and work both the Representative of God to man and the Representative of man before God, and therefore (Eph. 2^{14}) peace between the two. The glory of this Mediator consists in the fact that He not only is what He is as such, and does what He does as such, but that He is also revealed, i.e., reveals Himself, as the One He is and in what He does. Here again, therefore, we have both a being, namely, that He is revealed, and an action, namely, that He reveals Himself.

The same distinction and conjunction are to be seen in the first two parts of the doctrine. In the first He is the true Son of God who became what we are, going into the far country, and as such He suffers as the Judge judged in our place, as the High-priest offering Himself as the sacrifice. In the second He is the true Son of Man returning to His Father's house and He acts as such, namely, as the royal man who is the object of the pure divine good-pleasure. Similarly in this third part we have now seen that He is revealed, that He is the light of life (as we have shown in the second sub-section under this title), but that He also reveals Himself, Himself shining as this light (as developed in the third sub-section under the title " Jesus as Victor ").

In this twofold consideration we have done justice to the intention behind the distinction of the older dogmatics between the doctrine *De persona* and that *De officio mediatoris*. The only thing is that in the first two parts we have not dismembered the two *Loci* as the older dogmatics did by treating them separately, but have conjoined as well as distinguished them, explaining not only the action and work of Jesus Christ by His person and being, but also His person and being by His action and work. It is for this reason that in the preceding sub-section we have had to lay such emphasis on the historicity of the prophecy of Jesus Christ and finally to recount its history so far as it can be recounted. Yet even in doing this we could not avoid constant reference to the being of this acting Prophet, to the living Jesus Himself as the primary Subject of the events to be narrated. It is as He shines, and shines victoriously, that He is the light of life. And He is the One who shines victoriously because He is the light of life.

From the christological sphere in the narrower sense as thus traversed again, we shall have to press on in the following sections to an understanding, from the particular standpoint of this third part of the doctrine, first of the sin of man in encounter with the glory of the Mediator Jesus Christ, then of the vocation of man as the immediate result of His divine-human, prophetic being and action, then of the Christian community as a provisional, earthly-historical correlate to His being and action in its mission in and to the world, and finally, in relation to the individual Christian, of Christian hope as the final and supreme fruit of reconciliation in its self-revelation. In all these developments we can press on only from the starting-point here established, and there is hardly a step where we shall not have urgent cause to return to this starting-point and to realise how far we do actually begin here and how far everything that is to be noted in detail is actually to be understood in the light of it.

All the same, we have to press on. We shall not, then, be dealing any more with Christology in the narrower sense. We must enter the anthropological sphere, the sphere of our own life and the life of man generally. Or perhaps we should say rather more exactly the remaining sphere of our own life and the life of man generally. For the christological sphere is not to be found only in God, or somewhere in heaven, but at a specific point in the great field of human being and occurrence. It is here that reconciliation is enacted, and therefore reconciliation in its character as revelation, the prophecy of Jesus Christ, the shining of light in darkness. The present question concerns its effects on the remaining places in this great field which surround the christological sphere in the narrower sense, and are subordinate to it. Negatively, our answer must be in terms of sin as falsehood, and positively in terms of vocation, sending and hope.

But to make the transition to this wider sphere—as must now be attempted in this fourth and last division of the christological section—we shall have to interpose an intermediate discussion. The same course had to be adopted in the first two parts of the doctrine. The corresponding sub-sections were there entitled " The Verdict of the Father " (IV, 1, § 59, 3) and " The Direction of the Son " (IV, 2, § 64, 4). The theme of the transitional discussion now demanded is simply how far and in what way the being and action in the christological sphere can actually have effects, results and correspondences in this surrounding sphere of our own history and that of man generally. In other words, how far and with what right can we or must we proceed, on the basis of what is to be said of the being and action of Jesus Christ, to pronouncements concerning a being and action established and determined by it in our own life and that of the race as a whole ? To what extent is there a real and conceivable way from the one to the other, from Him to us ? It cannot be taken for granted that the justification and sanctification of man which took place there in Jesus Christ will take place here in our lives as our justification to be grasped in faith and our sanctification to be expressed in love. It cannot be taken for granted that Jesus Christ as Head has in human history and society a body in the form of His community, that He gathers and upbuilds His people. It cannot be taken for granted that man will be convicted of his pride and sloth and therefore of his sin in his encounter with the obedience of the Son of God and the lordship of the Son of Man. And in the present context it cannot be taken for granted that the shining of the light of life as the being and action of Jesus Christ will demonstrate its range and power in occurrences in the very different sphere in which we exist, even in the circle of which this shining light is the centre, and therefore in the

4. The Promise of the Spirit

vocation of man, the sending of the community and the hope of the Christian, or perhaps quite simply in the judgment of human falsehood. The step from the one to the other is too immeasurably great to be in any sense taken for granted. Hence it is quite unfitting that from a picture and concept of His being and action as Prophet we should go on at once to draw lines and consequences in relation to our own sphere, that we should immediately copy His divine-human appearance (or what we think we see and understand as such) on a reduced scale and in shadowy outline in our concept of our own being and action and that of man generally, that we should speak of correspondences to His history in ours or in that of the whole race as though it were the most natural thing in the world that there should be these, that a way from the one to the other should be open at once to our thinking and speaking. Between Jesus Christ as the Word of God and what becomes of this Word when we think we can receive and accept and assimilate and attest and pass it on, there yawns a deep cleft. Who are we other men, the rest of humanity, that the question can even arise, not of an artificial, but of a true and genuine continuity of this Word, and therefore of a real presence of the prophecy of Jesus Christ, of a shining of His light among and in and through us, in our receiving and attesting of His being and action? For here among us everything is so very different from what it is there with Him. We ourselves are so very different from Him. The grace of the light of life shining in and through Jesus Christ, even if we are remotely aware of it, is one thing, but quite another is the fact that it should shine among and in and through us, that shining victoriously in darkness it should do so in our darkness. If this is the case, if the one grace of Jesus Christ includes the fact that we may receive and attest its Word, if from this third standpoint which now concerns us other statements may be made about reconciliation than the christological in the narrower sense, then there is every cause for new attention, astonishment, gratitude and praise of God in this all-embracing work of His. If we do not face the question involved, but regard the answer as self-evident, it can hardly play any significant part in our thinking and speaking. If we do not see that we are first halted at this point, we cannot advance legitimately and therefore solidly, but only surreptitiously and in appearance. We must know what we are about when we dare to advance at this point. To consider this is the task of the fourth and final division of this christological section.

It is to be noted that we are not yet going in the direction indicated. We are still moving in the christological sphere in the narrower sense. We have still to show to what extent there is an exit from this sphere in the direction indicated, and to what extent it is legitimate, compulsory, possible and necessary, in relation to the being and occurrence which fill this sphere, to proceed in this direction.

namely, to what extent the being and occurrence which fill this sphere constrain us as such to move outwards into our own sphere. As at the corresponding points in the first two parts of the doctrine, we have thus to begin by showing that the decisive answer to our question is already given in the being and action of Jesus Christ, in the fulfilment of His atoning work, so that we have only to emphasise this afresh, understanding it as the answer to our present question. In other words, to find our answer we must turn again to His being and action as such.

In the glory of the Mediator as such there is included the fact that He is in process of glorifying Himself among and in and through us, and that we are ordained and liberated to take a receptive and active part in His glory. In this respect as in others, namely, in the glory of His mediatorial work, Jesus Christ is not without His own. He is who He is as He is among them, the saving and illuminating centre of which they form the circumference saved and illuminated by Him. Virtually, prospectively and *de iure* all men are His own. Actually, effectively and *de facto* His own are those who believe in Him, who know Him, who serve Him and who are thus the interconnected members of His body, i.e., Christians. In this as in all other respects He is, and His work takes place, in fellowship with them, for them, among them, in them and also through them. He Himself, and in His person and work God, is always their Lord and Head. The relationship is always established, maintained and controlled by Him and is thus irreversible. But it is a real relationship. He is always in fellowship with them. Where He is, they are. To see Him is also to see those who belong to Him, His own surrounding Him. It is impossible to believe in Him except in company with them. It is impossible to love Him without loving them as those who are also loved by Him. It is impossible to hope in Him without hoping for them. He is not a Head without a body, but the Head of His body and with His body. Even in the eternal divine decree of election He was not alone, but the One in whom as their Firstborn and Representative God also elected the many as His brethren because He also loved them in Him before the world was created and established. Hence He did not will to be the eternal Son of the eternal Father for Himself, but for us men. Nor did He become man for Himself, as though to be of divine essence as this one man, but in order to confirm His election as our eldest Brother, and therefore our election to divine sonship. He was God and became man as God in Him reconciled the world to Himself and fulfilled and sealed His covenant with all men. Thus His humiliation as the Son of God took place *propter nos homines et propter nostram salutem*, in fulfilment of our justification before God. And His exaltation as the Son of Man took place in order that He might draw us all to Himself (Jn. 12^{32}), in fulfilment of our sanctification for God. With those who in the wider or narrower sense, virtually

4. The Promise of the Spirit

or actually, are His own, He thus forms a unity and totality. There is, of course, strict and irreversible super- and subordination. There is a strict and indissoluble distinction of position and functions. The centre cannot become the circumference nor the circumference the centre. But in this order and distinction there is a totality. He can as little be separated from them as they from Him. We can only misunderstand the whole being and action in the christological sphere if even temporarily or partially we understand it as exclusive instead of inclusive or particular and not at once universal in its particularity. Hence all the required and necessary looking away from the world and all men, even from the Church and faith, in short from ourselves to Him, can only be with a view to seeing in Him the real world, the real man, the real Church and real faith, our real selves. To be sure, we see them in all their differentiation and distinction. But we also see them in the communion which He Himself has established, in the communication which He Himself has actualised, with this very different Other, and therefore in their reality as promised, given, maintained and controlled by God in Him.

This, then, is the basic answer to our question which is contained in all genuine knowledge of the being and action of Jesus Christ but now demands fresh emphasis. He Himself is not merely there in His own place, but as He is there in His own place He is also here in ours. He is the One who is on the way from there to here. Hence, as He is for Himself, He is also among and for and in and through us. He is and acts on His way from His own particular sphere to our surrounding, anthropological sphere. We mistake His whole being and work if we do not see its direct connexion to ours and therefore the direct connexion of ours to His; if we do not see, therefore, the continuity which He Himself has established and realises between His sphere and our sphere, or the sphere of human life generally. The reconciliation which has taken place in Him, in His person and work, is as such an occurrence which reaches beyond its own particular sphere, which embraces our sphere, the sphere of human life generally, which comprehends every man virtually, prospectively and *de iure* and the Christian actually, effectively and *de facto*, which assigns to him a receptive and spontaneous share. Even in relation to the high-priestly and kingly offices of Jesus Christ, and therefore in the first two parts of the doctrine, we cannot really see or understand or explain the atonement, the person and work of Jesus Christ, without having to consider in detail the problem or rather the reality of the outreaching, embracing and comprehensive character of this occurrence. This is the general christological answer to our question.

But the glory of the Mediator; the being and action of Jesus Christ as the Revealer of the name hallowed in Him, the kingdom drawn near in Him and the will of God done in Him on earth as in heaven; the light of life victoriously shining in Him; the Word of God and His grace spoken in Him; in short, His reconciling being and action in His prophetic office, is obviously the specific aspect and determination of this occurrence in which its outreaching, embracing and comprehensive character is not of course grounded—for it is grounded in all the determinations of this occurrence—but is certainly effective and recognisable in a particular way and as it were *ex officio*. We say *ex officio* because we are here concerned with the particular determination of the *officium mediatorium* as *officium propheticum*, as His being and action in self-declaration. In His glory He radiates His being and action for the world out from Himself into the world in order that it may share it. In His revelation, shining as light, He discloses and manifests and announces and imparts Himself, moving out from Himself to where He and His being and work are not yet known and perceived, to where there is not yet any awareness of the alteration in Him of the situation between God and man, to where the consequences of this alteration have not yet been deduced, to where the sin of man, his pride and sloth, already overcome in the justification and sanctification of man accomplished in Him, still maintain a foothold, in a twofold sense *per nefas*. In His revelation, as Word, He goes out into the darkness of ignorance in which sin necessarily retains place and power, and the life of those whose deliverance and salvation are accomplished in Him, who as His brothers are the children of God, but who are not yet aware of the fact, cannot assume the form corresponding to this accomplishment until He comes to give them this awareness and therefore to make possible this form. In His prophetic Word, in self-declaration, He does not remain aloof from those who dwell in darkness. He goes or comes to them to shine in and for them as the light of life, of their life already actualised in Him, in order that the place and power of sin, from which they are already liberated and separated in Him, should be destroyed in them too, in order that the alteration of the situation between God and man, which has validly taken place for them, should be effective and manifest in them too, in order that they, too, should grasp the grace of God which in Him is fully and unreservedly addressed to them already, in order that they, too, should thus begin to live by this grace. This is the outreaching, embracing and comprehending of reconciliation in its prophetic determination. It expresses itself. Its peculiar feature in this determination is that it shares with the world the fact that it is the world already reconciled with God. By this impartation it awakens and allows and commands it to know and experience and take itself seriously as such, to act as such, and therefore to exist as the reconciled and not the unreconciled world. It tells all those who do not yet know it that what has taken place among them is their own justification and sanctification, and in so doing it gives them the freedom to live in faith and love and calls them to tread the path of freedom. It reminds Christians of the fact that it is in this that

4. *The Promise of the Spirit*   281

they are Christians and thus marked off from others, that they already know this and have this freedom, that they should not be seduced from this path of freedom or grow weary of pursuing it. This expressing, imparting, telling and reminding, which are not just verbal and intellectual but supremely real and powerful, are the new and particular feature of reconciliation in its form as revelation, of the glory of the Mediator, of the being and action of Jesus Christ in His prophetic office. As the Bearer and in the discharge of this office, in the whole teleology and dynamic of His divine-human person and act, in which He declares to the world no other or less than Himself as the One who is with it and for it as its Lord and Saviour, He is the Word which is not just empty, but which as His own Word is the Word which enlightens, awakens and quickens the world around, lifting it to its feet and setting it on the march. As this Word, Jesus Christ Himself in His movement from His own sphere to ours, from there to here, is the illuminating centre in the light of which we who are the circumference may be bright. As it is His Word, His being and action for the world and men and ourselves become His real penetration to the world and men and ourselves. This is the specific christological answer to our question which we must now consider in greater detail.

A first and primary point is that it is the reference to the living Jesus Christ risen from the dead which makes it possible and necessary for us to give this particular answer to our question. The particular event of His resurrection is thus the primal and basic form of His glory, of the outgoing and shining of His light, of His expression, of His Word as His self-expression, and therefore of His outgoing and penetration and entry into the world around and ourselves, of His prophetic work. It is to this event that the New Testament witness refers, and on this that it builds, when it speaks of the universality of the particular existence of Jesus Christ, of the inclusiveness of His specific being and action, of the continuity in which He has His own special place but reaches out from it to embrace ours too, to comprehend us men, to address and claim and treat and illumine us as His own people which we are in virtue of His being and action, and thus to find a form among us and in us.

The testimony of the New Testament witnesses, their διακονία καὶ ἀποστολή (Ac. 1^{25}), in which the disciples for their part turn to Jews and Gentiles, is testimony to His resurrection (Ac. 1^{22}) as His self-attestation in respect of the universality, inclusiveness and continuity of His particular being and action, of its outreaching, embracing and comprehensive character. Not for nothing was it the Resurrected who at the end of St. Matthew's Gospel (28$^{17f.}$) came among the disciples who partly knew Him but partly still doubted, and said to them : " All power is given unto me in heaven and in earth. Go ye therefore (i.e., because I am the One, and to make known the fact that I am the One, to whom all power is given), and teach all nations . . . and, lo, I am with you alway, even unto the end of the world." It is by the resurrection of Jesus Christ

§ 69. *The Glory of the Mediator*

from the dead that God in His great mercy (1 Pet. 1³) " hath begotten us again unto a lively hope." It is as Christians are "risen with him" (Col. 2¹²) and " quickened " with Him (Eph. 2⁵) that they are what they are, and not in any other way. " If Christ be not risen, then is our preaching vain, and your faith is also vain. Yea, and we are found false witnesses of God . . . ye are yet in your sins " (1 Cor. 15¹⁴, ¹⁷). It is on this basis that the New Testament knows Him as the living Jesus Christ and therefore as the Messiah of Israel, the Lord of His community and the Saviour of the world. It is on this basis that it knows Him as the One who reveals Himself as Messiah, Lord and Saviour, as the Mediator in His glory, as the true Son of God and Son of Man in His self-attestation, as the Reconciler in His declaration as such.

We have to realise that with the Church of every age, if we attempt a positive answer to this question, we can think only on this basis and begin with this event, presupposing that it has actually happened in its relationship to the life and death of Jesus Christ as such but also in its distinction from them.

In His life and death as such, and therefore before this event, Jesus Christ was who He was: the Elect of God in and with whom His own are also elect; true God and true man, not for Himself but for the reconciliation of the world; High-priest and King *pro nobis* and *pro me*; Messiah, Lord, Saviour and Mediator of His own, not without them but for them and with them. His work, His being and action, were not augmented by His resurrection. How could they be? His work was finished. Yet without this event following His life and death, His finished being and action, this alteration of the situation between God and man as accomplished in Him, would have remained shut up in Him, because it would have been completely hidden from the disciples and the world and us, being quite unknown and therefore without practical significance. Without this event it would have lacked the glory and revelation and therefore the prophetic character of His being and action. His life would still have been the life of the whole world, but it would not have been light shining in this world and illuminating it. How, then, could it have reached the world as its life? What would it have meant for it? The grace addressed to all men in Jesus Christ would not have been for any of them Word or news or *kerygma*. How, then, could it be powerful for any of them? How could it be lived by any of them? He would then have been for us what He was, and have done for us what He did, in strict isolation and remoteness from us, without reaching us. And we for our part would be what we are, and do what we do, in strict isolation and remoteness from Him, without being reached by Him. The world reconciled to God in Him would then be practically and factually unreconciled as though nothing had happened, for it would be in no position to know Him as its Reconciler and therefore itself as the reconciled world, and thus to wrestle positively or negatively with what had taken place for it in Him, and to reconstitute itself as such. In such case, there could not possibly be

4. The Promise of the Spirit   283

events in our anthropological sphere like the justification, sanctification and vocation of man, the gathering, upbuilding and sending of the community and the faith and love and hope of the Christian. Between Jesus Christ and the world around there would stand the unbridgeable gulf or the unscaleable and impenetrable wall of His death with no communication either way. Without this event beyond His life and death which destroys His death, He could not be the One who comes to us as He who has lived and died for us, but only the One who in His death has gone infinitely far from us like anyone else who dies. He would then be a past and dead Mediator and Highpriest and King and Lord, etc., unknown and therefore without significance to us as such. Without this event He would have been what He was and done what He did quite in vain so far as we are concerned. This would be the situation if this event had not occurred.

But it has occurred. Now is Christ risen from the dead. As the living One He has been called out from the host of the dead and buried, of those who have gone, of those who are past and forgotten, of those who are unknown and of no significance to us. He has closed the gulf and stormed the high wall between Him and us. And this means that He not only was what He was for the world, *pro nobis* and *pro me*, and not only did what He did as the Son of God and Son of Man, but also that, according to the distinctive Easter term, He appeared in this being and action of His, coming forth and showing Himself as the One who is alive beyond the frontier of death, as the light of the world, as Word to all, as reconciliation revealed and not hidden, as salvation manifest and not concealed, as not merely the reality of the alteration accomplished in Him but also its eloquent truth. In the event of His resurrection from the dead, His being and action as very God and very man emerged from the concealment of His particular existence as an inclusive being and action enfolding the world, the humanity distinct from Himself and us all. In it He expressed Himself from without for us. In it He gave Himself to be seen and understood and known as the saving, upholding, sustaining centre of His circumference, as the salvation of all creation and therefore of us all. In it He thus established without, for us, the freedom to turn to Him, to place ourselves on the foundation of peace laid by Him, to breathe His air, to share His life. To know Him as ours, as our Lord, and to know us Christians as actually, effectively and *de facto*, and all men as virtually, prospectively and *de iure* His, is thus to know the power of His resurrection and therefore the power of this particular event. In Him there took place in a way which is basic for all the men of every age and place the disclosure and self-attestation of Jesus Christ, and in them there was granted the freedom to know Him, and in Him His being for, among and in them, and therefore theirs with and in Him. This knowledge is Easter knowledge. Its basis, theme and content are the life and death of Jesus

Christ in which He gave Himself to the world, to His community and therefore to us as Reconciler, Deliverer, Brother and Lord, uniting Himself with us and us with Himself. But the basis, theme and content of this knowledge are His life and death for us on the assumption of the particular knowledge of its revelation and declaration, in its character as Word and prophecy. In this character Jesus Christ and His being and action in His life and death have penetrated to us in the particular event of His resurrection, thus becoming truth in their reality, and as truth reality for the world, for the community, *pro nobis* and *pro me*.

It is thus with good reason that from the very first the main Christian festival has not been Christmas, nor Good Friday, but Easter. This does not mean that what took place in the birth and suffering and death of Jesus Christ is underestimated. It means that it is given its supreme value. For this knowledge of the being and action of the One who was born in Bethlehem and died on Calvary, the knowledge that He is not dead but that He lives for us and among us and in us, and that we may live with and in Him, has its origin in what took place on Easter Day as His emergence from the concealment to the revelation of His being and action for us, among us and in us. The freedom to keep Christmas and Good Friday is grounded in the freedom in which we keep Easter, i.e., in which we may know the One who was born and died for the world, for the community and for us as the One who lives for us, among us and in us.

This, then, is our general and detailed christological answer to the question of the possibility and legitimacy of a transition from the sphere of Jesus Christ Himself to our own general sphere of human life.

What have we done in giving this answer? As announced, we have first emphasised afresh the supreme answer to the question which is already given in the being and action of Jesus Christ, in the fulfilment of His work of reconciliation, if it is seen and understood aright. We have first recalled in general terms that He is never in any respect without His own, men, Christians, but that always in all respects He is what He is and does what He does with them, in them and through them. He Himself is and acts inclusively, and therefore in this transition from Himself to the world, to us. And in the realisation of this transition, as we have also maintained in detail, He is also light, Word and prophecy, the Revealer of His being and action, the declaration of the atonement made in Him, of the alteration of the situation between God and man accomplished in Him, for the world around, for and in and through us.

These two assertions may be regarded as an initial answer to our question. But we cannot make them without remembering that they can have force only in relation to the living Jesus Christ, as statements about Him, and in attention to His self-declaration. They are statements of Easter knowledge on the basis of His Easter revelation. Their power can be only the power of His resurrection. For it is in this that His being and action have disclosed themselves for

4. The Promise of the Spirit

and with and in and through us. In this there has taken place His announcement of the reconciliation fulfilled in Him. In this His prophecy is initiated in its primal and basic form. In this there took place first that exit, transition and entry. In relation to a dead Jesus Christ, known to us only in a more or less clear but then clouded recollection or through a more or less powerful ecclesiastical tradition, these statements would never even have occurred to us, and we certainly could not have made them with the definiteness with which we have done so. Whatever else we might know or not know concerning Him, we could know nothing of His inclusive being and action embracing the world, the Church and ourselves, nor of Him as the declaration of this inclusive being and action. He would then be hidden from us in His outreaching, embracing and comprehending. We could have only hazy conjectures or make only arbitrary assertions concerning His movement from there to here or the connexion between Him and us. A precise and conscientious affirmative can be given to the question of this movement and connexion only in the power of His self-witness as the living One, and therefore as the Resurrected from the dead. It can have its origin only in this event. It must maintain an awareness of its origin in this event. It will not loose itself from this event either in the fact that it is ventured or in the way in which it is ventured. That Jesus Christ and His own, He and we, do belong together as unity and totality, and that this is so as and because He reveals and declares Himself as the One who is for and with and in and through them—this positive answer to our question has validity and force as it has an Easter character given by reference to the living Jesus Christ and the occurrence of this event. Only as ventured with this character has it any real validity.

But this means (1) that, while the two christological assertions with which we started, the general and the particular, are correct in themselves, they are not adequate as a positive answer, or as the authentication of a positive answer, to our question. Even if it be assumed that, so far as this is possible generally and briefly, we have made them fully and correctly, the fact remains that not even the most apt and excellent statement concerning the universality, inclusiveness and continuity of the being and action of Jesus Christ, nor the best statement concerning the prophecy of Jesus Christ in which He Himself actualises them, can possibly be thought adequate to indicate the movement from Him to us, His being among and in us, which is the theme of our present enquiry. Theological clarity and cheerfulness are excellent gifts of God when we enjoy them, but they must not cause us to make the mistake of using the theological and specifically the christological statements which we ourselves can and should make to fill up the space in which only the living Jesus Christ in His self-revelation can affirm what we think we can and must say concerning Him. No Christology can reproduce either the Easter event in which He has come forth alive from the dead both to be and to be revealed and knowable as the One He is, nor Himself as the living One who attests Himself authentically in His being and action for and among and in us. It can be Easter Christology in preaching, teaching, worship, pastoral care and dogmatics only if it does not attempt such reproduction and if its declarations leave place, and indeed finish up by yielding place, to His self-declaration, just as the resurrection accounts of the Evangelists and Paul never narrate the event as such but always record and bear witness to the appearances of the Resurrected. Easter thinking and speaking about the interrelationship between Jesus Christ and the world around, about His outgoing and incoming into this world and to us, are thinking and speaking which, with due respect and glad anticipation, count upon the sovereign presence and action of the Resurrected Himself and therefore His own declaration, not trying to conceal or replace these, but yielding them place, in order that He Himself may come from this place to our place, and thus make this transition real and therefore true. If our christological assertions are sustained and determined and filled by this respect and anticipation, then they are reliable as theological statements, and we need not be mortally concerned about the elements of incompleteness and incorrectness which even at best will cling to them, since they can be valid and helpful as a positive answer to our question concerning this exit, transition and entry. In this respect matters are exactly the same as we maintained at the end of the previous sub-section with reference to our argumentations concerning the question of the certainty of the victory of the prophecy of Jesus Christ in its relation to the reality of this prophecy.

But this means (2) that this positive answer to our question has force and validity, i.e., an Easter character, if we never cease to be astonished that we can and should give it. It is not, then, that we falter for a moment before giving it, and then, when the solution to the problem is happily found, we cheerfully proceed to further thought and utterance, drawing deductions, making applications, finding illustrations and in short treating the matter as though it were under our mastery. If we really see and understand it, it is never under our mastery, and therefore we can never cease to be astonished. To emphasise afresh, from what we already know or think we know of Jesus Christ, the answer: " Lo, I am with you alway," is always to be set before the event, and to have to remember the event, in which all knowledge of Him has its origin. We think again of Lessing's problem of leaping the "ugly ditch " between history and faith. We think of the great difficulty of conceiving the possibility of the transition. Yet it is not these things, but the incomprehensible nature of the reality of its accomplishment in this event, which not once but whenever we think and speak of it brings us up short before the

4. The Promise of the Spirit

fact that it really is accomplished, that the way is open from the one side to the other. Hence we must be content to be brought up short continually if we have genuine knowledge and can thus proceed to genuine thought and utterance. The Easter event, or the New Testament accounts of the appearances which follow it, may be interpreted in different ways. This question need not detain us here. But however we interpret it, there can be no doubt that it was the event of a new and special act of God in which it took place and was manifested that the Living was not to be sought among the dead and buried and departed who may be mourned for a time and then forgotten. He was not to be sought among them because He was not among them. He was risen from the dead. He lived with full power to present and attest Himself. He " appeared " and acted and spoke. In this power He accomplished His communion and communication with His own and thus revealed His being and action for and among and with them. We count upon this special act of God, upon this life, upon this self-presentation and self-attestation, upon the action of the Resurrected from the dead in this special act, when we answer positively the question of this transition. If we really know what we are about in this, if we do it with true knowledge, we do it in the freedom grounded on this act of God, and on the basis of this event ; for in this event it has its origin as genuine knowledge. But this being the case, we cannot but do it with astonishment. We are startled at the nature of the reality to which we refer and on which we rest. We are surprised by the unexpected thing which enlightens and motivates us. We are thankful for the grace which frees us to go further. We adore as we make use of this freedom. Unless we hear the Halt which is here required of us, there can be no Forward. A positive answer to our question is made a valid and tolerable because an Easter answer only as it proceeds from a hearing of this Halt and therefore of this Forward.

The question whether or not this astonishment is contained and expressed in our words and statements is a critical one. On the surface many assertions may appear to be identical. Only if there is this astonishment, however, can there be serious, fruitful and edifying Christian thought and utterance in the Church and its theology. Otherwise there will be that which may seem to be learned and edifying but is basically and in its effects banal, trivial and tiresome. And it is worth asking whether this distinction is not more incisive and more serious in practice than all the distinctions of confessions and movements in Christian theology and ecclesiology, and does not cut right through them all with its greater depth and relentlessness. We may be Protestants or Catholics, Lutherans or Reformed, to the right or to the left, but in some way we must have seen and heard the angels at the open and empty tomb if we are to be sure of our ground and to say anything true or significant about this thing which is so vital for us all, namely, the matter of this transition.

From the relationship of a positive answer to our question with the resurrection of Jesus Christ, it also follows (3) that we not only can but should be sure of our ground in the matter of this transition. If we believe at all, we cannot half believe in the presence and action of the living Jesus Christ, in the fact that He is with us alway, even unto the end of the world. We can speak of this only in distinct and not in ambiguous words and statements. Naturally, we are not thinking here of the passion of a so-called conviction, let alone of any spiritual rhetoric. We are thinking of a certainty which may be deeply concealed and indiscernible because it cannot be expressed as such but only indicated indirectly, namely, the certainty that in the light of its origin in the Easter revelation only a positive answer can be given to our question, a positive answer being self-evident on this basis. There is a place for doubt, for the dialectic of Yes and No, for the attitude of perhaps and perhaps not, for hesitation whether things might be so. But this place is merely the forecourt where we think we are dealing with possibilities such as the obvious possibility that an unknown Jesus Christ might exist at a distance from the real world but could not have anything to do with us, or the opposite possibility which at least deserves consideration that He does perhaps have something to do with us because He is present and active within the world. Face to face with such possibilities, it is inevitable that we should hesitate. But the situation is quite different when we know that in the Easter revelation a decision has been taken which makes it impossible for us to be ceaselessly and therefore hesitantly occupied with possibilities because we are now concerned only with the reality of the way on which Jesus Christ strides into the world and to us as the One He is for the world and therefore *pro nobis* and *pro me*, not remaining alone but already present among us and with us. If it is clear that a positive answer to our question can be based only upon the reality of the living Jesus Christ manifested and known in this way, but that it really is based upon this as God's own act, then this positive answer, however it may be worked out in our thought and utterance, necessarily acquires and has the stamp of the axiomatic, the first and the last, and therefore the self-evident. In this matter we think and speak in terms of Easter if we no longer think and speak about this exit, transition and entry, but on the basis of them as bound and liberated by a decision which was not our work but has been taken in a way which is normative for our work. Our part is simply to have regard to this decision and to follow it. In so doing we shall certainly be conscious of the many sins of thought and word of which we are guilty. But we may also take comfort that in virtue of this origin of our knowledge it is constantly brought to light, but also protected. The decisive thing is that we should find ourselves set before, but also committed to and liberated for, the task of following the decision taken in God's own act, of taking all our own decisions of thought and word in the direction, in the clean and healthy atmosphere, of the decision made with the

4. The Promise of the Spirit

resurrection of Jesus Christ from the dead, in the love which drives out fear and leaves no place for legitimate or necessary doubts.

It is to be noted that this third determination does not contradict the second, namely, that the Easter certainty of a genuine positive answer to our question does not contradict the astonishment with which alone it can be made. The certainty is indeed rooted in the astonishment, and in the astonishment it continually becomes certainty. Hence we are confronted at this point by the same dividing line which runs through all Christian thinking and speaking, through all ecclesiology and theology. In all confessions and movements the ultimate test is whether, in the given freedom and the imposed obligation of the Easter revelation, with all the astonishment of certainty as to its origin, our theology, for all its human frailty and exposure, moves with steps that are sure and not unsure, not pursuing a zig-zag course but moving straight ahead on the way disclosed and appointed. The ultimate test is whether in this twofold determination, confronted by the living Jesus Christ, it has a purpose and future as Easter theology or ecclesiology.

It may be surprising but it is quite unavoidable that we should now admit that the real difficulty in this positive answer to our question is not behind us but still ahead. It is just because of the final point mentioned in our discussion that this is so.

For the full extent of the difficulty emerges when we take quite seriously the resurrection of Jesus Christ as the basis and confirmation of the answer now given. To take quite seriously does not mean merely to reckon with the accomplished nature of this event, or to try to think seriously in the light of it, but to realise, to perceive, to be quite clear what this event implies when properly understood, namely, what is implied by it as the self-declaration, accomplished in this new and specific divine act, of the being and action of Jesus Christ in His preceding being and action, as the expression of the reconciliation of the world to God effected in His life and death, as the revelation of the name of God hallowed in Him, the kingdom come, the will of God done on earth as in heaven, in short, as the prophecy of Jesus Christ in its primal and basic form and therefore in its distinctive immediacy and perfection. Immediacy and perfection are not proper to it in any of its indirect and derivative forms, e.g., in the witness of Scripture or the witness of the Church following the witness of Scripture. But they are proper to it in the self-witness of the living Jesus Christ and therefore in the event in the course of which He has appeared to His own as the One who is alive from the dead and therefore as theirs, as the Lord and Saviour present and active among and with and in them and therefore implicitly among and with and in the world, making peace between heaven and earth. This event, and therefore what has taken place in it, i.e., the appearance of the living Jesus Christ, of His being and action in its form as accomplished declaration, as spoken Word, as immediate and perfect revelation, are not taken seriously if we allow ourselves any subtractions or restrictions in estimating their scope. Whatever the results may be, whatever obvious questions may arise, we must accept the prophecy of Jesus Christ in the immediacy and perfection with which it encounters us in this event, in the self-attestation of the living Jesus Christ.

We hardly do justice to the Church or theology in almost any age and form if we reproach it with having failed to note that this is something to be taken seriously. We need only refer to the emphasis on the Easter festival already mentioned. Or we might allude to the conscious replacement of the Jewish sabbath by Sunday as the first day of the week, and the celebration of this κυριακὴ ἡμέρα (Rev. 1^{10}) as the day of the Lord's resurrection after the sabbath and thus a kind of recurrent Easter. But even though there is a lively or revived recollection of the significance of Easter, it has still to be asked whether there is any serious consideration or understanding of what has really to be celebrated on Easter Day or its weekly repetition, of what makes this day the Lord's day primarily and supremely for the Christian world, yet not for this alone, but for the world as a whole, for all men. Is it really perceived what distinguishes the Easter liturgy in the Roman Missal and the Easter festival in the consciousness of other Christians? In Christian piety and worship and preaching and instruction and theology, the resurrection of Jesus Christ is constantly regarded as merely one particular saving event among the many others which constitute the so-called history of salvation. It may be proclaimed as the solemn demonstration of Christ as Lord of life and death, and therefore of His deity. It may be envisaged as the crowning of His human life by the transcending and conquering of His death. As in the Liberal theology and preaching of the 19th century—and with a little good will we may regard even this as a genuine if ill-advised concern—efforts may be made to bring it home to the modern man by magnifying it as the model or even as an example of all incomprehensible renewals in the sphere of the creaturely life of nature and spirit, and particularly in that of individual human existence. To be sure, the fiery heart of the matter is seen in the best utterances of the Reformation theology of the 16th century. We need only read and ponder Luther's Easter hymns, or the *Heidelberg Catechism* under *Qu.* 45 : " What benefit do we receive from the resurrection of Christ ? " to which the answer is given : " First, by His resurrection He has overcome death, that He might make us partakers of the righteousness which by his death He has obtained for us. Secondly, we also are now by His power raised up to a new life. Thirdly, the resurrection of Christ is to us a sure pledge of our blessed resurrection." This is all true. But ought not the consideration of this matter to have extended beyond the benefits to a realisation of the particular greatness and scope of its objective occurrence as such ? And would not this have perhaps revealed that its occurrence, in giving us a positive answer to the question of the unity of Jesus Christ with His own and indeed with the world, carries with it certain consequences in face of which we must consider this positive answer afresh if we are to understand it rightly ? It may well be that fear of these consequences has a good deal to do with the fact that the Easter event and the Easter message are not taken more seriously than is usually the case.

What are these consequences ?

Let us try to be clear what it means if it is true that in this event there has taken place the self-declaration of Jesus Christ, of His being and action in the relationship between God and man, and therefore the revelation of the reconciliation of the world with God, the immediate and perfect prophecy, by a new and specific divine act, of the divine-human High-priest and King. Let us have no

4. *The Promise of the Spirit*

reservations on the ground that what has taken place is perhaps too great for the measure of our being and understanding, nor prudent fears of the questions raised. These will come later. But they can properly come only when we first realise on what basis and with what reference they can be put and answered. Our first and unconditional objective must be to see and know what the Easter message no less unconditionally says.

In a first and very general formulation of its declaration, we venture the statement that the Easter event, as the revelation of the being and action of Jesus Christ in His preceding life and death, is His new coming as the One who had come before. As is made quite clear by the accounts in the Gospels, the One who now comes afresh and appears to His disciples is none other than the One who had come before. He is " Jesus Christ yesterday " (Heb. 13^8), the One who yesterday acted and suffered and was finally crucified in His existence as temporally limited by His birth and death, with all the power and range and significance of this event for the whole world, but still enclosed yesterday within the limits of His existence, concealed and unknown in the world reconciled to God in Him, not yet exercising the latent power and range and significance of His presence and therefore putting into effect what was done in Him for all men and for the whole created order. This One who came before now comes afresh in the Easter event. He is " Jesus Christ to-day," in all His being and action of yesterday, and its whole power for the world, new in the fact that to-day, His death and the empty tomb behind Him, He moves out from the latency of His being and action of yesterday and from the inoperativeness of His power, appearing to His disciples and in them potentially to all men and the whole cosmos, declaring Himself, making known His presence and what has been accomplished in Him for all men and for the whole created order, putting it into effect. With its manifestation and self-declaration, the fact of there and yesterday now becomes the factor of here and to-day. And in virtue of this event, newly come in His self-revelation as the One who came, Jesus Christ will not cease to be this factor and to work as such. Hence " Jesus Christ for ever " (Heb. 13^8). As this factor, as the Prophet, Witness and Preacher entered into the world, as the light of His mediatorship, of the atonement made in Him, shining from this place, He is the living Jesus Christ, who has death behind Him, the light which shines in the world and can never be extinguished. And the world for its part is what it is enabled to be in the presence of this factor, in encounter with Him, in the shining of His light, in the determination given it by Him.

The citation in 1 Tim. 3^{16} from what is probably a liturgical text old even at the time of the composition of the Epistle should be allowed to speak for itself in this connexion : " He was manifest in the flesh, justified in the Spirit, seen of angels, preached unto the Gentiles, believed on in the world, received up into

§ 69. The Glory of the Mediator

glory." The passage is introduced into the Epistle as a comprehensive definition of what is " by agreed confession " (ὁμολογουμένως) the one great " mystery of (Christian) godliness " (μέγα τὸ τῆς εὐσεβείας μυστήριον). Its six clauses can hardly be understood as a list of successive saving events such as we have in the oldest versions of the Christian creed. They are rather six references from different standpoints to a single event which can only be that of the resurrection or self-declaration of the living Jesus Christ as the divine act. All the references apply to this. If the passage is really a hymn, it must surely be an Easter hymn, or part of such a hymn.

It is not merely possible but imperative that what took place in the Easter event, the fresh coming of Jesus Christ as the One who came before, should be summed up under the New Testament concept of the *parousia* of Jesus Christ. However the New Testament writers may apply the term in other respects, or refer to it without application, the concrete perception with which they do so is that of the resurrection of Jesus Christ, just as conversely their notion of the resurrection is strictly identical with the full range of content of the concept of *parousia*.

The word παρουσία (cf. for what follows the article by A. Oepke in Kittel) derives from Hellenistic sources and originally means quite simply " effective presence." A *parousia* might be a military invasion, or the visitation of a city or district by a high dignitary who, as in the case of the emperor, might sometimes be treated so seriously that the local calendar would be dated afresh from the occasion. The term was also applied sometimes to the helpful intervention of such divine figures as Dionysius or Aesculapius Soter. What is signified by the term, if not the term itself, is familiar and important in the thinking of the Old Testament. From His place, whether Sinai, Sion or heaven, Yahweh comes in the storm, or enthroned over the ark of the covenant, or in His Word or Spirit, or in dreams or visions, or simply and especially in the events of the history of Israel. To the men of His people He comes finally as universal King in the unfolding of His power and glory. The coming of " one like the Son of man with the clouds of heaven " (Dan. 7[13]) ; the coming of the righteous and victorious Messiah-King abolishing war and establishing peace (cf. Zech. 9[9f.]) ; above all the recurrent Old Testament picture of the coming God of the covenant Himself manifesting Himself in movement from there to here—all these constitute materially the preparatory form of what in the New Testament is called παρουσία in the pregnant technical sense, namely, the effective presence of Jesus Christ.

What is formally meant by the word is best seen from the fact that in the later New Testament (especially the Pastorals, yet also as early as 2 Thess. 2[8]) it is found in close proximity to, and sometimes replaced by, the term ἐπιφάνεια. In its Hellenistic origin at least ἐπιφάνεια denotes the making visible of concealed divinity. In 2 Thess. 2[8] both terms appear in a way which is not just plerophoric (so W. Bauer) but materially instructive. With the breath of His mouth the Lord Jesus will slay a hidden but one day manifested ἄνομος, destroying him τῇ ἐπιφανείᾳ τῆς παρουσίας αὐτοῦ. What else can this genitive conjunction mean but that the epiphany of Jesus Christ is the manifestation of His *parousia* or effective presence, or conversely that His *parousia* takes place in His epiphany and therefore His manifestation ?

As far as I can see, there are no passages (not even 2 Tim. 1[10]) where either term refers abstractly to the first coming of Jesus Christ as such, i.e., to His history and existence within the limits of His birth and death, of Bethlehem and Golgotha. In relation to these there would be no point in speaking either of

4. *The Promise of the Spirit*   293

ἐπιφάνεια (manifestation) or of παρουσία (effective presence). In them He is not even " manifest in the flesh " (1 Tim. 3¹⁶), and none of the other references in this passage can really apply to His pre-Easter existence as such. To be sure, the Word then became flesh, and His whole work was done in all its dimensions. But the incarnate Word was not yet revealed and seen in His glory (Jn. 1¹⁴). This took place in the event of Easter. In this event we certainly have the coming of the One who came before in that sphere. But it is now His coming in effective presence, because in visible manifestation in the world. It is now His coming in glory as the active and dominant factor within it. It is thus His new coming as the One who came before. It is now His " coming again," and in spite of Oepke I do not see how we can avoid this expression as we have provisionally and generally explained it.

We must now continue that, as concerns the scope and content of this event, the New Testament knows of only one coming again of Jesus Christ, of only one new coming of the One who came before, of only one manifestation of His effective presence in the world corresponding to His own unity as the One who came before. This does not exclude the fact that His new coming and therefore His manifestation in effective presence in the world takes place in different forms at the different times chosen and appointed by Himself and in the different relationships which He Himself has ordained. Everything depends, of course, upon our seeing and understanding the one continuous event in all its forms. But in the time of the community and its mission after the Easter revelation it also takes place in the form of the impartation of the Holy Spirit, and it is with this that we are particularly concerned in this sub-section. It will also take place in a different and definitive form (of which we shall have to speak in eschatology), as the return of Jesus Christ as the goal of the history of the Church, the world and each individual, as His coming as the Author of the general resurrection of the dead and the Fulfiller of universal judgment. In all these forms it is one event. Nothing different takes place in any of them. It is not more in one case or less in another. It is the one thing taking place in different ways, in a difference of form corresponding to the willing and fulfilment of the action of its one Subject, the living Jesus Christ. Always and in all three forms it is a matter of the fresh coming of the One who came before. Always and in different ways it is a matter of the coming again of Jesus Christ.

The Easter event is only the first form of this happening. From the standpoint of its substance, scope and content, it is identical with its occurrence in the forms which follow. It is no less significant than these, nor is it to be depreciated in relation to them. On the contrary, the one and total coming in its other forms has its primal and basic pattern in the Easter event, so that we might well be tempted to describe the whole event simply as one long fulfilment of the resurrection of Jesus Christ. There are, of course, similar temptations in relation to the second and third forms of the event.

§ 69. *The Glory of the Mediator*

We shall not attempt to reduce it in this way, since in so doing we should wander too far not only from the speech and terminology but also the material outlook of the New Testament. Thus, there can be no question that in all its forms the one totality of coming again does really have the character, colours and accents of the Easter event. There can also be no question that this is only the first if also the original form of this one totality.

If we allow the New Testament to say what it has to say, we shall be led in this matter to a thinking which is differentiated even in its incontestable unity, formally corresponding to that which is required for an understanding of the three modes of being of God in relation to His one essence in triunity: *una substantia in tribus personis, tres personae in una substantia.*

When the matter is usually spoken of in the New Testament under the terms *parousia* or epiphany, the reference is usually or chiefly to the third and final form, to the eschatological form in the narrower traditional sense, of the return of Jesus Christ, i.e., to His manifestation and effective presence beyond history, the community, the world and the individual human life, and as their absolute future. But reference to this climax of His coming dominates New Testament thought and utterance even where it is materially concerned with the subject without using these particular terms. We can hardly deny or explain this away in such typical passages as the *parousia* passages in the Synoptists, or the Thessalonian Epistles of Paul, or 1 Cor. 15, or the Apocalypse with its final ἔρχου κύριε Ἰησοῦ (22^{20}). Even the Gospel of John, which seems particularly to invite us to do this with its placing of both the gift of eternal life and the judgment in the present, resists it inasmuch as it is rather strangely the only book in the whole of the New Testament to speak of the last day (ἐσχάτη ἡμέρα) when Jesus will awaken the dead (6$^{39, 40, 44, 54}$) and His Word spoken to men will judge them (12^{48}); and it is advisable not to solve the implied difficulty of interpretation by critical amputation. According to the New Testament, the return of Jesus Christ in the Easter event is not yet as such His return in the Holy Ghost and certainly not His return at the end of the days. Similarly, His return in the Easter event and at the end of the days cannot be dissolved into His return in the Holy Ghost, nor the Easter event and the outpouring of the Holy Spirit into His last coming. In all these we have to do with the one new coming of Him who came before. But if we are to be true to the New Testament, none of these three forms of His new coming, including the Easter event, may be regarded as its only form. The most that we can say is that a particular glory attaches to the Easter event because here it begins, the Easter event being the primal and basic form in which it comes to be seen and grasped in its totality.

Yet, as we must plainly distinguish the resurrection, the outpouring of the Spirit and the final return of Jesus Christ, so we must understand and see them together as forms of one and the same event. A no less sharp warning must be issued against an abstract separation of the three forms of the new coming of Jesus Christ for which there is no basis in the New Testament. How else could we distinguish them except within the unity of the whole and therefore on the assumption of one event in these three forms?

Oepke is surely right when he says of the so-called last discourses in John that in them the "coming of the Resurrected, the coming in the Spirit and the coming at the end of the days merge into one another," and when he also says

4. *The Promise of the Spirit*

of the Synoptic Jesus that it is impossible to decide to what extent He made a clear distinction between His resurrection and His *parousia* in its final form. Yet may it not be that we can very definitely decide that He, or the Synoptic and also the Johannine tradition concerning Him, did not in fact make any absolute distinction between them at all in respect of either matter or form ? What do we learn from the well-known passages (considered in detail in *C.D.*, III, 2, pp. 499 ff.) in which Jesus unmistakeably prophesies the manifestation of the kingdom of God ἐν δυνάμει (Mk. 9$^{1f.}$), the coming of the Son of Man (Mt. 10^{23}, 26^{64}), or at least the sign which directly precedes (Mk. 13^{30} and *par.*) within the lifetime of those around Him ? If we may eliminate in advance what is in its way the greatest triviality of any age, what are we to make of the assumption which underlay a particular school of Neo-Liberal theology, and which is unfortunately encountered only too often outside the narrow circle of this school, namely, that Jesus was deluded ? If we find in the coming of the Resurrected, His coming in the Holy Spirit and His coming at the end of the age three forms of His one new coming for all their significant differences, there need be no artificiality in explaining that these passages refer to the first and immediate form in which His coming did really begin in that generation as the Easter event and in which the two remaining forms are plainly delineated and intimated. We are then forced to accept the statement of W. Michaelis which Oepke contests : " The resurrection . . . is the *parousia*," or again the statement of R. Bultmann (with particular reference to John's Gospel) : " The *parousia* has already taken place," although we must be careful to make the proviso that these statements are not to be taken exclusively but need to be amplified by the recollection that this is not the whole story. The outpouring of the Holy Spirit is also the *parousia*. In this it has not only taken place but is still taking place to-day. And as it has taken place in the resurrection and is taking place to-day in the outpouring of the Holy Spirit, it is also true that it will take place at the end of the days in the conclusion of the self-revelation of Jesus Christ.

It is thus impossible to relate a concept of the eschatological which is meaningful in the New Testament sense merely to the final stage of the *parousia*. Eschatological denotes the last time. The last time is the time of the world and human history and all men to which a term is already set in the death of Jesus and which can only run towards this appointed end. In the Easter event as the commencement of the new coming of Jesus Christ in revelation of what took place in His life and death, it is also revealed that the time which is still left to the world and human history and all men can only be the last time, i.e., time running towards its appointed end. In this sense the Easter event is the original because the first eschatological event. The impartation of the Holy Spirit is the coming of Jesus Christ in the last time which still remains. As we shall see, it is the promise, given with and through the Holy Spirit, by which the community, and with it the world in which it exists and has its mission, may live in this time which moves towards its end. Hence the new coming of Jesus Christ has an eschatological character in this second form too. If the *parousia* is an eschatological event in its third and final stage as well, this means specifically that in it we have to do with the manifestation and effective presence of Jesus Christ in their definitive form, with His revelation at the goal of the last time. It will consist again in a coming of Jesus Christ, and at this coming this last time, too, will reach the end which is already set for it in His death and revealed in His resurrection. The happening of the *parousia* is thus eschatological throughout its course. And it is this, as already indicated from the very first by the Easter event, because already and particularly in this event the term set to time in the death of Jesus Christ is revealed and the character and stamp of the last time is given to all the time which remains.

> When we treat of the unity of the three forms or stages of the one event of the return of Jesus Christ, it is perhaps worth considering and exegetically helpful, again in analogy to the doctrine of the Trinity, to think of their mutual relationship as a kind of perichoresis (cf. *C.D.*, I, 1, p. 425). It is not merely that these three forms are interconnected in the totality of the action presented in them all, or in each of them in its unity and totality, but that they are mutually related as the forms of this one action by the fact that each of them also contains the other two by way of anticipation or recapitulation, so that, without losing their individuality or destroying that of the others, they participate and are active and revealed in them. As the Resurrected from the dead Jesus Christ is virtually engaged already in the outpouring of the Holy Spirit, and in the outpouring of the Holy Spirit He is engaged in the resurrection of all the dead and the execution of the last judgment. The outpouring of the Holy Spirit obviously takes place in the power of His resurrection from the dead, yet it is already His knocking as the One who comes finally and definitively, and it is active and perceptible as such. Similarly His final coming to resurrection and judgment is only the completion of what He has begun in His own resurrection and continued in the outpouring of the Holy Spirit.
> To be sure, this is a view which is never systematised in the New Testament or presented in the form of instruction. But this does not mean that we are false to the Bible, or obscure its statements concerning the *parousia*, by adopting this view. Are we not more likely to throw light on them if we advance it with the necessary prudence yet also boldness? Are there not many passages in the New Testament which with their apparent contradictions cannot be satisfactorily explained except on the assumption of such a view? This is not a key to open every lock. But it is one which we do well not to despise.

We have now tried to understand the distinctive feature of the Easter event in the great context in which it stands and from which it must not be wrested. May we not say even in this respect that to a large degree it has not been taken with the seriousness appropriate to it, being hardly at all, or only very partially, seen and understood in this context? But after this attempt to clarify and enlarge the horizon, we must now return to this distinctive feature as such. What is specifically contributed in the resurrection of Jesus Christ as the commencement of His new coming as the One who came before, and therefore in the revelation of His reconciling being and action in its primal and basic form as the entry into His prophetic office?

We may begin (1) by stating that His self-declaration, and in it His coming into the world, to us and all men, has taken place once for all and irrevocably in His resurrection. It has done so no less uniquely and irrevocably than that which is proclaimed in it, namely, the reconciliation of the world to God, His high-priestly and kingly

4. The Promise of the Spirit

work, and therefore the justification and sanctification of man as they have already taken place in His life and death. In His new coming, in His arising from the hosts of the dead, it took place that the alteration of the situation between God and man accomplished by Him was actualised by taking place immediately and completely in noetic form also as the prophecy of Jesus Christ, by being brought out of concealment and revealed and made known to the world, by being thrust before every man and thus made a factor in the existence of the world and every man, so that account has necessarily to be taken of its presence and efficacy. This is what cannot be reversed now that it has taken place and has done so once and for all.

In Jesus Christ God has not merely acted as man's Judge and Liberator, restoring and renewing him. In so doing He has acknowledged this action in the resurrection of Jesus Christ. And this means supremely that He has publicly bound and committed Himself to man. He has given him the document written in His own hand and signed with His own seal, so that there can and will be no going back for God Himself in respect of the decision for the world and man taken and fulfilled in Jesus Christ. In virtue of what He has said in raising Jesus Christ from the dead, He Himself in all His divine being and action, in all His directing and controlling, in all the exercise of His sovereignty and lordship, can and will act only as the One who is bound to man, who has espoused his cause in the life and death of Jesus Christ, who has humbled Himself to him to save him, and exalted him to His own right hand. The resurrection of Jesus Christ is the pronunciation of the great divine Yea and Amen to which God will be as faithful as He is to Himself and after which everything which can and may be expected to follow from Him can consist only in repetitions, developments and confirmations. Hence we need not fear the being and rule of a *Deus absconditus* limiting and even questioning the being and action of God in Jesus Christ. It is to be noted that what we have here is not just a Yea and Amen which God has said and confessed, but a Yea and Amen which in saying He has also effected and which He has confessed by putting into effect and introducing as a factor. What we have is a divine noetic which has all the force of a divine ontic. He has spoken in acting. Hence He has spoken unequivocally, once for all and irrevocably. The document of the being and action of Jesus Christ, of the being and action of God in Him, is before us in all its validity, so that the world and all men may legitimately refer and appeal to it. This is the first distinctive and decisive thing which has taken place in the resurrection of Jesus Christ and which in it may be regarded as accomplished and therefore inviolable, exposed to no doubts and entangled in no problems. As God's particular act the resurrection is the particular Word of the faithfulness of God, to cleave to which the world and man are not merely allowed and required, but urged and compelled, as an implicate of their own existence even before they have perceived it, and whatever they may make of it.

But this leads us at once to the second thing which has taken place in the resurrection of Jesus Christ. It did not take place in a heavenly or supra-heavenly realm, or as part of an intra-divine movement or a divine conversation, but before the gates of Jerusalem in the days of Tiberius Caesar and therefore in the place and time which are also ours, in our sphere. As it took place, it became a link in the chain of cosmic occurrence. Here, in the world, there was revealed and made known in this event what took place for the world in the life and death of Jesus Christ, namely, the alteration of the situation between God and the world by the reconciliation of the world to God accomplished in Him. To this world and to us men, without distinction of time or place and without regard to our attitude towards it or the character of our existence as conditioned by it, God has sworn open fidelity in not merely doing what He has done for us in Jesus Christ but also revealing and making known among us what He has done. We do not refer to a creaturely self-disclosure, revelation or making known, but to the Word of God spoken to the creaturely world in this event within it. And this means that in it—we must not be unsettled by any secret Docetism in this respect—something has taken place in and therefore to the world and to all men with the same uniqueness and irrevocability with which God has confirmed Himself in this event, in this pronouncement of His Yea and Amen. In this respect, too, the divine noetic, God's self-declaration as the One He is in the being and action of Jesus Christ, the prophecy of the divine-human Mediator, has the full force of the divine ontic. The Word of God does not return to Him void (Is. 55[11]), but is effected as it is spoken and stands fast as He commands (Ps. 33[9]). This means, however, that after the declaration of its reconciliation to God effected in this event the world is not the same as it was before. Or better and more comprehensively, since this declaration has a retroactive force when it takes place within it, it is not the same as it would necessarily have been had it not taken place. Now that Jesus Christ is risen from the dead, no man who has lived or will live is the same as he would have been if Jesus Christ had not risen. The fact that Jesus Christ is risen means that the world is not reconciled as it were in secret or in its absence. No, it is the world to which its reconciliation is not just publicly proclaimed but, as it is proclaimed, is also publicly imparted. Whether consciously or unconsciously, it stands in the light of it. Nor is this a light like others. As distinct from others, its shining is with power. It incorporates into itself. It has thus given the world not merely a new appearance but a new character and form. No matter, then, how man may twist and turn, the Word of God, and in and with it his reconciled being in virtue of this Word, are suggested to and imposed upon him, as we have said, as an element

4. *The Promise of the Spirit*

in his own existence, not by nature, nor in virtue of a merit which he brings or may win, but by grace, in virtue of the pronouncement which has been made in the resurrection of Jesus Christ and which applies to him. It is assigned to him by the Word of God. Whatever he may make of it, the act of God is appropriated to him. He could more easily divest himself of his own being than of the fact that he is not just man, but that as such, since Jesus Christ is risen, he is determined by and addressed on the basis of what Jesus Christ has done and accomplished for him. He may miss this, or hear it and not obey, though he would do better both to hear and obey. But even before he can hear and obey he is a man who is addressed on this basis and altered by this address. And all the alteration of his being and thought and speech and action which will necessarily follow this address if he hears and obeys can only be related to, and proceed from, and demonstrate the fact that he is addressed and altered in the resurrection of Jesus Christ, being comparable to the opening of the eyes of one who is raised again from the dead. In the Word of God which comes to him there is already actual, in a way which is valid for the whole world and therefore for him too, that which he will later practise when he begins to believe and love and hope. The second thing which has taken place in the resurrection of Jesus Christ is thus not merely the alteration of the situation between God and man and man and God as treated already in relation to the high-priestly and kingly offices of Jesus Christ, but the real outworking and manifestation of this alteration in His prophetic office. The second thing which has taken place is the alteration of the world itself and man himself, which irresistibly demands, of course, a third alteration, namely, a transformation of the world and especially of human being and thought and speech and action.

Let us pause for a moment at the affirmation of this twofold occurrence. In the resurrection of Jesus Christ there has taken place God's solemn declaration of His faithfulness to the world and man. And in it there has taken place a new and positive determination which comes to the world and man with this declaration. In making this affirmation we recall that the Easter event is only the first form of the new coming of the Jesus Christ who came before in His life and death, and that we have thus to see and understand it in relationship to the impartation of the Holy Spirit and the final appearance of Jesus Christ for the resurrection of the dead, the last judgment and the creation of a new heaven and a new earth. But if we understand it in this context, and therefore in the light of the progress of His coming again, we have spoken too modestly of what took place at the commencement. We must speak of it more definitely. For in the light of this progress we cannot know or state too definitely that at its very commencement and therefore in the Easter event it has taken place once for all and irrevocably that God has acknowledged the reconciliation of the world to Himself accomplished in Jesus Christ, and that the world and every man has therefore received a new and positive determination. That this is the case is guaranteed by the present impartation of the Holy Spirit and by the final, consummating work of the prophecy of Jesus Christ to which we may look forward as enlightened by the Spirit. Hence we can and should conclude that the new creation has taken place in the resurrection of Jesus Christ. And the fact that it has done so is to be taken rather more seriously than is often the case in our thinking about Easter or Sunday, or in the normal Christian celebration of Easter or Sunday.

Yet as we try to take the Easter event seriously in this sense, there arises—not from without but from within, from a correct understanding of the matter—a first form of the question which has to be put in this context. We have emphasised that it has happened once for all and irrevocably. " Irrevocably " is straightforward enough. Where the Word of God does not merely declare His act (the act of reconciliation accomplished in Jesus Christ), but as this declaration (as the act of revelation of Jesus Christ) it is itself His act, there can be no question of revocation or withdrawal, and we have the firmest possible ground under our feet. But what is meant by " once for all " ? " Once " is plain enough. It means that this is a specific event which cannot and does not need to be repeated. This declaration has been made. Jesus Christ has appeared to His disciples as alive after His death. How could we say unequivocally that this has happened at all if we did not say that it has done so then and there once ? But " once for all " ? When we necessarily say " once," as when we say in the past tense that this happened, do we not tend to underline the distance or remoteness of this unique event from those which take place at other times, making it an independent event which has happened ? How, then, can we say " once for all " if we take seriously the fact that the Easter event has happened ? When we find assurance and comfort and joy in relation to the Easter event of the exit, transition and entrance of Jesus Christ from His own sphere to ours and that of the world, does there not open up again and with true seriousness the gulf (perhaps identical with the " ugly ditch " of Lessing) which seems to separate Jesus Christ in the uniqueness of His existence and work, and obviously of His prophetic work in this primal and basic form, from us and our world and *vice versa* ? Like the events of salvation, does not their revelation in the Easter event lie behind us in the hazy distance ? Are we not elsewhere, unreached and therefore unaffected by what has taken place in it ? In short, as we emphasise that God's acknowledgment of the world and the new and positive determination of the world thereby effected have taken place once, are we not brought back again to the beginning, i.e., to the question to which we were able and obliged to give a positive answer in the light of this event ? Or can and should

4. *The Promise of the Spirit*

we stick to this answer because it is legitimate and justifiable and necessary to say of this event that it has happened not merely once, but once for all? We shall meet the same question from other angles and in other formulations, and therefore we do well to postpone for the moment what is to be said in reply.

Our next step (2) must be to formulate more precisely what has actually and effectively taken place in the Easter event between God and the world, between God and us, and to the world and us. Here again we must try to take it in all seriousness, and cannot be content with even the most correct preliminary descriptions, but must see and appreciate the matter in its whole breadth and scope. At its very commencement in the Easter event, the return and self-declaration of the One who came before was not limited like that which according to the Evangelists, and in anticipation of this event, took place even in the pre-Easter existence of Jesus, e.g., in His miracles, in the perception and confession of Peter at Caesarea Philippi, and especially in the transfiguration. " We beheld his glory " (Jn. 1^{14}). It is surely illegitimate to place any restrictions on this witness. What the disciples came to see in the appearances of the Resurrected was no more and no less, but initially just the same, as what will one day be manifest to all eyes. They saw the full extent of His work and influence as achieved in His life and death. In its totality, universality and definitiveness it then passed into the reality of world-occurrence, of human existence both in detail and as a whole, of the cosmic being and life which are the presupposition and sphere of human existence. It was incorporated into this whole. In the midst of this whole, and therefore, as this took place within it, in a new and positive determination of this whole, there took place God's faithful acknowledgment of the creature which had fallen away from Him but which He had not forgotten or abandoned and which was not therefore lost to Him. Our first task is relentlessly to see and follow the lines which open up from this point.

The determination given the world and man by this event is a total one. The reconciling work of Jesus Christ is not just accomplished, but has gone out into the reconciled world as a shining light comparable with the leaven hid among three measures of meal (Mt. 13^{33}). This means that the leavening of the whole, the determination and alteration of the world and humanity by the kingdom of heaven in all its power and glory, is not merely possible but actual and in process of fulfilment. The fire which Jesus has come to kindle on earth (Lk. 12^{49}) is not the little fire of a religious, moral or political agitation or movement. It is the fire of the work which He has done in place of all men, and God in Him on behalf of all men. It is the fire of God's self-humiliation in Him and man's exaltation in Him. It is the fire of the judgment executed in Him and the grace triumphant in Him. This fire now burns and cannot be extinguished. The love with which God loved the world cannot remain external. The world is now the world loved by Him in His only-begotten Son. Man is now the man justified and sanctified in Him, and called by Him. But this means that the sin of his pride and sloth are forgiven, covered and annulled with the removal of the sin of his falsehood. And the death to which he has fallen victim is now the death from which he is delivered, which he can have behind and under him, since Jesus Christ, and he too as elect in Him, is risen from the dead to new life. He is now the son of God, since the eternal Son of God has come to his side as his true Brother, and is revealed and confirmed in his proximity, and as it were hand in hand with him, as the Son of the Father and his Brother. He is now the heir of eternal life and as such already has a share in his inheritance, because Jesus as the One who lives eternally has not merely associated with him but addressed him in His resurrection as one with him. And since the One who for our sake and in our place was rejected and tormented has been shown to be the Beloved of God in whom He has loved us from all eternity and therefore as the Liberated in whom our liberation is accomplished, all tears are indeed wiped from all eyes, and sorrow and crying and pain can have no more place among us (Rev. 21^4). And in view of the happening which all creation could witness on Easter Day, was not the sighing of all creation (Rom. 8$^{19f.}$) already heard, its unrest and anxiety stilled, its liberation accomplished? Was it or was it not the case that what Jesus alone had seen as the One who came before (Lk. 10^{18}) was now revealed to all eyes whether they saw or not, namely, that Satan had fallen from heaven like lightning, or positively (Mk. 9^1) that the kingdom of God became visible, and came into effective action as this link in the chain of world-occurrence, not under certain restrictions or diminutions, but in total power?

Is this all imagination? It is certainly sung in our Easter hymns. We say of sin that the Son of God has " abolished " it in His resurrection : " Now the night of sin is ended " ; " O time of joy, O happy day, When sin has yielded up its prey, When all our guilt is set aside And we by grace are justified." Or of death that " it hath lost its sting " ; " Now the power of death is slain, Innocence hath come again, And being without end." Or of Satan : " With might and main the serpent fought, When Christ took up the fray, With force and subtlety he wrought, Yet could not win the day. What though the Victor's heel he struck, He could not stand the battle's shock, And his own head was trampled." Or of the cosmos : " For this great comfort, Hero strong, The world doth raise its grateful song " ; " Sun and earth and all creation, All that suffered tribulation, Praiseth Thee this day of joy, That Thou didst its foe destroy." Or comprehensively : " The ancient serpent, sin and tomb, Fear and pain and final doom, Jesus Christ hath met and slain, Risen to-day from death again " ; " Exalted high, the Lord's right hand, Hath triumphed in this hour ; On foes which made defiant stand, It hath come down with power " ; " Death, devil, hell and sin, surprised, Are crushed by our triumphant Christ, Their wrath hath lost its terror." Or with positive application to the individual : " In Jesus' resurrection strong, To Sion's city I belong ; My peace is made with God above, I'm crowned

4. *The Promise of the Spirit*

with righteousness and love." In short: "Thanks be to God, our triumph sure, Is made by Jesus Christ secure, Victorious in the fight." Thus far our Easter hymns, and in tenor and even in wording they simply repeat what the New Testament said quite expressly long before. Our Easter preaching, whatever terminology or language we might use, is surely to be tested by whether or not it maintains the level reached in the hymns. But the question remains where is it led, and with it Christianity in its faith and conduct, if it does maintain this level. Where do we really stand if we take all this seriously?

To continue, the determination given the world and man in this event is a universal one. What took place in this event applied, of course, to Jesus Christ Himself, and then primarily in the forty days which followed (Ac. 1^3) to the little band of disciples, to the narrower and wider apostolic circle, to the men of the community called into being by this event. These men saw the kingdom of God coming in power. They found themselves addressed and claimed as justified and sanctified in the revelation of the work accomplished in the life and death of Jesus. They were taken up into the victory of life over death. Their tears were wiped away. Their liberation for eternal life and therefore for service in this life had taken place. This does not mean, of course, that the final goal and end was simply to set them in possession and enjoyment of this new being and in the corresponding action. The resurrection of Jesus is not a private satisfaction prepared for them. The Easter accounts have not only not suppressed but almost gone out of their way to emphasise that the personal results of the event were of little value, no great credit attaching to their astonishment, hesitation and doubts in face of it. From their own standpoint, we should have to say that the fruit of the happening is rather meagre according to the New Testament. But obviously their own personal deliverance and transformation were only incidentally and preliminarily the goal of this happening. Regardless of any personal results, the form in which it came to them was that of the missionary command: "Go ye into all the world." It was for this that the Resurrected appeared. In the reception and execution of this command they could enjoy the fruits of His appearing in their personal being and action, becoming different and better in themselves. But the real goal and end of the resurrection of Jesus and its attestation was His going out into the world, into all the world, just as the reconciliation revealed in this event was the reconciliation of the world and not just the satisfaction of the little flock of believers. The first-born right of this little flock cannot be overestimated, but it is linked with the first-born duty laid upon it in and with its prior selection. And this duty is a missionary duty. What does it mean to be given this duty? We must beware of arrogant identifications. The sending of the community or of Christians—of which we shall have to speak expressly in a later section—is not as it were the means by which the salvation of the world accomplished in Jesus Christ and revealed in His resurrection must be imparted to the rest of men and the whole cosmos, so that in this work we have a kind of repetition, representation and multiplication of the Easter revelation. No, the mission of the community has its ontological ground, its practical basis and its sure point of departure in the universalism of the Easter revelation itself, in which the impartation of salvation to the whole world has already been effected by the One who alone has authority and power to do it. Heaven and earth, angels and men and all creatures, are already in the resurrection of Jesus Christ set in the penetrating and transforming light of His person and work; they are already seized by that fire; they are already taught by Him, by the commencement of His prophetic work, how things stand with them on the basis of what took place in Him and by Him. By His living presence and action in the midst, they are already accused and judged but also comforted and cheered. They already take and have a part in the accomplished reconciliation, in the fulfilled covenant—a part which He has willed to give and given them as He rose from the dead among them. He appeared to His disciples, but to them as the first representatives of all. In their person He thus appeared to the whole of humanity and to the world. Their first-born right was that He appeared to them. But He appeared to them in the place of all. By anticipation all were included in them. Hence there was implied the first-born duty imposed with the right. In relation to all the others who in contrast to them did not yet know, had not yet heard or had not yet listened, how could they fail to recall what was said in power to all, summoning them to see with their own eyes the light of life already shining upon them and engulfing them, to know themselves as those who are already taught and accused and judged but also comforted and cheered in the Easter revelation of their Lord and Saviour, and to take up their lives as those who already stand in His light? What could they say to all—not in any individual power of revelation but in the power of witnesses of Jesus Christ solemnly ordained and commissioned to this ministry—except what He Himself had said to all in their person, namely, the powerful Word of God for and to the whole cosmos as received by Him? In the Easter event is grounded the necessity of Christian mission. A Christianity with no mission to all would not be Christianity. For it would not derive from this event. It would not be gathered and upbuilt by the Jesus Christ risen for all. Christianity has no option. Its only freedom is the wonderful freedom to turn in witness to the all to whom He has already turned in His resurrection. But again in the Easter event there resides the only possibility of Christian mission. It cannot replace, but only presuppose, His prophetic work, the immediacy and perfection with which it has begun in His resurrection and will continue from this point. It can only confess to all

4. The Promise of the Spirit

men and to the whole world that in its dimension as revelation, too, the work of Jesus Christ took place and takes place for them and to them. Christianity would deny what it has to confess if it were to ascribe any power of revelation to itself. And it would inevitably break under its arbitrary, self-imposed burden if it were to try to replace the Word of its Lord by its own word instead of attesting this Word. It has the freedom to fulfil its duty of mission in the knowledge that its Lord has long since preceded it with His Word in His resurrection, and that He is always well ahead of it, so that in this respect, too, it has only to follow Him. This is what must be said concerning the universal character of the determination given to the world in the resurrection of Jesus Christ.

At this point we note a weakness in even the best of our Easter hymns. It is perhaps connected theologically with the remarkably late discovery of the prophetic form of the work of Jesus Christ and consequently of the Christian duty of mission. As we have seen, these hymns can sometimes bring out the scope of the Easter event for the whole world. But they do this only occasionally, and they do not show what it necessarily implies for those who see this universal scope, namely, the imperative of Mt. 28$^{19f.}$ Even in their earliest forms, and more particularly in the 17th and 18th centuries, they tend to gravitate in the direction of the personal awakening, comforting, orientation and hope made possible and effected for Christians by the resurrection. In other words, they present a first-born right which is not also as such a first-born duty and therefore the duty of mission. In this respect, therefore, well-instructed Easter preaching must not only see to it that it does not fall short of them, but actually seek to go beyond them. This might well mean, of course, the introduction of a disturbing note. For reference would have to be made not merely to the necessity but to the sole possibility of the outgoing of Christians to the world in subordination of all the action required of them to the Word already spoken to the world by Jesus Christ Himself. And this would be very surprising to many good Christians. But it is quite imperative if the Easter event is to be taken as seriously as it deserves irrespective of the questions thereby raised.

And now from the same central point we must trace another necessary line. The determination given to the world and men in the resurrection of Jesus Christ is a definitive one. Definitive means that it holds good not merely for the beginning but for the end and for the course between. We may expect the progress and powerful conclusion of this determination, but not its replacement by another. What Easter brought, what it brought into the world, what it imparted and incorporated into the world, what it made our own, is life on the basis of accomplished reconciliation and the fulfilled covenant, the peace and joy of the life disclosed and granted to the creature in fellowship with its Creator, of eternal life. It is life procured for the world and us in the high-priestly and kingly work of Jesus Christ and revealed and therefore imparted in His prophetic work. It is life lived with Him, in the power of this whole work of His, in the fellowship of faith in Him, of love for Him and of hope in Him. The gift of this life, given in virtue of His radiating light, is thus in the form of its commencement the gift of Easter Day. But it has a continuation and it moves towards a conclusion and consummation. In its continuation and conclusion it will be given to the world and us otherwise than at its commencement. But it will not be replaced by another gift. For there is no greater, higher or better gift. There is good reason to look for other forms of this gift. In its first form, as the gift of Easter, it invites and commands us to do so itself. But there is no sense in looking for its replacement. If I know—as I may do on the basis of Easter—that Jesus is my confidence and Saviour in life, the question whether this satisfies us is answered as soon as it is raised. For if I know this, I not only should but may and can be satisfied with the very fact that I am " in life " in and with Him, and can desire nothing better. Neither humanity nor the cosmos as a whole can be given any more excellent determination than that which is given with the planting of the seed of the resurrection of Jesus Christ. For what has still to happen is simply the growth and fruition of this seed. With this first Word of the grace of God the last is implicitly spoken as well. If we look back to the resurrection as the beginning of the return of the Lord, we already look forward to the end of His return in His final manifestation. The determination then given to the world and us is on a small scale, but with no less totality, the same as will then be given conclusively on a big scale. To this extent it did not then receive a provisional determination which may be materially changed and will later be replaced. It received its definitive determination. This naturally implies that it cannot be disturbed or destroyed by any intervening obstruction or opposition. The world and man cannot slip or be pushed back again behind this new beginning. The movement thus initiated cannot be arrested. On this basis, and in spite of every circumstance, the world can only move forwards. Nor can it do so in a direction which is accidental or according to its own preference. It can move forwards only in the direction indicated by this event. The positive stamp impressed on the world by the fact that God has spoken His last Word in speaking His first cannot be expunged by sin, death or the devil, nor can it be replaced by a negative. That which God has given to it will be maintained and vindicated in the history of His creation in spite of every problem and difficulty. If we take the Easter event as seriously as it is taken in the New Testament, and if we try honestly to think in the light of it as is again done in the New Testament, how else can we regard the matter ?

But we may easily be betrayed into considerable difficulty if we see it in this way, i.e., if we reckon with the fact that there is no other or higher determination beyond that which is given to creation on Easter Day, because this already includes the highest in itself ; and that there is no opposing determination, because no such could have any power against it. Can this really be its definitive as well as its

4. The Promise of the Spirit

total and universal determination? Where do we stand if this is the case?

We again pause for a moment. Assuming that we take them seriously, we have only to consider the three concepts with the help of which we have tried to understand the determination of world reality and human existence by the resurrection of Jesus Christ and we are confronted at once by the second form of the question which necessarily arises in this connexion. We recall that it is a total determination, which means that in the sense of the Easter hymns there is no power which is not victoriously assailed and profoundly shaken and radically swept aside and condemned to impotence by the power of the resurrection. We recall that it is a universal determination, which means that it has already penetrated and reached and affected and seized the whole cosmos and every man, so that its Christian attestation must hurry after the prophetic work of Jesus Christ, but cannot do more than hurry after it. And we recall that it is a definitive determination, which means that the first Word spoken in the resurrection of Jesus Christ also includes the last, so that we must be directed by it in every respect, and need have no anxiety as to the progress of this happening in the sphere of the world and our own existence. But the problem is how we can do justice and hold fast to this overpowering insight. Is there not more shown us in the Easter revelation than we can see? None of the three concepts is selected arbitrarily. None is dispensable. They belong together, mutually supplementing each other. This is clear enough. But to each and all of them, both individually and in concert, nothing less is opposed than what seems to be the form of world reality and our own existence. No faith, love or hope can obviously carry us so easily over the obstacle of the almost complete invisibility of this determination. We may have various kinds of inklings, or regard certain postulates as legitimate and necessary for the establishment of these concepts, or experience individual insights in the given direction. But these do not really help us forward. That is, they do not answer the question why, seeing there is no doubt that we must confidently ascribe this total, universal and definitive power to the Easter event, its efficacy should not be manifest very differently in the form of the world and our own existence. Why do we need at all the help of inklings, postulates and insights of this kind? Why may we not everywhere know its power indisputably and irresistibly because directly? What remains of the positive answer sought and found in the Easter revelation to the question of the exit, transition and entry of Jesus Christ and the Word of reconciliation? What is meant by the efficacy of His prophetic office if in this respect we can only confess our dilemma, namely, our inability to follow even in thought, let alone in life, the knowledge disclosed in the Easter revelation? Can we maintain this positive answer in view of the fact that from this aspect, too, we necessarily discover that it is again radically qualified and called in question ?

Our final step (3) is to maintain the absolute newness of the form in which Jesus Christ in the Easter revelation imparts Himself, His mediatorial work, the life of the reconciled creature as the fruit of His work, to the world and us. We have said from the very first, but must now emphasise, that in this commencement of His coming again we have to do quite unmistakeably with the genuinely and radically and absolutely new coming of the One who came before.

He came as the same as the One who came before, as the Servant and Lord, the Priest and King, who lived and died among men within the limits of His time, in the poverty and fulness in which He was known or unrecognised or completely unknown before, corresponding exactly to the image in which He had more sharply or faintly impressed himself upon, and still lived in the recollection of, the more immediate or distant circle of those around Him, either to their joy or discomfiture, in illumination or warning. In other words, He came exactly in the form of the being and action which had been His being and action in the world like those of any other man. In this previous being and action He had been the suffering and active Mediator between God and man. It was as such that He now came anew in the work of His revelation.

Yet if only we will let them say what they do say, it is quite plain and unequivocal from the Easter records, for all their obscurity and difficulty, that He did not come in the form of an extension of the previous being and action actualised and completed by Him, as may be more or less concretely and palpably the case with other men when their work is done. Nothing could be more inappropriate than to compare His new coming with the Alpine glow following a day of sunshine. He did not come in the form of a preservation of His picture in the memory, or perhaps its endowment with new significance. It was not merely that He continued to exert the influence which He had previously had and which still remained. It was not merely that there persisted the thought of Him, or a previously uncertain but now strengthened conviction of the correctness and importance of His message, or faith in His person, mission and work as previously weakened and shaken by His death but now given fresh impetus, or an experience once mediated through Him but now presenting itself in new colours and contours. These things would not really be a new coming, a true *parousia*, as the coming again of the One who came before and then departed. Only rhetorically could they be described as such, and neither the Easter records nor the other passages in the New Testament which look back or refer to Easter give us any ground for this type of linguistic extravagance. Where is there a single scrap of evidence to support the view that the New Testament community lived in virtue of a reviving impression

4. The Promise of the Spirit

of Jesus, or in virtue of its own renewed and strong and strangely persistent thoughts and convictions about Him? What grounds have we for thinking that shortly after His death it miraculously attained the freedom to believe in Him with so strong a faith that it not only could and should believe in this faith or its marvellous origination, but it could also summon Jews and Greeks to faith in this new faith? Where do we find this? What is there to suggest that it might seem possible or legitimate or even obligatory to interpret the statements of the New Testament in this way? There did not merely recur a recollected picture of Jesus; He Himself came again. This is what the Easter records tell us. And this is explicitly or implicitly the basis, theme and content of the whole faith and message of the New Testament. The event of Easter Day was that He Himself came again, and that He summoned and awakened men to faith in Him rather than faith in their own faith, and to the proclamation among Jews and Greeks, not of their faith, but of His name and action, of the kingdom drawn near in Him.

But the fact that He who had come before came again was and is His radically and totally and absolutely new coming in the fact that it was His coming from beyond the frontier of all creaturely life as the Resurrected from the dead. This means, however, that He came back from the place from which none other has returned, from the tomb in which He was laid "earth to earth," from the place where all others permanently disappear from human sight when their hour comes. And according to the context of the Easter records in Matthew and Luke, we must also add that in coming thence He also went to the place where none other has gone, to heaven, which in the Bible denotes the hidden and inaccessible dwelling-place of God in the sphere of His creation. It was on the way from the one to the other that there took place the commencement of His return. It was in this transition that He appeared to His disciples, revealing both Himself and what God has accomplished in Him as the One who came before. It was in this form that He spoke to them as the Fulfiller of reconciliation and the covenant, as the Messiah of Israel and Saviour of the world, as their eternally living Lord. It was in passing in this form that He announced Himself as the One who would be with them to the world's end. It was in this form that, encountering them as the Resurrected from the dead, He Himself, and not a recollected picture of Him, established, kindled and created their faith in Him and became the basis, theme and content of their proclamation of His name and person and work. It was in this form that, accompanying them for a short stretch, presenting Himself visibly and audibly, making this unique transition from earth to heaven, He was not only seen by them as they had seen Him before, but they beheld His glory and there shone upon them the light of His life, and of their own life in Him.

§ 69. *The Glory of the Mediator*

It is self-evident that they could not record in any other way His appearances in this form and therefore the commencement of His return. It is self-evident that even if they had known and been able and willing to apply them, they could not have used historico-scientific or psychological or even existential categories to grasp or describe this event. It is self-evident that any attempt subsequently to verify them in these categories is forced materially to interpret what is obviously for them the miraculous origination of their faith in Jesus Christ as the new and better commencement of the movement of their own thoughts and convictions around the influence of His life now realised *post festum*, and formally to devaluate it as saga or legend fashioned by the mythological thinking of an age of magic, if not to descend to the various bizarre pragmatic explanations which have been suggested from time to time. Along these lines, however, it is quite impossible to see what the Easter records actually tell us in their obscure and contradictory and confusing way, and what they obviously mean to tell us, because this is what, come what may, they have to tell us as the presupposition of the whole faith and message of the New Testament. What can be seen along these lines can never be what the New Testament had to attest at this point, and does actually attest, as an event which has happened and has been perceived in place and time, namely, the appearance of Jesus Christ to His disciples in this form, the commencement of His return in this inconceivably exalted transition. It would be well if especially those who undertake to expound its assertions historico-critically would content themselves with as precise a statement as possible of this content which cannot be verified by historico-critical methods.

It is surely obvious that if in the Easter event our concern is with what the New Testament clearly envisages when it speaks of it, namely, the coming of Jesus Christ risen from the dead, then in all our attempts to denote and describe the new and distinctive character of this coming we cannot grasp too firmly or emphasise too strongly its particularity in face of all other conceivable realities.

Death is far too radically serious and sharp a limitation of all human being and action, and of creaturely existence generally, for us to try to understand the resurrection and return of a man from the dead, and his appearance after death, merely as a human or creaturely possibility integral at some deep physical or metaphysical level to the material or spiritual cosmos. To say death is to deny any future to the one who existed. Death is the frontier of human and all creaturely being beyond which it can only have been, beyond which there is no one and nothing save God the Creator, beyond which the creature is divested of all its own time and strength and ability and possibility and can be, if at all, only from God and for God.

Since, then, God alone can be its future, the life of a creature after death cannot in any sense or circumstances be anything other than its life from God and for God, i.e., the life which is not its own but is given to it by God. God alone is above death and after it. He alone has immortality (1 Tim. 6^{16}). If a creature is to have immortal life, i.e., the life which defies and overcomes death, which leaves it behind, which is no longer threatened by it, then in no circumstances can this be simply its autonomous continuation in life. It can be

4. *The Promise of the Spirit*

only its new life from God and with God. It can be only the eternal life which is given it by God after the manner of His own life. Its corruptible and mortal, therefore, must as such, as that which it was between birth and death, put on the incorruptibility and immortality which are proper only to God (1 Cor. 15^{53}). Its present form is not, then, dissolved or done away or destroyed, which would mean death, or a future without God. It is taken up into the new form which is not proper to it in its creatureliness but is given to it as that of God its Creator. The past state upon which it enters with death, and which is manifest in death, is thus taken from it by the fact that God, who was its only but true future even in its corruptibility before death and its corruption in death, is present to it in death itself. As what it was before death, it may thus be present and live eternally even after death in the power of His presence, i.e., not of itself, but in the power of the presence of God.

But if this is the case—and cost what it may we must push through our analysis of the Easter event to this point—then the question arises what is meant by the return from death after death of the man Jesus. There can be no doubt that in the great presupposition of the faith and message of the New Testament indicated in the Easter records we have to do with the concrete, visible, audible, tangible new presence of the man Jesus who was crucified, dead and buried. What we have here, then, is a perceptible and active presence and appearance which, if it is temporary and therefore limited in time, is within this short span comparable with the presence and appearance of a man who has not yet died. But it is the presence and appearance of One who has obviously crossed the frontier beyond which there is no future outside God, and who cannot therefore have before Him any other life but life from and with God and after the manner of God, i.e., eternal life. This means, however—and there can be no easier way of grasping the significance of what took place at Easter—that the frontier was also crossed in the reverse direction. The One who had come before, who had been crucified, dead and buried, who had perished like all flesh, came again among His disciples and participated in the existence of men who were still moving forward to death, of perishing creation in all its corruptibility, of world-occurrence in its spatio-temporal contingency and limitation. But there can be no question of a continuation of the life of man after death in his own strength or according to his own capacities or possibilites. Only the presence of the God who alone is immortal and transcendent can be the future of his this-worldly existence terminable by death. What is implied, therefore, by this new coming of the man Jesus ? What is meant by this new coming of a man who is mortal and has obviously died like all others, if His only possible life after death is the this-worldly life which has now been terminated by death but which by participation in the sovereign life of God is delivered from all past or future perishing, being made eternal by the omnipotence of the grace of God, and therefore participant in the immortality and transcendence of God ?

The radically new thing in the coming again of the man Jesus who obviously died on the cross was not a prolongation of His existence terminated by death like that of every other man, but the appearance of this terminated existence in its participation in the sovereign life of God, in its endowment with eternity, in the transcendence, incorruptibility and immortality given and appropriated to it in virtue of this participation for all its this-worldliness. He came again in the manifestation or revelation of His prior human life as it had fallen victim to death as such, but had been delivered from death, invested with divine glory, and caused to shine in this glory, in virtue of its participation in the life of God.

But to grasp the radical newness of His coming again, of His appearance in the glory of God, we must add at once that this was not just a mental appearance in the experience or intellect of the disciples as illumined by a vision or such like. It was His new appearance in the psycho-physical totality of His temporal existence familiar from His first coming. It was His new appearance in which He Himself met them on their own path in space and in the time which still remained to them after death, being present spiritually, of course, but also corporally as the same man He had been before, preceding, speaking, eating and drinking with them as with His fellows and as He had done before. In His participation in the glory of God, in which He was previously concealed from them, He now appeared to them on this short stretch of their life after His death, concretely participating also in their concrete temporal existence and in the concrete temporal existence of all creation. He was different in respect of His revelation as the true Son of God and Son of Man existing in the world. But He was not different in respect of the fact that, no less in this revelation of these days than previously in His concealment as the true Son of God and Son of Man, He existed among them and therefore concretely in time and space in the world. He was not different in respect of the fact that even and especially in this revelation He spoke and acted among them and therefore in the world, coming again not in semblance only but in reality.

If we are not to be guilty of Docetism in our exposition of the Easter story, to grasp and estimate the new feature in this coming we must see and accept the fact that the glory of God is here present in the personal, real, visible, audible and even tangible coming again of this man. Both as true God and also as true man Jesus Christ was again present in the midst of world-occurrence. Not only did God break out from His transcendence, but He broke into the this-worldliness of His creation. Here, as His temporal and spatial life, there shone in the resurrection of Jesus Christ, in His appearing as

4. The Promise of the Spirit   313

the Resurrected from the dead, the light of His eternal life. His temporal and spatial life shone as His eternal life. This was the shining with which He came again from the dead—the Jesus of yesterday to-day.

This, then, is the new thing in the return of Jesus Christ in its commencement, in its first form. This is what is envisaged and intended by the New Testament when it refers to His resurrection, when it knows Him on the basis of this event, when it knows Him on this basis even in looking back to His prior life and death as in all the four Gospels, when on this basis it believes in Him and confesses Him as the living Lord, and proclaims Him as the Messiah of Israel and the Saviour of the world. Let us make no mistake! This is the basis of the whole faith and message of the New Testament and the whole of the Christian community gathered and upbuilt upon them. The community exists as it derives from this source, from this new coming of its Lord. We need waste few more words at present concerning the difficulty of conceiving and representing this event. It sets before us the mystery of the revelation of God, in which the prophetic work of Jesus Christ is enveloped in this primal and basis form, and is plainly distinguished from other revelations and prophecies.

When one analyses the Easter event without reinterpretations or reservations as we have tried to do, not making the task easier by explaining the resurrection of Jesus Christ as the realisation of a general physical or metaphysical possibility of the creature or a purely mental event, but keeping to the New Testament witness as it stands, one appreciates at once that this event does not fit into any known or conceivable world-view, and that, as in the case of the existence of God (which is really the point at issue here too), any attempt to integrate it into such a view can only lead to its denial. It does not fit into any world-view, however, because, although like the reconciliation of which it is the revelation it has taken place in and for the world, and forms a link in the chain of general world-occurrence by which the world is supremely affected both in general and in detail, yet it did not derive from the life of the world either in heaven or earth, nor was it a natural or spiritual product of creation, but it took place only in the act of God the Creator who is the Lord of heaven and earth, of the natural and spiritual cosmos, of life and death. In other words, it occurred only as God came forth from His transcendence and entered our this-worldly sphere. As this act of God to and for the world, it cannot be integrated into nor provided for in any world-view, whether scientific, ethical, aesthetic, nor even mythological. Gods and their attributes and functions and acts and sorrows, together with ideas and concept of divinity, may well have a place in the various world-views under different names. But the same cannot be said of the act, the effective grace, the glory of the transcendent God in this-worldly reality as brought before us in this event. This is what makes it just as difficult to conceive and represent this event as it is to conceive and represent what is revealed in it, e.g., reconciliation itself, or the covenant, or peace between God and the world, or the very existence of the God who is at work in reconciliation and therefore in this revelation and therefore in the raising of Jesus Christ from the dead. God does reveal Himself in this event. But He could not the more effectively maintain and emphasise the mystery of His action generally, and specifically of His gracious act of deliverance, than by willing to reveal, and actually revealing, Himself and His work in this way, i.e., in this event.

Our present concern, however, is not with this aspect of the matter. The only point of referring to the mysterious character of the Easter occurrence is to protect it against clumsy misunderstandings or misinterpretations, or more positively to bring out the absolute newness of its structure. We must keep this plainly in view if we are to realise the scope and significance of this event. To take up again our earlier statements, it was an event which happened once for all and irrevocably, proclaiming, confirming and validating the effected reconciliation of the world to God and giving to and impressing upon the world and every man the total, universal and definitive determination corresponding to this completed reconciliation. But what does all this mean if this event consisted in that absolutely new coming of Jesus Christ ? What does it mean if it consisted in the fact that in those days, as a man among men, He did not merely live His temporal life as an eternal, His this-worldly as an otherworldly, His mortal as an immortal, His human as a divine—for He had done this as the One who came before—but actually revealed His life as such, living it visibly, audibly and tangibly in time and space in this form ? What was the result for the world that it had this within it, that the link of this event was added to the chain of events, or better that this seed of life, obviously so very new and different in relation to any known form, was mightily implanted in the life of the cosmos, not merely as the existence of the man Jesus in the glory of God, but as the phenomenon of His existence among the other phenomena of cosmic life ? What does it mean for the situation and status of other creatures, for ourselves, to be brought into direct proximity to this phenomenon and set in the light which shines from it ? What does it signify for all creaturely existence, action, passion, life and death that among all the commonplace or catastrophic, important or unimportant, glad or painful tidings of its progress and decline, note has also to be taken of the published news that Jesus Christ is truly raised again ? We best see its relevance if we simply hear or read it as one item of news among others, as though it were a headline in the daily paper : Jesus Christ is risen. But what are we to make of all the other items if we take note of this ? How does it stand with all other happenings if this has really happened, not in the safe distance of a world of ideas, but in direct proximity, in no less concrete reality ?

Once we realise the absolute newness of the structure of the Easter event, the only answer that can be given is that in it, in the appearance of the man Jesus in the glory of God, it has happened to the world that its future, goal and end as the world reconciled to God, its future of salvation, has become directly present as an

4. *The Promise of the Spirit* 315

element in its own existence which is new but no less concretely real than any other element.

What can and will become of the world now that God has reconciled it to Himself ? In the light of the revelation of this divine action, and the alteration which has taken place in it, it is obvious that, since God has had mercy on it in Jesus Christ and corrected the situation between it and Himself, it is no longer a lost world. But this cannot be all. It is not all. For in the light of this revelation it is no less clear that as this reconciled world it cannot continue as before. It cannot continue in this antithesis of a temporal and eternal, this-worldly and other-worldly, corruptible and incorruptible, human and divine life. It cannot continue in the downward movement to death which is implied in this antithesis, which distinguishes its form as the unreconciled world, which stamps it as the form of death, but which can no longer characterise nor control its form as the reconciled world, being made impossible by the alteration of the situation effected by God. Its reconciliation carries with it a call to advance. Reconciling it to Himself, God has given it a corresponding future : its redemption from that downward movement and that bitter antithesis ; or more positively its redemption as the making eternal of its temporal life, the transcending of its this-worldly, the investing of its corruptible with incorruption, the clothing of its humanity in divine glory, the perfecting of its creation by the new creation of its form in peace with God and therefore in and with itself.

How do we know this ? We do not know it on the ground of arbitrary surmise or speculation, but from the revelation in which not merely the accomplished reconciliation as such, but also God's will and purpose and plan in this action are not concealed but manifested and made visible, audible and tangible, i.e., in the resurrection of Jesus Christ from the dead. For it took place in this event that in the appearance of the one man Jesus in the glory of God there was made immediately present as a new but concretely real element in the existence of the world the goal given to the world in and with its reconciliation to God, its future of salvation as redemption from the shadow of death and the antithesis which pursues it, its future of salvation as its completion by the creation of its new form of peace, its being in the glory of God. Within world-occurrence there appeared in Jesus Christ, who as the one Son of God was the basis and goal of all divine election and creation and as the one Son of Man the Firstborn of creation and the Head of all other men, the life of all creation and all men already made eternal, already taken up into the beyond in all its this-worldliness, already invested with incorruption in all its corruptibility, already lived from and with and for God in all its humanity. This future determined for the world in and with its reconciliation became its true and concrete present. There did not merely

§ 69. *The Glory of the Mediator*

begin there a new era and movement within the existing form of world-occurrence. There struck the last hour of its existing form and the first of its new form necessarily following and corresponding to accomplished reconciliation. The old form was broken off, the new introduced, by the initiative, movement and act of God Himself. What took place on Easter Day was already the end of the being of the world and man in its previous form of death and the beginning of their being in the new and eternal form of life given them in God. Man in all his sin and misery (and the world with man) had behind him, in the resurrection of Jesus Christ, the death to which he had fallen a prey and towards which he moved, and before him his existence from God and with God and for God. What came upon the world and man in the resurrection of the man Jesus, in His appearance in the glory of God, was this presence of its future salvation ordained as the fruit of its reconciliation. The news of the presence of this future, of this to-day of the last and first hour, of the dawn of the redemption and consummation, is the Easter message. And the presence of the future in this event is the new seed of life planted in world-occurrence on Easter Day. It is the personally written and sealed and permanently valid document of the faithfulness of God transmitted into our hands with its total, universal and definitive content. We are now those who possess this document and may appeal to it and must live by what it tells us. And all creation is the creation which by the execution and presence of this document is set in the light of the presence of its future of salvation.

This, then, is how matters stand with the coming again of Jesus Christ in its commencement, in its first form, as now seen in this third statement from the standpoint of the complete newness of the form in which Jesus Christ in His revelation has imparted to the world and us Himself, His atoning work and the life of the reconciled creature as its fruit. For the sake of clarity we must develop more explicitly what is merely stated in this context. For the moment, however, we must pause to consider the question which arises with particular urgency at this point and which includes the question which confronted us earlier.

In relation to our final depiction of the future of the reconciled world already made present in the Easter event, we can first formulate this question as follows. How was it possible that the world's future already made present there in that event should not at once engulf the whole world like a tidal wave, engulfing with its presence all the men of all times and places whose future had become present there in the appearance of the risen Jesus Christ? How was it possible that the light of life, of the fulfilled covenant, of the accomplished reconciliation, which dawned there, should not at once penetrate into even the remotest corner, or that the seed of life implanted there in world-occurrence and the existence of all men should not spring up without

4. The Promise of the Spirit

delay and bring forth in every dimension the fruit of fulfilled redemption and consummation ? How was it possible that this goal of the will and purpose and plan of God for His creature should be reached there in the appearance of the one man Jesus in a way which in Him is valid for all like the atonement made by Him, but in effect should be reached only in Him, whereas for the rest of the world, beginning with His disciples as witnesses of His resurrection, it can be only a goal which is manifest, indicated and certain, yet unattainably distant in virtue of the frontier of death which still divides Him and them ? How could it be that He and not they or any other man should be invested with incorruption in His corruptibility, having death behind Him, being delivered from the form of death and set in living fellowship with the living God who alone is immortal ? How could it be that this event, so laden with incomparable force, should not yet have by a long way the corresponding total, universal and definitive effect, but that time and world-occurrence in time should seem to go forward, and should still seem to do so even yet, as if nothing had happened, as if the last and first hour had not struck, as if Christ were not risen ? How could it be that in spite of and even in their revelation the redemption and consummation corresponding to and necessarily following the accomplished reconciliation should not yet take place in this world in and to which the revelation is given, or even in the narrow circle of men who are participant in it ? How could all this be ? This is the question which faces us when we try to take seriously the Easter event, and especially when we try to take it quite seriously in its radical newness, in its " eschatological " content and character in the strictest sense of the term.

In this respect we must take care that we do not try to meet the question merely with answers which have the twofold characteristic of certainly being in their own place and manner very correct and important but in this very correctness and importance of leading back again to the question which they are designed to answer and in some sense do so.

We may rightly point out (1) that what really oppresses the world and us in spite of the Easter event, or rather in the light of a true appreciation of it, is not really a lack or failure or absence of its efficacy but simply the fact that this is not evident to us, and therefore its apparent absence. The last and first hour has really struck in the resurrection of Jesus Christ. The future of salvation is really present in it. Not reconciliation alone, but the ensuing redemption and consummation, have really taken place in it for the world and us in all their reach and depth. If we could see with God's eyes, we should realise that in spite of appearances everything is already very different, all things being made new and set right. The only thing is that we cannot see in this way. The actual alteration of our existence, of all things, of the whole being of the world, is hidden from us in the sense that it cannot be observed or experienced except in this event, in the living Jesus Christ Himself. The alteration of our situation effected in Him is concealed as it were by a veil which our eyes cannot penetrate. Do we not walk by faith and not by sight (2 Cor. 5⁷)? Is not our life hid with Christ in God (Col. 3³)? Yet its concealment, and the fact that we cannot " see " in this concealment, does not alter in the very least the fact that in this concealment (with Christ in God), in which we can know it only by faith, it is really our own life, fully and radically renewed on the basis of and in correspondence with the reconciliation accomplished in Him.

Why should not this be true? Why should it not have to be recognised as true in its own place? Even if this is so, however, the question has still to be asked why is it only our hidden life with God? Why cannot it be seen and observed and experienced as our life? Why cannot we lay our hands on its reality except in the Easter event or in Jesus Christ Himself? Why cannot we know directly our own existence and that of the whole world in the light of the eternal life of Jesus Christ? Why cannot this existence be lived out as our life in the future of salvation made present and therefore in the redemption and consummation? Why may it be known only under that veil when the Easter event means the removal of the veil which covers the reconciliation accomplished in Jesus Christ and its fruit? Why may it not be known openly and unequivocally and visibly and tangibly as our own life and that of the world by this fruit and therefore under the new heaven and earth as the life of men in the glory which corresponds to the covenant of peace concluded between God and the world? Why should not this glory be visibly, audibly and tangibly present in the man Jesus risen from the dead, not merely as His own future, but as ours and that of the whole world? Why are we still held at a distance from Him? Why do we have to believe in that which could then be seen and was actually seen? Why do we have to be among those who, unlike Thomas (Jn. 20²⁹), are blessed because they believe even though they do not see? Ought we not to put such questions? Do we not have to put them, as I believe, on any serious consideration of the resurrection of Jesus Christ?

The further answer (2) is also meaningful and legitimate, as a variation upon the first, that what confuses us, but ought not to do so, is the fact that in the Easter event we have to do only with a commencement of the revelation of reconciliation and its fruit in the ensuing redemption and consummation, but not with this revelation in its full development. In other words, we have to do with the return of Jesus Christ in its first but not in its final and conclusive form. The future of salvation both for ourselves and the world is already present in the resurrection of Jesus Christ. It is present in all its fulness. But this does not mean that it has ceased to be the future in another sphere outside this event, i.e., in the sphere of our

4. The Promise of the Spirit

own existence and that of the rest of the world. Hence, even though it is present and we may be joyous and strong in the light of this event, we have still to wait also with patience and hope. We cannot look back upon this event, therefore, without having still to look forward to the event in which it will be repeated and renewed and consummated in another form, namely, in the coming again of Jesus Christ in evident lordship over the creatures of all times and places and for the evident judgment of the quick and the dead and their evident subjection by His judgment. From the first event we have still to look to the second in which the light of the life which has appeared in Him will penetrate and fill even the remotest corner of the cosmos, in which everything mortal and corruptible will put on and enjoy immortality and incorruption, and in which God will become and be all in all. We still cannot do more than wait for this event, for the future of salvation in this conclusive and completed form. We can still see it as it were only in a narrow chink in its first form. We have still to believe in its second, coming, final and completed form. To this extent, even though we are the children of God, we do not yet know what we shall be (1 Jn. 3^2). This tension exists, and cannot be relaxed. Nor should it be. For on the basis of what we are in the light of Easter Day we may and should look and move towards what we are not yet but shall be in the still awaited presence of the future of salvation. From the one we have the freedom—and why not also the joy?—to be on the way to the other with all men and all creation.

It is surely obvious that, to an even greater degree than in the first form, the answer is correct and cogent in this second version, and must be duly honoured in the appropriate context. But it does not really set aside our initial question. For if we make this answer, and are satisfied with it, the question simply recurs in a new form. For how could the revelation of reconciliation and the ensuing redemption and consummation, as this took place in the Easter event, be only the commencement and not also the goal and totality of this event, i.e., its full development in every time and place and above and beyond every height and depth of creation? How could the return of Jesus Christ in its first form need a final form to conclude it? How could it even be capable of such repetition and renewal? How could the world's future of salvation become present there but only there, still remaining future elsewhere? How could time still remain after this event, a time of so much obviously unredeemed and imperfect human and creaturely being and occurrence? How could hope and patience still be demanded of us after this event? How could we be asked to wait for the still outstanding repetition of it in a more complete form? Why did it not itself become that to which we only look forward as its repetition and completion? Why, apart from what we see through that small chink, are we so fully dependent on faith? Why the need to speak in terms of "only" and "still" and "not yet"? Why is it, and to what end, that we must tarry in this tension between then and now and one day? Why is it that our freedom and joy can only be to accept this tension and thus to be continually on the march? What is the basis and meaning of the fact that Jesus Christ did not so come again once that all further coming again is superfluous? Why is it that we and all creatures have still a long way to go to the home to which we belong, to the time when we shall enjoy our eternal life on the new earth and under the new heaven, to the investing of our corruptibility with incorruption? Why have we still to wait? These are not improper or unbiblical questions. Paul often put questions of this kind. The Apocalypse is plainly occupied with them. Indeed, they are found explicitly or implicitly in the whole of the New Testament testimony and characterise the assurance with which the New Testament bears witness to its subject. We cannot suppress them if we take the Easter event seriously and do not fail to see that the last and first hour did indeed strike in it. For it cannot be taken for granted that between the rising of the Easter light, between the Word of God then spoken and its fulfilment, between what was actualised then in the man Jesus, and in Him, as the First-born of creation and the Head of His people, on our behalf and for all humanity and the world—between this actualisation and the actuality of our own existence and that of the whole world, there should be the fact or even the possibility of this distance and difference. This unsettling and impatient question may not be the last word. But it is not an unjustifiable question. It has a real basis in the resurrection of Jesus Christ. Hence the unrest and impatience manifested in it, although they can and should be quashed and turned into rest and patience, are not to be rejected as superfluous or even harmful. Would to God that with a more serious attitude to the Easter message there were in Christendom more of the unrest and impatience which—whatever else may have to be said —are necessarily expressed again and again in questions of this kind!

But our attempt to make answer (3) may also take a very different direction. Rightly again, we may put the counter-question. In the unrest and impatience kindled by the Easter event, do we not fail to see the wood for the trees? In other words, do we not overlook that which has already visibly and continually followed from the resurrection of Jesus Christ in the form of effects upon world-occurrence and the lives of countless individuals? Do we not miss the present and ever new events and realities in which it finds living correspondence and representation even on this side of His coming again in its conclusive form? In this connexion may we not think of the presence of the future of salvation which took place in world history in the proclamation of the living Lord and Saviour awakened and authorised by the Easter event? May we not have regard to

4. *The Promise of the Spirit*

the powerful historical impact which this proclamation had made, to the many direct and indirect ways in which it has determined and stamped human existence and thus confirmed in fact its eschatological character and content as the Easter message ? Did not and does not the return of Jesus Christ proceed in the twofold event of the Christian *kerygma* and the Christian faith created by this, and above all in the gathering and upbuilding of the Christian community ? As the Church has its origin in the commencement of the self-revelation of the Lord, of reconciliation, of the covenant and the kingdom, and as it moves towards the completed form of this self-revelation, is it not in its own existence, in its inward and outward form and activity, one long anticipation of the future and still outstanding fulness of the redemption and consummation ? Is it not the fulfilment of the promise of the Resurrected : " Lo, I am with you alway " ? Is it not the other world in this world, the incorruptible within the corruptible, eternal life in temporal, divine in human ? Is not the Church itself the eschatological fact *par excellence* ? In other words, is it not the case that in it that which took place once and once for all in the Easter event, as the exit and entry of God into the world, may still be noted and experienced, and still takes place continually, in the existential reaching and claiming of countless individuals both within its own sphere and without ? Were there not and are there not enough both of great and small who in the words of Ps. 34[8] can and must testify : " O taste and see that the Lord is good " ? Is not every administration of baptism and the Lord's Supper, every statement and especially every active or passive exercise of Christian confession, every common or personal prayer in the name of the Lord, every action or task undertaken and fulfilled in the Church in His name whether in weakness or strength, whether well or badly (and usually half-way between), every small or smallest suffering accepted or victory daringly achieved in His name, an indication that He did not rise in vain or ineffectively, that He has set for human and creaturely existence a goal to which it must irresistibly move, already orientated on what will be, already representing and pointing to what will come, and all on the basis of the fact that it was then present already in the resurrection of Jesus, all moved by the impact and impulsion then received by human and cosmic being, then given and imparted to it ?

Who can doubt that in its way this is all correctly seen and weighed and stated, that this answer has also to be considered at this point ? It can certainly be given otherwise than with the fatal and misleading note which it has largely acquired particularly though not exclusively in Roman Catholicism, the more so the heavier the emphasis laid on the ecclesiastical institution or the pious individual. It can genuinely refer to the work of the Holy Spirit and thus to the decisive thing which has to be said on this whole question. But even if this answer

§ 69. The Glory of the Mediator

is given and exploited in the best sense, the question will necessarily remain an open one. For where on this side of the resurrection of Jesus Christ are there genuine Christian actualisations in which the presence of the future of salvation which took place in the resurrection of Jesus Christ may be unequivocally seen and known and experienced in a way which is even approximately similar to that of the resurrection itself and is not exposed to some measure of haziness and doubt ? Where in the Christian *kerygma*, Christian faith, the Christian community, the life and activity of even the purest Church and its noblest and best members, does the risen Jesus Christ Himself really meet us and therefore the other-worldly in the this-worldly, the incorruptible in the corruptible, eternal and divine life in the temporal and human, and therefore the reality of redemption and consummation ? To maintain that in Christianity and the Church we have to do with the eschatological fact, do we not have to make use of the loudest assertions and wildest interpretations, so arbitrarily and artificially puffing up what meets us, namely, the being and activity of the Church and Christians, that we cannot possibly carry real conviction ? Can we ever persuade the world that what it sees in the Church and Christians is really an anticipation of the goal, of the future of salvation, towards which it, too, may look and move ? Are even the most impressive forms and products of our Christian and ecclesiastical life adequate for this ? Will anyone, either Christian or non-Christian, cleave in life and death to, or live and nourish himself by, that which stands before him and which he actually experiences in this sphere ? Nowhere, perhaps, does our Christian and theological thought and utterance need to be so thoroughly demythologised than at the point where it is really concerned with the eschatological character of the existence of the Church and Christians, and most of all perhaps where it thinks it must translate itself into existentialist categories. Can the Christianity and the Church which really derive from and are grounded in the resurrection of Jesus Christ ever be anything better than the place where, from out of and beyond all the required representations of Jesus Christ, the kingdom, the covenant, reconciliation and its fruit, men can only cry and call out : " Lord, have mercy upon us ! Even so, come, Lord Jesus " ? Is not perhaps the surest test of genuine Christianity and Church life whether the men united in it exist wholly in this expectation and therefore not at all in a supposed present possession of the glorious presence of their Lord ? Will not His truly promised and therefore undeniable presence among them necessarily show itself in the fact that they exist as those who know an honest and basic lack, and thus hope for His conclusive appearing and revelation and their own and the whole world's redemption and consummation, looking and marching towards it in Advent in a movement from Christmas, Good Friday and especially Easter ? What other time or season can or will the Church ever have but that of Advent ?

4. The Promise of the Spirit

A survey is required of the way which we have so far traversed in this sub-section before we pursue it to the end and come to the decisive statement in this context. In relation to our more narrowly christological consideration and presentation of the " glory of the Mediator," i.e., of His prophetic ministry and work, or His work of reconciliation in its prophetic character, our concern is with the basic problem of the reach or relevance of His prophecy for the world reconciled to God in Him, for the existence and nature of the man justified before God and sanctified for God in Him. What does it signify for this world and this man that the existence of the Son of God and Son of Man, Jesus Christ, is the Word of God spoken to them as well as the work of God accomplished for them? What does He establish among them as this living Word spoken to them and revealing the reconciliation already effected for them? In the two preceding sub-sections we have tried to understand the fact that in His prophetic being and work as this Word He is the light of the world and shines as such within it. Our present task has been to see and understand how far He really is the light which illuminates them, irradiating, filling, determining and refashioning with its shining. To avoid any semblance of uncertainty we have first had to make the general and analytical statement that He would not be the Mediator Jesus Christ in His glory if what He did, He did somehow and somewhere for Himself alone and not from the very first to His own, to men, and in and to the world. The true Mediator Jesus Christ not only is light, and shines as such, but is from the very first the light which enlightens and effectively determines the world, His Word being declared with all the power of God in the world reconciled to God in Him. Any who speak otherwise do not know what they are saying. But we could not be content with this general statement. It had and has to be made in relation to the living Jesus Christ who reveals Himself as such, and therefore to the Resurrected from the dead. We have thus had to regard His resurrection as the event in which His glory moved out to grasp the world and us men, in which it became and made history, in which He who came before but was concealed now came again and declared Himself and His work in the world. Trying to grasp the singularity of this event of His coming again in glory as seriously as possible from every aspect, and thinking and speaking synthetically rather than analytically, we have found in this event the concrete answer to our question, namely, that in that event then and there it took place that Jesus Christ was declared and became effective as the Word of God in the world reconciled to God with all the power of God and therefore once for all, totally, universally, radically and with definitive newness. But we have necessarily made the strange and disturbing discovery that in the resurrection of Jesus Christ, in which we have undoubtedly found the answer to our question, the answered question raises itself again with new vigour in face of this primal and basic form of the self-revelation of Jesus Christ as the eternally living Mediator, Saviour and King, in face of the wonderfully illuminating power peculiar to this event. It raises itself as the question of the operation of this power and therefore of the enlightening of our own and all created existence as it does actually take place in virtue of this event. Now it is to be noted that this question does not originate in man's sombre and sceptical assessment of himself and the world, but at the point where he is summoned to be confident and comforted in relation to himself and the world. It does not derive from unbelief, but from faith in Jesus Christ as the light of life lighting up, enlightening and irradiating the world with its shining. It does not derive from ignorance, but from recognition of the superior power with which God Himself then and there in that event has revealed to the world its atonement accomplished in Jesus Christ and thus spoken to it the redeeming and consummating Word. It does not derive from anxiety that the near return promised by Jesus has failed to materialise, but from joy at the fulness with which it has taken place in the resurrection. Hence it does not derive from the notion that His resurrection has too little power of enlightenment, which could only be the view of someone who did not or would not take it seriously, but from a shattering appreciation of the immeasurable power of enlightenment active in and flowing from it. This is not really lacking. Nor is it insufficient. The problem is that it is too great. That is, it is too great to be limited to the one event which took place then and there. In full and all-transcendent plenitude it is the power of this event. But it is too high, too deep, too comprehensive to be the power of this one event alone. As the power of this one event it points beyond it. It bursts through its isolations. It transcends its spatial and temporal limits. It must work itself out in another event filling and controlling all times and places. As the power of this one event, it anticipates that other, all-embracing and conclusive event. It makes and characterises Easter Day as the day of the proclamation and indeed the commencement of the day of all days, of the last day, of the day of the final return of Jesus Christ. To see His return in the event of this one day is to be given willy-nilly an expectation of the last day which recapitulates and judges but also fulfils all history. Hence the question or questions which crowd in upon us. Why has the self-revelation of Jesus Christ in the world and in our lives taken place only at that point? Why has it remained invisible elsewhere, so that outside that event its perception can be only a matter of faith and not of sight? In other words, how could it commence there without at once reaching its goal everywhere and perfectly? Or in other words again, what is the basis and meaning of the fact that in what may be called its relatively visible reflection in the world and our lives, i.e., in the Christian *kerygma*, and Christian faith and the Christian community, we have only more or less clear

4. The Promise of the Spirit

signs but not the thing itself in the fulness of the form peculiar to it on Easter Day? It is true that these questions do not destroy or even disturb the recognition, based upon that event, of the transcendent and embracing power of the self-revelation of Jesus Christ in its outreach to the world and the individual. But it is also true that there can be no evasion or concealment of these questions. For they are not imported from without nor do they derive from historicism. Like the recognition, and together with it, they are based upon the Easter event itself. In short, not merely the answer to the question of the effectiveness of the Word of God spoken in Jesus Christ, but the question which is raised again and even more urgently as we find our answer in the knowledge of the Easter event, has final necessity, integrity, dignity and importance, deriving as it does from the same source.

But where do we stand if this is the case? And how are we to proceed if our last word is not to be the mere assertion of a strange contradiction?

Our best course is to be confident that the contradiction which does actually confront us is not accidental but expresses an intrinsically meaningful and correct reality or order superior to and underlying the contradiction, so that we need not merely accept it with resignation but seriously respect and even joyfully assent to it.

Assuming that we are indeed authorised and commanded to proceed with this confidence, the first consequence is that we see basically why we cannot escape this contradiction, why we must give up all attempts to overcome or resolve it, why we must reckon with it without bewilderment or concern, why we must see and understand the world and ourselves in the light of it. We know that the contradiction itself is light and not darkness. We can radically accept the fact that the Easter event is the answer to our question which can and should be accepted without reservations or doubts or qualifications, and that in relation to the redemption and consummation already actualised in the revelation of the accomplished atonement matters do really stand as we sing in our Easter hymns. We can be radically prepared to admit the question or questions which result from the fact that the Easter event is too great to be exhausted in a single Easter occurrence. We are basically forbidden to try to escape the unsettlement caused by these questions, i.e., the necessity of looking from the one Easter Day to the very different one, to the day of the Lord of the last judgment and final fulfilment, no matter how true or good may be the reasons which we produce in favour of such evasion. These things are all basic or radical because our knowledge of the matter or order reflected in the contradiction depends upon our not concealing or disturbing the mirror of this contradiction as such by weakening or denying either the given answer on the one side or the implied question on the other. This knowledge is possible only as we fearlessly recognise and appreciate both the answer and the new question and therefore the contradiction as such. This radical acceptance on both sides is the first result if we are authorised and required to proceed with confidence.

Nor do we lack good reason and cause to proceed with confidence and therefore to accept the contradiction of which we are conscious. For both sides of the contradiction derive from the same source. Whether we think of the source of the given answer or of the newly raised question, we are concerned in both cases with the self-revelation of the one living Jesus Christ. He is the Hero of Easter Day, and as such He is too great to be merely the Hero of a day. He gives us the answer as He enlightens the world and ourselves from this point, as He is in this event the powerfully spoken Word of reconciliation and therefore also of redemption and consummation. But He also raises the new question whether and how it is really enough that He enlightens the world and ourselves only from this point, that He is the Word of God spoken only in this event. He invites us to trust that this contradiction is not accidental but necessary, namely, that it expresses a meaningful and correct substance, that it is not a phenomenon of intervening disorder but of genuine order chosen, willed and arranged by God and therefore by Himself, and therefore to be respected and allowed as a contradiction. He demands that we should proceed at this point, reflecting on the substance mirrored in the contradiction and the order recognisable in it. But what do we mean by substance and order in this connexion ? How can we perceive or even suspect anything of this nature in the contradiction, and thus make it the object of our reflection ? Concretely, He Himself, the living Jesus Christ, is the substance and order in question. He expresses, reflects, declares and reveals Himself in that contradiction. He is both the One who answers and the One who questions. He gives Himself to be known as both. He lays claim to confidence on both sides. And as He awakens and deserves confidence, we must take it that we are authorised and commanded to proceed here with this confidence.

If in His revelation as the Resurrected from the dead Jesus Christ encounters us as the One who really answers (as He alone can and does answer in the power of God), and yet also as the One who really questions anew (as He alone can and does question anew after the given answer) ; if in this statement and contradiction we have to do with His Word and self-declaration, then this necessarily means that He Himself encounters us as the living One in the concrete sense that, since He can and will and must both radically answer and no less radically re-question us in divine freedom, superiority and necessity, He obviously finds Himself in movement or on His way as the divine-human Mediator, striding from His commencement to the goal already included and indicated in it. He moves from His com-

4. *The Promise of the Spirit*

mencement, i.e., from the reconciliation already accomplished in Him, to the accomplishment of which there also belongs its revelation in His rising again from the dead. As He comes from this commencement, He can and will and must and does give a radical answer. But He does not stand or sit at the place where He gives it. He clearly moves forward from this place, from this commencement. Although it has taken place even as revelation in His resurrection, His work in its form as revelation is not ended or concluded. As the Revealer of His work He has not yet reached His goal. He is still moving towards it. He is marching from its beginning in the revelation of His life to the end of His not yet accomplished revelation of the life of all men and all creation as enclosed in His life, of their life as the new creation on a new earth and under a new heaven. In His prophetic work He moves from the one Easter Day to the day of all days, to the last day, to the day of His final and conclusive return. In the commencement of His work He already has this goal. The reconciliation of the world to God in Him was effected with this end in view. By way of anticipation, it is already reached in His resurrection, in Him as the Subject of the Easter event. The eternal light has already gone out into the world. The new and future redeemed and perfected world is already present. In this commencement, however, the goal is not yet reached except in Him. It is not yet reached in the situation of the world and man. It does not yet have the form of a world enlightened and irradiated by His revelation, of a redeemed and perfected man. It is to this goal which is still to be reached outside Him, to the revelation of His own glory as the glory of the world reconciled in Him, of the man justified and sanctified in Him, that He moves in and from this beginning. In this conclusion of His return He Himself is still future. On the basis of the commencement in which it is already anticipated, He will certainly complete this revelation. But He has not yet completed it. He is on the way, moving and marching from the commencement to the completion. It is in this way, at this stage of His being and activity, that He encounters us in His resurrection. And as the One who is on the way from this commencement to this goal He can and will and must be and give a radical answer and yet also pose a no less radical question. The answer is grounded in the fact that the presence of the future of salvation is already actualised in Him. The new question is grounded in the fact that, although He will certainly actualise it for and in us as the presence of the future of salvation of all creation, He has not yet done so, but in this respect His intrinsically perfect work is still moving towards its consummation.

It is for this reason that in the preceding sub-section we described the history of the prophecy of Jesus Christ, of His light victoriously shining in darkness, as a history of victorious conflict both in its overwhelming beginning and its continuing progress, but we could not go on to speak of its end. For it has not yet reached the end. Now that we have so closely studied the resurrection of Jesus Christ as the beginning, the primal and basic form, of His prophecy, we are in a better position to appreciate how the New Testament witnesses came to know and proclaim Him as Victor from the very outset, in the commencement and continuation of His conflict, and also in what sense we are summoned to accept this insight and further this proclamation. Yet on the basis of this very resurrection we are also in a better position to appreciate the reason for the incompleteness of His conflict. For we know that as light shining in and fighting against darkness He is not yet at the end but on the way to it from this beginning. We cannot retract a single word concerning the certainty of victory with which we can and should accompany His warfare. From what we have seen of its commencement we ought perhaps to have expressed ourselves more strongly rather than more weakly in this respect. On the other hand, it has become no less evident that, since He Himself is only on the way to the end included in this beginning, our task is to accompany Him with this certainty along the way which leads to this end, in His moving towards it, and therefore in the warfare which is not yet concluded.

It is indeed a fact that the world reconciled to God in Him is far from being a redeemed and perfected world, that wickedness, evil and death are still rampant in it and in each individual, that there is still within it a whole sea of "deserved" and "undeserved" suffering, that we must still fight, and can only fight, under so many errors and in so much weakness. Who can overlook or deny this? But it is only the reflection or epiphenomenon of the fact that our reconciliation and that of the world to God in Jesus Christ is indeed accomplished, and even perfectly revealed in His resurrection, yet that it is not yet at the goal in its character as revelation, but is still on the way, Jesus Christ Himself in His prophetic work as light being still engaged in conflict with the darkness which contests the peace established in Him. It is not we nor the world but He Himself as the living Word of God spoken to the world and us who first comes up against this fact. It is He first who is surprised and startled that it is not removed. It is He first—the One in whom reconciliation is already accomplished— who with a displeasure and clarity very different from ours sees that all creation is still bound and tortured. It is He first who with a pity which is not idle but active, angry, militant, aggressive and therefore genuine, takes pity on its aberration and confusion, its infirmity and misery. It is He first who bears the burden of persisting wickedness, the resultant evil and the death which darkens everything. He does this now as the Resurrected from the dead as once He undertook and did it in Gethsemane and on Golgotha, with all the affliction and pain which this entailed and which He did not refuse. It is not for nothing that Jn. $20^{20f.}$ speaks of the wounds borne by the Resurrected

4. The Promise of the Spirit

and proving to the disciples His identity with the Crucified. It is as the One who came before that He has come again, risen and alive. It is as the One who fulfilled the judgment of God by submitting to it, accepting the crown of thorns as His royal crown, that He effected reconciliation and was manifested in the Easter event. It is as this One that He illuminated and irradiated the world in this event. It is as this One that He is Victor from the very outset, and proves Himself to be so in opposition to the darkness which mounts and intensifies as a result of the death-throes of the defeated enemy. He first, who alone is a match for and superior to this enemy even in the last round of the conflict, sighs and weeps and entreats and prays, as He previously did, in the open battle which has not yet been carried through to final triumph. In short, it is not in the first instance the world, or the Church, or an individual man suffering under and either rebelling against or in some way enduring the conflict, but He Himself, the Resurrected, who is still on the way, still in conflict, still moving towards the goal which He has not yet reached. This is what we have to remember in face of that fact. He first, the Reconciler, Redeemer and Fulfiller, from the very outset the true Son of God and Son of Man and in all His being and action as such the Victor, the One in whose appearing on Easter Day the redeeming and consummating final day of God announced itself and actually dawned—He first is still a Warrior and Pilgrim on the way to that goal. He is this first, as the Head of His people and the First-born of all creation. It is not the case, then, that He is warring and wayfaring in company with the pilgrim people of God, with humanity and the world in their movement towards that goal, with ourselves as we sigh and long for the liberation of the children of God. The converse is rather true that it is in company with Him that all expectant humanity and the world, as it still lacks the presence of its future of salvation, the whole people of God in its desert wanderings, and therefore we ourselves, still find ourselves on the way and therefore in strife and conflict. That He is not yet at the goal but still on the way is not because the world, the community and we ourselves are not yet there and do not yet live in the presence of our future of salvation. It is not that in accepting solidarity with us He adapts Himself to our situation. On the contrary, the "not yet" in which the world, the community and we all exist has its basis in the fact that it is the good will of Jesus Christ Himself to be not yet at the goal but still on the way, so that the rest of creation has no option but to participate in and adapt itself to His situation. It is not because darkness is still there, and the defeated enemy still has power and opportunity to lash out in its death-throes, that Jesus Christ is forced to fight him as the Protector of the peace made by Him, that the history of His prophecy must continue, until He is finally pleased to put an end to the struggle and therefore to this history by a final and conclusive return and revelation. On the contrary, it is because Jesus Christ, as we have seen, is the victorious Aggressor, and because it is His good will to act and show Himself as Victor in the fight against darkness, as light illuminating and irradiating the world, that power and opportunity are given to the enemy to make his fatal resistance, that darkness may exist, that the conflict of light against it is not ended, that its goal and end, and therefore the goal and end of the history of the prophecy of Jesus Christ, are still future and not yet present. It is not in view of what is for various reasons the very provisional nature of the situation of the world, the Church, the community and ourselves, that Easter Day could not at once and as such be the last day, that the revelation of the reconciliation of the world and men could not immediately be the fulfilment of their redemption and consummation, that the first return of Jesus Christ could not be immediately His last. On the contrary, the provisional nature of our situation has its true basis and determination in the fact that it is the good will of Jesus Christ to move from the commencement of His revelation to its completion, not causing the commencement and the completion to coincide, but Himself first to be provisionally who He is and to do provisionally what He does, giving Himself time and place for combat. The world, the community and we ourselves have thus no option but to participate in the fulfilment of this good will of Jesus Christ, to tread with Him the way which He wills to take, to fight with Him the battle which He wills to fight, in short, to follow Him. Since He precedes us, and it is His good will to act as He does, the only possible thing for the world, the community and ourselves, and indeed the only right thing, is to follow Him, to accompany Him on the way to His goal, in His movement from here to there, from the first to the final form of His coming again, in His still incompleted conflict, concerning the issue of which there is no doubt, but in which He still wills to engage.

We speak of the meaningful substance and legitimate order expressed, revealed and declared in the contradiction between the answer given in the resurrection of Jesus Christ and the question raised again in it. Our first explanation of these terms was to the effect that the living Jesus Christ Himself is the substance and order manifested in this contradiction. But we can now say more precisely that the good will of the living Jesus Christ to precede us on this way from His beginning to His goal, in the ongoing fight of light against darkness, and to determine us for discipleship on this way and in this fight, is the substance and order declared in this contradiction, superior to yet also underlying it. This good will of His demands, awakens and establishes the confidence which orders and authorises us to think further in relation to this contradiction. We have already taken an important step in this direction. But it cannot be the last.

Is it not right and even necessary to consider how far we really have to do with a good will of Jesus Christ in this substance and order? Is it adequate to say that as His will it is obviously good in this respect too, and that we should love and respect it as such? In the last resort, it must certainly be admitted that it is a good will as His will. Yet while this is finally true, we cannot shrug off the question how far it is good merely in this way. We owe it to the dignity of this final answer at least to try to understand what is meant by good at this point. There is always the threat of an open or secret rejection of this final answer. Over all that we have considered and stated there might so rapidly and forcefully spread the shadow of the suggestion that we might conceive of a better will of Jesus Christ than that which He has actually undertaken to fulfil and is now fulfilling. And this might easily lead to the query whether the will which He is actually fulfilling can really be regarded and described as good in relation to what might be thought at least to be better. Why did He will to interpose between His own beginning and His own end this way and warfare and time with its " still " and " not yet "? Why did He will to cause the history of His prophecy to continue instead of bringing it to a triumphant conclusion? Why, when order and peace had been established between God and man in His life and death and powerfully enough proclaimed in His resurrection, did He will to entangle Himself first, and with Him the world, the community and ourselves, in the conflict against a darkness still somehow remaining, against sin, evil and death as somehow still persisting forces? Why did He not will His commencement to be at once His goal, His self-revelation in the world at once its redemption and consummation, Easter Day at once the last day, the day of the Lord, of His conclusive return and revelation, of the last judgment and the final fulfilment? Why did He will for Himself first, and therewith for the creation reconciled in Him, to set this distance still be to overcome between the one day and the other? Why did He Himself will to be still a Pilgrim and Warrior, thus entailing that the world, the Church and ourselves should not be at peace at home but unsettled in an alien land, and therefore directed to look for and hasten unto " the coming of the day of God " (2 Pet. 3^{12}), the day of His final victory? Is there not another will which might be called better than the one which He has actually undertaken to fulfil and is still fulfilling? In relation to it, can we seriously regard as good that which He is actually enforcing and pursuing when we think of all the dark and painful and dreadful things which its fulfilment involves? What are we to say to all this? How far is this His good will alongside which there cannot possibly be a better?

The answer is quite simply that it is His good will because it has as its aim the granting to and procuring for the creation reconciled to God in Him both time and space, not merely to see, but actively to share in the harvest which follows from the sowing of reconciliation.

In willing this and not something supposedly better, Jesus Christ confirms Himself and His whole being and action. From all eternity He is not alone, but He is the Elect of God in whom and with whom creation is also elect, not in order that it should vanish and dissolve in Him, nor to be merely the object of His work, but in Him and through Him to be free. He came down from God to be its Reconciler and to take the place of man, not in such a way that man is deprived of the meaning and right of his own existence, but rather in such a way that both are restored to him in the relationship to God reconstituted by the intervention of Jesus Christ for him, so that as a man justified before God and sanctified for Him he is lifted up from the ground and set on his feet. And now the good will of Jesus Christ in the matter which here concerns us is that the world, His people and ourselves should not be merely the objects of His action but that we should be with Him as independently active and free subjects when it is a question of this harvest, of the redeeming and consummating declaration of His life as given for us, of the illumination and irradiation of the world by the reconciliation effected and revealed by Him. He Himself who is alone the Head and Lord will naturally speak the last and decisive Word in this respect too. But first He allows the creation reconciled in Him to speak. He has not yet spoken His last and decisive Word because in this respect, too, He does not will to be alone or without us, because He does not will to go over our heads, because He wills to give us a share in His work in our independence as the creatures of God summoned to freedom, as those who are justified and sanctified in Him. And so He wills to give us time and space for this participation in His work. He wills to preserve the world, to cause it to persist, in its present and provisional form, in order that it should be the place where He can be perceived and accepted and known and confessed by the creature as the living Word of God. He wills to be invoked and proclaimed in His community in the world as the assembly where this knowledge and confession take place. He wills that each man should exist and also be sustained in his limits, in order that he may be a witness to the reconciliation accomplished in Him, to the future of salvation already present in Him. All this would have been impossible, however, if He had made that supposedly better choice. There could have been no way or distance between the beginning and the end, no continuation of the history of His prophecy, but only the immediate and direct dawn of the last day of His glory in and with His resurrection from the dead. This might have been very wonderful if He had so willed it. But there is no doubt that He would not then have willed a world sharing in His work, a community knowing and confessing Him, and ourselves as His witnesses. Or He would have willed the world, the community and ourselves only as objects and spectators of His activity, majestically ignoring the freedom of the creature for any

4. *The Promise of the Spirit*

activity of its own, and sovereignly depriving it of any opportunity to demonstrate this freedom, being quite uninterested in any such demonstration. In such circumstances He might well have shown Himself to be wonderful, majestic and sovereign, but He would certainly not have been gracious. Far from corresponding to the election, reconciliation and covenant fulfilled in Him, He would have contradicted them, showing to the world and men only the kind of lop-sided favour which European nations used to exercise without consulting them to the peoples of their colonies. He would not in any sense have been truly kind or good. No, in the sense of the grace and kindness of God His good will is obviously that which Jesus Christ has actually realised and still realises in the work of His prophecy. He did not will to ignore or pass by ourselves, the community and the whole world (not even to our supreme salvation, which is in Him alone and can come only from Him). He willed to have us at His side and in His discipleship in our own free work. He did not despise but expected the joy and gratitude and praise of creation. He required it in all its littleness. He did not wish to exclude or suppress it. Hence He did not will that He Himself or creation should be already at the goal. He willed rather that it should be on the way to the goal with Himself. The way between the commencement and the completion of His presence, the distance between Easter Day and the day of the consummation of His return, the ground which He has still to traverse and creation with Him, is the great opportunity which He has given creation freely to enter His service. It is senseless to try to contest the fact that He willed to give it this opportunity. This is not merely because it is senseless to resist His will in any case, but because His will to do this is obviously His good will. His gracious, merciful and patient will, His will in which God's condescension to creation, His faithfulness to His covenant-partner and His power in the fulfilment of its reconciliation to Himself are displayed in the fact that the Mediator sent by Him takes the creature or man so seriously that on the basis of his reconciliation and its revelation He allows and commands him to serve Him, and gives him time and place and opportunity for this free action.

We are now coming to the true relevance of this sub-section and therefore of the whole of this christological section of the third part of the doctrine of reconciliation.

Our initial question concerned the exit, transition and entrance into our anthropological sphere of the light of life or the prophecy of Jesus Christ. Our deliberations have shown us something of the external form at least of the relationship between this prophecy and our own sphere. His coming again as the Revealer of the reconciliation effected in Him includes this sphere or time of ours within itself. As His coming again has its beginning and goal, it also sets for this time or sphere its beginning and goal. In its first form as the Easter

§ 69. *The Glory of the Mediator*

event it took place before this time, and in its last form as the conclusive appearing of Jesus Christ it will take place after it. In its two forms, therefore, it is both the *terminus a quo* and the *terminus ad quem*, the before and after, of this time. It determines what takes place in it in the twofold sense that it derives from its occurrence in the Easter event and moves towards its occurrence in which the future of salvation of the reconciled world is made present. The superior dynamic of its occurrence on this basis determines the direction of what takes place in our sphere. Now its beginning is not its end. Its occurrence in the first form is still separated from its occurrence in the last. If the prophetic work or self-revelation of Jesus Christ is not hindered or interrupted, it is not yet concluded but still in process of realisation. It moves from its beginning to its end. Hence its occurrence maintains and even creates time and place and opportunity for world-occurrence, for the being and activity of man in our sphere. It has begun. But it is still in movement to its end. It is between the then of the Easter event, and the one day of the final appearing of Jesus Christ. It is " still " in process and " not yet " completed. It thus opens up for the creature which is reconciled but not yet redeemed and perfected a field on which it can and should demonstrate and express its freedom. This freedom is its freedom as the creature which is reconciled to God and which with Jesus Christ Himself moves from and to the revelation of its reconciliation. But it is its most genuine freedom. It is given time and place and opportunity to demonstrate and express it by this distance between the occurrence of the coming again of Jesus Christ in its two forms. The opening up of this field, which would not have been possible had the prophecy of Jesus Christ reached its end with its beginning, is the good and kind and gracious reason for this distance.

Even in relation to this external form of the relationship our sphere cannot be called remote from or alien to the prophecy and revelation of Jesus Christ and the reconciliation effected in Him. It cannot be regarded as distant from the living Word of God. With what takes place in it, it stands in the very centre, surrounded by the coming again of Jesus Christ as this still takes place, and therefore by His self-revelation, and therefore by the declaration of the love of God and the salvation of the creature. It is by this declaration that its structure and limits and orientation are decided both behind and before. It does not exist without it. With all that takes place in it, it has persistence and possibility only in virtue of the fact that it takes place within this space between the beginning and the end, and that having taken place in its beginning it is still on the way to its end. With all its occurrence, it owes its existence, persistence and possibility to the fact that the fulfilment of the return of Jesus Christ and therefore of His self-revelation entails the creation of this field on which the creation reconciled to God can and should demonstrate

4. *The Promise of the Spirit*

and express its freedom. The world, which is this sphere of ours, is not then a world which is unqualified in relation to the prophecy of Jesus Christ. On the contrary, it is supremely qualified in relation to it. And this is especially true of the man who lives in it and characterises it as his world. Nor is this merely because we are dealing with the world which is reconciled to God or the man who is justified before God and sanctified for Him. It is also because the world and man are so decisively and comprehensively determined by the revelation of their reconciliation as this is still in process of fulfilment. It is because they have their place and existence and structure and persistence in virtue of this continuing revelation.

It might well be asked whether a more precise relationship between the two is either possible or conceivable. At any rate, the light of life, the prophecy, return and self-revelation of Jesus Christ are not identical with our sphere, with the world and man. How could Jesus Christ, the living Word of God, be equated with the world and ourselves? We have here two distinct things. They co-exist in their encounter. Hence the question of the exit, transition and entrance into our cosmic and human sphere of Jesus Christ or the light of life is still an open and unanswered question for all our perception of the closeness of the relationship.

If we are to make our final answer to this question meaningful and significant, we must first consider some of the external conditions necessary for the demonstration and expression of human freedom in our sphere.

There are obviously some which are given in cases where man can exist in fruitful encounter with the ongoing revelation of Jesus Christ from its commencement in the Easter event, and therefore in the knowledge of His person and the work of atonement effected in Him, in acceptance and apprehension of His justification and sanctification, and therefore in faith and love. There are others which obtain in relation to those to whom the revelation of Jesus Christ comes from the same commencement and objectively with the same validity and strength, but for whom—in unfruitful encounter—its light shines in vain, its trumpet sounds in vain, to the extent that we do not find in them any corresponding perception of their reconciliation, or serious acceptance of their existence as reconciled creatures, or what might be called faith and love. In accordance with the truth which is His, God alone finally distinguishes between the two, between fruitful and unfruitful encounters, in short, between the Christian world and the non-Christian. But the distinction itself is true and valid. And the external and objective conditions for the demonstration and expression of human freedom are not the same in the two cases.

In addition, however, there are certain general conditions which apply to both, and we may begin with these.

First, there are the positive conditions under which both Christians and non-Christians exist on this field in virtue of the fact that according to the revelation made to all and valid for all they are reconciled to God in Jesus Christ. In the sphere prepared for them by their Creator, and according to the good nature which He has given them, they may realise their possibilities, use their powers, move within their limits and perform the great or little actions corresponding to their capacities, on the basis of the fact that the divine work of reconciliation in its powerful revelation has not reversed nor destroyed nor even in its goodness diminished the first divine work of creation, but rather confirmed and brought it to light. The sun of God shines on the just and the unjust. To both it is given and still allowed to be men, and to be men who as such can move and develop under God's sun like all other creatures after their kind. No less wonderfully, time is allowed and given them. For the revelation of their reconciliation is still moving to its end. Time has not yet become eternity. In its extension from the past into the present and future, it may still continue. We are thus allowed to go our ways as the Son of God and Man goes His way from His beginning to His end. As we do so, we may fulfil our lives in the realisation of our possibilities continually chosen by us. All of us, believers or unbelievers, have time and place within the great context of this revelation of the love and loving act of God as it moves from its beginning to its end. All of us have an opportunity which we may freely grasp. From the purely factual and objective standpoint, therefore, our creaturely existence as such has a teleology. Even in itself it cannot be wholly without meaning, plan or purpose. The distinctive yearning, willing, striving and planning in which each creature as such makes use of its freedom are not without final basis or supreme necessity and justification. For it makes use of its freedom in analogy to the teleology of the revelation of accomplished reconciliation. It thus follows a direction which is not condemned but confirmed from this standpoint.

But there are also certain general conditions which are very incisive and critical. The reconciliation of the world with God, and in it the justification and sanctification of man, have taken place and have been publicly declared in the resurrection of Jesus Christ. But this declaration is not yet complete. The reconciled nature of creation has still to be revealed, i.e., its redemption and consummation. This means, however, that the declaration is still exposed to the power of evil, which is broken in the accomplished reconciliation, but which can still mount its assaults and temptations and acts of violence. The defeated enemy is still capable of attack in his dangerous death-throes, and we for our part are still vulnerable to his efforts. Whether we are Christians or non-Christians, we still know sin in its form as pride and sloth. It is no longer our master ahead. But behind us, on our heels as it were, it still has some

4. *The Promise of the Spirit* 337

dominion as our past reaching into our future. We are still moving towards the time when it will be destroyed as it deserves and we shall live in righteousness and true holiness. It still afflicts our being in time as such. Hence, whether we are Christians or non-Christians, we have our time only as a time which continually passes. It is given us from morning to evening, from youth to age, as a time for truly reconciled being. But it steadily escapes us, and therefore, however long, it is always dreadfully short, far too short, in relation to what its fulfilment should be and never is. Hence the being of all creatures in the time allotted them is not merely passing but actually passes. Its goal is its end. It is a being which moves towards death. From its very commencement as life it is a dying. No creatures are spared either the final sealing of this dying or its anticipation in the greater or lesser sufferings of this time. However we demonstrate and express our freedom, we can do so only within this limit, on this side of the sharply drawn line of death which is visible from the very first and which will alone be visible at the last.

These, then, are the positive and critical conditions which apply to the existence of all creatures in our sphere.

How does it stand in detail with creatures which will and must demonstrate and express their freedom without the knowledge of Jesus Christ, without enlightenment by the Easter event, and therefore without realising that their reconciliation with God is accomplished? Jesus Christ has died and risen again for them too. He is their Lord and Head and Saviour too. In Him they, too, are reconciled to God. His Word comes to them too. They, too, live under the condition given to our whole sphere by His return and revelation. What must be said of the qualified nature of the freedom of all creatures in the midst of His prophetic work applies in all its fulness to them too. By the goodness of God the Creator they, too, in their divinely given nature may thus be and do what they can be and do in accordance with this nature. Time is given to them too. Meaning and future are given to their aspirations and strivings. They, too, may express their freedom as reconciled creatures. Yet they, too, are exposed to the powerful attack of the evil which is vanquished but not yet destroyed or banished. They, too, have only a short and transitory time. The law of death is fulfilled in them too. And all this is in order that they, too, may on this side demonstrate their freedom as creatures reconciled with God. But how, when they do not see the light of life which enlightens them, the light of the resurrection of Jesus Christ from which all being and activity in our sphere derive and to the eternal illuminating and irradiating of which they move? How can they see themselves as creatures reconciled to God? How can they come to affirm their freedom as such? How can they demonstrate and express it as their freedom? Yet if they do not do so—and they certainly will not if they do not know Jesus Christ—this means that the conditions prescribed for them as for all other creatures lose their meaning and become different in their case. Since they do not know the Jesus Christ who in His revelation strides from its commencement to its goal, it is concealed from them that our sphere as the sphere between the two, and limited and conditioned by them, is the time and place in which we may go with and after Him from this commencement to this goal. This is something which can be known only by those who realise that they are men reconciled in Jesus Christ, and who thus express the freedom which they are given. If this is not the case with us, as it cannot be apart from the knowledge of Jesus Christ, the time in which we exist is not a before and behind but the first and last, the one and absolute time. Since it lacks a before and behind, a beginning and end, we are without direction in this time and sphere of ours. We are not directed either from or to anywhere. We can move only with the sorry freedom of prisoners, thinking and speaking and acting at random. Whatever we may choose under the conditions which are prescribed as conditions for the demonstration of our freedom, of the freedom of those reconciled to God, is quite different now that we do not know Jesus Christ and cannot exercise this freedom. There is neither whence nor whither, neither why nor wherefore. All that is left is the naked structure of the sphere which is our first and last, our one and absolute reality. There remain only the forms of the sovereign fate which dominates both ourselves and our willing and choosing within this sphere of ours. Their validity and reality simply confirm afresh and on all sides that our existence has neither entrance nor exit. They merely imply that we are in such and such condition, that we have so much time, that we must somehow come to terms with the evil within and around us, that time not only slips through our fingers but carries us away with it, that the process of death is inexorably at work in our own and all life. In these circumstances the conditions themselves are not subject to any condition. They are infinitely constant relationships, orders and forces, and as such presuppositions to which we are wholly and always subject. They are the indestructible walls of our prison. Our supposedly free action is only within these walls whose significance is simply to be these walls, so that our existence can have no other significance than to be existence within them. Enclosed within them, we are not merely not yet redeemed, but totally unredeemed. "There is no peace for the wicked." This statement describes their ontic situation as well as their noetic, their external as well as their internal, their objective as well as their subjective. It tells us that the conditions prescribed for all creatures are their judgment. Nevertheless, it is true for them, too, that the work of Jesus Christ precedes and follows all being and occurrence in our sphere and therefore their own ignorant and enslaved existence, that He Himself is not conditioned by the valid and effective conditions

4. The Promise of the Spirit

which are their judgment, but is their Lord. They can find no hope in their freedom actualised in bondage. But He is their hope too. For He is on the way from His commencement to His goal. No competition is offered to His work by any situation which arises and persists in our sphere, however objectively or subjectively corrupt. This work cannot be destroyed or arrested. It consists in His giving Himself to be known by those who do not know Him, in His opening of the eyes of the blind and the ears of the deaf, in His bringing of light to the people that walks in darkness in one of those prison cells, in His calling of them out of bondage into freedom. For although He is not known by them, above all and decisively He has already accomplished their reconciliation to God. He alone therefore, but He invincibly, is the hope even of the ungodly, even of creatures which, lacking illumination by the Easter event, can exercise their freedom only in bondage.

How about those who may live as enlightened by this event? How about Christians? We must probe rather deeper in this respect.

It would be excellent if in relation to Christians we could simply reverse everything that we have said about non-Christians, describing them quite unequivocally as men who may know Jesus Christ and therefore themselves as reconciled in Him, who may thus grasp and exercise their freedom as such, and therefore for whom the positive and critical conditions of creaturely existence at the heart of the occurrence of revelation are not prison walls, but boundaries open both behind and before to mark the stretch on which they may be on the way in harmony with the prophetic work of Jesus Christ, and thus on both sides meaningful conditions of their meaningful because teleologically orientated and impelled existence.

Is it possible to attempt this kind of direct reversal? Is the situation of Christians within the sphere of the conditions given to all really so very different from that of non-Christians? It would not be advisable, but false, dangerous and illegitimate, to try to contest that it is basically and factually different, that the difference between knowledge and ignorance of Jesus Christ as concerns the situation of man in his sphere is comparable only with the distinction between heaven and earth. For all the common features, everything is totally different, not merely subjectively in the thought and outlook and conduct of the men, but objectively in the form of the orders and relationships which determine them. For the eyes of the blind are now opened and the ears of the deaf unstopped. Man himself is made bright in the light of the resurrection of Jesus Christ. He can affirm His justification before God and sanctification for God as already taken place. He can live in this affirmation. He exists with the non-Christian in the same provisional sphere with all the presuppositions which are also limitations. He lives in the same world. But this sphere or world is a different one, not merely in his own conception and opinion, but in fact. In this same world everything is conditioned and controlled on the basis of the commencement of the revelation of Jesus Christ, towards its completion, and by the dynamic of its course. Hence it must serve the demonstration and expression of his freedom. Within this sphere he may thus look back with gratitude and forward with a hope which overcomes fear. Journeying between the times, he may humbly rejoice in his present. In anything else that may be said, we must insist, and never lose sight of the fact, that as the man who knows Jesus Christ is undoubtedly a very different man from the one who does not know Him, so his situation is very different in the common sphere of the world. For a true perception and understanding, everything depends upon our not reducing this difference to a mere peculiarity of thought, outlook and conduct, but recognising and maintaining that already here and now, in the sphere of the " still " and " not yet," the Christian exists as the creature of God which is good and reconciled, though it is not of course redeemed and perfected, but still threatened. Hence on his way between Easter Day and the general revelation and resurrection, he is under the law of a new and different world established in the accomplished reconciliation. He already lives in the power of the kingdom of God drawn near. On the old earth, he is already on the new, and under the old heaven already under the new. Where the prophetic work of Jesus Christ does not take place in vain, but is fruitful, this is its subjectively and objectively real work, to be seen and understood in the first instance as unreservedly true and actual.

Yet when we have said this, and without retracting in the least, we must add at once in a rather more subdued key that there were reasons for beginning : " It would be excellent," and that we may well hesitate to interpret the situation of Christians as a simple reversal of that of non-Christians. To be sure, this is basically true, and must be stated in some such way as we have tried to state it. But it is equally true that what is to be said basically and materially of the existence and situation of Christians can be truly said only in relation to the actual fulfilment of their existence in their situation, i.e., only in relation to the history of Christians, and even this only with certain very serious modifications.

The first of these derives very simply from the fact that wholehearted Christians cannot without endangering their own being as Christians renounce their solidarity with non-Christians. This is not merely because we can none of us be Christians without at some point or in some way being very decided non-Christians. It is decisively because the blind and deaf and imprisoned, for whom the conditions under which all exist are conditions of bondage, are still our fellows, indeed, our brothers as men who like ourselves are reconciled to God in Jesus Christ. Can we then go our way, and rejoice in our present as wayfarers between the times, but forget these others

4. The Promise of the Spirit 341

who are held fast in their own place and are not on the way? Are we not directly affected by their misery? Is it not our misery that like Lazarus before the gate of Dives these others who are like us, and for whom Jesus Christ died and rose again no less than for us, exist alongside us in this direct proximity? In our own freedom do we not stand in the bondage of these others? Can we advance under this shadow without stopping to assist them? Can we breathe without sighing for them, perhaps because they do not feel their own misery? Can we find personal comfort in the knowledge of Jesus Christ without being deeply disturbed by the fact that these brothers who do not have this knowledge are so comfortless? And if Jesus Christ is the hope of the ungodly too, what other possibility can there be for Christians than to realise in this solidarity with the ungodly that Christ is their only hope as well? How can Christians dissolve or even deny their co-existence with non-Christians?

A further modification is suggested by the very dangerous imperfection of what makes Christians Christians and thus distinguishes them from non-Christians, i.e., of their knowledge of Jesus Christ, of their self-knowledge as creatures reconciled to God, of the freedom in which they actually move and express and reveal themselves as justified before God and sanctified for Him, of the certainty of their steps on the way marked out on both sides by the conditions valid and effective in that central sphere of ours. Even the best of Christians can hardly boast of an absolutely clear vision of Easter Day, of wholly lucid thought on the basis of it, of a comprehensive knowledge of Jesus Christ free from every form of defect or distortion. And they certainly cannot boast of a self-knowledge in which their reconciliation to God accomplished in Him stands fully before their eyes and is taken with fitting seriousness and consistency as the basic fact which renews and controls their existence. They all live only modestly and partially in and by the affirmation of the freedom which is given them as those who are justified and sanctified in Jesus Christ. They all tread cautiously if bravely on the way of discipleship which leads from the commencement to the goal and on which all the positive and critical conditions of their creaturely existence may and must be conditions of their freedom. But we must remember that every qualification which even the best Christian has to admit if he is sincere —and he could not be a Christian if he were not—implies a regrettable and removable lack and defect in the position in which he as a Christian is so very different from the non-Christian. Indeed, it implies more than this. Every great or small, qualitative or quantitative deficiency in his knowledge of Jesus Christ, his ensuing self-knowledge and his demonstration of his given freedom in consistent following of the way to which he is directed, signifies a tarrying in or regression to the situation and mode of existence of the non-Christian. In this deficiency he must recognise, if he is sincere, that he is not merely a poor or weak Christian but a decided non-Christian. In it he himself is blind and deaf; he himself is a prisoner; he himself is under the dominion of conditions which are simply the conditions of fate and bondage. There can thus be no trifling with the imperfection of our Christianity. It is no excessive Puritanism that the constant impulse of the New Testament is towards Christian perfection. The poverty and obscurity of our knowledge of Jesus Christ, the half-heartedness of our life in the given freedom, the uncertainty of pilgrimage, in short, the imperfection of our Christianity, signifies that it is only with one foot, and perhaps only with our toe-nails, that we are on solid ground, but that for the rest we dangle over the abyss in daredevil acrobatics. This will not do. But it is what we do. We cannot be Christians and non-Christians. But we are. What has to be said basically and materially concerning our being as Christians in these circumstances is thus valid only in the light of this very dangerous contradiction which is never resolved in our historical existence and situation as Christians. And it may be that in fact we are far more virulently and intensively non-Christians than Christians. Yet however that may be, to the extent that we may be Christians in spite of our non-Christianity, our real distinction from non-Christians will consist in the fact that we know that Jesus Christ Himself, and He alone, is our hope as well as theirs, that He died and rose again for those who are wholly or partially non-Christians, that His overruling work precedes and follows all being and occurrence in our sphere, that He alone is the perfect Christian, but that He really is this, and is it in our place.

Another and very different modification is also necessary in our viewing and understanding of the state of Christians. That which distinguishes and marks off their existence and situation from that of non-Christians makes it in many different ways a problem which the latter do not feel and cannot know.

First, Christians owe their great or less, their clear or less clear knowledge of Jesus Christ, and all that this entails, to the Easter event, to His self-declaration as the Resurrected from the dead, and to this alone. It is only from this source that the eternal light shines into the sphere in which Christians and all others exist. If they see what others do not see, namely, the prophecy of Jesus Christ, His revelation of the atonement made in Him, it is only from this point. Others who are not aware of this commencement of the revelation, the *parousia*, the prophetic work of Jesus Christ, know nothing of the strange necessity laid on Christians, of the venture, which is to them unavoidable, of looking back beyond all other events to this one event, of distinguishing above all the clamorous notes and words which fill their ears the one note sounded here, of listening to the Word spoken here, of opposing all distractions and keeping to the one instruction and direction given here, of treading within the

4. The Promise of the Spirit

common sphere with its many different ways the only possible way which is indicated here. Christians can do no other. They are Christians because, in strength or weakness, partially or totally, they can do no other. Their existence, their situation, their very all is grounded in and begins with the fact that Jesus Christ is risen. But can they succeed in existing in this concentration, in wrestling with the conditions imposed on them too with this absolutely one-sided orientation?

Secondly, Christians see in this commencement the goal, i.e., the presence of the future of salvation of their own and all existence. They cannot, then, look back to the beginning without looking forward beyond all other occurrence, events and forms to the last revelation and *parousia* of the same Jesus Christ which is there intimated, to the completion of His prophecy in the illumination and irradiation of all that was and is and will be, and therefore to the still awaited redemption of the world reconciled in Him. Necessarily therefore—and they would not be Christians otherwise—they live absolutely from the inauguration and absolutely towards the consummation of His prophecy under the conditions normative for them as for all men. They exist in the great tension which does not exclude but relativises, critically reduces and purifies all little tensions, their eye on this goal of the still awaited and conclusive coming of Jesus Christ. They are thus like arrows waiting to be shot from a bow stretched to the very utmost. What do other men know of this existence in tension, of the limitation of all other permissible and necessary expectations of the creature in this sphere by this one expectation which transcends them all? Non-Christians, who are still prisoners, have the advantage over Christians that they are spared this mode of existence. Will Christians persevere in it? Is it really tolerable? But they have no choice except actually to persist in this expectation.

Thirdly, from this commencement to this goal they are on a way, and in the freedom shown them in the knowledge of Jesus Christ and the ensuing self-knowledge they cannot halt nor sit down and rest, but only go forward under the conditions which limit them on the right hand and the left. They are Christians as or to the extent that they are really on the move as pilgrims. The dynamic of the teleology in which Jesus Christ goes His way in the performance of His prophetic work leaves them no option but continually to rise up and accompany or follow Him. For them as for all others there are pauses in relation to specific actions. From time to time they must cease working, and thinking, and above all talking. There are, indeed, pauses in the moral warfare. But in all these things they never cease to be claimed. There is no cessation of responsibility, no moratorium of Christianity, of the Gospel and its command. Their concentration on the commencement and straining towards the goal of the Jesus

Christ known by them find expression in the exertion to be always on the move from the one to the other—a tormenting situation which, almost to the envy of Christians, is not asked of non-Christians and not therefore known by them. But Christians cannot as such escape it. And perhaps it is not least in attempts to escape it that they so often play the dangerous game of being non-Christians. At any rate, the question forcefully obtrudes itself whether it is possible to live a life exposed as is the life of Christians to the incessant pressure of this call to advance.

A fourth point has also to be made in this connexion. It demands consideration because it introduces a concept which is decisively important for the further development of this third part of the doctrine of reconciliation. Men who are Christians in the knowledge of Jesus Christ, in the ensuing self-knowledge, and in expression of the freedom thereby indicated, are called as such in distinction from all others, i.e., called and commissioned to attest Jesus Christ in the world and among their Christian and non-Christian fellows. The existence of Christians in the world and on their way from the Easter event to the final appearing of Jesus Christ is not an end in itself, nor is the existence of the Christian community as the pilgrim people of God. The situation would be easier and brighter if the Christian could regard his difficult existence at least as his private affair, and make some tolerable arrangement for it within the limits of what is possible for him. But it is a public affair, and therefore the Christian is a public person irrespective of any modesty or reluctance he may feel in face of this requirement. He is a Christian only to the extent that he is obedient to his calling to be a witness and messenger of Jesus Christ. For as a Christian he moves with open eyes and ears from the commencement of Christ's prophetic work to the completion of this work. Accompanying Jesus Christ along the great course of His new coming, He is necessarily set in the service of His work, of the occurrence of His self-revelation. In deep subordination and discipleship, but with supreme resolution, he is commissioned to take part in it as a witness of the second, third or fourth degree. This participation in the prophecy of Jesus Christ is the meaning of the committal and responsibility with which he is on the way within the sphere of the preconditions valid and effective for all men. The prophets of the Old Testament described this participation as a "burden." It is so. It implies for the Christian on one side that he cannot regard himself—even in the brightest Easter joy or the most ardent longing for his redemption and fulfilment—as the meaning of his existence and situation, nor make it the goal of his pilgrimage even in the purest sense to seek and find himself, i.e., his personal life or perhaps himself in his distinctive individuality. It implies for him on the other side that he is there, and has life and breath, and may exist in the knowledge of Jesus Christ, in order that he may declare

4. *The Promise of the Spirit*

to the reconciled world which still moves in darkness the wholly new divine Yes pronounced in Jesus Christ, but also the unexpected and painful divine No pronounced in the same Jesus Christ, the coming of its new form and the passing of its old. It cannot be taken for granted that a man will agree that he cannot be a Christian without accepting this task. Whether he does or does not, decides whether his faith in Jesus Christ is genuine enough to permit and command him unhesitatingly to see and address the world as the world reconciled in Him, and not to be led astray either by obvious pleasure in his own personal security, by preoccupation with his own inner problems, by consciousness of his incapacity for the fulfilment of this task, or by the extreme improbability of any success commensurate with his efforts. Can and will his faith be genuine enough in this respect? Again we might say: Happy the non-Christian upon whom there is not imposed a task which is inwardly so demanding and outwardly so thankless! But the Christian has no option. Nor is he allowed to undertake it reluctantly, nor, once he has undertaken and tries to do justice to it, to become tired and cross. It is either discharged with relaxed joy and joyous relaxation, or not at all. Surely this is a real burden!

Can the Christian succeed in bearing this burden which in so many respects is so much heavier than that of the happy heathen, worldlings, non-Christians and ungodly of all kinds who are so radically exempted in these matters so long as they remain such? Will he persist in being sustained first and last and exclusively by the fact that Jesus Christ is also and specifically his hope?

In sum, this is how matters stand with the demonstration and expression of human freedom in the sphere left for us between the commencement and completion of the *parousia* and revelation of Jesus Christ and under the conditions prescribed for men in this sphere. This is the existence and the situation of non-Christians and Christians. The final thing which is true and is to be said of both is that Jesus Christ is their hope. It is to be said in different senses. He is known to the latter and unknown to the former. To the latter He is the trusted final ground to which they may always confidently return and on which they may always rest in all the frailty and vulnerability of the realisation of their freedom, in all the particular difficulty of their way. To the former He is concealed, invisible and inaccessible, having no correspondence in them, meeting no hope which seizes Him as their hope, taking comfort in and cleaving fast to Him. Yet factually and objectively, and not altogether ineffectively for all the concealment, He is their hope too. There may be great difference in the constitution and situation of the two within the common sphere. But there is agreement in the fact that this sphere of theirs as such is the field in this centre, so that whether they know Jesus Christ or not they do in fact come from the commencement of

His way and move to its completion, both being wholly in need although in different ways, and neither being utterly deprived of Him seeing He is their common Reconciler. For this reason and to this extent, whether known or unknown, He is the hope of both. In other words, in His conclusive appearing and revelation with all that was and is and will be, He will finally bring to light the existence and situation of both Christians and non-Christians, knowing and unknowing, free and bound, setting it in His light, judging it, but judging it righteously as the Judge in whom the reconciliation of the whole world with God has taken place. That He is the hope of all means that wittingly or unwittingly all move towards His appearing and judgment. Whether known now or unknown, He is the future of all.

But this conclusion indirectly includes our final statement in this context.

We do not make positive answer to our question concerning the exit, transition and entrance of Jesus Christ from His own sphere to ours merely by understanding the place and meaning and inner structure of this sphere of ours, or the existence and situation of man in relation to the conditions valid and effective within it. At the last moment this might prove to be an answer which is basically negative. In other words, it might be as follows. We in our sphere are certainly between the commencement and completion of His work and thus in close proximity to Jesus Christ. The great occurrence of His return, *parousia* and revelation precedes our existence in our situation in its first form and follows it in its final form. But so far as concerns the present place and time and opportunity which are allowed us for the expression of our creaturely freedom, it is perhaps interrupted or suspended. Our sphere is surrounded and affected by this occurrence and therefore by the presence and action of Jesus Christ. But it is omitted, by-passed or passed over, so that it constitutes a kind of vacuum in the centre of this event. It is thus in this vacuum, *remoto Christo*, that there takes place our Christian or non-Christian realisation of freedom. The light of Easter which has dawned in advance shines upon it only remotely and from outside, as does also the same light in its final and eternal radiance and glory. It does not shine among us and in us, but only upon us. There can be no exit and entry of the living Christ from His sphere into ours. There can be no question of His direct presence and action on the field on which we exist, either knowing Him and demonstrating our freedom as Christians or not knowing Him and not demonstrating it as non-Christians. Whether known or unknown, He stands and moves only on the margin of our Christian or non-Christian existence and situation. Apart from the legitimate and imperative backward and forward glance at His presence and action behind and before, we are with Him only in this indirect relationship, and primarily,

4. The Promise of the Spirit

properly and directly we are left to ourselves, to our own Christian or non-Christian being and nature and efforts. This means, however, that it is only indirectly, from the distance behind and before, but not primarily, properly and directly, that He is the Bearer of the authority and lordship to which we are subject in our sphere, the source by which we live and from which we have to draw for direction and orientation in our sphere, the supreme court with which we have to reckon and which we have to respect. What dominates primarily, properly and directly is the complex of the positive and critical conditions prescribed for man, and therefore in the first and final instance the subject existing under these conditions, i.e., man himself, a non-Christian if he does not know of the indirect relationship to Jesus Christ, a Christian if he does, but in either case man himself in his attempts to wrestle and come to terms with these conditions in good or bad expression of his freedom, man in his Christian or non-Christian self-understanding, man in his self-assertion hazarded and made either in knowledge or in ignorance of Jesus Christ. And naturally the Christian in particular is the representative, substitute, or vicar of the living Jesus Christ who is not Himself present and does not act or speak directly or personally in this vacuum. In this vacuum the only part or significance which Jesus Christ can have in practice is that which is conceded or left to Him by Christians, Christianity and the Church. In practice He can exercise His authority and power in this vacuum only in the form of the authority and power of these representatives, and speak His prophetic Word only in the form of their vicarious words. He may well be exalted and magnified by Christians as the Mediator, Lord and Saviour who has come and will come again. But in our sphere which is not touched by His coming again, the fact remains that there is a pause in His life and work. He Himself is not personally present and active. He does not prove, attest or express Himself as the One He is. He has temporarily relinquished the discharge of His function in favour of the Christian. And as this necessarily means for the Christian that in practice he is pointed to himself, to his own knowledge and self-knowledge, to the freedom thereby indicated, so for the non-Christian it means that to gain his sight and hearing, to become a Christian, he has the not very encouraging prospect of being referred to the witness of Christianity and the impression made by the clarity, cogency and credibility of the institutions and activities of the Church or of various Christian personalities, groups and movements. This is the result if our answer is finally negative.

With no attempt at detailed elucidation, it may be pointed out how many conceptions of the situation in the time between the resurrection of Jesus Christ and the conclusion of His new coming—the Roman Catholics are not alone in this respect—do rest openly or secretly on this negative answer to our question, on the notion of a pause in the prophecy of Jesus Christ, of a vacuum which is created by and persists with this pause and in which we now exist, of a Jesus Christ who speaks with us only on the borders of our sphere but is absent from the sphere itself, of the substitution of Christianity for His own living presence and action, of the very doubtful dignity and authority of the representative speech and action of Christianity. How much Christian self-deception and arrogance, how much Christian and non-Christian misery, has its root in notions of this kind and cannot be overcome so long as the root is left untouched ! If our question is to be answered in the sense of these notions and therefore negatively, then the well-known cynical epigram is true and cannot be contested, that " what Jesus Christ brought was the kingdom of God ; what emerged was the Church."

What we have considered and seen in this sub-section, however, has not prepared us for this negative answer or for a recognition of the correctness of such notions. Our understanding of the prophetic work of Jesus Christ in self-revelation, of His resurrection as the commencement of its fulfilment, and of our human existence and situation in the sphere left to us in the midst of this prophecy, have all inclined us to a very different conclusion. What place does this understanding leave for a kind of pause in the life and work of Jesus Christ Himself and the rise and persistence of that vacuum with all that it involves ? Provisionally and implicitly at least, we have already directly contradicted this whole conception in the statement with which we concluded our consideration of the situation of Christians and non-Christians in this sphere, namely, that Jesus Christ is their common hope. He is their hope, we maintained, because, as they all wittingly or unwittingly come from His resurrection, He is also their future, the Mediator and Reconciler to whose final appearing, and with it to the illumination of the whole world by His revelation and therefore to their judgment, they move forward in all the darkness and obscurity and problematical nature of their existence. But now, to bring out concretely both the futility of that conception and the positive answer to our question, we must emphasise that He *is* the hope of all. He not only was this in the Easter event, and will be at His final appearing. He is not only the hope which shines into their sphere from this beginning and end, impelling on the one side and enticing on the other. He is the hope which shines here and now, among and in them, at the point where they exist. As He once spoke and acted as their hope in the Easter event, and as He will do so again at His final appearing, so He does in the present at the place and time where they now are. Moving as their hope from the Easter event to His final appearing, He does not stop short at the field left them for the expression of their freedom, leaping across it to resume and continue His activity on the other side. He does not give rise to any vacuum in which He refers and therefore leaves them to themselves, He Himself being only a known or unknown figure on the margin. He is the hope of all here and now, just as present and active on the field on which they exist as He was when

4. *The Promise of the Spirit*

He began His prophetic work and as He will be when it reaches its goal in His final appearing. He is the hope of all as the way of His prophecy leads through this field and He Himself, the living Lord Jesus, treads this way. Whatever may have to be thought and said concerning the conditions under which we now exist, or concerning the darkness in which non-Christians and the obscurity in which Christians express their freedom, or concerning the acute and absolute or latent and relative problems of all human existence in this sphere, Jesus Christ Himself is present and active in it for us all, and therefore, as active Subject in His Word, He is the hope of all not merely from a far horizon or as an object of recollection and expectation to be contemplated and respected from a distance, but as One who is in the place where we are on the day which is our day. This means, however, that He is our hope in that His new coming as the One who came before, His coming again, His *parousia*, His revelation, goes forward without interruption and becomes and is an event in our sphere, so that for us and all men it really is quite directly a matter of accompanying its occurrence, of following Jesus Christ Himself from His beginning to His end. As we have already expressed it in an earlier context, His coming again does not merely take place in the first and final form, but also in this second and intermediate form in our sphere. It is in this form that as the One He was and will be He comes to us in our place and time, not tarrying here, for He hurries on the way to His goal, yet not abandoning us, but associating us with Him on this way, so that He may be really ours, and we His, as already here and now we are made His companions in travel on this way.

It is thus clear that there is no substance in the hypotheses mentioned, or in the conception developed in them. If the return, *parousia* or revelation of Jesus Christ is not interrupted, there can be no vacuum in the midst of its occurrence. It cannot be the case, then, that the expression of our creaturely freedom takes place in a sphere where there can be only a distant influence of the light of life, where our relationship to Jesus Christ can be only indirect, where it can be reduced to a mere looking back to His past presence and action and forward to His future, where primarily and properly we are left to ourselves, to our Christian or non-Christian will and achievement, where man must be in practice his own first and also final authority. There can be no question of Jesus Christ being even temporarily directed in His absence to let Himself be represented by an honoured Christianity and the holy Church, or of non-Christians having to wait to be impressed by the clarity, cogency and credibility of the witness of Christians. Jesus Christ cannot be absorbed and dissolved in practice into the Christian *kerygma*, Christian faith and the Christian community. He cannot be replaced by Christianity. He remains sovereign even in this respect. There is no pause or vacuum in the exercise of His prophetic function. He Himself is fully present and active. He does not really need any representatives, any anointed or unanointed, great or small, sacramentally or existentially endowed vicars. Thus all the self-deceptions and usurpations of Christians, and the ensuing troubles of Christians and non-Christians alike, are tackled and removed at the very root. Neither the Christian nor the non-Christian is left to himself in his creaturely freedom. He is confronted by the Mediator and Reconciler who comes again here and now and acts in face of and on him in His superior freedom. He is confronted by the Word spoken not only then and one day, but also directly here and now. And in this confrontation he is sustained, shielded, comforted, nourished and guided in all the obscurity of his way. As Jesus Christ in His to-day of Easter and of the last day encounters us in our to-day, He is with us all the days, and is the hope of us all.

But the time has now come when we should give its proper name to the new coming of the One who came before, to this middle form of His coming in which it is His coming to us in our intervening sphere. We may then conclude this whole enquiry and presentation by trying to see and understand His coming in this form.

In this connexion, we now see the relevance of the title given to this sub-section : " The promise of the Spirit." The return of Jesus Christ in this middle form, in which it takes place here and now, is His coming in the promise of the Spirit. This is His direct and immediate presence and action among and with and in us. In it He is the hope of us all. This reality, the promise of the Spirit, is the decisive answer to the question of this sub-section.

> Intentionally I do not say the reference to this reality to which we have now come in the course of our deliberations, but the reality itself. We can and must refer to it, as we now do. But no indication of it can be the answer which we have constantly sought to our question. Only the reality itself can be this. In this respect it resembles the certainty of the victory of Jesus Christ, of which we had to say at the end of the previous sub-section that it cannot be established by any argumentation, but only by His own self-declaration as the Victor He is. In the same way only the promise of the Spirit itself can prove that it is the answer to our question. We cannot make any contribution in this respect, but can only maintain that it sees to it itself.

In this reality there takes place the transition and entrance of the prophecy of Jesus Christ to us and to our sphere, and all we who exist in this sphere, whether Christians or non-Christians, are drawn into the history of salvation and given a part in it. On the basis of this reality we are justified in what follows in counting on the history of salvation, and particularly the history of its revelation in our own human and cosmic sphere.

The phrase " the promise of the Spirit " (Gal. 3^{14}, Ac. 2^{33}, cf. Eph. 1^{13}) has two meanings, and this is why it should be selected at

4. The Promise of the Spirit

this point. The one reality of the new revelatory coming of Jesus Christ in the middle form which now concerns us and which is denoted by this phrase, has a twofold sense commensurate with the particular situation in which it takes place, and although the two meanings are comprehended in the one phrase they can and must be distinguished. In either case it is a matter of the Spirit, of the Holy Spirit, and of promise : of the Spirit to the extent that the Spirit is the particular mode of the coming again and therefore the presence and action of Jesus Christ in the place and time between His resurrection and His final appearing ; and of promise to the extent that the distinctive feature of His being in our sphere does materially consist in the fact that Jesus Christ as the hope of all is present to us as the One who promises and is promised. We have seen already that the structure of this sphere of ours is determined by the fact that under commonly given conditions there exist two kinds of men, the Christians who know Jesus Christ and the non-Christians who do not. Jesus Christ in His return in this middle form of His prophecy is the hope of all, as He was the beginning for all on the basis of the Easter event, and as He will be the end for all in His final appearing as Redeemer and Judge. But coming into and passing through the sphere of these two kinds of men, He is the hope of all in different ways for the one kind and the other. For both He signifies " the promise of the Spirit." But He does so with a distinction which the twofold meaning of the phrase itself will perhaps help us to grasp.

" Promise of the Spirit " can mean (1) that the Spirit promises. In this sense, Jesus Christ in the power of His life as the Resurrected from the dead, in the glory of His coming again in its first form, gives to men the sure promise of His final appearing, of the conclusion of His revelation, and therefore of the redemption and perfecting of the world reconciled in Him, of its participation in the life of this new cosmic form, and therefore of its own eternal life. And in so doing He gives it the sure promise of His presence and assistance in its temporal being directed to this goal. On this reading it is presupposed that the Spirit, the Holy Spirit, i.e., Jesus Christ acting and speaking in the power of His resurrection, is present and active among and with and in certain men. And His present operation in these men is to give them the twofold pledge : the promise, intimation and guarantee of His coming as Redeemer and Perfecter, of the new cosmic form to be inaugurated by Him as the future of the world and their own ultimate future ; and the promise, intimation and guarantee of His presence and assistance in their temporal future, in the world which has not yet reached its goal but is only moving towards it, on their own way within the world-occurrence moving to this end. Our present concern—for we are dealing with this intervening state of the world and the men existing in it—is with the second aspect, i.e., the promise of the Spirit as the pledge of the living Jesus Christ given

§ 69. *The Glory of the Mediator*

to certain men for their temporal future, for their existence in worldoccurrence as it still continues, and therefore on this side of its and their ultimate future. This is not separated from the first and comprehensive and decisive because ultimate pledge. It is given in and with it. It is in a sense enclosed within it. Enclosed within it in such a way that the ultimate, too, cannot be separated from the penultimate, it, too, is given to them. These particular men become recipients, bearers and possessors of the promise of the eternal kingdom and eternal life, not only with the fulfilment, but already here and now. They already exist as such here and now in a distinctive way, as men who are determined and characterised by this promise, who are activated, capacitated and equipped by the fact that it is given them, who move towards its fulfilment here and now as they pass from every temporal present to the temporal future still allotted to them. The promise of the Spirit sets them on the way to this end, and accompanies them on it, as the sure pledge that this is the way, and that they may and should tread it, as the pledge of their freedom, as the command valid for them, as the permission given them, as the constantly imparted power to tread it. The mystery of grace, yet also the sober reality of their existence, is that they exist as recipients, bearers and possessors of the great and comprehensive and decisive because ultimate promise of the Spirit, in fellowship with its Giver, the Spirit Himself, touched and indeed filled by His power, and therefore by the power of the risen Jesus Christ, and therefore—for how could they fail even here and now to exist as such ?—under the determining, guiding, comforting, admonishing and strengthening power of the second promise which is enclosed in the first and which applies to their temporal future.

The recipients, bearers and possessors of the promise given by the Holy Spirit are Christians, men for whom Jesus Christ not only is who He is, the Son of God and Man, the Mediator, the Reconciler of the world and their own Reconciler, for whom He is present and active not merely in fact and objectively, but who also know Him as the One He is, who know His presence and work in subjective correspondence with His objective reality, who believe in Him and love Him as they know Him, who can repeat the confession of Jn. 20[28]: " My Lord and my God," and who in knowing Him know themselves as men reconciled, justified and sanctified in Him, and may thus make use of the freedom indicated to them in Him. As the Holy Spirit, i.e., Jesus Christ Himself in the power of His resurrection, addresses and gives to them His promise of the eternal kingdom and their eternal life, here and now in the world which is not yet redeemed and perfected, and as men who are not yet themselves redeemed and perfected, they awaken from their sleep and dreams to the knowledge, confession and freedom in which they may be Christians and exist as such. And as the Holy Spirit, i.e., Jesus

4. *The Promise of the Spirit*

Christ Himself in the power of His resurrection, sets them on their way in this world which is not yet redeemed and perfected, and accompanies them on this way with His promise of the eternal kingdom and their eternal life, He is their assistance in the Christian knowledge, confession, freedom and actualisation of freedom which they have to achieve daily and in successive situations. And as this assistance He continually permits and commands and helps them to become and be Christians step by step on this allotted way to the indicated goal, bestowing upon them in the twofold form and strength of His promise the gifts and lights and powers which they need for this purpose. He makes them Christians, and arms them to exist as such. In this sense, in this alteration, determination and characterisation of their human existence, Christians who are not yet redeemed and perfected, who are still on the way like others, but on the way after this manner, are already recipients, bearers and possessors of the promise, of the sure, yet not just sure, but in the power of its Giver the mighty promise of the Spirit, so that in the weakness of their flesh they are spiritual men. In this sense Jesus Christ is here and now the hope of these men, of Christians.

" Promise of the Spirit," however, can also mean (2) that the Spirit is promised. We shall attempt to show what this implies. Whether we think of it as the pledge of His final appearing, of the redemption and perfecting of the world reconciled in Him, of eternal life under a new heaven on a new earth, or as the accompanying pledge of His assistance in their temporal existence as it moves towards this future, the pledge given to men by Jesus Christ in the power of His life as the Resurrected, in the glory of His coming again in its first form, has not yet been successful in the case of certain men. That it is given them, too, is something which still stands ahead of them. They do not yet have it; they have still to receive it. This understanding presupposes that the Holy Spirit, i.e., Christ acting and speaking in the power of His resurrection, is not yet among and with and in certain men, i.e., that He is not yet present and active in them in the subjective realisation corresponding to His objective reality. The Holy Spirit Himself and as such is here a reality which is still lacking and is still to be expected. He is the content of a promise which is given but not yet fulfilled. What is lacking to these " unspiritual " men, as they lack the Spirit, is obviously His eternal and temporal, ultimate and penultimate, promise, and therefore their own qualification as its recipients, bearers and possessors, the determination, characterisation, endowment and equipment of their existence accomplished with this reception. As they have no promise of the ultimate future, the eternal kingdom and eternal life, they cannot have the enclosed promise in respect of their own existence in time as their immediate future. Not descrying the farthest horizon of being in the world and their own world, they cannot see the nearest horizons of their way. Pursuing this way as they, too, are allowed and commanded, they lack direction. Expressing the creaturely freedom which is conceded to them too, they do not have the ability to distinguish between the true way and the false, nor the command, permission and power to seek and find the true way and to tread it without fatigue or confusion. In all these things they are left to themselves, being referred to the caprice, accident or fate of their own inventions or obscure impulses. How can the Holy Spirit guide, comfort, admonish and strengthen them when He is not present? How can He do so among and with and in the men to whom He is not given and who do not therefore have Him?

We speak of non-Christians, of men for whom Jesus is who He is and is also present and active as for non-Christians, but who do not know Him as such, who exist as if He were not there, who do not accept the relationship in which He has set them because they do not realise that He has long since done so, who cannot then know, affirm or understand themselves or what they are in virtue of this relationship, who miss the freedom given them by it, who do not know how to make any use of it. It is not as though Jesus Christ did not die and rise again for them, or as though they were not reconciled, justified and sanctified to God and before Him and for Him. It is simply that they have turned away from this benefit so fully and unreservedly proffered to them, so that it is of no avail, but hovers as an unknown quantity in the clouds, remaining non-actual among and with and in them, being in a sense wasted on them. It is simply that in them the Holy Spirit comes up against closed doors and windows, not reaching or dwelling or working in those who do not know Jesus, not giving His twofold promise, not qualifying them as its recipients, bearers and possessors, not being able to determine and characterise their existence from within as the Ruler of their spirits, wills, hearts and minds. As they do not know Jesus Christ, they themselves cannot ask, seek or knock. How, then, can they find? How can it be given or opened to them? They will not yield their own spirits and wills and hearts and minds. How, then, can the Holy Spirit hold fellowship with them and give them all these things anew? One thing, however, they do not lack. And this one thing is more important than all that they do. For the Holy Spirit, as Jesus Christ is risen, is promised to them too, and with Him His twofold promise, His eternal and temporal pledge. They are not condemned to the unspiritual life in which they exist as non-Christians. Or if so, it is they who do it. And they themselves are not the final court. Even those who make out that they are the most hardened and obstinate of unbelievers are not condemned to this, nor are those who conduct themselves ever so wickedly under the domination of the only too human pride and sloth which control them and in abuse of their creaturely freedom. In the sphere at whose commencement Jesus

4. The Promise of the Spirit

Christ rose again there is no fate in virtue of which they can and must be only non-Christians and therefore ungodly. There is no such external fate grounded in the conditions and structure of this sphere, nor is there an internal grounded in themselves, and there is certainly not one imposed by God. Hence no aversion, revolt, resistance or outrage on the part of the non-Christian can alter the fact that he, too, exists in the world which God created good as the external basis of the covenant and therefore for this salvation, and which He has reconciled in Jesus Christ in fulfilment of this covenant and in realisations of the election in which he, too, is elect. He, too, is reconciled to God. Jesus Christ died for him. And He rose again for him. In the power of His resurrection He is his Lord and Saviour. This means, however, that the Spirit and His ultimate and penultimate pledge with all its indwelling power are promised to him. It cannot be simply said that he is not the recipient, bearer and possessor. It must be said that he is not yet these things, because he does not yet know Jesus Christ. And so we should not think or say absolutely of all the things he lacks that he simply lacks them, but that he still lacks them. This is the case. He is not yet within, not yet caught up in the living stream of life, not yet moved by the promise of the Spirit, not yet living by the lights and powers and gifts bestowed with this promise, but still without on the rocky banks of this stream. Or conversely, he is still within on a patch of desert, but not yet without in the surrounding meadows. Yet the stream already flows for him and the meadows are already there for him. The promise of the Spirit already avails for him and applies to him. Since Jesus Christ has risen for him, His power and that of the Holy Spirit are already on the way to him and on the point of reaching him, of indwelling him, of giving him the promise, of causing him to participate in its lights and powers and gifts, of radically refashioning and continually refashioning his existence. Nothing of what the Spirit does, effects and accomplishes among and with and in Christians is not ready like a harnessed stream to be effective among and with and in non-Christians. And when there comes the hour of the God who acts in Jesus Christ by the Holy Ghost, no aversion, rebellion or resistance on the part of non-Christians will be strong enough to resist the fulfilment of the promise of the Spirit which is pronounced over them too, which applies to them, which envisages and comes to them, or to hinder the overthrow of their ignorance in the knowledge of Jesus Christ and therefore of themselves as creatures reconciled in Him, or to prevent the discovery of their freedom as such, and therefore the beginning of its exercise, and therefore the Christian alteration and renewal of their existence. Their blindness and deafness still stand like a dam against the surging and mounting stream. But the stream is too strong and the dam too weak for us to be able reasonably to expect anything but the collapse of the dam and the onrush of the

§ 69. *The Glory of the Mediator*

waters. In this sense Jesus Christ is the hope even of these non-Christians.

This, then, is the new coming in our historical sphere of the Jesus Christ who once came in His own time as very God and very man. This, then, is His new coming in the glory and revelation of His mediatorial act, as the light and Word of life, in His prophetic office. In correspondence with the fact that it is the form of His coming between the commencement and the goal, and in correspondence with our historical place between, it is His coming as the hope of all men. We say this when we say that it is His universally relevant coming in the Holy Spirit and in the promise of the Holy Spirit. As He comes here and now in this form to us and all men, His second coming, His prophetic work, proceeds here and now without a break or pause, without the arising of a vacuum in which nothing happens and we and all men are left to ourselves without Him, in another sphere than that of His light and Word, being referred simply to recollection and expectation. As we have seen, the Easter event, which initiated His coming again in glory, His self-declaration, as the One who came before, was limited by His ascension, which in the language of the Bible speaks of His exit from the sphere which death limits for all creatures and His corresponding entry into the mystery of the living God. In this transition He appeared then and there to His disciples. Anticipating it in His own person, He indicated to them then and there the goal of His self-declaration as the Mediator between God and the world and therefore the ultimate future of the relationship and intercourse between God and the world, i.e., the redemption and consummation. In this form in which He was then and there present and manifest to His disciples, He is not now present and manifest to the world or to us who exist between this event and the ultimate future indicated by it. The form in which He is here and now present and manifest to the world in the time between these two times, the form in which He comes to us here and now, is the power of His coming in that first form, of the light which from it shines into this world of ours. It is the form of His coming in which He is the hope of all men, namely, the promise of His Holy Spirit.

There are many old and new prejudices and reservations in respect of the meaning and character of this new coming which takes place here and now in our sphere. These are shortsighted and restrictive because they weaken the material content. They are thus to be dispelled.

In this form (1) it is no less genuinely His own direct and personal coming, His *parousia*, presence and revelation, than was His coming there and then to His disciples in the Easter event, or than will be one day His coming in its final and conclusive form as the Judge of the quick and the dead. He is in heaven. He has entered the mystery of the living God. He is not present, then, as He was once as the

4. The Promise of the Spirit

One who came before, or as He was in the Easter event, at a specific and limited point in creaturely space. Nor is He extended over all points in creaturely space as maintained by the original Ubiquitarianism of the Lutherans. He is to be sought in heaven " at the right hand of God the Father Almighty " and therefore up above (Col. 3^1). This does not mean, however, that He is imprisoned there (for we remember that this is indeed the mystery of the living God). It does not mean that He is prevented from being and working and revealing Himself here too. How can He who is there not also be willing and able to be here too, and to do His work here ? The fact that He is there at the right hand of God means that He is in full possession and exercise of the freedom of action, the authority of rule and the disposal of grace of God Himself. It means that He exercises them here and now, in the sphere of existence left to us, on this side of the fulfilment of His prophetic work and in its progress to its goal, in the form of the power of His resurrection and the promise of His Spirit. Yet He does exercise them truly and properly and not improperly. In this form we have to do with His own direct and personal coming even though we still await the final form. In this form we are concerned in the full sense of the words with His *parousia*, presence and revelation.

In this form of His coming (2) He is no other, but the Son of God and Man, the Mediator between God and the world, in the totality and not merely a part of His being and existence. That He comes to us here and now in the promise of the Spirit does not mean then (as is rather incautiously maintained by *Qu. 47* of the *Heidelberg Catechism*) that He comes only in the power of His pure deity, His humanity being left in heaven. In His presence and activity in the promise of the Spirit, if it is really His promise of His Spirit and the power of His resurrection, there can be no question of a restitution of the separation between divine and human being which was done away in His incarnation. It was not in such separation, but in the unity of His divine and human natures, that He went to heaven, and entered the mystery of the living God, and now lives at the right hand of God the Father Almighty. When He came again in the Easter event, having crossed the frontier of death imposed on all creatures, He did not appear to His disciples as another and purely divine being, but as the One who had come before and lived among them and died on Golgotha. His coming in its final form will be His coming as this One. And in exactly the same way His coming in the promise of the Spirit between these two times is His new coming as this One who came before. In this form of His *parousia*, presence and self-revelation, He is in this mode the One who came before, very God and very man, the One whose unique life and death are attested in the New Testament, on the basis of the Easter event, as the reconciliation of the world to God accomplished in Him. As this One in

His totality He is here and now the hope of all men. How would He or could He be this if His presence and action in the promise of the Spirit were those of another, of a Word of God without and apart from the flesh assumed by Him? Even in the promise of the Spirit, however, He is this One, and as such the hope of the world. He is the incarnate Word of God, not abandoning this flesh of ours, not leaving it behind somewhere (even in heaven, in the mystery of God), but acting, speaking and revealing His glory in the flesh.

His working in this form of His coming (3) is qualitatively no less than it was in the first form and will be in the last. The promise of the Spirit is no more but also no less than the power of the resurrection of Jesus Christ operating in the time between the times. This power, however, is absolutely His power as Son of God and Man. It is the power of the atonement made in Him, which in its revelation, and in every form of its revelation, is no less but in the full sense just as powerful as it is in itself. For the prophetic work of Jesus Christ is no mere appendage or echo of His high-priestly and kingly work. It is an integral element in the whole occurrence. Hence if the promise of the Spirit is one of the forms of the prophetic work of Jesus Christ, then quite apart from the dignity to be ascribed to the Holy Spirit on a sound doctrine of the Trinity, we cannot possibly think less of His work than we do of that of Jesus Christ Himself. The Spirit is His Spirit, and therefore the Spirit of the Father, and therefore without any reservation or diminution the Spirit of God. His promise is, then, in both its senses the work of God. As the Spirit of the Lord (2 Cor. 3^{17}), the Spirit is Himself the Lord. To restrict His dignity or depreciate His work is thus to question God Himself. To reject Him in this time between is to reject God, i.e., the God who in this time acts and speaks in the Son by the Holy Ghost. Hence the famous hard saying in Mt. 12^{31} about the sin of blasphemy against the Holy Ghost which cannot be forgiven because it denies the presence of God as the source of a life of forgiveness. The *parousia*, presence and revelation of Jesus Christ in the promise of the Spirit are not confronted by another *parousia*, promise and revelation distinguished by the fact that they are more divine, more glorious, more effective to salvation, and therefore to be taken more seriously and valued more highly. If we do not have here the only form of the prophecy of Jesus Christ, but only the second and middle form, in this form the prophecy is the total proclamation of the total love of God and the total salvation of man. It is not because of the form, but of the men who may be and become the recipients of the Spirit and His promise, that the impression or notion arises that what is addressed and given us in this time between by God through the Spirit is less valuable, less helpful and even perhaps inadequate. The " sufferings of this present time " (Rom. 8^{18}) ; the fact that in this time we and all creation look forward with groaning (Rom. $8^{19f.}$)

4. *The Promise of the Spirit*

to the redemption and consummation and therefore to the coming of Jesus Christ in His final form ; the cry : " O wretched man that I am ! " in face of the contradiction in which even the Christian and apostle continually finds himself entangled (Rom. 7^{24})—these cannot mean that Christians have cause to complain of an inadequacy of the Spirit who is given them as the pledge and firstfruits of the ultimate future, or of His eternal and temporal promise, or of the lights and powers and gifts which are bestowed with it. The promise of the Spirit gives us no grounds for sighing. On the contrary, it is the power of the resurrection of Jesus Christ. There is repeated in it the anticipation of His final revelation. In it all things are already given to us and the world. From the standpoint of the Holy Spirit and His promise, of His presence and action, of the Giver and the gift, there can be nothing lacking here and now to those to whom it is addressed and given, unless it be the progress of the prophecy of Jesus Christ from its present to its future fulness, " from glory to glory." And indeed, according to 2 Cor. 3^{18}, even this is the work of the Lord who is Spirit, so that it can throw no shadow on the perfection of His work. This contention is indispensable to a right understanding of the human situation in this time of ours. The idea that it is a vacuum must be completely dispelled even in the form which suggests that it may be regarded and therefore accepted and endured as a " day of small things." If it really is this or worse, if our existence in it may be represented with some reason as sojourn or pilgrimage in a vale of tears, this is not because it is no longer the time of Easter and not yet the time of the end, but " only " the time of the Holy Ghost. For what could " only " mean in such a context ? If it is the time of the Holy Spirit given to Christians with His sure and powerful pledges, and promised to non-Christians with His equally sure and powerful pledges, then this settles the fact that in it, even on the assumption of the conditions set and obtaining for us men in the transition and therefore the limitation, vulnerability and weakness in which we now exist, even within world-occurrence moving to this goal and end, everything is of God and is therefore in order, i.e., in the special yet divinely ordained order appropriate to this time of transition. If we can and should long for the new order of the future world—and the Spirit Himself makes this unavoidable in His great promise for the last days—then we can and should also rejoice with unstinted gratitude in the order which is present already, being established by the presence and action of Jesus Christ in the promise of the Spirit. Not only was God glorious in the past, and not only will He be glorious in the final fulfilment of His promise, but He is glorious here and now in the promise of His Spirit, He Himself being present and active yesterday, to-day and to-morrow. In relation to Him there is no cause to bemoan or bewail or reject our present, but rather to extol and accept it from the heart. How can the joyful call to advance which we hear in it and which we should observe give to it a tragic aspect ? If it were really tragic, there would be a serious threat that we should not hear this call, but that in our expectant longing for the coming new world and its order we should be disillusioned rather than genuinely comforted and encouraged. If we do not honour the little, penultimate pledge as seriously given to us *hic et nunc* by the present and living Christ, we cannot appreciate or make much of the great and ultimate pledge for the eternal *illic et tunc*. In these circumstances, have we really received the Spirit and His twofold pledge, the temporal as well as the eternal, the eternal as well as the temporal ? If we have, how can we help being merry even here and to-day ? It is no contradiction to us that in the one hope in Jesus Christ our time is given us only for eternity and eternity only for our time.

Yet the question which we have already posed and answered once arises again. Why is it, in what sense, and on the basis of what higher necessity, that a history of the prophecy of Jesus Christ must arise at all in these three forms, and must still be in progress for us in this middle form ? Why must there be, between the Easter time and the definitive end time, this intervening time, the time of the promise of the Holy Spirit, the time of Jesus Christ as our hope ? Why was not the beginning immediately the goal, the goal already the beginning, the appearance of the living Jesus Christ to His disciples His *parousia*, presence and revelation to the eyes and ears of all creation and therefore their redemption and consummation ? We can no longer restrict ourselves to our previous answer that it was and is the goodness of God that to His own glory and the salvation of the creature He does not overlook the latter, but wills to give and gives it time and space and opportunity for the expression of its freedom within the context of His work. This is true. But we can now give the better and deeper answer that the return of Jesus Christ in this middle form, that His prophecy in its extension as ongoing history, that the reconciliation of the world to God as it is not yet concluded as revelation but still moves forward to its goal, has its own specific glory. We do not forget or depreciate the provoking and even dreadful riddle, indeed, it is daily and hourly before us both in great things and small, that in the form of the promise of His Spirit, Jesus Christ is dealing both in Christians and non-Christians with men who are not yet redeemed and perfected in a world which, while it is reconciled to God, is still wrapped in such thick darkness. Now this riddle is not as such solved or set aside. Yet supposing that it has a bright and perhaps luminous side on which it necessarily does not appear so dreadful but may be tolerated with unbroken joy ? Supposing that the great regime of the transition which characterises the " still " and " not yet " that cause so much human questioning and longing and sighing, which characterises our time and situation and our existence

4. The Promise of the Spirit

in them, is not at all negative as His regime, nor a mere burden which has to be cast off as quickly as possible, but a specific form of the greatness of the pitying love of God, a specific demonstration of the reconciliation of the world as it is accomplished in Jesus Christ? Is it then something negative, or does it include a lack, that Jesus Christ is here and now the hope of us all, or that He is thus present in the promise of the Spirit? We have seen that in this way He is no less real, that He is not another, that He is no less the One He was and is and will be. How can it be burdensome or a matter of embarrassment and unsettlement that He is present in this way? Why should we not have here a particular, and in its particularity a necessary, indispensable and true development of His glory, which deserves our praise and thanksgiving, so that instead of doubting and murmuring we should joyfully accept it? Can we reckon as a demonstration of the glory and humanity of God only the great final promise whose recipients, bearers and possessors we may now be, and not in like manner, according to its own truth and power, the enclosed, little, penultimate promise according to which He is on the way with us and we may be on the way with Him? Will the faithfulness of God only begin to be His total and as such effective faithfulness when this great and ultimate promise is fulfilled? Or does it not encounter us in its totality and power even in the fulfilments of the little, penultimate promise in which Jesus Christ is with us here and now, our Companion on the way through time, the Mediator, Saviour and Lord that He is, our Leader present all the days in the power of His leadership? What basis is there for the speculative wish or postulate that the first form of the *parousia*, presence and revelation of Jesus Christ should also have been its last? This would imply the impossible and blasphemous assumption that there ought not to have been the particular development of the grace, the deity and humanity of God in which Jesus Christ is the hope of all and therefore in the promise of the Spirit, but that God should have withheld from Himself and us His presence and action in the form of His provisional promise in time, and the demonstration of His power in our present, under the conditions and in the limitations and problems of our present, and in the vulnerability of our existence, refraining from being our God or having us as His people in this way. We have only to realise how great God is in the fact that He did not refrain from willing to give, and giving, and continuing to give the history of His dealings and fellowship with the world and us men, i.e., the history of salvation, this form as well, and we shall see at once how empty is this postulate, and be kept from raising this idle question even in dilettante fashion. The bright and luminous side of the riddle of our existence in transition, in the time of the " still " and " not yet," is the fact that Jesus Christ Himself is in transition, living, acting, speaking and working under the same sign, and that this is not even partially to His shame but to His distinctive glory, so that it cannot be to our hurt that He is present in the form of the promise of the Spirit, but to our full salvation. To Him there is really to be ascribed praise and thanksgiving even *e profundis* and in and under all the sighing for the progress and conclusion of His work. Unreservedly joyful praise and sincere thanksgiving must be given Him for the fact that He willed and arranged that we should have time and place and opportunity not merely for the expression of our creaturely freedom but for life in hope in Him as the hope of all men, for life under the promise of God and in the power of this promise.

We shall now try to see in very general outline what is this life under the promise and in the power of the promise of the Spirit as now made possible for us men.

Once we have freed ourselves from the prejudices and reservations which we have again dispelled, it is clear that this life stands under the one positive sign *par excellence*. Whatever may have to be said by way of complaint that we live under the conditions indicated, or that our day is no longer Easter Day and not yet the day of redemption and consummation, or that we are entangled in the thrust and counter-thrust of question, answer and new question, there can be no doubt that this present day of ours is also a day of the living Jesus Christ. It may well be also a day in which all of us, Christians and non-Christians alike, sin in evil thoughts and words and deeds as though we were not those who were justified and sanctified in His life and death. It may well be a day on which the earth is covered, as once before the flood, by so much merited and unmerited suffering. It may well be a day when no moment passes in which death does not make what seems to be an irrevocable end of some human life. It may well be a day of the devil and demons, of yielding but still resisting darkness. This is true. But it is not decisive. The decisive thing is that it is also a day of Jesus Christ, a day of His presence, life, activity and speech. Moreover—and this is what we have been trying to learn—it is concretely a day of His coming again in the full sense of the word, of His new coming in glory, here and now in this intervening time which is our place. It is a day in the history of His prophecy, of the ongoing work of His self-declaration of the revelation of that which, when He came before, He enacted and accomplished in His life and speech and action and passion and death in His time as the act of God for the world and for all men. In the first instance we are not contemporaries of the great and little personages of the history of the world or culture or even the Church, of their lives and acts and opinions, of their enterprises and achievements as more or less authentically reported in the press and by radio. In the first instance we are contemporaries of Jesus Christ and direct witnesses of His action, whether with closed or open or blinking eyes, whether actively or passively. More closely and properly than any other man—indeed, He alone closely and properly in the full sense—He is the Neighbour of every other man, the Good Samaritan for all of us who have so obviously fallen among thieves. And incomparably more important and incisive and significant than anything that may happen to the world in East or West, or to any one of us by way of good or ill and with or without our co-operation, is that which comes upon the world and each of us with the fact that Jesus Christ as the light of life, as the Word of the covenant of grace, but also as the future Judge of the quick and the dead, passes actively through the midst at every hour, the hope of us all in the promise of the Spirit addressed to all. And the part of all humanity and each individual in this positive sign of the middle period and situation of His *parousia*, presence and revelation is that wittingly or unwittingly we are alongside and with Him. His to-day is really ours, and ours His. Nor does this mean only that what He does to-day and what we do proceed along two specific and separated lines. He goes on our way and we on His. Hence He does not do what He does without us, nor we without Him. Our action is wholly ours, yet it is determined by His. There is thus no altering the fact that the events, forms and relationships of the public and private action which apparently (but only apparently) fills this intervening time, that our great and little successes and defeats and advances and retreats and enlightenments and obfuscations and joys and sorrows, stand in a relationship which may perhaps be suspected, not to say perceived, only infrequently by a few, which may be more near or distant, which may be one of opposition or concord, which may seem to be colourless and indefinite, but which is still a very real relationship to the movement in which He passes through our midst, striding through our time from His commencement to His goal. No man eats or drinks, wakens or sleeps, laughs or cries, blesses or curses, builds or destroys, lives or dies, outside this relationship. Whether we affirm, deny or ignore His prophetic work, whether we resist or further it, whether we serve or hinder it, we all take part in it as the occurrence which truly and properly fills this time of ours. He and He alone knows infallibly how we do this. The manner in which we have done, do and will do so is written in the book of life which will not be opened until the last day, and which will then perhaps contain many surprising data. The positive thing, however, about the lives of all of us here and now in our time is that we do actually take part in the *parousia*, presence and revelation of Jesus Christ as the hope of us all, in the promise of the Spirit addressed to us all. Nor do we do so merely incidentally and externally, but centrally and internally, though externally, too, as men who, existing in time, are encircled by the glory of the Mediator. It may be added that in this relationship to Him, whatever form it may take, we are indissolubly linked with one another. It may also be added that in it we are linked with all to whom He was present before our time as His way was also theirs and theirs His, but also with all those whose way He will share after our time. In the relationship to Him the history of present, past and future is thus a single whole in which nothing did or will escape Him, in which none could or can flee from Him or slip from His grasp, i.e., break free from the relationship. As He lives in relationship to us in our time, we live in relationship to Him together with all the men of our own and all times, there being no separation between them and us nor us and them. The day of His revelation in its final form will concretely reveal this. But since our day is a day of His revelation as the hope of us all, a day of the promise of the Spirit, it is already true and actual in this day of ours, and thus to be reckoned with in all seriousness and with all joy.

Was it not necessary to relate the statement that Jesus Christ is here and now our hope, quite expressly to all men, and therefore also to non-Christians, to the heathen, to the theoretically or practically ungodly? How could we limit the positive sign of life in the midst of the times to Christians? The main concern of the ongoing of the history of the prophecy of Jesus Christ which fills our time is with non-Christians. Their existence is a reminder of the darkness which resists it. It is for their sake that it must go forward, that Jesus Christ as the living Word of God is still on the way to-day. Their conversion from ignorance to knowledge, from unbelief to faith, from bondage to freedom, from night to day, is the goal of His prophetic work so far as it has a temporal goal. He wills to seek and to save those who are lost, who without Him, without the light of life, without the Word of the covenant, will necessarily perish. He is for them specifically this light, this Word. He goes after them. He is their hope. The promise of the Spirit is for them. Why not? It is true that they are not for Him that which corresponds to what He is for them. They do not see Him as the light which shines for them. They do not hear what He has to say to them about what He has done for them. They do not know Him as He knows them. They do not take up the relationship which by His *parousia*, presence and revelation is established and obtains between Him and them and them and Him. On the contrary, they adopt in relation to Him an attitude of indifference, aversion and obstruction. But this cannot alter the fact that He is for them. As such, His relationship to them and theirs to Him is a fact which cannot be altered or removed. For it is established and created by the fact that, as the One He is, He lives in the midst of our time and takes the most direct way to them. Hence He is not merely their hope as well, but their hope specifically. Christians have many reasons to see this. In days past were not they themselves non-Christians, or sleeping and even dead Christians, and therefore in fact and at bottom non-Christians? Is it not the

4. *The Promise of the Spirit*

case that they were not for Him as He was for them? Have they not every cause to be grateful that in spite of this, without their response of love, indeed, even when they were enemies (Rom. 5^{10}), He was for them, their hope, and the Holy Spirit was obviously promised to them in this way? Similarly, He is obviously promised in all His fulness to those who still confront them as non-Christians. Similarly, He is the hope of these others too. And supposing more importance is attached to those who are not yet Christians? Supposing they are more interesting to Him than Christians in His will and action? Supposing the greater weight of His will and action falls in this sphere? Supposing His light shines brighter here, and His Word is more living and active? Supposing the unconverted are sometimes dearer to Him than the converted? Supposing the knowledge of Jesus Christ which divides Christians from non-Christians, when imparted to the latter in fulfilment of the promise seriously given to the heathen too, brings forth among them more rich and varied and useful fruits than among those who already know Him, so that the last are first and the first last? Supposing the Christian is deceived when he adjudges his fellow a non-Christian, because the knowledge of Jesus Christ has already found a lodging in him in a form which the Christian and perhaps the man himself does not recognise? Supposing, finally, the Christian is deceived as to his own Christianity, being more of a non-Christian than a Christian, and basically perhaps not really being a Christian at all? In face of all these by no means irrelevant questions the Christian should be glad that he lives under the lordship of Jesus Christ who is the hope even of those who are not for Him as He is for them, and under the promise, and in the power of the promise, which is also given to non-Christians of every kind.

Remembrance of this should serve, not to diminish or restrict, but to increase and extend the gratitude, joy and responsibility with which the Christian may be such here and now under this positive sign and in accompaniment of the prophetic work of Jesus Christ, i.e., with which he may exist in the knowledge of Jesus Christ and as the recipient, bearer and possessor of the Spirit and of the lights, powers and gifts promised by Him. It is obvious that the positive sign under which our time and our life in this time stand means something more and different to him than it does to the non-Christian. Not only is this sign set up for him, but he knows it, and may live in and by this knowledge. As we have seen, life is not really made simpler or easier for the Christian. On the contrary, the fact that he may live as one who knows means that burdens are laid on him which others do not have to bear. For he knows his inescapable solidarity with all men and indeed all creatures in all their sorrow. He knows their increasing rather than decreasing debt and guilt in relation to both God and man. He knows the difficulty of the task which is set him, how thankless it is and how unlikely to be successful. To know Jesus Christ is to accept the Word of reconciliation spoken in Him and His prophetic work. It is thus to accept a Word which is new and strange to the world reconciled in Him, indeed, which is continually new and strange to the Christian himself. To know Jesus Christ is to appropriate this Word in opposition to what the world always thinks and says and practises, and above all in opposition to oneself. Hence to know Jesus Christ is from the very first, however modest or weak the knowledge, to take the side of Jesus Christ, to become a responsible subject instead of a mere object in His cause, to be prepared not merely to hear His Word but also to repeat or accompany it, however softly or clumsily. This is what makes the Christian so great but also so small. It makes him so great because it means that he does not merely belong to Jesus Christ as all men undoubtedly belong to Him, but that he does so in such a way that the work which Jesus Christ does in the world is the meaning of his work, and the fight which Jesus Christ wages in the darkness against darkness is the cause to which he dedicates himself. But it makes him so small; for he is appalled by the dominant condition of great and little human affairs, by his old godless and brotherless Ego which emerges as his first and most dangerous opponent when he appropriates the Word of Jesus Christ and sides with Him in this battle, and by the monstrous demand which is made of him that he should be a witness to Jesus Christ and therefore a little true salt, a small light in the darkness. Who is so painfully affected or smitten as the Christian by the dominant darkness around and in him, by the unredeemed and unperfected state of the world in its present form which is also and primarily his own, by the contradiction in what is already true but not yet actual, by the manifest dominion of sin and death, by the constantly renewed resistance of the evil in whose service he again and again finds himself? Who has such deep and necessary cause for sighing as he who has received the promise of the Spirit, in whom it is already fulfilled, who knows what others do not yet know, namely, that Jesus Christ alone is the hope of the world and therefore his hope, to whom the positive sign under which we may exist here and now is known and not merely imposed, who is thus permitted but also required to live with this knowledge? " What shall we then say to these things? " We do well not to say anything more or better than what Paul said in Rom. 8^{31}: " If God be for us, who can be against us? " But this we must say. And it is more and better than anything which has to be said concerning what makes the Christian great and small. It includes the twofold truth that it is indeed a hard and oppressive and humiliating thing to be a Christian, and therefore with Jesus Christ and His Word in one's heart to have to be against the whole world and oneself, but that it is also an incomparably glorious, comforting and proud thing to be a Christian and therefore to be at the side of Jesus Christ, to be not merely an object in His work but a subject in His service, to be not merely a hearer of His Word but a great or little, skilful or unskilful witness of this Word. How can the difficulty of the Christian way be avoided when the Jesus Christ who precedes on this way is none other than He who bore His cross to Golgotha ? But how can it fail to be a glorious way when the power which sets the Christian on it is that of the resurrection of Jesus Christ ? The God who reconciled the world and therefore the Christian to Himself, and who does not cease to reveal Himself as the One who did so, is for him in either case, on this way which is both difficult and glorious. This is what makes the life of the Christian possible, necessary and meaningful in this time. This is what makes him in all circumstances a positive man. His life is positive in the fact that from the very first it is one long calling upon God. He calls upon God representatively for those who do not yet do so, or do not seem to do so. He does not exclude but includes them when he prays to this God: " Our Father ! Hallowed be Thy name ! Thy kingdom come ! Thy will be done on earth, as it is in heaven ! " This God will not faint, neither be weary. He hears all those who call on Him in this way. " He giveth power to the faint ; and to them that have no might he increaseth strength. Even the youths shall faint and be weary, and the young men shall utterly fall : but they that wait upon the Lord shall renew their strength ; they shall mount up with wings as eagles ; they shall run, and not be weary ; and they shall walk, and not faint " (Is. $40^{28f.}$).

§ 70

THE FALSEHOOD AND CONDEMNATION OF MAN

As the effective promise of God encounters man in the power of the resurrection of Jesus Christ, man proves himself to be a liar in whose thinking, speech and conduct his liberation by and for the free God transforms itself into an attempt to claim God by and for himself as the man who is bound in his self-assertion—a perversion in which he can only destroy himself and finally perish.

1. THE TRUE WITNESS

The christological basis of this third part of the doctrine of reconciliation is now behind us. It reached its conclusion in our presentation of the promise of the Spirit. This is the particular form of reconciliation in which it is already achieved yet still takes place as a divine act of liberation accomplished here and now. It is its spontaneous self-declaration in the time still given to the world and us. It is the dawn and shining of the light of life, the living Word of God, the victorious coming of Jesus Christ in the history of His prophetic work. It is the Servant and Lord Jesus Christ still engaged in His work in His transition and entry into our human situation and history as these are basically altered by His life and death and generally illuminated by His resurrection from the dead. What does it mean for us, for the world already altered and illuminated by Him, for the men reconciled in Him and participant in His revelation, that in the promise of His Spirit He is not distant but near and among us, that He encounters us on our way, that He does so as the true Witness of our reconciliation accomplished in Him, of the fulfilled covenant of grace, in all the glory of His mediatorial work? The attempt to answer this question will form the content of the rest of this third part of the doctrine. We shall have to speak of the vocation of man, of the sending of the Christian community, and finally of hope as the gift and state of the individual Christian summoned by the Word of the living Jesus Christ.

But the first phenomenon which we meet with in this sphere, and therefore the first theme to which we must apply ourselves, is the man of sin. This man is the one who is reconciled to God in Jesus Christ. It is he whom Jesus Christ encounters and to whom reconciliation comes in the form of His prophetic work, i.e., in the promise of the Spirit. What does the doing of the prophetic work of Jesus

1. The True Witness

Christ mean for this man as such? The doctrine of sin must thus claim our attention for a third time. In the first part ("The Lord as Servant") we saw it as reflected in the high-priestly work of Jesus Christ. It appeared as the strange opposite of the humility with which the Son of God humbled Himself in obedience to the Father. It was the pride with which man exalted himself in an attempt to be as God, his own judge and helper. In the second part ("The Servant as Lord") it was set in the light of His kingly work. It thus appeared as the strange opposite of the exaltation and majesty of the Son of Man. It was the sloth in which man allows himself to sink and fall into the morass of his unnatural yet natural stupidity, inhumanity, dissipation and anxiety. In encounter with the prophetic work of Jesus Christ, as a negative reflection of the self-revelation and glory of the Mediator, as the darkness resisting the light of life, as the contradiction of the truth which reaches man, his sin appears in the guise of falsehood. We shall have to speak of it under this form in the present section. And as in the first part we had to speak of the fall which follows and is already enacted in the pride of man, and in the second of the misery implied in his sloth, so here we shall have to show that in and with his falsehood he necessarily finds himself on the way which leads to his condemnation.

As concerns the knowledge of sin, we start with certain assumptions explained in previous volumes. The Christian conception of sin as man's aberration and transgression is not to be gained from abstract norms of the good and just and holy and proper which are then adorned with the name of the Law of God, as though we thought we could construct it from general anthropological axioms and their implications, or by systematising and standardising certain biblical statements. The doctrine of sin cannot be established, expounded or developed independently of or prior to the doctrine of reconciliation. It forms an integral part of the latter. It derives subsequently and retrospectively from a knowledge of the existence and work of Jesus Christ as the Mediator of the covenant of grace. Sin may be known in its nature, reality, implications and consequences as it is opposed, vanquished and done away by Him. Only in this setting can we speak of it with Christian relevance. The Christian concept of sin is not to be gained in a vacuum, *remoto Christo*, but from the Gospel to the extent that the Gospel itself, as the good news of man's liberation by and for the free God, has also the character and form of the true Law of God, the promise of the grace of God containing His no less gracious claim, as the ark of the Old Testament covenant contained the tables of the Decalogue. In all its forms sin is man's perverted dealing with the stern goodness and righteous mercy of God addressed to him in Jesus Christ. It is their denial and rejection, their misunderstanding and misuse. It is man's direct or indirect enmity against the promise of God which as such is also His demand. Proving itself to be such

§ 70. *The Falsehood and Condemnation of Man*

it is unmasked, discovered and judged as man is confronted by the Gospel, by the living Jesus Christ in the Gospel. These statements of principle and method are expressly established and developed from the biblical, historico-dogmatic and systematic standpoint in the first part of the doctrine of reconciliation (*C.D.*, IV, 1 § 60, 1), and recapitulated in the second part (IV, 2 § 65, 1). They need not detain us in the present context.

With the conception of the Gospel and the Law which supports and integrates them (cf. my work *Evangelium und Gesetz*, 1935, and *C.D.*, II, 2, § 36–39), they belong to the basic substance of my dogmatics as hitherto presented. This does not prove that they are right. But I must declare in passing that I have not been convinced that they are wrong by what has been urged against them by theologians of Lutheran background and upbringing to whom they are particularly repugnant (e.g., W. Elert, P. Althaus, E. Sommerlath, H. Thielicke, W. Joest, and, in the *Antwort* of 1956, G. Wingren, and with particular circumspection Edmund Schlink). There are still far too many things which I cannot understand in the counter-thesis, advanced with varying degrees of sharpness and consistency by these authors, that the Gospel and the Law differ and are even antithetical in significance and function.

I do not understand (1) with what biblical or inherent right, on the basis of what conception of God, His work and His revelation, and above all in the light of what Christology, they can speak, not of one intrinsically true and clear Word of God, but of two Words in which He speaks alternately and in different ways to man according to some unknown rule.

I do not understand (2) the meaning of a supposed Gospel the content of which is exhausted by the proclamation of the forgiveness of sins and which is to be received by man in a purely inward and receptive faith ; nor of a supposed Law which as an abstract demand can only be an external ordinance on the one side but on the other is ordained to accuse man and therefore to indicate and prepare the way for the Gospel.

I do not understand (3) how there can be ascribed to the apostle Paul a conception of the Law of God in which he admittedly does not agree with the self-understanding of the Old Testament, or in plain terms contradicts it, the more so when this conception is so obviously false in the light of the Old Testament itself, and especially of what we now know (M. Noth, G. v. Rad, J. H. Kraus) of the Old Testament concept of Law in its positive relationship to the covenant of Yahweh. I am surprised how lightly this very disturbing problem of exegetical presupposition is taken.

I do not understand (4) how the concept of a supposed Law can be attained or exploited except (as in the 16th century, and with very serious consequences in the 17th, 18th and 19th) by appealing to the idea of a natural law and therefore of a general natural revelation, or by falling back on a most primitive form of biblicism ; and I am surprised that this dilemma has not been accepted as a warning.

I do not understand (5) how there can be achieved in this way what is at issue in the present context, namely, how the confrontation of man by this supposed Law can give him a serious, precise and inescapable knowledge of human transgression and therefore of human sin, or how far such a Law can have the divine authority and power to bring man into subjection to its judgment. Nor do I understand how or to what degree man is to find himself on the way to the Gospel by falling short of this Law.

Do I not understand Martin Luther if I do not understand these things ? I certainly do not understand the Luther of the conflict against the Antinomians, whom I also encounter with something of a shock in not a few of his earlier and

1. *The True Witness*

later writings. Nor do I understand that which subsequently developed as classical Lutheran teaching on this subject. But when we consider the varied wealth of the secrets enclosed in the Weimar edition, do we not have to admit that there is perhaps more than one Luther in this respect, and that there is a Luther to whom appeal cannot be made by the classical teaching or its modern expositors and exponents who oppose me in the name of it ? For my part, I might set alongside the critical contributions of Wingren and Schlink the essay of H. Gollwitzer which appears along with theirs in the *Antwort*, or more recently the book of Gerhard Heintze, *Luthers Predigt von Gesetz und Evangelium* (1958), from which I learn that, especially on the fairly broad lines of his exposition and application of the Decalogue, and specifically of the first commandment, Luther in his sermons on the Sermon on the Mount and the passion story could also follow a programme (*Nihil nisi Christus praedicandus*) in relation to which it might well be asked whether I am not quite a good Lutheran after all. But to maintain this, or at least to be able to appeal on my behalf to an authentic Luther, I should have to be as well versed in the intricacies of the Weimar edition as those who, equipped and claimed for this task both by nature and grace, launch their own Luther against me. Hence my only option is, either with Luther or against him, to stand by the insight which I have previously attained and proved.

On the basis of this presupposition we may say at once that the truth unmasks, discovers, accuses and judges the man of sin as such. But the truth which does this in all circumstances (whether men realise it or not) and irresistibly (whatever they attempt against it) is Jesus Christ Himself as the true Witness of His true deity and humanity, as the authentic Witness of the saving grace of God which has appeared in Him justifying and sanctifying man. It is Jesus Christ in and with the promise of the Holy Spirit, going with us men on our way through the times from His resurrection as in the promise of the same Spirit He also comes towards us on this way in intimation and anticipation of His final coming. He is the Law or norm of God confronted and measured by which man is shown up as a transgressor, and specifically as a deceiver and a liar. Of himself man certainly could not and would not regard himself as such. In encounter with Jesus Christ—and in virtue of the resurrection there is none who does not find himself in this encounter—the reality of the falsehood in which he exists acquires a recognisable being and perceptible form, and necessarily discloses itself for what it is. It awakens, lives and acts in opposition to Him. What characterises it as sin, and makes it immeasurably dreadful and reprehensible, as an event which cannot be comprehended in its reality, is that it is the denial, perversion and falsification of what is said to man as God's Word in Him, the Son of God and Man. This also reveals, of course, its limitation. Jesus Christ is a match for it. In relation to Him it can only be shadow and not true light. It can deny Him as the Word of God, but it cannot silence Him. It is a second thing which follows Him as the first, but it cannot be the last. It cannot absolutise itself. This does not make it any better. If it is only within this limitation, relatively to the truth in Jesus Christ and therefore transitorily, that it has power and significance, this does not alter in the slightest its character as

§ 70. The Falsehood and Condemnation of Man

sin or the condemnation to which the man of sin and therefore man as a liar has fallen victim. It must be seen and estimated and feared in the being and form, in the reality, which it has within this limitation, i.e., in the deeds and misdeeds of man.

Sin as sin against the grace of God is falsehood as it is also pride and sloth. But in its role as falsehood it operates on another level than in its forms as pride and sloth. In relation to these it is as it were in a third dimension. As lying, too, sin is an arbitrary, unfounded, unjustifiable and wicked breaking out from the reality of the covenant which on the basis of His eternal election of grace God has founded already in and with the creation of all things, which He has fulfilled to His own glory and man's salvation in the humiliation and exaltation, in the true deity and humanity, of Jesus Christ, and which He has thus established and unshakeably confirmed as the promise made to all men but also as the norm and criterion of all human conduct. In its form as falsehood, however, sin is specifically man's unfounded and inexcusable breaking out from this reality to the extent that it is also truth. It is the arbitrary obstruction with which man encounters the prophetic work of the Mediator between God and man. It is the darkness which he opposes to the light of election, creation and reconciliation, and in which, like Zwingli's cuttle-fish in the dark fluid emitted by it, he tries to hide himself from God, his fellows and not least himself. To be sure, he is guilty of falsehood in the pride in which, in contrast to the humility of the Son of God, he seeks to occupy the place of God and play a divine role ; as also in the sloth in which, in contrast to the majesty of the royal man Jesus, he seeks to divest himself of the dignity of his divinely given nature. Not for nothing have we continually had to insist in these first two parts of the doctrine of sin that it belongs to its reality constantly to try to conceal itself in the most diverse forms and to pretend that it is necessary, righteous and holy. Where and when is man prepared to admit that as a sinner he is a transgressor, that he is in the wrong against God, his fellows and himself, and that he is plunging into the abyss ? Proud and slothful, he is necessarily false as well. Covering over what he is and does, he obviously betrays the fact that in his pride and sloth he stands in relation to the truth, but in a relation of opposition to the truth which is not utterly strange but which comes to him, being unwilling to accept it, refusing all but negative dealings with it, withholding his recognition and seeking to escape it. This whole process is essentially the distinctive work of falsehood even in the first two forms. The specific function of falsehood is thus to be the common exponent in which they both necessarily betray and express themselves as sin.

But this does not by any means exhaust its distinctiveness. Independently of its co-operation with the first two forms, it has its own meaning and character. These derive from the fact that it is

1. The True Witness

not merely in the material, intrinsically timeless and constant opposition in principle of man to the grace of God, but in his historical encounter with the Word of divine grace addressed to him, that sin in this third form of falsehood becomes mature, virulent and open. In this encounter sin, too, forms itself into a word. If pride and sloth are the works, falsehood is the word of the man of sin. In this there is manifestly fulfilled its basic character as a counter-stroke to and caricature of the threefold office and work of Jesus Christ. In it there is also given proof of its lack of autonomy, independence or originality in relation to the will and work of God—a characteristic from which it cannot free itself in its downward flight to nothingness. The devil has nothing of his own to oppose to God, but only falsifying imitations, as we shall see very clearly in the present section. Within the economy of sin itself, however, falsehood must obviously be treated as a new form.

How does it arise? As the Lord of the covenant of grace fulfilled in Jesus Christ, God continues His action or work of reconciliation by speaking to man, by addressing him, by telling him what He is for him in His grace and what man may be for God in gratitude for His grace. He has already done this as the Lord of the covenant prior to its fulfilment, in the prophecy of the history of Israel which merely intimates the history of Jesus Christ, in the language of His acts in and to this elect people as articulated in human terms by the witnesses of the Old Testament. And in the prophecy of Jesus Christ as the Word of His fulfilled will and action there is still heard the voice of the rule of God as it moves to its fulfilment, the Word of the old covenant as the promise of the new, and of the new as the confirmation and therefore the power of the old. But the totality of the history of salvation concretely enacted once and for all, and thus completed and concluded, has as it were a spearhead in which it continually takes place as it is also a living Word speaking of and for itself beyond its own particular age. In this form it goes right into the world *post Christum* as this moves to its goal and end. In our temporal and historical sphere between the first and the final revelation of Jesus Christ, it comes to the men existing in this sphere. The revelation of Jesus Christ, His work as the true Witness of God in this intervening time, is the promise of the Holy Spirit. By this Word of God the man of this intervening time, with the man of the time of the Old Testament witness, is forced to make answer. And his answer is sin in the form of falsehood. It did not have to be this. God's Word discloses to him his justification and sanctification as they have taken place in Jesus Christ, and therefore the fact that as the man of sin he is displaced, vanquished, dead and buried in the life and death of Jesus Christ, so that he is freed not only for the reality but also for the truth of his reconciliation, for knowledge of it. As he did not have to persist in his pride and sloth, no more did he have to persist in his falsehood. He had only to give place to the Word of God encountering him as the promise of the Spirit, to give to it the place which rightfully belongs to it in his heart and conscience and whole existence, and he would immediately have found himself in agreement with it. His answer would then have been his own free, spontaneous and quite unequivocal Yes, corresponding to what is said to him by God. In this answer the time left to him, the Christian era as we might call it for once, could and would have acquired and had its true meaning for him. This is why this time is left to him as the time of grace. Responding in this way to God's Word, the man reconciled to God in Jesus Christ and made aware of this reconciliation by Him, could and would have moved towards the goal and end of this time in His final and conclusive revelation. That he may give this answer to God, freedom is also given him in this sphere. But he does not give it. In a way which is doubly nonsensical in view of the time of grace and the freedom granted to him, and doubly incomprehensible in relation to what is said to him, his answer is his falsehood, i.e., his attempt not to allow to be true that which is true between God and him, to set aside the truth which is told him by God, to produce instead his own truth, which as such, opposing and replacing the Yes which he owes to God and which God has made him free to utter, can only be his untruth. There are many signs that just as nonsensically and incomprehensibly he thinks that he can persist in his pride and sloth, and seriously tries to do so. But here sin takes on a character of its own in this third form. At this point it emerges as man's counter-revelation to the divine revelation of grace, and therefore as sin in its most highly developed form. To disclose it in this form there is needed the situation of the era dominated and determined by the prophecy of Jesus Christ, i.e., the Christian era, to which there also belongs the time of the prophecy of the history of Israel. Epigrammatically, and to be taken *cum grano salis*, we might say that falsehood is the specifically Christian form of sin.

Before we deal with man's falsehood as such, its nature and corruption, we must be clear what is the witness of the true Witness in relation and contradiction to which sin is kindled as falsehood or false witness, and by which it is accused, condemned and judged as such.

It is in the light and in virtue of the power of this witness that it becomes mature, virulent and palpable, that its seed and kernel sinks deep into man, not into his nature but into his unnatural obduracy, and that as man's answer it becomes his act. Man as the man of sin does not break free from God. Even in his untruth he can live only by the truth of God. He can only sin against it on the assumption that is is the truth, and speaks to him as such. His own truth, and therefore the untruth with which he answers it, can have only the form and content of a travesty of the truth. Only the truth im-

1. The True Witness

mediatedly and incontrovertibly unmasks him as a liar. It does this in the most simple way imaginable. If we think in terms of a complicated process of *pro* and *contra*, or if we try to grasp and present the encounter of the truth with man, and what takes place in it, in the form of a dialectical or even psychological analysis, we have obviously failed to see or understand what is at issue. As the truth is simply present as such, yet is not indolent but speaks, attesting itself to man as a Word directed to him; as it is quite nonsensically and incomprehensibly unwelcome to him; as in self-protection he advances his untruth against it; as he does not prevail against it but can only be a convicted liar in its presence, this totality does not form a nexus whose individual members and moments can be explained in terms of themselves and one another, and therefore understood and described pragmatically. On the contrary, it is a history which in fact takes place in this way and not another, and in which the truth is truth, and man man, and the two encounter and collide with one another. What takes place, then, is simply that the truth reveals itself as such to man, that he does not want it, that he advances against it his untruth, that it shows this to be what it is, that man is thus shown up as a liar and stands unmasked as such. What we have here is a history which, in the greater context of the prophetic work of Jesus Christ, and the even greater context of the history of reconciliation, can only be recounted, the systematics of which in all its dimensions is only grounded in itself as history, and which can be clearly seen only if we preceive its two decisive elements, the superior truth which reaches and strikes man, and the man who, reached and struck by it, is no match for it, but is detected and unmasked by it in his untruth. If it were not the truth, and did not reach man as such, it could not do this. But it is the truth, and reaches man. If he were not man, and were not reached by the truth, this would not happen to him. But he is man, and is reached by it. Hence it takes place irresistibly that it unmasks him and that he is unmasked by it, being convicted of his sin. We shall speak of the truth which unmasks him in this first sub-section, and of the man who is unmasked by it, of his falsehood as such, in the second.

"What is truth?" It is certainly not (1) an idea, principle, or system (whether constructed by the integration of views and outlooks or the combination of concepts, whether traditional in form or more original). Nor is it a structure of correct insights, nor a doctrine, even though this be a correct doctrine of the being of God, that of man, their normal relationship to one another and the establishment, restoration and ordering of this relationship. The truth certainly can and should be reflected in such a doctrine, and secondarily attested in this form. It demands to be taught as such, i.e., to be grasped, considered and understood with the greatest possible consistency, and to be expressed in tolerably correct, clear and logical thoughts,

§ 70. *The Falsehood and Condemnation of Man*

words and sentences. But even in the doctrine which is most correct, and most conscientiously attained and fashioned, we are already or still in the sphere of man and not yet or no longer in that of the truth of God which encounters him. Even at best, doctrine as the work of man is always a dubious and equivocal phenomenon. In the mouth of human teachers and the ears of human listeners it is always threatened by some measure of misunderstanding, deception, falsification and corruption. Even as a structure of insights which are wholly correct it can be or become falsehood. Indeed, falsehood loves to take the garb of doctrine, idea, principle and system. And the more divine an idea pretends to be ; the more radically a principle is carried through and asserted ; the more definitively a system claims to be the truth ; the more a doctrine seems to be abounding in correct insights, the more we have cause to suspect that what is trying to claim and enslave us is an idea, principle, system or doctrine of falsehood. We can be sure at least that no doctrine has of itself the power to unmask the sinner, i.e., the power of the event in which he is irresistibly detected and exposed as a liar. No doctrine has the power of which we shall have to speak in the next section, namely, the power of summoning him out of his falsehood to a knowledge and confession of the truth, to obedience and service. The truth alone has the power for both these things. But the truth which has this power is the speech, action and operation of the person of the true because primary Witness who encounters man in this history. Jesus Christ in the promise of the Spirit as His revelation in the sphere of our time and history is the truth. Doctrine thus participates or does not participate in the truth to the extent and in the measure that directly or indirectly it teaches Him or fails to do so. But He cannot be enclosed or confined in any doctrine concerning Him, not even the most correct Christology. As the origin and theme of all doctrine, He is also its Lord. He is not conditioned by nor bound to it, as it is conditioned by and bound to Him. He is sovereign in relation to it, and is thus the measure and criterion of all doctrine concerning Him and all other doctrine. It is as He encounters man and speaks to him, that man is unmasked as the man of sin. Not in the light of doctrine, but in His light, man is convicted of his falsehood.

" What is truth ? " It certainly cannot be expected (2) to encounter man as a phenomenon which is immediately and directly illuminating, pleasing, acceptable and welcome to him. He would not be who he is if the promise of the Spirit came to him easily and smoothly. The gate through which it comes to him, if at all, is not wide but strait, and its way to him is not broad but narrow. Basically, it is in harmony with him and it speaks to his innermost self. For it tells him about the reconciliation of the world to God which has taken place in Jesus Christ, about this as his own justification and sanctification, about the new birth which it implies for him, about the freedom and peace

1. *The True Witness*

of his true being as a new man in Jesus Christ. Yet telling him of these things, it is a new and strange and unsettling message compared with what he is in himself apart from this being of his in Jesus Christ, and with what he thus regards as pleasing, acceptable and true. It lacks the brightness and radiance which might cause it to seem true and acceptable. Indeed, the new man in Jesus Christ of whom it tells seems to be wrapped in obscurity compared with the old whom we know so much better and with whom we are naturally well acquainted. We need to pierce the obscurity, to penetrate the alien, threatening and uncomfortable aspect under which the truth draws near to man, if we are really to see it as the truth. We need to do something which is not at all self-evident, namely, to become other people. In the first instance, it does not address us; it contradicts us and demands our contradiction. Hence it does not commend itself. It is not welcome but unwelcome. It would certainly not be the truth if it did not have the tendency and power to pierce that obscurity, to penetrate that first aspect, to change us and therefore to open us to itself. It would not be the truth if the newness and strangeness in which it first encounters us were no more than the hard shell of a sweet and very precious kernel, if its aim and impulse were not to make perceptible and accessible to us the joy and peace of our true being as new men in Jesus Christ. But it would also not be the truth if it won us for itself by any other way than that of a powerful Nevertheless and Notwithstanding, if it did not encounter us in that hard shell, if it served up that insight on a platter, if it disclosed itself to us cheaply and otherwise than in a desperate conflict of decision. Things gained in this easy and self-evident way might well be kindly and good and even true within the sphere of a creaturely life, but they would certainly not be the truth of God. And they would be distinguished from this by the fact that they would entail no unmasking of man, no exposure of him as a liar, and therefore no summoning of him to a knowledge of the grace of God, to faith and obedience. That this is so in the case of the truth of God is grounded in the fact that this is identical with the true Witness Jesus Christ as the revelation of God's will and work for man enacted in Him. The glory of this Mediator, however, is a glory which is concealed in its opposite, in invisibility, in repellent shame. This Witness does not encounter man in a splendour which wins him easily and impresses him naturally. Raised from the dead by the power of God, He encounters him in the despicable and forbidding form of the Slain and Crucified of Golgotha. It is as the One whose way leads and ends there that He is the Reconciler of the world to God, the justification and sanctification of man. It is with Him as this One that our life is hidden and secured in God. And it is as this One that He comes again, revealing Himself in the world which moves to this end and goal and therefore in our sphere of time and history. The Word of the cross is thus the light of life, the saving revelation of God, the promise of the Spirit, in which He visits and accompanies and encounters man. It is as the Word of the cross that it has and exercises this power, and therefore primarily in this context the power to unmask the man of sin as a liar. To whom could it possibly appear welcome, acceptable or even tolerable? As it is this Word from which we think we can only turn away in rejection in view of the menace of its form, it is obvious that we should try to escape from it in falsehood, accepting instead a truth or untruth which it is easy to hold and affirm and which has the advantage that it enables us to think that we can avoid exposure. We can only think this. For in face of this Word there is for man, no matter what he thinks, no possibility of escape or concealment.

On the basis of these prior delimitations, we must now come to grips with the matter.

We turn again to our starting-point. The true Witness, and therefore the pronouncement, revelation and phenomenon of the truth, the truth itself, which unmasks man as it encounters him, is the living Jesus Christ present in the reconciled world in the promise of the Spirit and acting in and towards it in exercise of His prophetic office. Whether we name Him or not, we refer to Him when we make the following statements in respect of the true Witness as the Subject of this exposure.

This true Witness is the historical person of a concrete man. This man lives. He is present in the world in which we also live as the world reconciled to God in Him. He is at work in it, expressing the truth. He encounters us in it. He does this in a form commensurate with the sphere of our time and history, in the promise of the Spirit. But in this second form of His coming again as the Revealer, as also in the first (His resurrection) and the third (at the goal and end of all days), He does it as this man. He cannot be replaced by any distinct and distilled significance, power, influence or effects of His person and work. Nor can He be replaced by any truth which appeared in Him but may now be asserted independently, by any idea bound up with Him only as its first proponent, by any correct human doctrine concerning Him (as in the first of our preliminary observations). The Lord Himself in His Word is the promised and promising Spirit. Neither the truth nor its expression can be separated or even distinguished from Him. To be the true Witness, therefore, He does not need to be confirmed nor authorised by any other. To give force to His expression of the truth, He does not need to be interpreted by any generally known truth nor any specific, e.g., ecclesiastical truth deduced from His appearance. As He Himself lives and acts in the form of the promise of the Spirit, He is the true Witness. He is Himself the truth and its expression. And in His existence and life as such He unmasks every other man.

1. *The True Witness*

What is there about the existence and life of this man which makes Him the true Witness and therefore the light in which the darkness of falsehood is revealed and may be known as such ? The basic point to be made in this connexion is that the secret of the judicial power of truth exercised by this man consists in the fact that God exists in a relationship to Him and He to God which has no parallel on either side, which distinguishes Him from all other men, which enables Him to meet them on an equal footing and as a genuine man, and yet, existing in this relationship between God and Himself and Himself and God, necessarily to question, accuse and condemn them. Primarily, the unparalleled relationship of God to this man is that God unreservedly and totally stands surety for Him, that He makes His own cause the cause of this man, that He pledges and hazards His own glory for His glory, that He unconditionally entrusts Himself in all His grace and holiness and eternity and majesty to this man as though He were not a man but one with Himself. He does not will to be in the heights without also being in the depths of this man. He does not will to be God without Him, but only with Him. This involves a risk. There is no telling what might become of Himself and His deity in undertaking it. But He does not fear any of the imaginable dangers of this enterprise. He has no suspicions in relation to this man. He simply says Yes to Him. Nor is this a theoretical, anxious, external or provisional Yes. It is a practical, confident, internal and definitive Yes. He utters it without reservation, and it has unreserved validity. " Thou art my beloved Son, in whom I am well pleased " (Mk. 1^{11}). It is of no consequence to God to stand or fall with the existence of this man. For He will not fall. As surely as He is God, He will stand with Him. Hence there follows the corresponding relationship of this man to God. It is an exact reflection of the relationship of God to Him in which it is grounded and from which it derives. As God in His majesty stands surety for Him, so He in His lowliness stands surety for God. He makes the cause of God His own, and seeks His own glory only in that of God. He wagers on God with the same human boldness as God wagers on Him with divine boldness. He is confident that this wagering on God is the only possible, right and saving thing for Him as man. " My meat is to do the will of him that sent me, and to finish his work " (Jn. 4^{34}). This man for His part does not will to be man without God, but only with Him. He, too does this in face of, but without regard for, all the consequences and perils which this might involve. He does it with a Yes in which there is no hidden No. He does it with no fear of such an enterprise. He, too, is ready to stand or fall with God, and He cannot and will not fall. For as surely as He is a man, He will stand with God, just as God for His part will stand and not fall with Him.

It is as this is God's relationship to Him, and His to God, that this man is the true Witness. For in this relationship to this man

God is the true God, i.e., God in the authentic revelation of His divine nature, God as He is. And in this relationship to God man is true man, i.e., man in faithful confession of His humanity, man as he is. The meeting of this revelation of God and this confession of man is truth in the full sense of the term. For both, i.e., both God as He is and man as he is, are the one, whole truth. As this man exists in this meeting, in the unity of God and man, He is the truth, expressing it in His existence and doing His prophetic work in the world. And as He does this in expression of the truth, He encounters other men and in confrontation with them the expression of their existence is shown to be a lie. Their existence, too, speaks of a real relationship between God and man, but not of that between true God and true man. What is proclaimed in their existence is another God, another man and another relationship between them. And the untrue declaration of their existence is unmasked as such when they are confronted by this man, the true Witness, and by the true declaration of His existence. But before we can properly appreciate this, we must take some further steps in relation to our basic affirmation.

That relationship between true God and true man, true man and true God, is reflected in a twofold determination of the existence of the One who is the true Witness. His life as man, as the man who in the promise of the Spirit passes through our sphere of time and history, accompanying and encountering us, is one which is offered up by Him to God, which is set in the service of God, and which as such is approved, accepted and appropriately distinguished by God.

It is a life which is offered up to God. We may begin with the turning of this man to God, with His wagering on Him. To this there corresponds externally and visibly, in the attitude and action of His life, the fact that it is lived in the sphere of God's order and according to the direction of His command. How could it be lived merely inwardly, invisibly and passively in this great confidence in God? Or how could it be given only occasional and arbitrary expression. As the turning of this man to God is serious and total, He does not belong to Himself. He does not direct or control His own possibilities. Neither chance nor His own desires can rule what He thinks or speaks or does either generally or in detail. His practice in the continuing intercourse with God, His fellows and Himself is fashioned rather in analogy with the confidence which He has in the God who has so fully entrusted Himself to Him. It can consist only in a series of offerings, of acts of obedience, of achievements of service. What distinguishes the existence of this man, namely, that He has chosen God and God alone as His good, finds reflection in the fact that the practice of His life is an analogy of this choice, and thus consists in an actual series of choices and decisions which faithfully correspond to this choice of God. He justifies God concretely by concretely

1. *The True Witness*

doing for His part what is just in the sight of God. It is in doing this that He proves Himself to be the true Witness.

Again, His life is one which is distinguished by God. The turning of God to Him, His venture with this man, does not remain inward and invisible, but is made tangible and perceptible in God's directing and fashioning of His way. Here, too, there is analogy. God's Yes to this man, like this man's Yes to Him, is not abstract but concrete. He watches over Him. He cares for Him as for the sparrows or the lilies of the field, indeed, more than for them. He gives Him His daily bread and more. He does not merely sustain Him but opens to Him the whole treasure-house of creation. He quickens Him abundantly and superabundantly. He gives Him cause to be glad of life. He causes Him to prosper, to be successful, indeed, very successful, in what He does. He enables Him to accomplish His ends and see results. "Thou preparest a table before me in the presence of mine enemies : thou anointest my head with oil ; my cup runneth over. Surely goodness and mercy shall follow me all the days of my life " (Ps. 23$^{5f.}$, but how many other Psalms might be quoted, and we should not be in too big a hurry to give them a purely spiritual interpretation). In all these things, God shows and expresses that He is pleased with this man, that He seriously means to give Him a share in Himself, that He approves and accepts the life offered up and yielded to His service, that He can and will use it. To this man's existence as a true Witness there can and does belong the integral element that God deals with Him as the God who is well disposed towards Him, crowning Him with loving-kindness and tender mercies (Ps. 103^4).

But now we come to the decisive point to be seen and said in relation to this man as the true Witness. Betweeen the two given conditions of His existence which for their part reflect the meeting of God and man which constitutes His existence, there naturally stands an inner connexion. It is not for nothing that the life offered up by Him to God is the life which is distinguished by God. It would be the most dreadful and frivolous misunderstanding—the lie which opposes the true Witness—if we were to understand and explain this connexion of the two determinations in terms of a *Do* and *Des*, a *Credit* and *Debit*, a balance and debt. It consists rather in the fact that on both sides freedom is the form and character of the intercourse between true God and true man, i.e., of the intercourse which determines the existence of this man and in the fulfilment of which He declares the truth and is the true Witness. It is in this way and this way alone, in this reciprocal freedom, that this intercourse corresponds to the relationship between God and man and man and God by which the existence of this man is constituted.

The offering which corresponds to God's turning to this man, His act of obedience, His rendering of service, is His free act. It is not prompted, motivated or conditioned by the thought of a reward to be received from God. He does not undertake it for the sake of the distinction promised by God and to be expected from Him, nor with a view to the value and acceptability of this distinction, nor as a means to its attainment, nor as the payment of the price for which it is to be had, nor obviously for fear of the evils which might follow the neglect of this work or non-payment of this price, nor in avoidance of the penalty which might be exacted on any omission in this regard. His offering is His free act in the sense that He makes it only in knowledge of God Himself, in fear of Him, in delight in Him, for His own sake, and because He cannot let go of Him. It is made necessary only by the fact, in which it has also its only motivating basis, that God is God for Him, that He is in fact His Lord. It is His free act inasmuch as He does it with no other basis, claim or interest, and therefore gratuitously and for nothing, apart from this one basis.

In exactly the same way the distinction which corresponds to the address of God to this man, and with which He crowns Him, is God's free act. He bestows it without any consideration of merit. It is not a counter-achievement to the achievement required by Him and fulfilled by this man. It is God's great reward, but it is not a payment, a requital, a moral and legal obligation on the basis of a higher law. It is not an article which God must deliver to Him in virtue of the price of offering, obedience and service which He has paid. God does not owe Him anything. He does not have to distinguish Him. He does so on His own initiative, in His overflowing kindness towards Him. He does not have to approve and accept the life offered. He does not have to use His service. If He does these things, it is His supreme, but free wisdom and righteousness. He crowns the One who offers Himself, yet not because He does so, not in respect of a value which this action has for Him, not because of practical advantages which thus accrue to Him, but simply and solely in the sovereign good-pleasure which He has in Him and for the sake of the this man Himself. The distinction of this man is God's free act inasmuch as He does it with no other basis, obligation or interest, gratuitously and for nothing, apart from this one basis.

In this sense freedom is the form and character of the intercourse between true God and true man enacted in this man. This is what makes Him the Witness of the truth, the true Witness.

But this intercourse between true God and true man which takes place in Him who is the true Witness, the twofold determination of His existence visible in Him, can be regarded simply as a reflection of the conjunction or unity by which His existence is constituted and in which He is what He is and declares the truth as such. Hence the freedom which is the form and character of this intercourse has nothing whatever to do with chance or caprice. It is not an external and empty freedom, destitute of content. Returning to the original order of the two Subjects active in this intercourse, we may make the following assertions.

God crowns this man so freely because He is so free in His relationship to Him. There is here no question of a binding obligation. He makes disposition concerning Himself in this acceptance, this total, unhesitating, unreserved committal to Him. He crowns Him so freely because He is true God in this His positive relationship to Him. How can this true God fail to distinguish this man? How can He do so except in freedom? This is the truth of God attested in the existence of this one man as the true Witness.

Again, this man obeys God freely because He is so free in this relationship to Him. No question of a binding necessity arises. He Himself decides for the acceptance and committal in which there can be neither anxiety nor reserve. He offers Himself to God so freely because He is true man in this positive relationship to God. How can this true man fail to obey God, to offer Himself to Him? How can He do so except in freedom? This is the truth of man attested in the existence of this one man as the true Witness.

In sum, God does not have to be the God of this man, but He can be and He wills to be. Hence He crowns Him. Nor does the man have to be the man of God, but He can be and may be. Hence He obeys Him. In His freedom for man which mocks at all questions of payment, God is true God. And in His freedom for God which is quite unconditional, man is true man. And the conjunction or unity of true God free for man and true man free for God constitutes the existence of this One who is the true Witness. As free God and free man meet and are one in Him, He is the truth and declares the truth in relation to which every other man shows himself to be a liar.

Our concern has been with the basic structure of the one man, Jesus Christ, with the pure form in which He is the truth and declares it. We have been considering the twofold relationship between God and Himself as man and *vice versa* which constitutes His existence, the twofold act of offering on His side and crowning on God's which determines His existence, the twofold freedom of this act in which there is reflected, expressed and made known the freedom in which God is true God as the God of this man and man is true man as the man of this God. It is thus that we see what makes this man, conceived in His pure form, the true Witness, the Prophet of truth as the man Jesus Christ.

It would not be difficult to illustrate this line of thought both in general and in detail from the pages of the New Testament, whose witness to this Witness has obviously been our first source of instruction in this whole presentation. But this would take us far afield, and might involve mere repetitions of exegetical proofs already adduced in other parts of the *Church Dogmatics*. And I will admit that secondarily I have had before me in this field a noteworthy figure in the witness of the Old Testament who will be with us throughout the discussion.

§ 70. The Falsehood and Condemnation of Man

This figure is Job. " A witness of Jesus Christ," is how Wilhelm Vischer describes him in the sub-title to a little work devoted to him (1933, 6th ed. 1947). And indeed it would be difficult to read the Book of Job attentively without being aware of the fact that the figure of Jesus Christ as the true Witness unmasking the falsehood of man is delineated in it in distant, faint, fragmentary and even strange yet unmistakeable outline. At all events, in preparing the theme of this section, I first read Job and some of its many expositors, and then considered the subject and its development in the light of the text. If, then, I recall certain passages at the appropriate points in the section, it is less by way of illustration and more by way of indicating the actual sources of my whole line of thought.

We may take for granted an acquaintance with the main literary problem of the Book and the fairly generally recognised hypotheses in solution of it. Chapters 1–2 and 42 seem to be a folk-story concerning the rich Job who was sorely tried but remained faithful to God and was finally justified and blessed by Him. They constitute the framework for chapters 3–31, which are a poetical account of the speeches of Job and his three friends. These constitute the main portion of the Book though we should note that there are perhaps some inversions, especially in 25–26. Later there seem to have been added to these the poetical speeches of Elihu in 32–37, the poem of Behemoth and Leviathan attributed to Yahweh in 40–41, parts of 38–39 which deal with other remarkable features of the cosmos and particularly of the animal world, and finally the poem on wisdom contained in the last speech of Job in 28. At some time and by some person all this came to be seen and understood as the unity which it now constitutes in the Canon. We remember these problems and hypotheses as we now turn to consider the whole.

(We may note in passing the most famous of the recent books on Job: *Antwort auf Hiob*, 1953, by C. G. Jung. From the human standpoint this is a very penetrating study, and incidentally it throws a good deal of light on the psychology of the professional psychologist. As an attempt to explain Job and the Bible, however, it suffers quite hopelessly from the fact that according to his own declaration on p. 15 the author is quite " unashamedly and ruthlessly " giving expression to his very remarkable impressions. Hence he cannot possibly read and consider what is actually there, and his work is quite useless in this regard.)

We now commence our presentation, and we first turn our attention to a line which emerges at the beginning and end of the Book and on which we find what we have previously called the pure form of the true Witness.

Who is Job ? According to 1^3 he is a man of the east. That is to say, he has his home to the east or south-east of the Dead Sea. He lives outside Israel and probably in Edom, as seems to be indicated by the name Uz given to his country in 1^1. With his witness he thus belongs to the series of not infrequent figures in the Old Testament tradition who are outside the covenant of Yahweh but who still arise and work as true witnesses and prophets of Yahweh. In this case we have an Edomite, and this is the more remarkable and significant if we are not really dealing with a historical person but a figure of saga, as seems more likely. Why was not a member of one of the sacred tribes introduced for this purpose ? Instead we have a foundling, who is twice called " my servant Job " by Yahweh the God of Israel in conversation with Satan (1^8 ; 2^3) and expressly confirmed to be such at the end of the story ($42^{7,\ 8}$), and of whom it is attested that not merely in his own land but on the whole earth " there is none like him " in piety, sincerity, fear of God and hatred of evil. He is thus a unique figure in relation to whom God is quite sure of His cause—so sure that at the decisive point in His interview with Satan He suspends it on the faithfulness of Job in answer to doubting Satan, and gives the latter a free hand to expose him to the severest temptation. There is thus a kind of wager (1^{12}, 2^6) in which God—Yahweh the God of Israel—pledges His own honour against Satan and entrusts it into the hand of this Edomite. He does not hesitate for a moment to make this venture, to make Himself the One to whom Job will later appeal as his Witness and Recorder in heaven (16¹⁹), his Surety (17³), his Advocate and Representative (19²⁵), to accept such total solidarity with him as to compromise Himself. Job is a fallible man like all others. But God is infallible. Hence in the matter at stake, in that which God Himself guarantees, Job cannot and wil not fail. At the point of departure already we cannot expect anything other than the act of Job's faithfulness to this God as grounded upon the rock of this confidence of God in Job. He will not " curse " Yahweh. He will not say anything concerning Him which implies his separation from Him. He wil always say what is right about Him. Such an one is Job.

God's attitude to Job is indicated at the beginning and end of the Book by the blessing which He showers with such visible and palpable splendour upon his life. According to 1²ᶠ· he is the father of seven sons and three daughters, the owner of seven thousand sheep, three thousand camels, five hundred yoke of oxen and five hundred she asses, and the lord of a very great household, so that he may be called " the greatest of all the men of the east." We may also add what Job himself in his concluding speech, recalling this first time of blessing, says concerning the great and powerful around him : " Unto me men gave ear, and waited, and kept silence at my counsel. After my words they spake not again ; and my speech dropped upon them. And they waited for me as for the rain ; and they opened their mouth wide as for the latter rain. If I laughed on them, they believed it not ; and the light of my countenance they cast not down. I chose out their way, and sat chief, and dwelt as a king in the army, as one that comforteth mourners " (29²¹⁻²⁵). Again, when the time of temptation and torment passed, " the Lord blessed the latter end of Job more than his beginning " (42¹²ᶠ·). He was given a similar number of children, " and in all the land were no women found so fair as the daughters of Job " (who were given the attractive names : Little Dove, Sweet Savour and Little Rouge-Pot, 42¹⁴ᶠ·). In addition, his herds were doubled. Between this beginning and end the blessing of God is, of course, reduced to a dreadful minimum. He himself is spared in the first experiment arranged for him when his wealth and children are all taken from him (1¹²), and his life alone remains in the second when he is afflicted with an awful sickness (2⁶). This is not nothing, but it is certainly—or certainly seems to be—extremely little. Yet it must be remembered that Satan could have done nothing at all without God's permission, and that he is never allowed to destroy him. Even in the severest trials which he undergoes, Job is thus in the ruling and protecting hand of God, and is preserved by it. We see, then, that he has not ceased to be one whom God has previously blessed and whom He will bless again. Above all, we see that God has not ceased to be to him still the One He is shown to be in the radiant commencement and conclusion of his story.

To this there corresponds what we are told concerning Job's relationship to God, his practical commitment to Him, his obedience. It is not only in God's praise of him that we hear of this. In accordance with the purpose of the Book, we may again refer to the concluding speech attributed to Job (chs. 29 and 31), in which, with no intention of self-righteousness or self-boasting, he depicts and maintains the positive character of his life before and with God with a confidence quite unparalleled. " A picture of pure and exalted piety for which there is hardly a parallel in the Old Testament," is the verdict of one commentator (S. Oettli, *Das Buch Hiob*, 1908, p. 92) ; and with special reference to 31¹⁻³⁴, ³⁸⁻⁴⁰ another expositor (H. Lamparter, *Das Buch der Anfechtung*, 1951, p. 184) speaks of " the great and even classical model of piety in the Bible " rivalled in intensity only by the Sermon on the Mount. As declared with great solemnity, Job has not turned out of the way nor followed his eyes in such sort as to become a deceiver to his own advantage. He has not broken up any marriage, and has respected the rights of his manservants and maidservants. He has not scorned

§ 70. The Falsehood and Condemnation of Man

the widows and orphans, nor persecuted the righteous. He has not trusted in gold or possessions, nor been guilty of even the most incidental worship of the heavenly bodies. He has not even rejoiced in, let alone desired, the misfortune of his enemies, nor refused hospitality to any, nor unlawfully appropriated any of his lands. This is his confession before God, and at each point he invokes upon himself a particularly severe curse in case he has offended in any respect in spite of what he says. But he has not done so. The striking social and even political aspect of the ethics represented in 31 is even more noticeable in 29^{12-17}: "Because I delivered the poor that cried, and the fatherless, and him that had none to help him. The blessing of him that was ready to perish came upon me: and I caused the widow's heart to sing for joy. I put on righteousness, and it clothed me: my robe and turban were my right (so S. Oettli). I was eyes to the blind, and feet was I to the lame. I was a father to the poor: and the cause which I knew not I searched out. And I brake the jaws of the wicked, and plucked the spoil out of his teeth." In the last sentences of his concluding speech (31^{35-37}), Job strikes a note which can be understood only as the expression either of ungodly arrogance or of adamantine certainty of his practical commitment to God. Armed with his own declaration of his innocence and righteousness before God, he calls for the corresponding accusation against him. Where is it? He wants to see and read it. He wants to lift it on his shoulder like a trophy, and wind it round his head like a crown or turban. It will prove to be untenable at every point, and will thus speak more strongly for him than anything he might say. Adorned with this writing, he will meet God like a prince. His relationship to God, not merely in personal but in representative and even priestly terms on behalf of others, emerges in two very significant strokes in the prose narrative. In the introductory account we read that his grown-up children regularly met in each other's houses for a common meal. When this happened, Job sent a message that they should sanctify themselves, and he himself rose early the following morning and offered a burnt offering for each of them. " For Job said, It may be that my sons have sinned, and cursed God in their hearts. Thus did Job continually " (1^{4-5}). The last recorded act of Job is of a similar nature, for we read that he prayed for the three friends who unlike him had not spoken what was right concerning Yahweh but advocated the worst of all forms of falsehood, i.e., religious falsehood. And Yahweh accepted the intercession of Job on their behalf (42^9). It was as Job made this intercession, and Yahweh accepted it, that his own fortunes changed, and God gave him twice as much as he had had before (v. 10). In everything we shall have to say about lying and liars, we must not forget that the true Witness does not merely unmask them but also effectually intercedes for them, and in so doing comes to share in a new, visible, divine blessing. We may well say that this is the crown and innermost meaning of His obedience, of the righteousness before God which is so unmistakeably emphasised in the Book, of His whole way.

This brings us to the decisive point in this connexion, namely, that the relationship between Yahweh and Job has the character of freedom. Freedom is not caprice. The relationship could not be other than it is. The intercourse could not take a different course. Yet there can be no question of any necessity of the relationship or ineluctability of the intercourse. For it is all grounded in and fashioned by free electing and disposing on the part of God and equally free obedience on that of Job.

How does Yahweh come to be the Partner of the man of Uz in the drama of this history? He obviously is this with great seriousness and intensity. He manifestly could not be otherwise. But why is He? To the author of the saga, and the author or authors of the speeches, and the redactor of the whole, it seems to have been self-evident that they should not raise this question. It is simply a fact, based on the good-pleasure of Yahweh, that He is the God of this Edomite, that He finds in him His servant, that He recognises him as such, that he really is such. There can be no question of any material grounds for interest in Him. His conduct toward him shows this. It is one long demonstration of the boundless confidence which He has set in him and the fidelity which He has plainly sworn to him. But it is not, as the false and lying theology of the three friends presupposes and maintains, a moral or juridical law which is secretly above Him. Along the line of His unchangeable fidelity, it is His self-determined and to that extent free and royal conduct. Satan is quite right: "Hast thou not made an hedge about him, and about his house, and about all that he hath on every side ? thou hast blessed the work of his hands, and his substance is increased in the land" (1^{10}). And Yahweh will bless him similarly and even more abundantly at the end of the story. Yet the point is that He does not have to do so either at the beginning or the end. Without being untrue to Job, He can reduce His blessing to the bare minimum of preservation which Job would prefer to renounce according to $3^{20f.}$. He can give Satan, within a limited but very large sphere, a free hand in relation to Job. He can do so to such an extent that God Himself can and actually does appear to Job to be an enemy and persecutor. He did not owe him favour, nor will He do so. He can also allow disaster to fall upon him. On the other hand, He can also bring to an end the experiments of Satan and bring about a new turn in the fortunes of Job. He can leave it to Job to engage in conversation with his very dubious friends, and listen silently to his complaints and accusations, to their endless sermonisings, and to the justifiable or not so justifiable protests of Job against them. Yet in the time appointed He can also appear to him as the One He is in all the freedom in which He is faithful to him and all the faithfulness in which He is free in respect of him (42^5), in an astonishing series of questions ($38^{1ff.}$) making the answer in which, lending force to the protests of Job and making him a witness to the truth, He gives the lie to his friends, but in which he also puts Job in his place and shows him his limitations. He can and does do all these things as the free God who is also as such the Liberator of Job.

And how does Job come to be the servant of God ? The answer is that he simply is. And the freedom with which he is reveals itself in his conduct, namely, in the fact, contested by Satan but put to the proof by God, that he fears God for nought, disinterestedly, gratuitously, neither swayed by the maximum of blessing nor hindered by the minimum, as one who earns a reward nor one who receives a reward, on no other basis except that Yahweh is God, his God. The emphasis laid by W. Vischer on this "for nought" (*chinnam*) in the first allegation of Satan was to the best of my knowledge something quite new in explanation of the Book, but it is something which we cannot now dismiss. It is precisely this "for nought" which is the righteousness at issue in the righteousness of Job. For it is in this respect that it is wholly directed to the free God, that it acknowledges God to be in the right, and is therefore righteous. This is the nerve of his protests against the three friends, who do not tell the truth but are guilty of falsehood in every point because they are so in this one point, refusing to allow that there can be any question of this " for nought " between God and Job. Again, it is the critical factor in relation to which God Himself can finally attest that he has spoken the thing which is right concerning Him, and in the knowledge of which as the beginning of all wisdom Job had obviously to prove himself, not without being shamed. Yet it is plainly enough shown to be the secret of his conduct at the very beginning of the story in two much quoted verses which refer to his attitude when the storm of misfortune and pain broke over him. Sorrowfully tearing his clothes and shaving his head, he falls to the ground and worships, saying : " Naked came I out of my mother's womb, and naked shall I return thither ; the Lord gave, and the Lord hath taken away ; blessed be the name of the Lord " ($1^{20ff.}$). God would not be God if He were not free both to give and to take away. And when sickness comes, and Job takes a potsherd and sits among the ashes, he calls his wife " one of the foolish women " when she suggests that he should let go his integrity and curse God, for " shall we receive good at the hand of God, and shall we not receive evil ? " (2$^{2f.}$). Job would not be Job if he were not free to receive both evil and good from God. This implies that he fears and loves the free God as such, that in his conduct towards Him he has regard to His free disposing, that his conduct is free in consequence, that it is his free and gratuitous service of God, grounded in a fear and love of God which are decisively concerned only about God Himself and not His gifts. This free service of God is the programme of his action as it emerges from the very first and as it is a target for the scepticism of Satan. Yet it is also free in the sense that in fulfilment, though not in substance, the execution of this programme in time of temptation is not behind but still before him. It is a new step ahead. Job as a fallible man will not actually perform it without also doing wrong, and putting himself in the wrong, even though he keeps to the right. This is the meaning of his story according to the commentary given in his conversations with the friends. In it he moves through temptation to this goal and end in a new offering of himself and under a new blessing of God. He will make this forward step, and therefore keep to the right even though he also does wrong and puts himself in the wrong. Already the free servant of God, he strides through the hell of affliction to his liberation by and for the free God. And as this free servant of the free God he is from the very first, formally considered, a type of the true Witness.

We cannot say more than this. Job is not Jesus Christ, even on the purely formal consideration which is our present concern. As a remarkable Edomitish outsider, he belongs to the context of the witness of the history of Israel which is only moving towards the history of Jesus Christ. The interrelationship of conduct between Yahweh and him does not amount to the unity of God and man in the existence of Jesus Christ. The obedience of his offering is not equivalent to the natural obedience of sonship in Jesus Christ. The divine blessing under which he stands and with which he is again endowed is not the same as the fulness of power given to Jesus Christ. The doubts which he knows as in his human frailty he passes through the hell of affliction are very different from the infallibility with which Jesus is already Victor even as he goes to the defeat of Golgotha. And he is, of course, quite unlike Jesus Christ in the fact that, while the emphasised social character of his righteousness, and concretely his offerings for his children, and above all his intercession for his friends, make it quite plain that the life of God with him and his life with God have an import extending beyond his personal existence, yet there can be no question of any work of salvation being accomplished in the drama of his history, nor of his existence having any saving significance or necessity. The fact remains, however, that in spite of these dissimilarities there is so much similarity that in relation to this first and decisive aspect of his existence we may well speak of an analogy in relation to Jesus Christ, and with suitable qualifications Job may thus be called a type of Jesus Christ, a witness to the true Witness.

We must consider the man Jesus Christ, who comes as the true Witness in the promise of the Spirit, first of all in His pure form ; and we must never forget this in whatever follows. Yet it would be a kind of Docetism to stop here, or to be content with what has been said. This pure form is certainly the meaning and power of the existence of this man and His witness to the truth. As He exists in this pure form, He is the Mediator between God and us men in His prophetic work. It is the secret of His existence. In it He exists for God and before God as His eternal Word which became flesh, as His eternal Son who is also the Son of Man. In it He obviously exists also in His presence and revelation on earth, even in the promise of the Spirit as the form of His revelation in this time of ours. This does not mean, however, that He is revealed to us men, and may be perceived and apprehended by us, in this pure form as such. We know it as He expresses Himself in it in His revelation, as He manifests it in His prophetic work in the world. His prophetic work, and therefore the manifestation of His pure form, take place, however, in attestation of what He has concretely been and done in His history on earth. And they take place in time, within the world which is reconciled in Him but not yet redeemed. They take place finally among and to us sinners, who are justified and sanctified in Him, and with whom as such He is still on the way. He speaks His Word in a very different form of existence appropriate to its content, to its setting, and to us men as its recipients. To be sure, the pure form in which God alone sees and knows Him is in immediate proximity to us in this other form, for in both cases, whether before God or for us, He is One and the Same, and the former is manifested in the latter. In the latter, too, He is the eternal Word, the eternal Son of God. But in the divine and therefore the pure form He is near to us only in mystery, and therefore in concealment from every human eye. As He is among us and encounters us here and now, He bears a form in which the pure form is present and active only in a form which is hidden, obscure and puzzling. For us, for our vision and understanding, the knowledge of Jesus Christ in His pure form is an indirect knowledge, i.e., knowledge in this other form, which certainly has its secret and force in the pure form, but which is not as such identical with it, which is rather alien and quite dissimilar to it. It is knowledge *in contrario, sub specie aliena.* " When I was a child, I spake as a child, I understood as a child, I thought as a child . . . now we see through a glass, darkly . . . now I know in part " (1 Cor. 13$^{11f.}$). Indirect knowledge is that which arises when the person or object to be known makes itself known. It can be achieved only in consequence of self-declaration. And as the One who is to be known as the true Witness—we recall our second preliminary observation concerning the question : " What is truth ? "—Jesus Christ treads the narrow way through the strait gate of His other puzzling form appropriate to the content, the setting and the recipients of His prophetic Word. It is in this that He now passes through the midst of us in the promise of the Spirit. It is in this that He encounters and unmasks falsehood. He does it as the suffering Jesus Christ.

Passion was the action in which in His existence the name of God was hallowed, His kingdom came, His will was done on earth as in heaven ; the action in which God reconciled the world to Himself in the humiliation of the Son of God and exaltation of the Son of Man ; the action in which the justification of man (of every man)

§ 70. *The Falsehood and Condemnation of Man*

before God and his sanctification for him were accomplished. It is naturally to be expected, indeed, it is inevitable, that the revelation of this action should correspond to its content, and therefore that in practice the prophetic work of Jesus Christ should have the form of passion. It is the work of Jesus Christ the Victor, i.e., of the One who definitively in His own person bore for all men the sin which separates man from God, who robbed the devil of his right to them and death of his power over them, who introduced the new and free man. It is as this Victor that He has come again, revealing Himself to His disciples in the event of Easter Day. And it is as this Victor that He will come at the end of all days in His final, universal and definitive revelation. It is as this Victor that He also lives and acts and speaks in His intervening coming in the promise of the Spirit. But He is the Victor of Gethsemane and Golgotha. Hence in all its moments His coming again is His manifestation as this Victor, as the strange, unlikely, inconspicuous *Imperator* and *Triumphator* who enters, rules and triumphs in this form : elected by God as rejected of Him ; judging the world as judged by it ; superior to all men as despised by all : free as bound ; mighty as impotent ; eternally living as dead and buried ; completely victorious in complete defeat. He not only was, but here and now in His ongoing prophetic work He still is the suffering Servant of God, the King crowned with thorns. How else could He be that on which everything hinges—the same to-day as yesterday ? How else could He bear witness here and now to the reconciliation effected in Him, to Himself as the One who accomplishes, brings and guarantees salvation, and therefore to the name and kingdom and will of God ? How else could He declare the truth here and now ? He who trembled and shrank back in Gethsemane, who was betrayed by Judas, denied by Peter and forsaken by all His disciples, who was accused by the congregation of saints as a blasphemer and condemned by the civil authorities as a rebel, who was scourged and scorned before Pilate and Herod, who offered up His life, who shed His blood, who found Himself abandoned in death even and above all by His God—in this passion of His He is not only the reality but the true revelation of reconciliation to-day as yesterday. And it is as He attests the truth, Himself, in this form, that He unmasks us as liars. It is in this form of suffering, as the wholly Rejected, Judged, Despised, Bound, Impotent, Slain and Crucified, and therefore as the Victor, that He marches with us and to us through the times, alive in the promise of the Spirit. In this form He is at the core not only of the kerygmatic theology of Paul but also of the kerygmatic accounts of the Gospels. In this form— " unto the Jews a stumblingblock, and unto the Greeks foolishness " (1 Cor. 1^{23})—He has addressed His own, His community, and through this the world, from the time of His resurrection onwards and therefore from the very first. He has continually proffered Himself to the

Church and the world in this form. He encounters us in this form or not at all. To look past it is not to see Him. To miss the Word of the cross is not to hear Him. What is not included in the Word of the cross, but tries to assert itself as free Christian truth alongside or outside this Word, even though it may speak of the love and grace of the heavenly Father, the coming kingdom of God and service to one's neighbour, cannot possibly be His Word nor have the meaning and power which such words can have only if they are His Word. The denominator common to His Word in all its dimensions and contents, the one point of truth in all its declarations, is that it is the Word of the suffering Witness to the truth. It is as assailed, deserted and harried to death that He interceded and intercedes for us with God and for God with us. As such He is our peace, and the Messenger of our peace. As such He is to be distinguished from all false prophets, messiahs, saviours and apostles of peace, even though they allege His name. But it is obvious that in this respect He does not fit but completely contradicts the picture which man has of a bringer of good news, and especially of one who brings such conclusively good news, and proclaims himself as its content, as the liberator present in divine power. It was only too easy to despise the suffering and afflicted Jesus Christ as the Witness to truth, and if He is still the same to-day as yesterday the temptation is just as strong to-day and always to say : " Save thyself. If thou be the Son of God, come down from the cross " (Mt. $27^{38f.}$). What are we to make of Him if He is still to-day the One who yesterday died with the cry : " My God, my God, why hast thou forsaken me ? " (Mk. 15^{34}) ? What does it mean that it is only as this One who is rejected and abandoned by God that He is His Elect and therefore the true Witness of the kingdom of God come in His person ? Can we really accept the fact that it is this man who meets us to-day, with no answer to the scorn naturally heaped upon Him, and with only that question to His and our God on His lips ? How wonderfully high must be the truth attested by Him, and how terribly deep the human falsehood which He unmasks !

The fact that the Word of God is marked by the act of reconciliation as its content is the one thing which makes it necessary that the true Witness Jesus Christ should meet us in the alien form of His passion. But we can and must consider this necessity from another angle. The setting of His working, the place in which He encounters us, is the temporal and historical sphere between the reconciliation of the world to God (together with its revelation in His resurrection as the commencement of His return), and its revelation in the completion of this return as God's consummating work for the redemption of His creation. As all occurrence in this sphere, and all men within it, come from this commencement, they all move to this completion. The positive character and aspect of this sphere of ours consist in the fact that it is the particular sphere of the prophecy of Jesus Christ, of His presence, activity and speech in the promise of the Spirit, of the Gospel which is to be proclaimed to the whole world. But it has also a very serious and threatening character. It is not only the sphere of the light of life shining in Jesus Christ. It is also the sphere of the darkness which opposes it, of the humanity which is not yet enlightened, which is still in process of enlightenment, which is not yet redeemed for life with Jesus Christ. It is the sphere of the " not yet " by which the life of each individual within it is stamped. It is the sphere in which the sin which separates man from God is validly deprived of right or power in Jesus Christ, but in which it is still active as a threat and temptation in a way which has very destructive practical consequences in spite of its total deprivation of right or power. It is the sphere of the " still " which also determines the life of each individual within it. And if the light of life undoubtedly increases in this sphere, continually growing clearer and brighter, yet rather strangely—or not so strangely —we cannot say that the threat and temptation of this sin which has been overcome, removed, abolished and deprived of all right and power in Jesus Christ, are a threat and power which continually grow weaker. On the contrary, we are forced to see and say that in this time which moves towards the consummation of the glory of God and the salvation of man they assert themselves the more obstinately and intensively, intruding the more energetically and noticeably with their evil consequences. The sphere of our time and history is not, then, the theatre of a decrease of darkness, as we might suppose, but rather of its intensification and increase. The New Testament gives us not the slightest grounds for regarding the era *post Christum* as one when the human contradiction, the power of pride and sloth and above all of falsehood by which the world is characterised and determined, shows any signs of decrease, but rather as a period of its augmentation together with that of the Word of God. Nor do our own observations seem to point in any other direction. As and because the living Jesus Christ is present and active in our sphere, it is the theatre of a final and supreme development of the disruption and destruction already overcome in Him, and of increased obduracy on the part of the man of sin who is now seriously challenged and alarmed by his displacement as already effected in Him. With all the irresistibility of its movement, occurrence in our sphere of time and history has thus from first to last the character of genuine conflict. And it is the purpose and order of God that this should be the case. His will may be seen in the fact that Jesus Christ, and in Him He Himself, is the first Pilgrim and Warrior in this history with all its " not yet " and " still." His good will may be seen in the fact that for all its ambiguity and imperfection this history is man's opportunity under the promise of the Spirit to participate in reconciliation as an active subject, namely, as a recipient and bearer of the Word of reconciliation. And this good will of God inevitably includes the fact that the human sin which Jesus Christ has already deprived of all right and power still has in this sphere of ours a theatre in which to act with all its destructive consequences. It is still allowed this supreme effort and development, this act of aggression in the very presence of its Conqueror. Since it is directed as evil against God, it does not take place without Him that within its solidly and definitely described limits it can rage violently and lash out around it. But if this does not take place without God, does it mean that it takes place with Him? Does He not merely permit but will it? We could say this only in the sense of the saying addressed to Pharaoh in Ex. $9^{15f.}$ (cf. Rom. 9^{17}): "For now I will stretch out my hand, that I may smite thee and thy people with pestilence; and thou shalt be cut off from the earth. And in very deed for this cause have I raised thee up, for to show in thee my power; and that my name may be declared throughout all the earth." Evil is still allowed to run this dangerous course in order that the glory which God has secured by what He has done in Jesus Christ may be increased and truly magnified in the conflict waged personally by the same Victor of Gethsemane and Golgotha in the time and history now hurrying to their goal and end. And with the glory of God there is inseparably bound up the salvation of man, namely, that humanity, or many of its members, should have the opportunity under the leadership of this Victor, and as hearers and doers of His Word, of playing an active part in this conflict, in His prophetic work, and therefore secondarily in the divine act of reconciliation. This negative determination of our time and history, which is not without but according to the will of God, carries with it the implication that the form in which Jesus Christ the Victor is on the way with us, accompanying and encountering us, should be none other than that of the Victor of Gethsemane and Golgotha, and therefore of the suffering Servant of God, the afflicted Prophet. Continually and with intensified severity it takes place that He first should bear the contradiction and opposition of the beaten but not yet routed forces of the enemy, of the foe which tries to maintain itself more desperately than ever before, of the man of sin who has been deprived of all right and power but defends himself the more obstinately. He first must still take up and carry His cross. The Jesus who lives and is among us in our time is the One who is still harassed and forsaken, accused and condemned, despised and smitten. He has already fought and won as such, but He still does so as the true Witness, unmasking the falsehood of our time and therefore of us all. It would not be our time, this strange era *post Christum*, if He could be present in it otherwise than as the Man of Sorrows. To be sure, He is God's Hero, rescuing the world from its woes. But He is God's Hero in this form, the mighty Warrior in His very weakness. And continually and with intensified severity there comes upon Him the most bitter thing of all, that He is dealing not merely with the contradiction and opposition of evil, of the man of sin, of his pride and sloth and falsehood, that He is dealing not merely with what we call the devil, but that He has also to wrestle with the good will of God, recognising and honouring as His will, and therefore as His good will, the fact that the man of sin is not yet abolished, that this frightful liberty of action is still allowed him, that even though with restricted power the devil may still go about as His adversary, like a loudly roaring lion (1 Pet. 5^8). In correspondence with the present world as the setting of His prophetic work, Jesus Christ is thus not merely the One who suffers, but, as in Gethsemane and on Golgotha, He is the One who is smitten and afflicted by God, and it is in this way alone that He is the true Witness.

We are led to the same result as we approach the matter from a third angle. When we speak of the sphere of our time and history, we can and should think concretely of ourselves, of all the men living in it among whom each is an individual, but as such belongs to and represents the whole. It is we all in our predestined or free inter-relationships who quite personally experience the era *post Christum* with all its characteristics and perversions, with its unquenchable hope in Jesus Christ and its misery attributable to ourselves. We also fashion this era. Each of our collective and individual times is in its own way itself this strange era. It is to us as citizens, creators and victims of this time hastening to its end that the true Witness comes. Hence in relation to what each individual still is, He is a Witness to what he no longer is in Him. And in relation to what he is not, He is a Witness to what he already is in Him. In face of my or thy or our pride and folly, He is a Witness to my and thy and our justification before God and sanctification for Him. Within the dreadful isolation and alienation with which we mutually plague one another and make of God's wonderful creation a kind of forecourt of hell, and within our fruitless and impotent attempts to replace this by some tolerable kind of co-existence, He is a radiant and liberating Witness to our solid and definitive fellowship with God and therefore with one another. In what may be called both in the narrower and the broader sense the almshouses and prisons and hospitals and mental homes of our collective existence, the cemeteries of our more solid and more extravagant hopes, the specific inward and outward needs and stresses and pains which openly or secretly constitute our individual problems, and in which each suffers from but is also guilty of and responsible for the emergence of the hard and puzzling features of the present form of the world, He is the Witness to its limit, to its approaching end, and therefore to our liberation, redemption and completion. Jesus lives as this Witness to the name and kingdom and will of God among us. But in all the misery of a lost mass such as the humanity addressed in the Word of reconciliation, among men such as we are, how else can He live but in the form of the Suffering and Afflicted of Gethsemane and Golgotha ? He surely cannot live as One who was once there but is so no longer, who once had that form but has now put it off and left it behind as a butterfly does its chrysalis, who exists to-day only in the transfigured form of the divinely crowned Victor. In practice at least, it is to be noted that a living Christianity has always in its hymns and prayers, and above all in its administration of baptism and the Lord's Supper, experienced and seen and understood and expounded and proclaimed His presence within it and the world as the presence of the Crucified.

Even in the most questionable feature of the Roman Mass, namely, its character as a representation of the sacrifice of Golgotha, we must acknowledge that it does at least make this clear. And Evangelical preaching must never lag behind it in this respect.

To be sure, Jesus Christ exists also in the pure, divine form. This is the meaning and power of His form of suffering. But in it as such He may be seen and known only by God. He is a mystery to us. In His prophetic work on earth, in time, He is concealed in this pure form and exists among and for us in the form of suffering in which the pure form is at work. In the pure form, how could He really be among us or for us, in our place and situation, in our inescapable conflicts, unavoidable arrestations and irreparable defeats ? In it how could He be the man who speaks to us as those who are what we are ? Were not that form concealed in His form of suffering, He would not be the Brother by whom we find ourselves understood and whom we may also understand. Solely and abstractly as the eternal Word and Son of God, in the form in which the Father alone sees and knows Him, He would necessarily be remote and strange, and could give neither comfort nor direction for all His glory. We could not receive what He has to say to us concerning the burden of our sin and guilt and penalty which is lifted from us because it is borne by Him, concerning our justification and sanctification effected in the bitterness of His death and passion, and therefore concerning our hope, if He did not also tell us that He still bears this burden in all its reality and is thus with us when we have to carry our burdens and experience our sorrows. But He does say this. It is not merely that He was once " touched with the feeling of our infirmities " ; He is so still. It is not merely that He was once tempted as we are ; He is with us and before us, tempted as we are (Heb. 4^{15}). And when it says that " in the days of his flesh ... he offered up prayers and supplications with strong crying and tears unto him that was able to save him from death " (Heb. 5^7), this is more than recollection, for it speaks of His presence here to-day among us in all our confusion, aberration and abandonment, before all our locked prison doors, at all our sick-beds and gravesides, and, of course, with questioning, warning, restraint and delimitation, in

396 § 70. *The Falsehood and Condemnation of Man*

all our genuine or less genuine triumphs. He is still the Friend of publicans and sinners whose very family think that He is mad, who is accused of blasphemy and sedition, who is reckoned with malefactors and crucified with them, who is forsaken by His disciples and our God. All this is behind Him, yet it is also continually before Him. It is thus that He is among us and with us. " Slumbering and sleeping, We're safe in His keeping ; On our awaking, The glory is breaking, Of His mercy so freely bestowed." A man is merciful when he takes to heart the need of another. Jesus Christ has once and for all taken our need to heart. This was His passion. But although He did it once and for all, He did not do it once only. Risen from the dead, He lives and takes it to heart with undiminished severity. This is His passion to-day. And it is thus that He is the true Witness.

It is necessary that we should give point and emphasis to this whole line of thought in a concluding observation. Are we sure that Jesus Christ is really the true Witness in this way, in the form of His suffering ? Is He really the Witness of what is not merely true in fulfilment of a divine economy, and therefore not just provisional and relative and thus destined to withdraw and disappear in favour of another and higher truth ? In His form of suffering is He really a Witness of first and final and proper truth behind and above which there is no other, i.e., the truth itself, which is truth not merely for us here and now, but in itself from and to all eternity ? Is He this in His form of suffering in such a way that it is neither necessary nor possible, required nor legitimate, to look past the man of Gethsemane and Golgotha to another Proclaimer of truth who is perhaps only provisionally represented by Him ? Do we have to keep to Him ? Are we unable to escape Him ? Must we confess that we are liars before Him ? The question is almost suggested by the fact that we have had to distinguish the pure form of Jesus Christ in which God sees and knows Him from the form of suffering in which He encounters us as the true Witness. Before God and for Him, and therefore in proper truth, in the final court of appeal, is He then other than the man of Gethsemane and the Suffering and Afflicted of Golgotha ? Is He the latter only in a temporary manifestation and representation of the former ? Do we thus have to cling only provisionally and relatively to the latter, but seriously and properly to the former ? Should we really ask concerning the proper truth of the former, of the Word and Son of God in Himself and as such ? Our answer must be a most decided negative. In this respect, too, distinction does not mean separation. It is as the Word and Son of God that He exists as the man of Gethsemane and Golgotha. It is in His pure form that He is the secret, power and meaning of His form of suffering. He exists in this unity, and not otherwise. And in this unity He does not exist merely for us, as though He were a spectacle arranged for our benefit behind which there stands another reality, so that we have always good grounds for asking, and are indeed forced to ask, concerning another truth. Nor are there any grounds for the speculations attempted in this direction; nor the positivist scepticism entailed. In the unity between His pure form in which He is hidden from us and the form of suffering in which He is revealed, He exists primarily before the eyes and in the knowledge of God, and therefore properly, and from and to all eternity. That God alone sees and knows Him in His pure form does not mean that God knows Him only in this form, so that before and for God, and therefore in proper truth, He is an anonymous λόγος ἄσαρκος, quite different from the One who encounters us in the alien and puzzling form of His passion. This would carry the frightful implication that the mercy in which Jesus Christ comes to us as our Brother here and now in our world of sin and misery has nothing whatever to do with the mercy of God Himself, and that God does not participate, or does so only from a divine height and distance as a Spectator, in the events between Jesus Christ and us and therefore in His prophetic work. But this is not the case. For God and before Him, and therefore in eternal truth, His eternal Word and Son, known to Him alone in His pure form, exists as the man of Gethsemane and Golgotha known to us, and is present to us in this very form. It is the Crucified who was raised again from the dead and ascended into heaven, where He sits at the right hand of God the Father Almighty. It is as this One, the Suffering and Afflicted, that " he continueth ever, and hath an unchangeable priesthood, and is thus able to save them to the uttermost that come unto God by him, seeing he ever liveth to make intercession for them " (Heb. 7$^{24f.}$). The Lamb slain not only stood, but still stands, between the throne of God and the heavenly and earthly cosmos (Rev. 5^6), and according to the song in this chapter He not only was but is worthy to open the book and the seals, and to receive power and riches and wisdom and strength and honour and glory and blessing. This Lamb slain, this " priest for ever after the order of Melchisedec " (Heb. 7^{17}), is obviously more than a medium or vehicle or witness of a different and superior truth to be experienced through Him. He is the medium, vehicle and witness of His own truth and therefore of the truth beside and above which there is none other either on earth or in heaven, for us or for and before God. As a true Witness in this insurpassable and definitive rather than provisional and relative sense the suffering Jesus Christ, victorious in His suffering, pursues His prophetic task. It is as such that He comes to us. It is as such that He goes with us. It is as such that He encounters us. In His mercy God's own mercy is present and active. God Himself suffers with us as He suffers. And as the Witness to this truth on this incontestable basis Jesus Christ is also in this very form the man who is competent and strong to unmask us as liars.

§ 70. *The Falsehood and Condemnation of Man*

In relation to Job, too, we cannot stop at the pure form in which we have learned to know this typical witness to the truth. He appears as such only at the beginning and end of the Book. In the main central section, which at its redaction and reception into the Canon was already seen to be the decisive portion, he takes on a different form. It is not that he does not remain the same. As the same both in God's relationship to him and his to God, he will later reappear in the pure form which for the moment is concealed, and is thus in some way maintained and demonstrated even during the concealment. Yet the concealment in the central part of his story is radical. Readers are hardly prepared for the reappearance of the first form when they consider the debate with the three friends which constitutes the main part of the Book. Least of all are they prepared for it by chapters 32–37, when Elihu steps forward as an ostensible umpire and is equally angry with both parties. Many commentators have regarded his decision as one which precedes the Word of Yahweh Himself. They have described Elihu as a genuine agent of God preparing the ground for an understanding of His own Word. He has even been compared with John the Baptist. Intentionally or otherwise, however, he merely strengthens the impression that at the end of all these human words, apart from a few gleams of light in the speeches of Job, especially in the poem on wisdom, we are simply left in a blind alley from which there can be no exit except by the intervention and protest of a higher, indeed, of the supreme power. Before this intervention and protest, we are in no sense prepared to accept that Job is not only in the wrong but is also justified, and may thus reappear in the pure form in which he entered his way. The very commencement of this middle section is surprising. To be sure, the end of the second chapter gives us for the first time a seriously disturbing sense of Job's extremity of affliction in consequence of the experiments permitted to Satan. His three friends, who have heard of his misfortune, come upon the scene, "every one from his own place" (2^{11}); and according to the origins ascribed to them it is obvious that they, too, are men of the east and not Israelites. They have "made an appointment together to come to mourn with him and to comfort him." How they find and see him is described thus in $2^{12f.}$: "And when they lifted up their eyes afar off, and knew him not, they lifted up their voice, and wept; and they rent every one his mantle, and sprinkled dust upon their heads towards heaven. So they sat down with him upon the ground seven days and seven nights, and none spake a word unto him: for they saw that his grief was very great." As concerns Job himself, the last indication of his attitude had been given in 2^{10}, namely, that evil as well as good must be received from the hand of the Lord, which reminds us of 1^{21}. And as in 1^{22}, it is affirmed in 2^{10}: "In all this did not Job sin with his lips." We are thus surprised when in the introduction to what follows, in what is obviously the work of the redactor, we read in 3^1: "After this opened Job his mouth, and cursed his day," and the more so as we peruse the first complaint under this head in 3^{3-26}, which is not provoked by anything said by his silently sorrowing friends, but wells up spontaneously from Job himself. The appearance of mature resolution suggested perhaps by chapters 1–2 was obviously deceptive. Job has still a long way to go before he will reach the point where we find him again in chapter 42. With the fine sayings in 1^{21} and 2^{10} he has merely plotted the way, according to the obvious view of the redactor and apparently of the incomplete folk-saga reproduced in the Book. He has now to tread it. What it means that Yahweh takes as well as gives, that evil is to be received at His hand as well as good, must now be experienced to the bitter end. The step corresponding to those fine sayings must now be taken. This is the alteration in the situation and attitude of Job as now dramatically presented to us. Only now do we see how heavily he is hit by what has happened. The anxious question is raised whether he will endure. We realise, at least, how desperately hard it is for him to prove himself a servant of Yahweh, and how much he has still to learn as such.

1. The True Witness

The beginning of Job's complaint in the transition from the second chapter to the third is surprising in its depth and intensity as well as its suddenness. There is a certain impressiveness in the sympathy shown by the friends, and we are affected by the weight of Job's misfortune, but these fall far short of, and seem in no sense congruous with, the profound perplexity of Job as he does not merely contemplate and bemoan his affliction objectively, but must simply experience and suffer it. The poet now takes up the story, and as he understands the catastrophe which has come on Job according to the saga, it has affected him not merely externally but in his innermost and total life, radically challenging and questioning him. There is no place to which he can withdraw from what has happened and even survey it from without, let alone harness and master it either in life or thought. He is completely mastered and overwhelmed by it. " My sighing is my daily bread, and my roarings are poured out like water " (3^{24}). He can only exist in his suffering. And so ($3^{3f.}$) he can only protest, as Jeremiah did in words which are almost more extreme (20^{14-18}), against the fact that he must exist, against the day when he was born, and even further back against the night when he was begotten and conceived. If only this day and night, which are spoken of almost as personal enemies, could be struck out of the calendar and abolished and never have been ! " Wherefore is light given to him that is in misery, and life unto the bitter in soul ? " ($3^{20f.}$; cf. $10^{18f.}$). " Only so long as his flesh is on him does he have pain, and so long as his soul is in him does he mourn " (14^{22}). Why does he have to live ? If he had not been conceived or had died at birth, he would now have the peace of kings buried in the pyramids constructed by them ($3^{13f.}$), or of a hidden untimely birth (3^{16}). As he puts it later : " That it would please God to destroy me ; that he would let loose his hand, and cut me off ! " ($6^{9f.}$).

The question of the subject of Job's complaint in his later speeches, and in extreme form in this first one, is not so easily answered as might first be supposed. The general and comprehensive theme is clear enough : " Is not service the fate of man upon the earth ? are not his days like the days of an hireling ? As a servant earnestly desireth the shadow, and as an hireling looketh for the reward of his work ; so am I made to possess the months of vanity, and wearisome nights are appointed to me " ($7^{1f.}$). But what does this mean concretely ? The loss of his possessions and children ? We might expect so from $1^{13f.}$. And there is in fact indirect allusion to this at the beginning of his great concluding speech : " Oh that I were as in months past, as in the days when God preserved me ; when his candle shined upon my head, and when by his light I walked through darkness ; as I was in the days of my youth, when the secret of God was upon my tabernacle ; when the Almighty was yet with me, when my children were about me ; when I washed my steps with milk and butter, and the rock poured me out rivers of oil " (29^{2-6}). Yet the true subject of painful recollection in this chapter is neither his own lost possessions nor the family which flourished around him and was now destroyed, but the honour which he had had among young and old and which he now had no longer (29^{7-25}). And in the other speeches we look in vain for indications which might point us concretely in the direction of his loss of family and wealth. Is it his sickness then ? We are told in 2^7 that Satan " smote Job with sore boils from the sole of his foot unto his crown." And there are passages in the speeches (e.g., $7^{4f.}$, $19^{17f.}$) in which many commentators (e.g., G. Hölscher, *Das Buch Hiob*, 1934, p. 22, 45) think they see such a plain description of his illness that they even attempt a medical diagnosis and identify it as elephantiasis or *lepra tuberculosa*. I am not satisfied, however, that the interest, spirit and style of the poem permit us to read it so pragmatically or to try to gather from it such concrete items. The same holds good of the exposition of similar passages in the Psalms. There can be no doubt, of course, that the sickness is sometimes mentioned. But it hardly plays the role which might have been expected from 2^7. And new factors seem to be introduced as

§ 70. *The Falsehood and Condemnation of Man*

compared with chapters 1 and 2. He is forsaken and even despised by his relations and acquaintances and even his brethren (19^{13-19}). He sees himself threatened and maltreated by enemies : " Mine enemy sharpeneth his eyes upon me. They have gaped upon me with their mouth ; they have smitten me upon the cheek reproachfully ; they have gathered themselves together against me. God hath delivered me to the ungodly, and turned me over into the hands of the wicked " ($16^{9f.}$). And in 30^{1-15} we read of something for which we are not in the least prepared in 1–2, namely, of a strange proletariat of the desert, of a wild band of robbers, described in graphic phrases, under whose insults and probably outrages Job has also to suffer even though they are folk " whose fathers I would have disdained to have set with the dogs of my flock " (30^1).

It is obvious that Job sees himself struck by all these adversities and swept into the mounting stream of dissolution which relentlessly hurries him towards destruction, death and the underworld. In the first instance, for even this can only be a penultimate word, it is this being in dissolution which seems to be the bitter element in all his bitter experiences and to form the basic subject of his complaint. " Man that is born of a woman is of few days, and full of trouble. He cometh forth like a flower, and is cut down : he fleeth also as a shadow, and continueth not " ($14^{1f.}$). " My days are swifter than a post : they flee away, they see no good. They are passed away as the swift ships : as the eagle that hasteth to the prey " ($9^{25f.}$). " My days are swifter than a weaver's shuttle, and are spent without hope " (7^6). Why without hope ? Because Job realises that " thou wilt bring me to death, and to the house appointed for all living " (30^{23}). The way leads into " the land of darkness and the shadow of death ; a land of darkness, as darkness itself ; and of the shadow of death, without any order, and where the light is as darkness " ($10^{21f.}$; cf. 16^{22}). For " man dieth, and wasteth away " (14^{10}). When a tree is cut down, there is hope " that it will sprout again, and that the tender branch thereof will not cease " (14^7). But " man lieth down, and riseth not " (14^{12}). " As the cloud is consumed and vanisheth away : so he that goeth down to the grave shall come up no more. He shall return no more to his house, neither shall his place know him any more " ($7^{9f.}$). In this complaint all Job's complaints seem at a first glance to have their common centre. We must understand that he is not just oppressed by the fear of death. He does not bemoan his own future being in the underworld from which there is no return. Indeed, he has expressly desired that God would crush him, that He would snap off the thread of his life, that He would let him be in death rather than in this life ($6^{9f.}$; cf. 7^{15}). And even in relation to his being in death and the underworld, he hazards the bold thought, to which we must return, that God might there shelter and conceal him from the wrath which strikes him in this life, that He might post him there like a sentinel, make him wait to be relieved, and then remember him again some day ($14^{13f.}$). He does not bewail his future destruction as the goal of his ways, but the present which has this future, his being on this way, his sliding down this steep slope. If only he had not entered this way, or had now trodden it to the end ! It will not be dreadful to be at the end. On the contrary, it is dreadful to be here with only this end in prospect, to be on the way which leads only to this abyss, to this house from which there is no return. Job's complaint is against a life which only leads to death, which is only a journey into darkness, which is a mere passing and nothing more. " I loathe it ; I would not live alway : let me alone ; for my days are vanity " (7^{16}). This is the kind of life that his own has become under the pressure of his afflictions.

So far, however, we have not yet given the decisive answer to the question of the basis and substance of Job's complaint, of his true grief. We do not have to be Jobs to know the transitoriness of life as we lose possessions, family, health, security and honour. Others have experienced and pondered on such things, and, as it might appear, with more moderation, tranquillity and dignity than

1. *The True Witness*

Job could achieve. But behind all this, according to the great central portion of the Book and the Job poem proper, there stands in his case a very different grief which millions of other sufferers, the brave Stoics and their like, have never even experienced, let alone suffered, which is certainly reflected in the *descensus ad inferos* thus far depicted, but compared with which the latter and its individual elements can have only instrumental, subsidiary and relative importance. It is only from this other grief, and as they declare it, that the latter take on their specific significance and attain their unbearable sharpness. It is as the one who is stricken by this sorrow that the poet sees and understands this man of Uz sitting in the ashes, this man who has nothing left but a potsherd with which to scrape his sores. In relation to this very different sorrow he obviously feels no need, in the development of Job's complaint, to give any corresponding emphasis to the grounds of complaint specifically underlined in the basic saga (i.e., the loss of goods and children, and sickness), nor to attribute to him burdens for which there is no foundation in the prose narrative (e.g., the fact that his kinsfolk have abandoned and scorned him, the attacks of enemies and insult by the rabble). He is certainly afflicted by a mass of pain, but there is much more to it than that. If there is no doubt that the poem is related to the saga, that it is inspired by it and links up with it, there is also no doubt that the picture which is given of Job cannot be harmonised with that of the saga nor the words put in Job's mouth literally interpreted in the light of it in the sense of pragmatic history. At its heart the poem bursts through the framework of the saga, only returning to it at the end. As it contemplates as its own specific problem the true grief of Job, in its handling of the basic material it gives to Job's complaint a breadth and depth of almost mythical proportions. To be sure, it has not lost sight of the man of Uz. He can still be seen in his historical setting on the ashes bemoaning his fate with his sorrowing friends. And at the end the poem will return to the Job of the saga. But in between, in his speeches, he seems as it were to become more than life-size. He is unmistakeably endowed with the characteristics of that figure of the suffering righteous which is formally so distinctive of the whole witness of the Old Testament and materially so constitutively important for it, which we also meet especially in the prophet Jeremiah and the Suffering Servant of Isaiah 53, but also collectively in Lamentations and both individually and collectively in so many of the Psalms. The particular point of distinction of this figure in the Book of Job is, however, the very different one of the great affliction, pain and torture by which Job is visited, thus comprehending all the others in himself and putting them in the shade. This great sorrow has stricken with a centrality and intensity for which there are few parallels even in the Old Testament and none at all in the rest of the world's literature.

According to his speeches in the central section, his true sorrow in all his sorrows, and therefore the primary subject of his complaints, consists in the conjunction of his profound knowledge that in what has happened and what has come on him he has to do with God, and his no less profound ignorance how far he has to do with God. He is guilty of wrong in the conflict of his ignorance and knowledge, committing the fault which finds expression in the declaration of his grief, and which he will later have to acknowledge and bewail in dust and ashes (42⁶). To anticipate, this fault will not mean his disqualification as a witness to the truth. This is not because it is counter-balanced by that in which he is still in the right, namely, his constant knowledge that he has to do with God. It is because God Himself throws His own weight into the scales, dispelling the fault of Job, causing him to give up the conflict, and enabling him to experience, see and know to what extent he has to do with Him. We must return to this later. For the moment, however, we see this knowledge and ignorance of God in headlong collision and unbearable tension. This is the depth and essence of the suffering of the suffering Job.

He knows that he has to do with God. In this respect he is right. He sees

§ 70. *The Falsehood and Condemnation of Man*

and understands his losses, his sickness, his other adversities, the hopeless transitoriness of his life, to be the will and work of God, whatever else they may imply or he may make of them. Does he not realise that Satan, too, has a hand in them ? Rather strangely, this intervening figure which is so active in chapters 1 and 2 disappears as though he had never been in the central poetic section. A short, sharp look at him seems to have sufficed for the author of Job too. He does not recur either in the speeches of God or in the conclusion, not even for the tempting purpose of making the triumphant declaration that Yahweh has been successful in wagering on the faithfulness of Job. Satan is no problem to complaining Job, whether in respect of God's relationship to and intercourse with Satan, his existence among the sons of God (1^6), the wager, or his role in Job's own affairs. Job has simply to maintain the faithfulness on which God has wagered without looking aside to other issues. But he does this by not doing what Satan has wagered that he will do (1^{11}, 2^5), i.e., by not cursing God, by not separating himself from Him either in word or act, by not busying himself either with the strangeness and harshness of the course of the world and particularly of his own fate, the mysteries and terrors of its metaphysical depths, or the wickedness and folly of those who oppose him. He stands by the fine sayings of 1^{21} and 2^{10}, clinging in some fashion to Yahweh as the One who takes from him what He had previously given and from whose hand he now receives evil as he had received good. The movement may be strange and erratic, but he does receive it from Him. Hence in all his complaints he always thinks in terms of God's dealing, whether in the third person as a statement concerning His rule and action, or in the second as an address to the God who rules and acts in his life. He obviously has neither taste nor breath for abstract considerations or modes of speech. He has to do with Him, not merely in general but in relation to His special and personal action in respect of Job himself. In this there is manifested the relationship between God and himself, himself and God, which constitutes his existence. Satan is never taken into account even in the most outrageous forms and elements of his statements about God and addresses to Him. Job's concrete knowledge of God, and therefore the basic condition of his character as a witness to the truth, is thus unshakeable.

This concrete knowledge is of the fact that God is ruling and acting in his life. But Job's particular difficulty is that this knowledge is in tension and conflict with his no less concrete ignorance, which neither he, nor, as the poet plainly thinks, anyone else can overcome without the intervention of God Himself, of the extent to which God is at work in his life. There can be no question of God abandoning him. He does not abandon him, but keeps him inescapably in His grasp. Yet Job finds it impossible to see or understand in what sense he experiences this unbreakable clasp of His hand, or can understand it as His will and accept it as His work. He firmly sees his God and not another in what overwhelms him. But he does not understand Him in it. He does not recognise his God any more. He sees God, but as it were a God without God, i.e., a God who does not have the features of his own true God, who had become his Partner in free faithfulness, and whose partner he had similarly become, in blessing on the one side and righteous obedience on the other. He does not doubt for a moment that he has to do with this God. But it almost drives him mad that he encounters Him in a form in which He is absolutely alien. He suffers from the very faithfulness which means that God will not abandon him nor he God. He cries and beats against the fact, which he would like to escape, that he must keep to this God even though He comes to him in this alien form. He asks and asks again why does his God come in this form. He questions His right as His God to show Himself to him in this form. He opposes to this form of God the right of the relationship in which God stands to him and he to God. He adjures Him to acknowledge this right. And he has to experience the fact that all his crying and beating and attempting to escape, all his questioning and

1. *The True Witness* 403

doubting and protesting, is powerless against the iron fact that God does encounter him in this form. As he himself puts it, "thou art become cruel to me: with thy strong hand thou opposest thyself against me" (30^{21}). Thus Job is the man "whose way is hid, and whom God hath hedged in" (3^{23}; cf. 19^{18}). "For God maketh my heart soft, and the Almighty troubleth me" (23^{16}). "He hath also kindled his wrath against me, and he counteth me unto him as one of his enemies. His troops come together, and raise up their way against me, and encamp round about my tabernacle" (19$^{11f.}$). "For the arrows of the Almighty are within me, the poison whereof drinketh up my spirit: the terrors of God do set themselves in array against me" (6^4). "For he breaketh me with a tempest, and multiplieth my wounds without cause. He will not suffer me to take my breath, but filleth me with bitterness" (9$^{17f.}$). "He breaketh me with breach upon breach, he runneth against me like a giant" (16^{14}). "I was at ease, but he hath broken me asunder" (16^{12}). "Thine hands have made me and fashioned me together round about; yet thou dost destroy me" (10^8).

It is in face of this that Job raises his questions. "Is my strength the strength of stones? or is my flesh of brass?" (6^{12}). "Wherefore hidest thou thy face, and holdest me for thine enemy? Wilt thou break a leaf driven to and fro? and wilt thou pursue the dry stubble?" (13$^{24f.}$). "Am I a sea, or a whale, that thou settest a watch over me?" (7^{12}). "Why hast thou set me as a mark against thee?" (7^{20}; cf. 16$^{12f.}$). "What is man, that thou shouldest magnify him? and that thou shouldest set thine heart upon him? and that thou shouldest visit him every morning, and try him every moment? How long wilt thou not depart from me, not let me alone till I swallow down my spittle?" (7$^{17f.}$). "Is it good unto thee that thou shouldest oppress, that thou shouldest despise the work of thine hands?" (10^3). "Remember, I beseech thee, that thou hast made me as the clay, and wilt thou bring me into dust again?" (10^9). Occasionally, though relatively infrequently, these questions are accompanied by the request: "Are not my days few? cease then, and let me alone, that I may take comfort a little, before I go whence I shall not return" (10$^{20f.}$). "Turn from him, that he may rest, till he shall accomplish, as an hireling, his day" (14^6). But with the question or request there is above all the defiant protestation that he has kept the covenant with God. Or has he not done so? God should tell him where he has failed. "Let him take his rod away from me, and let not his fear terrify me: then would I speak, and not fear him; for I am not conscious of such things" (9$^{34f.}$). "I will give free course to my complaint against him; I will speak in the bitterness of my soul. I will say unto God, Do not condemn me; shew me wherefore thou contendest with me" (10$^{1f.}$). "Behold now, I have ordered my cause; I know that I shall be justified. Who is he that will plead with me?" (13$^{18f.}$). "My foot hath held his steps, his way have I kept, and not declined. Neither have I gone back from the commandment of his lips" (23$^{11f.}$). "Then call thou, and I will answer: or let me speak, and answer thou me. How many are mine iniquities and my sins? make me to know my transgression and my sin" (13$^{22f.}$). "Though he slay me, yet will I trust in him: but I will maintain mine own ways before him" (13^{15}). This challenge, which in the poem is Job's final word, culminates in the specific account of his previous action and conduct, and finally (31$^{35f.}$) in the almost insolent demand for a written accusation, which, since he knows from the very first its hollowness, he will wind around his head and thus attired encounter God like a prince.

Materially, however, Job's final word is to be found neither in the question nor request, nor even in the protestation, but in his constant sighing, which is both painful and angry and even scornful, at the obvious incongruity and impotence of all these forms of complaint, and especially of his protestation of innocence. The strange and dreadful element in the form in which God meets him consists finally in the fact that He does not enquire concerning the one with whom He has to do, concerning his guilt or innocence. He disposes and

§ 70. *The Falsehood and Condemnation of Man*

rules quite simply in accordance with the infinite right of His infinite might in face of which man can only maintain a horrified silence, or break out into violent protest, but concerning which he cannot speak with God since God will not allow this. " Oh that I knew where I might find him ! that I might come even to his seat ! I would order my cause before him, and fill my mouth with arguments. I would know the words which he would answer me, and understand what he would say unto me. Will he plead against me with his great power ? Oh if only he would regard me ! " (23³ᶠ·). But He does not do so : " Behold, I go forward, but he is not there ; and backward, but I cannot perceive him. On the left hand, where he doth work, I cannot behold him : he hideth himself on the right hand, that I cannot see him " (23⁸ᶠ·). " Lo, he goeth by me, and I see him not : he passeth on also, but I perceive him not. Behold, he taketh away, who can hinder him ? who will say unto him, What doest thou ? " (9¹¹ᶠ·). " If I speak of strength, lo, he is strong : and if of judgment, who shall set me a time to plead ? " (9¹⁹). " He destroyeth the perfect and the wicked. If the scourge slay suddenly, he will laugh at the trial of the innocent " (9²²ᶠ·). " If I wash my hands with snow water, and make my hands never so clean ; yet shalt thou plunge me in the ditch, and mine own clothes shall abhor me. For he is not a man, as I am, that I should answer him, and we should come together in judgment. Neither is there any daysman betwixt us, that might lay his hand upon us both " (9³⁰ᶠ·). " But he is of one mind, and who can turn him ? and what his soul desireth, even that he doeth. For he performeth the thing that is appointed for me : and many such things are with him. Therefore am I troubled at his presence : when I consider, I am afraid of him " (23¹³ᶠ·). If I lift up my head, " thou huntest me as a fierce lion : and again thou shewest thyself marvellous upon me. Thou renewest thy witness against me, and increasest thine indignation upon me ; thou exactest service from me " (10¹⁶ᶠ·). In short : " Behold, I cry out of wrong, but I am not heard : I cry aloud, but there is no judgment " (19⁷).

This relationship with God, then, is the true grief of Job and the real subject of his complaint. It would hardly be apposite to speak of a " controversy " with God. The whole point is that there can be no controversy with God. Job can only be in relation with Him as with One who has the strange and terrifying form of a relentlessly aggressive adversary before whom he is completely defenceless. To be sure, his true grief is only a transformation of the positive secret of his existence, of the covenant established once for all and irrevocably between God and himself, himself and God. It is only a specific modification of his existence as the servant of Yahweh. But what a transformation it is when God is for him only his most dangerous and implacable enemy refusing to let him go, and he cannot break free from Him but can only see himself as an enemy who is for no evident reason and with no obvious justification persecuted, threatened and ill-treated by Him ! Surely all ancient and modern sceptics, pessimists, scoffers and atheists are innocuous and well-meaning folk compared with this man Job. They do not know against whom they direct their disdain and doubt and scorn and rejection. Job does. As distinct from them, he speaks *en connaissance de cause*. They can easily enter into controversy with a God whom they do not know as their God. Job cannot do this. He can curse the day of his birth. But he cannot curse God. He cannot separate himself from Him He wishes he could. This is why he longs for death. This is why he hazards the bold conjecture whether God will perhaps grant him security before Him in the underworld. But he knows only too well—hence the futility of suicide—that even in death and the underworld he will still have to do with God, whether for good or ill. It is in the very proximity to God which is such a burden to him that he is for good or ill a contestant with God, a true " Israel " (Gen. 32²⁸) such as the amateur opponents of the good Lord can never be in their mild or more violent offensives against Him. It is in this proximity that he finds words

1. *The True Witness*

of repudiation compared with which all theirs are only pious platitudes. How strange it is that none of them has ever tried to learn from Job! If they had, they might have begun to realise at least what it is that they are attempting, and thus been able to give more forceful expression to their cause.

But what has happened in this specific relationship between God and Job, and Job and God, which forms his true grief and the real subject of his complaint? There has certainly been no dissolution or removal of the covenant relationship established in the prior free choice of God and the subsequent free choice of man. But there has been an incisive change within this relationship. Without being unfaithful to Job, God has exercised His freedom towards him by reducing to the cheerless minimum of actual preservation the blessing with which He had hitherto undeservedly blessed him. He has thus encountered him in a form in which He is unrecognisable as his God even though He has not ceased to be this. And if he for his part is not to be unfaithful to God, Job must follow this decision by rendering free if suffering obedience to the One who has become unrecognisable and is concealed in this alien form. What is the meaning and basis of this change? The answer to this question obviously gives us the answer to the question of the meaning and basis of Job's suffering which is the consequence of this change, and of the rights and wrongs of Job's complaint against it, and therefore decisively against the change in the form of God which underlies it.

There can be no doubt that from the standpoint of the free action of God and the problem of the corresponding free action of Job, this change is a partial action in their common history. For all its unshakeable solidarity, the covenant relationship between God and Job is not just a static factor. Its ontic is dynamic. That is to say, it exists as it achieves and maintains existence. That it exists in this way, and is thus capable and in need of change, does not contradict its nature. It is supremely in accordance with it, i.e., with the freedom of the divine and human choice in which it is grounded. A partial action in the history in which the relationship between God and Job takes place is the change wherein God executes this change of form in free decision and Job must follow the divine decision with an equally free human decision, i.e., to render suffering obedience to Him. God does not stand still. He takes a step forward. It is for Job to take a corresponding step forward. What God does is an expression of the free faithfulness in which He has turned to Job. To adopt the term used by Kierkegaard in his book of 1843, it is a "repetition" of the establishment in the same free faithfulness of His covenant with Job. Hence there is demanded of Job an expression of the free faithfulness with which he has turned to God, a "repetition" of his existence with the same free faithfulness in the divinely established covenant. What we have here is a partial action in their common history. The change within the relationship will not be final. But for the moment it remorselessly entails the fact that God, even though He will not let Job go, conceals Himself from Him by making Himself unrecognisable as his God, so that Job's part can only be that of freedom and therefore of obedience in suffering. He can achieve this only in the conflict and unbearable tension of knowledge and ignorance: of knowledge that he has to do with God even in this alien form; of ignorance how far He has to do with God in this form. This gives us the real complaint of Job. From complaint at his deprivation of the blessing of God, at his losses, his sickness, and the transitoriness of existence, which is only the starting-point, he rises to the true complaint which he launches on the basis of the known God against the unknown. In other words, it is in the name of God that he complains against God, i.e., against the strange form in which God encounters him, rejects him, disputes against him, and persecutes him as an unjustly disowned and ill-treated servant. Even though from the very outset he knows that he has neither competence nor power to mount this attack, yet he presses it to the bitter end. This is the remarkable and indeed honourable complaint of Job in all its rights and wrongs. It is honourable

406 § 70. *The Falsehood and Condemnation of Man*

because it is that of the form of obedience appropriate to the partial action of his history with God. He would not have been obedient if he had not raised this complaint and carried it through to the bitter end in spite of all objections. The first thing to be seen and said is that in it he accomplished the repetition required of him.

The clearly declared meaning of the Book of Job is that he put himself both in the right and also in the wrong in so doing. " Who is this that darkeneth counsel by words without knowledge ? " is Yahweh's own challenge to him (38^2). And Job accepts this judgment and confesses : " I have uttered that I understood not ; things too wonderful for me, which I knew not " (42^3). He thus recants, and repents in dust and ashes (42^6). Yet the wrath of God, as we read in v. 7 f., is not really kindled against him, but against the three friends, to whom it is twice said explicitly : " Ye have not spoken of me the thing that is right, as my servant Job hath." Hence Job is both in the right and also in the wrong in his complaint. We cannot possibly agree that he was wholly right in venturing that repetition, as Kierkegaard, who devoted regular dithyrambs to him as the consoling companion of his own melancholy, would have us believe. To be sure, we cannot distinguish between the sayings of Job, as some commentators think they have to do, subjecting them to mild censure here, applauding them there, and occasionally rejecting them as extravagant, erroneous and sinful. There are no grounds for any such procedure in the text. There are certainly passages, to be mentioned later, which plainly show us that Job is in the right. But they do not really belong to his complaint. As his words, they already anticipate the right which is not his own, but which is finally promised and given him by God. They are alien in the darkened landscape around them, as is Job's own existence as a servant of Yahweh in the East. They are foundlings, or meteors descending from another world. They are exceptions confirming the rule. In Job's complaint as such we cannot distinguish between right and wrong in such a way as to fix on any of his utterances and say that this is right or this is wrong. In their own way they all point both to the right and to the left, both above and below. It cannot be otherwise than that Job—*simul iustus et peccator*—is right in all his sayings as the servant of Yahweh, and in none of them as fallible man. We thus see him everywhere under the law which he has accepted and on the way of the expression and repetition required of him, yet everywhere, too, as a blind and deaf and lame man who can only stumble and fall and rise and stumble and fall again on this way. Inextricably intermingled are the glorious sincerity with which he strictly refuses to see white or grey where there is only black, to transform God in this incomprehensible form into God in a comprehensible, and on the other side the shamelessness with which he does not even request but demands as a right that God should put off this alien form and make Himself comprehensible, as though He were not his God even in this form. He rightly maintains as God's partner the cause which he has never abandoned but consistently championed. He rightly maintains his righteousness before God. But he blatantly sets himself in the wrong by arrogantly advancing this righteousness as a claim that God should be righteous before him, to his human eyes and according to his human thoughts and standards. In this we see, of course, the liberty of the child of God which may and must cling to the possession promised and assigned to it. But we also see the astonishing childishness which will not accept the fact that the possession is not yet given, that even though it is assigned it is still in the hand of the father, that the time of the actual handing over is his affair alone. We see the violent impatience of a man who, taking the kingdom of heaven by storm (Mt. 11^{12}), will not wait to receive it but wants to fix himself the time and manner of its reception and thus threatens at the very root the very freedom which he exercises. Everything is in order to the extent that there is a resolute, despairing reaching after God in spite of every obstacle. But the very reverse is the case to the extent that there is an obvious reaching beyond oneself and therefore an asserting of oneself against God which means opposition to Him. On the one side, Job respects the freedom of God both to give and to take. On the other, he does so with a resignation which defiantly insists that God ought really to have exercised His freedom very differently, i.e., in fitting deference to human freedom, as though this were not derived from God. How can we fail to see and distinguish the two aspects ? We certainly have to do with both right and wrong. And how entangled and confused they are ! If he were not on the way, he could not stumble and fall. Those who are not startled and forced to run away find it easy to maintain a dignified composure. He is shameless in his glorious sincerity, and he cannot really be sincere without being shameless. Why should he not maintain his real righteousness before God ? But how can he do so except by clamouring that God should be righteous before him ? Is not his very freedom as a child of God revealed in the violent impatience by which he most seriously jeopardises it ? Is it not the true children of God who even at best can be patient only with great impatience ? Reaching after God, what can he do but declare himself dissatisfied, and thus assert and reach beyond himself, reprehensible though this may be ? Is it not in the evil resignation of Job before God that we see his respect for the divine freedom ? Yet how fatal it is that he can show this respect only in the guise of this resignation ! What are we to say to all this ? In view of the unmistakeable positive aspect of his complaint as one who contests with God, are we to agree that Job is excused and even justified in relation to the negative aspect in which he contests *against* God and therefore *without* Him ? Is he forced to be a kind of superman doing evil that good may come (Rom. 3^8) ? This is the view we should have to adopt if Kierkegaard were right to rejoice that in his complaint Job abandoned as the " meagre comfort " of worldly wisdom his earlier affirmation : " The Lord gave, and the Lord hath taken away ; blessed be the name of the Lord " (1^{21}) ; that he no longer repeated this, but became instead " the mouth of the suffering, the sigh of the bruised, the cry of the afflicted," " an alleviation for all who are silent in their distress, a faithful witness to all the woe which can dwell in a lacerated heart." This is all true of Job, yet in the practice rather than at the cost of the confession. And if he proves himself thereby, this does not cover or atone for the fact that he does so only in repudiation, speaking with God yet also without Him, about Him and to Him. " The secret of Job, the vital force, the nerve, the principle, is that in spite of everything he is right. Asserting this, he demands that he should be treated as an exception to the rule ; and his endurance and power prove his authority to do so " (Kierkegaard). This is going too far. It throws everything out of focus. Ungodliness does not cease to be such because it is ungodliness in what is good. Not at all ! The piety and theology of the friends exposed and unmasked in confrontation with Job are in another sense ungodliness in what is good. We cannot deny that after his own fashion Job, too, is guilty in this regard. It is incontestable that the counsel of God was very much darkened by him as he fulfilled it, vindicating God in answer to Satan. But who can condemn him for this ? He who alone is qualified to condemn him has not done so. While putting him in his place, He has expressly conceded that in, with and under all that is wrong he has said that which is right concerning Him. Hence the warning and question cuts both ways. Who of us may or can or should lay his unclean human finger on the words of Job, whether *in peiorem* or *in meliorem partem*, as though he could be the umpire for whom Job very foolishly appealed (9^{33}) yet very wisely knew even as he did so that his appeal was futile ? There are no such umpires between God and man. Job himself could not try to be such. And we certainly cannot as we follow his history, his vindication, the repetition of his confession at the beginning of his way. He himself could not bring to a conclusion his strange dealings with God, nor can we as we consider Job's speeches alone, but only in retrospect of God's own decision. As the history continues,

§ 70. *The Falsehood and Condemnation of Man*

God Himself will intervene between Himself and Job. He will not justify him without humbling him. But He will not humble him, as he had not been humbled in all his misery and affliction, without also justifying him.

All that we can do is to read the drama of his history, and particularly of this partial action in which it is the drama of his suffering and complaint, with fear and pity, or rather with awe and love. It is the drama of the contestant with God, the Israel, who was not Jesus Christ, the sinless One made sin for us (2 Cor. 5^{21}), but only Job, who in his suffering and complaint, notwithstanding its obvious difference from those of Gethsemane and Golgotha, was still a witness to Jesus Christ, to the One who as the suffering, crucified, dead and buried Son of God and Man is the only true Witness, in face of whom the falsehood of man is shown to be mere wind and vanishes as such.

We now return for the last time to this only true Witness, to Jesus Christ in His prophetic work, in the promise of the Spirit, in which He is present to us in our sphere of time and history. As we have seen, He is present in His form of suffering, wherein the pure form in which God alone sees and knows Him active but also concealed. It is in this form that He is the true and authentic declaration of the truth, because in it He is Himself the truth beside which there is no other or higher truth whether on earth or in heaven, in time or from and to all eternity, for us or for God.

But how far—we finally ask—is He the truth which perceptibly expresses itself in this particular form? A Prophet speaks. A Witness speaks. He can be heard and is heard. In the words of Is. 52^{15}: " He shall astonish many nations ; kings shall shut their mouths at him." This is said of the suffering righteous of the old covenant. But for this to happen he must open his own mouth and say something. How does he do this? How can he? How can Jesus Christ speak in this form? If His passion is the form of His action here and now, is He not by definition a mute and silent Witness ? " He was oppressed, and he was afflicted, yet he opened not his mouth : he is brought as a lamb to the slaughter " (Is. 53^7). " He shall not cry, nor lift up, nor cause his voice to be heard in the streets " (Is. 42^2). But what will happen if this is so ? What a contrast there is between the wordiness and noisiness of humanity and the Church of Jesus Christ in their tireless and inexhaustible attempts at self-communication and self-expression in their various more or less legitimate and urgent affairs, and Jesus Christ as the Proclaimer of the reconciliation accomplished in Him, and therefore as the Crucified ! What a power of words on the one side, and what impotence on the other ! For where all others, ourselves included, have the desire and the breath to speak with as much force, articulation and circumstantiality as possible, the only way in which He can and will present His cause is by means of the sigh on the cross which comes down through the centuries. What a Prophet this is, what a Witness, what a Word which is so very different from all human words whether temporal or spiritual, irreligious or religious, which is not in any sense

1. *The True Witness*

one of the voices which may be heard in their common concert ! Assuming that there is such a thing as the *theologia crucis*, the Word of the cross, and that it denotes the reality of the prophetic work of Jesus Christ, what is meant by this *theologia* or Word ? And how can it do that of which we are speaking, namely, unmask as such the falsehood of man, and silence the man of sin as he talks so boldly and proudly in the great brawling and chattering of the world and humanity ?

A remarkable fact emerges as we tackle this question. Jesus Christ does actually speak. He does so in the promise of the Spirit as the Crucified. And as such He does not merely murmur or whisper, but through the centuries, and therefore here and now among us, He speaks with a voice " as the sound of many waters " (Rev. 1^{15}). He speaks so clearly and powerfully that when His Word goes forth all the non-Christian and Christian clamour of the world is reduced to a dying murmur. Even when they hear Him only from afar, others can only ask in astonishment whether it is possible that He should not be heard, and issue a summons to hear His voice. His Word is the sound which would fill heaven and earth even if there were no ear to hear Him. It did so even when specific individuals had not done so. It will do so even if they hear it no longer. Paul was thinking of His Gospel, which for him was identical with the Word of the cross, when in Rom. 10^{18} he quoted the passage in Ps. $19^{3f.}$ which speaks of the glory of God going through all the world and to the end of the earth even though there is neither speech nor language nor audible voice. This is how it is with this voice, with the Word of the Crucified, of the One who does not strive nor cry, who is not heard in the streets, who is at once drowned even by a toy trumpet. He speaks where all others think they do, but in reality only lisp and stutter. He has something to say, and says it, where all others want to say something but have nothing worth saying compared with what He says. He utters that which, when He is present, has to be uttered, and is therefore ineluctably uttered. In Him the truth is present, indeed, He is the truth, which, as He speaks, speaks by itself, about itself and for itself with its incomparable force, clarity and distinctness.

This is what emerges when the question is raised whether and how the man of Gethsemane and Golgotha, Jesus Christ in the form of His passion, has any voice or Word and therefore speaks and can be heard in the world as the true Witness. What answer can and should be made except that indicated, which at once transcends and supersedes the question, namely, that He does. He, this man, Jesus Christ speaks and makes Himself heard specifically in this form. Nor does He do so among and alongside many others and in more or less victorious competition with them. He alone does so. The real question is not where He is left with His voice and Word in relation to ours, but where we are left with ours in relation to His. This is the only possible answer. But it is not an idea which we can reach by deductive reasoning, nor an event of nature or history which we can reach by inductive. It is not a fact whose existence, operation and significance can be proved by information acquired of ourselves and then perhaps disproved by fresh information from another source. Hence no one can maintain what is at issue in this answer, or champion it against opposing assertions, as though it were his own stock of knowledge to be advanced or defended, whether as the content of personally established and tested religious conviction, or of an authoritative tradition in which he thinks he stands, or of an ecclesiastical authority to which he has committed and subjected himself. If intended and given in this way, the answer is false for all that it is correct. It is a lie like any others, and worse than others. Its whole freedom and power lie in and depend on the fact that it points to the miraculous power of God Himself, to the " arm of the Lord " (Is. 53^1) here revealed. Hence no discussion is to be feared and no discussion can be provoked or fostered. This is the truth speaking for itself. It is not an argument. It will thus prevent those who know and honour and love it as the truth from entering into argument or even the most laudable of exploitations. It can be made legitimately only in an obedience which advances no claim, only kerygmatically, only with the holy irresponsibility and defencelessness of the man who knows that in this matter, in relation to the miraculous power of God Himself, He knows nothing and has nothing to say, not even on the authority of his own faith. Only as man actually believes, and does so rather than says so ; only as he may and must say what he believes and knows ; only as there is no authorisation or assurance apart from that which God does not owe him but in fact gives him, though not into his hands or into captivity to his thought and utterance : only thus can the answer have meaning and power, acquiring them by means of the miraculous power of God to which it points. As distinct from any theory or factual record, it can only be attested, known and proclaimed. Only the truth itself and therefore God Himself can vouch for it. Directly or indirectly, it can properly be made only in prayer, in intercession that God Himself will vouch for it. But in prayer there may be given without hesitation, vacillation or doubt, without the slightest uncertainty, the answer that the crucified Jesus Christ does speak ; for as He speaks God speaks. We shall now try to develop this only possible answer in all its vulnerability and invulnerability.

As the Word of this man, the Word of the crucified Jesus Christ is distinguished from all other human words as God's Word by the fact that it is spoken out of the great, conclusive and absolute silence in which all the words of all other men reach their end and limit, namely, the silence of the death of this man. God alone as the only Lord of life and death can break this silence, and therefore speak out of this end and limit of all human words. For He alone is beyond this end and limit. If there is human speech out of and therefore in penetration of this silence, and therefore from this beyond, as such it can only be the speech of God. But the crucified, dead and buried man Jesus Christ does speak. Those who hear Him, hear God. Those who dare—who may do so because they must—to confess that they hear Him, that they do not merely hear a report or doctrine or anything else concerning Him but really hear Him, dare to confess that they hear God. Not hearing God, they would not hear Him, or would only hear something about Him. The Christian community dares to confess that it hears Him, the crucified, dead and buried man Jesus Christ. In so doing it confesses that it hears God, His voice and Word. We remember, however, that the speaking of this man out of the silence of His death, and therefore the speaking of God here and now, are not bound to any human hearing and confessing, even though they be those of the Christian community. This man and therefore God would speak even though there were no human hearing and no affirmation by human confession. His speaking is the basis of human hearing and confessing, not *vice versa*. Whether or not men hear and affirm by confession, the fact that it is uttered and breaks the silence of death distinguishes His speech from all other human speech as the human Word which is pronounced with the superior power possessed only by God, and therefore as the declaration of the truth, as the speech of the true Witness.

But we must press on to the immediate issue. Thus far we have described and understood it as the Word of God only in a formal sense, in its infinite but not its qualitative uniqueness and particularity as compared with all other human words. God is also the Lord of life and death, and the fact that the Word of Jesus Christ is the Word of God is disclosed also in the fact that it is spoken to break the silence of His death—for He speaks as the Crucified, Dead and Buried—and therefore to transcend the frontier of death which puts an end to all the speech of all other men. In other words, He speaks from the place from which God alone has the power to speak. Yet in itself this is not enough. It forms only an introduction to the real point which we have to see and consider. We are not dealing with any man who was put to death but who now speaks again ; we are dealing with this man. We are not dealing with any kind of miraculous speech ; we are dealing with the very definite declaration of this man who was put to death. We are not dealing with God as the One who gave Him His own power just to speak, i.e., to say anything at all out of the silence of His death ; we are dealing with God as the One who enabled Him to make a pronouncement with a specific content. He speaks of the work of God accomplished in His death, or, as we may and must also say, accomplished by Him as the One who suffered and died on the cross. He speaks of the reconciliation of the world to God effected in His death and passion.

§ 70. The Falsehood and Condemnation of Man

That is to say, He speaks of the judgment on the man of sin, of the displacement of this man which God has accomplished in His person, to which He had to subject Himself in obedience, and in achievement of which He has offered Himself up as the one obedient man in the place of all others. He thus speaks of the divine act of the justification of sinful man before God effected in His death. And He speaks of the introduction of the liberated man which in His person again God has accomplished as the beginning of a new human life in fellowship with Himself, and which He Himself could and did realise in pure gratitude as the first-fruits of all others and in the place of all others. He thus speaks of the divine act of the sanctification of man for God again accomplished in His person. He speaks of the conclusion of peace on both sides in which God fulfils the covenant between Himself and man on both sides, delivering man, and in him all creation, from his exposure to the assault of nothingness, and rescuing him for participation in His eternal life. No man or creature could be the doer of this deed, the accomplisher of this work, the lord of this history, just as none could be its own creator. God alone, in the incomprehensible love in which He is free and the incomprehensible freedom in which He loves, could do and accomplish this, has actually done and accomplished it, has acted as the Lord of this history. He alone can reveal this work. The crucified man Jesus Christ does this. Hence He speaks God's Word. Indeed, we may say more. In this action God has expressed Himself, His innermost being, His heart, His divine person, His divine essence, Himself as the One He is. As the One who has done this, He has distinguished Himself from the God or gods of all the general notions and concepts of divinity invented and projected by man. As the Doer of this act He is the one true God. He is this, therefore, in the death of the man Jesus Christ. In the death of this man, in Him the Crucified, He reveals not only the work done, but in and with this Himself, His divine person, His divine essence, in distinction from the nature of divinity in general or the divine forms in which this is seen and reverenced. God Himself is needed to reveal this work, and especially to reveal Himself, His divine person and essence. Who but God could or would reveal God? Hence the content of the pronouncement of this slain man is both the work and also the person and essence of God. The Word of this man, from the standpoint not only of its miraculous form but of its even more miraculous content, is the Word of God. As such it distinguishes itself from all other words. As such it has the might of the Rider on the white horse (Rev. 19[11f.]) whose eyes are as a flame of fire, on whose heads are many crowns, but who is clothed with a vesture dipped in blood, who thus judges and makes war in righteousness, and who is called Faithful and True, an obvious equivalent for the name which He alone knows and can make known, namely, the Word of God (ὁ λόγος τοῦ θεοῦ). It is as this Word of

1. *The True Witness* 413

the work and person and essence of God, which as such can only be God's own Word, that He is the declaration of the truth, the true Witness who as such speaks for Himself and beside whom there can be no other.

But now, in relation to the same question of the mystery of the identity of the Word of the Crucified with the Word of God Himself, we must take a new and strange step. As He speaks of the work of reconciliation and therefore of the person and essence of God, He speaks the Word of God, since God alone can speak of these. But it belongs decisively to this work of God, and therefore to the heart of God's person and essence, that His action in the conclusion of this peace, in the work of atonement and deliverance, in the justification and sanctification of man, should entail severity, pain and terror for the one man who was ordained and who give Himself to accomplish it. His death and passion are not an unfortunate accident or overruling fate. What men decree and execute against Him in supreme corruption and iniquity takes place according to the holy and gracious counsel of God. It is not merely permitted but directed by Him. It is God's will that in the death of this one man judgment should be fulfilled on all others, but that they should all be set up and set right, that the old man should be expelled and the new man introduced once and for all in the place of all, to His glory and to the salvation of all. But this means that it is God's will to cause this one man to pay the price. And the accomplishment of this good will of God means that as He does so, in accordance with the deserts of all He must turn away from and even against this One, against the Righteous and Holy elected by Himself to be His Servant, against the One who knows no sin but shows to Him only obedience and gratitude. The bitter implication is that He puts Him in the place of us all, that He makes Him His Lamb (Jn. 1^{29}) bearing the sin of the world, the Representative of all human transgression and corruption in all its forms, the One who bears responsibility for the great disruption of the relationship between Himself and us, and for all the disturbances of which our own lives are secretly or blatantly the theatre. The consequence is that this Elect of God as such must be the Rejected of God, delivered up by Him into the hands of the unrighteous and unholy, and, as ordained by Him, suffering and dying as a malefactor, not apart from but with and according to His good and merciful and kind but death-dealing will. The consequence is His not unjustifiable cry of pain which no arts of exegesis should be employed to mitigate : " My God, my God, why has thou forsaken me ? " (Mk. 15^{34}). It is at once the death-cry of the man who dies in Him and the birth-cry of the man who comes to life in Him. There is a notable difference between what He says in relation to the men, the Jews and Romans, to whom He is delivered and who bring about His death : " Father, forgive them ; for they know not what they do " (Lk. 23^{34}), and

§ 70. *The Falsehood and Condemnation of Man*

what He says in relation to God : " My God, my God, why hast thou forsaken me ? " No, He is not mistaken. There is reason for this dreadful question. It corresponds exactly to the situation. When the question is thus raised : " Who, who for my salvation, Hath brought this lamentation, And grief upon Thee now ? " it does not suffice to answer with the true enough confession : " I, I and my transgression." We must also refer to the will and act of God at work in this event. God has never forsaken, and does not and will not forsake any man as He forsook this man. And " forsook " means that He turned against Him as never before or since against any— against the One who was for Him as none other, just as God for His part was for Him as He never was nor is nor will be for any other. But the very fact that He was for Him—for Him as our Reconciler, Saviour and Mediator—necessarily entailed that He was wholly against Him as the One who took our place as the place of evildoers. Nor is it enough to say that we have to do here merely with this strange work of God. We have to do with God Himself, with the One who is active in this work, with His own person and essence. In the person of this one man Jesus of Nazareth, it is His own eternal Son, " Light of Light, Very God of very God, Begotten not made ; Being of one substance with the Father," who has come down as the Representative of the world and our common Substitute, offering Himself as such, and thus having to bear the wrath and curse of God and to suffer and die according to His will. But this means that God Himself is not a remote and aloof spectator or non-participating director of this event, of the dreadful thing which it includes and entails for this man. With the eternal Son the eternal Father has also to bear what falls on the Son as He gives Himself to identity with the man Jesus of Nazareth, thus lifting it away from us to Himself in order that it should not fall on us. In Jesus Christ God Himself, the God who is the one true God, the Father with the Son in the unity of the Spirit, has suffered what it befell this man to suffer to the bitter end. It was first and supremely in Himself that the conflict between Himself and this man, and the affliction which threatened this man, were experienced and borne. What are all the sufferings in the world, even those of Job, compared with this fellow-suffering of God Himself which is the meaning of the event of Gethsemane and Golgotha ? It is of this fellow-suffering of God Himself borne on earth and also in heaven to the greater glory of God and the supreme salvation of man ; it is of the God who has not evaded, and on the very grounds of His deity could not evade, this suffering with and for the world, that the crucified man Jesus Christ speaks. He speaks the wonderful Word of the wonderful God who has taken our guilt and ensuing misery that they should be no longer ours, thus concluding the peace the price of which He Himself willed to pay and did pay in the person of this man, and therefore in the person of His own Son, and therefore in His

1. *The True Witness*

fatherly heart. Who else but God could or would speak of this, declaring that He had done it, that He is this God, and that this God is the one true God? But the declaration of the Crucified is this declaration. And as such it is the Word of God Himself, the declaration of the truth, the testimony of the one true Witness.

Pursuing the same line of thought, we must now look back again from the content of the declaration of the crucified Jesus Christ to the problem of the special form of the true Witness. From the very first we have not concealed the fact that in the Jesus Christ who encounters us in His form of suffering we are concerned with a phenomenon which is strange, shocking and quite opposed to what we might for once call the natural feelings and desires and thoughts and beliefs and dreams of man. On the basis of what we regard as divine, who of us would look for the truth of God in this form? Who of us could or would acquiesce in the fact that we must find it in this form and this form alone? This is what continually isolates Jesus Christ in every age and place, so that we would rather avoid Him, and can make nothing of Him, and prefer to have no dealings with Him. This is what ensures that faith can never be a matter of course. "This shall not be unto thee" (Mt. 16^{22}). And above all, we cannot have dealings with a Christ like this. Man has always and everywhere felt at home with a form which presents itself as an embodiment of the fertility, the elemental wealth, the beauty, and the spirit of the cosmos and man, or conversely with one which expresses the demonically majestic terror of creation, as when we see the high mountains, or the ocean, or the original riotousness of terrestrial flora and fauna, which are the foci of certain artistic representations of the religions of Asia. But what is he to make of Jesus Christ the Crucified, in whom he has to do only with the one painful point, in whom there is no place for his crude or refined jesting, even for that which is possible in relation to the majesty of the terrifying? What is he to make of this suffering and dying man in all his nakedness, abandonment and rejection, with his hopeless complaint and mute accusation that this is how man deals with God and therefore with man, that this is how God and therefore man is betrayed, forsaken, rejected, ill-treated and put to death by man? How can we rejoice to see Him? What can we make of Him when He seems to hold up before us the reflection of our own human reality divested of all illusion?

It is most unfortunate that the fact that we do not willingly look to Him in this form is so obscured by the preoccupation of so much Christian art with this subject, and especially by the inane misuse of the symbol of the cross right into our own times.

But we have to see what Peter had to see, namely, that there is no flight or escape to another Christ in another and more radiant form, because it is in this form that He is the temporal and eternal truth which encounters us. He encounters us in this form, or not at all. But if this is so, we have to accept the total otherness and strangeness and isolation of God in Him and His isolation. He speaks remorselessly of the God whose thoughts are not ours, nor His ways ours (Is. 55[8]), who is not directed by us, by whom we ourselves must be directed, whom we can only recognise as our Lord and Judge, and before whom we must acknowledge the worthlessness or all our own thoughts and beliefs and dreams of what is meant by God or divine. It is of this God that the Crucified speaks. And He does so as this God alone can Himself speak of Himself. Hence the Crucified speaks the truth. But let us imagine for a moment that we do not wish to avoid Him as He encounters us in this form. We are ready to receive instruction—this instruction—from Him and therefore from God Himself concerning God. This means that we must be ready to be told by Him that we shall not find God where we think we should look for Him, namely, in a supposed height. It means that we must be ready to be told by Him that we shall find Him precisely where we do not think we should look for Him, namely, in direct confrontation with and at the very heart of our own reality, which, whether we like it or not, reduces itself with the crumbling and tottering of all our previous genuine or illusory possibilities and achievements to the one painful point where each of us is stripped and naked, where each is suffering and perishing, where each is engaged in futile complaint and accusation, where each is alone. The lonely man of Gethsemane and Golgotha, the lonely God, then comes together with lonely man isolated in his deepest need. Each of us can then say that in this place, even though he is forsaken and alone, he is not forsaken and alone, since the crucified man Jesus Christ, and in Him as the Son of God God Himself, has also stooped down and come to this place and been forsaken there. There among the smitten and abased, among whom we would prefer not to reckon ourselves, God has raised His throne (Is. 57[15]), the throne of the glory of His grace in which, at His own cost, He has made peace between us men and Himself, justifying and sanctifying as His covenant-partner fallen and wretched man, and saving him for eternal life with Himself. There God does not say No to man without bearing and experiencing Himself all the bitterness of this No in order that according to His own will and power He might, in, with and under this No, pronounce to him His own eternal, divine Yes. Hence it is only in the supposed height of man's own corrupt desires and wishes—a height which has to be destroyed and is already given up to destruction—that God is to man alien and remote and hostile. There in the depths of his naked and true reality God is His Neighbour and Brother suffering with him and for him. He is the Good Samaritan who shows mercy on him. This is what the crucified man Jesus Christ has to say to us, and does say, as the Word of God, since only God can say it. This is

1. The True Witness

what we are told if we do not close our eyes to the painful point at which we all find ourselves. It is the Christmas message in the midst of darkness. It is the invitation: " Come unto me, all ye that labour and are heavy laden, and I will give you rest." And whether or not we are prepared to open our eyes to our own reality and the presence, help and assistance of God in it, the crucified man Jesus Christ speaks the truth as the Word of God. Bearing witness to the truth, He is the true Witness who puts to shame all opposing witnesses as liars.

We pause for a moment. The subject of our enquiry is the possibility of the speech of the crucified man Jesus Christ as the true Witness. Our answer is one which at once transcends and removes the question. For we have only to point to the fact that this Witness does speak with a power, clarity and distinctness greater than any other, and this not in spite of the fact, but because of the fact, that He is the One who suffered, and was crucified, dead and buried. Inevitably, we have had to realise that this unilaterally and unequivocally positive answer, as a reference to what actually takes place, can only be a reference to the miraculous working of God which is beyond all human thought and speech, so that it can be given only in relation to its verification by the truth which is God Himself, and therefore only kerygmatically, only in the certainty of faith, only in this and not on the authority of our faith, only in confidence in the authority of its object, only in prayer to God for the confirmation which we cannot give of ourselves. In relation to the miraculous work of God, and as a reference to it, we may and must give this positive answer, and regard it as incontestable to the extent that in it we refer to God, though highly contestable to the extent that it is we who refer to God. But the miraculous work of God which is our concern consists quite simply in the fact that, as the crucified man Jesus Christ speaks, God Himself speaks, and therefore He speaks the Word of God. We have tried to bring out different aspects of this simple substance of our answer. We have heard this man speak from the place from which only God can speak. He does not do so merely as others. Others can speak by their influence. Indeed, there are some who speak only by this influence and therefore after their death. But He speaks with living power as and by God Himself, not only in His death, but from His death, by His death, and from out of the silence of His death. Again, we have heard Him declare what only God can declare as His own work, i.e., the effected reconciliation of the world to God, peace between Him and us, our justification and sanctification, and God Himself as the Doer of this work, God's person and essence, who and what He is, and what He wills and does as such. We have heard Him speak, as only God can do, of the mystery of this act, of His divinely willed and accomplished offering, surrender and sacrifice of Himself as innocent, obedient and grateful man, of His bowing beneath the No which God

§ 70. *The Falsehood and Condemnation of Man*

pronounced in order to utter the mighty Yes of His conclusion of peace, of His suffering in the place of those to whom God willed to say Yes and has thus to say No as well, of the mystery of the divine action in this mystery, of the suffering which God took to Himself in placing it on His eternally beloved Son according to His purpose, of His own wounding by that which according to His will had to fall on Him for His own glory and for our salvation. Hence we have finally heard Him speak of that concerning which God alone can speak, which can be only the declaration of His Word, namely, the inconceivably real unity of the supreme strangeness yet supreme proximity with which God encounters us in His form as the man of Gethsemane and Golgotha, the direct connexion between the utter lostness of man and his utter salvation as presented and brought home to him in the reflection of His form as this man. The miraculous work of God in this matter is this speaking of His Word, of the Word which He alone can speak, but which He really does speak when the crucified man Jesus Christ speaks. In relation to this we have had to give at once this answer, very conscious of its contestability as a human declaration, of its indispensable need to be verified by God and His free utterance, and therefore of the impossibility of making it otherwise than with invocation of His name, yet with confidence in the incontestability of its basis. We have had to give the answer with which we started, namely, that the Crucified speaks indeed, that He does so with unparalleled force and clarity and distinctness, that He does so as the incomparable true Witness, inasmuch as His Word is also the Word of God.

In development of this answer, however, we have still to take a final step. Our constant formulation has been that He speaks or utters or declares a definite Word of His own which as such is the Word of God. We have hitherto assumed that He is also heard, and can be heard. Nor have we done more than suggest this assumption in terms of the qualifying assertion that since He speaks the Word of God His utterance is not conditioned by whether or not it is heard by various individuals. This is the main point at issue. In this as in other respects God is a great Lord with many strange lodgers in His household upon whom His gifts seem to be lavished in vain. He does indeed speak to many ears which are closed and deaf. If He summons all to hear, this does not mean that He is the prisoner of a necessary reciprocity between His divine speaking and our human hearing. As the beginning of His speaking does not coincide with the beginning of our hearing but precedes it—for if He had to wait for the beginning of our hearing, how could He begin to speak?—so the fact that it no longer finds a hearing among us does not mean that His speaking comes to an end. Whether He is heard or not, He speaks in His own freedom and power. When God speaks; when the crucified man Jesus Christ speaks, He does so—for what else does speaking mean, and how else should we know that He speaks?—not merely with the intention of being heard by us, but also with the power to make Himself heard. He does not actually speak without being heard. He thus speaks audibly. There is already a reciprocity between His divine speaking and our human hearing which, if it is not necessary and does not limit or condition His speaking, has actually been created and takes place in the power of His free act. Without this assumption we could not have given the positive answer we did to the present question. Our whole development of this answer could be undertaken only on this assumption. As we maintained continually, we have seen or heard these things. And our whole assumption is that we have actually heard what is said. We must now study the assumption as such.

How does it come about that the true Witness Jesus Christ is heard by us, that His Word and therefore the Word of God is accepted and understood and taken to heart by us? How can this happen? We must be very clear that His audibility cannot consist in the audibility, receptibility or comprehensibility of a human explanation, articulation and application of His Word, of a doctrine such as that which we have attempted from different angles in what precedes. However relevant and well-grounded such a doctrine might be, it can be heard as such, and apperceived with varying degrees of insight and assent, without there being even remotely a hearing of the true Witness and the Word of God spoken by Him. Conversely, there can be a hearing of the true Witness and therefore of the Word of God without the apperception of such a doctrine. Indeed, in its humanity and vulnerability such a doctrine might even be a serious hindrance to the hearing of His Word. Such a doctrine can explain, articulate and apply the Word of the cross and therefore the Word of God in human speech in a way which is more or less apposite, felicitous and helpful. In so doing it can attest it, inculcate it in specific concretions, and set it in the light of relative comprehensibility. But it cannot be a substitute for it. It cannot try to be itself this Word. Even though it be the purest doctrine, it is not this Word. To hear the Crucified and therefore God Himself is to hear Him, either with or without such a doctrine of this Word, and sometimes perhaps even in spite of it. Possibly the doctrine is of service, helping us to hear Him. But it cannot in any circumstances do more than this. It is good or bad to the degree that as genuine *doctrina* it points beyond itself and summons us to hear, not itself, but Him. Thus really to hear Him is to go beyond all doctrine and to hear that which doctrine as such can only intend, envisage and indicate, namely, that to which it can only " refer " (for, as we have said from the very first, we are dealing with the miraculous work of God Himself). The goal and yet also the limit of this reference is that with its help, or perhaps in spite of it, He Himself is heard. In every case, then, He Himself

§ 70. *The Falsehood and Condemnation of Man*

replaces it. Let us assume that we really heard Him when we spoke continually of what we heard or saw ; that we heard Him speak out of the silence of His death ; that we heard Him speak of the act of God in the reconciliation effected in Him, of the mystery of His self-offering and sacrifice, of the fellow-suffering of God as the mystery of this mystery, of the distance and proximity, the height and depth of God in this form of His suffering ; that we heard Him speak, at the point where only God can speak, of the things of which none other can speak save God. Let us assume that we heard Him. But if so, what we heard was immeasurably greater than all the indications with the help of which we have tried to understand and take account of the fact that we have heard, and of what we have heard. If so, it was the Crucified and therefore God Himself who spoke to us beyond all these and similar indications which could not do more than indicate. And if so, the power in which we heard, and to our own astonishment could hear, was not the power of these indications, explanations and descriptions, but His own power, the power of the Crucified and therefore of God Himself, the power of His own Word, which cannot be comprehended in any human word, which in its reality transcends all the words of human indication, which leaves them behind and judges them, yet also heals and orders them. If so, we did not empower ourselves by our little speaking, but were empowered by Him in the overflowing wealth of His speaking. If so, He spoke His truth to us, or better into us, in a way which is infinitely better than we could ever say it to ourselves even with the best will and the closest attention. If so, we no longer had the option of possible or obligatory openness to our own speaking or that of others as speaking concerning His truth. We apperceived it as those apperceived by it. The power of our hearing was simply the power of His speaking, as the power of His speaking became that of our hearing. It was the work of the Holy Spirit that we heard and therefore could hear.

This final sentence brings us to the point at which we may survey and sum up the whole of the third line of thought which we have now concluded and along which we have described Jesus Christ as the true Witness, and especially His speaking as such. It is in the work of the Holy Spirit that He is present in our sphere of time and history as this speaking Witness, that He strides through it as such, that He acts and operates in it, that He encounters us men of this sphere with His promise and claim. The work of the Spirit promised by Him, yet also continually promising for His own part, is the form in which He comes to us and is present with us here and now after the first form of His coming again in His resurrection from the dead and before its final form in His revelation at the goal and end of all history. In what has preceded we have more than once had to point to a presupposition the presence of which we could in no sense make the subject of theory or

1. *The True Witness*

calculation, and would be wrong to attempt to do so, because it is not a presupposition which even Christians can achieve of themselves, but one in which it can be only a matter absolutely and exclusively of God's free act of grace and revelation present in a way which we cannot control, though known and experienced by us in its accomplishment. This presupposition is the activity of the Holy Spirit. It is in this that Jesus Christ comes to us here and now, as the man who came once and then came again first in His resurrection from the dead, as the man of Gethsemane and Golgotha, as the Crucified. It is in this form that He is the truth, and so declares it that it is received as such. It is in this form that He speaks the Word of God and what He says is heard as such. It is in this form that He is present to us and active among and in us as the Prophet, the true Witness. In this form, or not at all! And it is in the work of the Holy Spirit that in this form He is the speaking truth, that He audibly speaks the Word of God, that He is active as the Prophet, the true Witness. The work of the Holy Spirit is distinguished from what are in their own way the real works of other very active spirits by the fact that in it Jesus Christ as the Crucified, and therefore the Word of God, and therefore the truth, speaks out and is declared and active. The Holy Spirit is simply but most distinctly the renewing power of the breath of His mouth which as such is the breath of the sovereign God and victorious truth. It is the power in which His Word, God's Word, the Word of truth, is not only in Him, but where and when He wills goes out also to us men, not returning to Him empty but with the booty or increase of our faith and knowledge and obedience, and not remaining with Him on its return but constantly going out again to us to bring back new gain, and thus establishing communication between Him and us and initiating a history of mutual giving and receiving. As Jesus Christ the Crucified speaks His Word as the Word of God, the Word of truth, in the power of this operation, He comes to us, acting as the Prophet and speaking as the true Witness. It is obvious that in this final development we are referred again to what we previously called the miraculous work of God which cannot be attained by any human contemplation or comprehension, thought or utterance, nor enclosed in any theory, namely, the majestic autonomy and freedom of His grace, which is the mystery of the existence and work of the true Witness. Confronted by Jesus Christ as the Witness existing and active in this mystery, the falsehood of sinful man is necessarily unmasked and disqualified.

We turn for a third time to the Book of Job, whose distinctive course we are relating secretly and indirectly to our own way. We shall have to do so a fourth time when in the second sub-section it will be our task to state and describe as such the falsehood discovered by the true Witness Jesus Christ as it emerges in its classical and sublimest form, i.e., as that of piety, in the speeches of the three friends of Job. But first we must again consider Job himself, the issue of his passion, the decision concerning the justice or injustice of the complaint so violently made by him and so tenaciously upheld in conversation with the friends. This is depicted at the end of the Book in the intervention of Yahweh, in His speeches, and then by way of confirmation in the resumption of the popular saga with its account of the rehabilitation and new blessing of Job. Yet it is also plainly intimated in certain elements in the preceding complaints of Job not so far considered.

We remember that the theme of Job's complaint was the change in the divine form which found concrete manifestation and expression in the blows of fate which he had suffered. God had obviously adopted this new form in exposing him to these blows. His wrath and curse had replaced His blessing. Where God had previously been the Friend and Helper of His elected and electing servant, He has now become his Enemy and Persecutor. Job does not doubt that he still has to do with the same God who had elected him, and whom he had elected, even in this dark portion of the history of his co-existence with God, even in this painful alteration of God's attitude towards him. Yet he cannot see to what degree he has to do so. His complaint thus rises against God in this hiddenness like the unceasing surge of the ocean against the sea-coast. Questioning, petition, protest and finally the cry of bitter resignation succeed one another. Rightly or wrongly ? As we have seen, an equal case can be made out on both sides, for the same utterances seem to support both views when read and understood in their context. In trying to hold fast to God, and actually holding fast to Him, as the One who acts in this way, how can he understand or acquiesce in the concealment in which He now encounters him, in His existence as *Deus absconditus* ? Yet how can he reject this concealment without making himself guilty, even in his clinging to the *Deus revelatus*, of knowing better than God, of being more just than He, of hurling defiance against God for the sake of God ? Both questions necessarily crowd in with equal force upon the reader of Job's speeches. In what the poet causes Job to say he is given no materials by which to decide. Obviously, it is not intended that such materials should be given. Job is depicted as in the straits of a dilemma from which he cannot escape. There is no way back as the friends recommend. But there is no way forward that he can see, though he would like to press on. Yet decision is plainly demanded. For it is necessary that Job should be in the right, even though he is also in the wrong, if in the continuation of the story he is to prove to be God's true witness against Satan, faithful to the law which he has accepted and moving forwards with God. The matter cannot be left in the undecided state which is plainly the situation at the end of Job's last speech in chapter 31, and which does not seem to be materially altered by the ensuing speeches of Elihu. If things were left like this, we could not know whether Job was right or wrong in relation to his three opponents. It might, of course, be suggested that in chapters 3-31 we have an independent text which really intends to leave matters like this, both as between Job and God and also as between Job and his friends, thus indicating the indissolubly problematic existential situation of man at peace and yet also at odds with God. But we cannot be satisfied with this if we consider the whole span of the Book. The overriding purpose of the whole is to show that this situation is intolerable and that it is in fact resolved. Whatever view we take of the interposition of the speeches of Elihu, we must agree that they themselves do not accomplish nor even prepare the way for this. In a way which is dramatically disruptive, or dramatically most effective, they merely prolong the existing stalemate. A decision is finally reached. Job shows himself to be the witness of Yahweh, taking the new step forwards with God. For all that he is so wrong in his complaints, he is right in the upshot, and he is wholly right in relation to his human opponents. In regard to them, he shows himself to be a witness to the truth, and they are revealed to be liars. But this decision is not reached in a new development in the thought and utterance of Job, though there are signs of

1. *The True Witness* 423

such a development. Nor is it reached in the finally illuminating verdict of a fourth or fifth human contributor to the discussion. It is reached when Yahweh Himself intervenes and His Word is uttered and received as spoken by Himself. It is reached when God ignores the three friends, and Elihu, and Job, and all that even Job has thought and said, and gives His own answer to His servant "out of the whirlwind" in two speeches which may originally have been independent but for all their distinction have the same common purpose ($38^{1f.}$ and $40^{7f.}$). And that it took the form it did is emphatically confirmed with no less popular than serious realism in the account of Job's rehabilitation and restoration in $42^{7f.}$. It is to be noted that Job did not pass through the straits of the dilemma. In his complaint he could only be the one who knew better and was more just at the cost of incorrigible defiance and therefore of putting himself in the wrong. He has now to confess that he is guilty of this. He is not shown to be right, therefore, by finally passing through the straits and thus being able to justify himself. He is shown to be right as Yahweh Himself comes striding through from the other side, as Yahweh Himself encounters him in the straits, as He answers his questioning, petition, protest and resignation, as He puts him in the wrong but in so doing acknowledges him to be faithful to and in accord with his election, thus justifying him, and doing so in a visible and tangible way, as the concluding narrative shows. As the recipient of the self-witness of God, as the one who is made worthy by His answer, as the one who is humbled yet also justified by Him, Job shows himself to be the man God had wagered he was in opposition to Satan, namely, His true witness.

Before considering the conclusion to which the story of Job is brought by the decision pronounced and fulfilled by Yahweh Himself, we must first cast a backward glance on the occasional but significant passages which in the middle of Job's complaints and without arresting them, though hardly in keeping with them, point forward to this final decision like lights which suddenly flash out and then disappear immediately. We shall first quote them directly. "Also now, behold, my witness is in heaven, and my record is on high. My cry goeth up to God, and mine eye looketh up with tears to him ; that he should decide between man and God, between him and his partner" (16^{19-21}). "Lay down now, put me in a surety with thee ; who else will strike hands with me ?" (17^3). Most famous of all: "I know that my *go'el* (advocate? avenger? redeemer?) liveth, and that he shall stand at the latter day upon the earth : and though after my skin worms destroy this body, yet shall I see God : whom I shall see for myself, and mine eyes shall behold, and not another" (19^{25-27}). Or again, some words which we have considered already, and in which Job voices the idea and request that God might shelter him from His wrath in the underworld and thus keep him safe until He later remembers him : "All the time of my service would I fulfil, until my relief came. Then shouldst thou call, and I would answer thee : thou shouldst have a desire to the work of thine hands. Thou shouldst number my steps, and not have regard to my sin. My transgression would be sealed up in a bag, and thou shouldst sew up mine iniquity" (14^{13-17}).

For a proper understanding of these passages, it is as well that we should take note of a development in 27^2 where Job introduces a speech (the text seems to be in confusion) which constitutes his final answer to Bildad, the youngest of his three opponents : "As God liveth, who hath taken away my judgment; and the Almighty, who hath vexed my soul." From this oath we see that the God who encounters him in this incomprehensible, strange, terrifying and hostile form is a God who lives, as is also apparent in the other passages, which speak of Him as living, as standing on the earth (19^{25}), as living in heaven (16^{19}), as being a Witness to Job, as being his only Guarantor (17^3), his Advocate, Avenger and Redeemer (19^{25}). But the fact that this God lives is what makes it impossible for Job, so long as breath remains in him, to yield to his friends and to cease his cycle of questioning, petition, protest and resignation, substituting deception

§ 70. *The Falsehood and Condemnation of Man*

instead at this painful point. Job cannot as it were look behind this God who acts towards him in this manner, or look away to another who gives him no cause for complaint. " Who else will strike hands with me ? " What he demands of God is not that He should make Himself known outside or alongside His unknowability, but in this unknowability; that He should show Himself a trusted Friend even in His hostility. The astonishing assumption of these utterances is that even as His Opponent He is still his Advocate and Guarantor, and therefore for him even as He is against him. In explanation it is thus better to refrain from following H. Lamparter (p. 108), who in reminiscence of Luther speaks of a flight from the " strange " to the " true " God, or S. Oettli (p. 59), who speaks of a cleavage in his idea of God, of an inspiration imparted to him in terms of which " the terrible enemy under whose strokes he is crushed cannot be the true God of righteousness," of his flight " from a God of terrors who sinks behind him to the God who must and will finally acknowledge him as his servant." Nor can we agree with Oettli again (p. 66) when he says that the God of wrath who pursues him under the guise of Satan dissolves into nothingness as an empty illusion. Nor can we accept the view of G. Hölscher that in these passages Job obviously penetrates behind the notion of God as an angry demonic being, or a mere God of force and might and justice, to a " deeper and more personal basis in God," to a " God of love and faithfulness." The remarkable feature in these passages, that which distinguishes them from those around as intimations of the speech of Yahweh Himself, is the very fact that Job is not contemplating a Satanic guise etc., but God Himself meeting him in darkness, terror and wrath, that it is at His hands that he suffers and yet to Him that he appeals and in Him that he seeks comfort. In this respect it is perhaps more apposite and helpful to recall the words of Goethe (in *Tasso*) than those of Luther : " And so at last the sailor lays firm hold, Upon the rock on which he had been dashed." The passages in 14^{13-15} and 19^{25-27}, the eschatological bearing of which we cannot discuss in this context, make it perfectly plain that Job is looking to the point where the obscurity of the divine rule encounters him at its most impenetrable, to the approaching darkness of his being in death, in the underworld, with the hope in c. 14 and the certainty in c. 19 that even there he will have to do with the God who holds His hand over him, seeing Him as his *go'el*, not through the spectacles of another, but with his own eyes. That this has taken place by the decisive Word of Yahweh is what he will confess expressly at the conclusion of the Book (42^5). In the same way Jacob-Israel had stood up against and struggled with the man who encountered him at the ford Jabbok and who wrestled with him until the breaking of the day : " I will not let thee go, except thou—mine opponent—bless me " ; and had finally been blessed by this opponent and could thus finally confess : " I have seen God face to face, and my life is preserved " (Gen. $32^{24f.}$). A flight from God to God ? We may accept the phrase. But if so, it means a flight from the God unknown in His unknowability to the God whom we hope or are sure is known in the same unknowability. There is thus no cleavage in Job's thinking about God ; there is fulfilment and unification. Among more recent expositors, it seems to me that R. de Pury (*Hiob, der Mensch in Aufruhr*, 1957, p. 23 f.) is the most perspicacious : " The remarkable thing about this Book is that Job makes not a single step of flight to a better God, but stays resolutely on the field of battle under the fire of the divine wrath. Although God treats him as an enemy, through the dark night and the abyss Job does not falter, nor invoke another court, nor even appeal to the God of his friends, but calls upon this God who crushes him. He flees to the God whom he accuses. He sets his confidence in God who has disillusioned him and reduced him to despair. . . . Without deviating from the violent assertion of his innocence and God's hostility, he confesses his hope, taking as his Defender the One who judges him, as his Liberator the One who throws him in prison, and as his Friend his mortal enemy."

1. *The True Witness*

This is a hard saying. But we should not soften it if we are to see and understand that at this point the distant but definite limit of Job's complaint comes into view in company with its final necessity. Job's complaint cannot cease as his accusation against the God who encounters him with hostility. It cannot set its own limit. It can never exhaust nor empty itself, and thus can only be endless. It is this, not only before these passages but after. What the passages tell us, however, is that in its immanent endlessness it can neither begin nor continue without clinging to the One to whom and against whom it is directed with the certainty, grounded in Him alone, of His decision not only against but also for the man who hopes and trusts in Him. Of His decision! Job's word in these passages is not the Word of God, and therefore it is not the taking of His decision. He can only keep his ear open for God Himself to speak His Word. He can only wait for God to take His decision. It is of this waiting with open ear that these passages speak in, with and under Job's complaint. But truly to wait with open ear he must not leap ahead. He must follow with complete openness the change in God's attitude towards him, and thus look to the point where God finds Himself here and now in relation to him on the basis of this change. He must thus look steadily into and not past the hostility with which God encounters him. It is only from the point where God finds Himself in relation to him, where his grief has its origin and his complaint its basis, that a limit is set both to his complaint and his grief. It is not set by the word and work of Job. It is not set, therefore, in these remarkable interruptions of his complaint. He hopes, yet also knows, that it will be set by the Word and work of the God who is now so hostile to Him, and that this will take place where and when and how God Himself decides. He knows this no less surely, indeed, more so, than he knows that his grief has its origin in His will, that his complaint has its basis and necessity in Him, and is not therefore to be abandoned. He looks to the one and only God who " even now " (16^{19}), even in the hostility of His attitude, is the same as He will be, who will set that limit in His own time and manner, who is thus his Witness, Advocate and Guarantor, who even now is for him as He is against him. In this way, and this way alone, Job is a real Israel, a witness of the truth, and as such also a witness of Jesus Christ.

From a different standpoint, are we perhaps to regard the poem on wisdom in $28^{1 \cdot 17}$ as another intimation of the decision to be awaited from God Himself ? It is at least worth considering in virtue of its originality, its poetic power, and the impressive concentration of its message. It certainly does not belong to the original body of the central poetic section of the Book, but has been inserted from another source. We have also to ask whether it was really the intention in the final redaction to include it at this point, ostensibly as part of the concluding speech of Job, since in what is in any case a very confused context from the literary standpoint it has no obvious connexion with what precedes or follows. But however that may be, the reason for its inclusion is not difficult to see. It is much easier, indeed, than in the case of the speeches of Elihu. It is clearly to be regarded as a preparation for the decision towards which the Book is moving to the extent that its message consists plainly and simply in the statement that wisdom is accessible to God alone (with the corollary that it can come from Him alone), wisdom being here understood, as it was intended to be understood in the context in which the poem is set, quite concretely as the possibility of giving to the complaint of Job a true and appropriate answer which will both establish and yet also limit it. For God alone knows and can therefore give this answer. That to which man may profitably attain by his own investigation and activity, along paths where neither the eye nor the foot of even the most gifted animals can follow him, is indicated in vv. 1–11 in a vivid description of ancient mining as obviously known at first hand by the author. " But where shall wisdom be found ? and where is the place of understanding ? Man knoweth not the way thereto ; neither is it found in the land of the living " (vv. 12–13). It cannot

§ 70. The Falsehood and Condemnation of Man

be purchased by even the most precious things in the earth (vv. 15-19). Hence the refrain in v. 20: " Whence then cometh wisdom, and where is the place of understanding ? " " The depth saith, It is not in me : and the sea saith, It is not with me," we have learned already from v. 14. And now we are told : " It is hid from the eyes of all living, and kept close from the fowls of the air. Destruction and death say, We have only heard the fame thereof with our ears " (vv. 21-22). In a word, it is inaccessible to man or any creature. Positively, the exclusive statement may be made : " God understandeth the way thereof, and he knoweth the place thereof " (v. 23). He has used it indeed in His work of creation (vv. 24-26) : " Then did he see it, and declare it ; he prepared it, yea, and searched it out " (v. 27). This is the message of the poem. In contrast to the other products of the wisdom literature, it speaks neither of the nature of wisdom nor of its theoretical nor practical significance. It does not praise nor commend it. In the original form it does not seem even to contain the wellknown saying that the fear of the Lord is the beginning of wisdom (Prov. 1^7, 9^{10} ; Ps. 111^{10}), which for all its intrinsic merits has here a conventional ring and therefore weakens the effect, having been probably added as v. 28 by an apprehensive scribe. What the poem itself says is simply that wisdom and its place and way are known to God alone, that they are accessible to and may be controlled by none but Him. In the depth of the dilemma to which the previous history of Job had led him, and as a warning against further speculations along the lines of the answers attempted by the three friends, this statement is quite meaningful in the context, and understood as a parallel to and amplification of the passages already adduced it might well be regarded as a saying of Job himself. It certainly maintains at this point that there can and will be only one way out of the dilemma, and that this will not be from below upwards but from above downwards, not as the way of man but solely as the way of God.

Thus prepared, we come to the heart of the matter, the act of God in which the decision is made in cc. 39-42. It does not consist in God's lifting of the visor as it were, in His reversing the change in His attitude to Job, in His transforming the unknown form in which He encounters him as an alien and enemy back into the form in which He was previously known to him. God made no mistake in the step forwards which He took in the history of His co-existence with this man. Hence He does not need to withdraw. It is not merely that after the raging of the sea and howling of the wind the welcome face of the sun shines forth again. It is not merely, in even more banal terms, that everything turns out for the best. Certainly the story seems to have a happy ending in $42^{7f.}$, when there is an apparent reversal and the three friends as well as Job are blessed again. But it is obviously not the purpose of the Book of Job merely to tell how God first caused Job to become poor and forsaken and sick, but then made him rich again and gave him more children and restored his health (which is not even mentioned). The new and greater joy which follows his grief is only the concrete attestation, necessary in its own way, of the fact that the complaint of Job, which poses the problem of the Book, is effectively answered by God, that it thus reaches its limit, that its injustice is revealed by God, but also the justice in its injustice. The act of Yahweh in which this takes place, however, consists in the fact that, without lifting His visor and prior to any change in the fate of Job, He speaks to him. There is no theophany at the conclusion of the Book of Job, even though we read in 42^5 (cf. 19^{22}) : " Now mine eye seeth thee." He has seen God as God has spoken to him and he has heard His Word. And in distinction from the words of the three friends, the Word of God heard by him does not consist in an interpretation, in a doctrinaire explaining away, in an illuminating apprehension of the strange and terrible form in which He has encountered him. On the contrary, we read that " the Lord answered Job out of the whirlwind " (38^1 ; 40^1). This " out of the whirlwind " has been regarded as the addition of a redactor suggested by the depiction of an approaching storm in the preceding last speech of Elihu

1. *The True Witness* 427

(37¹⁴ᶠ·). But even if this is true, it still emphasises the fact that the answer of God does not mean that God suddenly reveals Himself to Job as the " God of love and faithfulness " or something similar. There is no such self-interpretation in the content of either of the two speeches introduced by these words. It is not in removal of His concealment but from within it, not in setting aside His unknowability but (according to all our previous findings) both in it and in confirmation of it, that God reveals and makes Himself known to Job. That this God whom Job had sought in vain in his sequence of questioning, petition, protest and resignation now finds His accuser; that He who is vainly asked to speak now speaks of Himself, this is the act of Yahweh which sets Job in the wrong in his complaints and accusations. It is to be noted, however, that as God persuades and convinces and overpowers him, as He makes Himself known in His unknowability and thus sets him in the wrong, He also shows him to be right both before Himself and before men. As God says of Himself what He does say in His speeches, and as Job allows to be said to him what he may and must allow to be said, he is put in his place by God, and yet, because it is God who does this, he is put in a good place. The equilibrium of his right and wrong is broken. He is put in the wrong, but what is more important he is decisively, subsequently and effectively put in the right as the one who has persistently waited with open ears to hear this, so that even in respect of his very wrong complaint and accusation his character as the servant of God which he was from the very first, and did not cease to be, is recognised. Thus the perennial nature of the relationship of the election and the covenant between God and himself, himself and God, is revealed and made public by the One who is Lord and Judge in this relationship.

Do we have here the operation of a *Deus ex machina* as in so many colourful dramatic fables? Are we dealing with a God who is sometimes otherwise engaged or simply forgetful but finally resumes His divine activity, or a God who like the sea-god Neptune in Mozart's *Idomeneo* finally softens in view of the confusion caused by His wrath and thus takes appropriate action to restore the situation? But Yahweh does not need to be carried by any *machina* or brought on the scene from without. He was there from the very first. Indeed, He was always the dominating figure. He does not need to remember Job. He was never otherwise occupied than with His servant. He does not need to change His attitude towards him. He has only to speak to him. He has only to make Himself known as the One He was and is even and precisely in this alien form, as the One who has never left the scene but always dominates it. That Job needs Him to do this is what constitutes his wrong. Surely he comes from the divinely given knowledge of God as the One whom he has chosen. Surely it is neither possible nor permissible for him as the elect of God to become the accuser of God in repetition and expression of his knowledge of God. Yet the fact that as this accuser he still hoped and was certain that God would make Himself known afresh and thus do what He now did; the fact that in despair he called on God to do this, and waited with open ears for His answer—this constituted the right of Job subsequently and effectively recognised to be such. God has only to speak to Job, to answer him, and to do so in such a way that He makes Himself known as the One He always was and is and will be, for a distinction to be made between his right and wrong, and the right to triumph unequivocally over the wrong. And God did speak to Job. He did answer him. He did make Himself known. This is the act of Yahweh at the conclusion of the Book of Job.

There is reason to underline the fact that it is the act of *Yahweh*. It is obvious, and cannot be an accident, that this proper name of God in the Old Testament, the name of the covenant God of Israel, is predominant in the explanatory opening chapters (1–2), being always used except in a few more general references, but that in the whole of the central section, whether in the speeches of the friends and Elihu or even in the complaints of Job himself, it is replaced by the generic

§ 70. *The Falsehood and Condemnation of Man*

names Elohim and Shaddai, only to recur quite suddenly in the introductory verses to the divine speeches in 38¹ and 40⁶ and to become predominant again in c. 42. Thus Yahweh, the Lord of Israel and its history, the God of Abraham, Isaac and Jacob, is the God whose servant is Job the Edomite. Yahweh is the One who makes the transaction with Satan which is the first turning-point in the history of Job, and who speaks the Word of decision which is the second. Yahweh is the One who finally proclaims the right of Job and transforms his great grief into even greater joy. Yahweh is the ruling Subject in the history of Job. But He is this unquestioningly in the predication indicated by the names Elohim and Shaddai. Yahweh, the Author of the special election of Israel and also of Job, is God, and therefore the Most High and the Almighty who is both illimitable and incomparable. It is not in relation to the Subject Yahweh that the problem of Job arises. He would not be Job, the elect of Yahweh, if there could be any problem in this respect. As this Subject God is always known to him. It is in relation to Him that he knows and clings to the fact that in what befalls him he has to do with God. It is on the basis of this knowledge that he disputes with God. The disputing or problem, however, arises from Yahweh's being as Elohim and Shaddai, from the majestic and almighty operation of Yahweh in relation to him. In this predication and activity which are undoubtedly intrinsic and proper to Yahweh, He is unknowable to him. In respect of this predication and work he does not know how far he has to do with God in what befalls him. The right of Job is his unwearying demand for the self-declaration of Yahweh even in this being and action of His as the Most High and the Almighty. His wrong is his repudiation of the Most High and the Almighty which, since Yahweh is the Most High and the Almighty, and unknown to Job is acting as such, is necessarily directed against Him as the One concealed in this predication and work. And the answer which Yahweh gives to Job necessarily consists in the fact that Yahweh makes Himself known as Elohim-Shaddai, as the One who even in the enigmatic character of the rule of His majesty and omnipotence is still the God of the particular election of Israel and therefore of Job, and therefore the Lord with whom he cannot dispute (39³¹ᶠ·) and whom he cannot try to set right, but in face of whom he can only keep silence. " I am the Almighty God " (Gen. 17¹)—I and none other. Far from the Word uttered by Yahweh provoking or even fostering division in Job's thought of God, it restores and re-establishes the unity which is so severely threatened. The divine Subject acknowledges in His Word His intrinsic and distinctive predication and work, and thus gives Job the freedom to abandon as inappropriate and indeed impossible for the elect of Yahweh the accusation against this predication and work which is unwittingly directed against Yahweh Himself. It is for this reason that the divine speech at the conclusion of the Book of Job is to be described emphatically as the act of *Yahweh*.

As is apparent not merely from the new beginning in 40⁶ but from the minor variations in theme, we have here two different compositions which have been brought together from obviously different sources. (The question suggests itself whether there did not once exist a whole corpus of Job literature of which a selection has now been assembled in the present Book.) The fact that God speaks, and that He does so with Job himself, ignoring the three friends, is important enough in itself. In an existentialist poem of our own age He would no doubt have made His impression upon Job, if at all, by means of an unbroken and majestic silence. But this cannot be the case between Yahweh and His elect. As Job spoke urgently to Yahweh, so He now speaks most impressively to Job. Yet we cannot agree with commentators (e.g., S. Oettli, p. 115 and H. Lamparter, p. 230) who seem more or less inclined to regard the fact that God spoke to him as more important than what He says according to the poems. How can we estimate the value of a Word without observing its content ? There is, of course, an understandable urge to try to evade the Word at issue by devalu-

1. The True Witness

ing its content in favour of its actual utterance. What attentive readers of Job, already startled by so many strange features in the earlier chapters, are not plunged into new and serious bewilderment when they come to chapters 39-41 ? We can only agree with R. de Pury (p. 32 f.) : " This answer raises more questions than it answers. . . . Can we imagine using it at the bed of a dying man, or in the home of a woman who has lost her husband and children ? . . . We are disappointed. . . . Is God making fun of Job and us ? Or is the author of the Book of Job making fun of God ? " What we read is at a first glance poles apart from what we might have expected Yahweh in His identity with Elohim-Shaddai to undertake by way of self-interpretation in answer to the complaint and accusation of Job. Mere counter-questions are hurled at the questioner Job. Nor are these theological in nature. They are questions of natural information filled out and underlined by express descriptions. In the first speech (cc. 38-39) they concern the sphere of heaven and earth, from the depths of the sea to the Pleiades and Orion, and including various rather strangely selected examples from ordinary zoology. In the second (40-41), hovering on the borders between zoology and mythology, they concern such monsters as Behemoth and Leviathan, which are described in such terms that with a little good will we may accept the common view of expositors that they are based on the hippopotamus and the crocodile. But what is the meaning and relevance of all this ?

In the first instance, we can only say, as indeed we must if we keep to the text, that Job apparently grasped its very practical significance for him. There can be no doubt that he understands and accepts these strange addresses as an answer to his question, and an answer which has such radical force that he finds the complaint completely exploded by them and therefore abandons it. There can be no doubt that according to the view of the poem God makes Himself known to him thereby even in His unknowability, that Yahweh is completely revealed in His identity with Elohim-Shaddai, his bitterest enemy as the Friend for whom he has asked so long in vain. He replies as follows to the questions addressed to him by God in these speeches : " Behold, I am vile ; what shall I answer thee ? I will lay mine hand upon my mouth. Once have I spoken ; but I will not answer : yea, twice, but I will proceed no further " (40^{4-5}) ; and when he has heard the speech on Behemoth and Leviathan : " I know that thou canst do every thing and that no thought can be withholden from thee . . . therefore have I uttered that I understood not ; things too wonderful for me, which I knew not. . . . I have heard of thee by the hearing of the ear : but now mine eye seeth thee. Wherefore I abhor myself, and repent in dust and ashes " (42^{2-6}). We thus have an unconditional surrender of the same Job who could not and would not yield a handsbreadth to the highly theological argumentations of his friends. What is there to enforce such a change ? Where has his eye seen the Lord ? It is in the cosmology and zoology presented with such continual questions, in the first animal book with its successive pictures of lions and ravens, in the hippopotamus or crocodile of the second address. And it is his surrender in face of this divine revelation which is graciously accepted by God, which is recognised as a confirmation of his faithfulness, and this with such retroactive force that later, in spite of his admitted wrong, he is justified even in relation to his complaint. As distinct from his friends, he, the servant of Yahweh, has spoken what is right about God (42^8). And he has done so after his instruction and conversion through these addresses.

As readers of the Book, we must obviously resolve to follow at all costs the understanding with which Job unmistakeably heard these addresses. If we fail to understand the Book at this critical point, we must admit that we do not understand it at all. But what is there to understand ?

A not unimportant indication of the content of the Word of God here spoken is perhaps to be found in its very surprising form. Theological instruction in the most pregnant sense is to be imparted, namely, instruction by God, and

430 § 70. *The Falsehood and Condemnation of Man*

therefore by the One who is supremely, properly and in the long run uniquely competent to give it, concerning the supreme and deepest theme of theology, i.e., God Himself. But this incomparable theological Doctor refuses to handle this incomparable theological theme with the gravity which we might think suitable to His person and to the subject. He might speak of Himself on the same level as Job and the friends, namely, on that of ecclesiastical and academic theology. He might preach and lecture, and how well He could do it! But He does not have to do this. He has the transcendent freedom to speak very differently, and the humour to make powerful use of this freedom. He does not begin to operate on the expected level. He moves off at what seems to be an unexpected tangent to every thoughtful person. He permits Himself to ignore all that has been said about Him. But there is a deep seriousness in His humour, for in so doing He succeeds—for Job at least—in speaking intelligibly and convincingly. What sovereignty is already expressed in the fact that this Teacher can manage to speak in this way, and to do so with such resounding success!

But as we further consider the form we note that this sovereignty is also expressed in the fact that in accordance with His power to do so He chooses to speak of Himself by not speaking of Himself, revealing the mystery without even indicating that it is His mystery. In the boldest of digressions, He speaks of very different things, of heaven and earth and sea, and more specifically of ordinary and extraordinary specimens from the animal kingdom. He lets these other things speak, and causes them to speak, not in the form of natural theology, but simply and yet eloquently of themselves. He obviously counts upon it that they belong so totally to Him, that they are so subject to Him and at His disposal, that in speaking of themselves they will necessarily speak of Him and His mystery. He is so sure of them as His creatures—as sure as He is of Himself—that He has only to open the great book of nature and show Job a few pages to be sure at once of the service which the creatures will quite simply render Him in His self-manifestation. They have only to declare their own existence and nature and they speak indirectly but very effectively of Him, not merely indicating His mystery but revealing it. For it is not they who do it, but God who enables them to speak in His own self-declaration, summoning in the first address the dry land and the sea, the dawn of day and the night of death, the snow, the hail, the rain, the dew, the clouds and the lightning, the lion, the raven, the coney, the wild ass and ox, the stork, the horse and the falcon, and then in the second address those two formidable monsters. These all speak for Him. God causes them to do so. It is a hazardous venture perhaps, but God undertakes it and succeeds. He is such a sovereign theological Doctor that to speak of Himself He can be silent concerning Himself, and even cause His creatures to speak concerning themselves rather than Him, and yet in so doing succeed in speaking with irresistible clarity and cogency concerning Himself, so that Job at least understands immediately and exactly what He has said concerning Himself.

Finally, the form of this Word of God indicates the content in the fact that the declaration consists only in questions expressly or tacitly directed to Job. He is addressed and taken seriously by God as a free man. He is not therefore overwhelmed nor belaboured nor smitten to the ground " in a piercing sense of his own nothingness," as represented in more than one exposition. He is not confounded either by the sight of heaven or ocean, or by Behemoth or Leviathan. What is said to him is not enforced upon him in an authoritarian and dictatorial manner. He must say himself, first what is his own position in relation to the natural and animal kingdom displayed before him, then, as he reflects on this, what is his place in relation to God, and finally and decisively in the context of the present issue who and what God is in relation to him. God thus answers Job's question to him by inviting and requiring him to answer the question put with such strange indirectness. He answers Job's appeal to him by making an

1. *The True Witness* 431

appeal of His own to Job. The Word spoken to him does not merely come to him, or pass over him and away like a monstrous roller. It comes right into him. Indeed, it is to be uttered by himself as his own word, as the confession of his own heart and lips. God allows everything to depend on this recognition and confession. What a risk! Job might do no more than gape at the book of nature unfolded before him. He might perhaps find aesthetic enjoyment in some of the forms, and be shocked by others. He might simply close his eyes in disgust. He might make nothing of it all or misunderstand it. He might make no answer at all, or only the answer of silence, to the question put to him. God would then have wasted His time with him. He would have beaten the air. The lesson would have failed. No decision would have been reached. For it was essential to such a decision that Job himself should answer, and answer correctly. Otherwise he would have resumed his old complaint and accusation, and could have continued it *ad infinitum*. Indeed, he would have had to do so. At the end of the Book God Himself would then have been the true and great loser. But so great is the sovereignty of the Teacher who undertakes this instruction that He does not fear this risk. So free is God that He dares to have dealings with the free man Job. We might almost say that He again wagers on Job and wins again as Job's answer shows.

The content of cc. 38–41 corresponds to this form. In what they declare, Yahweh affirms His freedom in face of Job. Yahweh is also Elohim-Shaddai, the Most High, the Almighty. As the Friend of Job, his sworn Covenant-partner, He is also the Sovereign on whose election and faithfulness he may and must rely, of whom he cannot ask enough, but who has reserved His own total rights in respect of the mode of His rule over and with him, so that it is not to be expected of Him that He will necessarily encounter him in accordance with his own thoughts and ideas and standards and desires and presuppositions. As His elect, Job can only serve him " for nought " (1^9), i.e., with no claim that His rule should conform to some picture which he has formed of it. He is necessarily untrue to his election if on the ground of the non-conformity of God's rule with the picture which he has of His wisdom, righteousness and love, he resists what these actually are in accordance with the nature and will and counsel of God. Yahweh has the freedom to encounter him as he has done according to Job's complaint, in that alien and hostile form. In it He does not cease to be, nor is He any less, his Friend, his sworn Covenant-partner. This is what is indirectly declared in cc. 38–41 in the form of mere descriptions of the cosmos created by Yahweh, who is also Elohim-Shaddai, and now summoned to bear testimony to Him.

The cosmos which Yahweh calls upon to testify is, of course, an echo of the voice of His own Word concerning His autonomy of power which is operative in these forms and in which He evades the power of man even though the latter feels it, His immanent autonomy of purpose which man cannot catch or follow in his own explanations, even though he attempts to do so, and His most concrete autonomy of will, respect for which is the presupposition of all the realisation of man's freedom in his own sphere. In this autonomy He always in some degree encounters, confronts and opposes man in a way which is sinister, strange, disquieting and even terrifying. He does not ask for his understanding, agreement or applause. On the contrary, He simply asks that he should be content not to know why and to what end he exists, and does so in this way and not another. He simply asks that he should admit that it is not he who plans and controls. He simply asks that he should concede that he has nothing to do with his course and direction. For what does he know of the foundation of heaven and earth, of the alternation of day and night, light and darkness, sunshine and rain, of the feeding of the young lions and ravens, of the purpose and possibilities of such animals as the mountain goat, the wild ass and ox, the stork and falcon, which simply roam or fly at large and defy all attempts at domestication or practical use, of the horse too, which was in the same category in ancient Israel, snorting and champing, " swallowing the ground " in the gallop, leaping all obstacles and only the more enraged by hostile trumpets ? Finally, what can he say if he comes up against Behemoth or Leviathan, created by God no less than he (40^{15}) ? " Will he make many supplications unto thee ? will he speak soft words unto thee ? will he make a covenant with thee ? wilt thou take him for a servant for ever ? Wilt thou play with him as with a bird ? or wilt thou bind him for thy maidens ? Shall the companions make a banquet of him ? shall they part him among the merchants ? . . . Lay thine hand upon him . . . thou shalt do it no more. Behold, the hope of him is in vain : who then is able to stand before him ? " ($41^{3f.}$). This, then, is the message of the cosmos. It is to be noted that what is brought forward in these speeches of Yahweh is not His blind superiority to man, but His questioning whether man can really think that the cosmos is his cosmos and belongs and listens to him. Can he really think that it is ordered according to his ideas, wishes, purposes and plans, that it must be the *theatrum* of his *gloria* and guarantee his *felicitas* or at least his *securitas* ? Not of itself, but as God causes it to speak as His creation, the cosmos puts to man a question which he can only answer in the negative. The result is that within the created world man is confronted by innumerable great and small factors in face of the autonomy of which he must bow for good or evil, respecting the mystery of creation itself and thus being enabled to live as a genuinely free man within it as within a house which God Himself has built and assigned to him.

Here then, uttered and audible only between the lines in cc. 38-41, not as the declaration and question of the cosmos, but clear and perceptible in this as its echo, and immediately and accurately accepted and understood by Job, the Word of God is spoken. Beyond all the majesty and power which are only lent to creation, but reflected in them, Yahweh Himself is seen directly in it by Job. He is seen in the autonomous power and purpose and will of the Creator and Lord of all this creation which has its own power and purpose and will, as the free Sovereign, as Elohim-Shaddai, whose good-pleasure is the source and meaning and measure and limit of all wisdom, righteousness and love, as the One who in His freedom has elected Job, and been elected by him. It is He whom Job hears in the echo of the voice of creation, and sees in the mirror of its forms : He whose goodness is sovereign, not occasioned nor conditioned by Job in respect of its mode or exercise, nor to be judged by Him, since it wells up of itself alone, and shapes itself alone, and for this reason is true and genuine and eternal goodness, the goodness of the unshakeably faithful God of the covenant. What He asks Job is whether He has ever known Him except as this free God, even when His ways with him seemed to be more clear and agreeable and pleasant than they are now. Has he forgotten that He is this free God ? Has he not asked after Him as such ? If not, how could he as the elect ask after Him as the electing God ? Has he not complained before Him and to Him ? But what right had he to accuse when he could not speak but only be silent before the question of the wild ass or Leviathan ? What better knowledge or what better wisdom, righteousness and love could he suggest than that given by Yahweh ? If he could only close his mouth in face of the mystery of creation, could he open it in face of the mystery of Yahweh its Creator and Lord otherwise than to sing His praise ?

This is Yahweh's answer to Job out of the whirlwind. This is His appeal to Job's freedom to know His freedom and to love and praise Him in His freedom as Elohim-Shaddai. Has Job maintained his freedom to do this, his freedom for the freedom of God, when God's hand lay heavily upon him and he did not know how to come before Him except with complaint and accusation ? Has he demonstrated it ? Yes or no ? This explanation of Yahweh's question is not given, of course, in the texts which reproduce His speeches. But we are forced to give it in view of what we are told later of the attitude of Job and

1. *The True Witness* 433

that of God. In the texts we are simply given the questions hurled at Job in relation to his competence as regards the mystery, i.e., the autonomous power and purpose and will of the cosmos. We are given no express declaration of Job in relation to his incompetence as regards this mystery of creation. It is tacitly presupposed that he sees and confesses this. Above all, however, the texts do not tell us that Job was given any explicit theological instruction. That the freedom of the Creator is implied by the independence of the cosmos is an obvious conclusion, but it is not even indicated in either of the two divine speeches. They leave the matter open. It is clearly for Job to draw the conclusion, namely, to confess that as he is incompetent in respect of the independence of the cosmos, so he is in respect of the freedom of Yahweh and His rule as Elohim-Shaddai, and thus to confess that he is the faithful and free elected covenant-partner of Yahweh. And it is an astonishing fact, in view of the fulness of the preceding speeches, that we are told practically nothing concerning the corresponding reflection and confession of Job. There is nothing more palpable than the brief indications in $40^{3f.}$ and $42^{1f.}$. The reader is simply confronted by the fact that in and with the strange answer of Yahweh, conceived and formulated in cosmological, zoological and mythological terms and consisting in pure questions, the long awaited decision in the case of Job is taken. He is confronted by the fact that at a single leap as it were Job has been radically instructed and converted theologically, not only accepting the independent features of the cosmos and admitting his incompetence in respect of them, but acquiescing in God's freedom towards him. Above all, he is confronted by the fact that in spite of all the wrong which Job has committed and confessed, God recognises him as His servant who has remained faithful to Him and proved his faithfulness afresh in this very admission. He is thus confronted by the fact that Job has not really lost but maintained his freedom to know Yahweh's freedom towards him, and demonstrated it by admitting the wrong of his accusation. In other words, Yahweh Himself is justified, or rather justifies Himself, in the confidence which He put in him. He did not err when He counted upon it that even in the most painful experience of His majesty and power, even in the most bitter complaint and corresponding accusation, Job would still cling to Him and not cease to invoke Him as His Witness, Pledge and Advocate. He did not err when He was confident that as the free God He could deal with him as a free man, and thus expect him to hear and understand and take to heart His Word even in that strange and bizarre form, even in its concealment in the self-declarations of creation. Finally, He did not err when, again respecting his human freedom, He dared to speak it in the form of a question which he himself must answer. In all these things, in His whole demonstration and use of His royal freedom, Yahweh maintained and practised His own right against Job, yet also for him and through him, even in Job's realisation and decision, suddenly and promptly induced by His Word, that he must give Him the glory as the free God, that he must bow to the rule of His freedom, and that in this very submission he must be, and continue to be, His faithful yet free man, His elect and genuine covenant-partner. Note that he must continue to be. He has been, for otherwise he would not have been capable of this realisation and decision. Even in his great trial, even in doing wrong, he has been. He stumbled, but he did not fall. His realisation and decision were a repetition and confirmation of the position in which he was set by Yahweh in relation to Him, and which he never left. Yahweh wagered on him, and did not lose but won. Hence it was essential that there should be a confirmation of his right in simple confirmation of the choice to which Yahweh remained unshakeably true even in the strange form in which He encountered Job. The final passages of the Book of Job confront us with this complex of facts. They do not analyse it. They do not show the sequence and relationship. They simply maintain that the step forwards in the history of the reciprocal co-existence of God and Job, which is what is at issue in all that precedes, is finally taken and manifested in the fact that God spoke to Job and Job heard Him. They simply narrate this event. Thus the circle closes as it opened, namely, with man's liberation by and for the free God : by the free God, since it is He who is the Witness speaking against Job yet also for him ; and for the free God, since Job, set in the wrong by Him yet also in the right, proves to be the faithful witness of this God.

2. THE FALSEHOOD OF MAN

In this context, the falsehood of man does not interest us as a moral phenomenon and problem, but centrally as a spiritual, or rather as a supremely unspiritual and anti-spiritual phenomenon and problem, as the disguise or mask which the man of sin at once assumes when he is confronted by Jesus Christ the true Witness, and which is torn off again in the course of this encounter. The falsehood of man is the great enemy which resists the divine promise declared in the prophetic work of Jesus Christ, but which is at once smitten and routed by the immanent power of this promise, the power of the resurrection of Jesus Christ. We do it too great honour if we hesitate to say at once that it is the mask which is immediately torn from the face of the man of sin when Jesus Christ has dealings with him, that it is the enemy which succumbs at once to the power of the divine promise. On the other hand, we must certainly do it the honour of taking a sharp look at it even though it is only the impotent counterpart of the divine act of revelation in process of fulfilment in Jesus Christ. For we need to be warned against what is in practice the imminent rather than the remote danger of confusing this divine act with the act of the man of sin which is falsehood in this encounter, and as such something much more evil and dangerous than lying in the purely moralistic sense. All the wickedness and folly of man in this time of ours between the first and the final forms of the coming again of Jesus Christ, in this age of the Holy Spirit, and all the affliction which he brings upon himself in consequence, find as it were their climax in this phenomenon and problem, in the falsehood of man, in its specific form as the untruth which impotently yet very really opposes the truth of reconciliation, of the covenant, of the justifying and sanctifying grace of God. The falsehood of man to which we must now turn is the untruth of man in relation to the truth of Jesus Christ encountering him.

A first and provisional affirmation must be that it consists in a movement of evasion. It thus presupposes man's distant or closer encounter with Jesus Christ and His truth. It cannot take form in a vacuum, or generally, but only in relation to Him. But it does take form in relation to Him. As the knowledge of faith and love and hope is possible and actual only in relation to Him, it is only in the same relation, as tares in the same field as the wheat, that falsehood arises. At an earlier point we called it the specifically Christian

2. The Falsehood of Man

form of sin. What we meant was that it is the form in which sin occurs in the Christian age which begins with the resurrection of Jesus Christ and which is determined by the action of the Holy Spirit and teleologically by the outcome of this action in the final appearance of Jesus Christ. It is the form of sin which properly speaking is possible and powerful only in this age. It takes place as man desires and attempts to avoid Jesus Christ as the true Witness encountering him. Man would rather escape this encounter. He fears the One who encounters him and the implications of the encounter. He starts back from what it will mean not to be his own but to belong to this Saviour and Lord, to be a man reconciled to God, to live in covenant with Him, to be justified and sanctified only but very really by the grace of God. He fears the upshot of all this. And so he thinks that he can and should evade the One who attests it all to him. It is to be noted (1) that in relation to the twofold act of the invasion of truth and the powerful rise of the knowledge of truth, it is an attempt to resist the former and to arrest and suppress the latter. It is to be noted (2) that it arises with an existing realisation of the significance of this twofold act. It is to be noted (3) that it arises on the presupposition that, since it is quite useless to try to offer any direct resistance to this twofold act in frontal opposition to the truth and suppression of its knowledge, the only possibility is that of evading the true Witness, of attempting to escape by flight the forcible impact and superiority of the truth and what it involves. Falsehood has no great solidity in this encounter. From the very first, it must shape its action in accordance with that of the truth, and not *vice versa*.

But the movement of evasion which man executes is remarkable and artful and yet also practicable enough. Strictly speaking, he only desires and attempts to execute it. Evasion means trying to find another place where the truth can no longer reach or affect him, where he is secure from the invading hand of its knowledge, and from its implications. But he obviously knows—and this is the further witness which he must involuntarily give to the truth even as the liar he is and the doer of untruth—that he cannot really escape it, that there is no such place. He must obviously be prepared for the fact that the true Witness is also superior to the extent that, having once encountered him, He will follow him to this new place and there set him in the same dilemma. The falsehood of man would be almost innocent in its gullibility and dilettantism, and would certainly not be the true and mature falsehood which anticipates real success, if man attempted to evade the encounter with that Witness and His testimony merely by pretending that nothing had happened and occupying himself with other interests and concerns. The serious and tenacious evader lurking in us all knows quite well that he must face the truth, that untruth can do its work only in face of the truth. But how can it pretend both to face the truth and to evade it? The discovery and undertaking of evasion even in face of the truth is the real masterpiece and artistic triumph of falsehood. The man of sin who really thinks realistically and perspicaciously asks himself why he should not try to employ the truth itself, and the knowledge of the truth, in the evasion of its attack and seizure of control. If it cannot be overcome, if it cannot be effectively resisted, if its knowledge cannot be arrested, and if there is no place in which to be rid of it, then it might well be the solution to canalise and transform its power. Hence he will not close his ears to it. He cannot do so, for it is already in his ears. But he will hear it only as he chooses to do so. He will not negate it. On the contrary, he will confirm it emphatically. But he will confirm it only in the sense in which he can regard it as tolerable and useful. He will understand and approve and grasp and champion it, but only in the form of a picture in the colours and contours of which it is divested of the distinctive menace which caused him to start back from it, only in a character in which it seems to be brought under his control, and promises to become his willing and powerful servant, consoler and helper. This is how falsehood speaks. This is the view of the man of sin. He does not question the truth. He does not oppose to it any antithesis. He does not persecute it. Nor does he ignore it. These are innocuous and irrelevant preparatory stages or accompanying phenomena of his real enterprise, or violent later reactions when it fails. In his real enterprise he kisses his Master as Judas did in Gethsemane. He is not against the truth, but with it and for it, appealing to it with sincerity and profundity and enthusiasm, constituting himself its diligent pupil and strict teacher, making it his business to defend and propagate and magnify it. He sets up a theoretical and practical system of truth. He forms parties in favour of truth. He establishes fronts on behalf of truth. He founds schools and academies of truth. He celebrates days and even whole weeks of truth. He organises formal campaigns for truth. He is so active in the cause of truth that compared with him Jesus Christ the true Witness seems to be only a waif and bungler who must surely be glad that He has found a patron and advocate to support Him so skilfully and powerfully. Surely, it is a masterly way of escape when man succeeds, or thinks he succeeds, in handling the truth by facing it as he must, and yet at the same time avoiding it, namely, by changing or transposing it into a translation of his own, into an improved edition, in which it looks most deceptively like itself, and yet by a hardly noticeable alteration of key and accent and origin and goal it is no longer itself, but has become the truth which is mastered by him instead of the truth which masters him, being given a pretty but very effective muzzle, so that it can still give a muffled bark but can no longer bite. To be sure, the liar does not deny the truth. He does this only when he is a beginner, or has grown feeble with age and enters his second childhood. In his prime the liar confesses the truth with the greatest emphasis and solemnity. He accepts the truth of God, the truth of man, Christian truth. The only thing is that it has become untruth, since in his mouth it can only be the truth which is taken in hand and inspired and directed by him, and uttered, heard, understood, explained and applied as such. The only thing is that its thrust is now intercepted and its impact blunted. The only thing is that it is now directed into exactly the opposite of its original direction. This is the accomplishment, or at least the attempted accomplishment, of falsehood, of the man of sin, in the Christian era which is the age of the Holy Spirit.

If he executes his movement of evasion well he can do it only in this way, with and for the truth, and as its opposite, as un-truth. This is the best of which he is capable in this field. The fact that this is so is another indication of how feeble and inferior and unoriginal he is in relation to the prophecy of Jesus Christ, and how far ahead of him this is. It is obviously this prophecy which prescribes and enforces the law of his action. He can live only by this prophecy, only by opposing it, and only by doing so boldly, relevantly and with prospect of success. He can thrive only as the Grand Inquisitor, only as the Antichrist who would like to be an opposing Christ but as such can act only as a substitute Christ. Even at the height of his inventiveness and power the man of sin can never achieve more than this sleight of hand. It may be seen at once that " one little word—a little word on the part of the One whom he would replace—can fell him." But he does achieve this. And who can deny that in its way and within its foreordained limits this supreme achievement is sufficiently notable, impressive, enticing, seductive, dangerous and destructive ? How can we overlook the dominant position to which *post Christum natum* he has attained at once with his supreme achievement and which he has continually strengthened and extended in ever new forms ? How can we overlook the thick layers of mist in which he has continually enwrapped himself in these years of the Lord and of salvation and which he continually spreads abroad to the dishonour of God and the perdition of man ? If he is not to be taken seriously in relation to Jesus Christ, he is to be taken very seriously indeed in relation to us men, and especially in relation to us Christians of this age. Nothing is more dangerous than the falsehood in which he manages, or at least tries and thinks that he manages, to use the truth to silence the truth, or the true Witness, by finding for Him a place, by championing Him, by making Him its Hero, Example and Symbol, yet all the time patronising, interpreting, domesticating, acclimatising, accommodating, and gently but very definitely and significantly correcting Him.

Rebus sic stantibus, we must thus be prepared to see the falsehood of man appear in a very earnest, respectable, devout and Christian form. Conversely, we must be prepared to have dealings with the falsehood of man where earnestness, respectability, devoutness and Christianity are seen with particular weight and impressiveness. It must be remembered that as un-truth it has taken and swallowed and so far as possible digested and assimilated the truth. It thus has it within itself. To be sure, it perverts it. And since the truth necessarily resists its perversion, it has it to its own judgment and final destruction. But it has it, and therefore it cannot fail to have the power of a certain faded lustre. The true and succulent lie always has something of the scent of the truth. In some manifestations of falsehood it is heavy with truth in the form of truisms, so that if we think we know and should describe it as falsehood we are bound to look like iconoclasts and must anxiously ask ourselves whether it is not we who are the liars, blaspheming holy things and holy people. Its aspect is in no sense an ugly mask by which we are warned easily and immediately of its dangerous and dreadful character and the eternal destruction which lurks behind it. If it betrays itself by such an aspect, it is still, or again, a primitive and sorry affair. The true and succulent lie has a radiant aspect of righteousness and holiness, of wisdom, excellence and prudence, of zeal, austerity and energy, yet also of patience and love for God and man. The instructed Grand Inquisitor or Antichrist who can commend his evil cause, and therefore the man of sin in the full power of his work, is a sympathetic and a seriously illuminating and convincing figure, not to be confused with such unsympathetic associates as Hitler, Mussolini or Stalin, and able to count upon finding many well-disposed people to applaud and follow him. It is his perverse relationship to the truth, his marching out in armour apparently very similar to the armour of God in Eph. $6^{11f.}$, which makes him so sympathetic, illuminating and convincing. There are thus good reasons why his sleight of hand is so successful, why it seems to be even more successful than the prophecy of Jesus Christ which it imitates, in order to free itself the more securely from it. If it lacks solidity, the fact that falsehood is so light means that it can cover a good deal of ground. How, then, are we to differentiate it from the truth ? Who is to make the differentiation ?

Naturally, it does not differentiate itself. It will take good care not to characterise itself as falsehood. Its whole concern is to conceal its true nature, to mask its true purpose. And if any think that we ourselves, who at very best are all men of sin, can of ourselves differentiate it from the truth, we must see to it that we do not go astray and simply publish and proclaim and represent as the truth what is perhaps only another form of falsehood. It is because no man, not even or least of all the Christian, is proof against this mistake of trying of himself, and in his own power, to differentiate it from the truth, that the falsehood of man, of which we are all the

2. The Falsehood of Man

victims and perpetrators, must be taken with such great seriousness. Yet the truth itself, Jesus Christ as the true Witness infallibly differentiates falsehood from the truth. At the very point where it arises, where it begins its sleight of hand, and therefore where the man of sin is confronted by Jesus Christ, it is seen to be falsehood, to be a perversion of the truth, and there is thus unmasked and exposed the dreadful nature of what the man of sin attempts as his supreme achievement, but also the impotence of this attempt. Jesus Christ neither is nor ever will be identical with the figure which in His name the man of sin causes to enter and to act under his patronage and advocacy. He is not ensnared by the Yes with which this man greets Him the more surely to deny Him. He escapes his grasp even as it is made, and leaves him only with His shadow, or with the caricature of His shadow, for the accomplishment of what he has in view. Whatever the man of sin may make of us, Jesus Christ does not allow Himself to be mastered nor dominated by him. The falsehood of man cannot make Him what it would like to think and proclaim and celebrate and employ and use, i.e., the One who is accepted and interpretatively adjusted by man the liar, the Grand Inquisitor, the Antichrist, the occupant of the throne of grace erected and adorned for Antichrist. In face of this whole enterprise, He does not cease to be Himself, to do His own work, to speak His own Word. In face of the falsehood of man, His truth does not cease to differentiate itself from this falsehood, to maintain its independence of it, to be the truth. The supreme achievement of the man of sin can make no difference in this respect. When it has had its day, and used it in its own fashion, it will ultimately founder on Jesus Christ and be completely destroyed. And the fact that basically even now it cannot but founder on Him is what will be revealed amongst many other things with the final coming again and manifestation of Jesus Christ. Among and in relation to us, falsehood may provisionally accomplish a great deal. But in relation to Jesus Christ as the Lord of our time, it does not have the solidity even for provisional success. As and because He, and therefore the truth, is independent in respect of it, He has and exercises the power to differentiate Himself from falsehood and falsehood from Himself, to divest it therefore of the attractive guise which it has assumed, to characterise it as the true and full-grown lie that it is, to condemn it as such, but also to reveal the limit of its validity and power and therefore of its perniciousness. It is not we who do this. It is He who does it. And as He does it, not ceasing to speak for Himself and thus to designate and characterise falsehood according to its true nature, all that remains for us to do is to hear His voice and Word, and therefore to be set by Him at the point where falsehood arises and is judged as such, but where faith, love and hope have their source as well, that we may there perceive its true nature and character, that we may see it in all its distinction from the truth, in

§ 70. *The Falsehood and Condemnation of Man*

all its infamy and menace, but also in its impotence, and that we may thus be liberated from the necessity of having to be its victims and perpetrators. If it is not taken seriously by Him, it need not be taken seriously by us. We need neither fear it nor love it. If we do have to take it seriously, it need only be in our withholding of all fear and love from it. The great and critical moments in the history of the commencement and the goal and conclusion of the return of Jesus Christ, in the history of the Christian era, the age of the Holy Spirit, but also in the history of the life of man in this time, were and are those in which there may be both generally and in detail, not by the perspicacity or profundity of man, but in the power of the Word of the true Witness again received by man, and therefore in the power of the Holy Spirit, certain provisional discoveries—preceding and intimating the final revelation of Jesus Christ—of the glorious, unsettling yet deeply consoling fact that even in its supreme form falsehood is only falsehood, and that its deceptive appearance of truth is very far from speaking the truth. The community of Jesus Christ and the individual Christian are constantly asked whether such moments are imminent, or have already occurred.

In the light of what we have seen of the true Witness, we may easily perceive in outline at least wherein falsehood consists in relation to Him. What does man fear when Jesus Christ encounters him? What is the oppressive and painful element in the truth which he would like to evade, and which, since he has to face it, he can evade only by reinterpreting and transforming the truth into untruth? What is it that falsehood seeks to silence, suppress and eliminate in the form of an acceptance in which it is manipulated and altered and denied? What is the truth which the man of sin hates, yet does not expel, but tries to absorb into falsehood as his supreme achievement, and thus to transform into untruth?

We may best begin by maintaining that one of the points at issue, and in a sense the whole point, is that truth encounters it quite simply and obviously in provoking identity with its Witness, Proclaimer and Revealer, and conversely that its Witness encounters it in direct identity with the truth. The truth which He attests is the reconciliation of the world to God, but this reconciliation as effected in Him. It is the covenant between God and man, but this covenant as fulfilled in Him. It is the justifying and sanctifying grace of God, but this grace as dwelling and effective in Him, as alive in His fellowship with man and the fellowship of man with Him. He attests this *truth* as He attests Himself. But He attests it as He attests *Himself*. We do not encounter Him without at once encountering this *truth*. But we do not encounter this truth without at once encountering *Him*. There would be no offence in the truth as such, in the idea of the gracious intercourse of God with man and the grateful intercourse of man with God. On the contrary, why should not this seem to be

2. The Falsehood of Man

acceptable and credible and even welcome? Nor could there be any objection to the existence of an extraordinary, authentic Proclaimer of this truth. On the contrary, why should it not be in order to encounter such? Boundless offence is caused, however, if in the person of this Witness we are directly confronted with this truth in a manner which does not allow of any distance or qualification, and if in this truth we are directly confronted with this Witness in a manner which does not allow of any differentiation between it and His person. The painful and scandalising thing which man wishes to avoid is the identity between this man and this truth, between this truth and this man. For in its identity with this man the truth makes an attack on him which it would not make if it were the mere notion of intercourse between God and man. And in His identity with the truth this man claims and indeed already possesses and exercises a power over him which He could not have, and which could thus be evaded, if He were merely its supreme manifestation or most impressive symbol. Since this man is identical with the truth and the truth with Him, the encounter with the truth and therefore with Him—we refer to the encounter with Jesus Christ—becomes an absolutely vital, binding, decisive and even revolutionary affair. That is why the man of sin would like to escape it. He cannot accept this identity, and since he cannot alter the fact of it he tries to reinterpret it, to transform it into non-identity. The truth may be accepted on the one side, the man who attests it on the other, and thus separated they cannot violate or offend him, nor cause him any discomfort, nor demand any decision. On both sides he will gladly affirm them. But in no circumstances can he accept them in their identity. In their identity he denies them both. He seeks to silence, suppress and eliminate their identity. This is the work of falsehood. It is by cleaving their unity that it tries to manipulate the truth and the true Witness. It is thus that it transforms truth into untruth and the true Witness into the untrue. It is thus that it seeks to reinterpret them. It goes without saying that if the truth is sundered from the true Witness, if it is made the mere idea of intercourse between God and man, then, however perfectly it may be thought out and presented, it is not the truth. And if its Witness its only its Witness, its manifestation and symbol, then, however highly He may be extolled as such, He is not the true Witness. To reject their unity is to reject the truth with the true Witness and *vice versa*. And this is what the man of sin is on the point of doing, not without a great seriousness of his own and therefore a pious lifting up of the eyes.

From rather a different angle, the offence which man takes in the encounter with Jesus Christ, and which he seeks to avoid in his falsehood, consists in the fact that the true Witness is the man of Gethsemane and Golgotha, and therefore the truth is the truth of His death and passion. This Witness is characterised and distinguished from all other witnesses, and the truth attested by Him from all other truths, by the fact that He is risen and lives and reigns and speaks as the One whose whole work led Him ever deeper into the shadow of the cross towards which He moved and which He actually bore and suffered in fulfilment of His work. His royal will is His readiness not to preserve but to give His life. His royal power is the weakness in which He surrenders Himself into the hard hand of God and at the same time into the hands of men. His royal panoply is the crown of thorns thrust on Him in mockery and contempt. His royal Word is His Word from the cross, the sigh with which He died. It is thus that He is the true Witness. And His truth, the truth attested by Him, consists in the fact that the reconciliation of the world to God took place when He (2 Cor. 5^{21}) was made sin by God that we might be the righteousness of God in Him, when He was treated by God as the sin of the world which He found impossible and intolerable, and therefore when He was rejected and destroyed as its Bearer and Representative. The truth is that the hallowing of the name of God, the coming of His kingdom, the doing of His will, the fulfilment of the covenant between God and man, took place in the shedding of His blood. The truth is that the grace of God which justifies and sanctifies us men has its essence and manifestation in the fact that He " humbled himself, and became obedient " (Phil. 2^8), obedient to the suffering of the death of a malefactor. Hence, to hear Him to-day is to hear the sigh of this One judged in our place. To see Him to-day is to see this One condemned, expelled and rejected in our place. To believe in Him is necessarily to realise that His place ought to have been ours. To love Him and to hope in Him is to be required, in remembrance of what we deserved and as a sign of fellowship with Him, to take up and bear our much smaller crosses, and not to be able to escape this requirement. The narrow way of the Christian who belongs to Him, which leads through the strait gate of discipleship, means neither more nor less for man than that in order to win his life he should give it up for lost and really lose it. It is thus that Jesus Christ is the true Witness and Himself the truth. It is with this offence and folly that He meets us, and not otherwise. This is what we cannot ignore in this encounter, yet also cannot of ourselves accept. This is what presents to the falsehood of man the challenge to render it innocuous, to work it over, to translate and reinterpret and transform it, to make it a less troublesome penultimate Word of God instead of His ultimate Word. Surely, it is well able to appropriate and domesticate even and especially the cross of Jesus Christ, and the Word of His cross: perhaps in such a way that the Word of His cross is changed into a word of the dramatic mortification which takes place and is fulfilled in man, of the reconciliation to God, his fellows and himself which is accomplished by himself in the suffering yet also the overcoming of the inward tension of his existence; perhaps conversely

2. The Falsehood of Man

by ascribing to it as the Word of the cross of Jesus Christ an objective significance and efficacy of such a magical power that there can hardly be conceived a surer way of sheltering the reality of one's own existence against its claim and assault ; perhaps by distinguishing from His death a true Gospel of Jesus Christ, His message about God and the soul and the soul and its God, about the fatherly goodness of God and the brotherly love demanded of men, as though these were the really valuable things, and by then understanding His death, which is also valuable in its own way, as the intrepid martyr-death of the Bearer of this message underlining the importance and the glory of the message itself ; perhaps in such a way that His death and passion are understood as a passing cloud which obscures His mission but is then victoriously dispelled as God co-operates with the work of human folly and wickedness for a supreme test ; perhaps more profoundly as the antithetical element, which will be the more certainly set aside, in a dialectic of world-occurrence, of the ways and destinies of all men, and even of the way and will of God Himself, in the movement of which the man Jesus Christ had also to participate and in the typical representation of which there is to be found His true significance ; perhaps more one-sidedly as an unforgettable indication of suffering, perishing and death as the true substance of the truth disclosed to man and to be recognised by him. Cannot all these things be heard, and more gladly heard than the Word of the true Witness and His truth in what is undoubtedly their genuine and original form ? Is it not perfectly plain that in all these reinterpretations man is trying to overcome the element of offence and to make it inoffensive, to create instead of the true Witness one who can not only be accepted but even given an honourable place, to discover behind His truth a truth which will be acceptable and by which he can continue to live without any terror, without any need for conversion and new beginning, without commending himself wholly and utterly into the hands of God ? Do we not recognise in them, not only many profound or less profound and therefore more acceptable because more superficial and artless speculations and doctrines, but also much passion music which is certainly gripping yet not finally disquietening because so beautiful ? Do we not see in them all the pictures of the crucifixion which move us perhaps but may still be admired at a safe distance from their theme, not to speak of the little crosses carried for adornment by our ecclesiastical dignitaries and Christian ladies, and, in short, all the great and small agencies of mitigation by the unrestricted production of which man thinks that he can succeed in making the narrow way broad, the strait gate wide, the new thing of God a practice of man, the great mystery of God little, and then supposedly great in its littleness ?

Again, however, the dreadful thing for the man of sin, and therefore for us all in our encounter with Jesus Christ, consists very concretely in the fact that it is God's Word which is spoken in the power of His Holy Spirit, which approaches and invades us in this power, and which claims us as those who are pledged to hear and obey. This is the Word with which we have to do. And this fact is the dreadful thing behind both the aspects mentioned. The solid and unbroken unity of God is the basis and mystery of the provoking identity of the truth there spoken and the Witness who speaks it. And the revolutionary love of God, which is present and at work both to kill and to make alive, is the basis and mystery of what is for us the most repugnant form of suffering and death of the Witness and the testimony with which we are confronted. It is God who here comes upon man, the Father upon His estranged child, the Lord upon His runaway servant, the eternally Holy One upon the transgressor, the eternally Merciful upon the abject, the eternally Living One upon the one who wants to live but cannot live alone or without Him, and in all these things the omnipotent Creator upon the creature which He has called out of nothing into being. This is what determines the order, character and course of their encounter. In it there is said to man what only God has to say to him. And it is said as only God will and can say it. And man must listen to it as he can listen only to God, and answer as he can answer only God. Only one thing can come in question on God's side in relation to man, namely, His grace and its command; and only one thing on the side of man in relation to God, namely, his gratitude and therefore his obedience. It is a matter of the work and event of fellowship which on God's side can take place only in the gift of His Holy Spirit and on man's only in the reception of this gift and the resolute and active conversion of the lost son. This is why we are shocked. We are not prepared quite so easily and self-evidently to be the lost son, nor to have to be converted. We do not want dealings with the Holy Spirit and His gift and the reception of this gift. Both seem to us absurd, the one as a miracle we cannot really expect and the other as a demand we cannot really concede. It is because we suspect these underlying factors that the identity of the Witness and His testimony is so alien and the Word of the cross so repugnant. Hence we should like to change things. But here is something we cannot change. Hence there is need that falsehood should again be enlisted to help us. Cost what it may, this order, character and course of our encounter with Jesus Christ must be reinterpreted and explained away. What must happen is above all that the meaning of this encounter as the coming together of two partners who are from the very first and unchangeably unequal, namely, God and man, should not be flatly denied but should be obscured as much as possible, being replaced by the less unsettling notion of a continuous co-existence of the two. It is thus to be understood, not as a history with a distinctive beginning, continuation and goal, but as the provisionally differentiated objective-subjective content of a provisionally fluid but basically solid and

2. The Falsehood of Man

therefore apprehensible relationship of correlation between God and man. But if there is to be the desired freedom from unsettlement, it cannot be left at that. If the distinction between the two partners cannot be denied, it must be made as loose as possible. God must be approximated and made as similar as possible to man, and *vice versa*. To this end, the distinction between the true Witness Jesus Christ and other men, in which that between God and man only too plainly forces itself upon us, must be relativised in such sort that man generally is regarded as a potential Christ. And in the process the truth attested by Him must acquire the character of something basically known to every man, something already realised by him, something which has only to be brought to his remembrance. We can no longer speak of it in the strict sense as a Word which must be spoken to man in its character as revelation, which he has not yet heard and which cannot be brought to his remembrance. There is no good reason why the state into which what was previously encounter has been transformed, and which may be very living and fluid in itself, should not be described objectively as an act of the life of God. But why should it not equally well be described subjectively as the most inward, spiritual, religious, ethical and existential act of the life of man? God and man become ambivalent. We may speak indeed of Father and child, Lord and servant, the Holy One and our sin, the Merciful and our misery, the Creator and us as His creatures, grace and gratitude, command and obedience. But are not these modes of speech, comparable to the two foci of an ellipse which as such are engaged in an irresistible movement of approximation to the centre of a circle in which their difference and therefore their particularity must finally disappear, in which even the inner movement in that state must finally be ended and there will thus be neither an act of God nor an act of man any more? Why should not the fellowship between the speaking God and hearing man in the gift and reception of the Holy Spirit be understood as this relative, fluid and on both sides provisional distinction yet interconnexion of two foci? And why should not the Holy Spirit in particular be understood as the impelling force of the process in which the two foci find their common centre and therefore hasten beyond mere interconnexion to fusion and therefore to the dissolution of their distinctions and particularities? This dissolution of distinctions is positively the blessed union of above and below, of there and here, of God and man. It is the point where God has no longer to speak nor man to hear from a distance. It is the point where God no longer has to give nor man to receive, where their conversation and history are both ended, where reconciliation, covenant, grace and the Jesus Christ active in and testifying to them may all be dispensed with even as ciphers, concepts and symbols, where prayer is ultimately superfluous even as a monologue. And this point is the vision and *telos* with reference to which, not of course in frontal attack upon truth (as emerges very plainly in this connexion) but in appropriation of it, man engages in falsehood, and hopes by means of it to escape the danger in which he finds himself in encounter with Jesus Christ. There are many practical attitudes which he may assume, and many conceivable manipulations which he may use, in the course of this attempt. We have already grouped them in somewhat schematic form. The plan and energy employed, and the apparent provisional result, namely, the tranquillising of the man disturbed in that encounter, are always the same. And at some earlier or later stage all of us take an active or passive part in this appropriation of the truth and its Witness, and therefore in the triumph of falsehood.

In the last resort, everything which falls to be said about that which is so dreadful to the man of sin in his encounter with Jesus Christ the true Witness, and which has thus to be concealed by lies, can and must be reduced to a single phrase, namely, that it is simply a matter of freedom. God confronts this man as the One who is incomparably free, and it is his own liberation by and for the free God, in which he himself is to be one who in his own way is incomparably free, which is at issue and which he is required to accept. God makes Himself known as his God, as his loving Father and Lord, Friend and Helper, who opens up to him the fulness of His treasures. But He does this in absolute independence of all presuppositions distinct from Himself, of all psychic or moral principles, laws, criteria or standards. More positively, He does so as Himself the presupposition of all presuppositions, the good and therefore the source and norm of all good. He does so in His self-determination and therefore in His freedom. Hence the identity of the Witness and the truth attested by Him, in which man is prevented *a limine* from occupying a place where he can make meaningful objections or even reservations in relation to this Witness and His testimony. Hence the Word of the cross as the form of this Witness and His testimony, behind and above which man cannot have recourse to any other, but by which he is referred and impelled directly to the only means of deliverance in the grace of God as the Lord of life and death. Hence the indissolubly differentiated relationship between the speaking of God and the hearing and answering of man, between the gift and the reception of the Holy Spirit as the fellowship into which God enters with man and man is taken up by God. In the encounter with Jesus Christ there takes place from all these different angles an absolutely sovereign grasping of man by God. It is sovereign inasmuch as man is left no possibility of encountering God from a position which is not that posited and secured for him by God Himself through His Word and Spirit. It is sovereign inasmuch as it leaves man no normative conception of goodness, truth, right, love, salvation, well-being, or peace, with which to encounter God, to consider Him, to accept or reject

2. The Falsehood of Man

Him, to wrestle with Him, to grasp or evade Him, to take up His cause or to argue with Him. At this point man is dealing with the wholly self-determinative God who controls the concrete content of all conceptions and is therefore alone normative. He is dealing with His love, but only as *His* love. In his thinking concerning Him and his ensuing attitude towards Him, he has to orientate himself by the rule, direction and control revealed in His revelation. In his own deciding he has to follow the decisions in which God gives him information and direction concerning Himself, and therefore concerning man. He has to cleave freely to this free God. Freely, for God's sovereign grasping of man is not an act of force to induce a *sacrificium intellectus et voluntatis*. On the contrary, it evokes and establishes the *intellectus* and the *voluntas fidei*. It is a matter of man's decision and therefore of his freedom in following the free God in obedience to His decisions. The concern of God active and visible in the encounter with Jesus Christ is His concern for the man who is himself to be freed, not for a puppet or chess-man. Man cannot determine himself for freedom. He cannot make himself free. God must do this. He neither is nor can be free without God. To be free, he must be born again by God's Word and Spirit. He must be born again to freedom and therefore to self-determination, i.e., to that which accrues to him as a responsible covenant-partner of the free and self-determining God, as His creature, as the one who is loved by Him. What is given him, and required of him, is the freedom of one who belongs to the free God and is freed by Him. Man's freedom means liberation from all the presuppositions conditioning and limiting God and himself. It means liberation from every arbitrary presupposition and therefore from himself. More positively, it means attraction and activity in relation to the information and direction received from the One who gives and requires his freedom. It means the courage and joy to make the only possible and meaningful use of it corresponding to its nature, i.e., the only use which can be considered in view of the fact that it is given and required by the free God. It is a matter of the freedom of God's covenant-partner, creature, child and servant elected by Him. It is a matter of the freedom to elect Him as elected by Him. It is a matter of the freedom of responsibility to Him.

The man of sin starts back from this free God and his own liberation by and for Him. Like a tornado, this God sweeps away all the assurances, props and supports which he seeks in relation both to God and himself, and therefore all his reservations and excuses, all his attempts to hold aloof from God, to maintain himself against Him, to secure a place of his own. How lofty is the being before and with God in which he is set! How rarified is the atmosphere in which he must learn to breathe in the only place where he can now exist as a free man freed by the free God! Surely he must try to find relief in the obvious reinterpretation, translation and transformation.

§ 70. The Falsehood and Condemnation of Man

The first and general possibility is that of systematising the event of the confrontation of the man who is to be freed and the free God as this takes place in encounter with Jesus Christ. It is that of trying to change this confrontation into a co-ordination, a system of two essences, a divine, infinite and absolute on the one side and a human, finite and relative on the other, foundation and support for this co-ordination being found in the relationship or equality of the one essence with the other in virtue of a principle which is superior to and comprehends them both. The freedom of God and man may then be reduced to the obviously incontestable contingency of their actual co-existence in this order. The meeting of the free God and the man who is to be freed is then neutralised, softened and smoothed from the very outset by the order in which both already co-exist, by the principle which establishes and controls this order, and in virtue of which the infinite is no less referred to the finite, the absolute to the relative, and therefore God to man, than *vice versa*. In it there can be no more question of a true giving and receiving or commanding and obeying. Man's confrontation with God in this order and under the control of this principle can no longer have any decisive significance or the character of a liberation of man by and for the free God. There cannot take place in it the passing of the old or emergence of the new. This elimination of the freedom of God and man, this depriving of the confrontation of God and man of all force and tension by the notion of an order overruling and comprehending them both, is the general alleviation which the falsehood of the man of sin has in view.

In detail the freedom of God may then be changed into the factuality and normativeness, which are not denied but very highly esteemed, of a supreme and therefore divine being. This being is one which *via eminentiae* may be conceived and regarded as the sum of all human notions of the good, the true and the beautiful, of love, righteousness and wisdom, endowed with spatial and temporal infinitude and with power over spatio-temporal and therefore finite being and occurrence. And it is one which *via negationis* may be recognised as the sum of the limit and transcendence of all finite being and occurence, as the sum of a being independent of that of all other entities, as the sum of what is knowable only in its unknowableness to our knowledge which is orientated on the finite and therefore itself finite. However strongly the factuality and normativeness and therefore the majesty of this supreme being may be emphasised, it obviously has nothing whatever to do with the freedom of God, because as the majesty of this being it is limited and constricted by the positive and negative presuppositions with the help of which man attempts to define it. Within the sphere of this kind of terminology there can be no question of God as a Subject who is self-determinative in His nature and attributes. Indeed, the question arises whether in this

2. The Falsehood of Man

being discovered and determined *via eminentiae* and *via negationis* we really have to do with God at all and not with the ideal picture of the being, order and mystery of the world as seen and understood by man, and finally with the ideal picture in which man tries to see and understand his own being and its order and mystery. Who but man himself has given this picture its factuality and normativeness and therefore majesty ? There can be no doubt at least—and this is the goal of the man of sin—that the majesty which is substituted for the freedom of God, and perhaps proclaimed and extolled under this name, can be easily maintained, considered, contemplated, pondered and even sincerely honoured without even the slightest implication of that sovereign grasp of God upon man. This supreme being has too close an affinity to the supreme content of man's understanding of the world and himself for man not to have plenty of scope for dealing with it as he could never deal with the free God, for genuine wrestling with it, for ascribing or denying to it specific attributes, for accepting or rejecting it *in toto* according to his own findings, for confessing or denying its existence, or perhaps adopting an attitude of interested neutrality in this regard. A sphere for what, in his ignorance of both God and himself, he regards as his own freedom is what the man of sin wants to secure for himself. And it is to accomplish this, and in repudiation of the free God, that he imagines the false but solemn, tranquillising and even soporific idea of God as the supreme being.

With the same end in view, man cannot accept the freedom for God given and required by the free God. How can there be any such freedom if God is not the free God and is not capable of that sovereign grasping of man ? Instead, there is imagined the foolish freedom of man to do or not to do according to his own inscrutable pleasure. The most excellent and powerful work of this freedom consists in the repudiation of the free God and the fabrication of a substitute in the form of that supreme being. It is here that it manifests and characterises itself as the most profound opposite of freedom. What is man ? He is, or regards himself as, the being which, alongside many others and as their crown and completion, is capable of this repudiation and fabrication in the exercise of the good-pleasure which he regards as his freedom. His particular contention is that he is in the glorious position of being able to imagine and create a God under this or some other name, or even none at all. If he can do this, what can he not do ? And since he can do many other things, why not this ? But if he can imagine and create a God, how close, how similar and perhaps how equal he must himself be to divinity ! It is to be noted that the Promethean attitude in which he seeks to boast of this divinity or divine likeness of his, and thus to bid defiance to the gods, is a relatively insignificant because naive form of his falsehood. As an atheist in the sense of the modern atheism affected in the West, the man of sin is far from seeing how best to prosecute his evil cause. Falsehood is mature and dangerous when it carries through its attempt to introduce a substitute God with the consciousness and in assertion of the majesty of this supreme being, and therefore with an estimation and, in order to give this force, a sincere feeling of the dependence of man on this being, a deep and serious reverence and humility before it, and at the same time a confession of the littleness of man in comparison with it. Only then is this enterprise and its imagined result, the substitute God of one's own invention, impressive, credible and serviceable to ward off the danger of a freedom which has first to be given to man but is then required of him as such. If in this its most excellent work man exercises what he regards as his freedom with an appropriate religious modesty and reserve, with the attitude of one who knows his ignorance, of one who worships in the dust, then he may be satisfied that he is doing his work in the most relevant and therefore the best way, and he can and may rightly ask that his course should not be confused by the intervention of Another, of the free God who is not invented, endowed or jealously guarded by him, but who determines Himself and lays His sovereign grasp on man. He can and may ask that he should not have to expose himself to liberation by and for Him. He has already done all that is necessary. He has freed himself for what is in keeping with an orderly relation to God, and at the same time for a corresponding orderly attitude in every other respect. He can then confidently trust his own judgment. He can persuade himself at every point, convincing himself that he is not against God but for and with Him, and therefore that he is genuinely and properly man even on a specifically Christian reckoning, the only thing being that he is without the free God and liberation by and for Him, but instead thinks that he can maintain and assert himself and therefore his own lack of freedom in relation to this God. If the man of sin could only succeed in carrying through his enterprise at this point, resisting liberation by and for the free God; if the Kremlin and the Vatican could only agree instead of fighting one another, then the game would be almost won against the true Witness Jesus Christ and His testimony.

We need not continue our analysis, but may conclude by stating that the falsehood of man as here envisaged is not simply identical with the untruth active in all human unbelief, superstition and error. Objectively, we certainly have in these general phenomena the artificial negation of truth disclosing itself as such and thus ostensibly triumphing. Hence we have in them manifestations of the falsehood of the man of sin. But the fact that they are this is an assertion and judgment which are possible and justifiable only in comparison with the prophecy of Jesus Christ and therefore on this basis. They arise and exist in the sphere in which He, too, is present as the true Witness. They stand in His light, and it is in this light that their nature as

2. The Falsehood of Man

falsehood is revealed and may be seen. Yet human unbelief, superstition and error may be regarded only as secondary phenomena, as potential or latent falsehood, where they arise and exist in the same sphere as Jesus Christ and are thus undoubtedly measured by Him, but do not take place in direct encounter with Him or as elements in the direct history of man with Jesus Christ. Jesus Christ has not yet met all men. Not every man as yet exists in direct and immediate historical relation with Him. And it is only in these circumstances that the man of sin is revealed and expresses himself according to his true nature. Only here does falsehood reach maturity. Only here does he lie subjectively and not just objectively, actually and not just potentially, consciously, intentionally and by design and not just in fact. Only here does he find serious cause and reason to be afraid of the truth, to try to evade it, and, since he is unable to do this, to have resort to the artifices of falsehood. Only here is he both guilty as a liar, which was always true, and also makes himself guilty, his lie being a responsible action of which he is well aware. Only here, in the Christian form of falsehood, which we have had in view, do we come up against the primary phenomenon of falsehood. It is here that that which as falsehood not only slumbers in secret in the man of sin, but objectively and factually emerges quite clearly enough in his works of unbelief, superstition and error, now breaks out and is operative and revealed in concentrated form. And the recognition of this primary phenomenon carries with it an insight into the false nature of all human unbelief, superstition and error, and their appropriate judgment as such. Since the latter is unavoidable, so, too, is the evangelistic and missionary task and duty of the Christian community. But even as the presupposition of all Christian evangelistic and missionary work, this judgment can be accurate, true and powerful only in the thinking and utterance of those who are perfectly clear and are prepared to confess that they themselves are the ones to whom it applies first, that in them as Christians the unbelief, superstition and error, and therefore the falsehood of man, have their true and original form. Thus in asserting the secondary phenomena as they perceive them in all men, they will be kept from all pride, never throwing stones at others, but with them and for them, and thus authorised to tell them the truth, looking to the justification and sanctification which they also need, which they need first, and which they can as little as others ascribe to themselves.

By way of a second conclusion, we may add a word concerning the phenomenon and problem of the common lie, i.e., of falsehood in the moral sense. We do not understand it, nor can we effectively resist it, if we do not see that it, too, has its origin, its corrupted essence and its temporary existence around the pious form of falsehood and as its epiphenomenon. The worst of weekday lies has its roots in the even worse Sunday lie, the profane in the Christian. As man becomes a liar in the encounter with Jesus Christ, he becomes a liar at every point. According to the law of intercommunication, when he comes to fear the great, primary and central truth, at the same time and in the same way he necessarily comes to fear the little, secondary and peripheral truths, and since he cannot escape these either, to live with them he must try to translate and transform them into untruths. As he secretly transforms God and himself, and especially divine and human freedom, into a picture in which he can be the master instead of having a master, in which he can be bound instead of free, so he does with what is said to him as a secondary and provisional truth by the historical reality of the world and his own position and task in their narrower and larger context. The original alteration irresistibly carries with it that of the whole panorama. What is not there, must be there; and what is, must not be. Is it not true, and is it an accident, that in no historical sphere has common lying flourished so grandly as in the Christian era? Why? Obviously because man in this era is exposed to a relatively much stronger unsettlement and constriction by the painful truth of God than in any other sphere. Wrong and misery have always been present, and therefore there has naturally been a plenitude of lying and deception in the lives of individuals. But when and where has the critical and salutary truth, which, since God overrules, even secular human reality can audibly and intelligibly proclaim, been so massively and purposefully transformed into untruth in the public utterances of the great human societies, as here where secular reality not only can speak, but does actually acquire the muffled yet unmistakeable voice of an echo in virtue of the actual presence and action of Jesus Christ? When and where, obviously in violent reaction against this voice, have society, business, states, their governments and parties, the classes and races (two terms of very doubtful origin), so boldly strutted across the stage with continually new and more refined and striking fictions than in world history *post Christum*? When and where has there been opened such a gigantic maw of lying as the so-called " press," which to-day with its exaggeratedly bright or gloomy imparting of news, its interpretations, insinuations, commendations and calumniations in the service of a one-sided interest, at once the slave and the master of public opinion, is *the* word which is drummed into the ears of all of us every day, and is obviously meant to be " impressed " upon our minds and hearts and consciences? And all this is planned and contrived by baptised and more or less believing Christians, not in a heathen world, but in more or less close confrontation with the Gospel of Jesus Christ. In it all the Christian churches in some way have a hand, at least in the sense that from their own standpoints they all accept as true the fictions spread abroad by these various authorities and help to pass them on to their members and the rest of the world with their blessing

2. The Falsehood of Man

and in edifying garb. But this reminds us that there cannot truly or finally be any Christian ill-will towards these authorities and their fictions, since all these things take place within the sphere of the great, primary and central, i.e., the pious lie which is indeed the Christian lie, which is the primary phenomenon by which they are incited and activated and of which they are the epiphenomenon. If we do not recognise the lie at the centre, we shall hardly see it on the periphery. And if we do not resist it at the centre, we shall certainly not do so on the periphery. The relationship between the two cannot be broken. Christianity has again good cause to beat its own breast before it can describe as falsehood the falsehood of the world, the common lie, and before it can make honest use of the truths of the world. There must be light in itself before there can be more light in the world. In itself and at this centre, however, there will necessarily be accomplished the destruction of the pious lie and therefore the spreading of light, for here the man of sin is confronted directly and immediately by Jesus Christ the Witness of the truth, for whom he is no match even though he deploys his most subtle stratagems. Concerning the spreading of light in the world, and the destruction of the common lie, we need not be finally anxious in the light of the promise which speaks with living power at this centre. Nor, if we look in this direction, need there be lacking in us the courage which we need in the service of this spreading of light and therefore in conflict even with the common lie.

We now turn for the fourth and last time to the Book of Job, and this time to the three friends who conversed with him, Eliphaz the Temanite, Bildad the Shuhite and Zophar the Naamathite. In other words, we turn to the speeches in which, after the dreadful silence which they share with him for seven days (2^{13}), they answer his complaints and accusations, trying to impart instruction, comfort and admonition, but obviously unable to do so, so that they have finally to be told by Yahweh ($42^{7f.}$) that His wrath is kindled, not against Job with his complaints and accusations, but against them, because in contrast with His servant Job they have not spoken that which is right concerning Him. In more recent exposition it has been rightly observed that their intervention is as it were the continuation, development and even the fulfilment of the satanic assault made upon Job under the permissive overruling of God. What the Bible has to say concerning human falsehood in its original form as the pious lie finds classic documentation in the speeches of these friends. If we read them attentively, we have especially to reckon with the fact that it is most difficult to distinguish the true witnesses from the false and therefore truth from untruth. Indeed, only Yahweh Himself can do this at the end of the Book. For these men are unquestionably good, earnest and religious. And in marked contrast to the violent utterances of Job, which border at times on blasphemy and the denial of God, they unquestionably speak good, earnest and religious words. Indeed, at certain points their words are golden, being incomparably better adapted for instructional, pastoral, liturgical and homiletical use than those of the one whom God finally confirmed as his servant and recognised and visibly established as a witness to His truth. Even if we start with the clear declaration that they did not speak that which was right, and therefore spoke of God under the wrath of God, so that we have really to regard them as representatives of

§ 70. The Falsehood and Condemnation of Man

falsehood, we certainly cannot treat them with a severity like the holy severity of God to which they apparently fell victim. There is certainly no cause for the attitude : " God, I thank thee, that I am not as these Pharisees." We must not overlook the fact that they are introduced as the friends of Job, the witness of God, who may be of very doubtful quality but who are at least sincere and wish him well. They certainly have no idea that they are agents of Satan and the worst tempters of Job. They speak in all good faith, though unfortunately in so doing they speak, as may well happen, that which is basically perverted and dangerous. Above all, we must not overlook the fact that the final attitude of God towards them is not that of His wrath, nor is His conclusive Word to them that of judgment. It is the command that they should go to Job and, in order to avert the threatening judgment (" lest I deal with you after your folly " 42^8), take with them a burnt offering of seven bullocks and seven rams, the intercession of Job and the statement that God has accepted this being the last news that we are given concerning them (42^9). This does not alter in the least the judgment on them and therefore the need to read critically their well-meaning and intrinsically very striking and excellent speeches. It must be said rather that the material judgment on them acquires its final sharpness from the fact that only sacrifice and intercession can save them from the proper consequences of what they have properly deserved as friends and thinkers and speakers of this kind. The friends of Job are such interesting figures theologically just because on the one side such excellent people who are on such friendly terms with the true witness undoubtedly incur the guilt of the real falsehood of the man of sin, and yet on the other the ground does not open beneath their feet to swallow them up as in the rebellion of Korah, but the patience and goodness of God, even if not without the intercession of the servant and true witness of God, are maintained in relation to them, so that in the event they too—is not this a final proof of the magnifying of the divine and human freedom which is so characteristic of this Book ?—are enfolded by God's active readiness for the remission of sins. We shall have to remember this when we speak of the condemnation of man in our concluding sub-section.

Our first contention must be that what the friends say in their attempt to instruct and convert Job reads very well in itself. We should not be dealing with the falsehood of man if it openly betrayed itself in the speeches of these men. We can learn from them that the man of sin can present his evil case far better than might have been expected. If they are wrong, as they are, it is in such a way that they are also right, just as Job is right in such a way that he is also wrong. And first of all, in our brief survey of their position, we must see and recognise that they are right both in the theological propositions which they advance and also in the way in which they apply them to answer Job. The statement most emphatically made by all three is that, whether or not man understands and approves it concretely, God in His sovereign overruling is always holy, righteous and wise, and therefore is always to be glorified. This is both right and important. So, too, is the statement that His overruling has secretly, and yet also in large measure openly, the character of a judicial action in which each is rewarded according to his works, so that the pious may hope for mercy but the godless will sooner or later be overtaken by merited destruction. So, too, is the statement which almost has a ring of the Reformation, namely, that there is none righteous before God, and therefore none who has any right to be surprised at the severity of what may befall him, or to complain or even rebel against it. So, too, is the injunction that the best thing for a man to do when he is overtaken by the severity of God is to cling the more genuinely to Him, to allow himself to be directed by Him, and to accept His discipline. So, too, is the promise most impressively formulated by Eliphaz ($5^{8f.,\ 17f.}$) that the God who makes sore also binds up, that the God who wounds also heals, that from Him there may definitely be expected final deliverance from every need, redemp-

2. *The Falsehood of Man* 455

tion from death and a happy issue to all affliction. So, too, are the references, in amplification of this theme, to the temporary nature of the successes and triumphs of the ungodly which are such a puzzle to the godly in time of suffering. Very correct, too, are the urgent warnings to Job to think of the majesty of the divine wisdom and the consequent limits to his human knowledge, and therefore not to give free vent to his complaints and entreaties, nor to be so arrogant and omniscient and defiant in relation to God and his three friends, as if his fate were the problem of all problems and his violent attitude the key to its solution, nor to throw the alleged and perhaps in fact very doubtful justice of his cause into the scales, but rather to be converted—which is surely necessary—and thus to learn afresh the goodness of God as one who is humbled by Him. What fault can we really find with all these things ? Hardly a statement which they make is not in its own way meaningful and does not have parallels not only in the rest of the Old but also in the New Testament. And many of their sayings leave nothing to be desired not only in thoughtfulness and perspicuity but also in noteworthy profundity. Indeed, when Yahweh speaks His concluding Word, is not Job actually brought very close to the point which Eliphaz, Bildad and Zophar obviously have in view and to which they try so very earnestly if unsuccessfully to direct him ? Does he not actually confess that he is guilty before Yahweh and thus place himself at this point, hence conceding at last that they are right ? Is this really human falsehood ? In these three fine men do we not have those who in their own way are also genuine witnesses ? In their speeches do we not have at least in detail clear declarations of truth ?

Already, however, the manner in which Job, the man who according to God's judgment speaks what is right concerning Him, reacts against these speeches, points in rather a different direction. It is not merely that he does not yield an inch to them in substance, but that he actually continues his complaints and accusations without deviation until the intervention of Yahweh Himself. It is not merely that what he alleges represents no concession to their teaching, with the exception of a few passing references, but that he sovereignly ignores what they say to him. Indeed, his speeches are full of statements in which he sharply and bitterly rejects their exhortation. " God forbid that I should justify you," he cries out in 27^5 ; his tongue would utterly deceive if he were to do so. He compares their efforts to a stream which is frozen in winter and dried up in summer ($6^{15f.}$), and himself to a thirsty caravan approaching it from a distance and vainly hoping to find water there. What scorn he pours upon them ! " No doubt but ye are the people, and wisdom shall die with you " (12^2). " How hast thou helped him that is without power ! how savest thou the arm that hath no strength ! how hast thou counselled him that hath no wisdom ! and how hast thou plentifully declared the thing as it is ! To whom hast thou uttered words ? and whose spirit came from thee ? " ($26^{2f.}$). And what categorical statements he makes ! " But ye are forgers of lies, ye are all physicians of no value " (13^4). " Miserable comforters are ye all " (16^2). " Your remembrances are like unto ashes, your defences to shields of clay " (13^{12}). Nor is this all. In their speeches he finds himself tenfold scorned, insulted, maltreated, tormented, lacerated and crushed ($19^{2f.}$ and 22). Instead of having pity on him as one smitten by the hand of God, in defence of God they speak perversely and deceitfully, championing the cause of God, conducting His case against him, persecuting him as God does ($13^{7f.}$, $19^{21ff.}$). It is for this reason that he accuses and threatens them : " Is it good that he should search you out ? or as one man mocketh another, do ye so mock him ? He will surely reprove you, if ye do secretly accept persons. Shall not his excellency make you afraid ? and his dread fall upon you ? " ($13^{9f.}$). " Be ye afraid of the sword : for wrath bringeth the punishments of the sword, that ye may know there is a judgment " (19^{29}). Probably these last references give us an indication of the answer to the question why Job cannot accept the material content of the speeches of these worthy men, let alone be

456 § 70. *The Falsehood and Condemnation of Man*

fully satisfied by them, but must resist them so resolutely and even bitterly. And in so doing perhaps they help us to see why Yahweh Himself finally accuses them of not speaking that which is right concerning Him.

The fact that Job does not enter on a material discussion as such shows us that he is not opposing the actual content of their statements and trains of thought, nor even their possible relevance to his particular case. He knows very well that what they represent is, as Bildad reminds him in 8⁸, the wisdom of the fathers, and according to 12¹² he has no thought of evading this. Indeed, he tells them expressly that it is not their doctrine which separates them from him. "But I have understanding as well as you ; I am not inferior to you : yea, who knoweth not such things as these ? " (12³). " Lo, mine eye hath seen all this, mine ear hath heard and understood it " (13¹). " I have heard many such things . . . I also could speak as ye do : if your soul were in my soul's stead, I could heap up words against you, and shake mine head at you. But I would strengthen you with my mouth, and the moving of my lips should assuage your grief " (16²ᶠ·). Put yourselves in my place : " Mark me, and be astonished, and lay your hand upon my mouth " (21⁵). And obviously because they do not do this : " O that ye would altogether hold your peace ! and it should be your wisdom " (13⁵). Hence the difference between them and him—do we not have here again an indication of the direction in which we are to seek ?—consists in the fact, and obviously in this fact alone, that they and he are at very different points. If he were as they, and they as he, he could give them the true and important instruction which they now give to him. He knows it by heart, and has nothing against it. But if they were as he, or could imagine themselves in this condition, he would not tell them what they tell him, true and important though it is. They would see that it has nothing whatever to do with that for which he makes his complaint and accusation, with the question whether it is right or wrong, nor with the witness which he does not cease to bear in his particular situation. But he is not as they are, nor they as he. They speak the truth in their situation, but he in his can only treat it as falsehood and therefore reject it.

Our starting-point is the fact that the situation in which the friends find themselves, and from which they see Job according to his accusation, is only in their imagination and not in fact the standpoint of God, i.e., a place which not only enables and permits but even requires them to be against Job, not only in a human cause and with human authority, but in the cause of God and with divine authority, because they are in alliance with Him. Their representations which would be incontestable if they made them from this place, rest on the assumption that, on the basis of the tradition in which they stand and with reference to which they address Job, and on the basis of their own experience and reflection, they have information about God to which they have only to refer back to be able to speak appropriately concerning Him, i.e., information about His nature, that He is always wise and righteous, and about the degree to which He is in action always faithful to this nature of His in His action and rule, and is thus to be feared and loved as God. In His majesty and omnipotence, as Elohim Shaddai, and therefore in the very aspect in which He is so obscure to Job, He is to them an open book, from which they have only to read to their friend, who obviously is not at the moment able to read for himself, and they may rightly expect that he will hear the truth which will answer all his questions and bring him to a better mind. And when he does not respond, but continues to ask about that concerning which they know and can give him such definite information, they think that they are justified and even laid under an obligation to protect the God they know so well against his complaints and accusations, and indeed to launch a counter-attack in His name, not merely contending for Him but contending with Him against Job, and this obviously in the interests of Job himself, in the severity and yet finally also the patience of seeking love. The

2. The Falsehood of Man   457

must contend against Job because they can view the intransigeance of his open protest against them only as his obstinacy against the majesty and omnipotence of God which they see so clearly as His wisdom and righteousness. To them in their belief that they are thinking and speaking for and with God, this is an attitude which they can only resist and attack in the hope of breaking it. And so in relation to what he has to suffer at the hand of God they torture him in the very worst fashion that one man can torture another, addressing him as from God, for the sake of God and in the name of God. Let us make no mistake. As Job himself said clearly enough, somewhere behind the laborious mildness which controls their instructions there is already prepared an *auto-da-fé* to be celebrated *ad maiorem Dei gloriam*. This is what disqualifies their speeches in advance, however full of content they may be. This is what robs them of power and makes them so unconvincing and even intolerable to Job. He, the true witness, does not stand alongside God, nor look over His shoulder. He does not have and cannot give information concerning Him. He does not think that he must represent and defend Him as an ally and advocate. Least of all does he believe that he should cast what he knows in the teeth of others, or even establish, comfort and assist himself. He simply stands before and under God. He clings fast and is faithful to Him inasmuch as, even at the risk of making a mistake, he does not cease to seek Him, i.e., to ask to what extent, with what majesty and power, He may still be his God. He cries out for the Word of God, for His new revelation, for the decision which will carry further his history with Him. He knows God as the One who knows him through and through, not as the One who is known through and through by him. He knows Him as his Advocate and Defender, not as the One who needs his assistance. Those who think otherwise, as do the friends of Job; those who imagine that they can think and speak from the standpoint of God, may be very right in what they say, as the friends of Job were right, but they are also grossly wrong. They think and speak in the garb of truth, but in this garb they think and speak untruth. Whatever might be said for or even perhaps against the true witness, as in Job's case, they represent the falsehood of man, and only a radical change of situation and attitude can alter the fact.

A second and not unrelated point to be noted is that the friends speak about God and Job in terms which are strikingly unhistorical. They preach timeless truths, truths which were once lit up as concrete Words of God and therefore as genuine truths in the context of the history of Israel, and which might perhaps shine out again and again in the context of definite happenings between God and man, but which in abstraction can only live on and bloom like cut flowers. Even when they address Job directly, they simply put before him deductions from these timeless truths. Their utterances should be compared in this respect with those of Job himself, as also with the contexts in which the truths represented by them are brought out in many of the Psalms. In Job's speeches we are plunged into the strain and stress of the ongoing history of Yahweh with him. Everything that he says, whether right or wrong, is baptised in the fire of a painful encounter with Him. Almost every word is related to the situation in which he now finds himself placed. At every point he is either describing the incomprehensible attitude of Yahweh towards him, or stating the substance of his grief and suffering and the complaint, question and protest which he must address to God. On the other hand, when we turn to the speeches of the friends, they do, of course, have something of the liveliness which is not lacking in the atmosphere of the class-room, and they have many well-weighed and perspicuous things to say on the problem, but they do not derive from the problem. They thus reflect a rather confused and indignant superiority as compared with the unsuitably violent utterances of Job. To be sure, the three friends do not speak about God merely on the intellectual level, but also on that of emotional and moral participation. And in relation to Job there is a sincere attempt at sympathy

§ 70. The Falsehood and Condemnation of Man

with him in his lot and in the state of excitement in which he finds himself. Yet the fact remains that they speak as those who are totally unaffected by the despairing struggle for the knowledge of God into which Job finds himself plunged by what has befallen him. They speak as those who are totally unaffected by the tension, which stirs Job so profoundly, between his knowledge that in this situation he has to do with Yahweh his God and his ignorance how far he has to do with Him. They obviously fail to see and understand that they have no awareness or categories for what is taking place between God and this man. They can only say to him—and this is what makes Job so impatient and truculent —that which it is always safe to say in such cases (for Job is for them only a case falling under a general rule), namely, that God is unconditionally wise and righteous, that one day the pious will surely reap their reward and the wicked their punishment, that all men are sinners, that none has any claim to preferential treatment etc. They obviously have nothing more illuminating or helpful to say, and are at such different points that they can never make any real contact, for the simple reason that the whole reality and therefore the possibility of an occurrence between God and man such as that with which they are dealing, the whole idea of the historicity of the existence both of God and of man, is so completely alien to them. And it is so completely alien to them because they will not accept it, because they prefer to limit their own relationship to God to their knowledge and acceptance of these permanently and universally valid statements concerning Him and their efforts to apply them to their own lives. Their whole aim is to convert Job to a similar relationship. And it is against this that Job struggles. What has their truth to do with the truth of God and man? This has no permanent and universal validity. The radiant claim to be always and everywhere valid is too closely threatened by the counter-claim that never and nowhere is it really valid. The real truth of God and man is valid when God and man are engaged in eye-to-eye and mouth-to-ear encounter. It is valid as the truth of the event of their common history. It is valid *hic et nunc*, as there is the meeting of God and man. In the speeches of the friends, and obviously in their whole theology, this meeting is not envisaged. Indeed, it is evaded. Earnestly though they think and speak, they utter truths which cost nothing and are worth nothing, which neither wound nor heal and which therefore involve genuine torture, which do not have to be confessed but may simply be stated with the necessary edifying patter and the demand for prompt conversion. They thus utter truths which from the very first are enveloped if not swallowed up by untruth. That is why with all their theological excellence they illustrate the falsehood of man as it emerges in confrontation with the true Witness.

Again and particularly they betray themselves as falsehood by their enclosing of the relationship between God and man in a fixed and orderly structure. What other alternative have they when they juggle away its historicity? They lay down at once as the presupposition and framework an omnipotence of God the rule of which man must make the best of since he is unable to resist it and incompetent to assess its purpose. They also lay down a wisdom of God which man must admire and honour even though, as is only natural, he cannot follow its paths. They lay down a holiness of God which is so pure and exalted that whenever a man realises that he is measured by it he must contritely see and confess his fallibility and his actual failings. Above all, they lay down an evident connexion and agreement, which God has ordained and established, which is therefore righteous, and which man must take into account and consider, between his piety and good conduct and the consequent reward which God will accord and give him on the one side, and his transgression, sin and wickedness and the terror and destruction of the penal judgment of God on the other. They thus lay down a moral world order established and maintained by God, a universal history which is also universal judgment separating the sheep on the right hand

2. The Falsehood of Man

from the goats on the left, so that each man may expect what he has justly deserved by his being and action, and each forges his own good or evil in clear fulfilment of the good and righteous will of God. But in these circumstances none can or should regard himself as innocent, or refuse to accept his share of the ills of world-occurrence as they not unjustly smite him. Those who have a good conscience in respect of their strivings should endure in the light of the bright outcome which they may finally expect. They should prove themselves upright in relation to all that they, too, have undoubtedly done wrong, and still do wrong, in relationship with God and their fellows. They should leave their ways to the extent that they were evil. They should set right what is wrong, making a new and better beginning, making progress and moving up a class in the great school of which they share both the severity and the benefits with other scholars. This is the kind of orderly structure which is discernible in the speeches of Eliphaz, Bildad and Zophar, and to the recognition and practical acknowledgment of which they try to win Job. How can we help but applaud them ? This is not just Judaism. *Mutatis mutandis*, it is also the wisdom of the Greeks, the Asiatics and the Africans. It is the common inheritance of thought and principle by which even the Christian Church has largely lived with much thankfulness, and still lives to-day. But the discrepancy between Job and his friends could hardly have been greater or sharper. For them there was a meaningful system of good and evil, of salvation and judgment, of failure and restitution. This existed from the very first. God was active merely as its Architect, Guarantor and Executor. Man was occupied merely in filling up the different columns of a questionnaire put to him and countless others with him. Job, on the other hand, saw a living, active and speaking God uniquely confronting a living man in his unique existence and responsibility. For the friends, everything was already integrated, and each event could consist only in the concrete confirmation of an ineluctably presupposed structure. For Job everything was open, active and in motion. From God's concrete being, action and speech as the Almighty, the Wise and the Righteous to man's equally concrete attitude and responsibility, whether good or bad, everything could be true only as it took place, only in the events of their encounter ; and it could show and prove itself true only as it became true. In the speeches of the friends we simply have the repetition of well-worn formulae and sacred clichés. In those of Job we have something original, new knowledge, the truth itself breaking through in all its virgin freshness. It is little wonder that no understanding or even conversation is possible between him and his friends. For these are not two theories or opinions first colliding but then amenable to clarification and compromise. The thought and utterance move on two completely different and mutually exclusive levels, so that the familiar and beautiful exhortation to listen to one another cannot possibly apply in this instance. There remains only the stark alternative. Either the friends are right and Job is utterly wrong in refusing to accept their advice, or Job is right and it is the friends who are utterly wrong. And the decision of Yahweh is that he is right and they are wrong, so seriously and totally wrong that they can be saved from impending destruction only by sacrifice and intercession. But the shattering thing about that in which they are wrong is that it is so impressively clothed in the garb of that which is right. They did not invent at random the orderly structure which they proclaimed as the truth. They pieced it together from the rags and tatters of the revelation known to them by tradition and experience and the knowledge which had impressed itself upon them. As a whole and in detail it is a counterfeit which fully resembles the truth. But, in the words of Job, they cannot construct anything better than defences and shields of clay with the elements and materials borrowed by them. The great skill of their work is unmistakeable. To this very day who is not inclined to think and speak in the categories of this structure which has such a powerful ring of truth ? But in it we are dealing with what Job describes as a

§ 70. *The Falsehood and Condemnation of Man*

brook frozen in winter and dried up in summer. The caravan is forced to go on as thirsty as when it reached it. The declaration of the Book of Job is quite unequivocal that in this structure we have to do with the falsehood of man.

For when men think and speak from this divine standpoint and therefore non-historically and within the framework of this orderly structure, there is no place in their utterances for two factors, namely, the free God and the man freed by and for Him. Yahweh as the free God of the free man Job, and Job as the free man of this free God, together in their divine and human freedom enter into the crisis in which God becomes so incomprehensible to Job even though He will not let him go, and Job becomes so angry against God even though he will not let Him go. It is in the sphere and exercise of this freedom that there takes place what does take place, the severity of God and the misery of Job, the silence of God and the crying of Job, and finally the self-revelation of Yahweh as the divine decision which closes the case, and the knowledge of Job. But this is what the friends who wish to give their assistance in this crisis can neither see nor understand. They cannot assist him because they lack all awareness or taste for either divine or human freedom, and therefore the decisive thing which is absolutely essential for true thought or utterance concerning either God or man. How, then, can they even discuss with Job?

The God of whom they speak never acts freely. He never acts in independent self-determination directed and characterised only by His own choice and love. He neither chooses nor loves. He does nothing for nought, *gratis*, according to His good-pleasure. He has no initiative in relation to man. From the very first He is just as responsible and committed to man as man to Him. In good or ill He can only react to him. He can only requite him, whether with salvation or perdition, with blessing or cursing. He owes both the one and the other. In relation to him He stands under a law distinct from Himself, the law of repayment, of reciprocal agreement, of reward and punishment. Basically, then, He is His own prisoner. He does not exist as the divine person in attributes determined by His own being, will and action, but as the personification and therefore the epitome of certain divine attributes in which He must be fundamentally perceptible to man in all His dignity, in which He must be amenable to and in need of testing and demonstration by man, which He must confirm and express in His being, will and action, and which He has actually confirmed and expressed according to the experience and insight of such clever and pious men as the three friends. He is not Yahweh and as such Elohim-Shaddai, as such righteous, wise and powerful in what is always a definite and limited sphere, as such operative and manifest in these His attributes. He is Elohim-Shaddai, righteous, wise and powerful in general and according to man's conception of deity in his positive and critical reflections; and only as such, as a special instance of His divine being, is He Yahweh, the Lord of the covenant. It is not with sovereignty, but only as bound in this twofold, i.e., external and internal way, that He ostensibly stands over man and confronts him. We say ostensibly because such an unfree God cannot really stand over him or confront him. He can be God only in the unfreedom of a man-God. Certainly this unfree God can be championed, as by the friends of Job. His historicity can be abstracted away as it is by them, and He can be honoured and loved in what is thought to be His true and non-historical essence. He can certainly be proclaimed and treated as the origin and exponent of that orderly structure, of that institutionalised truth, as again by the friends. If He could do so, He would demand that this should be the case. But this unfree God is not the God of Job. Hence he cannot really understand them when they speak of God, let alone accept their attempted persuasions in the name of this God.

Correspondingly, Job cannot recognise himself at all in what they are saying to him and therefore regarding the man confronted by God. A man freed by God is to them no less and perhaps even more strange a being than the free God

Himself. They know only the man who is free to try to set himself in the place of God and thus to speak down from heaven to his fellows. They know only the man who is free in the sense that he is not concretely claimed by any history enacted between God and himself. They know only the man who has the freedom to claim within the sphere of that orderly structure that which accrues and belongs to him. They know only the man who is free for himself, i.e., who is interested in his salvation, in the avoidance of perdition, in God, only for his own ends and not therefore for nought, *gratis*, for God's sake. They know only the man who is basically free from God and not concerned about Him at all. They know him only in the ignominious dependence and total unfreedom of this *Do ut Des* relationship. They do not know him as the one who is freed from this dependence by God, by His choice and love, in order that he may in return choose and love God for His own sake, because God is the God who first chooses and loves him. It is as and because they know nothing, and want to know nothing, of this free man who is just as terrifying to them as the free God, and perhaps more so, that the three friends are inevitably so very shocked by Job's obstinate protestation of his innocence, which in fact is nothing other than the freedom given him by God and exercised in relation to Him. And it is because this means everything to Job—together with the indissolubly related freedom of God—that he must insist upon this protestation even though it gives the maximum of offence and more. The freedom of both God and man is the truth as whose witness he confronts them. It is at this truth that they stumble and fall. We certainly cannot say that it is entirely absent from their speeches. As always happens in conflict against the truth, it is rather suppressed and replaced. Instead of the true freedom of God there appears a freedom which amounts only to a general notion of His unconditional power and majesty ; and instead of the true freedom of man a freedom which amounts only to the ascription to him of the light-hearted ability to think and speak from the standpoint of heaven, non-historically and within the framework of that orderly structure, and thus in the question of salvation or perdition to decide, as it is hoped, for salvation and not perdition, and in this context, but only in this context, to decide for God and not against Him. But this is indeed to change the truth into untruth. And as this is done in the speeches of the three friends, there is erected in them an unparalleled monument to falsehood, to the falsehood of the man of sin.

To be sure, this monument is only a by-product of the Book of Job. That it gives it only incidental notice is at once apparent from its striking omission of any attempt at differentiation or characterisation in its depiction of the three men and their utterances or of Job's attitude towards them—an omission which some expositors have ingeniously but only artificially and unconvincingly tried to make good. As compared with the sharply delineated figure of Job, they are only secondary characters with no particular individuality, and therefore, as compared with the highly unique revelation of the truth in the bearing, attitude and utterances of Job, the revelation of falsehood in their stereotyped speeches cannot be more than a *parergon* of the presentation which is the true aim of the poem. Yet it is a very clear *parergon*, and as such it demands an attention not always given it in exposition. For where the true witness enters, his very doubtful friends will soon appear. Where the truth of God and man is manifested, the falsehood of man will necessarily be revealed as well.

3. THE CONDEMNATION OF MAN

In the corresponding sub-section of the first and second parts of the doctrine of reconciliation we spoke of the fall and misery of man : of his fall, i.e., of the way in which in his pride he pays the guilt of his existence which he does not have to pay but which is cancelled only in the death of Jesus Christ ; and of his misery, i.e., of the way in which in his sloth he falls victim to the slavery of his existence which he does not have to throw off but which again is overcome only in the death of Jesus Christ. The threat entailed by and indeed enclosed in the falsehood of man must be described, however, by an incomparably sharper word. What he chooses and draws down upon himself with his falsehood is his condemnation. To be condemned is to be judged, i.e., to be judged by God. The man of sin in his fully developed form as a liar is the man who goes forward to his condemnation. It is his condemnation not merely because he will not accept the truth of his deliverance from guilt and slavery but because he tries to turn it into its opposite, desiring to live by and in the untruth into which he attempts to change the truth. It is his condemnation simply to be hopelessly guilty in his pride and hopelessly enslaved in his sloth. The threat under which he comes to stand and indeed places himself as he lies, is that he will be nailed to his lie, that he will be treated seriously as a liar, that he will be granted and finally assigned to a life by and in untruth as the portion which he himself has chosen, a life which as such can only be a lost life, and can only be described as such. A life in this condemnation is the evil which Yahweh seriously destines for the friends of Job and which they have themselves chosen as their future with their falsehood. We must now try to see how man comes to stand under this threat and what his situation under it implies.

Jesus Christ accomplished what man had no freedom, right, nor power to accomplish, namely, the reconciliation of the world to God, the deliverance of man from the guilt and slavery of his sin, his justification and sanctification, his acceptance into peace with God as the fellowship of Father and son. In accomplishing this, He lived and died as the true Son of God and the true Son of Man. No one and nothing can undo or reverse this free act of the free grace of the free God in which there has already taken place the birth of a new and free man. And in the Word of the same resurrected and living Jesus Christ, in the power of the promise of the Holy Spirit, there is continued right into our own time that which once took place in His life and death in the simple form of the truth of that reality, the light of that life, the disclosure that we were concerned in that free act of God and therefore in that birth of a free man, that it applies to us in our time, that we derive from our deliverance as it has taken place in Jesus Christ and indeed from our acceptance in Him into the fellowship of the children of God, that we here and now may live in and with Him as those who are saved and exalted to be the children of God by Him. This good news is the truth. But we start back from it as it comes to us. Why ? We have given certain reasons. We are startled by the identity of the Witness who proclaims it, of His truth, with the reality disclosed by Him. We are startled by the form of His passion, and therefore by the narrowness of the way and the straitness of the gate through which He bids us pass to be with Him. We are startled by the miracle of God and of the Holy Spirit to whom we are invited to entrust ourselves in this disclosure. We are startled by the freedom in which God acts for and to us according to this disclosure, and also by the freedom which He gives to us yet also requires of us. To be sure, these can and should all be reasons for rejoicing rather than starting back in horror. Yet the fact remains that when this disclosure is made we who are men of sin start back instead of rejoicing. How can the man of sin be made to see and understand to whom he owes his existence and the possibility of his continued existence after what has taken place for him in Jesus Christ? Who of us is in any position to understand even himself as the man of sin he is and must confess himself to be? By its very nature sin defies explanation or understanding. Both *ante* and *post Christum* it is man's impossible possibility which as such is not amenable to rational presentation. It is simply a brute fact. The man of sin exists in the manner possible to him. And as such he is startled by the Word of truth. And because he is startled by it, he must try to evade it, to keep it from his ears and mind, to reject it. But he cannot dismiss the promise of the Holy Spirit from the world either generally or in his own case. Once it comes, the encounter with it is inescapable. And because he cannot avoid it, he has recourse to falsehood, attempting as we have seen, and as illustrated in the speeches of the friends of Job, to turn the truth which oppresses him into untruth. It is thus that he comes under the threat of condemnation.

For in refusing the Word of truth he refuses his pardon. And what is his attempt to turn the truth into untruth but a foolish attempt to turn his pardon into its opposite, into judgment and condemnation? The process must be exposed with merciless clarity. The promise of the Spirit, the Word spoken to man by the risen and living Jesus Christ as the Prophet of the truth of God, is as follows. Thou art no longer the man of sin whose figure and role thou dost still assume. That man is set aside and overcome. He is dead. Thou canst be that man no longer, not just because thou hast put him to death, but because thou hast done so in My death and passion. I have lived,and died for thee. In Me thou becomest and art another man justified before God and sanctified for Him : thou in Me as the Son of God and Man who exists in thy place as thy Saviour, Head and Lord ; thou as My brother and therefore a child of God, who has acted and decided and spoken through Me, as thine. Freedom is thus established, proclaimed and given by Me : perfect remission from the guilt which thou in thy pride hast taken on thyself ; full liberation from the slavery to which thou in thy sloth hast sold thyself ; unconditional authorisation and wholly adequate empowering for a real life accepted and

464 § 70. *The Falsehood and Condemnation of Man*

accepting and therefore joyful, for a life which cannot be lost because it is lived with God and eternally. This is the Word spoken to man in its identity with the One who speaks it. This is the Word of His cross, the Word of God, the promise of the Spirit. Whether it pleases him or not, whether it cheers or startles him, this is its substance, promise and claim. Wholly and utterly and in every respect it is his pardon which is declared by the true Witness of the truth. This and this alone, but in all its fulness, is what he hears from Him. And it is to this that he reacts when he lies and thus attempts to change the truth into untruth. What can this attempt signify and be, then, but a foolish effort to change his pardon into its opposite, its divine validity into a divine validity of the condemnation which would certainly overtake him, the proud and slothful wretch, the bankrupt debtor and slave of sin that he is, were not Jesus Christ his Saviour, Head and Lord ? To lie is to try to substitute for the election of man fulfilled by God a rejection which is not God's will for him and which according to God's Word is averted by His act. The decisive purpose of lying is that the free God should be replaced by One who is externally and internally bound, and that the man freed by and for God should be replaced by one who in his self-determination is " selfless " in the worst sense of the word, i.e., incapable of genuine self-determination and therefore unfree. Lying is denial of free grace as the truly divine reality and possibility, and repudiation of free gratitude as man's only possible response to it. Lying is the rash attempt to set up a situation between God and man in which Jesus Christ does not exist as the Mediator between them. Lying is the provocation of God in which man wantonly tries to set himself at the point where only God's naked wrath will strike and destroy him. What man actually utters when he lies, even if he does not put it in words as is unfortunately so often the case, is no other than the dreadful cursing of himself : " Well, I'll be damned ! " This means, however, that in and with the lie there comes into view and action again the man who in Jesus Christ, and therefore in the eternal election and historical act of God, has been displaced and overcome and put to death, i.e., the man of sin who, as he denies and rejects God, his fellows and finally himself, can only be denied and rejected and judged and damned by God, and can thus exist only in logical self-destruction, being doomed ultimately to perish and be lost. As man lies, he conjures up the shade of this dead man and thus places himself under this threat. But he does actually lie. Thus the time determined by the return of Jesus Christ in the promise of the Holy Spirit, this time of ours, is characterised not only by this promise, but also by the falsehood of man which in this sphere, in the very encounter with the prophetic Word, arises and spreads itself abroad in its most dangerous form. Our time, and all of us in it, stand not only in the light of life, but also in this shadow of death, under the threat which acquires power and is an active and

3. The Condemnation of Man

therefore unquestionable reality in virtue of falsehood. The lying man as such, set in the situation corresponding to his imaginations and pretensions, can only be the man who is judged and condemned by God and is therefore lost.

He stands under the threat and danger of being damned. His condemnation hangs over him like a sword. Less than this cannot be said in relation to his falsehood. With it he has brought himself into this danger, leaving the point where he is totally and definitively pardoned and therefore safe, taking up the position where he can expect no pardon but only condemnation, and thus standing under this sword. His condemnation is not yet pronounced. There is still only the threat and menace of it. But these are real enough. By reason of his falsehood his situation is determined by the prospect and expectation of condemnation. By reason of his falsehood this and this alone is his future. The moment God nails him to his fatal exchange of places, to his falsehood, to his cursing of himself, the sword will inevitably fall, his condemnation will become a present reality and he can only be lost. God has not yet done this. But in virtue of man's falsehood everything points to the fact that He will do so, that He might just as well do so to-day as to-morrow, and that man therefore can only be damned and lost. This is the first thing which has to be said. Naturally more than this cannot be said. The threat has not yet been fulfilled; the sword has not yet fallen. Fearful as it is, the danger is still only a danger. Man lies, but he is not yet damned and lost. From the standpoint of his lying, he can and should be every moment. But so far he is not. God has not yet willed to keep him to what he has attempted in his lying, to nail him to the exchange on the basis of which an end must finally be made of him. So far man still has time. This is the second thing which has to be said with the same seriousness. In the light of the inconceivable rise and domination of falsehood, and the many attempts to transubstantiate truth into untruth, it might often have been assumed during the course of the Christian era that the cup was full and the wrath of God must fall. Occasionally the same, indeed, the far more terrifying thought might have struck many of us in relation to our own participation in Christian falsehood. But in neither case has the end yet come. The condemnation which seems to be man's immediate prospect and expectation has not yet taken place. He is not yet lost as he should be according to his sin. The evil justly assigned by Yahweh to the friends of Job has not yet broken over them. The third point must be made, however, that the fact that what threatens has not yet taken place does not mean that it has no present significance and actuality. We cannot lie and then, because the dreadful end does not come and we are not damned and lost, carry on as if nothing had happened. It does not mean nothing to say: " Well, I'll be damned!" even though it is God's affair whether or when He will take seriously and put into effect this insane desire. What takes place immediately in and with falsehood—and it is quite enough—is that man is betrayed into the shadow of that threat and on to the steep slope at the end of which he will be damned. It carries with it a far-reaching alteration, if not for the worst, at least for the unmistakeable evil of being thrust on to this slope and having to spend the time which remains in this fatal movement. The man who lies is not spared this. It is not the case, then, that for the time being no direct harm is done by his evading the truth as suits himself. More especially, he does not find the peace and well-being which he tries to create by assuring himself against its attack and hiding from it as his first parents did in Paradise. In making this attempt, he assumes the figure and role of the man of sin and gives new actuality to his fall and misery. It may be only an attempt. The man of sin who lives again in him, and who has really been displaced, overcome and put to death in Jesus Christ, may be only an arbitrarily conjured shade. The falsehood of man may be only an undertaking which finally proves impracticable. The fact remains that this attempt has its consequences in which the future chosen by the man who lies, even though not yet present, is directly enough delineated and proclaimed. This future determines, characterises, burdens and obscures already the present in which he is not yet damned and lost but only moving to his condemnation and perdition. As he lies and deceives, even while he awaits further developments he implicates himself in a lost and false situation.

It is the same situation in which men exist whom Jesus Christ has not yet encountered to the extent that for some reason they have not yet been reached by the proclamation of the divine pardon. They, too, live as though Jesus Christ did not exist and the pardon issued and being issued in Him had no validity. Thus they, too, live on the steep slope on which man's condemnation is his only future and at the bottom of which they can only be lost as the debtors and slaves of their sins. They, too, live under the unpleasant conditions which mark the fatal movement in this direction. Falsehood as the specifically Christian form of sin thus has the first general result that, when the Christian transforms the truth revealed and proclaimed to him into untruth, he is betrayed, or relapses, or causes himself to relapse, into the same situation as that from which he had to be redeemed as Jesus Christ encountered him and as he could thus perceive and accept the divine pardon. It places him in a similar if not exactly the same situation as that of the blind and the deaf who have not yet had any opportunity to hear and appropriate this pardon, to be nourished by its truth, to live a new life in the true human situation created by the reconciliation of the world to God effected in Jesus Christ. In lying, the Christian resumes the old life of the blind and deaf among whom he was once numbered. He returns from the true situation disclosed to him to the untrue situation of "heathenism." The only thing is that the conditions under which man has to exist in it are undoubtedly made much more unpleasant for him by the fact that it is his falsehood which has placed him there. This cannot be said of the rest. It is relatively in their favour that they have had no opportunity of changing the truth into untruth. It has not yet encountered them. But it has encountered the Christian. He has changed it into untruth, and he is thus delivered up to their situation, in which he must exist as if Jesus Christ did not exist even though he calls and fancies himself a Christian. It is obvious that the results for him are relatively more serious. His situation is not merely untrue; it is lost and false. And this means that even in this situation he is accompanied and not let go by the recollection of the unfalsified truth which encountered and seized him but which he tried to escape and therefore falsified, by the suppressed knowledge that according to this truth everything could and should be different. Since he has put himself in this situation artificially, it can never be natural or self-evident that he should be there. In it he can never enjoy the relative innocuousness and security of those who have no inkling of the true situation but can only regard the untrue as normal. He has more than an inkling of the true situation. It has been disclosed to him. Hence he can no longer be in his element in the untrue. Under the burden of Christian falsehood he finds it harder to be deprived of freedom from the guilt and slavery of sin than non-Christians who have never heard of this freedom, but have so far been spared the encounter with truth, the fear of it, and the temptation to falsify it. Hence the fact, which often calls for notice, that "the children of this world" (Lk. 16^8) are in their status and sphere wiser than "the children of light," i.e., that in the fatal human situation in which Jesus Christ seems to be absent, no matter how unpleasant or difficult this may be for them, non-Christians are relatively better able both morally and technically to make do, to help themselves and to conduct themselves calmly and cheerfully, than are Christians who have been in encounter with the truth and have denied and falsified it.

Nor should we forget an additional factor in the case of Christians, namely, that in relation to these others with whom they are now in the same boat they necessarily have a guilty conscience, and if not, they are actually encumbered by the fact that the falsification of the truth which is their work and not that of the others is one reason, if not the main one, why the light of the Gospel does not shine more brightly in the world, so that they can be surrounded by countless men to whom the divine pardon has either not been attested at all, or not been attested in a way which is credible and convincing. "You have not come over and helped us" (cf. Acts 16^9). You could not help us. How could the friends of Job have even the desire, let alone the power, to do evangelistic or missionary work? And even if they had, how

§ 70. *The Falsehood and Condemnation of Man*

could they even interest anyone in the cause of God and man, let alone win him for it ? How can a Christianity in which there has been so much and such powerful spiritual and common lying force a way for the truth and therefore for the message of freedom into all the spheres in which it has not yet been proclaimed and heard ? With all its individual members, it is burdened by this heavy responsibility. That is to say, Christians have not merely to suffer what all must suffer in the untrue situation in which Jesus Christ seems to be absent, but whether they think of it or not—and they ought to think of it— they must also exist under the accusation of the suffering of all the others who have not yet heard the divine pardon because of their arbitrary repudiation and insane attempt at falsehood.

We are reminded of the prophet Jonah fleeing from Yahweh and His commission ($1^{3f.}$). On board the ship from Joppa to Tarshish he was down below fast asleep when because of him the storm threatened to engulf the ship and its crew. But the lot fell on him. And the upshot was that to save the ship and the crew, the rest hesitantly—and even with vows and sacrifices—yet also resolutely threw him into the sea, and the storm was abated. The only thing was that Jonah openly confessed his guilt to these pagans and himself advised them what to do, whereas, when the world threatens to cast Christianity overboard, it is seldom ready to admit that the general misery which has brought this about can have anything whatever to do with its own guilt, but usually sees all the failings in the evil world, and, far from being prepared to denounce its own sin and make free restitution for its fault, it normally protests most vociferously against any open threats of ejection.

The real unpleasantness and misery, however, of the untrue situation of man and the lost and false situation of the Christian under the threat of damnation, is that his whole being is given an aspect which deforms, distorts and corrupts its true reality. In its reality his world is the world which is created good by God and reconciled to Him in Jesus Christ. And in his own reality he is the man created good by God and justified before and sanctified for Him in Jesus Christ. This is true. And in the true human situation the aspect under which his reality will represent itself to man will necessarily correspond to this truth. But how can he live by and in this truth when he tries to change it into untruth ? In making this attempt, he is betrayed into the untrue, false situation in which his reality represents itself to him under an aspect which contradicts rather than corresponds to the truth. It has not really changed, or been replaced by another reality. The falsehood of man has no power to alter or even to set aside the reality of God and man in Jesus Christ. It has only the power, and this only to the extent that it is given or left to it by God in His wrath, to be man's punishment as well as his sin by causing the aspect under which this reality represents itself in man to contradict rather than to correspond to the truth which man himself is seeking to transform into untruth. The reality discloses itself to him in an image which is defaced, distorted and corrupted. In this

3. The Condemnation of Man

image it has not changed itself or the truth. Nor has it disappeared from it. For the truth which man tries to change into untruth is always the truth. But as the unconquered and unconquerable truth which it still is in this image, it punishes the man who tries to subject it to this process by representing itself and the reality of his being in such a way as to correspond to the untruth into which he seeks to transform it. Unavoidably it encounters him in this distorted image. We cannot stand on our heads, if we attempt and are able to do so, without seeing everything other than it is and in distortion of its true reality. Everything is upside down and the wrong way round. Man is thus forced to live with this distorted image which he has set up by his falsehood and which corresponds to it. As he sees things, so they are, not in themselves, but for him. So, then, he must have and experience them, and so they must have their effect on him. The distorted image has as such reality and power in relation to the one who stirs it up by his falsehood. It controls, determines, limits and characterises his existence. He is forced to have and to experience the world and himself in the defaced, distorted and corrupted form in which they represent themselves to him in this image. He exists in a subjective reality alien to and contradicting his objective reality. He is still the man whom God created good and who is reconciled to God. He has not been allowed to fall. He has not slipped out of the grasp of the divine power and mercy. But as this man he is obviously punished by God. In accordance with his untruth and falsification, he finds himself in an untrue and falsified situation. He is a bewitched man in a bewitched world. We are not speaking of the worst thing. He is only moving towards this in this situation and bewitchment. To be sentenced, condemned and lost is the worst thing. But it is bad enough to be moving towards this. It is bad enough to be under the dominion of the all-distorting image, to have to stand under the provisional judgment of the truth changed into untruth by human falsehood.

The pathology of the man of sin is not part of the true subject-matter of dogmatics. We should not tarry in the depths of even the provisional judgment to which he has fallen victim. To realise the seriousness of the situation, it is enough to point briefly to these depths without trying to plumb them, to recall in a few sentences the well-known painfulness of the situation in which man finds himself when he exists as though Jesus Christ did not exist, and into which the Christian in particular arbitrarily manoeuvres himself by means of his falsehood.

The false image in which his reality represents itself to him, and under the dominion of which he has to live, has no centre. That it lives by the reality, and therefore not without the truth, is shown by the fact that man cannot refrain from seeking a centre or meaningful source of his being, from trying to give himself such a centre. But the perversion of the truth into untruth in which the reality represents

§ 70. *The Falsehood and Condemnation of Man*

itself in this image, shows itself in the fact that this seeking is a restless probing in which it seems legitimate and imperative to set one thing after another in the centre, to make one thing after another the necessary origin of his being, to see, understand, think, act and behave now in the light of one thing and now another, in short, to try to live always in a certain *euphoria* and also a certain assurance, yet always to be disillusioned, always to be ready to change the zealously adopted standpoint, to burn to-morrow what is worshipped to-day. It is a probing in the different phases of which he always finds himself finally thrust back to some point on the periphery. In this dominating image there is lacking a centre which he has not to posit, which is posited already, which cannot be lost, but which is once for all to be respected.

Having no centre, however, the image is also without any periphery. Having no definite because given source, the being of man has no definite because given goal. It has no limit nor law. The image in which the reality represents itself is not without truth to the extent that it is concerned with possibilities which he is encouraged and summoned to realise. But he realises them—and it is here that we see that the truth changed into untruth is the origin—only in a general way, with no precise reference to even his own specific and genuine possibilities. He thus hastens forward without guidance or direction, abandoned to the control of this image, with neither plan nor goal nor limit, scurrying hither and thither, with no definite orientation, open on all sides, ready for anything, and therefore not really free, but the prisoner of his own empty demand for extension, and therefore of his inner caprice and external fate.

Again, there is no real co-existence. The image in which his reality represents itself seems to indicate and disclose such a coexistence to the extent that it is not without truth. But since it reflects only the truth changed into untruth, this co-existence dissolves at once into a mere proximity and finally hostility. It lacks any unifying force, and thus the relation of man to his fellows oscillates between a commitment to various interests which makes them seem indispensable as instruments for various purposes, through practical indifference in which their existence is only a neutral factor, to open or secret enmity in which they become annoying, disruptive and dangerous figures against whose existence and self-expression he can only adopt a defensive and offensive attitude. A similar oscillation characterises his relation to other creatures, to the great and little cosmic realities which in their totality form the sphere in which he may fulfil his role and enact his history as man. In this respect, too, everything seems and is equally possible, from bold grasping and enjoyment as though this sphere belonged to him and only awaited his skill to make it useful, through ungrateful remoteness in which he is unaffected by its light and shade and uninterested in what

3. The Condemnation of Man 471

it offers, living in it as though he did not really do so, to the provoking discovery that this house, too, has limits and walls, and therefore to the attempt to break through these, to disappointment or vexation at the failure of this attempt, and then to sorrowful resignation in which the whole is experienced only as cosmic evil and is found to be tolerable or intolerable as such. Why the one or the other, or the one after the other, or perhaps an endless alternation between them? No answer can be given. The image in which the reality of man represents itself in his untrue situation provides no answer but continually leads him astray. In relation both to his fellow-men and to the cosmos it speaks only of a co-existence which is constantly transformed into an empty proximity and even hostility.

In general terms, this is the great painfulness and profound falsity of the human situation under the dominion of the false image in which his reality appears in accordance with his falsehood. There is here no steadfastness and therefore no certainty nor sure advance. We always seem to be dealing with the truth and with man's life before and in it. But the truth always escapes him, and so, too, does his life, like a butterfly slipping through the fingers of a child. Life involves an unceasing dialectic, in which he is pushed and rocked backwards and forwards by an alien, irresistible movement, being caught up in a constant change and alternation, in sheer ambiguities, in a relativity and convertibility of all antitheses, which make pointless any will to abide, indeed, any will at all and therefore any consistent action. Do we live in a strange but very puzzling and therefore unsettling harmony with the plenitude of phenomena, or in a glorious but ultimately fatal isolation from them? Is it really worth while to move over from attractive caprice to rigid morality? But is it worth while to follow the opposite path from Pharisaism to Bohemianism? Is it better to hasten than to wait? But why should it not be better to wait than to hasten? Is there any self-assertion which does not finally result in despicable self-surrender, or self-surrender which is not perhaps an extreme form of despicable self-assertion? Is there any desire which is not anxiety, or does not finish up as such? Conversely, is there any anxiety, even the profoundest, which does not have the glow of desire or concupiscence and threaten at any moment to break out into a consuming fire? Is there a humour which can laugh without weeping, or a seriousness which man can assert without laughter? Should we pursue religion? Why not? But why not equally a sober or enthusiastic secularism? Can we seriously try to be conservative or progressive? Reaction always provokes revolution, and revolution reaction. In this antithesis, and all the other alternatives, is there a wise mean, a neutral abstention from choice? Yes, but only at the cost of surrendering activity to inactivity, in which everything perhaps calls for even more clear and active decision. Only at the cost perhaps of declining responsibility in the

§ 70. The Falsehood and Condemnation of Man

most important questions and thus becoming even more useless than the most useless demagogues and zealots on the right hand and the left. Is not all contending for the rights and freedom of the individual burdened by the fact that it does violence to fellowship, and all contending for fellowship by the fact that it does violence to the rights and freedom of the individual? Is there any faithfulness on the one side without the reverse of open or secret unfaithfulness on the other? Is there firmness without severity, enthusiasm without fanaticism, soberness without aridity, love without tyranny? Is there building up without pulling down? Is there a Yes without the bitter and in some way unjust No which causes injury to someone? Is there any prudence which at some level is not cowardice, any sympathy, however sincere and well-meaning, which is not offensive? Can we comfort ourselves with the reflection that all things, with the sure and certain dangers which they bring, have their own time in which they can and should be ventured afresh? But if so, when is the time for one thing and when for another? Who authorises or commands me to select this and reject that as even temporally expedient, let alone as right or wrong for higher and more lasting reasons? Who is really at the helm? What authority has this or that old or new principle, or the third person in whose goodness and power I trust, or finally I myself? Yet every time I select or reject, and make the ensuing movement, I have to do with an act of my own most inward life, and perhaps with one which may have decisive and incalculable consequences for others, for human good or ill on the widest possible front.

What more can we say? The situation is so profoundly indeterminate, when to all these questions only provisional and relatively right and important answers can be given, when the very answers hasten to their own dissolution, when the last word seems to rest with the sorry figure of Pilate and his question: " What is truth? " It is so obviously an untrue, and in the case of Christians a false and falsified, situation under the lordship of an image in which the very different reality willed and realised by God is present only in a way which is concealed, defaced, distorted and corrupted, because man, when he is confronted by it and by the revelation of the truth, does not joyfully and thankfully face and accept it, but rather tries to conceal it. In these circumstances, he does not see or have or experience anything—either the world or himself—as it is, but only as it is not.

The painfulness of the situation is concentrated, and finds its most striking co-efficient and exponent, in the problematical nature of human speech. In themselves and as such, speaking and hearing are a wonderful possibility in the realisation of which the human situation could and should and would become really human. What should take place in human speaking and hearing is the utterance, declaration and revelation of human reality with a view to its indication,

3. The Condemnation of Man

impartation and communication to others and with the final purpose of the communion or fellowship of the one with the others. But when man not only resists the truth but changes it into untruth, when he wills to live in untruth, human reality cannot be uttered or expressed or declared or revealed, and therefore it cannot be imparted or communicated, in his speech. His speech can only lack this determination. All human speaking and hearing suffer from this, and not least, but first of all, those which are Christian. If speech is " the house of being," the occupier seems to have left without giving any definite address. This is why it is so tremendous a task, constantly to be resumed and accepted with resignation, not only to say, even in our own thoughts to ourselves, let alone to others, that which we really intend to say in the way intended, but also to hear that which others both say and intend to say, i.e., to interpret or even to discern the dream with which they are occupied when they say it. This is why human speech especially is the arena of such ceaseless misconceptions and errors, and also of so many more or less intentional great or small concealments and distortions, and also of so many tragic and comic misunderstandings for which both speakers and hearers must usually share the responsibility. This is why the truth is inexpressible when referred to our human speaking and hearing, and yet only a cheap wisdom and sorry consolation can meet the situation by holding and declaring that silence is the better part, i.e., by either renouncing altogether the realisation of this most human of all human possibilities or by undertaking it only with the greatest hesitance and resignation. This is why fellowship in human reality, which must and may be the final goal of speech, is never attainable by man of himself, his speech serving rather to promote alienation and disunity between man and man, and therefore inhumanity.

And we have to remember that this whole painful and perverted being, perception and experience which are the lot of man in the situation created by his falsehood are only his being under the threat of the condemnation which this falsehood entails. The condemnation itself implies God's acquiescence in the cheerless disintegration of man's existence and situation. It implies His allowing man to glide headlong down that slope and finally to be lost. To be damned is to be committed to an eternity in which we are rejected by God and therefore lost. It is to have to be finally what we wish to be when we change truth into untruth and live in and by this untruth. This sword has not yet fallen. This worst thing has not yet taken place. But it is indeed bad enough to have to exist under the threat of damnation. Human life stands under the warning sign, the painfulness of which we have briefly indicated.

This is something which has to be said. It concerns the mystery of iniquity which cannot be overlooked or explained away, which is supremely real and active in its own fatal manner, in the era *post*

Christum, in our own time. It is very disturbing to have to say and confess this. And it applies to us all. Yet we cannot say or confess it correctly without finally thinking of the limits within which it is true and applies to us all. It is the important negative subsidiary clause of an even more important and dominant principal clause. Inescapable though it is, it is true and applies to us only as conditioned and limited by this principal clause. We have also to see and consider a great sign which stands before but also after the acknowledgment of this small one. It is not for nothing that in this section we have dealt much more basically and explicitly with the true Witness to the truth than with the falsehood and condemnation of man. Quite literally, it is not for nothing. That He exists and lives and works is the principal sentence which forms the presupposition or limit without which the statement we have just made would have no basis as a subsidiary clause and could not be understood.

What is the bearing of this ? When talking of the falsehood of man which carries with it his condemnation, and first his existence under the threat of condemnation, we have always been careful to speak only of man's attempt to change the truth into untruth. That man wants to do this ; that he tries to do it ; that this attempt is the culmination of his sin in its specifically Christian form ; and that it entails and encloses that change for the worse and expectation of the worst, is all obvious enough. But when we really consider the matter, it is even more obvious that, although this attempt is resolved, planned and taken in hand, it can never succeed or reach its goal. The falsehood of man is ultimately only his falsehood. It may take many forms, but it can never be more than this. Startled by the truth which encounters him in the true Witness, man may imagine a truth according to his heart's desire, a pseudo-truth. With great power and cunning he may project, allege and impose this by false pretences. He does this, and in so doing he accomplishes something. Untruth as such is thus introduced by him as a factor which is real and effective enough in its own way and within its own limits. And he himself is the man responsible for its reality and effectiveness. It is he who burdens himself with the ineluctable consequences of the untruth produced by him for his own situation. He now is what he has to be in the contradiction between his subjective and his objective reality. Yet he cannot accomplish the one thing which he really has in view. He cannot change the truth into untruth. He cannot dissolve the truth, or cause it to disappear, in untruth. It seems as though he can do this in the deception which is real and effective enough in its own way. But this deception does not even touch the truth, let alone alter it, or rob it of its power, or expel it from the world. It touches and alters only man and his situation. Not can it expel even man himself from the world and therefore from the sphere of truth. He may use great strength and cunning in advancing it,

3. The Condemnation of Man

but the truth is still valid for him and still applies to him. It is the fixed star which shines unchanged above all the clouds created by him, pursuing its own course without deviation. As compared with untruth, it has the insurpassable advantage of having behind it and for it the divinely willed and created and ordered and determined reality of man in the person of its true Witness, Jesus Christ, and therefore the love with which God has actively loved and loves and will love the world and man in this One, and the fellowship of the free God with the man freed by Him and for Him. As compared with falsehood, it has the decisive advantage of being the light, the Word, the revelation, the glory of this God and this man. That this weighs in its favour means that it cannot even be disturbed, let alone outweighed, by any revelation which the falsehood of man may bring against it. Man can stand on his own head, but he cannot make the truth do so. He can only attempt to change it into untruth.

Nor is this all. The truth is identical with the living Jesus Christ, its true Witness. It is identical with the personal work of His self-declaration as the self-revelation and self-impartation of the reconciliation effected in Him. It is identical with His prophecy, with the promise of the Spirit, and therefore with the present reality of God and man in this time of ours. It does not merely stand superior like the fixed star above man and his attempt to change the truth into untruth. The history between it and the man who make this attempt continues. It goes into offensive action against this attempt in all its superiority to untruth. Thus the man who produces untruth is continually confused, unsettled and attacked by it. It continually falls upon him in this undertaking. It is not true therefore—how could it be ?—that the era *post Christum* is a sphere which is effectively controlled or even blockaded by human falsehood. It is also and much more the sphere in which the manoeuvres of lying man are constantly disrupted and thwarted as by an invisible hand. This man cannot live undisturbed, or project, allege and impose what he desires. To his different attempts in this direction, in a way which is always unexpected and most unwelcome, limits and conclusions are set beyond which he grows tired of what he has undertaken and final abandons his efforts. Great and little, insignificant and yet sometimes also spectacular manifestations of the truth surprise him and pierce like lightning the clouds produced by him, overthrowing him completely even though he may later resume his attempts in another form. These provisional indications show him that the last word belongs to them and not to him, that the time will come when his efforts will have had their day and will be ended, that even now his successes are doubtful, vulnerable and transitory. On a strictly sober view of our time we must also see that in an astonishing way provision is made to rouse sleeping men and Christians, to interrupt their evil dreams, to bring about the recognition that they were and are and will be dreams,

476   § 70. *The Falsehood and Condemnation of Man*

to light up again the reality. It is most astonishing when we consider the men and especially the Christians to whom this happens, and yet it is not in the least astonishing but supremely natural when we consider who is present among us " with His Spirit and gifts."

The fact that the truth not only has an insurpassable advantage over falsehood but is on the offensive against it has an unmistakeable significance and effect on the false and illusory situation of man under the threat of approaching condemnation. What makes this situation so painful, as we have seen, is the defacing, distorting and corrupting image in which reality must represent itself to those who try to change truth into untruth and under the dominion of which they can experience it only in the bad form indicated. But as the truth cannot be violated, altered or expelled by the falsehood of man, the reality of the free God and the man freed by Him and for Him cannot be violated, altered or expelled by the image in which it must represent itself to lying man as the ground of so much pain. And as the truth is on the offensive against the falsehood of man, so this reality is on the offensive against the dominion of this perverting image and therefore against the unavoidable evil and painfulness of man's situation under its lordship. As the reconciliation of the world to God, the justification and sanctification of man, is the reality, and indeed the living and present reality in Jesus Christ the true Witness of its truth, a limit is set both to the falsehood of man and also to his decay and destruction, to the disintegration of his existence under the dominion of the pseudo-reality of that image. War is declared on them and they are checked. We cannot withdraw or erase anything that we have said concerning the process of disintegration. But we cannot describe it without recalling that its course is also determined and conditioned by the reality of God and man in Jesus Christ which is not affected by but resists it. It would be ungrateful and shortsighted if we were not to recognise that on this basis it is constantly opposed by sustaining, unifying, positive factors and forces. It may be very powerful and its effects far-reaching, but it can operate only under this counter-pressure. The manifestations of the truth are followed—for " the truth shall make you free "—by manifestations of the freedom of God and man. If the human situation is bad enough, it cannot be denied that it might be worse, and that it is not worse because it is continually shot through by these manifestations of the truth and freedom, because it is determined in fact not only by its great painfulness but also openly or secretly by so much that is good and beautiful descending from above rather than arising from below. For not only *intra* but *extra muros ecclesiae* there are also lights in the darkness, clarities in confusion, constants in the oscillating dialectic of our existence, orders in disorder, certainties in the great sea of doubt, genuine speaking and hearing even in the labyrinth of human speech. They are all very wonderful and unexpected and unforeseen.

3. The Condemnation of Man

They are always completely new when they come. But they are never wholly lacking to us men and Christians in our time. We should always hope for them and pray for them. For the reality of God and man in Jesus Christ is superior to the pseudo-reality to which we are delivered by our falsehood. Nor is it idle in respect of it, but on the offensive against it. Inevitably, the experience of the limits of our bad situation, and of the good and the beautiful which are not withheld from us, but rather, to be more exact, are lavished upon us, will always be in fact the new and unexpected work of grace and its revelation. God does not owe us this gift and experience. It can only be a matter of free grace and therefore of liberations by and for the free God, whether in great things or small. But the secret of the continuation under threat both of Christianity and of humanity generally is the fact that they may continually experience the unexpected work of grace and its revelation, so that in spite of all the apparently unavoidable consequences of falsehood, and the corresponding despotism of that perverted image, they may again and again be nourished and live by this unexpected work.

A final word is demanded concerning the threat under which the perverted human situation stands, in spite of its limitation by the powerful and superior reality of God and man, to the extent that from below it is also continually determined by the falsehood of man in a sinister but very palpable manner. Can we count upon it or not that this threat will not finally be executed, that the sword will not fall, that man's condemnation will not be pronounced, that the sick man and even the sick Christian will not die and be lost rather than be raised and delivered from the dead and live? This question belongs to eschatology, but two delimitations may be apposite in this context.

First, if this is not the case, it can only be a matter of the unexpected work of grace and its revelation on which we cannot count but for which we can only hope as an undeserved and inconceivable overflowing of the significance, operation and outreach of the reality of God and man in Jesus Christ. To the man who persistently tries to change the truth into untruth, God does not owe eternal patience and therefore deliverance any more than He does those provisional manifestations. We should be denying or disarming that evil attempt and our own participation in it if, in relation to ourselves or others or all men, we were to permit ourselves to postulate a withdrawal of that threat and in this sense to expect or maintain an *apokatastasis* or universal reconciliation as the goal and end of all things. No such postulate can be made even though we appeal to the cross and resurrection of Jesus Christ. Even though theological consistency might seem to lead our thoughts and utterances most clearly in this direction, we must not arrogate to ourselves that which can be given and received only as a free gift.

Secondly, there is no good reason why we should forbid ourselves, or be forbidden, openness to the possibility that in the reality of God and man in Jesus Christ there is contained much more than we might expect and therefore the supremely unexpected withdrawal of that final threat, i.e., that in the truth of this reality there might be contained the super-abundant promise of the final deliverance of all men. To be more explicit, there is no good reason why we should not be open to this possibility. If for a moment we accept the unfalsified truth of the reality which even now so forcefully limits the perverted human situation, does it not point plainly in the direction of the work of a truly eternal divine patience and deliverance and therefore of an *apokatastasis* or universal reconciliation? If we are certainly forbidden to count on this as though we had a claim to it, as though it were not supremely the work of God to which man can have no possible claim, we are surely commanded the more definitely to hope and pray for it as we may do already on this side of this final possibility, i.e., to hope and pray cautiously and yet distinctly that, in spite of everything which may seem quite conclusively to proclaim the opposite, His compassion should not fail, and that in accordance with His mercy which is " new every morning " He " will not cast off for ever " (La. $3^{22f., 31}$).